METHODS, STRATEGIES, AND ELEMENTARY CONTENT FOR BEATING AEPA, FTCE, ICTS, MSAT, MTEL, MTTC, NMTA, NYSTCE, OSAT, PLACE, PRAXIS, AND TEXES

CHRIS NICHOLAS BOOSALIS

California State University, Stanislaus

with

CHARLES JACKSON
SAM A. MARANDOS
ERICA SEROPIAN CARDEY
LESLIE HEROD

PEARSON

Boston ■ New York ■ San Francisco
Mexico City ■ Montreal ■ Toronto ■ London ■ Madrid ■ Munich ■ Paris
Hong Kong ■ Singapore ■ Tokyo ■ Cape Town ■ Sydney

Senior Series Editor/Series Editor: *Traci Mueller*
Series Editorial Assistant: *James P. Neal, III*
Marketing Manager: *Jennifer Armstrong*
Production Editor: *Beth Houston*
Editorial Production Service: *Walsh & Associates, Inc.*
Composition Buyer: *Linda Cox*
Manufacturing Buyer: *Andrew Turso*
Electronic Composition: *Omegatype Typography*
Cover Administrator: *Joel Gendron*

For related titles and support materials, visit our online catalog at www.ablongman.com.

Between the time website information is gathered and then published, it is not unusual for some sites to have closed. Also, the transcription of URLs can result in typographical errors. The publisher would appreciate notification where these errors occur so that they may be corrected in subsequent editions.

Disclaimer

This book offers expert and reliable information regarding the exams and content that it covers. It is sold with the understanding that the purchaser/user will verify all of the information about these exams since said information is subject to change. The purchaser/user also recognizes that no promise of success can reasonably accompany the purchase/use of this book. All information about the exams addressed in this text is taken from publicly available materials and materials available as a matter of the public record. The author and publisher specifically disclaim any liability that is incurred from any and all types of use/misuse and/or application/misapplication of the contents herein. AEPA, FTCE, ICTS, MTEL, MTTC, NMTA, NYSTCE, OSAT, PLACE, and TExES are registered trademarks of National Evaluation Systems, Inc. MSAT and PRAXIS are registered trademarks of Educational Testing Services, Inc.

Library of Congress Cataloging-in-Publication Data

Boosalis, Chris Nicholas.
    Methods, strategies, and elementary content for beating AEPA, FTCE, ICTS, MSAT, MTEL, MTTC, NMTA, NYSTCE, OSAT, PLACE, PRAXIS, and TEXES / Chris Nicholas Boosalis.
      p. cm
    Includes bibliographical references and index.
    ISBN 0-205-42560-7
    1. Teaching—United States—Examinations—Study guides. 2. Reading (Elementary)—Examinations—Study guides. 3. Teachers—Certification—United States. I. Boosalis, Chris Nicholas. II. Title.
LB1762.B66 2006
370'.76—dc22

                                                     2005042187

Printed in the United States of America

10 9 8 7 6 5 4 3 2 1   09 08 07 06 05

Dedications

*For Beatriz Velasquez—the finest educator I have ever known
and someone who dislikes these exams as much as the next person.*

—Chris Nicholas Boosalis

*To my husband, Greg. Without his unwavering support and encouragement
this project, as so many other things, would never have been possible.*

—Erica Seropian Cardey

*This book is dedicated to three people who taught me to strive,
focus, grow, change, and accept: Carmen Jackson, Lamar Jackson,
and William Barnes. Each of them in their way are reflected in my life
and work, and I bless them for it. I would like to acknowledge the help
of Chris Boosalis without whose help and drive this project would have
languished. I would also like to thank my students throughout the years for
helping me to mold and change many of the concepts presented here.*

—Tony Jackson

*I dedicate this work to my beautiful wife of thirty-five years who put up
with me all this time and to my three wonderful children—Anthony, Peter,
and Demetria—and new family members—Carl Berry, Carl Saumuel Berry,
and Vannia Marandos. May they all prosper and have a wonderful future.*

—Sam Marandos

To all teachers who are taking this test—study hard and best of luck.

—Leslie Herod

CONTENTS

CHAPTER TEN

The U.S. Constitution and the Bill of Rights   282

SECTION FOUR   ELEMENTARY SCIENCE   286

CHAPTER ELEVEN

Physical Science   286

CHAPTER TWELVE

Life Science   313

CHAPTER THIRTEEN

Astronomy and Earth Science   346

SECTION FIVE   ELEMENTARY MATH   362

CHAPTER FOURTEEN

Elementary Mathematics   362

CHAPTER FIFTEEN

Algebra and Functions   386

This text offers serious preparation for serious candidates. It is designed to provide comprehensive, in-depth support to test-takers, college instructors, and preparation leaders alike. This text addresses everything that one must know prior to the exam, including the secrets of a passing score (Chapter 1); the written portions (Chapter 2); the multiple-choice portions (Chapter 3); and the content of elementary education in the remaining chapters: language arts, social studies, science, math, and the humanities. Here is how this book will help you:

- *Test-Takers.* Preparing for these exams can be challenging and worrisome. There is a lot of information to learn in a very short amount of time, not to mention the daunting format of the test that you face under strict time restrictions. Our singular goal is to ensure that you learn *what to know* before the test and can practice *what to do* on the day of the test.
- *College Instructors.* This text will offer you a way to ensure that your students have "covered the material" that is most often tested on the exam. We promise that this text will reduce the burden that these exams place on your shoulders so that you can return to the real profession of preparing future teachers to teach real children real skills, not just to pass a state exam.
- *Preparation Leaders.* This text is written to be immediately practical to candidates and to those charged with preparing them. The goal is to help you to help others through time-management models, essential strategies, aligned content, and activities that incorporate state standards for the content areas that will make preparation both comprehensive and easy.

WHICH TESTS DOES THIS BOOK COVER?

The formats, contents, and strategies address the following exams in detail:

- *Arizona Educator Proficiency Assessments* (AEPA—Elementary): Language Arts, Mathematics, Science, Social Studies, the Arts.
- *Colorado's Program for Licensing Assessments for Colorado Educators* (PLACE—Elementary Education): Language Arts and Literacy, Science, Mathematics, Social Studies, Humanities, Wellness and Physical Education.
- *Florida Teacher Certification Examinations* (FTCE—Kindergarten–Grade 6): (1) Language Arts, Social Science, Science and Technology, Mathematics, Physical Education, Human Development, The Arts. (2) (FTCE—Reading K–12).
- *Illinois Certification Testing System* (ICTS—Elementary): Language Arts, Mathematics, Science, Social Studies, Health, Physical Education, Fine Arts, Professional Knowledge.
- *Multiple Subjects Assessments for Teachers (PRAXIS)* (MSAT—Content Knowledge): Literature and Language Studies, Mathematics, Visual and Performing Arts, Physical Education, Human Development, History/Social Studies, Science. (MSAT—Content Area Exercises): Literature and Language Studies, Mathematics, Visual and Performing Arts, Physical Education, Human Development, History/Social Studies, Science.
- *Massachusetts Tests for Educator Licensure* (MTEL—General Curriculum [formerly elementary]): Language Arts, Mathematics, History and Social Science, Science and Technology/Engineering, Child Development, Integration of Knowledge and Understanding.

- *Michigan Test for Teacher Certification* (MTTC—Elementary Education): Language Arts, Mathematics, Social Studies, Science, The Arts, Health, Physical Education.
- *New Mexico Teacher Assessments* (NMTA—Elementary Education): Language Arts, Elementary Education, Mathematics, Social Studies, Science, Reading.
- *New York Teacher Certification Exams* (NYSTCE—Multi-Subject CST): English Language Arts, Mathematics, Science, Social Studies, Fine Arts, Health, Fitness.
- *Oklahoma Subject Area Tests* (OSAT—Elementary Education): Subtest 1: Reading/ Language Arts/Social Studies. Subtest 2: Mathematics/Science/Health/Fine Arts.
- *Texas Examinations of Educator Standards* (TExES—Generalist EC–4): English Language Arts and Reading, Mathematics, Social Studies, Science, Fine Arts, Health, Physical Education.

IS OUTSIDE READING REQUIRED?

We encourage outside reading from methods courses, journals, or from other selected sources. The most valuable information will come from your state standards and any text that your state has adopted to align with them. We encourage you to align other resources with the organization of this book, which is designed to correspond with the exam content.

WHERE IS THE SAMPLE EXAM?

Sample exams are very, very tricky. Our research demonstrates that practicing on contrived sample exams, especially the multiple-choice portions, is not only ineffective but also harmful. The items that other manuals include really are nothing more than someone's "best guess" about what the items will be like. Practicing on those items only gives one a false sense of security. If you do a little online reading about other preparation manuals and what candidates say about them, you will see what we mean in a very short time.

The only practice exams that we will endorse at this time and recommend that you purchase are the ones that come from the company that developed your test itself. Visit your state's department of education or go directly to the test's official site for information on how to obtain the study guide for your exam.

WHY DO PEOPLE FAIL THESE TESTS?

People fail these tests for three reasons.

1. No time-management plan.
2. No strategies to tackle the written, constructed-response, and multiple-choice questions.
3. No knowledge of content.

Problem One: Time Management

National Evaluation Systems (NES) and Educational Testing Service (ETS) exams truly require preparation. The more you know about what to expect on the day of the test, the better you will do. Students who see one of these tests for the first time and who have not been prepared for that initial shock may be at a great risk of failure. Mismanaged time really is a formula for failure. Chapter 1 details specific time-management models that you are sure to find helpful. If you follow the time stipulations carefully, completing the exam with time to spare will be a realistic goal for you.

Problem Two: Strategies

You need to have strategies for tackling the written and multiple-choice sections of the test. The written and multiple-choice sections must be done in a particular order to maximize your chances of passing. The day of the test *is not the time* to begin thinking about what to do on the test and how to do it. With a time-management plan and proven strategies for the written and multiple-choice sections, your chances of passing the test have just moved from possible to likely. Chapters 2 and 3 of this text detail strategies to beat all of the essay and multiple-choice questions on the exam.

Problem Three: Content

Knowledge of NES or ETS content, although important, does not determine success or failure. If you do not know the content, you'll have a difficult time with the terms and concepts. Also, you'll probably fail. But ignorance of content does not tell even half of the story of why students don't pass the first time. Candidates who have extensive experience in the content of the test that has been earned in reading-methods classes and through direct experience in elementary classrooms have failed the test multiple times. The reasons? Problems one and two above. Without a time-management plan and solid strategies, the odds of passing the test on the first attempt are probably worse than flipping a coin (not even 50/50). Your success depends on how you prepare for the exam and what you do on the day of the test. This book is devoted to assisting you in passing the test on your first attempt. The content material included in this book is directly applicable to the essay and multiple-choice questions that you will see on your exam.

After studying hard and following my directions, time management, written responses, multiple-choice questions, and exam content will no longer be an issue for you. *And then you will beat the exam!*

ACKNOWLEDGMENTS

All of the authors wish to thank our editor, Traci Mueller; and our reviewers Christine Buel, Nyack College; Scott Fike, D'Youville College; Dale Oswalt, Olivet Nazarene University; Russell M. Thatcher, Oklahoma Panhandle State University; and our friends at Allyn and Bacon. The authors also wish to thank Stefanie Dimotakis and John Mitchell for their suggestions on Copernicus and haiku.

Real Scores, Real Strategies

This chapter presents important information about your exam, its format, how it is scored, and how exactly to beat the test. Beating the test means learning how to manage your time on the essays (if any), the multiple-choice questions, and knowing the precise number of questions that you must answer correctly in order to pass the test. Let's begin with the exam formats and other information before describing how to approach your test specifically.

WHAT FORMATS OF NES EXAMS EXIST?

NES exams come in two varieties: Subtest and Comprehensive. Explanations of each type of exam follow.

Subtest Exams

Subtest exams test your knowledge of elementary content by pairing two or more content areas together and asking you to pass each subtest individually. Each subtest has its own independent score assigned to it, and you can take only one during a session or a combination of them. OSAT exam is a subtest exam.

OSAT: Two Subtests

Your scores may remain valid for only a certain amount of time, so you typically must pass each subtest within a given period of time or repeat the whole thing again. Consult your registration bulletin for more information.

Comprehensive Exams

Comprehensive exams test all content areas at once. For example, you will see language arts, math, science, social studies, and so forth in one large exam. You must pass the whole exam with the content areas combined or you will need to repeat the whole thing again, even if you did well on one or more content areas. Comprehensive exams can include both multiple-choice and essay questions or multiple choice questions only.

- ■ With essays: AEPA, MTEL, NYSTCE, OSAT
- ■ No essay: FTCE, ICTS, MTTC, NMTA, PLACE, TExES

In this text you will learn how to beat either variety, and the descriptions provided will be about your exam in particular.

WHAT FORMATS OF ETS EXAMS EXIST?

The PRAXIS (Professional Assessments for Beginning Teachers) Series contains two separate exams. One is a standard paper-and-pencil exam called Multiple Subjects Assessment for

Teachers: Content Knowledge. The MSAT: Content Knowledge has 120 multiple-choice questions from a variety of areas and lasts two hours. The second exam is called Multiple Subjects Assessment for Teachers: Content Area Exercises, and it contains eighteen essays from a variety of areas and lasts three hours.

HOW DO YOU PASS THESE TESTS?

Here are the most important things to know in order to pass the exam (*Note:* This information pertains mainly to NES exams; ETS exams function differently and require a different explanation. Familiarize yourself with the information below, but be sure to review the specific information about the MSAT (PRAXIS series) described later in this chapter.

1. Understand your real passing score.
2. Approach noncompensatory scoring carefully.
3. Compensate for null multiple-choice questions.

Real Scores

NES reports its passing scores in terms of a scale. For example, they tell you that a passing score is 220 on a 100–300 point scale. These numbers are no fun to see, because you don't know exactly how many questions that you have to answer in order to pass. The rationale for the scale is unimportant, but the real passing score is. For example, if I tell you that you have to answer seven out of ten questions correctly to keep your job, then you're going to pay very careful attention to the questions you answer until you've answered seven of them correctly. Anything beyond seven doesn't matter. The scaled score obscures this real passing number, but we have found ways to uncover each of them for your test. You will learn about them shortly, after understanding the next two important areas: noncompensatory scoring and null questions.

Noncompensatory Scoring

Noncompensatory scoring means that you cannot use one content area to compensate for another. This applies to both subtest and comprehensive exams. Take a subtest exam like OSAT for example. Subtest one pairs language arts and history together, and you have to get a **combined** score of 220 in order to pass; however, you cannot get every language arts question correct and completely miss history and still pass. There are **mandatory minimums** assigned to each content area within a given subtest or comprehensive exam. You will learn all about the minimum scores when we address your test directly, and you will also find that information absolutely essential in how you approach and ultimately pass your exam.

Null Scores

NES uses you as a guinea pig. They try test questions out on you, which accounts for the high numbers of people who leave the test session saying: *Some of the questions had two right answers!* That's probably true, because they are the null questions. Null questions do not count toward your score and are impossible to identify. Though you cannot identify them, you must learn how to survive the multiple-choice section effectively. If not, you will end up spending too much time on questions that do not count toward your score; and you may also end up retaking the test because of these questions.

HOW ARE PASSING SCORES CALCULATED?

NES exams have either multiple-choice questions only or multiple-choice questions with essays. The multiple-choice questions are scored by machine. You can have them rescored for a fee if you think they've made a mistake, but you're pretty much stuck with the score that you get. Worse, there are null questions that do not count toward your passing score. The essays are *always* scored, so it is critical that you complete any and all essays that you see. They will be rated by two or more people according to a three- or four-point rubric. It is critical that you write the way NES wants you to write these essays. When we discuss problems with passing NES exams at the end of this chapter, you will learn all about the basic NES skills required for your elementary exam.

IN WHAT ORDER DO THE MULTIPLE-CHOICE QUESTIONS APPEAR?

Some of the exams have as many as 225 questions that address all of the stated content areas (language arts, math, science, etc.) The order of the questions can be by section, group, or jumble. Ideally, you'll see just one *section* of math, science, or social studies. That will enable you to focus on one content area at a time and start with your strongest area. *Group* questions might alternate five to ten questions: five math, five science, five art, and so forth. They are more difficult, because you have to shift your train of thought back and forth. The worst scenario is the *jumble,* where questions appear as one content area after another or are simply randomized. Thankfully, we have worked out a plan for you to make any question order survivable through a strategy called *the Tally Strategy.* It will be specific to your exam.

HOW SHOULD I APPROACH A TEST WITH ESSAYS?

Since the exam includes multiple-choice and essay questions, you have to decide how to approach each of these areas. You have two basic options. The first is to simply complete the essays first and then do the multiple-choice questions. Why? Because the essays will be scored for certain, and you want to earn points on them. But there is a better approach: The "Two Step."

The "Two Step" is the preferred method for all exams with essays. The first step is to survey and outline each of the essays and then do the multiple-choice questions for a defined amount of time. A four-hour exam would be divided as shown in Table 1.1.

TABLE 1.1   Multiple-Choice with Essays

FIRST	SECOND	LAST
• Outline All Essays • Analyze Data	• Do Multiple Choice • Do Gimmies & 50/50s	• Finish All Essays • Guess Away!
30 Minutes	2 Hours	1 Hour

After outlining the essays, you then complete as many of the multiple-choice items that you can answer easily. You then return to the essays and finish them. The multiple-choice questions that you just finished may be packed with terms, activities, and content that could be useful to you. Because of the abundance of possible clues that might be contained in the multiple-choice questions, you may be able to actually use the test against itself. This approach is recommend for everyone and proves its effectiveness time and time again. Spend any remaining time on the hard multiple-choice questions by either answering them or guessing on them.

THE HYBRID APPROACH

A hybrid approach simply means that you survey the written sections first, answer or outline the case next, answer or outline short answers two and three after that, and then outline or answer short answers one and four last. After outlining or answering the written questions, you complete the multiple-choice questions, saving enough time to return to the short answers that you only outlined because you couldn't figure them out completely. The remaining time is spent filling in any written-response outlines with the information that you have "borrowed" from the multiple-choice questions.

Table 1.2 is offered as an example, if you find yourself needing to use your own "hybrid" approach. It is based on a four-hour exam.

TABLE 1.2   A "Hybrid" Approach

ESSAY ONE	ESSAY TWO	GIMMIES	50/50s	GUESS AWAY
30 Min.	*30 Min.*	*120 Min.*	*40 Min.*	*20 Min.*
Time Spent	Time Spent	Time Spent	Time Spent	Time Spent

Scribble this table in your test book (if allowed) to keep track of your time as you take the test. It is your responsibility to figure out the times that are applicable for each section if you intend to use this model, since it is impossible to predict when the question might only inspire an outline from you and not a full response.

DIVIDING AND CONQUERING THE MULTIPLE-CHOICE QUESTIONS

Most people simply start with the first question and then work through items one by one. That does not work very well for any of these exams. When you take the test, you will quickly realize that some of the questions are really obvious and some are quite impossible. You will also note that some the questions are very, very long because they rely on data sets and others are really short and easy to complete. These facts indicate that you cannot simply start with item one and continue through the questions. You are going to have to employ a different approach that will allow you to move through the test efficiently.

Divide and conquer is the best approach to the multiple-choice questions. Imagine that you have one hundred minutes to complete fifty-two items. What you do is divide the questions into five sections, spending no more than twenty minutes per section (see Table 1.3).

TABLE 1.3   Dividing and Conquering Multiple-Choice Questions

SECTION 1	SECTION 2	SECTION 3	SECTION 4	SECTION 5
Items 1–10	*Items 10–20*	*Items 20–30*	*Items 30–40*	*Items 40–52*
20 minutes	**20 minutes**	**20 minutes**	**20 minutes**	**20 minutes**

You look at items one through ten first and pick out the ones that are the easy questions. Do them first. Then, spend time on the ones that are 50/50s (ones that you can get with some effort). Finally, skip the items that are real time wasters and move on to the next section. If you have time at the end, you can go back and work on the time wasters if you want, but you will probably end up guessing on them.

THE TALLY STRATEGY

These tables will be very important to you, since you need to keep track of your test's mandatory minimum scores while also accounting for the null questions. For example, a one hundred item test with five content areas will have only a certain number of questions that count and a certain number of required correct answers for you to be declared "subject matter competent." Table 1.4 provides an example:

TABLE 1.4   Tally Table for Hypothetical Exam

	LANGUAGE ARTS	SCIENCE	MATH	SOCIAL STUDIES	ARTS
NUMBER OF ITEMS	20	20	20	20	20
SCORED ITEMS	15	15	15	15	15
REQUIRED ITEMS	**12**	**12**	**12**	**12**	**12**

Though you will see twenty items per content area, only fifteen of them count; thus, you will actually answer **five** questions for absolutely no reason. To ensure that you pass, you have to answer a minimum of **twelve** questions correctly. Therefore, you must answer about **five additional questions** correctly to be certain that you reach the minimum score and do not end up answering too many "null" questions.

The tally tables will look like this for each exam (see Table 1.5).

TABLE 1.5   Hypothetical Tally Table

	LANGUAGE ARTS	SCIENCE	MATH	SOCIAL STUDIES	ARTS
REQUIRED ITEMS	**17**	**17**	**17**	**17**	**17**

As you complete the exam, mark the number of questions that you feel certain you've answered correctly in the blank space in the *tally table* that you will draw in your test booklet or on the scratch paper you'll receive. Doing so ensures that you have attempted a sufficient number of questions to surpass the mandatory minimum score stated for your exam.

HOW DO I PASS *MY* TEST?

Each exam addressed in this text will be described to you in detail. They are listed alphabetically by state for your convenience. You will see the amount of time that you have to complete your test. In addition, you will also learn what the **real** required score is for each content area of the test. For example, you may see one hundred questions, but only eighty of them will count. Furthermore, each content area, be it language arts, math, science, and so forth has a minimum score assigned to it. You will see exactly the number of questions that you have to do with care to compensate for both the null questions and the mandatory minimums for each content area to ensure that you increase your chances of passing your exam to the fullest extent possible. Please verify the information below in the registration bulletin available for your exam.

Arizona Educator Proficiency Assessments

AEPA—Elementary (Language Arts, Mathematics, Science, Social Studies, The Arts). Each test session lasts four hours. Your score is reported on a scale from 100 to 300, with 240 as the minimum passing. The AEPA elementary includes approximately 100 selected-response questions and one written-performance assignment (see Table 1.6).

As Table 1.6 shows, you will see about 100 multiple-choice questions that vary depending on the weight of the content area. Furthermore, you will see one essay that is tied to one

TABLE 1.6

SUBAREAS	APPROXIMATE WEIGHT	90%	10%
		APPROXIMATE MULTIPLE-CHOICE ITEMS	ESSAYS
I. Language Arts	17%	21–23	
II. Mathematics	17%	20–22	
III. Science	17%	20–22	1
IV. Social Studies	17%	20–22	
V. The Arts	12%	14–16	

Source: NESINC (2003). AEPA 2003–2004 Registration Bulletin

content area (integration of knowledge and understanding). That language signals a unit plan or two extended lesson plans of some kind.

Table 1.7 shows you how to spend your time on AEPA.

TABLE 1.7

FIRST	SECOND	THIRD	LAST
Survey Essay	*Do Multiple Choice*	*Finish Essay*	*Guess Work*
• Outline It • Begin Data Analysis	• Do Gimmies • Do 50/50s	• Fill in Outline • Add Jargon • Add Content	• Do Time Wasters • Check Grammar
10 Minutes	**180 Minutes**	**30 Minutes**	**20 Minutes**

First, you should survey the essay. You can spend up to ten minutes on it. This leaves you with 180 minutes to answer the multiple-choice questions. Divide the sections as shown in Table 1.8.

TABLE 1.8

10–20	20–40	40–60	60–80	80–100
36 Minutes	36 Minutes	36 Minutes	36 Minutes	36 Minutes

Table 1.9 shows the number of questions that you must answer correctly in order to pass the test.

TABLE 1.9   Tally Table: AEPA—Elementary Education

LANGUAGE ARTS	SCIENCE	MATH	SOCIAL STUDIES	ARTS	ESSAY
16	16	16	16	12	1 Essay

Colorado's Program for Licensing Assessments for Colorado Educators

PLACE—Elementary Education (Language Arts and Literacy, Science, Mathematics, Social Studies, Humanities, Wellness and Physical Education). The test session lasts four and one-half hours. Your score is reported on a scale from 100 to 300, with 220 as the minimum passing. The PLACE elementary exam contains approximately one hundred multiple-choice questions. As Table 1.10 shows, you will see about one hundred multiple-choice questions that vary depending on the weight of the content area.

TABLE 1.10

SUBAREAS	APPROXIMATE MULTIPLE-CHOICE
I. Language Arts and Literacy	21–23
II. Science	20–22
III. Mathematics	20–22
IV. Social Studies	20–22
V. Humanities, Wellness, and PE	14–16

Source: NESINC (2003). PLACE Registration Bulletin 2003–2004

Here is how to approach the PLACE exam (see Table 1.11).

TABLE 1.11

FIRST	SECOND	THIRD	LAST
Gimmies	*50/50s*	*Time Wasters*	*Guess Away!*
200 Minutes	**30 Minutes**	**30 Minutes**	**10 Minutes**

Table 1.12 shows how to spend the crucial first minutes.

TABLE 1.12

1–20	20–40	40–60	60–80	80–100
40 Minutes	40 Minutes	40 Minutes	40 Minutes	40 Minutes

Table 1.13 shows the number of questions that you must answer correctly in order to pass the test.

TABLE 1.13

LANGUAGE ARTS	SCIENCE	MATH	SOCIAL STUDIES	HUMANITIES, WELLNESS, AND PE
17	16	16	16	12

Florida—Florida Teacher Certification Examinations

FTCE—Kindergarten–Grade 6 (Language Arts, Social Science, Science and Technology, Mathematics, Physical Education, Human Development, and The Arts). The test session lasts five hours, though you need to verify that information with your state's test representative. The Kindergarten–Grade 6 exam contains approximately 225 multiple-choice questions. No constructed response question accompanies this test. The score scale is most likely 100–300 with a scaled score of 240 as the minimum passing score, though you will need to verify that information with the Florida Department of Education (see Table 1.14).

TABLE 1.14

SUBAREAS	APPROXIMATE MULTIPLE-CHOICE ITEMS*	NUMBER REQUIRED TO PASS*
I. Language Arts	90	72
II. Science and Technology	35	28
III. Mathematics	35	28
IV. Social Studies	35	28
V. Humanities, Wellness, and PE	35	28

*Estimate based on other NES exams.

Table 1.15 shows how to spend your time.

TABLE 1.15   Time Management

FIRST	SECOND	THIRD	LAST
Gimmies	*50/50s*	*Time Wasters*	*Guess Away!*
220 Minutes	**30 Minutes**	**30 Minutes**	**20 Minutes**

Table 1.16 shows how to spend the crucial first minutes.

TABLE 1.16

1–20	20–40	40–60	60–80	80–100	
20 Minutes	20 Minutes	20 Minutes	20 Minutes	20 Minutes	
100–120	**120–140**	**140–160**	**160–180**	**180–200**	**200–225**
20 Minutes	20 Minutes	20 Minutes	20 Minutes	20 Minutes	20 Minutes

The Table 1.17 shows the number of questions that you must answer correctly in order to pass the test.

TABLE 1.17   FTCE Tally Strategy

LANGUAGE ARTS	SCIENCE	MATHEMATICS	SOCIAL STUDIES	HUMANITIES
72	28	28	28	28

FTCE—Reading K–12:   The test session lasts two and one-half hours. The Reading K–12 exam contains approximately 120 multiple-choice questions. No constructed response question accompanies this test. The score scale is most likely 100–300 with a scaled score of 240 as the minimum passing score, though you will need to verify that information with the Florida Department of Education.

Table 1.18 shows how to spend your time.

TABLE 1.18   Time Management

FIRST	SECOND	THIRD	LAST
Gimmies	*50/50s*	*Time Wasters*	*Guess Away!*
120 Minutes	**30 Minutes**	**15 Minutes**	**15 Minutes**

Table 1.19 shows how to spend the crucial first minutes.

TABLE 1.19

1–20	20–40	40–60	60–80	80–100	100–120
20 Minutes	20 Minutes	20 Minutes	20 Minutes	20 Minutes	20 Minutes

Illinois—Illinois Certification Testing System

ICTS—Elementary (Language Arts, Mathematics, Science, Social Studies, Health, Physical Education, Fine Arts, Professional Knowledge). The test session lasts five hours. The elementary exam consists of 125 multiple-choice test questions. A score of 70 or above on a 0–100 point scale is a passing score. If you have to retake a test, you must retake the whole thing. No constructed response question accompanies this test.

Table 1.20 below shows the content areas, their assigned weight, and the approximate number of multiple-choice questions.

TABLE 1.20

SUBAREAS	%*	SCORABLE MULTIPLE-CHOICE ITEMS*	NUMBER REQUIRED TO PASS*
I. Language Arts	23%	25–29	20
II. Mathematics and Science	22%	24–28	20
III. Social Studies	15%	16–18	12
IV. Humanities, Wellness, and PE	15%	16–18	12
V. Professional Knowledge	15%	16–18	12

Source: NESINC (2003). PLACE Registration Bulletin 2003–2004.

*Estimate based on other NES exams.

Table 1.21 how to approach the ICTS.

TABLE 1.21   Time Management

FIRST	SECOND	THIRD	LAST
Gimmies	*50/50s*	*Time Wasters*	*Guess Away!*
240 Minutes	**30 Minutes**	**20 Minutes**	**10 Minutes**

Table 1.22 how to spend the crucial first minutes.

TABLE 1.22

1–20	20–40	40–60	60–80	80–100	100–125
40 Minutes	40 Minutes	40 Minutes	40 Minutes	40 Minutes	40 Minutes

Table 1.23 shows the number of questions that you must answer correctly in order to pass the test.

TABLE 1.23   ICTS Tally Strategy

LANGUAGE ARTS	MATH/ SCIENCE	SOCIAL STUDIES	HUMANITIES	PROFESSIONAL KNOWLEDGE
20	20	12	12	12

Multiple Subjects Assessments for Teachers (PRAXIS Series)

MSAT—Content Knowledge (Literature and Language Studies, Mathematics, Visual and Performing Arts, Physical Education, Human Development, History/Social Studies, Science)

MSAT—Content Area Exercises (Literature and Language Studies, Mathematics, Visual and Performing Arts, Physical Education, Human Development, History/Social Studies, Science).   Both MSAT Content Knowledge and Content Area Exercise exams are produced by Educational Testing Services (ETS). Because ETS has different types of agreements with each state in which the exams are given, you must visit their website before preparing for the exam.

Familiarize yourself with the number of questions required to pass each of the exams for your state. You will find that all of the strategies that have been described for other exams will work for these exams, too.

The **MSAT Content Knowledge** exam contains 120 multiple-choice questions. The areas and distributions of the questions are shown in Table 1.24.

TABLE 1.24

SUBAREAS	%*	SCORABLE MULTIPLE-CHOICE ITEMS	NUMBER REQUIRED TO PASS
I. Language Arts	20%	24	
II. Mathematics	20%	24	
III. Visual and Performing Arts	10%	12	
IV. Physical Education	7%	8	
V. Human Development	7%	8	
VI. History/Social Studies	18%	22	
VII. Science	18%	22	

After reviewing Table 1.24, visit the ETS website, locate your state's requirement, and write the number of questions required to pass the exam for your state in the space provided above (far right column).

Since you will have two hours to complete the exam, your best approach to the multiple-choice questions is shown in Table 1.25.

TABLE 1.25   Time Management

1–20	20–40	40–60	60–80	80–100	100–120
20 minutes	20 minutes	20 minutes	20 minutes	20 minutes	20 minutes

Table 1.26 will be a useful guide for you to use as you answer questions on the exam. Remember that you will have to visit the ETS website, locate your state's testing requirements, and complete the tally table with the number of questions required to pass each section.

TABLE 1.26   MSAT Tally Strategy

LANGUAGE ARTS	MATH	VISUAL ARTS	PE	HUMAN DEVEL.	HISTORY	SCIENCE
24	24	12	8	8	22	22

The second exam, **MSAT Content Area Exercises,** consists of eighteen essays given over a three-hour period. Table 1.27 below shows the areas the number of questions.

TABLE 1.27

SUBAREAS	NUMBER OF ESSAYS
I. Language Arts	3
II. Mathematics	3
III. Visual and Performing Arts	2
IV. Physical Education	2
V. Human Development	2
VI. History/Social Studies	3
VII. Science	3

Table 1.28 show how much time you should spend on each of the essays during the testing period.

TABLE 1.28   Time Management

LANGUAGE ARTS	MATH	VISUAL ARTS	PE	HUMAN DEVEL.	HISTORY	SCIENCE
3 Essays	*3 Essays*	*2 Essays*	*2 Essays*	*2 Essays*	*3 Essays*	*3 Essays*
30 Minutes	**30 Minutes**	**20 Minutes**	**20 Minutes**	**20 Minutes**	**30 Minutes**	**30 Minutes**

Massachusetts Tests for Educator Licensure

MTEL—General Curriculum (formerly Elementary) (Language Arts, Mathematics, History and Social Science, Science and Technology/Engineering, Child Development, Integration of Knowledge and Understanding). Each test session lasts four hours. There are approximately 100 multiple-choice items on this test. Your scores are reported in a range from 0 to 100, with a score of 70 representing the passing score. This passing score is derived from a combined score from the multiple-choice items and the two essay questions. The multiple-choice portion accounts for 80 percent of your exam, while the essays account for 20 percent (see Table 1.29).

TABLE 1.29

SUBAREAS	WEIGHT	80% APPROXIMATE MULTIPLE-CHOICE ITEMS	20% NUMBER OF ESSAYS
I. Language Arts	17%	21–23	
II. Mathematics	17%	20–22	
III. History and Social Science	17%	20–22	
IV. Science and Technology/ Engineering	17%	20–22	
V. Child Development	12%	14–16	2
VI. Integration of Knowledge and Understanding	20%		

Source: MTEL Registration Bulletin 2003–2004 & MTEL Test Objectives.

As Table 1.29 shows, you will see about one hundred multiple-choice questions that vary depending on the weight of the content area. Furthermore, you will see two essays that are tied to one content area (integration of knowledge and understanding). That language signals a unit plan or two extended lesson plans of some kind.

Table 1.30 shows the best approach to the MTEL.

TABLE 1.30

FIRST	SECOND	THIRD
• Survey the data • Outline the essays	• Do multiple choice questions • Spend twenty-minutes per section	• Finish the essays and use terms and ideas from multiple choice if possible • Spend twenty-five minutes per essay
10 Minutes Each	180 Minutes	40 Minutes Each

Divide the sections as shown in Table 1.31.

TABLE 1.31

1–20	20–40	40–60	60–80	80–100
36 Minutes	36 Minutes	36 Minutes	36 Minutes	36 Minutes

Table 1.32 shows the number of questions that you must answer correctly in order to pass the test.

TABLE 1.32   MTEL Tally Table

LANGUAGE ARTS	MATH	SOCIAL STUDIES	SCIENCE	CHILD DEVELOPMENT	INTEGRATION
16	16	16	16	12	2 Essays

Michigan Test for Teacher Certification

MTTC—Elementary Education (Language Arts, Mathematics, Social Studies, Science, Arts, Health, and Physical Education).   Each test session is four and one-half hours in length. The MTTC Elementary exam consists of approximately 100 multiple-choice test questions. Your correct number of scorable test questions is placed on 100 to 300, with a score of 220 representing the passing score. There is no essay question on this test.

Table 1.33 shows the content areas, their assigned weight, and the approximate number of multiple-choice questions. As with other NES exams, as many as twenty-five questions will be thrown out. The number required to pass this test is a high estimate to account for the null questions and the mandatory minimum scores that accompany each content area.

TABLE 1.33

SUBAREAS	%	SCORABLE MULTIPLE-CHOICE ITEMS*	NUMBER REQUIRED TO PASS*
I. Language Arts	24%	21–24	22
II. Mathematics	20%	17–20	18
III. Social Studies	15%	12–15	13
IV. Science	15%	12–15	13
V. The Arts	13%	10–13	11
VI. Health and Physical Education	13%	10–13	11

Source: NESINC (2003). MTTC Registration Bulletin 2003–2004.

*Estimates based on similar NES exams offered elsewhere.

Table 1.34 shows how to approach it.

TABLE 1.34

FIRST	SECOND	THIRD	LAST
Gimmies	*50/50s*	*Time Wasters*	*Guess Away!*
240 Minutes	**30 Minutes**	**20 Minutes**	**10 Minutes**

Table 1.35 shows how to spend the crucial first minutes.

TABLE 1.35

1–20	20–40	40–60	60–80	80–100
40 Minutes	40 Minutes	40 Minutes	40 Minutes	40 Minutes

Table 1.36 shows the number of questions that you must answer correctly in order to pass the test.

TABLE 1.36   MTTC Tally Table

LANGUAGE ARTS	MATH	SOCIAL STUDIES	SCIENCE	ARTS	PE
22	18	13	13	11	11

New Mexico Teacher Assessments

NMTA—Elementary Education (Reading Instruction and Language Arts, Literature and The Arts, Mathematics, Science, and Social Studies).   The test session lasts four hours. Your score is reported on a scale, though the particular scale being employed has not been specified. Based on other NES exams, the scale will probably range from 100 to 300, with 220 or 240 as the minimum passing score. You will need to verify the scoring information on this test independently.

The NMTA elementary exam contains approximately 100 multiple-choice questions. As Table 1.37 shows, these multiple-choice questions vary depending on the weight of the content area. Based on the stated weights, the Table 1.37 shows the number of questions that you are likely to see for each content area.

TABLE 1.37

SUBAREAS	APPROXIMATE WEIGHT	NUMBER OF QUESTIONS
I. Reading and Language Arts	28%	28
II. Literature and the Arts	12%	12
III. Mathematics	23%	23
IV. Science	17%	17
V. Social Studies	20%	20

Source: NESINC (2003). NMTA Registration Bulletin 2003–2004.

Table 1.38 the best approach to the NMTA:

TABLE 1.38

FIRST	SECOND	THIRD	LAST
Gimmies	*50/50s*	*Time Wasters*	*Guess Away!*
180 Minutes	**30 Minutes**	**20 Minutes**	**10 Minutes**

Table 1.39 shows how to spend the crucial first minutes.

TABLE 1.39

1–20	20–40	40–60	60–80	80–100
40 minutes	40 minutes	40 minutes	40 minutes	40 minutes

Table 1.40 shows the number of questions that you must answer correctly in order to pass the test.

TABLE 1.40

READING	LITERATURE	MATH	SCIENCE	SOCIAL STUDIES
22	10	17	15	16

New York Teacher Certification Exams

NYSTCE—Multi-Subject CST (English Language Arts, Mathematics, Science, Social Studies, Fine Arts, Health, and Fitness). The test session lasts four hours. The NYSTCE—Multi-Subject exam contains approximately ninety multiple-choice questions, with one constructed response assignment (see Table 1.41).

TABLE 1.41 NYSTCE—Multi-Subject CST

SUBAREAS	% OF QUESTIONS	90% APPROXIMATE MULTIPLE-CHOICE ITEMS	10% ESSAYS
I. English Language Arts	21	19–21	
II. Mathematics	18	16–18	
III. Science	13	12–15	
IV. Social Studies	15	14–17	
V. Fine Arts	8	8–11	
VI. Health and Fitness	8	8–11	
VII. Family and Consumer Science and Career Development	7	6–9	
VIII. Foundations of Reading: Constructed-Response Assignment	10	10 pts.	1

Sources: NESINC (2003). NYSTCE Registration Bulletin 2003–2004

Table 1.42 shows the best approach to the exam.

TABLE 1.42

FIRST	SECOND	THIRD	LAST
Survey Essay	*Do Multiple Choice*	*Finish Essay*	*Guess Work*
• Outline It • Begin Data Analysis	• Do Gimmies • Do 50/50s	• Fill in Outline • Add Jargon • Add Content	• Do Time Wasters • Check Grammar
10 Minutes	**180 Minutes**	**30 Minutes**	**20 Minutes**

Divide the sections as shown in Table 1.43.

TABLE 1.43

1–20	20–40	40–60	60–80	80–90
36 Minutes	36 Minutes	36 Minutes	36 Minutes	36 Minutes

Table 1.44 shows the number of questions that you must answer correctly in order to pass the test.

TABLE 1.44   NYSTCE Tally Table

READING	SCIENCE	MATH	SOCIAL STUDIES	ARTS	HEALTH	FAMILY	READING ESSAY
17	16	16	16	9	9	9	1 Essay

Oklahoma Subject Area Tests

OSAT—Elementary Education (Subtest One: Reading/Language Arts/Social Studies; Subtest Two: Mathematics/Science/Health/Fine Arts).   Each OSAT subtest session lasts four hours. You have the option of spending those four hours on only one subtest or on both of them, if you take subtests one and two in one shot. Your score is reported on a scale from 100 to 300, with 240 as the minimum passing. If you do not receive a passing score on both Elementary Education subtests in one shot, the passing score on one subtest will be saved for up to two years from its original pass date. After that, you get to redo the whole exam. You will see both multiple-choice questions and an essay question on this test (see Table 1.45).

TABLE 1.45

ELEMENTARY EDUCATION TEST	SELECTED-RESPONSE QUESTIONS	CONSTRUCTED-RESPONSE QUESTIONS	MULTIPLE-CHOICE WEIGHT	ESSAY WEIGHT
Subtest 1: Reading/ Language Arts/Social Studies	55	1	85%	15%
Subtest 2: Mathematics/Science/Health and Fitness/Fine Arts	55	0	100%	0

Source: NESINC (2003). Certification Exams for Oklahoma Educators: Faculty Guide.

Let's look at each subtest in greater detail. On subtest one, you will be tested on reading, language arts, and social studies and see a total of fifty-five questions; however, the range of scorable questions can be as many as twenty or as few as eleven. The number of questions that you must answer correctly will also vary because of the scorable item variance (see Table 1.46).

TABLE 1.46

SUBAREA NUMBER	SUBAREA TITLE	85% APPROXIMATE NUMBER OF SCORABLE SELECTED-RESPONSE ITEMS*	15% ESSAYS
1	Reading	11–20	1
2	Language Arts	11–20	
3	Social Studies	11–20	

* Estimates based on similar NES exams.

Remember that you will also see one essay on subtest one related to reading instruction. The essay will count for 15 percent of your passing score. The rubric has four criteria and each criterion is worth two points. You need a score of three to ensure passage of the test, though you can do as bad as a two if your multiple-choice scores are adequate.

Let's look at subtest two next. Subtest two embodies math, science, health and fitness, and fine arts. Like subtest one, you will see fifty-five multiple-choice items but no essay. The scorable items vary wildly as shown in Table 1.47.

TABLE 1.47

SUBAREA NUMBER	SUBAREA TITLE	APPROXIMATE NUMBER OF SCORABLE SELECTED-RESPONSE ITEMS*	CONSTRUCTED RESPONSE QUESTIONS
1	Math	11–20	
2	Science	11–20	
3	Health and Fitness	1–10	
4	Fine Arts	1–10	

* Estimates based on similar NES exams.

Three time-management plans will be offered to you. The first plan is for taking subtest one only. The second plan describes how to take subtest two only. The last plan shows you how to do both subtests together. (*Note:* In all cases, you are advised to register for all of the subtests and to take them at once the first time. In the first place, you may end up finishing—and passing—all of them at once. If not, you will have had the opportunity to look ahead at the other subtests to get a sense of what you know and do not know and you can prepare accordingly.)

Plan A: Taking Subtest One Only.   In this scenario, you elect to take **only one** of the two subtests during a five-hour period. Since the time-management models are the same for both subtests one and two, we will only apply the strategy to subtest one (see Table 1.48). Please extrapolate the information to subtest two.

TABLE 1.48

FIRST	SECOND	THIRD
Outline Reading Essay	*Do Multiple Choice*	*Finish Essay*
• Identify Form • Analyze Data	• Answer Gimmies • Answer 50/50s	• Terms from Multiple Choice • Fill in Content • Guess on Remaining Multiple-Choice Items
15 Minutes	**180 Minutes**	**45 Minutes**

After outlining the essay for 15 minutes, spend the next 180 minutes on the multiple-choice questions. Divide your time as shown in Table 1.49.

TABLE 1.49

Subtest One: 55 Questions

1–10	10–20	20–30	30–40	40–50	50–55
30 Minutes	30 Minutes	30 Minutes	30 Minutes	30 Minutes	30 Minutes

Nail the gimmies and the 50/50s. Pull terms and content from the multiple-choice section into your essay. Spend no more than forty-five minutes on the essay, and use any remaining time to guess on multiple-choice questions that you could not figure out.

Plan B: Taking Subtest Two Only.   In this plan, you only take subtest two. Because there is no essay, the approach is a bit different (see Table 1.50).

TABLE 1.50

FIRST	SECOND	THIRD
Gimmies	*50/50s*	*Time Wasters*
• Find Gimmies • Answer Them	• Spend Time on 50/50s • Skip Time Wasters	• Attempt Time Wasters • Guess Away!
180 Minutes	**40 Minutes**	**20 Minutes**

During the first step, spend 180 minutes cycling through the questions. Nail the gimmies. Use Table 1.51 as a guide.

TABLE 1.51

Subtest Two: 55 Questions

1–10	10–20	20–30	30–40	40–50	50–55
30 Minutes	30 Minutes	30 Minutes	30 Minutes	30 Minutes	30 Minutes

Table 1.56 shows you how many questions you must attempt with care in order to pass the test.

Plan C: Taking Both Subtests One and Two.   In this scenario, you attempt both subtests at once. If this is your first attempt, you are advised to give them both a shot. Begin with subtest one, since it has the essay (see Table 1.52).

TABLE 1.52   Subtest One

FIRST	SECOND	THIRD
Outline Reading Essay	*Do Multiple Choice*	*Finish Essay*
• Identify Form • Analyze Data	• Answer Gimmies • Answer 50/50s	• Terms from Multiple Choice • Fill in Content • Guess on Remaining Multiple-Choice Items
15 Minutes	**90 Minutes**	**20 Minutes**

After outlining the essay, do the multiple-choice questions. Nail the gimmies and attempt the 50/50s. Use the "divide and conquer" model shown in Table 1.53. (*Note:* The time is very tight on this exam, so be extra careful with which questions you intend to answer or skip when taking two subtests simultaneously.)

TABLE 1.53

Subtest One: 55 Questions

1–10	10–20	20–30	30–40	40–50	50–55
15 minutes	15 minutes	15 minutes	15 minutes	15 minutes	15 minutes

Return to the essay. Finish it in twenty minutes or less. This will leave you with enough time to make a solid effort on subtest two. Table 1.54 below reflects how to handle the second test.

TABLE 1.54   Subtest Two

FOURTH	FIFTH	LAST
Gimmies	*50/50s*	*Time Wasters*
• Find Gimmies • Answer Them	• Spend Time on 50/50s • Skip Time Wasters	• Attempt Time Wasters • Guess Away!
90 Minutes	**15 Minutes**	**10 Minutes**

Since you have no essays, use your time to your advantage to find the gimmies first and then attempt the 50/50s. Spend your time as shown in Table 1.55.

TABLE 1.55

Subtest Two: 55 Questions

1–10	10–20	20–30	30–40	40–50	50–55
15 minutes	15 minutes	15 minutes	15 minutes	15 minutes	15 minutes

The last ten minutes should be spent on the time wasters or guessing. The tally table below summarizes the required number of questions that you must answer with care to ensure the best opportunity to pass the test.

OSAT Tally Tables.   Tables 1.56 and 1.57 summarize the content areas, the number of scorable questions, and the points that you must earn to pass each subtest.

TABLE 1.56   Tally Table

OSAT: Subtest One

READING	LANGUAGE ARTS	SOCIAL STUDIES	ESSAY
16	16	16	2–3 Points

TABLE 1.57   Tally Table

OSAT: Subtest Two

MATH	SCIENCE	HEALTH	ARTS
16	16	16	8

Texas Examinations of Educator Standards (TExES)

TExES—Generalist EC–4 (English Language Arts and Reading, Mathematics, Social Studies, Science, Fine Arts, Health, Physical Education).   The test session lasts five hours.

The score scale is 100–300 with a scaled score of 240 as the minimum passing score. The generalist exam contains approximately 225 multiple-choice questions. No constructed response question accompanies this test. Table 1.58 shows the content areas, their assigned weight, and the approximate number of multiple-choice questions.

TABLE 1.58

SUBAREAS	%	APPROXIMATE MULTIPLE-CHOICE ITEMS*	NUMBER REQUIRED TO PASS*
I. Language Arts and Literacy	40	90	72
II. Science	15	35	28
III. Mathematics	15	35	28
IV. Social Studies	15	35	28
V. Fine Arts, Health and Physical Education	15	35	28

Source: NESINC (2003). TEXES Registration Bulletin 2003–2004.

*Estimates based on similar NES exams.

Table 1.59 shows how to spend your time.

TABLE 1.59

FIRST	SECOND	THIRD	LAST
Gimmies	*50/50s*	*Time Wasters*	*Guess Away!*
220 Minutes	**30 Minutes**	**30 Minutes**	**20 Minutes**

Table 1.60 shows how to spend the crucial first minutes.

TABLE 1.60

1–20	**20–40**	**40–60**	**60–80**	**80–100**	
20 Minutes	20 Minutes	20 Minutes	20 Minutes	20 Minutes	
100–120	**120–140**	**140–160**	**160–180**	**180–200**	**200–225**
20 Minutes	20 Minutes	20 Minutes	20 Minutes	20 Minutes	20 Minutes

Table 1.61 shows the number of questions that you must answer correctly in order to pass the test.

TABLE 1.61

Texas Tally Strategy

LANGUAGE ARTS	SCIENCE	MATHEMATICS	SOCIAL STUDIES	OTHER
72	28	28	28	28

Major Essay Formats and Strategies

This chapter covers the essay portions of the exams plus valuable information for candidates who face multiple-choice–only exams. All test-takers need to learn the data analysis methods covered here. Many of the multiple-choice questions are structured just like the essays and require answers that follow the forms described in this chapter. Understanding these formats and their functions will help you to pick out correct answers on the test. In short, whether your test has essays or not, this chapter is an important one for you to read and understand.

EFFECTIVE WRITTEN-RESPONSE OUTLINES

Table 2.1 shows essay forms that you should memorize for the written portion of the test.

TABLE 2.1

CASE STUDY	UNIT PLANS	LESSON PLANS	COMPARATIVE ESSAYS	MATHEMATICAL PROOFS
¶ Strength One	¶ Content	¶ Need	¶ Discussion	¶ Proof One
¶ Strength Two	¶ Activity One	¶ Lesson Plan	¶ Example	¶ Proof Two
¶ Problem + Need A and B	¶ Activity Two	¶ Benefit	¶ Conclusion	¶ Explanation
¶ Need A + Lesson Plan + Benefit	¶ Benefits			
¶ Need B + Lesson Plan + Benefit				

Let's look at the function and purpose of each essay.

- Case studies ask you to analyze a variety of data sets to write a complex essay. Because case studies tend to be the longest pieces of writing, we will begin with them.
- Unit plans have you write cross-curricular lessons with activities for learning in the content areas.
- Lesson plans may require you to analyze data sets and then write a three-paragraph essay that identifies the need present in the data; a lesson plan for the identified need; and finally, a statement of the benefit of the activity.
- Comparative essays have the following formula: Paragraph one presents the central idea or ideas; paragraph two offers the comparison; and paragraph three posits the conclusion. You will see this format applied to the science portion of subtest two, where one question about the validity of a scientific claim is evaluated and another question about plant and animal physiology is analyzed.

■ Proofs are germane to the math portion of subtest two. You will be traveling back in time to seventh- and eighth-grade algebra and geometry to remember how to write up proofs of algebraic equations and calculate linear equations. The format of the proof includes the formula you will be using in the first paragraph, the first part of the proof in the second paragraph, and the second part of the proof in the final paragraph (if it is a two-part question).

QUESTION ONE: WRITING THE CASE STUDY

Writing the case study is easy, once you know how to do it. Here is an example question.

This case study focuses on a student named Bob. The data sets below describe his reading performance during the early part of third grade. Using this data set, write a response in which you apply your knowledge of literacy development to this case. Your response should include three parts:

ITEM ONE: State three strengths and/or needs reflected in the data.
ITEM TWO: Write two lesson plans for this student.
ITEM THREE: Explain how these lesson plans will help the student's development.

You have three tasks in your writing. For **Item One,** you have to identify strengths and needs drawn from your analysis of the student data to be presented next. **Item Two** requires you to write two lesson plans for this student based on findings from your analyses of the student data. Finally, **Item Three** asks you to state two benefits of the activities that you have offered for **Item Two.** Presumably, you must not only identify all three elements correctly, but also organize the answer so that evaluators can find them quickly and unmistakably to receive full credit.

Analyze the data sets on the following page.

You have four sets of data to consider for the case. The easiest item to look at is the student's test scores, because they reveal a definite trend of where the student's strengths and needs are. Starting with fluency, the test scores show that the student decodes text at grade level. This suggests that he should have enough attention left over for comprehension. Also, the test scores, the teacher and student dialogue, and the student's writing sample demonstrate that this student has literal comprehension. However, there appears to be a lack of inferential comprehension. You can see this because the student did not grasp the fact that the character in the story is on the verge of anger because his cousin is coming over. Plus, the student's test scores show that vocabulary and making inferences may be areas that would help him to improve his inferential comprehension.

This basic analysis tells you that he has particular strengths and a major need. The next step is to begin to formulate your essay around the strengths and needs that you have identified. The schematic shown in Figure 2.1 is one that you might want to memorize to help you with this task. You should receive scratch paper to use for this purpose during the test.

The numbered items show the items that you will put in each of the paragraphs. Numbers one and two identify the strengths in the student's data (decoding and literal comprehension), number three is the paragraph that states the major problem (inferential comprehension of narrative text), and the numbers four and five contain the lesson plans for the areas that need attention to help the student develop inferential comprehension (vocabulary development and making inferences).

Now, you are in a position to write the essay. The essay will be organized according to the outline for the case study that was described earlier. Table 2.2 below shows the proper organization and content for the case. The outline appears in the left column and the answer appears in the right column. Each part will be explained to you.

Read **Item One** again carefully. You should notice that you're supposed to identify two strengths *and/or* needs. That's important information for how to structure the essay. What you

Data Set for Case Study

Super Bowl Sunday was a day that Bob had been waiting for. It took forever for the day to arrive, and Bob looked forward to watching his favorite team, the Bull-dogs, play the most important game of the season.

For weeks, he had cheered his team on. With his mother's help, he even called a radio program to offer the team support. Now, finally, the day arrived. His family even told him that it was his day the night before.

"Bob," his mother called, "I need to talk to you." Bob approached his mother. "Your cousin Martin is coming," she said. "His mother is very sick, and we need to look after him for a couple of days."

Bob was indignant but said nothing. He knew that Martin had a disability and that he would scream louder than even Bob could if he didn't get his way—he also knew that Martin couldn't help it. Martin's favorite program was Star Trek, and it was on at the worst possible time.

Assessment Area	Bob's Scores	Goal
1. Decoding	3rd Grade	3rd Grade
2. Spelling	6	5
3. Main Ideas	4	5
4. Inferences	1	4
5. Polysyllabic Words	3	5
6. Prefix/Root/Suffixes	1	5

Teacher/Student Dialogue

Teacher: Tell me what you were reading about.
Chris: It's a story about a boy name Bob who's going to watch the Super Bowl.
Teacher: What else can you tell me?
Chris: The name of the team is the Bulldogs. Oh, and his cousin Martin is coming.
Teacher: What can you tell me about Martin?
Chris: He likes Star Trek.
Teacher: Is there anything special about Martin?
Chris: Yes. He can scream louder than Bob can.
Teacher: How does Bob feel about Martin coming over?
Chris: Happy, because they get to watch the game together.

Writing Summary

This is a story about Bob. Bob likes football. He is going to watch the Super Bowl with his cousin, Martin. Martin is coming over because his mother is very sick. They are going to watch the game and have fun, because Martin can scream louder than Bob can.

FIGURE 2.1

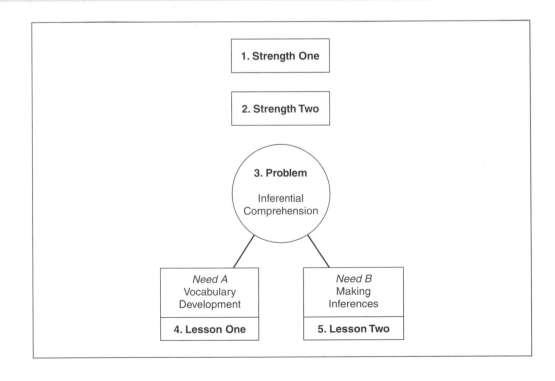

TABLE 2.2

Strength One	The student's test data show that he can decode at grade level. This means that he reads with adequate fluency and accuracy and that he should have enough attention available to try to comprehend what he is reading.
Strength Two	The teacher/student dialogue, his writing sample, and his test scores show that he does comprehend what he read literally. For example, he is able to identify factual information from the teachers oral questions, and he can even summarize these ideas in writing.
Problem Need A Need B	However, the student has a major problem with inferential comprehension, since he could not infer the problem that the main character is having with the fact that his cousin is coming over during the Super Bowl. This may be because he has no strategies available to him to comprehend higher-level vocabulary words. Also, he may not have any strategies that will help him to monitor his own understanding as he reads text.
Need A Lesson Plan Benefit	To help the student comprehend higher-level vocabulary words, the teacher should combine structural analysis with contextual analysis. First, she should build on his syllabication strengths and teach him how to analyze the syllables for prefixes, suffixes, and roots. Then, the student should practice this strategy on selected words to ensure that he can do it. Next, the teacher should show the student how to reassemble the word and check the context of the sentence to confirm the meaning of the word. These activities would help the student to comprehend unfamiliar vocabulary words and would greatly increase his chances to comprehend text inferentially.
Need B Lesson Plan Benefit	The student also needs to learn how to use self-questioning to monitor his own understanding while he reads. The teacher should use the passage and model how to ask questions during the reading. For example, she could model how to ask, "What is Martin like? Is Bob really happy about his coming over? Why does the last sentence say that this is the worst possible time for Martin to come to stay?" Learning how to ask and answer these questions will help the student to monitor his own understanding of the passage as he is reading the text.

will do is use the first two paragraphs of the essay, and the first sentence of the third paragraph, to answer **Item One** completely (see Table 2.3).

TABLE 2.3

¶ Strength One	The student's test data show that he can decode at grade level. This means that he reads with adequate fluency and accuracy and that he should have enough attention available to try to comprehend what he is reading.
¶ Strength Two	The teacher/student dialogue, his writing sample, and his test scores show that he does comprehend what he read literally. For example, he is able to identify factual information from the teachers oral questions, and he can even summarize these ideas in writing.
¶ Problem	However, the student has a major problem with inferential comprehension, since he could not infer the problem that the main character is having with the fact that his cousin is coming over during the Super Bowl.

The first paragraph of the essay states the first strength the data indicate. You include evidence to support your claim and where you found the information:

The student's test data show that he can decode at grade level. This means that he reads with adequate fluency and accuracy and that he should have enough attention available to try to comprehend what he is reading.

In the second paragraph, you state the second strength:

> The teacher/student dialogue, his writing sample, and his test scores show that he does comprehend what he read literally. For example, he is able to identify factual information from the teachers oral questions, and he can even summarize these ideas in writing.

Finally, the first sentence of the third paragraph conveys the major problem that the students is having:

> However, the student has a major problem with inferential comprehension, since he could not infer the problem that the main character is having with the fact that his cousin is coming over during the Super Bowl.

To this point, you have satisfied all of the principle parts of **Item One:** to locate strengths and/or needs in the data. Before you can answer Items Two and Three that ask for the lesson plans and the benefits, you have to finish the third paragraph. It serves a specific function, so pay careful attention to the next discussion.

Let's look at the balance of the third paragraph and its structure and function (see Table 2.4):

TABLE 2.4

Problem	However, the student has a major problem with inferential comprehension, since he could not infer the problem that the main character is having with the fact that his cousin is coming over during the Super Bowl.
Need A	This may be because he has no strategies available to him to comprehend higher level vocabulary words.
Need B	Also, he may not have any strategies that will help him to monitor his own understanding as he reads text.

Remember that the first sentence of this paragraph states the student's major problem Since the major problem is with inferential comprehension of narrative text, your next task is to identify and state two related needs for fluent decoding reflected in the data. These needs are in comprehending higher level vocabulary words and in monitoring his understanding as he is reading. The reason that you must identify two "smaller" needs to the big "problem" is that paragraph three is really an outline for paragraphs four and five. To establish the outline, you simply state two small needs (subneeds) present in the data that are related to this major problem of fluent decoding. In this case, the two needs (A and B) that are related to fluent decoding and are found in the balance of paragraph three:

Need A: This may be because he has no strategies available to him to comprehend higher level vocabulary words.
Need B: Also, he may not have any strategies that will help him to monitor his own understanding as he reads text.

Establishing this outline is essential for answering the next two items. Let's look at Items Two and Three again from the question to be sure that we're on track:

ITEM TWO: Describe two instructional designs to help foment the student's reading development by targeting the needs you reported; and
ITEM THREE: Explain the benefits of these activities for the student's reading development

To answer **Item Two** (e.g., two instructional designs) and **Item Three** (e.g., two benefits of these designs) of the case study question, you are going to use paragraphs four and five of the essay. The topic sentences for each of these paragraphs will be taken from the smaller needs that you identified in the third paragraph. You are going to write two separate lesson plans for them and then state the benefits of these lessons. Let's look at the structure and function of paragraph four (see Table 2.5).

TABLE 2.5

Need A Lesson Plan Benefit	To help the student comprehend higher level vocabulary words, the teacher should combine structural analysis with contextual analysis. First, she should build on his syllabication strengths and teach him how to analyze the syllables for prefixes, suffixes, and roots. Then, the student should practice this strategy on selected words to ensure that he can do it. Next, the teacher should show the student how to reassemble the word and check the context of the sentence to confirm the meaning of the word. These activities would help the student to comprehend unfamiliar vocabulary words and would greatly increase his chances to comprehend text inferentially.

Look at the opening sentence carefully: "To help the student comprehend higher level vocabulary words, the teacher should combine structural analysis with contextual analysis." This sentence in paragraph four simply restates **Need A** from paragraph three. Next, the essay includes the **first instructional activity** that you must state for Item Two:

> First, she should build on his syllabication strengths and teach him how to analyze the syllables for prefixes, suffixes, and roots. Then, the student should practice this strategy on selected words to ensure that he can do it. Next, the teacher should show the student how to reassemble the word and check the context of the sentence to confirm the meaning of the word.

Finally, paragraph four closes with the first benefit that you must identify for Item Three:

> These activities would help the student to comprehend unfamiliar vocabulary words and would greatly increase his chances to comprehend text inferentially.

At this point, you have provided **one required instructional activity** and **one required benefit.** You are halfway through completing Items Two and Three of the case study. To complete the rest of the case study, you'll be using the fifth paragraph. It is structured exactly as paragraph four was (see Table 2.6).

TABLE 2.6

Need B Lesson Plan Benefit	The student also needs to learn how to use self-questioning to monitor his own understanding while he reads. The teacher should use the passage and model how to ask questions during the reading. For example, she could model how to ask, "What is Martin like? Is Bob really happy about his coming over? Why does the last sentence say that this is the worst possible time for Martin to come to stay?" Learning how to ask and answer these questions will help the student to monitor his own understanding of the passage while as he is reading the text.

Like paragraph four, paragraph five restates a need from paragraph three (in this case, it is **Need B**): "The student also needs to learn how to use self-questioning to monitor his own understanding while he reads." This is followed by the **second required instructional design:**

> The teacher should use the passage and model how to ask questions during the reading. For example, she could model how to ask, "What is Martin like? Is Bob really happy about his coming over? Why does the last sentence say that this is the worst possible time for Martin to come to stay?"

The last task is to identify a related benefit of the activity that you have prescribed. The last sentence of the paragraph accomplishes that task: "Learning how to ask and answer these questions will help the student to monitor his own understanding of the passage while as he is reading the text."

At last! You have completed the three required tasks in the case study assignment using a five-paragraph essay. You identified two strengths in the first two paragraphs. You identified a major problem in the first sentence of paragraph three, along with two smaller needs. You identified two instructional activities related to the major identified need in paragraphs four and five. Finally, you identified two benefits related to the instructional designs that you wrote up in the final sentences of paragraphs four and five.

QUESTION TWO: WRITING UNIT PLANS

Understanding how to develop units of instruction will also be valuable for the test. Table 2.7 provides an example.

TABLE 2.7　Example Unit Plan Guidelines

GUIDELINES

1. Select topics that can be explored through different disciplines (e.g., *The Growth Cycle*).
2. Define clear phases for the activity. The first phase might emphasize one content area before another. For example, the students might "do the science" for the growth cycle first, and then use language arts activities on the same topic or theme in the second phase of the activity.
3. Select activities that the students to explore the topic in a deep way. For example, a science experiment would be an appropriate way to explore the growth cycle in phase one, and a research-based language arts activity that utilizes each phase of the writing process in the second phase would be appropriate.
4. Set the time for each phase and balance the activities throughout the unit.

Table 2.8 is an example unit that exemplifies each of these principles.

TABLE 2.8　Example Unit Plan

1. Science and language arts can be used in an interdisciplinary on the growth cycle for upper-elementary students.
2. During the first phase of the unit, I would emphasize exploring the growth cycle through a science experiment. First, I would develop small, manageable groups of students who would receive different kinds of seeds, soil, water, and fertilizer for the experiment. The would plant the seeds in different ways and create three different conditions for them. Some seeds would be planted in one container and receive only water for nourishment. The seeds in another contain would receive water and fertilizer. The seeds in the last container would receive water, fertilizer, and sunlight. The each group of students would care for each plant over a three-week period and measure growth on charts, draw illustrations of the changes, and note characteristics in their learning logs.
3. As the plants change, students would also develop research projects about which plants will grow best and why they believe that this is so. These hypotheses would be used as the basis for a written report that would utilize the writing process. Working in small groups, students would research the growth cycle, the role of soil, water, fertilizer, and sunlight in plant growth through classroom resources, the library, and the Internet. They would write up what they have learned about each topic, along with whether their early hypotheses about which plants would produce the most growth and why. The would apply editing for organization and polishing for style and grammar to their writing in preparation for the publishing-phase of their reports.
4. The final product for the unit would incorporate each group's research on the growth cycle and the role of each of the factors in the growth of the plants. Students would use the growth charts that they had kept, the drawings that they had made, and the written descriptions that they had noted to create visual displays of their findings which could then be presented to the class. They could also create a classroom science journal that would incorporate the students' findings on the growth cycle and how different conditions affect the growth of plants.

QUESTION THREE: WRITING LESSON PLANS FOR DECODING

You may be asked to write a lesson plan for either decoding or comprehension instruction. Let's look at these types of lessons next (see Table 2.9).

TABLE 2.9

QUESTION	SPELLING ITEMS	CHILD'S SPELLING
Based on your analysis of the spelling data write an essay that demonstrates the following. First, state the need reflected in the data. Second, describe instruction to remedy the need you have identified. Third, state the benefit of the instruction you described.	cat rat hat mat sat	kt rt ht mt st

You have three tasks to complete in this essay. First, you have to identify a need seen in the student's data (to be presented next). Second, you must create a lesson plan that would help the student to overcome the difficulty that she or he is having. Finally, you must be able to describe the benefit of the activity that you have identified. As you saw with the case study, you must not only identify all three elements correctly, but also organize the answer such that evaluators can find them quickly and unmistakably to receive full credit. (*Note:* Objectives and prior assessment will be omitted from this lesson plan and the one for comprehension, since the question does not call for one. If your question asks you to define a learning objective on the test, please make sure that you include one.)

Your task is to write a lesson plan to help the child transition from this stage into the conventional stage. This will require you to know appropriate activities for this need. Table 2.10 provides a sample answer to the question.

TABLE 2.10

FORM	CONTENT
¶ Need	The spelling data reflect that the child is in the phonetic stage. While able to encode initial and final consonants of words, she is not yet able to encode words using common rime patterns.
¶ Lesson Plan	Strategy: Begin by focusing on easily encoded words with common rimes (e.g., mat, sat, hat, etc.) Materials: Magnetic Letters: M, S, H, R, C, B Magnetic Letter Combination: AT White Board Dry Erase Pen Steps: 1. Distribute letters to the child and read each one aloud together, including the rime, -AT. 2. Tell the child, "I want you to put one letter in front of AT and read the word." 3. Work together to make words, until each of the letters is used. 4. Leave the consonant letters above the white board and write the rime AT on the board. 5. Ask the student to write as many AT words beneath the rime as she can from memory, using the consonants as prompts.
¶ Benefit	This lesson will help the child begin to encode medial and final sounds heard in words, because she has been taught to write words by a common word family.

As the sample answer shows, you are going to use three paragraphs for the essay. The first paragraph takes care of the "need" that the question requires. The second paragraph poses the instructional design requested. Finally, the required benefit is stated in the third and last paragraph. Each paragraph will be explained to you in detail.

Paragraph One: The Need

The first paragraph of the lesson plan is for the need:

> The spelling data reflect that the child is in the phonetic stage. While able to encode initial and final consonants of words, she is not yet able to encode words using common rime patterns.

It is important for you to be able to identify the correct need in the data, or you will be off in a misdirection for the rest of the essay. Be sure that you study the content of Chapter 2 carefully and that you know the models well to avoid such a problem.

Paragraph Two: The Lesson

The second paragraph of the essay describes the lesson plan that you will use to help the child with the need that you have identified. Because it is a spelling problem that is best addressed through a hands-on activity before practicing how to write the words, develop a lesson design as shown in Table 2.11.

TABLE 2.11

PREPLANNING
1. Distribute letters to the child and read each one aloud together, including the rime, -AT.
2. Tell the child, "I want you to put one letter in front of AT and read the word."

TEACHER MODELING
3. Work together to make words, until each of the letters is used.

GUIDED PRACTICE
4. Leave the consonant letters above the white board and write the rime AT on the board.

INDEPENDENT PRACTICE
5. Ask the student to write as many AT words beneath the rime as she can from memory, using the consonants as prompts.

This pattern is likely to be appropriate for all lesson plans that are used to address student needs.

Paragraph Three: The Benefit

The final paragraph states the benefit: "This lesson will help the child begin to encode medial and final sounds heard in words, because she has been taught to write words by a common word family." In brief, the benefit must explain and summarize how the activity that you have proposed in the second paragraph to remedy the need identified in the first paragraph will work.

QUESTION FOUR: WRITING LESSON PLANS FOR COMPREHENSION

On the next page is an example of a comprehension-related question:

Question

Based on your analysis of the teacher and student conversation, write an essay that demonstrates the following. First, state the need reflected in the data. Second, describe instruction to remedy the need you have identified. Third, state the benefit of the instruction you described.

Data Set for Comprehension

Did you know that the ocean stays warm long into the night? You might think that it is because the sun shines on it all day, which makes it hot. But even on cool and cloudy days, the ocean's temperature can still be warm after dark. How can that be?

The reason is that the sun's light is made up of waves. The waves are neither hot nor cold. The light waves penetrate the surface of the ocean and charge it, much like a battery. At night, the ocean releases all of the energy that it has been storing all day long. That's what makes the water feel warm at night.

Teacher: Can you tell me what you were reading about?
Student: It's about the ocean.
Teacher: What does it say about the ocean.
Student: It says that it stays hot long into the night.
Teacher: Does it tell you why it stays hot all night?
Student: Yes. It says that the sun shines on it all day and that it heats up the water.
Teacher: Can you read this part for me? (Points to third sentence of second paragraph.)
Student: "The light waves penetrate the surface of the ocean and charge it, much like a battery." Oh, maybe it is something else that makes the ocean stay warm at night.

Like the previous question, you have three tasks in your response. First, you have to identify a need that is present in the student's data. Second, you must create a lesson plan that would help the student to overcome the difficulty that she or he is having. Finally, you must be able to describe the benefit of the activity that you have identified. The lesson plan that you write must address a need in comprehension (see Table 2.12).

TABLE 2.12

FORM	CONTENT
¶ Need	The student is able to comprehend expository text literally but not inferentially, because she did not understand that the sun charges the ocean like a battery at night which causes it to stay warm after dark (she thought that the water just stayed warm).
¶ Lesson Plan	Strategy: Begin by focusing on using details from the text as the basis for making inferences. Steps: 1. Model the process of making inferences using a passage and reveal your thinking process to the student. 2. Show the student how to focus on the details of the text to create mental pictures of what the text is saying (e.g., How is the ocean like a battery? Why is that detail important?) 3. Continue posing questions to the passage that move into deeper inferences (e.g., if the ocean is like a battery, what happens to the energy that it collects?) 4. Work together with the student to assemble evidence to support the inferences you've been making. 5. Select a passage that requires making inferences and have the student practice the technique on the passage.
¶ Benefit	This activity would help the student improve her inferential comprehension of expository text because she would learn to use details from the text to make logical inferences about its meaning.

This response requires a need, a lesson plan, and a benefit. Following is an analysis of each paragraph.

Paragraph One: The Need

The first paragraph focuses on the need and satisfies part one of the question: "The student is able to comprehend expository text literally but not inferentially, because she did not understand that the sun charges the ocean like a battery at night which causes it to stay warm after dark (she thought that the water just stayed warm)."

Paragraph Two: The Lesson

The second paragraph of this essay describes a "Think Aloud" that is meant to help the child acquire inferential comprehension (see Table 2.13).

TABLE 2.13

PREPLANNING
1. Model the process of making inferences using a passage and reveal your thinking process to the student.

TEACHER MODELING
2. Show the student how to focus on the details the of the text to create mental pictures of what the text is saying (e.g., How is the ocean like a battery? Why is that detail important?)
3. Continue posing questions to the passage that move into deeper inferences (e.g., If the ocean is like a battery, what happens to the energy that it collects?

GUIDED PRACTICE
4. Work together with the student to assemble evidence to support the inferences you've been making.

INDEPENDENT PRACTICE
5. Select a passage that requires making inferences and have the student practice the technique on the passage.

Paragraph Three: The Benefit

The final paragraph of the sample essay states the benefit of the activity that one has proposed for the need: "This activity would help the student improve his inferential comprehension of expository text because she would learn to use details from the text to make logical inferences about its meaning." In sum, the structure of the third essay is the same as the first one, and all of the items must align or you will not receive as high a score as you should.

QUESTION FIVE: METAPHORS

A hypothetical question on language arts appears next. It tests your knowledge of literary devices.

Metaphors are common features of novels, short stories, poems—even film. For example, Alfred Hitchcock used many visual metaphor to comment on the human condition. In *North by Northwest,* for example, the main characters walk atop the sculptured heads on Mount Rushmore—much like head lice—perhaps conveying the *auteur's* sentiments about humanity and our position in the world. Using your knowledge of literary conventions, write a response in which you describe the use of metaphor in literature. Be sure to cite specific evidence from the text that you select for your discussion.

Step One: Identify the Question

The question is asking you for two important things. First, you have to describe what a metaphor is, and then you need to support your contention. To do that effectively, you must draw on your own knowledge of metaphor from literature and provide an adequate answer to the question. You will learn about such devices in Chapter 4 when we describe *metaphor* for you as an implied comparison between story elements and ideas outside the story through symbols.

Step Two: Analyze the Data

Begin with your definition and apply this understanding to a story that may employ metaphor, *The Old Man and the Sea,* for example (see Figure 2.2).

FIGURE 2.2

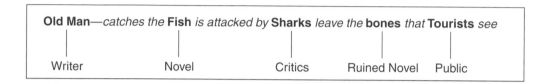

Using this example as an guide, you simply write the essay following the format of a discussion essay.

Step Three: Write It Up

Just like before, you write your answer in a way that will enable evaluators to find what they are looking for quickly and unmistakably.

Definition

Metaphors are an implied comparison between the characters, the setting, or the themes in a story and "real life" accomplished by way of symbols.

Example

Hemingway's *The Old Man and the Sea* provides an example. In the story, the old man catches the fish of a lifetime. While making the long journey back to shore, he winds up eating from his prize—worse, it is later destroyed by sharks. At the end of the story, only the bones are left. Tourists, who know nothing of the Old Man's struggles, comment that a storm must have blown the carcass ashore.

Conclusion

Metaphorically, Hemingway might be commenting on the human condition, though he himself said that it "was just a fish story." The Old Man could symbolize Hemingway, the prized fish could symbolize his novel. The sharks (humorously) might be critics, while the tourists represent the public who only sees what's left of the shredded novel. Extending the metaphor is easy: All human beings have trials that no one (only ourselves) can understand or appreciate—all that is seen is what is left of us, perhaps damaged and destroyed, once the struggle is over.

QUESTION SIX: U.S. CONFLICTS

Using your knowledge of U.S. history, select a war or conflict and:

1. Cite two causes of the conflict.
2. Elaborate upon the causes in detail.
3. State its conclusion and the effects it brought upon our nation.

Step One: Identify the Question

In this question, you are to identify a conflict from U.S. history, expound (elaborate) upon one of the causes, and then state its effects. The outline that you will create next will help you to answer the question (see Figure 2.3).

Step Two: Outline It

FIGURE 2.3

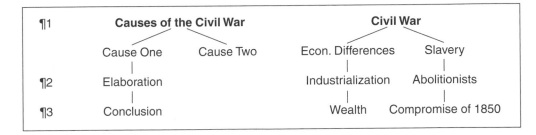

Step Three: Write It Up

Following the format, write up the outline that you created to answer the question.

Causes

The Civil War figures prominently in U.S. history. One major cause of the Civil War was the industrialization of the North, leaving the South still an agricultural region. Another major cause was the rift between the North and the South over the question of slavery.

Elaboration

The first of these causes was significant because the North had an advantage over the South in terms of wealth and continued population growth. The North was able to build factories and mass produce manufactured goods. The stream of new immigrants provided the workers necessary to keep up with its ever-expanding economy. The South, on the other hand, remained agricultural with its dependence on tobacco and cotton. Very few immigrants came to the South and workers were few. Thus, the South became more and more dependent upon slave labor.

Effects

These differences were at the heart of the conflict between the North and the South. Industrialization caused the North to become more wealthy, its economy was ever expanding and growing, and its population continued to grow. The population growth also gave the North the political advantage of having more representation in the House of Representatives and also more votes in the Electoral College. The South's dependence upon slavery made it necessary for Southerners to try and expand their lands into the new territories of the west. However, the Compromise of 1850 put a damper on their efforts by calling for settlers of that territory to vote whether they wanted to be a free state or a slave state. In the case of Kansas, many Northerners and abolitionists moved to Kansas to ensure that Kansas became a free state. This caused a rift between the two sides and blood was shed. Abolitionists also had been attacking the practice of slavery in the South through newspaper stories and the Underground Railroad. For these reasons, the Southerners went on the defensive and felt that they had to fight for their way of life.

QUESTION SEVEN: ASTRONOMY

A major change in scientific thought occurred that moved us from a geocentric universe to a heliocentric one. Using your knowledge of astronomy, briefly describe both ideas and cite one reason that one theory supplanted the other.

Step One: Identify the Question

In this case, you evaluate the validity of an argument. Here, you are asked to compare and contrast two competing theories in astronomy. In deciding how to write the essay, you must first identify each theory and then state why one theory is preferable to another theory:

- Ptolemy's position on our solar system.
- Copernicus's position on our solar system.
- Role of Galileo's invention of the telescope.

Step Two: Outline It

Given the above, your outline might look like that shown in Figure 2.4.

FIGURE 2.4

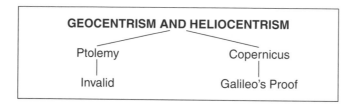

Step Three: Write It Up

The next step is to write the outline using the content of science.

Ptolemy's Position

Geocentrism was the belief that all the universe, the moon, sun, and five ancient planets, circled the earth. This idea was concocted by Ptolemy in 140 A.D. He believed the planets exhibited a retrograde motion. He also believed that the planets and other objects in the universe that circled earth were attached to epicycles that explained the brightness seen on earth. The belief at this time was that a prime mover had control over everything in the universe and the Earth was supposed to be the middle of the universe by divine right.

Copernicus's Position

Heliocentrism is the belief that all objects in the universe are measured with the sun at the center. This idea was theorized by Copernicus in 1543. He believed that the sun was in the center of the universe and the planets orbited the sun. He also believed that the moon orbited earth and all of the planets had a circular orbiting pattern that they followed. His observations conflicted greatly with those of Ptolemy, and Copernicus' predictions were more accurate using this heliocentric model.

Heliocentrism Wins

Why heliocentrism over Geocentrism? With the invention of the telescope, Galileo was able to disprove Ptolemy's theory of Geocentrism. Galileo was able to see that Jupiter had moons. This meant that not all objects in the universe circled the Earth. He was also able to see the imperfections in the sun and moon. With the progression of time and the invention of more powerful telescopes, scientists have been able to show that Copernicus' theory of heliocentrism is correct.

QUESTION EIGHT: GEOMETRY AND THE PYTHAGOREAN THEOREM

Often, you will be asked to demonstrate a formal geometric proof and to explain a separate proof in paragraph form. Consider the sample problem below.

Use the diagram and information to answer the two questions that follow.

Given the drawing and the information below prove that the triangle formed in the circle is a right triangle and then calculate the length of side AC.

Given

AC is a diameter of the circle.

An inscribed angle is equal to ½ of its included arc.

Figure ABC is a triangle.

Line AB = 6

Line BC = 8

Using your knowledge of geometric proofs, complete each of the following tasks:

- Write a geometric proof that demonstrates that ABC is a right triangle
- Write an essay that demonstrates how to calculate the length of side AC using the Pythagorean Theorem.

To receive full credit on this essay, you have two tasks. First, you must write a formal geometric proof to prove that triangle ABC is a right triangle. Second, you must write an essay that explains how to calculate the length of AC using the Pythagorean Theorem. Let's do each item one step at a time, beginning with Item A from the question above.

ITEM A: The Geometric Proof of Triangle ABC

You're going to write the geometric proof first. To determine that ABC is a right triangle, you have to demonstrate that one of the angles is of 90 degrees. This will satisfy Item A and enable you to answer Item B, applying the Pythagorean Theorem (you can only apply the Pythagorean Theorem to a right triangle). Here are the steps for writing a geometric proof that demonstrates that ABC is a right triangle.

Step One: State the Given Information from the Sample Problem. First, look at the "Given" information in the sample problem. "Given" in geometry means that the statements are assumed to be true for the purposes of the question. Simply transfer this information from the problem to the first part of your proof (see Table 2.14).

Step Two: State Any Information That Is Not Given. Remember that you are trying to prove that triangle ABC is a right triangle. The next thing that you must do is state the information that will help you to accomplish this task. Look at the drawing, and note that the triangle is inscribed inside of a circle. You should know that circles have 360 degrees (see Figure 2.5).

TABLE 2.14

STATEMENT	REASON
AC is a diameter of the circle.	Given
An inscribed angle is equal to ½ of its included arc.	Given
Figure ABC is a triangle.	Given
Line AB = 6	Given
Line BC = 8	Given

FIGURE 2.5

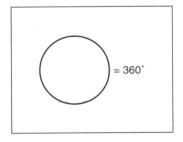

FIGURE 2.6

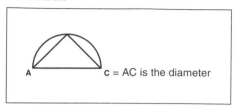

FIGURE 2.7

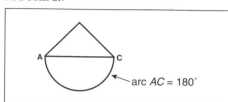

You also know that diameters (here: line AC) divide circles into two equal parts, and that line AC is part of triangle ABC (see Figure 2.6).

You should also know that semi-circles have 180 degrees, ½ of the circle itself, and that arc AC is of 180 degrees (see Figure 2.7).

Table 2.15 provides basic geometric definitions that, although unstated in the sample question, will never change. Write them down in your proof.

TABLE 2.15

A circle contains 360 degrees.	Definition of a circle.
A diameter divides a circle into 2 equal parts.	Definition of a diameter.
arc AC is a semicircle equal to 180 degrees.	Definition of semicircle.

Step Three: Prove That ABC Is a Right Triangle.   Since right triangles contain an angle of 90 degrees, you have to find a right angle to prove that triangle ABC is in fact a right triangle. Here is how you do that. Since arc AC is a semicircle equal to 180 degrees, ½ of it is equal to 90 degrees. Do you see angle B in Figure 2.8? Its angle includes the 180 degree arc AC, so half of the arc is equal to 90 degrees.

Therefore, you simply write this, as in Figure 2.9.

FIGURE 2.8

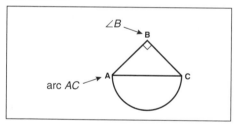

FIGURE 2.9

$\angle B = 90°$	An angle is equal to ½ of its included arc.

At last! You have found your right angle! This means that triangle ABC is a right triangle. Finish your proof by stating the obvious (see Table 2.16).

TABLE 2.16

Angle B is a right angle.	Definition of a right angle.
Triangle ABC is a right triangle.	Definition of a right triangle.

ITEM B: The Essay on the Pythagorean Theorem

> Write an essay that demonstrates how to calculate the length of side AC using the Pythagorean Theorem.

This must be written in essay form. You will use three steps to complete this item.

Step One: Import the Information from Your Proof.   Remember that the Pythagorean Theorem is used to calculate the lengths of the sides of right triangles. If it doesn't have a right angle, then you can't use the Pythagorean Theorem. Since you are writing an essay, start to sketch it out on your scratch paper. Note that you have just proved (see Table 2.17):

TABLE 2.17

Angle B is a right angle.	Definition of a right angle.
Triangle ABC is a right triangle.	Definition of a right triangle.

This information will be essential to your written response to the question.

Step Two: Perform the Calculation.   The next step is perform the calculation by hand on scratch paper before you write the essay. First, write the Theorem down:

$$a^2 + b^2 = c^2$$

Second, substitute the length of each side of the triangle for a, b, and c, recalling that c is always the hypotenuse.

$$AB^2 + BC^2 = AC^2$$

Now, substitute the numerical lengths of each side into the equation. Note that we had to use a variable for the hypotenuse (side AC):

$$6^2 + 8^2 = c^2$$

Now, solve for c^2.

$$36 + 64 + c^2$$
$$100 = c^2$$
$$\sqrt{100} = \sqrt{c^2}$$
$$10 = c$$

Therefore, line $AC = 10$

Step Three: Write It Up!

TABLE 2.18

ITEM A: The Geometric Proof of Triangle ABC

STATEMENT	REASON
AC is a diameter of the circle.	Given.
An inscribed angle is equal to ½ of its included arc.	Given.
Figure ABC is a triangle.	Given.
Line AB = 6	Given.
Line BC = 8	Given.
A circle contains 360 degrees.	Definition of a circle.
A diameter divides a circle into 2 equal parts.	Definition of a diameter.
Arc AC is a semicircle equal to 180 degrees.	Definition of semicircle.
B = 90°	An angle is equal to ½ of its included arc.
Angle B is a right angle.	Definition of a right angle.
Triangle ABC is a right triangle.	Definition of a right triangle.

ITEM B: The Essay on the Pythagorean Theorem

Since triangle ABC is a right triangle, the Pythagorean Theorem $a^2 + b^2 = c^2$ may be applied to it. Using substitution, we can restate the Pythagorean Theorem as $AB^2 + BC^2 = AC^2$. Substituting for a second time, the values for each side can be added to the equation $6^2 + 8^2 = c^2$. The square of 6 is 36 and the square of 8 is 64. Their addition results in $100 = c^2$. To find c one must take the square root of c^2. Whatever operation is done to one side of the equation must be done to the other side. The square root of 100 is 10. Therefore line AC has a length of 10.

QUESTION NINE: PHYSICAL EDUCATION

Aerobic and anaerobic exercises play important roles in one's physical conditioning. Using your knowledge of the principles of physical education, write a response in which you describe activities associated with both types of training and the related benefits to a person's health each activity brings.

Step One: Identify the Question

This question asks you for simple definitions and benefits of two different kinds of physical activities. The associated questions are:

- What are examples of aerobic exercises and their benefits?
- What are examples of anaerobic exercises and their benefits?

The question can be answered in two complete paragraphs on both types of physical activities.

Step Two: Outline It

The outline is straightforward, as you simply identify different activities and their attendant benefits (see Figure 2.10).

FIGURE 2.10

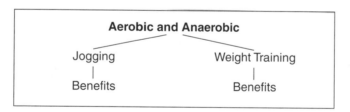

Step Three: Write It Up

Aerobic Exercises and Benefits

Aerobic exercises are activities like walking, running, jogging, and riding a bicycle. These activities are termed *aerobic* because they not only increase the heart rate, but also sustain that increase over a long period of time (aerobic exercises last at least twenty minutes). People consume more oxygen when they perform aerobic activities, and that increase of oxygen helps to burn fat that the body has stored. In addition, the elevated heart rate strengthens one's cardiovascular system. Finally, aerobic exercise is also good for relieving stress, a major factor in coronary heart disease.

Anaerobic Exercises and Benefits

Anaerobic exercise are activities like lifting weights, doing pull ups, and stretching out. These activities are of a short but very intense duration, where one exerts energy and then rests for a period of time. Stronger muscles are the reward of anaerobic exercise, though one does not burn as much stored fat because the heart rate is not elevated for a long enough period of time. There are, however, positive metabolic effects, because stronger and bigger muscles consume more calories. In addition, anaerobic activities are helpful in stress relief, so there is some additional benefit of reducing coronary heart disease through anaerobic exercise, too.

QUESTION TEN: HUMAN DEVELOPMENT

Human development questions can also follow the discussion format that you have just seen in PE. Consider the following question.

> Researchers of psycholinguistic development posit that children learn language in stages and through hypothesis testing during language acquisition. Using your understanding of child development, describe one aspect of language acquisition that reflects these psycholinguistic elements and include how they do so.

Step One: Identify the Question

Here, you are asked to trace elements of psycholinguistic development that reflects both stages and hypothesis testing during language acquisition:

- Provide evidence of a stage of language development.
- Provide evidence of hypothesis testing.
- State how they illustrate psycholinguistic language acquisition.

Step Two: Outline It

FIGURE 2.11

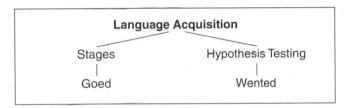

Step Three: Write It Up

> **Language Acquisition Stages**
>
> Psycholinguistic development shows that children learn aspects of their first language in definable and recognizable stages. After acquiring the past tense inflectional morpheme *-ed,* children tend to learn how to apply it appropriately in stages of acquisition. On their way to producing the correct form for many verbs that have irregular past tense conjugations, many children pass through these steps:
>
> Stage One: I goed to the story yesterday.
> Stage Two: I wented to the store yesterday.
> Stage Three: I went to the store yesterday.
>
> It is important to note that corrections during stages one and two often do not take, and even if they do, the child continues to produce this incorrect forms for a while.
>
> **Paragraph Two: Hypothesis Testing**
>
> Each stage that precedes the correct formation of the past tense at stage three is the result of hypothesis testing. The child believes he or she is actually producing the correct form when making the error. At first, the child simply overextends the inflectional morpheme *-ed* to any verb to make it a past tense verb. They do so because many of our verbs in English are formed this way. At stage two, the child overgeneralizes this inflectional ending to include the correct irregular forms of the verb (*wented, runned, boughted*). The child hypothesizes that both forms must work together somehow to properly form the past tense, so combining both elements seems like a very safe bet.

QUESTION ELEVEN: ART HISTORY

> Different periods of history reflect different forms of artistic expression (and vice versa). Using your knowledge of art history, describe the characteristics one finds in Impressionism versus Expressionism, then select one of these art forms to describe in terms of its historical context.

Step One: Identify the Question

In this question, your task is to compare and contrast two forms of artistic expression, before selecting one form and offering a sketch of the historical context surrounding its development.

- State the characteristics of Impressionism.
- Contrast those characteristics with Expressionism.
- Select one of the two forms of expression and describe its historical context.

Step Two: Outline It

Here, you are asked to draw distinctions between Impressionism and Expressionism. You can use two paragraphs for that task and simply discuss the historical context of one of them (Impressionism, in this case) (see Figure 2.12).

FIGURE 2.12

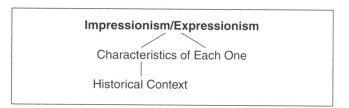

Step Three: Write It Up

Impressionism

Impressionism is a late-nineteenth-century French movement that features studies of light in the composition of the work. Claude Monet is a famous Impressionist artist. His pieces, sometimes bright, others soft, feature portraits of the natural world. When one views Monet's work, it is almost as if one is looking at the world at a distance or through a softly focused lens: Although the features of the landscape and the figures in them are discernable, degrees of light and color are the clear subjects of study that preoccupy his style.

Expressionism

Expressionism is an early-twentieth-century style with German roots. Expressionist works differ from the Impressionist style in two fundamental ways. First, although light and color are featured in Expressionism, too, they can be severe and overwhelming—nearly drowning out any discernable features or forms the artist captures. Secondly, Expressionism is a highly subjective style, because mood and introspection dominate the style, where the artists paint their inner perception of the external world.

Impressionism's Historical Context

Impressionism precedes Expressionism chronologically and can be seen as an initial step away from formalistic and traditional painting that emphasized form over more elemental studies of light and color. Although Impressionism might be less subjective in its presentation (the features of the subjects and the setting are still discernable), it is still a clear departure from more rigid styles of artistic expression.

Multiple-Choice Strategies and Applied Content

DIAGNOSTIC TEST

Before you learn the short cuts for the exam, you need to take a diagnostic test to find out just how strong your multiple-choice skills really are. You'll be asked to. You will see that how you do the test is just as important as what you do on the exam. You can have only one and one-half minutes per question, so please time yourself on this portion of the test. Get in the habit of checking your watch, as you would do on the actual test, and maybe even writing down your start time and end time to get an exact idea of how long it takes you. Turn the page and try out some questions from elementary language arts. Please do them even if you have already passed the language arts portion of your exam, since the skill set is the same for all of the other subject areas. Give yourself only six minutes to do these questions.

Read the traditional poem below and answer the two questions that follow.

Paddy West's

E're years before in London Town
I come to Paddy West's house.
He gave me a dish of American Hash
and he called it Liverpool Scouse.
He said, "There's a ship that's wantin' hands
and on her you'd quickly climb
The mate is a jackel the boatswain's worse,
but she will suit you fine.

Take off yer dungaree jacket,
and let me tell the rest,
Let's think of them cold nor'westers[1]
that we had at Paddy West's.

Now when I'd had a feed me, boys,
the wind began to blow.
Ol' Paddy sent me up to the attic,
the main royal[2] for to stow.
But when I got up in the attic,
No main royal could I find—
So I turned myself to the window and I furled the window blind.

Now Paddy he piped "all hands on deck!"
their stations for to man
His wife stood in the doorway with a bucket in her hand.
And Paddy he cries, "Now let her rip," and she flung the water my way, crying

"Clue in the fore t'gan'sl, boys,
she's taken in a spray!"

Now seeing she's bound for the south'ard
oh to Frisco she was bound,
Paddy he takes a length of rope
and he lays it on the ground.
We both stepped over and back again
and Paddy he said, "That's fine.
And if they ask was you ever at sea
you can say you've crossed the line[3]."

"There's just one thing for you to do
before you sail away. That's to step around the table where the bullocks underlay. And when they ask was you ever at sea you can say ten times round the horn[4] and by gracious you're an old sailor since the day that you was born."

"Put on y'er dungaree jacket,
And walk out looking yer best,
And tell'em you're an old sailor man
That's come from Paddy West's."

[1]Very cold ocean winds
[2]The main sail on a ship
[3]Crossed the equator in a ship
[4]Rounded the African continent in a ship

(continued)

1. In the poem, Paddy West's house is analogous to:

   A. A training facility.
   B. A diploma mill.
   C. A house of ill-repute.
   D. An apprentice's shop.

2. The narrator of the poem is best described as:

   I. A neophyte in search of training.
   II. An experienced sailor reflecting on his past.
   III. Feeling bitter about having been tricked by Paddy West.
   IV. Waxing nostalgic for Paddy West and his experiences there.

   A. I only
   B. I and IV
   C. III and IV
   D. II and IV

3. A first-grade teacher is planning a big book activity for her students. First, she selects the text and gathers the materials that will be required for the activity. She decides to use an easel and a pointer for the activity. Since the students have been working on big book readings for several weeks now, she decides to let the children take a direct role in the activity. After deciding to have the children take turns identifying the parts of a book, including the cover, the title, and the author's name, she considers what to do next. Which of the following items best reflects what the students could do next?

   A. React and comment on specific parts of the text that the teacher will preselect.
   B. Review the story's components (setting, purpose, etc.) after it has been read.
   C. Demonstrate their knowledge of the correct direction in which to read.
   D. Discuss the type of text that was read.

4. A kindergarten teacher writes the following sentence on the board:

   Today is Friday, January 29, 2002.

   She then reads the passage to the students, pointing to each word as she reads. Next, she reads the passage aloud with the children, pointing to each word as the group reads together. Using your knowledge of early reading activities, which response best represents the skill that the teacher is targeting?

   A. Reading text with proper intonation and fluency.
   B. Understanding that individual letters represents individual sounds.
   C. Recognizing that days of the week should be capitalized.
   D. Understanding direction in which text is read in English

Answers: 1. B,   2. D,   3. C,   4. D

Self-Assessment

What you did to answer the questions is just as important as having the correct answers. See if you fell victim to any of the following traps.

1. You did the questions in order, starting with the first question and ending with the fourth question.
2. You spent longer than two minutes per question.
3. You read the "Paddy West" poem first before reading the question items.
4. You couldn't do the question with the Roman numerals in it quickly—or at all.
5. You didn't do question number four first.
6. You didn't write on the test.

If any of the above items were true for you, then you have habits that need to be changed. Doing the questions in order and spending longer than two minutes per question are traps that many unsuccessful students fall into. As a result you might lose valuable opportunities to do easy questions and questions that are actually scored. Remember that not all of the multiple-choice questions count on the test. Just imagine if items 1–3 on the diagnostic test were the ones to be thrown out. Basically, you may have spent all of that time reading the poem and answering the questions for nothing.

Do not expect to do the questions in order; instead, know the raw score required to pass the test and skip through the exam effectively on your way to a passing score. Manage your time carefully as you work throughout the exam. If you spent longer than two minutes per question, you might want to reconsider your approach. Time probably evaporated, because you spent time reading the poem first before reading the questions. Reading the test items first is really important, because you can decide immediately whether you are going to attempt the question, skip it for now, or guess on it later. If you do decide to attempt the question, at least you'll know what you're reading the passage for. However, if you read the poem first, then you're reading for pleasure—and that's not how to approach a test.

If the Roman numeral question gave you trouble, then you probably need to learn the strategies to beat them. Roman numeral questions may or may not appear on the test. They are used on many exams, so you might as well learn how to do them just in case. Besides, the odds are that you will have to complete some pretty weird-looking questions anyway. Plus, all of the questions will require some degree of "figuring," so learning how to do these questions will give you some insight about how to do other kinds of odd questions. You'll learn how to do them a bit later.

At this point, think about how you really performed on the four questions. If you got all of them correct—great! But remember that only question four counted. Therefore, please think about the strategies that you used to arrive at those correct answers, since better ones may be available.

MULTIPLE-CHOICE STRATEGIES

Here are several important strategies that will help you make the exam work for you.

Read the Item First

Recall the sample test. Reading "Paddy West's" first before reading the questions is not the best approach. If you go back to that passage and the questions, it should be apparent that it might have made the task of understanding the poem easier if you had read the question items first. Doing so will enable you to decide whether you are going to do the question now, later, or not at all. You will of course be answering every single question, but some might be answered with a simple bubble and nothing more. Use this strategy for math, social studies, science, or any other subject area on the test.

Do the Easy Ones First

Divide the test into sections, and find the questions that are short and easy to understand. "Paddy West's" is a question that you might want to skip and answer much later, since it takes time and effort to try to read each question item and figure out how it applies to the question.

Do the "Unattached" Questions First

Attached questions are ones that are tied to data sets, such as the "Paddy West" exercise. Then, there are questions that are not attached to a big piece of data that you can just answer and quickly move on.

Use Strategies on the Odd Looking Ones

Do the weird-looking questions strategically. You will see plenty of these questions; in fact, the rest of this chapter is devoted to them. In the diagnostic test, the second question was certainly strange. Roman-numeral questions also fall into this category.

Take the time to review the question below, which appeared as the second question in the diagnostic test.

The narrator of the poem is best described as:

   I. A neophyte in search of training.
   II. An experienced sailor reflecting on his past.

(continued)

> III. Feeling bitter about having been tricked by Paddy West.
> IV. Waxing nostalgic for Paddy West and his experiences there.
>
> A. I only
> B. I and IV
> C. III and IV
> D. II and IV

The best approach is to look at the Roman numeral items first and shorten them as follows:

I. A **neophyte** in search of training.
II. An **experienced sailor** reflecting on his past.
III. **Feeling bitter** about having been tricked by Paddy West.
IV. **Waxing nostalgic** for Paddy West and his experiences there.

Next, apply the shortened items to the passage. Since the narrator is obviously not a neophyte (beginner) and is not expressing bitterness, items one and three are out.

I. A **neophyte** ~~in search of training.~~
II. An **experienced sailor** reflecting on his past.
III. **Feeling bitter** ~~about having been tricked by Paddy West.~~
IV. **Waxing nostalgic** for Paddy West and his experiences there.

Turn now to the answers and eliminate any item with a one or a three in it:

~~A. I only~~
~~B. I and IV~~
~~C. III and IV~~
D. II and IV

A, B, and C are eliminated because they contain the items eliminated from the Roman-numeral items. This leaves D as the only correct response.

Guess Strategically

The way that you should approach the exam after having answered every one of the easy questions first would be to find the questions that you think you can do with some effort. That might require doing the questions strategically as explained earlier or simply trying to eliminate as many wrong answers as possible before guessing on the remaining possibilities. For questions that you know you will never be able to answer, consider just picking the same letter each time. For example, if you have five questions left, use either b or c on all of them.

LEARNING HOW TO APPLY CONTENT

The content of each subject area is vast, and it will not be enough for you to learn simple definitions for each domain on the test. You will have to find ways to apply the content of each subject area in ways that combine different domains and subareas of the test together. *How* you learn the content will be just as important as *what* you learn in preparation for the exam. You need to learn the content of any subject area in terms of a *system* or a *sequence*. *Systems* include collections of concepts that can be compared and contrasted, like plant and animal cells in science, Jacksonian and Jeffersonian democracy in history, and metaphors and similes in language arts. *Sequences* can be thought of as the order of operations in math, time lines in history, and psycholinguistic sequences in child development. This will help you with certain kinds of questions on the test.

Language Arts

Systems and sequences are important for particular kinds of language arts questions. Consider the following.

> The key feature of an effective phonemic awareness activity includes:
>
> A. Letter–sound associations.
> B. Whether the child can track print.
> C. Picture–sound associations.
> D. Whether the child knows where to start reading or not.

Systems lie beneath both the question and the answers here, because items A–D demand that you choose between phonemic awareness and phonics. Thus, the content is best learned like this (see Table 3.1).

TABLE 3.1

PHONEMIC AWARENESS	PHONICS
• Oral language is used.	• Printed language is used.
• Pictures are used but not text.	• Letters, word families, and text are used.
• Segmenting sounds are goals.	• Fluent decoding of print is the goal.

Differentiating phonemic awareness from phonics is part of the domain and content area descriptions for this test, so learning the systematic differences of each is of central importance. A sequence is also present, since phonemic awareness comes before instruction in phonics, but it plays a lesser role in this question.

Systems and sequences also play a role in answering other kinds of language arts questions. Consider the following question.

> A second language learner writes the following sentence during a Language Experience Activity.
>
> *Where Chris is today?*
>
> Which of the following best reflects the child's current stage of interlanguage?
>
> A. Transfer-influenced syntactic development.   C. Developmentally ordered development.
> B. Orthographic stage syntactic development.   D. Transitional stage syntactic development.

After reading the data set and considering the content, it is easy to see that answer C is the correct one.

The question is actually about interlanguage, which is a term from second language acquisition that describes how one's first language affects learning the second language and what happens once a learner is immersed in learning the new language (see Table 3.2). The

TABLE 3.2   Interlanguage

TRANSFER FROM SPANISH TO ENGLISH	DEVELOPMENTAL ORDERS IN ENGLISH
Syntactic Transfer:	*Wh- orders:*
"House White" shows influence from Spanish where adjectives follow nouns.	Where cat? Where the cat is? Where is the cat?

first answer, transfer-influenced, is incorrect because the word-reversal is not influenced by the first language. The remaining items, orthographic and transitional, pertain to spelling and not to this example. Once again, knowing the content will help you make the multiple-choice questions work for you and not against you.

Some questions are immune to both systems and sequences, because they are the null questions.

> KWL is most effective for developing which reading skill?
>
> A. Developing predictive abilities prior to reading.
> B. Fostering active reading through posing questions.
> C. Elaborating knowledge after reading.
> D. Extending understanding after reading one passage and beginning another.

Unfortunately, all of the answer items are correct. *KWL* is a reading activity that stands for what you know, want to know, and have learned. Each of the items fit the bill for this activity, so take a guess and move on.

Social Studies

Let's turn to a few questions from social studies now to see how systems and sequences affect how you prepare to answer questions in this subject area. The types of systems and sequences to know in social studies include political and cultural structures and time lines and event sequences. Consider this question:

> Which of the following statements best characterizes the *Enlightenment* period?
>
> A. It is best characterized for its *Romanitas*—the love of all things Roman, including art, language, and philosophy.
> B. It is best characterized as a movement of the 14th century.
> C. It is best characterized by its most famous authors: Machiavelli and Locke.
> D. It is best characterized as the period that brought about development of the scientific method.

To answer this question, learning major historical events and their relationships will be helpful. The content would be organized and learned as shown in Table 3.3.

TABLE 3.3   Medieval History

THE RENAISSANCE	AGE OF ENLIGHTENMENT
• Mid-14th century Italian movement. • Interested in classical literature of Greece and Rome. • Concerned with the humanities. • Petrarch's love poems. • Machiavelli's leadership rules. • Realism in painting.	• 16th and 17th century European movement. • Produced the scientific method. • Inquiry based on proof. • Applied the scientific method to nature, government, law, etc. • Freedom of thought and natural rights.

If you take the time to outline the content this way, then it will be much easier to answer the question and to see why item D is correct. Systems and sequences will also help you to survive rather bizarre questions like this one:

A shared characteristic of ancient Athenian culture and the Qu'anish people of the Ural region includes which of the following items?

    A. They are best remembered for their contributions to the *Renaissance,* particularly in the area of the development and application of the scientific method to law, government, and humanity.

    B. They both included city–state systems and a similar form of governance which led to later contributions to western culture.

    C. They shared polytheism as a religious world view and incorporated this view into the art and literature of their time.

    D. Athenian culture borrowed heavily from the Qu'ans leading to advances in writing, art, and literature found in Athenian society.

The correct answer to the question is C, though it is impossible to know that. Before you see why this is so, please remember the following. Ideally, you would simply skip a question like that on the first pass through the test; however, you may find that you must answer several such questions in order to reach the raw score that you need to pass the mandatory minimum assigned to a given content area.

To figure out this Athenian/Qu'anish question, you have to focus on the culture that you probably know. In this case, it is the Athenians since there are no Qu'ans that we know of. You might ask why include such a hypothetical question at all. On the exam you will see plenty of cultures that you have never heard of, and you have to have a strategy to get through these questions.

In this case, try to think of Athenian society and the different systems that you could describe (see Table 3.4).

TABLE 3.4   Athenians

Political System: Emerging democracy

Art: Evolving and complex literary tradition

Science: Evolving and complex scientific tradition

Religion: Polytheism

Admittedly, the above is a very raw sketch of Athenian society, and that may be all that you can muster on the day of the test—but it may be all that you need! What you are trying to think of is a point that can be generalized to the unknown and unknowable Qu'anish peoples. Polytheism is probably the most applicable element of the other three ideas, since politics, arts, and sciences might seem more particular to Athenian society only. In sum, try to find the element that is most generalizable from one system to another if you encounter questions.

Null questions also populate social studies.

Many Latin American countries have democracies that closely mirror the U.S. or European forms of representation. Which of the following items best describe Colombia's form of democracy?

    A. It is republican form of democracy with federal, state, and district levels.

    B. It is a democracy about the same age as that of the United States.

    C. It is a Federalist system with city, state, and federal representatives.

    D. It adopted a Jeffersonian form of democracy.

Here, all of the answers are arguably correct. Simply guess and move on.

Science

Systems and sequences in science are a pretty natural consideration, since there are many kinds of systems to consider: physiological systems, astronomical systems, biological systems, and so forth. Understanding how to apply the content from these systems will be helpful to you on the test. Consider the following question:

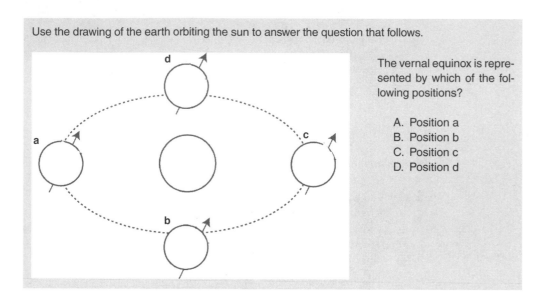

Use the drawing of the earth orbiting the sun to answer the question that follows.

The vernal equinox is represented by which of the following positions?

A. Position a
B. Position b
C. Position c
D. Position d

Item D is correct, because it shows the earth in springtime during the spring (vernal) equinox (when day and night are equal). The other positions of the earth show different seasonal occurrences for North America (c. the winter solstice—longest night; a. the summer solstice—longest day; and b. the autumnal equinox).

Learning systems and sequences will also be helpful if you are asked questions about cells systems and how they fit into different classification systems.

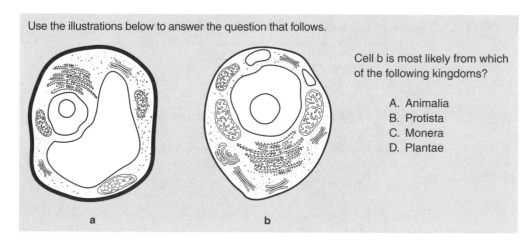

Use the illustrations below to answer the question that follows.

a   b

Cell b is most likely from which of the following kingdoms?

A. Animalia
B. Protista
C. Monera
D. Plantae

Very quickly, you must identify the parts of each cell and understand their differences. If you have learned the systems well, then labeling each type of cell should be easy (see Figure 3.1).

After labeling the images on the test, it should be obvious to you that that the cell a is a plant cell, because of the presence of the cell wall and the vacuole alone, and that cell b is an animal cell. Your choices on this list of items A–D really leave you with only one option (item A), since it is the only animal kingdom cell present on the list.

FIGURE 3.1

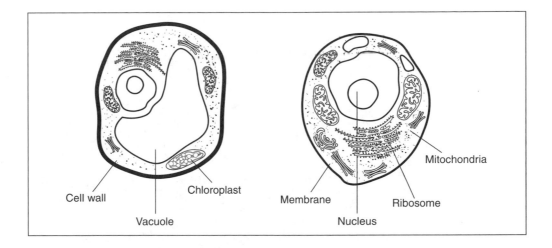

Null questions may also appear in science. Consider the following:

Match the line with the kingdom and its correct description:

Line One	Fungus	yeast, mold, mushroom	A. Line One
Line Two	Plantae	moss, ferns, seed plants	B. Line Two
Line Three	Moneran	bacteria and blue-green algae	C. Line Three
Line Four	Protoslst	one celled algae	D. Line Four

Each answer is correct for each kingdom.

Math

Sequences will be important in math, particularly when considering the order of operations you must perform to solve certain questions.

Use the information below to answer the following:

An Astrologist charges a fixed $10 copay and $5 for every hour (or fraction) of "work."

Which equation best illustrates the charges over a period of hours?

A. x = 5y + 10   C. x = (10 + 5)y
B. x = 10 + 5 + y   D. x = 10y + 5y

The question asks you to identify a linear equation that best fits the description. Here, the only correct answer is A because it captures the hourly charge (five dollars) times the number of hours (y) plus the copay (ten dollars). The rest of the items do not work for the description. Table 3.5 shows what the equation looks like over a period of time.

TABLE 3.5   10 + 5 (hours) = ?

TIME	1	2	3	4	5
Equation	10 + 5(1)	10 + 5(2)	10 + 5(3)	10 + 5(4)	10 + 5(5)
Amount	**$15**	**$20**	**$25**	**$30**	**$35**

This information is useful for answering the next question:

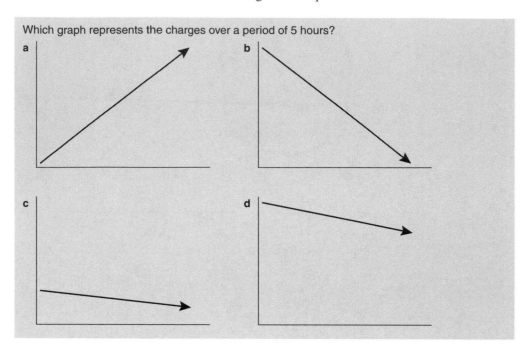

Using the data chart, it is easy to see that only graph a is correct, because the numbers ascend over time as shown in Figure 3.2.

FIGURE 3.2

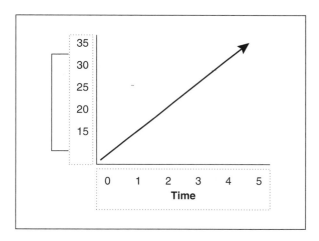

The other graphs show subtraction from a number over a period of time.

Geometry is another area that might require you to farm your knowledge of systems and sequences more fully. Consider this question.

Use the information below to answer the following question.

Figures a and b can be combined to form a cone with a height of 10 and a volume of 30. Using this information about each figure, determine which of the following statements is true.

A. The perimeter of b is 10.
B. Figure b is a right triangle.

C. The area of a is 11.
D. The sum of the area of a and b is 60.

Item A is easy to dispense with, because the perimeter of the triangle is certainly greater than its height and involves adding each side together. Item B is also easy to remove from the list, because it is not possible to make a cone out of a right triangle. The next items are not so easy to get rid of, because you have to perform the calculations in their proper sequence to know if they are true or not. Let's start with item C. To know if this answer is true or false, you must apply the formula for finding the volume of a cone.

Volume = 1/3 (Area of Base × Height of Cone)

Using the information from the question, you simply plug the information into the formula to determine the area of the base (figure a):

30 = 1/3 (A × 10)
3 = 1/3 (A)
9 = A

Thus, Item C is out, because A does not equal eleven. Now, it is true that you do not have to go any further with item D, since it is the only option left. HOWEVER, remember that you are looking for a minimum number of questions to answer correctly, and this might be a null question. Let's check item D just to be sure—obviously this cannot be true, since 9 and 10 do not equal 60. Unfortunately, you have performed all of the operations correctly but you did not find any correct answers here. The point in including this question is to reassure you that you will probably find questions for which there are no answers. Try to check your answers as you complete them—and use the tally tables described in Chapter 1!

A more obvious null question appears below.

A man has three children each with different sports interests. The first son loves golf, the second billiards, and the third water polo. He builds a pool so his third son may practice water polo. The pool is 20' by 40' and is 10' deep. Before the pool is filled the first son in a fit of jealousy fills the pool 1/3 full of golf balls. Not to be outdone the second son fills the pool 1/3 full of billiard balls. In the spirit of fun the third son fills the last 1/3 of the pool with water polo balls. Each golf ball has a circumference of 1½ inches, each billiard ball has a radius 2/3 of an inch and the water polo balls have a diameter of one foot. How much space is left in the pool for water?

A. 4592 cubic gallons   C. 5543 cubic quarts
B. 9583 cubic liters   D. 666 cubic inches

Consider skipping such questions until the end, because this one simply takes too much time.

Humanities

Let's look at physical education, child development, and the arts to see how systems and sequences can help you here.

This is a question from *physical education.*

Anaerobic activities are best characterized by which of the following characteristics?

  I. Walking, running, and jogging.
 II. A lower intake of oxygen resulting in higher metabolism.
III. Intense bursts of energy.
 IV. Relief from stress.

A. I only   C. II and III
B. I and II   D. III and IV

This is an easy question to answer, if you have learned the systems in physical education. The answers indicate choices between aerobic and anaerobic exercise, and the content is organized as shown in Table 3.6.

TABLE 3.6

ANAEROBIC	AEROBIC
• Weight lifting, isometrics, stretching. • Intense bursts of energy. • Relief from stress.	• Walking, running, and jogging. • Energy burned over a period of time. • Relief from stress.

You can easily eliminate Roman Numeral I and II from the list, because I pertains to aerobic exercise and II is absurd. Roman Numerals III and IV are the only possibilities left, making item D correct.

The next question is from child development, where a sequence is possible:

A child of 5;6 who is a monolingual English speaker produces the following utterance when his father leaves the room.

Where Daddy going?

Using your knowledge of child development, select a response that *best* describes the characteristics of this child's statement.

A. The utterance shows normal syntactic development for a child 5;6 and no interventions should be considered at this time.
B. The utterance shows inadequate semantic development for a child of 5;6 and interventions should begin immediately.
C. The utterance shows that dyslexia may emerge as the child becomes literate, given the word reversals in spoken language.
D. The utterance shows inadequate syntactic development for a child of 5;6 years of age and interventions should begin immediately.

To answer this question correctly, you have to have some sense about the sequential order of psycholinguistic development (see Table 3.7).

TABLE 3.7

BABBLING	HOLOPHRASES	TELEGRAPHIC STAGE	SYNTAX ORDERS
4 Months	*1–1.5 years*	*1.5–2 years*	*2–4 years*
Babbling consonants and vowel sounds.	Mommy Daddy Hungry	Cat no here. Milk all gone.	Where Chris? Where Chris is? Where is Chris?

Items A–C are incorrect. The syntax (grammar) should already be in place at this point, and semantics (meaning) and dyslexia (letter reversals) are not indicated by the data set. The only available answer is D, because it shows that the phrase does reveal a developmental problem given the sequence contained in the table.

Questions from the *arts* also depend upon systems and sequences, particularly major periods of art and time lines.

Use the table below to answer the question that follows.

Line One	Impressionism	This academic style from 17th century France centered on the use of light in art.
Line Two	Dadaism	This Vietnam-era style incorporated art, poetry, and music to protest events taking place in the 1960s.
Line Three	Expressionism	This style from Germany probes the artist's impressions and interpretations of the outside world.
Line Four	Cubism	This 1950s style is most concerned with accurate representations of the outside world, particularly in portraiture.

Which line correctly identifies the period of art with its description?

A. Line One   C. Line Three
B. Line Two   D. Line Four

One strategy that you should employ is to sequence the periods first to see if any items can be eliminated based on where they fall on the time line (see Figure 3.3).

FIGURE 3.3

1	2	3	4
Impressionism mid-1800s	Expressionism Late 1800s	Cubism 1907	Dada 1916

Based on the sequence, you can eliminate Lines Two and Four from the table, leaving only Lines One and Three: Impressionism and Expressionism. The systems beneath these historical periods will help you to answer the question (see Table 3.8).

TABLE 3.8

IMPRESSIONISM	EXPRESSIONISM
Impressionism is a light, spontaneous manner of painting which began in France as a reaction against the formalism of the dominant Academic style. Its naturalistic and down-to-earth treatment of its subjects has its roots in the French Realism of Corot and others. The hallmark of the style is the attempt to capture the subjective impression of light in a scene.	Expressionism is a style of art in which the intention is not to reproduce a subject accurately, but instead to portray it in such a way as to express the inner state of the artist. The movement is associated with Germany in particular, and was influenced by such emotionally charged styles as Symbolism, Fauvism, and Cubism.

Given the content, the only available answer is Line Three, since impressionism is **not** an academic style.

Null questions and time wasters can also be found on the arts portion of the test.

The Mellonville Stomp and the Lindeyville Hop have what steps in common?

A. Left, Right, Left, Left, Stomp   C. Left, Hop, Right, Stomp
B. Right, Right, Left, Left, Hop   D. Stomp, Stomp, Stomp, Stomp

Elementary Language Arts

DOMAIN ONE: ENGLISH LINGUISTICS

The major content areas of this domain include the terms and processes of English linguistics (content area one), along with how children and adolescents acquire English as a first and as a second language (content area two).

CONTENT AREA ONE: ENGLISH LINGUISTICS

Table 4.1 presents the terms and concepts at a glance. Familiarize yourself with the terms and some simple examples, before reading further and trying to learn the content in-depth.

TABLE 4.1

	PHONOLOGY	MORPHOLOGY	SYNTAX	SEMANTICS	PRAGMATICS
TERMS	The Study of Sound Units	The Study of Units of Meaning	Lexical/ Nonlexical Categories; Grammar	Word/ Sentence Meaning	Speech Acts; Discourse Theory
EXAMPLE	Consonant and vowel sounds in English	Tense markers like *-ed* or *-ing* or whole words like *cat*	Parts of speech; sentence types	The difference in meaning between the auxiliary verbs *need* and *want*	Apologizing, refusing, or interacting "at the bank" or "at the store"

Table 4.1 captures the elements of linguistics. *Phonology* is the study of sound units and functions, like consonant and vowel sounds in English. *Morphology* is the study of how sounds come together to make meaning, as how we tell the difference in meaning between the one collection of sounds like /bat/ and /pat/. *Syntax* is about grammar and how we structure sentences in speaking and writing to make meaning. *Semantics* is the study of meaning itself, where one studies the fine shades of meaning between words like *need* and *want*. Finally, *pragmatics* looks at very large language practices, like the act of apologizing or refusing, or how we use language differently when negotiating a transaction at a bank or buying fruit at the store. The next few sections will explain each of these areas in greater detail to assist you in learning what you need to know for the test.

The most important areas on which to focus in this section are the phonological processes that affect the sounds of the English language. You will be treated to background information that is necessary for you to understand phonological processes, but it may not be tested directly on the exam. Therefore, do not let the amount of information intimidate you; focus instead on the larger concepts in this section.

Phonology

Phonology describes the study of speech sounds in languages, including sounds in the English language, intonation patterns, and stress patterns (Carr, 1993). When studying speech sounds, linguists represent speech sounds between two forward slashes: /s/ and /z/. Please note that these representations are no longer the letter names "es" and "zee." They are the sound equivalents of "ssssss" and "zzzzzz." Here's a helpful example: Say the words *cats* and *cars* aloud to yourself and pay careful attention to the final sounds in each word. Here is what you should have said:

/kats/   /karz/

When these words are written, both of them have the letter "s" at the end of them; however, when they are spoken, these words have a different final sound. Why? Because the consonant sounds /t/ and /r/ affect what /s/ sounds like through a process of *devoicing* and *voicing* (to be explained shortly). In short, *phonology* is not only the study of individual sounds, but also the *linguistic processes* that affect what we hear in words when they are spoken.

Consonant and Vowel Sounds.   Consonant and vowel sounds differ. For the test, you need to know why they are different. Let's stay with our first example, *cats* and *cars*. The first sounds in each word are /k/ and /a/. As if you didn't know, the former is a consonant sound and the latter is a vowel sound. They are different because consonant sounds are made through high degrees of friction and obstruction, whereas vowels are made with the mouth open and the tongue in a different position. To get a sense of this difference, say the following sounds to yourself:

Consonant Sounds: /p/ /b/ /t/ /d/ /k/ /g/ (puh, buh, tuh, duh, kuh, guh)
Long Vowel Sounds: /A/ /E/ /I/ /O/ /U/ (Letter Names)

Here is what you should notice. In the consonant line, you made the sounds using different combinations of your lips, teeth, tongue, and throat. While in the vowel line you made the sounds by altering the position of your tongue in your mouth and the shape of your mouth. In short, some consonant sounds are made by stopping the air that comes out of your mouth, while vowel sounds are formed without obstructing the air coming out of you. That's the nature of the difference. What you need to understand for the test is more complicated, however, since you have to know much about the terms *voicing, place of articulation,* and *manner of articulation* and how they apply to both vowel and consonant sounds.

Voiced and Voiceless Consonants.   Say the consonant sounds again from the previous example, but this time, place your hand gently across your throat.

Consonant Sounds: /p/ /b/ /t/ /d/ /k/ /g/ (puh, buh, tuh, duh, kuh, guh)

You should notice that some of the consonant sounds made your throat vibrate while others did not. Here is what the pairings look like:

Voiceless: /p/   /t/   /k/
Voiced: /b/   /d/   /g/

If you try the pairs again, you should notice that each pair of sounds is made in exactly the same place in your mouth and in the same way; however, one sound makes your throat vibrate while another does not. You may not care much about that, but think about the impact voicing makes on what we understand. Say /pat/ and /bat/ to yourself. The only difference between how the sounds in these words are made is voicing—and that affects what we understand. If this difference did not exist, then there would be no difference in the spoken sentence: *Hand me the bat* or *Hand me the Pat.* Our understanding of the spoken sentences hinges on whether the initial consonant sound is voiced or not.

Let's now learn about our first linguistic processes: *voicing* and *devoicing.* Recall that the *s* at the ends of *cats* and *cars* has two possible sounds: /s/ or /z/. This is because the consonant that comes before the /s/ will affect whether it sounds like /s/ or /z/. Here is the rule for voicing and devoicing /s/:

- If /s/ follows /t/ or /k/, it is *unvoiced* as in *cats* and *trucks.*
- If /s/ follows any *voiced consonant,* then it sounds like /z/ as in *cars, goes,* and *runs.*
- If /s/ follows /sh/ or /ch/, then it sounds like /ez/ as in *washes* and *churches.*

These possible sounds for /s/, including /s/, /z/, and /ez/ are called *allophones,* because they are related to one another and emerge depending on the environment in which they are found.

Now, try saying the long vowel sounds again, this time with your hand on your throat.

Long Vowel Sounds: /A/ /E/ /I/ /O/ /U/ (Letter Names)

In each case, your throat vibrated, because **all vowel sounds are voiced**—there is no unvoiced counterpart; instead, there are short vowel counterparts for each of the long vowels:

Short Vowel Sounds: /a/ /e/ /i/ /o/ /u/ (ah, eh, ih, oh, oo)

Place and Manner of Articulation (Consonants).   You need to learn the terminology associated with where sounds are made in the mouth and how to describe the characteristics of the sounds we make (beyond mere voiced and voiceless sounds). We will start with *place of articulation.* Table 4.2 shows the terms associated with where sounds are made in the mouth.

TABLE 4.2   Places of Articulation (Consonants)

LABIAL	INTERDENTAL	ALVEOLAR	PALATAL	VELAR	GLOTTAL
With the lips	*Between the teeth*	*Right behind the teeth*	*With roof of mouth*	*With soft palate*	*In the throat*

Nothing demands an example more than does Table 4.3. Say the sounds within each category and note what happens to your lips, teeth, and tongue as you say them.

TABLE 4.3   Examples of Articulated Consonants

LABIAL	INTERDENTAL	ALVEOLAR	PALATAL	VELAR	GLOTTAL
With the lips	*Between the teeth*	*Right behind the teeth*	*With roof of mouth*	*With soft palate*	*In the throat*
/b/	/th/	/t/	/sh/	/k/	/h/

You should notice that different combinations of your teeth, tongue, and lips are used to make these sounds. Below is a summary of each type of place of articulation. Please say the sounds so that you can associate them with different places in your mouth. Pay particular attention to your lips, the shape of your tongue, and different places in your mouth as you learn the sounds associated with the terms below (Anderson, 1985).

- *Labials* are made with your lips, like /b/, /p/, /f/, /v/, /m/, /w/.
- *Interdentals* are made between the teeth, like /th/ in "thin") and /th/ in "these."
- *Alveolars* are made right behind your teeth, like /t/, /d/, /s/, /z/, /n/, /l/, /r/.

- *Palatals* are made with the roof of your mouth, like /sh/ (ship), /zsh/ (azure), /tsh/ (witch), /dz/ (gym).
- *Velars* are made with your soft palate, like /k/, /g/, /ing/.
- *Glottals* are made in the back of your throat: /h/.

You will need to memorize these terms. Using a combination of note cards, sound associations, and oral practice making the sounds will help you. You need to learn the terms associated with the different quality of the sounds above, before putting both *place* and *manner of articulation* together.

Manner of Articulation (Consonants).   The major *manners of articulation* appear in Table 4.4. Remember that "manner" refers to the *characteristic and quality* of the sound. Try to associate the definition with the *sounds* listed in the table.

TABLE 4.4   Manners of Articulated Consonants

STOPS	FRICATIVES	NASALS	LIQUIDS	GLIDES
Stops the air	*Vibrates the air*	*Out the nose*	*Fluid air*	*Evaporating air*
/p/ /b/ /t/ /d/	/f/ /v/ /th/ /s/ /z/ /sh/	/m/ /n/	/l/ /r/	/w/

We describe the sounds in Table 4.4 based on their characteristics. *Stops,* for example, stop the air coming out of the mouth. Say *pat, bat, tap, dog, king,* and *go* and you have the idea. *Fricatives* make the air vibrate. Try *fat, valley, thin, that, sat, zap, ship, witch,* and *hat* for illustration. The nasal sounds, both of which are in *man,* send the air out the nose, whereas *liquids* sound very fluid and "liquidy." Say "luscious" and "lugubrious" a few times to get an idea. Finally, *glides* have a quality that sounds like the air evaporates after it leaves your mouth. Try just the sound /w/ (e.g., "wuh, wuh, wuh"), and that description should make sense to you.

In short, *place of articulation* and *manner of articulation* describe where in your mouth the sounds are made (*place*) along with the quality the sound produced (*manner*). Let's put it all together before learning about the processes associated with making sounds in English.

Place, Manner, and Voicing of Consonants.   Table 4.5 sums up place, manner, and voicing for you. You should try copying the table down and filling it in until it is memorized. (*Note:* The voiced consonants are in **bold** and appear right below its unvoiced counterpart.)

TABLE 4.5   Summary of Place, Manner, and Voicing

MANNER	PLACE OF ARTICULATION					
	Labial	*Interdental*	*Alveolar*	*Palatal*	*Velar*	*Glottal*
Stops	p		t		k	
	b		**d**		**g**	
Fricatives	f	th (thin)	s	sh		h
	v	**th (this)**	**z**	**dsh**		
Nasals	**m**		**n**		**ing**	
Liquids			**l**			
			r			
Glides	**w**			**y (yellow)**		

Vowel Place and Manner of Articulation.   Vowels are different from consonants because they pass out of the mouth and/or nose with very little obstruction. Say the letter names A, E, I, O, and U aloud, and you should notice how your tongue and oral cavity form different shapes to make the sounds. Thus, the position of your lips and tongue cause minute changes that cause different vowel sounds to emerge. The Table 4.6 shows the place and manner of articulation of some common short and long vowels. (*Note:* Long vowels say their names and are shown in capital letters below.)

TABLE 4.6   Place of Articulation (vowels)

| TIP OF TONGUE | POSITION OF TONGUE IN MOUTH | | |
	Front of mouth	*Middle of Mouth*	*Back of Mouth*
High	feet /E/		shoot /oo/
Mid	mate /A/	but /u/	should coat /O/
Low	let /e/	mat /a/ cot /aw/	caught

The place of articulation of vowel sounds depends on where the tongue itself is placed (position of the tongue) and where the tip of the tongue is pointing (high, midway, or low). Try saying the words again and note the position of your tongue in your mouth.

Manner of Articulation (Vowels).   The sound quality of vowels is described as being *tense and diphthongized* or *lax*. *Tense vowels* include some vowel names, like the /o/ in *coat*. You can also hear tense, dipthongized sounds like the /oi/ in *boy* and the /ow/ in *cow*. *Diphthongs* are easy to identify because there are two sounds heard when you say them. Say *boy* and *cow* again, and you should hear two vowel sounds in each word. There are even *triphthongs* in English where three separate vowel sounds are heard in words: *loyal, liar, power*. Lax vowels are all of your short vowels: /a/—*pat*, /e/—*pet*, /i/—*bit*, /o—*hot,* and /u/—*but*.

Linguistic Processes.   What happens to sounds after we make them? Different *combinations* of sounds affect what we hear when we listen to spoken words or words in sentences.
     Flapping is a common process in U.S. English. For example, say the word *butter,* first slowly then quickly. Try it a couple of times. If you pay careful attention to the way that you probably pronounced each word, then you should have noticed the following:

Slow Speech Non-Flapping:	butter—/buter/
Rapid Speech Flapping:	butter—/buder/

In the case of *butter,* rapid speech affects the phonemes we hear in the word. The linguistic process is called *flapping* where the voiceless stop /t/ becomes a voiced stop /d/ in rapid speech

Aspiration.   Aspiration is another common linguistic process. Hold a piece of paper against your lips and try saying this pair of words: *pit* and *spit*. Pay attention to how far the paper moves away from your lips as you say the words. You should notice that the paper moved *away* from your lips when you said *pit* but hardly moved at all when you said *spit*. Why? Because the combination of phonemes in each words affects how they are pronounced:

Aspirated:	pit—/p^hit/
Unaspirated:	spit—/spit/

Aspiration affects stops in the initial position of words and syllables. In the word *pit,* for example, you make an "explosive" sound when the voiceless stop /p/ heads the word. *But when the phoneme /p/ follows a voiceless phoneme like /s/, then it is not aspirated.*

These minor processes affect pronunciation and accents in English. For example, it is easy to identify a speaker of British English because they tend not to flap their stops; instead, they aspirate them.

U.S. English: butter—/buder/
British English: butter—but^{h}ah/

Other languages (neither British nor U.S. English) tell the difference between words based on aspiration. As a Khmer speaker explained in class one day, aspiration in her language differentiates words that would sound exactly the same to a monolingual English audience:

Khmer—Unaspirated /p/:   *pong—/pong/—*"to wish"
Khmer—Aspirated /p/:   *pong—/p^{h}ong/—*"also"

She added that it was difficult for her to learn English in the beginning because she kept hearing all of the aspirated consonants in English and wondered what was happening! The four linguistic processes that you should know for the test are *assimilation, deletion, devoicing, epenthesis,* and *metathesis* (Anderson, 1985; Hyman, 1975; Wolfram and Johnson, 1982).

- **Assimilation.** In rapid speech, many words that we say sound different than they do in slow speech. The example of flapping in the word *butter* is an example of assimilation. Here, one sound becomes absorbed into another in rapid speech. The phonemes /t/ and /d/ are the most commonly assimilated sounds. Say the words *water, rotting,* and *putting* first carefully then very rapidly and you can see the process of assimilating /t/ into the "flapped" /d/ at work.

- **Deletion.** In rapid speech, we sometimes delete entire phonemes or syllables in spoken words. This explains how *contractions* formed in written languages. The spoken verb phrase *I am* said rapidly sounds like /im/. Here, we delete the short vowel /a/ from the phrase in rapid speech and later (to the unease of many grammarians and college professors) inducted this form into written English. Deletion also explains the mismatch between what we write and what we say. The name of the fourth day of the week is spelled *Wednesday* but is usually pronounced /wensday/. In this case, we have completely deleted a part of the syllable in the word that was once pronounced /owdensday/ named after the Saxon god of war, Odin. The linguistic process of deletion in spoken speech, then, accounts for many of the odd spelling patterns found in English and one's difficulty in learning how to spell many words, since there is often a great mismatch between what we say and what we write. Deletion is responsible.

- **Devoicing.** You have already learned about how consonants that precede /s/ can affect whether it sounds like /s/ or /z/. The phoneme /t/ is either voiced or unvoiced depending on the whether the consonants that it follows are voiced or unvoiced. Say *runned* and then *worked* to yourself. You should have said /rund/ and /werkt/. In the former, the /t/ sounds like /d/ because /n/ is a voiced consonant; in the latter, /t/ sounds like /t/, because the /k/ sound is unvoiced.

- **Epenthesis.** Just as we delete many phonemes and syllables in words when we speak rapidly, we also insert sounds that are not normally there. Say the words *something, warmth,* and *length* slowly and then rapidly. You may have said the following during rapid speech (not everyone does this): */sumphing/, /warmpth/,* and */lenkth/.* If your slow and rapid speech shows differences, then you are guilty of *epenthesis,* where you insert other sounds where they are not normally heard in slow speech. Again, this affects how children spell words in the beginning: Since they tend to spell by words based on what they say, these words may often be seen as *sumphing, warmpth,* and *lenkth* in the early stages of spelling development. Misspelling of words like *athelete* are also the result of epenthesis.

- **Metathesis.** In some regional variations of English in the United States, *metathesis* is common. If you have ever heard a speaker pronounce *asks* as /aks/ (e.g., *I need to **aks** you a question*), what you are hearing is the linguistic process of metathesis. Put simply, the final phonemes /s/ and /k/ are "swapped" one for the other, creating an identifiable regional accent when one hears a speaker *metathesizing* sounds in their speech.
- **Palatalization.** Some spoken words shift sounds in regional speech. *Williams* can be heard as /*weyams*/, where the liquid /l/ becomes a palatal /y/ sound.

In summary, these linguistic processes affect what we hear in slow and rapid speech. These processes can affect how we spell and the regional accents that we have.

Morphology

Morphology is the study of the smallest units of meaning in a word (Katamba, 1993). Just as there are phonemes in each language (individual sound units), there are also morphemes (individual units of meaning). Sometimes, morphemes can be as small as one sound. Take /s/ for example. This phoneme also functions as a morpheme in English, because it makes words plural (cars) and possessive (Chris's). Not all sounds or letters are morphemes by themselves. The letters *p, e, l, h, n,* and *t* do not mean anything all by themselves; however, if you arrange them differently and add a few more letters to the combination, you get a singular morpheme: *elephant.* If you add the letter *s* to this singular morpheme, you get **two morphemes:** elephants (elephant + s). To understand these concepts fully, let's learn about free and bound morphemes next.

Free and Bound Morphemes.   There are two types of morphemes to know for the test: free and bound (see Table 4.7).

TABLE 4.7   Free and Bound Morphemes

FREE MORPHEMES	BOUND MORPHEMES
• Stand-alone words: 　　Cat 　　Chris 　　Runs	• Attached to stand-alone words. • Inflectional suffixes like -s, -'s, and -ed. • Derivations like -tion, -ize, and -al. • Root words like *tele* and *form.*

When you think of free morphemes, just imagine any combination of letters or sounds that can stand alone and have meaning. The words *car, Chris,* and *frog* are free morphemes. Bound morphemes, on the other hand, cannot stand alone and have meaning. The morpheme, -s, for example, only makes sense when functioning as plural marker (car**s**) or as possessive indicator (Chris's) or as a indicator of third person singular for verbs (run**s**). It has no meaning when it is all by itself. For the test, you may have to be able to tell the difference between *inflections, derivations,* and *root words.*

Counting Morphemes.   You may be asked to count free and bound morphemes in words. The word *duck* represents one morpheme. When spelled, it has four letters in it (*d, u, c, k*); but when spoken, it has three phonemes: /d/, /u/, /k/. Together, these sounds and letters combine to make **one morpheme,** even though it has four letters (graphemes) and three phonemes.

The word *ducks* has two morphemes: One is free and the other is bound. See if you can identify them. You should have identified *duck* as the free morpheme and the plural marker -s as the bound morpheme, because the former can stand alone and the latter cannot. Try the same thing with these words: cars, Chris's, works, working, and worked. The bound morphemes are -s, 's, -s, -ing, and -ed. The words car, Chris, and work are all free.

Let's now consider a different combination of letters. Say, *ptffs* aloud. *Ptffs* represents **no morphemes,** because this combination of letters means absolutely **nothing** in English. There is nothing *free* or *bound* about the word. The plural marker *s* doesn't mean anything either in this case, because the *base word, pttfs,* doesn't mean anything either.

In summary, one way to count morphemes in words is to look for the base word and for any endings that might represent separate morphemes.

Affixes are either prefixes or suffixes and can be counted as morphemes. There are two major groups of affixes that you need to understand for the test. As shown in Table 4.8, the first group of countable affixes are called *inflectional suffixes,* and the second special group is called *derivations affixes* (both prefixes and suffixes) (Wysocki & Jenkins, 1987).

TABLE 4.8 Affixes

INFLECTIONAL	DERIVATIONAL

• Plurals: books, cars, wishes
• Possessives: Mike's, Chris's
• Comparative: bigger
• Superlative: biggest
• Verb tense: walks, walked,
  walking, chosen
• Third singular: He runs,
  walks, stops
	• Prefixes: un-, re-, inter-, de-
	• Suffixes: -able, -tion, -al,
	  -ize, -ment

Inflections make nouns plural or possessive; they make adjectives comparative or superlative; they make different tenses and mark subject/verb agreement. What they do not do is radically change the meaning of a word or its grammatical category, because that is the job of the *derivational prefix* or *suffix.*

Read the sentence below and pay careful attention to the word in bold.

The speaker was rebuked for his position on **internationalization.**

In the word *internationalization,* there are five morphemes. One of them is the base word *nation* and the rest are *derivational prefixes* and suffixes. Let's count all of the morphemes in *denationalization.* In addition, watch as the meaning of the word and its grammatical category changes as prefixes and suffixes are added to the word (see Table 4.9).

TABLE 4.9 Applied Structural Analysis

1	2	3	4	5
Prefix	*Base Word*	*Suffix*	*Suffix*	*Suffix*
• inter- • between	• nation • state	• -al • adjective • marker	• -ize • verb • marker	• -ation • noun • marker

The process of counting derivational morphemes and analyzing their meaning in words is called *structural analysis.* In this example, *internationalization* has a number of important derivational affixes in it that radically alter the meaning and grammatical category of the free morpheme, *nation:*

- ■ *nation* to *national* (noun to verb)
- ■ *national* to *nationalize* (adjective to verb)

- *nationalize* to *nationalization* (verb back to noun)
- *nationalization* to *internationalization* (national unity to international unity)

Derivational affixes tend to retain the same meaning across words. The meaning of the prefix re- is stable across a variety of words, including rewrite, reread, rething, and so forth. Some affixes, however, can be **both** inflectional and derivational. The suffix -er in the word bigg**er** is an inflectional suffix because it makes the adjective *big* the comparative adjective *bigger;* however, in the word teach**er**, -er is a derivational suffix because it changes the verb *teach* into a noun meaning "one who teaches."

In summary, derivational affixes are far more powerful than simple inflectional suffixes. Derivations can change a words meaning or its grammatical category, whereas inflections can only make nouns plural or possessive or verbs past or present. Let's turn now to the final kind of bound morpheme: the root word.

Root words are similar to derivational affixes, in that they are all bound morphemes. They cannot stand alone and mean anything. But unlike prefix and suffixes, they *carry the meaning of a word by themselves* and *other letters attach to them to convey meaning* (prefixes and suffixes are like leeches, since they attach themselves to words and alter them *parasitically*). Consider the root word *ann* (from the Latin, meaning "year") and *tele* (from the Greek, meaning "to send").

- **ann-**   **ann**ual, **ann**iversary, **ann**um, **ann**uity
- **tele-**   **tele**vise, **tele**x, **tele**port

In each case, *ann* and *tele* function as root words, because they carry the meaning of the word, even though they are *bound* (derivational affixes are not this powerful; they can *alter* meaning, e.g., *re-televise,* and alter a word's grammatical category, but they do not carry most of a word's meaning like a root word does). In addition, when looking for root words within words, you are actually studying a word's *etymology:* its history, meaning, and origin.

One caution is required when counting both root words and derivational affixes. Some syllables in words may look like either root words or derivational affixes, when they are in fact neither. Consider *chimpanzee.* If we divide *chimpanzee* into syllables: chim / pan / zee, you might be tempted to count the syllable *pan* as the derivational morpheme *pan* (meaning "across"). You would be wrong in doing so, because the syllable within *chimpanzee* does not function as a bound morpheme, since the entire word represents one free morpheme.

Syntax

Syntax describes the grammar of any language. For the test, you need to know the distinction between *descriptive* grammar and *prescriptive* grammar. Descriptive grammar describes a language the way that people use it without judging whether the utterance is correct or incorrect. Descriptive grammarians, for example, are less interested in whether *Who should I say is calling?* or *Whom shall I say is calling?* is the correct form, but are more preoccupied with how one transforms *I shall say who is calling* into the question form. Prescriptive grammarians, however, are concerned with correct usage, and that is why we will review the eight parts of speech, phrases, clauses, and sentences.

Let's learn about descriptive grammar first. Since descriptive grammar will probably amount to only one question on the test, we will not spend a great deal of time on it. Descriptive grammar uses two key terms that you should know for the test: deep structure and surface structure. Surface structures are the sentences that we produce; deep structures are the underlying sentences that we use to make our utterances. Consider the following utterance.

Whom are you addressing?

A wh- question, like the one above, is a surface structure, because it is what one says to ask the question. The utterance has a deep, beginning structure that starts out like this:

You are addressing whom.

This deep structure has an order: subject / verb / object, which looks like this (see Table 4.10).

TABLE 4.10

SUBJECT	VERB	OBJECT
You	are addressing	whom

To arrive at the surface wh- question, one moves through a number of *grammatical transformations.* Watch as the utterance moves from deep to surface structures (see Table 4.11).

TABLE 4.11   Wh- Movement

DEEP STRUCTURE	**You are addressing whom.**
Wh- Movement	**Whom** you are addressing _____.
Inversion	Whom **are you** addressing.
Surface Structure	Whom are you addressing?

This pattern holds across all interrogatives (who, what, where, why, when). The point of this discussion is that descriptive grammar and deep structures appear across languages, and there are some interesting commonalties that hold across languages. For example, there are nouns, verbs, adjectives, and adverbs across languages, so that any idea that can be expressed in one language can also be expressed in another language.

Another important notion is that some deep structures appear to be part of a "universal grammar" because the are found cross-linguistically. The subject / verb / object pattern is one that is found in many languages and may be part of a neurological deep structure that all of us as learners of language arrive on Earth predisposed to use. Consider the an utterance in English and then in Spanish (see Table 4.12).

TABLE 4.12

	SUBJECT	VERB	OBJECT
ENGLISH:	*I*	*have*	*a dog.*
SPANISH:	*Yo*	*tengo*	*un perro.*

Since this subject / verb / object pattern is very stable in English and in other European and Romance languages, it seems to be a reliable deep structure that is shared across many languages.

Since the bulk of your questions about English grammar will be of the prescriptive kind, let's spend some time reviewing traditional grammar, starting with the eight parts of speech.

Recognizing the Eight Parts of Speech.   For the test, you may be asked to identify any number of grammatical terms or to identify the parts of speech within written sentences. Page length will not permit a full review of English grammar, but we will present the major areas that you need to know for the exam. The eight parts of speech are *nouns, pronouns, verbs, adjectives, adverbs, prepositions, conjunctions,* and *interjections.*

Nouns.   Nouns name persons, places, things, ideas, animals, qualities, and sometimes actions that we perform (e.g., **Swimming** is fun). The following are the major terms and examples, associated with nouns; they are ideal candidates for flashcards.

- *Common nouns* name unspecific persons, places, things, ideas, etc. For example, men, cars, and policies are all unspecific, common nouns.
- *Proper nouns* name specific persons, places, things, etc., and are usually capitalized. For example, *Chris Boosalis* is a proper name, so it is capitalized, as is his place of birth (*Minnesota*), ethnicity (*Greek*), and title of the book he is writing (*Beating Them All!*).
- *Concrete nouns* name things that we can see, feel, taste, touch, and/or smell and can be either common or proper. For example, *cars* is a concrete, common noun, but *Colgate*, the brand of toothpaste, is a concrete, proper noun.
- *Abstract nouns* name things that we cannot experience through the five senses. They can also be common or proper. The feeling *love* is a common, concrete noun, but *Einstein's Theory of Relativity* is not only proper but also *very* abstract.
- *Collective nouns* name groups of people or collections of things. For example, *team* refers to a group of people, but *herd* refers to a group of animals.
- *Compound nouns* are made up of two words, like *heating duct, air horn,* or *Batman.*
- *Singular nouns* name individual people, places, or things, and *plural nouns* name more than one noun.

One important note concerns spelling plural nouns. Fortunately, you can just make some noun plural by adding the *inflectional ending* -s to the end of the word, such as *cars, bats, trucks.* Here are more spelling patterns that you should be aware of for the test (just in case):

- Some nouns, however, take -es, if they end in *s, x, z, ch,* or *sh,* like *basses, axes, fezzes, churches, wishes.* This is also true for many words that end in -o, like *potatoes* and *tomatoes;* however, there are enough exceptions to this rule for words that end in -o that you should probably consult a dictionary to be sure on the spelling (*pianos, radios,* etc.).
- Other nouns change their spelling when adding -s. For example, some words that end with a consonant + y add -ies to form the plural (*harmony* → *harmonies*), unless the word ends with a vowel + y (*monkey* → *monkeys*).
- Most nouns that end with the letter *f* simply take -s to form the plural (*tiff* → *tiffs*), though there are exceptions (*wife* → *wives; leaf* → *leaves*).
- Some nouns take *ablaut* forms in the plural, where they change their internal spelling. *Mouse—mice, foot—feet, goose—geese* are examples.
- We preserve the etymology of some words that we spell in English. For example, *thesis* in the plural is *theses, medium* is *media* (like print media), *datum* is *data,* and *analysis* is *analyses.*
- Possessive nouns are formed by adding's or s', depending on whether they describe individual or group ownership. To show that one person has possession of a book, one writes *Chris's book;* however, if there were multiple authors with the first name Chris, then one would write *Chris' book,* since the book belongs to all of the authors named Chris.
- *Gerunds* are verbs with the inflectional affix -ing attached to them. They are used as nouns to describe activities that we like or dislike to perform. For example, ***Thinking*** *is my favorite thing* to do or *I hate **running*** are two example of gerunds functioning as nouns.

Having described nouns and the terms associated with them, let's move now to pronouns, words that are used to replace nouns in sentences.

Pronouns.   Pronouns, like regular nouns, name people, places, things, both concrete and abstract, but they are used to replace nouns to help eliminate redundancy. Consider the following paragraph without pronouns.

Isaac Eziquial Montague Williams worked at the post office. Isaac Eziquial Montague Williams enjoyed working at the post office. Isaac Eziquial Montague Williams retired from at the post office when Isaac Eziquial Montague turned 65.

Pronouns eliminate the need to say nouns over and over again. They are sensitive to the position they occupy in sentences, the number of things they are replacing, and the function they are performing. Pronouns must also have an *antecedent,* the person or thing that defines what the pronoun in a sentence or paragraph means:

Isaac Eziquial Montague Williams worked at the post office, and **he** enjoyed it.

In the sentence above, the pronoun *he* is used to replace the rather lengthy name *Isaac Eziquial Montague Williams.* Thus, the *antecedent Isaac Eziquial Montague Williams* defines who **he** refers to in the example sentence above. Without clear antecedents, sentences can be confusing, as the next sentence is meant to illustrate to you.

The **man** walked the **dog,** and **he** was happy.

Who is happy? The man? The dog? Because he might refer to either potential antecedent, one cannot say for sure. This is also called structural ambiguity, because you cannot immediately tell to whom the pronoun *he* is referring.

Table 4.13 captures the major categories of pronouns that you need to know for the exam, and explanations follow the table.

TABLE 4.13

Pronouns replace nouns and require an antecedent.

ANTECEDENT NUMBER	SUBJECTIVE	OBJECTIVE	POSSESSIVE *Subjective*	*Objective*	REFLEXIVE
Singular	I	me	my	mine	myself
Singular	you	you	your	yours	yourself
Plural	we	us	our	ours	ourselves
Plural	they	them	their	theirs	themselves
Singular	he	him	his	his	himself
	she	her	her	hers	herself
	it	it	its	its	itself

The first column, antecedent number, simply means that you must ensure that your pronouns agree in number with whatever noun they are replacing. For example, singular, first person pronouns include *I, me, my, mine,* and *myself.* Singular, second person pronouns are *you, you, your, yours,* and *yourself.* Plural, first person pronouns (if you're included in a group) include *we, us, our, ours,* and *ourselves.* Plural, third person pronouns (if you're not included in a group) include *they, them, their, theirs,* and *themselves.*

To understand pronouns, you need to understand subjective and objective positions in sentences. When a pronoun acts as the subject of a sentence (the thing performing an action or under description) is uses the subjective case:

- I am here.
- You are here.
- They are here.

Subjective case pronouns must agree with their antecedents both numerically and conceptually. Consider the following absurd sentences:

- The **team** is here, and **he** is happy.
- The **idea** is a good one, so **she** should be carried out immediately.

Each of the sentences above is problematic. In the first sentence, the antecedent and pronoun do not agree in number; and the second sentence simply sounds ridiculous.

If the pronoun receives the action (direct object) or benefits from it (indirect object), its form sometimes changes:

- He called me. (not *I*)
- He called you. (no change)
- He called them. (not *they*)

The same thing happens with possessive pronouns. They change depending on their position in the sentence (see Table 4.14).

TABLE 4.14   Possessive Pronoun Cases

SUBJECTIVE	OBJECTIVE
My book is taking too long to write. **Our** work is hard.	That book is **mine**. That book is **ours**.

Reflexive pronouns direct actions or descriptions back to the subject of the sentence.

- I tend to keep things to myself.
- The dishwasher works by itself.

There are other types of pronouns that you need to know for the test (see Table 4.15).

TABLE 4.15   Other Types of Pronouns

INTERROGATIVE	DEMONSTRATIVE	INDEFINITE	RECIPROCAL
Who/Whose/Whom What Which	this/that these/those	everyone everybody nobody no one	each other one another

Interrogative pronouns usually head sentences that ask questions.

- Who are those people?
- Whose dog is that?
- Whom is she speaking to?
- What are they doing?
- Which one should I buy?

Demonstrative pronouns indicate which person or object is being described and its distance from the speaker:

- That is a nice suit.
- This is a nice suit.

- These are fine shoes
- Those are fine shoes.

That and *this* do have subtle differences. *That is a nice suit* and *This is a nice suit* reflect potential differences in distance: *That* indicates the speakers greater distance from what he or she describes, and *this* indicates a closer proximity. The same idea is true for *these* and *those*. In actual speech, these differences are pretty much arbitrary and moot, since many speakers use them interchangeably.

Indefinite pronouns refer to things and people in a general and collective sense.

- Everyone is here.
- Everybody is here.
- No one is here.
- Nobody is here.

There is virtually no difference between everyone/everybody and no one/nobody.

Reciprocal pronouns refer to actions or descriptions that apply to plural and collective groups of people and things.

- We must love **one another.**
- Be kind to **each other.**

The difference between *one another* and *each other* is very subtle: *One another* seems more general than each other, because *each other* seems to include the speaker and whomever he or she is speaking to in the statement. Once again, the distinction seems pretty arbitrary in actual speech.

Verbs.   Verbs make statements, ask a questions, or give a commands or directions (as shown in Table 4.16).

TABLE 4.16   Verbs

BEING	ACTION	AUXILIARY	TRANSITIVE	INTRANSITIVE	INFINITIVE
is, am, seems, feel	run, walk, stand, feel	has, have, had, be, am, is, are, will	take, make, bring	run, walk, sleep	to be, to run, to walk, to stand

Being and Action Verbs.   The first distinction to make is between *being* and *action* verbs. Being verbs describe or qualify the subject of a sentence:

Chris **is** a 35-year-old male teacher.

In this sentence, no action is taken; instead, Chris, the subject of the sentence, is described in terms of being: age, gender, and profession. Contrast this sentence with the next one that describes action:

Chris **walks** his dog, Krusty, in the morning.

Here, Chris undertakes the act of walking his dog. It is a concrete action. There are also abstract actions, like *Chris* **swears** *to tell the truth, the whole truth, and nothing but the truth.* Note that some verbs can be **both being and action verbs**. Compare the next two sentences:

- Chris **feels** sick.
- Chris **feels** his dog for ticks.

In the first sentence, *feels* functions as a being verb, since one cannot physically touch the adjective following the verb *sick;* the use of *feels* in the second sentence is an action verb because a physical act is taking place (touching the dog to find ticks).

Auxiliary verbs clarify when an action takes place, took place, or will take place. In other words, they tell us present, past, and future, along with really fine shades and degrees of time (the progressive and perfect tenses). We will deal with these tenses in greater detail in a moment. For now, just consider this sentence.

Chris **will** walk his dog in the morning, and Krusty **will** be happy.

In the sentence above, the auxiliary verb *will* tells us that an action will take place in the future (walking the dog), in addition to the resulting, future effect on the dog (happiness).

Transitive and *intransitive verbs* may also appear on the exam. Here is how to identify and describe them. Transitive verbs require an object in order to make sense. A *direct object* is a something that benefits from the action performed in the sentence:

Chris **writes books** in the morning.

In this case, the act of writing produces something, in this case a book. Here, *writes* is a transitive verb because it acts upon something (a direct object), and the sentence makes sense when it is read. Transitive verbs may also take things called *indirect object,* something that benefits from the action being performed:

Chris writes a letter **to Beatriz.**

The act of writing in the sentence above produces a direct object (letter). The beneficiary of the letter is the one who receives the product (Beatriz), making her the indirect object of the action.

We can easily contrast transitive verbs with intransitive verbs. Intransitive verbs need no objects to make sense. Consider each column of sentences in Table 4.17 and ask your self which ones make sense and which ones do not.

TABLE 4.17

A	B
I take.	I run.
I make.	I walk.
I bring.	I sleep.

The statements in column A make no sense to you because the verbs have no objects after them; however, the sentence in column B make perfect sense, since they can stand all by themselves without objects. Please note that *run* and *walk* from column B can also be transitive if you want them to be transitive. Simply add an object to them:

- I run machines for a living.
- I walk my dog in the morning.

Sleep, on the other hand, cannot be transitive because no object will make sense in the object position.

- I sleep sharks.
- I sleep raisins.
- I sleep coconuts.

Table 4.18 shows *infinitive forms of verbs.* You will learn more about infinitive verbs later in the section on phrases. For now, simply understand that infinitives are the *pure, unconjugated* form of the verb.

TABLE 4.18

INFINITIVE FORM	BARE INFINITIVE
To Be	Be
To Walk	Walk
To See	See

Infinitives appear after many verbs, like *need* and *like:*

- I need **to work** today.
- I like **to work** on writing.

Bare infinitives appear after other verbs, like *must* and *shall:*

- I must **work** today.
- I shall **work** today.

We move now from this general discussion of verbs to something more specific: tense.

Verb tenses in English are important to know for the test (just in case), and there are plenty of them. Learn the simple ones first: past, present, and future (see Table 4.19).

TABLE 4.19

	PAST	PRESENT	FUTURE
Regular	I walk.	I walked.	I will walk.
Irregular	I was here.	I am here.	I will be here.

Conjugating present, past, and future tenses of verbs depends, first, on number of persons undertaking the action or being described. Second, conjugation depends on whether the verb is regular or irregular. Space will not permit us to present every conjugation available for regular and irregular verbs, but free lists do exist on the internet. Table 4.20 provides a very brief example of person and regular and irregular conjugations in the present, past, and future tenses.

TABLE 4.20

PRESENT TENSE	REGULAR	IRREGULAR
First Person	I walk.	I am here.
Second Person	You walk.	You are here.
Third Person	He, she, or it walks.	He, she, or it is here.
First Person Plural	We walk.	We are here.
Third Person Plural	They walk.	They are here.

For regular, present tense verbs, only third-person singular varies, since you must add the inflectional suffix -s to properly conjugate it. On the other hand, the irregular verb to be varies wildly according to person (see Table 4.21).

TABLE 4.21

PAST TENSE	REGULAR	IRREGULAR
First Person	I walked.	I was here.
Second Person	You walked.	You were here.
Third Person	He, she, or it walked.	He, she, or it was here.
First Person Plural	We walked.	We were here.
Third Person Plural	They walked.	They were here.

The past tense for regular verbs is accomplished by a simple addition of the inflectional suffix -ed. Once again, the irregular verb *to be* varies depending on the number of persons in question (see Table 4.22).

TABLE 4.22

FUTURE TENSE	REGULAR	IRREGULAR
First Person	I will walk.	I will be here.
Second Person	You will walk.	You will be here.
Third Person	He, she, or it will walk.	He, she, or it will be here.
First Person Plural	We will walk.	We will be here.
Third Person Plural	They will walk.	They will be here.

We represent the future tense in English through the auxiliary verb *will*. For both regular and irregular verbs, one simply adds the auxiliary plus the bare infinitive form of the verb. For example, the sentences above look like this: *will + (to) walk* or *will + (to) be*.

Participles are formed in two ways: by adding -ing or -ed. The -ing form describes the progressive tense (to be described next), and the -ed form makes the past tense.

I am work**ing.**   I have work**ed** here before.

There are irregular forms of past tense participles, too. Consider *wear:*

I **have worn** that suit several times before today.

Both present and past participles can function as adjectives as shown in Table 4.23.

TABLE 4.23

What a **tiring** job it is to write. (*Tiring* describes the job.)	The **worn** dress looks horrible on her. (*Worn* describes the dress.)
This job is **tiring.** (*Tiring* is a predicate adjective.)	That dress is **worn.** (*Worn* is a predicate adjective).

The final type of participle is the perfect participle. It's form is easy to recognize, because it uses *having* and the past participle form of a verb:

- **Having typed** for four hours, my fingers hurt.
- **Having worn** these shoes for two days, my feet hurt.

We will have even more to say about participles when we discuss phrases toward the end of this section on syntax.

Progressive tenses describe actions that began in the past and are either (a) happening now, (b) finished completely, or (c) starting at some point in the future (see Table 4.24).

TABLE 4.24

PRESENT PROGRESSIVE	PAST PROGRESSIVE	FUTURE PROGRESSIVE
I am walking.	I was walking.	I will be walking

The difference between the simple and progressive tenses are subtle but important. To say *I walk* means that you are capable of walking or that is one of your means of transportation. *I am walking,* on the other hand, means that you are now, at this moment, walking.

Perfect tenses describe actions that were completed in the past and may or may not happen again (see Table 4.25).

TABLE 4.25

PRESENT PERFECT	PAST PERFECT	FUTURE PERFECT
I have walked here before (and I'm doing it now).	I had walked there before (but not now/any more).	I will have walked for four hours when I get there.

The perfect tenses, particularly present and past perfect, vary in speech. You will hear many speakers use them interchangeably, saying *I have walked here before* and *I had walked here before* with no distinction in meaning.

The *perfect progressives* are the most complicated of all and describe the past, present, and future (see Table 4.26).

TABLE 4.26

PRESENT PERFECT PROGRESSIVE	PAST PERFECT PROGRESSIVE	FUTURE PERFECT PROGRESSIVE
I have been walking now for four hours.	I had been walking there before (but not now/any more).	I will have been walking for four hours when I get there.

Adjectives.   Adjectives modify or qualify both nouns and pronouns. *Modify* simply means describing nouns in the following terms:

- Color: The **blue** car is here.
- Condition: The **dirty** blue car is here.
- Number: **Three** dirty blue cars are here.
- Comparative: That car is **dirtier** than that one is.
- Superlative: That is the **dirtiest** car I have ever seen.

Note the final two examples, comparative and superlative. Comparative adjectives are formed by adding the inflectional ending -er to the end of the adjective, and superlatives are formed by adding -est. There is an exception to this rule. If the word has more than two syllables, then the adverbs (to be discussed next) *more* and *most* are used instead of the inflectional affixes -er and -ing (see Table 4.27). (*Note:* The incorrect statements are the * items.)

TABLE 4.27

COMPARATIVE WITH MORE	SUPERLATIVE WITH MOST
*The first test was challenginger than the second one. The first test was more challenging than the second one.	*It was the terrificest play I've seen. The was the **most** terrific play I've seen.

When adjectives follow being verbs, they are called predicate nominatives:

- He looks **sick.**
- He seems **tired.**
- She is **joyful.**
- She is **nice.**

Determiners are another type of adjective. *A, the,* and *that* are the most common types of determiners; they tell us whether a noun is specific or nonspecific:

- A car hit a man (nonspecific).
- The car hit the man (more specific)
- That car hit that man (very specific)

Some determiners must agree with the nouns they modify. Your choice of using **a** and **an**, for example, depends on whether the noun that follows it has a vowel sound at the beginning or not.

- a car, a bike, a rock
- an apple, an orange, an omelet

Some words, like *herb,* take *an,* as in *an herb.* The formal pronunciation of the word omits the initial consonant sound, even though British English **does** pronounce *herb* with an /h/ sound at the beginning.

In short, adjectives modify nouns and pronouns; adjectives, the subject of our next discussion, modify everything else.

Adverbs.   Adverbs define, qualify, or limit a verb, adjectives, other adverbs, phrases, clauses, or whole sentences. As you can see from the definition, adverbs do a lot of modifying. Here they are in action:

- Verb: I wrote *quickly.*
- Adjective: I have a *very* small dog.
- Adverbs: I see *very* well.
- Phrases: The book is *right by the door.*
- Clauses: *Since you didn't complete the work,* I cannot pay you.
- Sentences: I like pizza; *however,* the doctor said I can't have it.

Here are the functions they perform in various sentences.

- Location (here, there): The cat runs **here** and **there.**
- Manner (sloppily, neatly): I painted the house **neatly,** but mowed the lawn **sloppily.**
- Degree (very, hardly): I am **very** happy, though I am **hardly** surprised.
- Time (now, later): I want the project finished **now** rather than **later.**
- Negation (not): I'm **not** going there, and I'm **not** coming here.

Prepositions.   Prepositions show relationship between a noun and its object to other words in a sentence. Propositions tell us where things are (*at, above, near, far*). Prepositional phrases tell us when things will happen (*in the morning, at noon*), and describe nouns in greater detail (*in the red car, in the green shirt*). Here are ten common prepositions: *in, on, near, far, before, after, for, to, with, without.*

Prepositions require a noun to have meaning. The noun is called the *object of the preposition,* as in:

- in **the car**
- on **the floor**
- near **my house**

Together, the preposition and its noun are called a *prepositional phrase.* Prepositional phrases can perform the functions of *adverbs* and *adjectives* depending on what they are describing or qualifying (see Table 4.28).

TABLE 4.28

- **Adverbial Prepositional Phrases**
  Turn **to the left.**
  (indicates in which direction one must turn)

- **Adjectival Prepositional Phrases**
  The man **in the blue shirt** is holding a gun.
  (specifies which man among others is holding a gun)

The easiest way to distinguish between types of prepositional phrases is to decide whether the prepositional phrase is modifying or qualifying a noun or a verb. If it modifies a noun, then it is adjectival; however, if it modifies a verb, then it is adverbial.

The preposition *to* is a special case. In English, *to* can be a preposition or it can act as an *infinitive marker.* Here is how to tell the difference:

A. I went **to** the store.
B. I like **to** dance.

In sentence A, *to* is a preposition. You know this is true, because of the noun phrase *the store* that is the object of the preposition. In sentence B, on the other hand, *to* is an infinitive marker, since like takes infinitive phrases and because *to* is attached to a verb (dance).

Conjunctions. Conjunctions link words, phrases, or clauses together.

Conjunctions connect small things like words together and may also join larger pieces of sentences together, including phrases or clauses. There are three types of conjunctions that you should know for the test (see Table 4.29).

TABLE 4.29   Common Conjunctions

COORDINATING	CORRELATING	SUBORDINATING
and, but, nor, for, or	either/or both/and neither/nor	when since because

Coordinating conjunctions balance words, phrases, or clauses together:

- Words: *Chris **and** Mike are here.*
- Phrases: Chris and Mike ran *in the park **and** in the field.*
- Clauses: *Chris and Mike ran in the park,* **and** *they swam in the lake.*

Each of the sentences above uses a conjunction to join words, phrases, and clauses together. Your selection of the correct conjunctions depends on what you're trying to express:

- Balance: Chris **and** Mike
- Choice: Chris **or** Mike
- Exclusion: Not Chris **but** Mike

Correlating conjunctions show positive or negative relationships between words, phrases, or clauses.

- Words: **Either** Chris **or** Mike will do the work.
             Neither Chris **nor** Mike will do the work.
- Phrases: **Neither** working at the store **nor** saving all my coupons helps.

Correlating conjunctions require parallelism. *Parallelism* simply means that whatever words or phrases or clauses that the conjunctions are correlating must be in the same form.

- Not Parallel: Swimming and to run are my favorite activities. (incorrect)
- Parallel: Swimming and running are my favorite activities. (correct)

Subordinate conjunctions, like *when, since,* and *because,* show orders and contingencies, where one thing or idea depends upon some other, superior idea. *Subordinate conjunctions* are easy to identify: although they look like independent sentences, they make no sense if they are by themselves. The subordinate clauses are in bold; the independent clauses (the ones that can stand alone) are italicized.

- **When I get home,** *I will eat.*
- **Since you didn't come to work,** *you going to be fired.*
- **Because you didn't come to work,** *you're fired.*

In sum, conjunctions exist to link words, phrases, and clauses together in a coherent way. Let's turn now to the shortest part of speech that we have: the interaction.

Interjections.   Interjections show emotion (surprise, awe, disappointment, excitement, etc.).

Interjections capture emotion—*any* emotion. They are short and use a comma if the expression is matter-of-fact or an exclamation point if the expression is emphatic.

- Pain: **Ouch!**
- Joy: **Yea!**
- Interruption: **Oh,** pardon me.

To this point, you have reviewed the eight parts of speech: nouns, pronouns, verbs, adjective, adverbs, prepositions, conjunctions, and interjections. You will now learn about how these words become organized into *phrases, clauses,* and finally, *whole sentences.*

Phrases.   Phrases are groups of words that do not stand as sentences by themselves. We can describe phrases in terms of their simplicity or complexity. *Simple phrases* are called noun phrases, verb phrases, and prepositional phrases (see Table 4.30).

TABLE 4.30   Simple Phrases

NOUN PHRASES	PREPOSITIONAL PHRASES	VERB PHRASES
The man in *the blue hat* . . .	The man *in the blue hat.*	I *ran very, very, very quickly to the store.*

There are two *noun phrases* in the example. The first noun phrase is *the man* and the second one is found in the prepositional phrase *in the blue hat*. In brief, noun phrases contain the *central noun* and all of the articles (*the*), adjectives (*blue*) used to describe it. Look at the prepositional phrase now. The phrase *in the blue hat* is *adjectival* because it describes the noun *the man*. Verb phrases, like noun phrases, contain the verb and all of the adverbs and prepositional phrases used to describe it. The verb phrase *ran very, very, very, quickly* describes not only what action took place (*ran*) but also how the action was carried out (*very, very, very quickly*) and in which direction (*to the store*). Direction is conveyed through an adverbial prepositional phrase, because it describes the action further.

A Note on Noun Phrases. Noun phrases perform many, many functions. We have already seen how they can be objects of prepositions (**in** *the blue hat* and **to** *the store*), but there are a few more ways that they can exist in sentences (see Table 4.31).

TABLE 4.31   Noun Phrases

SUBJECTS	*The man who is standing right here* wrote the book.	The entire noun phrase, including the words that describe where the man is standing, is the subject.
PREDICATE NOMINATIVE	Bob is *the man who is standing right here.*	The noun phrase in italics is predicate nominative that functions as descriptor that further qualifies the subject, *Bob*.
DIRECT OBJECTS	I brought *a really delicious pumpkin pie.*	The noun phrase is part of the predicate and is a direct object that tells us what I brought.
INDIRECT OBJECTS	I brought a really delicious pumpkin pie to *my sick friend.*	The noun phrase, my sick friend, is the object of the preposition (*to*). The prepositional phrase functions as an indirect object telling us to whom I brought the pumpkin pie.

The other variety of phrases are more complex and perform a variety of functions as shown in Table 4.32.

TABLE 4.32   Complex Phrases

PARTICIPIAL PHRASES	GERUND PHRASES	INFINITIVE PHRASES	APPOSITIVE PHRASES
The man **wearing the blue suit**	Running in the morning with my wife . . .	To run in the morning . . .	The teacher, **Mr. Johnson,** is here.

Participles are the progressive and past tense forms of verbs. As you learned earlier, they are formed using the inflectional affix -ing (if it is progressive) and -ed if it is past tense (unless it is an irregular verb). We discussed how participles function as adjectives (*the* **driving** *rain*) and as a predicate nominative (*The day was* **tiring**). Participles can also function as whole phrases that function as adjectives to further describe nouns.

- The man **wearing the blue suit** is mysterious.
  (The present participle further describes the man.)
- **Agitated by her coworker's lack of work,** she considered alternatives.
  (The participial phrase in above further describe Chris's state of mind.)

One additional example of a participial phrase is the perfect form. You can spot them immediately, because they begin with *having:*

Having thought about your plan, I have decided against it.

This perfect participial phrase further describes the subject's state of mind.

Gerunds are the *-ing* forms of nouns. They function as subjects and convey a sense of action at the same time. The sentence *Running is my favorite activity* shows how gerunds can function as subjects. You may be asked to tell the difference between a gerund phrase and a participial phrase. To do so, ask yourself if the -ing form of the verb functions as a noun or as an adjective. If it is a noun, then it is a gerund; if it is an adjective, then it is a participle:

- *Running in the morning with my wife and small dog* is the best part of my day.
  (The gerund phrase acts as a complete subject of the sentence above).
- *Running out of control,* the robot became dangerous.
  (The participial phrase describes the robot more adjectivally).

Infinitive phrases are marked with *to + verb,* as in *To run in the morning is fun.* Infinitive phrases act as parts of speech (nouns, adjectives, and adverbs) as sentence subjects, objects, predicate nominatives, and adverbial/adjectival modifies. They come in two varieties: present and perfect. Here they are in action (see Table 4.33 and 4.34). Perfect infinitives are more nebulous; they describe things that took place before the action in the sentence.

TABLE 4.33   Present Infinitives

- *To run in the morning* is fun. (subject)
- I like *to run in the morning.* (direct object)
- My goal is *to create life in this jar.* (predicate nominative—it follows a being verb)
- The worst way *to do* things is the hard way. (adjective describing *things*)
- I was happy *to see* you. (adverb qualifying the adjective *happy*)

TABLE 4.34   Perfect Infinitives

A. I appear *to need a different brain for this task.*
B. I am sorry *to have forgotten my pants.*

If you are asked to identify perfect infinitives, just ask yourself if the infinitive phrase describes an action happening prior to whatever is being described in the sentence. For example, sentence A describes the need for a past condition to complete a present task; sentence B describes a past act of forgetting that now affects a present situation (rather painfully).

Appositive phrases are the final type we will describe before moving on to clauses. Appositives are easy to identify because they are offset with commas and function as adjectives to further describe nouns:

- The teacher, *Mr. Dobbs,* is here.
- The car, *a brand new Toyota Solara,* is what I want for my birthday.

Sentence Clauses.   Sentence clauses are much larger than phrases. They have a subject and verb and because of these features they can be mistaken for sentences. Clauses can either stand independently or be dependent upon other clauses in the sentence. Another type of clause, the relative clause, is termed restricted or nonrestricted depending on whether the information it adds to the sentence is essential or nonessential to the meaning of the sentence. Let's look at each type of clause next.

Independent Clauses.   This is part of a sentence that can stand all by itself and has a subject, verb, and maybe an object or predicate nominative. You can identify an independent clause because it makes sense all by itself. You will see an example of and independent clause when we discuss dependent clauses.

Dependent Clauses.   This part of a sentence cannot stand all by itself, even though it has a subject, verb, and maybe an object or predicate nominative. You can identify a dependent clause because it does not make sense all by itself; instead, it must be clarified through another, independent class. They are introduced by a subordinating conjunction, such as *because, when, if, since, when,* and *so.*

The following are examples of independent and dependent clauses. Their order here is arbitrary. (*Note:* The dependent clause is in **bold.**)

- I could not work today, **because I was sick.**
- **Because I was sick,** I could not work today.

In each of the examples above, the dependent clause cannot stand by itself. It makes no sense to say: *Because I was sick* (period). This would result in a sentence fragment. You may be asked to identify problems in writing, and this is certainly one of them. Just read the data and look for any incomplete-sounding ideas. When you find them, they will probably be due to a lonely dependent clause that lacks an independent clause for meaning.

Relative Clauses.   These clauses provide more information about nouns and use *that, which, who,* and *whom.* Like dependent clauses, relative clauses cannot stand alone. (*Note:* The relative clauses are in bold.)

- The man **that I know from school** is here.
- The man **whom I know from school** is here.

Note that the difference between a subordinate clause and a relative clause is the word used to introduce it (subordinating conjunctions introduce dependent clauses, and words like *that* and *who* introduce relative clauses.

You may also be asked about restricted and nonrestricted relative clauses. If the clause is restricted, then you offset the clause with commas; if it is nonrestricted, then you do not use commas. Restricted simply means that the information is essential to one's understanding of the sentence.

Restricted Clauses: The girl who came in first won the race.
Nonrestricted Clauses: The boy, who is next to Bob, won the race.

The relative clause *who came in first* is essential information in the restricted clause example above. No commas are used to offset the information because it is essential to the meaning of the sentence. The relative clause *who is next to Bob* in the nonrestricted example is offset with commas, because it is incidental information. In both cases, the relative clauses simply add more information about the nouns to which they are attached, yet their degree of purpose affects whether they are treated as being restricting or nonrestricting in their function.

Sentence Types.   There are four of types of sentences to recognize for the exam: simple sentences, compound sentences, complex sentences, and compound-complex sentences. (In Table 4.35, subjects and main clauses are underlined once; predicates and subordinate clauses are underlined twice.)

Please keep in mind that some sentences have only compound subjects or predicates, which does **not** make them compound sentences.

- **Chris and Mike** are here. (compound subject)
- Chris and Mike **ran and jumped.** (compound predicate)

TABLE 4.35

SENTENCE TYPE	EXAMPLE
Simple sentences: One Subject + One Predicate	Simple sentences are straightforward.
Compound sentences: Two Main Clauses	One sentence contains a subject and verb, and the second sentence contains another subject and verb.
Complex sentences: Subordinate Clause + Main Clause	If the sentence has a main clause and a subordinate clause, it is complex.
Compound-complex sentences: Two or More Main Clauses and a Subordinate Clause	If the sentence has two main clauses and a subordinate clause, it is compound and it is complex.

Kernel Sentences.   There are five major categories of kernel sentences to know for the exam. Thy include declaratives, interrogatives, exclamatory, conditionals, and imperatives (see Table 4.36).

TABLE 4.36   Kernal Sentences

Declarative	Today is a very nice day.
Interrogative	Where are you going? Do you need a ride?
Exclamatory	You're late again!
Conditional	If you don't work hard, you won't finish.
Imperative	(You) Shut up.

Each of the examples should be obvious to you. Declarative sentences make simple statements of fact, and interrogatives pose questions using a wh- or *do* form. Exclamatory sentences make emphatic observations or statements and use an exclamation point. Conditionals pose contingencies that will either be satisfied or not satisfied. Finally, imperatives make commands and use the understood you for the subject.

Semantics

Language is arbitrary. Why do we call a frog a frog and a rose a rose? There is no reason beyond our mutual agreement that *that is what we are going to call those things.* Semantics is the study of these assigned labels that we attach to everything in the English language and how we assign meaning to things (Kemporson, 1977). The areas of semantics to know for the exam include denotation, connotation, structural meanings, etymology, and the effect of context. Each area is discussed below.

Denotative meanings of words are their dictionary definitions. Consider the denotative meaning of the word *cool.* The literal meaning of this word that one might encounter in any dictionary is "below room or body temperature." The *connotative* meanings associated with *cool* are beyond this narrow definition:

- He is very *cool.*   (hip)
- She is *cool* to the idea.   (feels negative)
- The officer *cooled* the thief.   (knocked unconscious)

Connotative meanings are all of the assigned meanings of the word that move beyond the literal definition of the word. Many words in English acquire these other meanings through use.

Meaning is built into many words through their internal structures. You learned about his earlier when we discussed morphology and how derivational affixes and root words contribute to a words meaning. Certain derivational prefixes can drastically change the meaning of a word. Recall the base word *nationalization*. Its meaning will change depending on the prefix we assign to it.

Denationalization
Internationalization

The additions of *de-* and *inter-* to *nationalization* radically alter the meaning of this base word. Prefixes do not have to alter the meaning so drastically though. Some prefixes offer very subtle changes to a word's meaning:

- It was so dark that his features were *undistinguishable.*
- Janet is *indistinguishable* from her twin Christine.

The prefixes *un-* and *in-* provide very subtle distinctions for how we use *distinguish* in certain sentences. Please note that this discussion does not mean that we can attach prefixes and suffices to words any way that we want, because some constructions are quite *unpossible,* like:

inspectabulatious
preremarkablinglouser

Structural analysis is used to teach children vocabulary using prefixes, suffixes, roots, and base words. Table 4.37 shows an example of the process of structural word analysis applied to the word *antidisestablishmentarianism.*

TABLE 4.37

PREFIX	PREFIX	BASE WORD	SUFFIX	SUFFIX	SUFFIX
anti-	*dis-*	*establish*	*-ment*	*-arian*	*-ism*
Opposed to	*the removal of*	*the state*		*believers of*	*a philosophical position*

Word Types. You may also be asked about four different kinds of words, including homophones, homographs, synonyms, and antonyms (see Table 4.38).

TABLE 4.38

Homophones	site, cite, sight
Homographs	subjéct and súbject
Synonyms	happy, joyful, merry
Antonyms	happy vs. sad; calm vs. stressed

Homophones are words that sound the same but their spellings indicate the differences in their meaning and how they are used in sentences. Homographs are words that are *orthographically* (e.g., written) the same way but are pronounced differently. The examples reflect two sets of words whose meanings change, depending on whether the medial vowel is long or short (*lead* vs. *lead*) or whether the stress is placed on the first syllable or the second (*subjéct* and *súbject*). Synonyms and antonyms are words that are related to one another either by meaning roughly the same thing or having meanings that are in opposition to one another.

Many synonyms, like *sloppy, messy, dirty, disorganized, disarrayed,* and *disheveled,* can be analyzed for their fine shades of meaning. Table 4.39 shows an analysis of semantic features, a common classroom activity for vocabulary.

TABLE 4.39   Semantic Features Analysis

	DISORGANIZED	DISARRAYED	DISHEVELED
• Characterizes a person's behavior	X		
• Characterizes a person's appearance			X
• Characterizes the order of objects	X	X	
• Describes the condition of a location			

Context plays a role in which words we select for reading. This is especially true of homographs. Consider the following:

- He **leads** a group of scouts through the forest.
- He needs a number two **lead** pencil for the test.

Context determines whether you read lead with a long or short vowel. When *lead* is a verb, the vowel sound is long; when it is a noun or adjective, it is short. The same is true for homographs that involve stress shift:

- Give me a **minute** while I think of the answer.
- I looked at a very **minute** sample under the microscope.

Context determines whether the stress is on the first or second syllable: on the first syllable, *minute* means "a moment in time" while on the second syllable, it means "very small."

In multiple-meaning words, context also tells you how to interpret the word either denotatively or connotatively:

- He **hammered** the nail into the board.
- He got really **hammered** last night.

Clearly, the meanings of the word *hammer* in each of the sentences above are different, and that difference is determined by sentence context.

Pragmatics

Pragmatics is the study of language use in social situations (Levinson, 1983). Linguistics look at use at the micro and macro levels. At the micro level, one looks at speech acts, styles, and registers. At the macro level, linguists analyze discourse (conversation) within social contexts (language used in the classroom, at the bank, etc.). The registration bulletins for all of the exams list only a few descriptors for this area of linguistics, so we will only present the major areas for you. Let's look at speech acts first.

Speech acts include requests, commands, statements, and any other functional kind of utterance that you can think of. Linguists discuss all utterances in three ways: illocution, locution, and percolation. Illocution is the kind of speech the utterance happens to be (a command, warning, refusal, apology). Locution refers to the surface meaning of the utterance. Percolation is the underlying effect of the utterance. Table 4.40 shows these levels applied to an example utterance.

TABLE 4.40

If you don't stop following me, I'll call the police.

- Illocution: Warning.
- Locution: Leave me alone.
- Percolation: There will be trouble if my condition isn't met.

Speech acts get much of their illocutionary, locutionary, and percolationary effect from the phonology, morphology, and semantics we select when speaking. This is because we vary our styles when we communicate, particularly in the level of informality or formality (Cohen, 1996). Consider these examples In Table 4.41 at face value.

TABLE 4.41

Gimmie the pencil!	*Would you please lend me a pencil?*
• Illocution: Command.	• Illocution: Request.
• Locution: I need a pencil.	• Locution: I need a pencil.
• Percolation: Hurry up!	• Percolation: Formal, polite request.

Although both of these utterances have the same locution (*I need a pencil*), they accomplish the goal of satisfying the locution differently. *Gimmie a pencil* is a command with the effect of hurrying the holder-of-the-pencil up. It is also *informal,* because the phonology and syntax are reduced ("give me" becomes "gimmie"), and it is said as an imperative (exclamatory) sentence. Conversely, the second sentence, *Would you please lend me a pencil?* is a *formal* request. The phonology is not reduced and and grammatical correct forms are used ("Would you . . ." and "lend"). The entire request is modified by *please,* marking it as a polite request.

Informal and formal styles are part of registers (Joos, 1967). Registers are appropriate speech styles that we use in different social situations and vary depending on formality. We vary our phonology, morphology, syntax, and semantics depending on whom we are speaking with and in what situation. There are four registers to consider:

- Intimate: Couples' speech (**baby cakes, lover, sweetie pie**)
- Casual: Speaking among friends and family. (**Gimmie the pencil.**)
- Formal: Speaking among coworkers, employers, etc. (**Would you please** . . .)
- Frozen: Languages used on signs and in ceremonies. (**Dearly beloved** . . .)

These registers affect the choices we make when speaking. For example, the way that we speak to an intimate partner is probably different from the way that we might address a principal or school administrator. Look at the utterances in Table 4.42 and consider how the utterances vary linguistically.

TABLE 4.42

	PHONOLOGY	**MORPHOLOGY**	**SYNTAX**	**SEMANTICS**
Casual	I like runnin'.	It ain't unpossible.	She goin' home.	He fly an' phat.
Formal	I like to run.	It is impossible.	She went home.	He is quite acculturated and rather attractive.

The casual and formal registers affect all of the elements of linguistics. Casual speech permits phonological reductions (*to run* becomes *runnin*), questionable morphology (*impossible* becomes *unpossible*), grammatical reductions (*she went* becomes *she goin'*); and casual semantic lingo (using *fly* and *phat*). These casual speech characteristics are not found (usually) in formal speech styles.

Each of these speech acts, registers, and styles vary according to *genre*. Genres are social situations that require particular speech acts, registers, and styles (Halliday, 1978). Table 4.43 below shows a familiar genre and offers some comparisons of the register and vocabulary found therein.

TABLE 4.43

GENRE	AT A SHOWER	AT A FUNERAL	AT BURGERWORLD	AT AN INTERVIEW
REGISTER	*Casual*	*Formal*	*Casual*	*Formal*
VOCABULARY	All things baby (first steps, remembrances)	dearly departed; this great man/woman/cat	burger, fries, coke	experience, abilities, salary
SPEECH ACTS	Declarations and Expressions	Declarations and Expressions	Requests and Refusals	Requests and Explanations

Each genre uses different styles, registers, and speech acts, not to mention vocabulary. If we are native speakers of English, then we probably have expectations for each of these areas. Our knowledge of the appropriate use of language in a variety of social genres is called *communicative competence*. As defined by Hymes (1972), communicative competence is something that we acquire through experience (e.g., the language of the home, workplace, school, etc.). Using the wrong register, style, or speech act during a formal job interview (calling the interviewer *sweetie*) can reveal one's communicative *incompetence*. Communicative competence and knowledge of social genres will be more of an issue when you learn about the needs of English Language Learners in content area two.

Sociolinguistics

Sociolinguistics is the study of register and genre variation within a culture and between cultures (Fasold, 1984; 1990). Intraculturally speaking, consider the language that brain surgeons use when betting on a putt at the local golf course versus the language that they use when separating conjoined twins in the operating room. Clearly, the registers will vary sociolingustically, given the linguistic demands that these activities present: registers, styles, and speech acts will be very different indeed.

In the *inter*cultural sense, we can look at sociolinguistic differences across cultures (Barnlund, 1989). Doing business in Japan versus in the United States is an frequently cited example of the differences in styles between two cultures, especially in the way that refusals are conveyed. In the United States, the phrase *We'll think about it* might actually mean just that: *We will consider the offer and get back to you on it*. For the Japanese, this phrase usually is a flat and firm refusal. Cross-cultural communications are very important, given the different ways that speech acts can be carried out in different cultures.

Face is another sociolinguistic consideration. Some cultures value harmony to a great degree, such that ensuring that members do not lose face (i.e., become publicly shamed) is highly valued. *Top of the World* (Ruesh, 1991), a novel about Inuit Alaskans, has confrontations phrased in a like manner:

> *Someone* had better stop talking or *someone else* is going to hurt them.

For the tribe described in the novel, using the third person when confronting another person allows for a high degree of face-saving, since threats are spoken indirectly.

For the test, you will need to be aware of several other aspects of sociolinguistics, including linguistic relativity, idiolects, issoglosses, sociolects, and dialects. These areas will probably constitute only one or two questions on the exam, therefore, you will only learn about the most important aspects of this area.

Linguistic relativity asks the question, *Does one's language limit or broaden their experience of life?* The Sapir–Whorf hypothesis would answer the question in the affirmative. Certain Inuit tribes in Alaska and Canada have a couple hundred words for snow. There is snow that is good for hunting, snow that is good for building, and snow that can kill you. I grew up in a part of Minnesota where there is just as much snow as one finds in Alaska, but I can only come up with about five words for snow (besides snow): sleet, slush, powder, fluff, and *sparkly.* Sapir–Whorf would argue that my experience with a snowy world is limited and that the Inuits have a much broader and therefore "better" appreciation of their word because of their extensive linguistic repertoire.

This example seems innocuous, but it isn't. Bernstein (1964) had a similar idea about linguistic relativity. He looked at elaborated and restricted codes among the social classes in England. Elaborated codes are the varieties of English spoken among the educated upper class members, and the restricted codes are the varieties of English spoken by the lower class members. He reasoned that speakers of the restricted code must have restricted thoughts, given their restricted and limited language, and speakers of the elaborated code have much broader and deeper thoughts due to their higher variety of language.

The counterargument to Sapir–Whorf and Bernstein is descriptive linguistics (rather than relative linguistics). Here, any language variety can express any thought that the human mind can conjure up. Although one's vocabulary may be limited, it can grow and expand through experience and understanding. Therefore, all language varieties are equal; only our perceptions of language varieties vary (sometimes unfairly).

These considerations bring us to other sociolinguistic considerations about the language of individual speakers (idiolects), social groups (sociolects), and regional varieties of English (issoglosses and dialects).

Idiolects characterize the language that we, as individual speakers, use when speaking. All of us have our own verbal ticks (saying, "uh-huh" or repeating phrases) and our own way of expressing ourselves. For example, I had a friend who said, "on the thing" all the time as filler speech. "On that thing, I'm going to get on that thing just as soon as I'm done getting on this thing." That is an example of an idiolect.

Sociolects characterize the language used by subcultures, ethnic enclaves, social classes, and speech communities. Teens use language in interesting ways that can be described as a sociolect. Peer groups exert a great influence on many children's speech patterns, and "teen talk" has its own terminology that separates it from the adult world. The most recent additions include *phat, bling-bling,* and *shnizle. Can* is also becoming an adjective, as in *That's so can!* Teen sociolects can be further reduced into different social groups. The language that athletes use may not be the same as what one hears in other social groups. Consider the following terms:

- Spange (spare change), squat (temporary home) used by homeless teens.
- Sketchy (unstable), grind (skateboard move) used by the "skater" crowd.
- Freds/Wilmas and Barneys/Bettys (unattractive and attractive people) used by the "popular" kids.

Note too that sociolects are highly volatile and that phrases can be "in" one day and "out" another. "Valley talk" that was popular in the 1980s is seldom heard nowadays, unless one is speaking "nostalgically." Phrases like *Gag me with a spoon* seem to have gone the way of *far out, wowie zowie,* and *twenty-three skidoo* before it. "Teen talk" has an ever-changing quality about it that seems to change the moment that "too many outsiders" catch on to it.

Sociolects vary greatly and mark individuals based on the language that they use. Ethnic enclaves can develop their own sociolects, too. Studies of African American communities note that the auxiliary *be* has acquired a new tense for some speakers of this sociolect. *I be scared sometimes* is used systematically to express temporality, and the feature is particular to speakers of this variety of English (not necessarily African Americans).

Social classes also speak sociolects. The most famous study of this phenomena is by Labov (1972). He looked at the way that different social classes use English in social settings and the attendant class effect. Informal speech involves phonological reductions (as you now know). Sometimes, when we say *running* casually, we say *runnin'*. That reduction happens because casual speech is usually rapid speech, and we must reduce the language to speak quickly. Lobov looked at another reduction: dropping the sound *r* at the ends of syllables in the way that a phrase like *fourth floor* would be spoken as *foath floah* (a common reduction in New York English). He found that upper class speakers would say *foath floah* in casual speech but not in formal speech; *however,* members of the lower class would say *foath floah* both in casual speech and in formal speech. This indicated that the most formal speech of the lower classes is the casual speech of the upper classes. Although one variety might not be better than the other, some people may look upon us with derision based solely upon the sociolect that we speak.

Jargon is another variable of one's sociolect. The terminology that medical professionals use is different from what auto repair technicians use (see Table 4.44).

TABLE 4.44

MEDICAL PROFESSIONALS	AUTO MECHANICS
Scalpel	Cross Point
Stethoscope	Allen Key
Sphygmomanometer	Impact Wrench

Work place terminology is important because it reveals who is an insider and who is an outsider. For example, hearing your doctor say, "Hand me the pointy thing," during your next operation might not inspire much hope for your survival. Language and our perception of another person's competence seem to go hand-in-hand.

Issoglosses and *dialects* are above the level of the sociolect. An issogloss is a variation of English that differs between cities or closely connect areas (state borders), whereas dialects are regional variations, like the difference between Midwestern and Eastern English and Northern and Southern English. There are identifiable differences in phonology, morphology, syntax, and semantics.

In Minnesota, there is an issogloss that exists in the phonology of natives of Minneapolis and the natives of St. Paul. It can be heard in the short vowels of certain words (see Table 4.45).

Issoglosses can also mark a person as being from one state or another. This is true for certain words that are particular to Minnesota but not heard in the adjoining state of Wisconsin. The variation is not so much phonological but semantic, as the words for certain nouns are different (see Table 4.46).

TABLE 4.45

MINNEAPOLIS	ST. PAUL
Irish /irish/	/ireesh/
Plaza /plaza/	/PLA-za/

TABLE 4.46

	MINNESOTA	WISCONSIN
Water Fountain	Drinking Fountain	Bubbler
Soft Drink	Pop	Soda
Tuna Casserole	Hot Dish	Tuna Casserole
Rubber Band	Rubber Binder	Rubber Band

Dialect differences are much broader than issoglosses. They often involve differences in syntax and semantics, but the differences are most apparent in phonology. Consider this example of Midwestern, Southern, and Eastern pronunciations of these words (see Table 4.47).

TABLE 4.47

	MIDWEST	SOUTH	EAST
car	car	cawer	ca
bar	bar	bawer	ba

Southern speech tends to lengthen vowels. The phrase *My dog died* might sound like "Mah dawg diahed" because of this phenomenon. Similarly, some speakers in the eastern states tend to drop the /r/ from spoken words, giving their speech patterns a very distinctive and identifiable sound quality.

Dialect differences a can also appear in syntax and semantics. Some Southern English speakers use "might" as a "double auxiliary":

■ I might could come tomorrow.
■ I might could do it.

In the Midwest, one hears *you guys* in casual speech quite frequently, and in Texas *y'all* (perhaps singular) and *all y'all* (perhaps plural) is the common casual form; these differences also mark one as being from one part of the United States or another.

Generation Change. In immigrant communities, there are often generational changes that results in a phenomenon called *hypercorrection.* When immigrants arrive to the United States, they bring their native phonologies with them. When they learn English, they often have an accent because their first language lacks features found in English. In sections of New Jersey, many immigrant groups lacked the sound /er/ in their first language, resulting in their pronouncing *girl* as /goil/. Their children, who learned English as a first language, noticed something was wrong with this pronunciation and dropped /goil/ from their vocabulary using the common form /gerl/ instead. But the second generation did something very interesting: They *hypercorrect* their parents' misuse of the /oi/ sound. This resulted in the second generation pronouncing **anything** with /oi/ in it as /er/ (see Table 4.48).

TABLE 4.48

GENERATION ONE		GENERATION TWO	
Girl	/goil/	Girl	/gerel/
		Oil	/erl/
		Toilet	/terlet/

Generation language change does not have to be due to the hypercorrection of an error. Notice how the auxiliary *shall* has all but disappeared from our language. If you listen carefully to the speech of the elderly, you may hear them using *shall* far more frequently than younger people do. In a generation, *shall* just might disappear altogether from English, in the same way that *thou* (the formal you) most certainly has. It seems that the most formal aspects of the language tend to be lost from the language, and the casual speech of yesterday becomes the formal speech of tomorrow.

Historical Change. English, as we speak it today, did not begin like this. It has had three major periods: old, middle, and modern. The transition from old English to middle English is marked by the Norman Conquest of 1066. During this period, the great vowel shift occurred, where many long vowel sounds became short, and short vowels became long. This shift affected not only the way that words sounded, but also the syntactic forms of them. The original word for *mouse* and its plural form lend an example.

Before the vowel shift, the singular for mouse was *mussi* and the plural form was *mussen.* After the vowel shift, the singular form became *mouse,* and the plural form went from *mussen* to *mice.* The same thing happened with *goose* and *geese.* Other shifts occurred and affected the way that we spell words today (see Table 4.49).

TABLE 4.49

	OLD ENGLISH	**MIDDLE ENGLISH**	**MODERN ENGLISH**
Name	/nama/	*/name/*	*/nAm/*

The old English pronunciation of *name* was a two-syllable word, /nama/. After the shift, it was still a two-syllable word, but with a different vowel in the second syllable: /name/. In the modern English period, it became the word that we say today: /nAm/ with the long vowel. The problem with this word occurred when we first began writing English. In the late 1500s, Mulcaster and Coote decided to regularize English spelling and published a book on spelling rules. They decided that long vowels for certain words would be marked by adding a *silent e* to the end of them: *name* and *like* are examples, because they could be spelled in a variety of ways (nayme, naim, etc.) before the *silent e* rule. This rule was applied across many words with odd-sounding vowels, resulting in the exceptions that we have today: *love, have,* and *done.*

CONTENT AREA TWO: FIRST AND SECOND LANGUAGE ACQUISITION

Here you will learn about first and second language acquisition in terms of phonology, morphology, syntax, semantics, and pragmatics. There are a few terms that are common to both first and second language acquisition, but others belong to second language acquisition only. Let's look at the commonalties first.

Common First and Second Language Terms and Concepts

■ *The Critical Period.* One important universal is the notion of the critical period for acquiring a first language (Lenneberg, 1967). Some researchers of first language and second language acquisition hypothesize that children who learn their first languages after (maybe) 3 years of age will miss an important window of opportunity to learn their language. Animal studies of song birds suggest this idea: When young birds are kept from learning songs after a particular age, they are then unable to acquire them. Since we cannot ethically isolate a child from learning his or her language until age 10 to see if the same idea is true, we can only assume that there might be a critical period for learning a first language.

Occasionally, examples from horrible life circumstances do arise. Two famous cases exist (Curtis, 1977). The first is from France, where a child was discovered living in the wilderness who presumably had no interaction with language from the time he was lost until the time he was found. Since he learned French after age 5, the quality of his language acquisition was rather poor. In the United States, a preadolescent child named Genie (a pseudonym) was discovered living in absolute isolation in a room of a house. Her family never interacted with her verbally (hardly emotionally either) and she had no spoken language. The quality of her language, especially her phonology and syntax, was very poor. In fact, she sounded as if she were a hearing-impaired person when speaking English, even though her hearing was not damaged. Both of these cases show that there may be a critical window for learning English as a first language, in spite of the fact that we may never know if the French child or Genie herself experienced brain damage that subsequently affected their language development.

The critical period may also affect second-language acquisition (Asher & Garcia, 1969). The onset of puberty may account for the difficulty non-native speakers have in losing their accents. Because the brain lateralizes (assigns specific areas of the brain to perform particular functions) it may not store the second language in quite the same way. In addition, the phonology for one's first language may be fixed, and that will also play a role in how one sounds when speaking the new language.

■ *Developmental Stages.* Some aspects of first and second language acquisition are subject to nearly identical developmental stages (Pfaff, 1987). For example, learning *wh- questions,* like *Where is Chris going?,* happens in a particular order by both children learning English as a first language and adolescents and adults learning English as a second language. These shared stages are thought to indicate that there is a psycholinguistic aspect to language acquisition (e.g., it is **not** a matter of simply memorizing the correct forms).

■ *Developmental Orders.* Like developmental stages, certain aspects of first and second language acquisition occur in an order. Consider how the morpheme /s/ is acquired: The plurals (cars) occur before the possessives (*Chris's*), and the third singular -s (*runs*) is acquired last. Again, this fact lends credence to the shared psycholinguistic aspects of first and second language acquisition (Larsen-Freeman, 1976).

■ *Hypothesis Testing.* First and second language learners test out their current level of language acquisition against reality (Bley-Vroman, 1986). For example, when a child says *goed* to form the past tense of *go,* he or she does so with the belief that he or she is correct. Only later does he or she change this assumption through exposure to the correct form. Second language learners do the same thing, for example, when English learners say *wented* to form the past tense.

Particular Terms and Concepts Related to Second Language Acquisition

■ *Silent Period.* The silent period is an interval that occurs before English language learners start producing language (Hakuta, 1974; Huang and Hatch, 1978). During this time, the learner may only produce memorized chunks of language—or no language at all—for months as they adjust to a new language and a new environment. The notion is that learners do not start producing language until they feel comfortable enough to do so (Krashen & Terrell, 1983).

■ *Transfer Phenomenon.* Adolescent and adult language learners bring their first language with them when learning the second language. This fact can both hinder and help second language acquisition (Odlin, 1989). Transfer can occur when the English language learner "defaults" to their knowledge of their first language and applies phonology, syntax, semantics, and so forth to the task of speaking and understanding the second language (Newmark, 1966). If the first language interferes with the learning or producing the second language, then it is called *negative transfer.* An example of negative transfer is when a learner whose first language is Spanish says *house white* instead of *white house,* mainly because they use Spanish syntax to produce the English form. *Positive transfer* occurs when the first language helps the second language. Cognates are found across many languages. Many of the names of the months in Spanish are the same in English: Febrero/February, Marzo/March, Abril/April, Junio/June, Julio/July, Agusto/August, Septiembre/September, Octubre/October, Noviembre/November, Diciembre/December. These similarities may make learning the names of the months easier in the second language because they are similar to what is found in the first.

■ *Interlanguage.* As coined by Larry Selinker (1972), interlanguage is the distance between the first language and the second language. Errors reveal how far the learner is moving from the first language and into the second language. Generally speaking transfer errors (resulting from negative transfer) show less progress in the second language, whereas errors resulting from developmental stages and orders (errors that occur when children learn English as a first language) show more progress (Taylor, 1975). The reason is that transfer errors suggest that the learner is relying heavily on the first language, while developmental errors demonstrate that the learner is moving into the second language more fully.

■ *Fossilization.* This refers to second language learners who get stuck at a particular level in English and cannot seem to progress beyond a particular level. Fossilization is most obvious in one's accent and seems tied to the onset of puberty. In families with children who arrived in the United States after the age of 15 and with younger children who were subsequently born in the United States, the older children may have very profound accents while the younger children speak with no accent at all. Fossilization and the age of arrival appear to play a role in how one will ultimately sound in the second language.

First Language Acquisition

Developmental stages and orders dominate first language acquisition at virtually all of the linguistic levels (see Table 4.50) (Ingram, 1989; Owens, 1984).

TABLE 4.50   First Language Acquisition

PHONOLOGY	MORPHOLOGY	SYNTAX	SEMANTICS	PRAGMATICS
Sounds are acquired in an order.	Inflections are acquired in an order.	Grammar is subject to stages.	Meaning is acquired in an order.	Family Language Peer Language Social Language

Phonology.   All babies babble the same from birth, regardless of where they are born. For example, newly born children in the United States, China, or Russia all babble the same sounds over and over again, the most common sounds being /b/, /p/, /s/, and /k/. This suggests that these sounds are universal to human beings, since all "normally developing" children start out with the same set of phonemes right from birth.

Newborns, regardless of their place of birth or ethnicity, can distinguish between pairs and strings of phonemes (Elmas, 1975). *Diachronic listening studies* show that children can tell the difference between *voiced* and *unvoiced consonant* sounds like /p/ and /b/ when they hear them. These studies are conducted by having a newborn listen to a string of *phonemes* like the *unvoiced stop* /p/ over and over again while their heart beats are measured. Then, the *voiced stop* /b/ is introduced and the heart rate is measured. Many studies show that the child's heart rate increases when the new phoneme is introduced, and this physical response suggests that the child can demonstrate an understanding of the appreciable (yet subtle) difference between each type of phoneme.

Universal babbling and diachronic listening studies suggest that children are predisposed to learn languages, since they babble from birth (though indistinguishably) and can even tell the difference between pairs of sounds. Humans, it seems, are "hard wired" to acquire the ability to speak, given these innate abilities of producing and distinguishing sounds. Consider also that race and ethnicity play no role in how well one acquires a language—it is done right from birth. Around age 0;6 (please read as "6 months"), the sounds one hears in a child's babbling changes, probably because the environment is providing the child with *input* to be acquired. For example, if we compare the babbling of children in the United States with Chinese and Japanese babies, differences begin to emerge (see Table 4.51).

These differences are important, because children begin to babble differently after 6 months of age. Because Chinese is a *tonal language* and Japanese is a very *syllabic language*

TABLE 4.51

BORN IN THE U.S.	BORN IN CHINA	BORN IN JAPAN
Babbling voiced and unvoiced stops.	Babbling voiced and unvoiced stops *and tones.*	Babbling voiced and unvoiced stops *and syllables.*

(meaning that these language use tones and syllables to distinguish words and meaning when speaking), children begin to note and acquire these differences even before they begin to use language to communicate. Obviously, the differences between the languages continue to grow remarkably from this point forward.

In English, the following phonemes tend to be acquired before others (Lock, 1983).

- Six Months: Voice and unvoiced stops (p, b, t, d, k, g)
- Two Years: Voiced and unvoiced fricatives (f, v, s, z)
- Four Years: Voice and unvoiced infrequent fricatives (thin, than, ship, azure)

Please note that the terms *acquired* and *learned* will be used interchangeably here; however, there is a distinction in second language acquisition. Both terms indicate that the child can produce sounds *when she or he wants to produce* them (e.g., when saying words). It takes time for children to be able to produce and control these sounds. On their way to producing these sounds, children do quite a bit of *consonant reducing* and *deleting* (see Table 4.52).

TABLE 4.52

TARGET	CHILD	
stop	top	(initial sound deletion)
try	ty	(medial deletion)
sleep	sweep	(initial blend reduction)

In the beginning, the child may think that he or she is producing the correct form; later, they may become aware that they are unable to articulate the sound correctly and may display frustration at this inability.

Morphology.   Inflectional affixes are acquired in a particular order that is common to all children learning English as a first language (Brown, 1973). As mentioned earlier, children tend to learn the plural -s before the possessive -s. Third singular -s (runs, hits, jumps) tends to be last. The reason is probably because the plurals and possessives are concrete and third singular is abstract: It is easy to understand plural and possessive forms, but third singular -s is more for decoration; therefore, this third singular form is learned later.

Learning how to form the past tense morphologically occurs in stages. First, the child learns the form -ed to make the past tense, and then *overgeneralizes* this inflectional ending to any verb to make the past tense (see Table 4.53).

Table 4.53 shows how a child might move from one stage of hypothesis testing to another on the way to learning how to correctly form the past tense for irregular verbs in English (*go/went, run/ran, sit/sat*). Please note that the forms that the child uses in stages one through three (*goed* and *wented*) are seldom heard in the environment since the child's caregivers (parents and teachers) probably use the correct forms of the verb when speaking to the child, yet the child uses these incorrect forms *anyway* because they make the most sense to him or her. Overgeneralized forms (*goed*) and hypercorrected forms (*wented*) are common here.

TABLE 4.53

STAGE ONE		STAGE TWO		STAGE THREE	
Overgeneralization		*Hypercorrection*		*Uptake/Self-Correction*	
Parent:	What did you do yesterday?	Parent:	What did you do for your birthday?	Parent:	What did you do for your birthday?
Child:	I **goed** to the store.	Child:	I **wented** to the zoo.	Child:	I **wented** to the zoo.
Parent:	You **went** to the store?	Parent:	You **went** to the zoo?	Parent:	You **went** to the zoo?
Child:	Yes. I **goed** to the store got a toy.	Child:	Yes. I **wented** to the zoo and saw lions!	Child:	Yes. I **went** to the zoo.

Syntax. Developmental stages affect the acquisition of English syntax. Below are the most common areas (Bloom, 1994; Cairnes, 1996; Chomsky, 1969).

Holophrases occur around 12 to 18 months. These are one-word utterances that the child uses to mean a variety of phrases. For example, the word *me* can mean a variety of things: I'm hungry, I'm tired, I need to be changed, I'm really hot in this jumpsuit—could you please take it off? Often, the child's caregiver is able to understand what the child wants based on a single word either by intonation or simple trial and error.

The *Two-Word Stage* occurs shortly after the one word (holophrastic) state when children put two words together. *Chris car, kitty here,* and *no wash* are probably things that I said at this stage when I was a child, and so did you. The important idea to note is that a grammar is emerging at this stage, though it is very reduced and stripped down.

The *Telegraphic Stage* occurs when the child strings words together with a discernable grammar. *Daddy go, Milk all gone,* and *I now tired* are examples of the telegraphic stage. In each case, there is a subject and a verb form in the utterance; and it is becoming structurally correct, though the utterances lack "unessential" elements like determiners, prepositions, and so forth.

Compound Subjects and Adverbial Modifiers are in place and in production about kindergarten. For example, *Mike and Chris ran and jumped far* is a viable sentence at this stage, while prepositional phrases as modifiers may be in place by the end of kindergarten. This is because spatial concepts for words like *in, on, near,* and *far* must be established first before attaching a spoken or written label to them.

As the children improve in their language, they go through other stages. *Question and Negation Forms* as shown in Table 4.54 are examples that emerge around age 2 (Kilma & Bellugi, 1966).

TABLE 4.54

DO + QUESTION	WH- + QUESTION	NEGATION
You like?	Where go?	No run.
You do like it?	Where you go?	I no running.
Do you like it?	Where you did go?	I'm not running.
	Where did you go?	

The orders for learning the *do, wh-* question, and *negation* forms are quite universal for children learning English as a first language. The orders seem inescapable (linguistics do not bother studying these forms anymore, because they are so common). These orders suggest that there is a psycholinguistic aspect to learning English as a first language. In the first place, children are not hearing phrases such as "you like" or "where go" or "no run" in the environment, *yet they produce them.* Some kind of linguistic structuring must be taking place in the child's mind for these odd forms to be produced on the way to learning how to correctly form the syntax of each of these statements.

Semantic Acquisition.   The meaning of certain words and phrases are acquired in an order. In the beginning, children overextend and underextend the meanings of words. For example, a "woof-woof" may be any animal with four legs and a tail (dogs, cats, beavers, lions, etc.), and "kitty" may only refer to the *child's cat* and to no other catlike animal. *Subordinate clauses* and *passive voice sentences* are among the last things to be acquired. These elements can be acquired as late as fourth grade, if not beyond. The problem is understanding the meaning that these sentences convey. A sentence like

> If I had run for just twenty-five minutes longer, then I would have won the race and I would not have to be here writing this book.

is a pretty complicated sentence to understand (for anyone), and it makes sense that the form is acquired late.

Passive and complex constructions are also acquired quite late (Turner & Rommetveit, 1967).

    A. Cookie Monster ate the cookie.
    B. The cookie was eaten by Cookie Monster.
    C. I will have been standing here for five hours when the clock strikes three.

Because position dominates in understanding what sentences mean, sentence A is easy to understand. The agent (subject) carries out the action on the goal (object). However, sentence B is tricky, and a child might act out the sentence with a puppet by having the *cookie* eat *Cookie Monster* instead of the other way around. The child might believe that the first position of the sentence always contains the agent, so he or she acts upon that belief. Again, position is what the child might rely upon for meaning and thus accounts for why passive sentences are acquired later. The last sentence is highly complex and requires knowledge of time and contingencies to be fully understood. Cognitively speaking, some children may not be ready to understand such a sentence without the experience and knowledge of time.

Pragmatic Acquisition.   Acquiring a sociolect also occurs in an order. The child typically learns the "family language" first, meaning that they acquire the variety of English that their parents speak, along with the caregiver's idiolect and the regional issolect and dialect. At school, peer groups exert a greater influence, especially during adolescence, and aspects of the child's language may move away from what his or her parents and teachers speak. Later, when the child grows up and moves into the workplace, the language of that environment will tend to dominate as he or she tries to accommodate themselves into that world.

Second Language Acquisition

Adolescent and adult second language acquisition share similar developmental orders and stages present in first language acquisition, but there is the additional characteristic of positive and negative transfer. This is because second language learners bring a complete (or nearly complete) linguistic system to the second language learning experience. You will see how these factors play a role in learning a second language at each linguistic level.

Phonology.   Recall that transfer is particular to second language acquisition. For second language learners, more negative transfer issues emerge when second language learners encounter English (Gass & Selinker, 1983), because the first language has sounds that are different from what one finds in the first language. Subsequently, the English sounds that English language learners produce are negatively affected. For example, the Spanish phoneme /s/ is often heard as /es/. This affects the way that English words are pronounced:

- ■ Smoke   /esmok/
- ■ Cereal   /eserial/

If the first language lacks similar phonological processes, then the first language may interfere with the pronunciation of English words. The phoneme /th/ at the ends of English words is often heard as a /t/ for this reason:

- ■ English: with
- ■ Spanish Influence: /wit/

Final consonants are often voiced at the ends of words that native speakers of English devoice:

- ■ English: /werkt/
- ■ Spanish Influence: /werk-ed/

In short, negative transfer issues are most apparent at the phonological level, perhaps because of the critical period cited earlier (where the brain has already specialized phonology before introducing the second language).

Morphology.   There is a similar developmental order to learning English morphemes that you saw in first language learning. The plurals tend to be learned before the possessives and third singular comes in last. These stages tend to be moved through quickly, because adults can grasp the abstractions more quickly than children can. Overgeneralizations of -ed are common, too, and *goed* and *wented* are common developmental errors at this level as a result of hypothesis testing.

Syntax.   Both transfer and developmental errors are common when learning English syntax. As cited earlier, Spanish speakers who place the adjective after the noun are relying on their first language syntax to produce English. Developmental orders for questions (do and wh-) are common here. A similar pattern is present for negation, though the form *no sing* is ambiguous, since speakers of romance languages form negation with *no* + verb (one cannot readily see if this interlanguage error is the result of transfer or development). Conditional sentences and passive voice sentences are acquired later, just as you saw with first language acquisition.

Semantics.   Transfer may also occur when the learner thinks there is enough similarity between words in the first language and words in the second language.* This strategy will work for true cognates in each language but not for false cognates. Because English has many influences, including German, French, and Spanish, learners can often draw upon their first language to get at the meanings of words. By proxy, German, French, and Spanish borrowed many words and roots from Greek and Latin, so there has been much filtering into the language that accounts for so many true cognates found in English and other languages (see Table 4.55).

TABLE 4.55

ENGLISH	GERMAN	SPANISH	FRENCH	GREEK (DIMOTIKI)
School	Schule	Escuela	Ecola	Scholeio
Number	Nummer	Numero	Nombre	Numero
Cat	Katze	Gato	Chat	Gato

*Kellerman, E., & Sharwood-Smith, M. (1986). *Cross linguistic influence in second language acquisition.* Echisford: Pergamon.

Morphemes, too, are similar in many languages. Greek and Latin morphemes are found in both English and Spanish, and they can be affected by positive transfer (see Table 4.56).

Negative transfer can hinder semantic development, particularly where false cognates are concerned. False cognates are words that look very similar to words in English, yet have very different meanings (see Table 4.57).

TABLE 4.56

	ENGLISH	SPANISH
in-	inept	inépto
im-	impossible	impossible
-able	insupportable	insuportable
pre-	precede	predecir

TABLE 4.57

ENGLISH WORD	SPANISH WORD
embarrassed (ashamed)	embarasada (pregnant)
molest (criminal act)	molestar (annoy)

Idiomatic expressions are also challenging and can be subject to developmental errors. While at a college party, an exchange student wished to express how the group was "really partying" hard and how much fun he was having. He climbed on to a table and announced: *We ALREDY party now!* Such expressions might be hard for second language learners to grasp at first, so be sure to look for errors in idiomatic expressions in the data on the test.

Pragmatics.   Pragmatics is also a part of second language acquisition (Bates & MacWhinney, 1981). You have learned about different registers of social speech in different genres of language use. For example, two friends who are playing poker (the genre) will probably use an informal speaking style (register) during the game. Their requests will be informal, direct, and maybe even jovial (if they are winning). This type of language use may not be appropriate during a funeral, though.

Language learners need to learn about these different genres and the registers within them. Making requests, for example, must be taught directly, but so must the appropriate level of formality required. Consider the following:

- Lemme see that article.
- Give me the article.
- Excuse me, may I please see the article?
- Pardon me, but would you be willing to allow me to view that article for just a moment?

Each of the sentences above mean the same thing: They make a request. But *how* each utterance achieves that goal is different.

Theories of Second Language Acquisition

You may be asked questions about the major theories of second language acquisition. They fall into three general categories: behavioral, natural, and sociolinguistic.

Behavioral Theories.   Behaviorist B. F. Skinner (1957) proposed that languages are learned just like any other behavior: through rewards and reinforcement. As children grow, the environment provides them with input, and they learn the language through rewards and reinforcements that their caregivers provide to them. Hearing the words *cat, dog, run,* and so forth over and over again provides the child with the stimulus need for acquiring the words. As the child repeats what he or she hears correctly and is praised or rewarded for doing so, long strings of stimulus and response chains are formed. Thus, human language is something that is modeled and reinforced for the child from birth and beyond.

Natural Order.   Stephen Krashen is the major theorist of the natural order of learning a second language (Gass & Selinker, 1994). Because English has developmental orders in it,

Krashen theorizes that language can be acquired in the same natural way. He also hypothesized that learning and acquisition are not the same thing. When one develops a vocabulary in a second language, they do so through acquisition: They obtain the language without consciously trying to do it, much like children do when growing up. Language learning, on the other hand, is very effortful and unnatural (but necessary): It is for learning formal grammar, standard forms of the language, and the like. One view is not better than the other; instead, each area serves a different purpose: Acquisition is for obtaining the language naturally; learning is for developing the capacity to correct one's grammar when writing or speaking. There are other important principles to know in this area.

- **The Monitor Model (Larsen-Freeman & Long, 1991).** The monitor is what we use *learned* language for. When we study grammar rules and do grammar exercises, we are *learning* (not acquiring) language. The monitor is what we use to fix our errors when *producing* the language. Think of the monitor as a quality control specialist whose task is to ensure that the utterance is grammatically and socially acceptable. This job can be done well only if the learned information is correct and can be applied to the utterance.
- **The Input Hypothesis.** Krashen (1985) believes that learners must have comprehensible input to acquire language. That is, input that is at and just a bit beyond their current level of competence in the language. This is captured in the *i + 1* model. Think of it this way: If you have a learner who can comprehend the plural forms, then your goal is to move them from the plurals to the possessives (and later, third singular -s). Acquiring language occurs naturally through exposure and experience (not direct instruction) through input that has been modified by the speaker to be understood by the learner just above the learner's current stage of development. The silent period occurs because the learner is building up competence through comprehensible input.
- **The Affective Filter Hypothesis (Krashen, 1981).** The affective filter can be characterized as the degree of resistance one has toward learning the language. Generally, if the student is full of anxiety or anger toward the speaker of a given language, then learning is probably going to be made more difficult. Teachers, too, can raise students affective filter. If the teacher displays negative attitudes toward the learner's primary language and native culture, then the student may feel shame and anger and acquisition may not take place. A highly affective filter will impede one's receiving comprehensible input, the necessary ingredient for acquisition.
- **First Language Literacy.** Krashen (1983) also posits that children need to be literate in the first language to make the process of acquiring the second language easier. He theorizes that first language skills will transfer to the second language positively. For example, the concept of reading, of letter patterns, direction of sentences, and the meaning of stories will make sense in English if those ideas are grasped first in the native language. The same is true for narrative text schema and other elements of literature (plot, setting, character, etc.).

We can summarize Krashen's (1983) theory by stating that one acquires a second language through input that teachers make comprehensible. In addition, one's affective filter (resistance to learning) must be low enough to allow the input to enter.

Sociolinguistic Theories: BICS and CALP.   Some researchers, James Cummins (1979) in particular, make a distinction between **Basic Interpersonal Communication Skills** (BICS) and **Cognitive Academic Language Proficiency** (CALP). BICS amounts to social language, and the idea is that learners will acquire interpersonal language rather quickly—the language for playing and working with others on the playground and in the classroom. CALP, on the other hand, is the language of academics. Understanding metaphor and entropy, for example, is more cognitively demanding *in this view* than making a request for a date on Friday night. Teachers need to be aware of this distinction and try to ensure that both BICS and CALP develop equally. If not, then the learner may be very socially proficient but remain academically challenged. One must be careful to instruct both social and academic language to English language learners so that both aspects develop equally. (See Communicative Approach for BICS and CALLA for CALP in the next section.)

ESL Methods

ESL instruction has the ultimate aim of mainstreaming English Language Learners into the "regular" classroom. This means that absolute beginners who are learning English must be taught quickly enough to move them into an academically demanding classroom where they must learn not only the English language but also academic concepts, like metaphor, mathematical functions, and scientific methods. Following are general ESL methods that appear on the test.

Audio Lingual Method and Grammar Translation. Pattern drills and memorized dialogues typify the audio lingual method, where the constructed features of language are reduced to memorized chunks of information and practiced through repetition. Imagine a worksheet with a sentences (perhaps out of context) for students to read and repeat along with a tape recording:

- **I want** to learn English.
- **I want** the anesthesiologist to stay in the room during the appendectomy.
- **I want** a library book.

These approaches are very behavioral, given the emphasis on memorization and stimulus–response. The rest of the approaches take a more "naturalistic" approach to the acquisition of English.

Language Experience Approach. LEA activities will be described in detail in content area six. For now, understand that a method of teaching English language learners to associate spoken and written language can be accomplished through LEA activities. Here, the teacher and the student discuss an experience and the experience is written down (usually one sentence in length). If the learner cannot write yet, then the teacher writes the sentence down. In either case, whatever the learner says is what is written in print (errors and all): for example, "I goed to the store this yesterday."

The principle behind LEA is this: *What was discussed is written, and what is written is read.* Later, the errors can be corrected, but error correction is not the focus of early LEA; instead, the goal is to help the learner make the link between spoken and written language. The same is true for conceptual knowledge. For example, if the teacher is instructing the theme of friendship and loss, it may be necessary to try to relate to the students' own notions of this experience first. The student can be asked to think about what it was like to leave friends from the home country when emigrating to the United States. This way, the student can relate a real experience to the text and not struggle with both the language and the content simultaneously.

Total Physical Response. TPR is a method of instructing basic ESL (Asher, 1969; 1982). You model concrete actions and present concrete objects to language learners to help them make the connection between spoken language and the things they describe. Imagine that you have a group of absolute beginners and that you want to teach them basic commands like *stand up, sit down, turn left,* and *turn right.* Using TPR, you model each of these commands from the learner by saying the command and demonstrating the action. Then, you work with the learners to guide them in both saying and acting out the command. Finally, you say the command and have the learner demonstrate the action.

TPR is useful for teaching more complicated commands and nouns. Consider the following (see Table 4.58).

TABLE 4.58

COMMAND	NOUN
Touch your	Nose
Show me your	Hair
Where is your	Arm

Here, the teach models and guides the learner in learning these commands and requests, along with the concrete nouns.

Other TPR activities use labels around the classroom. Every concrete object in the room is labeled with a readable index card (e.g., clock, chalk board, light switch, desk, etc.). These labels become part of TPR activities that are carried out daily as part of the morning routine.

Realia.   Realia means using concrete objects, materials, and observable experience to teach abstract concepts. Think of how you would teach words like *sweet* and *sour* without realia. The task is much easier if you bring in a lump of sugar and a slice of lemon. That's using realia! Only using words to describe abstractions is ineffective for many learners, but especially for ELLs whose skills in the target language may be limited. In short, realia.

Communicative Approaches.   These activities include having students learn an applicable language on a continuum from the easiest to the more difficult tasks. The continuum begins with the most *concrete* use of language (using present tense, immediate social situation) to more *abstract* uses of language (using past or future tense, expressing wants and desires in more abstract social situations). Consider the following examples and their linguistic demands on the speaker.

- Discussing what one does in the morning.
- Discussing their favorite activity.
- Discussing what they did for their last birthday.
- Discussing what they would and would not like to do on summer vacation.

The first activity is the most concrete. It asks the student to talk about what they do in the morning (e.g., wake up, eat breakfast, dress for school, etc.). The rest of the utterances are more abstract and involve more complicated utterances. The last item, for example, requires expressing choices using lots of modals, which is beyond the concrete linguistic demands of simply discussing what one does in the morning. Other types of communicative activities include having students answer questions about what they like to do and then develop a list of their own questions to be posed to their classmates. As students work together to find and write down answers to their questions, they can work on both oral and written language development simultaneously.

If you have taken any foreign language classes during your college career, then you are probably already familiar with the communicative approach. First, you learn vocabulary in a given social situation, like being *at the bank* or *in the classroom.* You probably saw lots of pictures and vocabulary with an English translation. Then, you practiced a dialogue of some sort in the target language before learning a simple grammar point. The rest of the lesson then had you applying both the contextualized vocabulary and the grammar point in a variety of reading, writing, speaking, and listening activities. An example of the communicative approach for English language learners is shown in Table 4.59.

The point is to teach vocabulary and grammar within a defined social context, so that it is immediately applicable and usable by the learner. This approach is much different from the audio–lingual method where the vocabulary can be decontextualized and the grammar points quite obscure.

TABLE 4.59

GENRE	VOCABULARY	DIALOGUE	GRAMMAR POINT	COMMUNICATION
At the bank	would like loan money	Hello. I would like a loan. Why would you like a loan?	Future will + verb would + verb	Listening Speaking Writing

Natural Approach. Krashen and Terrell (1983) synthesized approaches like LEA, TPR, realia, and communicative approaches into a singular method called the *Natural Approach*. It is based on the *Natural Order Hypothesis* described under the ESL theories section. Briefly, the natural approach relies on comprehensible input, exposure to rich vocabulary in context, listening and reading over speech production, and an anxiety-free learning environment to keep the affective filter low. The goal is to move students from no skills in English to an intermediate stage over a period of time (greater than one year). Learners also move from basic communication skills to more academic skills before transitioning into sheltered content classroom (described next) or into mainstream classrooms.

The approach divides learners into four groups: preproduction, early production, speech emergence, and intermediate fluency. Preproduction learners are not producing any language yet (or only chunks), so they are taught using high levels of TPR, realia, and modeling. They are not expected to produce language at this point, but rather to receive and "build up" their comprehension through comprehensible input. Early production learners have some speech that is emerging on its own (they are now ready to produce language) and instruction begins to ramp up to include wh- questions, and so forth. At the speech emergence state, learners then perform more linguistically demanding activities, such as predicting, comparing, and describing. Finally, when they are intermediately fluent, they learn to handle academic tasks in English and prepare to move into a sheltered or mainstream classroom. The natural approach model is shown in Table 4.60.

TABLE 4.60

PREPRODUCTION	EARLY PRODUCTION	SPEECH EMERGENCE	INTERMEDIATE FLUENCY
• TPR modeling • Yes/no questions • Pictures • Realia • Simplified language	• TPR with responses • Role playing • Wh- questions • Labels and realia • Simple response • Expectation	• Predicting • Comparing • Describing • How and why questions • LEA • Listing, charting, graphing	• Essay writing • Analyzing charts and graphs • More complex problem solving and evaluating • Pre-writing activities • Literary analysis

As the learners' communicative abilities increase, the teacher talk decreases. In addition, the scaffolds move from TPR to more academically oriented tasks (e.g., writing essays, analyzing charts, etc.). Checking listening skills also varies from the pre-production stage to the intermediate production stage. For example, in the pre-production stage, one could have students demonstrate comprehension by carrying out concrete tasks. For example, asking students to place an "x" inside, to the left of, on top of, and beneath a box on a piece of paper will tell you whether the student understands basic commands and prepositions.

Similarly, one can read a story and have students select pictures that best reflect what was just described orally. Again, in all of these tasks it is important to target only the skill in question and not others. For example, it would be inappropriate to have students write notes or summarize the requests in writing during the listening comprehension task. That is because one would be assessing two competing skills at once, which would be unfair to the student and cloud your knowledge of the students listening skills. Plus, such an assessment might be beyond the students' current level of language.

Checking speaking skills will also vary across the language levels. In the preproduction stage, little beyond memorized greetings might be expected. Later, informal conversations might be the focus. In all cases, the task must match the purpose. Having the student complete a dialogue about a conversation, for example, does not match the purpose of seeing if the students can carry on a conversation. Only a truly informal conversation between the teacher and the student can accomplish that.

Cognitive Academic Language Learning Approach (CALLA).   CALLA activities teach students academic content as they learn English. This approach is also know as sheltered English instruction. Academic content is modified and taught to English language learners, like metaphors in literature, the Pythagorean Theorem in mathematics, and expressionism in art, though specially designed academic instructional designs. As you can see, the focus is on learning the content of a subject (math, science, social studies, language arts, etc.), rather than on simple English language communication skills (see BICs and CALP earlier in this section).

Following are CALLA activities that address academic content and English language development (Chamot & O'Malley, 1986).

Preview/Review.   This method preteaches (previews) vocabulary and academic concepts in a lesson before actually undertaking instruction (Lesslow-Hurley, 1990). This way, the students will not be lost in the language they are struggling to acquire while trying to also understand an academic concept like *entropy* in a science class. In addition, realia and pictures may also be used to introduce the topic in advance. For example, before listening to a brief lecture on plant and animal cell similarities and differences, students will be shown pictures of both types of cells, along with the labels that describe each part. The pictures will provide concrete support (a scaffold) to students before they learn unfamiliar information in the lecture. The lesson ends with a review of the vocabulary and academic concepts to ensure that the student has learned both areas through the lesson.

Visual cues and realia-based demonstrations are very helpful. They are *advanced organizers* and provide concrete referents that summarize and support the information that one is going to explain verbally. Here, students' minds will be prompted to think about what the lecture is going to be about. In addition, they will also have a support system upon which they can rely that is **not** based on the language of which they may only have a thin grasp. They will have a visual support to guide them through the lesson.

Study Skills.   Teaching study skills is also important. When asking ELLs to carry out a task in a science classroom, it may be beneficial to have the students write the steps down first so that they can have a scaffold to carry with them into the task. Without the list, the students may find it difficult to remember all of the spoken words that they have just heard in a language that they have not yet mastered. Keep in mind that note taking is a part of study skills; this is not an appropriate way to measure listening skills in general, because it adds an additional skill of writing to the task thereby clouding what the student can and cannot do when listening to directions.

CALLA Assessment.   Finding ways to assess ELL students' knowledge of content is important. This type of assessment is different from traditional assessment, in that the teacher must find a way to reveal what the student understands about a subject without testing their language skills at the same time. These assessments may include many demonstrations or other nonlanguage based means of assessing what the child understands. This extends to the first language. If the child supplies words correctly from the first language into the section language to describe the content, then it shows that the child is actively engaging the material. What the student must learn is how to express the same idea in English, though that would be done through separate instruction and assessments. CALLA assessments ensure that the student will not be unfairly assessed on both language and academic skills simultaneously and that they can show what they really know about a subject without being limited by their English learner status.

A sample CALLA lesson that utilizes these principles is shown in Table 4.61.

TABLE 4.61   CALLA Science: Teaching a Sheltered English Lesson on Ocean Life

Preview: Introduce the academic content using lots of visuals and charts that are not language dependent. For example, when teaching the difference between mammals, crustaceans, and cephalopods, use pictures, objects, and other hands-on materials to convey the differences among these different elements of sea life.

Teach Vocabulary: Teach the vocabulary to associate with the objects and the concepts using speech, print, and modeling. Have the students use labels to identify different pictures or have them draw the items in their journals before attempting to read the content.

Guided Practice: Provide students with a scaffold for the reading. The scaffold should offer more support to the text as they read and look for information. The scaffold can be a visual outline of the paragraph or a cloze activity (fill in the blank) where the students supply the correct label in the text using the vocabulary that they have learned.

Review: Close the activity by reviewing the outline or the cloze activity and reteach the vocabulary that had been introduced. *Assess the students in the same way that the lesson was delivered:* having the students label pictures, complete cloze activities, or draw and label items in their journals.

Constraints on Second Language Acquisition

The final area that we will consider pertains to constraints on language learning. How well one learns English as a second language is dependent upon a variety of factors. Assuming that the environment provides all the input that a learner needs, along with plentiful opportunities to learn, the following factors appear to play a role in how well one will acquire the language.

Age (critical period) **does** have an impact on how well one learns a second language. In general, adolescents and adults learn the basics of the language faster than children because they have access to deeper analytic functions. But children learn the language better in the long run, because adolescents and adults fossilize more quickly. *Fossilization* means that they get stuck at a particular level in the language and have an accent that they cannot lose or they must speak only in the simple present, past, and future tenses because more complicated tenses remain too elusive. Fossilization may occur because of *brain lateralization,* where certain brain functions are assigned to particular sides of the brain (language acquisition being one of the functions). In short, children may acquire the language more slowly, but they tend to learn the target language more completely than adults do. In short, before puberty, less fossilization; after puberty, more fossilization.

Motivation itself is an important ingredient in learning a second language, though it is unclear what kind is best. There are two types of motivation to consider. The first is intrinsic and internal; the second is extrinsic or instrumental. The distinction is simple. Intrinsic/internal motivation is based on a deep desire to participate with other speakers of the target language. Intrinsic/instrumental motivation, on the other hand, is more utilitarian: One wants to learn the language to get something (e.g., better grades, jobs, etc.).

Learning style, too, is important but not a great determiner. Those learners who are easily frustrated and cannot handle ambiguity may spend a great deal of their time being angry while learning the second language, whereas students who can tolerate degrees of uncertainty may learn more comfortably. However, learning style is not an absolute indicator of how well or poorly one may ultimately learn the target language.

CHAPTER FIVE

Literacy

DOMAIN ONE: ENGLISH LINGUISTICS *(continued)*

CONTENT AREA THREE: LITERACY DEVELOPMENT

The easiest way to view content area three is to make a distinction between learning to read and reading to learn (O'Mally, 1998). Just imagine that learning to read is where you teach all of the foundational skills to a child, so that later they can read to learn independently *just as you are doing right now in preparation for the test.* There is a model associated with this content area, and it is important for you to commit it to memory (see Table 5.1). We will go into this model in detail throughout this chapter.

TABLE 5.1 Literacy

KINDERGARTEN	FIRST	SECOND	THIRD	FOURTH	FIFTH+
Concepts about Print Phonemic Awareness					
	Decoding Instruction		Fluent Decoding		
	Vocabulary				
Regular Sight Words		Irregular Sight Words	Syllabication	Structural Analysis	Etymology
Listening Comprehension		Reading Comprehension			
		Literal	Inferential		Evaluative

To begin, learning to read is to occur in kindergarten through third grade. Look at Table 5.1 and notice that *concepts about print* and *phonemic awareness* are taught early on in kindergarten. From late kindergarten through grade three, children start learning beginning, intermediate, and advanced phonics. *Regular* and *irregular sight words* are also instructed during the reading-to-learn stage, though in separate activities. Heavy emphasis is on skills instruction, particularly in the areas of learning to decode print and the foundations that precede that ability. By the end of grade three, children are expected to be *fluent decoders of text,* so that they can begin to focus on higher level vocabulary and reading comprehension. Comprehension instruction is mainly through listening comprehension activities to grade two.

Reading to learn occurs in grades four and above. Here, students learn how to gain knowledge independently from a variety of narrative and informational and scientific texts. To do so, they will need *vocabulary instruction* that starts with syllabication and moves on to etymology. In addition, students will also need **comprehension instruction** so that they can understand a text literally, inferentially, and critically (evaluative comprehension). This means that they will need instruction in strategies that will allow them to work with text independently and to demonstrate that they have understood what they have read, regardless of whether the text is a short story or an article on gene therapy.

Concepts about Print

Concepts about print (CAP) includes all of the functions of a book. Since humans are not born as readers, we must learn about all of the principle parts of a book before it can be used as a tool for learning. This a top-down process, where the largest concepts are taught first (Gray-Schlegal & King, 1998):

1. Book Concepts: Title, Picture, Author's Name, etc.
2. Sentence Concepts: Where to start, direction, return sweeps
3. Word Concepts: Word boundaries, first and last letters, word reading
4. Letter-names: The names of upper- and lowercase letters out of sequence.

Memorize the order above. The highest level of CAP is letter naming, where children see an upper- or lowercase letter and says its name. This ability is extremely important, because children will later attach a variety of sounds to the letters that they say by name. Consider the letter *s*. First, they will learn the name of the letter, /es/. Later, they will learn to attach other sounds to it when they see it in print, as in cat/s/, dog/z/, and wash/ez/. Letter–sound associations cannot happen until they can see a letter and say its name, though. Please recognize that letter–sound associations take place in separate activities and after *phonemic awareness* (the subject of our discussion after CAP) is in place.

CAP instruction involves big book readings, and all elements of CAP can be modeled this way (Park, 1982). As the teacher reads to a group of students, she points to each word as it is read aloud. This is a very common way to make the association between spoken and written language, since we were not born simply knowing this relationship. Using a pointer or having the child read with her finger to track print is a common technique to teach directionality, though it must be discontinued later on as it may interfere with fluency.

Reading aloud to students is important, because it exposes them to book language and helps to provide them with a rich oral vocabulary. In addition, it also begins to teach them about story grammar or schema: the elements and organizational framework of a story. Though they cannot read on their own yet, the students will begin to acquire ideas about plot, setting, character, and so forth at this point, which will greatly assist them when they begin to read and try to comprehend these elements independently. Assessments can also follow oral reading, where students' literal comprehension of a story that has been read aloud to them can be assessed. Students can be asked to order story panels or to draw pictures of the events in the story and the teacher can see what the children have and have not understood.

Language experience activities can also be used for CAP instruction. For emergent readers, language experience approaches are common to help them develop reading readiness. It targets requisites for reading, like language and conceptual development. These approaches have children experience something, like going to a zoo or grocery store, and then creating a story about it. This activity helps them to develop oral language expression and to develop the foundations for reading, like *concepts about print,* where one links spoken and written language together (e.g., directionality, word concepts, word boundaries, distinguishing words from letters, etc.). Early in development, the child might not understand that written words represent what we say in speech, so this concept will have to be taught explicitly (Taylor, 1992).

Language experience approaches can also be part of early reading assessment. By having children discuss an experience and write it down, you can see their current level of concepts about print (directionality, word boundaries, letter sounds), spelling development, and letter formations. During early LEAs, student utterances are written down word for word, errors and all. If the child says, *I goed to the store today,* then that is what is written. Why? Because the goal is to make the connection between what is spoken can be written.

After the sentence has been written down, the child can "read" the sentence with the teacher and point to each word as it is read:

I   goed to   the   zoo   today.

Corrections can be made, as in the example above. Here, the child has *syllabicated* today into /to/ and /day/. The teacher can indicate that the word is to be read as whole by pointing at the word and running the finger beneath the word while saying it. Then, the student can practice the skill. This way, the student will understand how to read a multisyllabic word correctly.

Later LEAs can target corrections to fix goed/went confusions. The utterance is written on note cards and amended as you see below:

I   goed   to   the   zoo.

went

Morning message activities are also a form of language experience. Here, the teacher writes a "message" on the board each morning and has the students "read" the sentence with the teacher: Today is Friday, March 11, 2004.

Students can take turns reading each word aloud with a pointer with the students or the teacher can simply model the reading for the students before having them choral-read the text. Such an activity will teach the students many aspects of CAP, including capital letters at the start of sentences (*Today*) and for proper nouns (Friday, March) and correct placement of commas and periods. Furthermore, students learn about directionality, word boundaries, and letter names. In sum, morning message activities incorporate all aspects of CAP and are appropriate choices if you are asked to identify a proper activity for fostering CAP development with young children.

Note too that you may be asked questions about using multisensory techniques to teach letter formation often involving environmental print. Examples of environmental print include familiar logos seen often in the child's world. This is good for teaching letter recognition, along with copying the alphabet through multisensory techniques and metalinguistics. Copying the alphabet, for example, targets the motor skills necessary for legible handwriting and may also help them to memorize the letter patterns. Accompanying multisensory techniques, such as writing in the air, in sand, or tracing sandpaper letters while saying them aloud, are effective for helping to distinguish easily confused letters like *p/b, d/q*—letters that are orthographically similar. Finally, metalinguistics also play a role in teaching children how to form letters. Telling the difference between making a *b* and making a *d,* for example, might occur by having the child associate language with the formation: stick and circle for the letter *b* and circle and stick for *d* might help them distinguish them when printing them on paper.

In summary, children with caregivers who read to them at home will be at a distinct advantage because they arrive to school with many concepts in place. Families should be encouraged to read with their children for this reason. Having students take books home to read with their families is an excellent way to foster family literacy. In addition, second language learners from literate households may have the same advantage, regardless of home language, because these concepts transfer. Regardless of the language, many aspects of CAP will transfer and students will learn the schema of narrative text, because these concepts are common to all linguistic groups. Developing a list of books to be found at the local library is another way to foster family involvement in literacy. This will also ensure that the messages that one receives from school are consistent with what one hears in the home.

Phonemic Awareness

Phonemic awareness is the understanding that words are made up of individual sounds (Yopp & Yopp, 2000), and is considered to be the earliest predictor of a child's ability to read (Adams, 1990). Studies of children with reading difficulties indicate that they have very poor phonemic awareness, so the rationale is that if phonemic awareness is addressed early on, then reading difficulties may be avoided later on.

Phonemic awareness is a foundational skill that prepares a child to associate individual sounds to individual letters through direct instruction in first grade. This cannot happen unless children learn to distinguish sounds within words, and that is not easy. When we speak, individual sounds in words, and even whole words in sentence, run together making it hard to distinguish one sound from another. Early on, children must be taught to distinguish one sound from another until they can actually break a spoken word into its individual, constituent sounds in an activity called segmenting (Ball & Blachman, 1991). The order of assessment and instruction for phonemic awareness is as follows:

- Matching Sounds
- Substituting Sounds
- Blending Sounds into Words
- Segmenting Sounds from Spoken Words

The whole point of phonemic awareness is to teach children to segment spoken words into individual sounds like this:

Spoken Word: *cat*   /k/ /a/ /t/

Phoneme counting is an important activity to understand for segmenting. Having the child listen to a word, say it slowly with the teacher, and then count the sounds in it is a very typical activity. Do be careful when reading test data. If you are asked to count phonemes on the test, do not be fooled when looking at letters. Remember that phonemic awareness deals with sounds not letters and that some letters are not heard in words (see Table 5.2).

TABLE 5.2

book	/b/ /u/ /k/	three sounds
cake	/c/ /A/ /k/	three sounds
rain	/r/ /A/ /n/	three sounds

Since trying to segment a spoken word like /kar/ (car) into its constituent sounds can be hard (it seems to have only two sounds, /k/ and /r/), teachers use Elkonin sound boxes for instruction. Using a picture of a car, sound boxes drawn beneath it, and markers for the children to move into the boxes, teachers can instruct segmenting like this (see Figure 5.1).

FIGURE 5.1

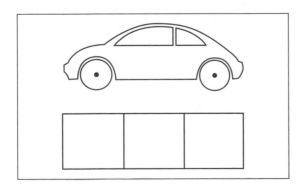

In this activity, the student looks at the picture and says the word, /kar/. With the teacher's help, the child moves markers up into the boxes while saying each *sound* (not letter) in order to make the sound segments concrete. Doing so helps the child "see" the sounds in the word and understand that spoken words are made up of individual phonemes.

Assessment of phonemic awareness can take place formally, where the teacher reads or shows pictures to the child and asks him or her to identify initial sounds or to segment the spoken words into individual sounds. Results can be compared with other students in the class and needs can be targeted through small group or individual instruction. Assessment can also be informal, in which the teacher simply asks a child to identify the sounds heard at the beginning, end, and middle of the child's name or in a simple, three-phoneme word like /mat/.

Games are frequent devices to teach children to become aware of sounds. The easiest starting point is with the child's own name or the names of other children. Children can be prompted to guess the names of their classmates after the teacher prompts them with a sound, or they can identify the initial sounds heard in their own or others' names when they are spoken (e.g., what do we hear at the start of Chris's name?). Such an activity will promote the notion that words are made up of individual sounds, even though we really only hear strings of sounds at once in spoken speech. Reading rhyming books or patterned books aloud to children can cue their awareness to sounds in the English language, too.

Be sure that you do not confuse phonemic awareness for phonics instruction. Phonemic awareness deals with sounds only and readies a child to associate individual sounds to letters; however, pure phonemic awareness activities do not use print (Williams, 1980). Phonics activities may import a sound from phonemic awareness, but they always include print.

As a final note on both concepts about print and phonemic awareness, please note that they are taught separately but consecutively.

- 9:00 A.M.   Concepts about Print Instruction
- 10:00 A.M.   Phonemic Awareness Instruction

Decoding Instruction

Decoding instruction begins when the letter naming and segmenting are in place. Children in first, second, and third grade move through the process of learning to decode text. Look at Table 5.3 and familiarize yourself with the patterns. Pay particular attention to the distinction between phonics and regular and irregular sight word instruction, since they are separate areas of instruction.

TABLE 5.3

LEARNING TO READ			
KINDERGARTEN	**FIRST GRADE**	**SECOND GRADE**	**THIRD GRADE**
	Beginning Phonics		
		Intermediate Phonics	
			Advanced Phonics
Regular Sight Words		Irregular Sight Words	

Phonics instruction is distinct from sight word instruction. Consider the following sentence: <u>The</u> cat sat <u>on the</u> mat. This sentence contains two types of words. The sight words are underlined and the decodable words are not. Sight words are words that cannot be decoded easily. *The,* for example, ought to be pronounce /tuh-he/ or /th-eh/, but it isn't. So, sight words must be recognized and this ability must be taught.

Decodable words are those that the child can decode by looking at the letters and then seeing and saying the patterns: c -at, s -at, m -at. In order for a child to be able to read the sentence above, he or she will need to be able to recognize and automatically say the sight words, while also looking at the decodable words and "cracking" their code.

Sight Words

Sight words are words that cannot be decoded easily, because the combinations of letters do not correspond to regular phonics rules. There are two categories of sight words: regular and irregular. Regular sight words are taught very early. They are words like *a, an, the, saw, was, here, there, on, by,* and so forth, and are called "regular" because they are both frequent and quite short. Irregular sight words are different. The words *though, threw, through, throughout,* and *thought* are examples. The pronunciation patterns are not stable across the words, even though they look very similar. They are hard to syllabicate, too, so normal decoding strategies may not apply to them. Emergent and developing readers must learn to recognize them automatically based on repetition or memorable features that distinguish one sight word from another sight word. Look at Table 5.4 and note the span of instruction across the early grades.

TABLE 5.4

LEARNING TO READ			
KINDERGARTEN	**FIRST GRADE**	**SECOND GRADE**	**THIRD GRADE**
Regular Sight Words		*Irregular Sight Words*	
a, an, the, was, saw, here, there, to, on		though, through, thorough, throughout	

Although the words are certainly not precise by grade level, you should note that the sight words that children are expected to recognize grow more and more complex as the time at school increases. Highly irregular sight words like *aforementioned* and *heretofore* would be very late, given their complexity and infrequency in print.

One activity that will help students to learn sight words is to teach by feature and to underline each of the sight words as they appear in text to draw attention to it (Hennings, 2002). Visual discrimination is most effective, because their attention is focused on these irregular words. Having students try to pronounce words like *though* and *throughout* is ineffective because the words do not follow regular phonetic patterns. Thus, another sense (like sight) must be used to teach these words, so that children can automatically recognize them in text.

Assessing sight words can take place with a list of words out of context and then in context. For example, sight words like *when, then, the, an,* and *who* can be assessed orally in a column and then in the context of a sentence. This way, the teacher will isolate the words that she wants to know if the child can recognize, and she will also see if the child can identify the words outside of and within context.

Word walls are another common method. As children encounter sight words in print, they can be written or tacked to the word wall. The words can then be used in separate sight word activities (writing them down, sorting them by feature, etc.) or used as cues when reading them in context.

Decodable Words

Decodable words are those words that the child can decode based on their letter combinations. Consider *cat, sat,* and *mat.* These words fit logical patterns, and if one can recognize the letter, the sound, and the common pattern -*at,* they can say the word. Children can be taught to recognize -*at* and then learn to manipulate index cards with the letters *c, s,* and *m* to form the words *cat, sat,* and *mat* in decoding activities.

The way that sight word and decoding instruction mesh is as follows. First, recall the sample sentence that contains both sight and decodable words in it: *The cat sat on the mat.* As you now understand, children will need to know both sight words and decodable words to decode the text. Imagine instruction to read the sentence to look like this:

- 9:00 A.M.   Sight Word Instruction (*the, on*)
- 10:00 A.M.   Decodable Word Instruction (*mat, cat, sat*)
- 11:00 A.M.   Practice (*The cat sat on the mat.*)

Decoding instruction needs more discussion. You need to understand beginning, intermediate, and advanced phonics instruction for the test. Look at Table 5.5 and note the progression of instruction. Though some of the terms might be unfamiliar to you, just try to get a sense of the progression for now.

TABLE 5.5

LEARNING TO READ			
KINDERGARTEN	**FIRST GRADE**	**SECOND GRADE**	**THIRD GRADE**
Letter Names Sound Segments	*Beginning Phonics* Letter Sounds Onsets/Rimes		
		Intermediate Phonics Blends/Digraphs Vowel Patterns Phonics Rules	
			Advanced Phonics Syllables Fluent Decoding
Regular Sight Words		*Irregular Sight Words*	

Look at kindergarten first, and recall that students are supposed to leave kindergarten knowing their letter names and their sound segments. They will then be able to associate the letters and sounds together in first grade during beginning phonics instruction. This is important because many letters in the English alphabet do not follow the alphabetic principle. The alphabetic principle is that one letter represents one sound. That works for words like *Ape* and *Ace,* since the letter *A* says its name in each word. But now think of words like *apple, ant,* and *aunt.* As you can see, there are many variant sounds associated with just this letter, so that makes learning to read English, a phonetically irregular language, challenging.

Table 5.5 also shows that instruction moves from letter–sound correspondence to onset–rime instruction during beginning phonics instruction to more complex elements of print during intermediate and advanced instruction (blends, digraphs, rules, and polysyllabic words). The goal is for children to fluently decode print by the end of third grade, so that instruction can then focus exclusively on comprehension. Note that sight word instruction parallels decoding instruction and also increases in complexity.

Beginning Phonics Instruction.   As you know, decoding instruction begins with letter–sound correspondence and then moves on to decoding simple onsets and rimes in simple consonant–vowel–consonant (CVC) words (e.g., *cat, sat, hat,* and *mat*). Learning to decode words like these focuses on consonants first, because they are easiest to recognize especially in initial position. Early decoding activities teach children to decode words by word family using simple onsets and rimes. Onsets are the first consonant or consonants in a syllable, and the rime is the vowel you hear in the word plus any consonants that follow it. Consider the common onsets and rimes shown in Table 5.6.

TABLE 5.6

ONSETS	RIMES
C	-at
M	-an
T	-ake

Look at all of the simple, monosyllabic (one-syllable) words we can make from these onsets and rimes: *cat, can, cake, mat, man, make, tan, cake, make, take*. Beginning phonics instruction focuses on these decodable words using these easy-to-generalize patterns. Along with sight words, the decodable words can be used in simple decodable sentences that children can begin to decode independently.

Phonics instruction increases in complexity, moving far beyond decoding simple onsets and rimes.

Intermediate Phonics Instruction.   During this phase, more complicated letter patterns and positions are used for instruction. Although initial positions of letters are easy to recognize, final and medial positions (in that order) are more challenging. Furthermore, letter combinations become more complicated. There are two types of letter combinations to know for the test: blends and digraphs. Blends are two or more consonants together, and each consonant can be heard. Digraphs bring two or more letters together to make only one sound. To help keep blends and digraphs straight, just remember that the "bl" in *blend* is a blend (you can hear the *b* and *l*), and the "ph" in *digraph* is a digraph (you hear only one sound, not *puh-huh*). Examples of each type of combination are shown in Table 5.7.

The examples in Table 5.7 contain consonant digraphs and blends. The digraphs are *th* and *th*. Note the position of each digraph. The test maker wants you to understand that digraph position presents its own challenges to children learning to decode digraphs: In the initial position, they are easier to recognize (**th**is, **sh**ip); and in the final position, they are more difficult (wi**th**). If you are asked questions on sequencing instruction, try to keep the "position" principle in mind.

Consonant blends in the example include *bl, st,* and *nd*. Again position plays a role in sequencing instruction because of the position principle. Activities to teach either digraphs or blends is the same as what you saw earlier with simple onsets and rimes. Index cards with the digraph or blend written on them can be paired with common onset to form words. This type of activity is appropriate for virtually all areas of phonics instruction.

There is another type of digraph and blend that you need to know for the test: vowel digraphs and blends. Vowel digraphs contain vowels that come together to make one sound; vowel blends, on the other hand, bring vowels together to form two or more sounds (see Table 5.8).

TABLE 5.7

CONSONANT DIGRAPHS	CONSONANT BLENDS
this	blue
ship	stop
with	bend

TABLE 5.8

VOWEL DIGRAPHS	VOWEL BLENDS
paint	coil
meet	sow
boat	boy
tow	royal

As Table 5.8 shows, vowel digraphs bring *ai, ee, oa* together to make long vowel sounds (the vowel letter names for *a, e,* and *o*). Vowel digraphs are difficult, because there are many variations in how the patterns are decoded. Consider *ow* for example. As a digraph, it makes *tow, row,* and *bow;* however, it also makes variants like *cow* and *sow* which are vowel blends (discussed next). The letter combinations *oa* and *ee* are relatively stable since their pronunciations do not vary wildly, but the rest of the digraphs have many short and long vowel associations attached to them. This makes vowel digraphs a challenging area of decoding instruction.

Vowel blends bring two vowels or letters together to make two or more distinct sounds. Say the words *coil, cow,* and *boy* to yourself. You should have noticed that you said more than just one vowel sounds when saying these words. That is because vowel blends are also *vowel diphthongs.* A diphthong contain two vowels that make up two distinct sounds. So, *coil, toy, ouch,* and *bow* (as in "take a bow") all have diphthongs in them. In fact, *coil* /koyul/ and royal /royul/ are *triphthongs,* since they have three separate vowel sounds in them.

Phonics instruction grows even more complex as it turns to phonics rules. Phonics rules are also called phonics generalizations, and they are dependable patterns that can be extended across many kinds of words.

The most reliable phonics rules to remember for the test are as follows:

- Consonant-Vowel-Consonant (CVC) and Consonant-Vowel-Consonant-Consonant (CVCC) Patterns: The medial vowel is usually short, as in *cat, sat, bet, set, mitt, sit, lot, hot, but, rut,* and *tack, sack, with.*
- CVCe (silent *e*) Patterns: The silent *e* makes the medial vowel long or say its name: *name, mite, cove, mute.* There are exceptions: *love* and *have.*
- Two Sounds of *C*: When *c* is followed by *e, i,* or *y,* it sounds like /s/: *cereal, city,* and *cytoplasm.* It is hard like /k/ elsewhere: *cat* and *cot.*
- Two Sounds of *G*: When *g* is followed by *y* or silent *e,* it sounds soft like /j/ in *gym* and *garage.* It is hard like /g/ elsewhere: *get, got, **ga**rage.*
- VV patterns usually make the first vowel long or say its name, as in *main, each, moan,* but there are many exceptions. The combination, *oo,* for example, makes *book, look, took,* but also *spool* and *fool.* Also, *ou* is makes the /ool/ in *through* and the /O/ in *though.* The most stable patterns to remember are *oa* and *ee,* since their long vowel associations (/O/ and /E/ respectively) remain constant (Bear, Invernizzi, Templeton, & Johnston, 2000).
- R-Control: Some words are hard to read or spell because the *r* is overpowering or says its name. Examples: *car, tar, bar, far, bird, curb.*

Before discussing advanced phonics instruction, let's close with the most common activity used to instruct all of the aforementioned areas: the word sort. Here, children sort word cards into two or more piles based on their sound. For example, when learning to read and write words based on the hard and soft *c* phonics rules, the children will sort the words *city, cereal,* and *cytoplasm* into one pile and *cat, cot,* and *cut* into another pile. This activity helps the children recognize patterns that help us when reading and writing both familiar and unfamiliar words according to these generalizable patterns (see Figure 5.2).

Such an activity will work for short onsets/rimes, vowel digraphs and blends, and the all of the phonics rules. Sight words, too, can be instructed in this way, even though they are not decodable. Sight word sorts have the children learning to automatically recognize sight words based on features that they can recall within the words (see Figure 5.3).

The point is to teach children to automatically recognize these words in isolation so that they can say them immediately when they see them in context.

Advanced Phonics Instruction.   The ultimate aim of decoding instruction is fluency. By third grade, all children are expected to be able to fluently decode print. Remedial instruction in problematic areas takes place until print is no longer an issue for them. This is because of a singular idea that we will revisit again: *Fluency enables comprehension.* If children cannot decode text fluently, then they spend their time making and correcting errors. Since their atten-

FIGURE 5.2

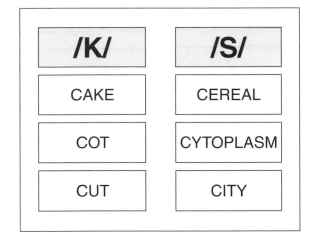

FIGURE 5.3

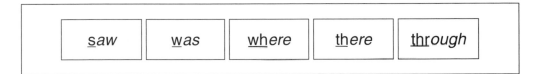

tion is occupied with struggling through the text, the idea is that they will not have enough attention left over to comprehend what they have decoded. Plus, decoding errors can simply interfere with comprehension. Decoding *car* for *cat* throughout a passage on kittens will leave the reader with a vastly different impression from what the author had in mind when she wrote the text. Thus, fluency is critical for comprehension, and that is why kindergarten through third grade instruction is so preoccupied with teaching children to rely on print.

Polysyllabic Words

Polysyllabic words are words with more than one syllable. To be fluent decoders, children must be able to handle these kinds of words. Polysyllabic words are challenging, because many of the words are made up of open and closed syllables. An open syllable is one without a consonant in the rime; a close syllable has a consonant in the rime. Let's look at the difference. Put your hand under your chin and say the following words: *mama, dada,* and *haha.*

Each time your chin dropped, you marked a syllable. Syllables are build around the vowels that we can hear in words. Each of the example words has two syllables: *ma / ma, da / da,* and *ha / ha.* Each of these syllables is open, because there is no consonant in the rime. Now say these words (hand under chin) for a contrast: *batman, catman,* and *antman.*

These polysyllabic words have two closed syllables in them, because there are consonants in the rime positions of the syllables: *bat / man, cat / man, ant / man.* Decoding polysyllabic words with open and closed constituents is important, because upper elementary text is filled with them. Consider the four types of polysyllabic words (Vacca & Vacca, 1989).

- Compound words like *Batman, toolbox,* and *weathermen.*
- Complex words with prefixes and suffixes like *unrecognizable* and *antidisestablishmentarianism.*
- Decodable words like *calculus* and *elephant.*
- Irregular words like *Wednesday* and *February.*

Being able to fluently decode polysyllabic words and complicated sight words (*throughout, however, therefore*) fluently is the requisite for moving from the learning-to-read stage into the reading-to-learn stage.

Some types of polysyllabic words are the result of adding certain inflectional affixes. Consider what happens when adding -d and -ing to some words (see Table 5.9).

TABLE 5.9

-ed	-ing
pin–pinned	pin–pinning
step–stepped	step–stepping

Doubling these consonants occurs in English to preserve the short vowel sounds in each of these words, *pin, step* when adding -ed and -ing. It is possible that you may see decoding data that has a child decoding words with these inflectional affixes like this */run/ /ed/, /pin/ /ed/,* or */step/ /ping/*. Obviously, these needs would have to be corrected; and the appropriate type of activity would involve word cards and would be performed like a word sort:

Here, each card would be read separately before being united and read as one word.

The teacher would return to text and ask the child to read words with these types of inflectional endings within the context of print.

Fluency

Fluent decoding of complex, polysyllabic text separates learning to read and reading to learn. Fluency is the ultimate aim of instruction and refers to smooth and accurate decoding of text. Once children can decode text fluently and accurately, then they are ready to focus on comprehending vocabulary and the text itself (Adams, 1990). Here is the reason: Children who cannot decode fluently will spend all of their time making and correcting errors. Furthermore, their attention will be occupied with errors, and they will not have enough memory left over to comprehend what they read. Therefore, K–3 instruction focuses on decoding text almost exclusively when teaching basic reading skills (Rasinksi, 2000; Stahl & Kuhn, 2002).

Fluency is defined as reading a text at a good rate of speed and with correct intonation. Reading accurately but too slowly, for example, may mean that the child is focusing too much on the print and not enough on meaning of the passage. Both areas could be separate targets of instruction if deficiencies are present in either aspect. After students become fluent, then they will be able to devote the majority of their attention to textual meaning and comprehension.

Three types of activities are appropriate for fluency. The first is for increasing speed. Repeated reading of familiar texts at the child's independent reading level is always appropriate, whether it is followed by a discussion, done in pairs, or performed with a tape recorder (Samuels, 1997). The second activity is for eliminating flat and monotone reading behaviors. Choral and echo reading activities where the teacher models how to read a passage that has been copied and highlighted to emphasize a rising and falling voice are appropriate (McCauley & McCauley, 1992). The last activity is for repeating behaviors, in which the child repeats words, phrases, or whole sentences. This behavior is usually due to lack of confidence (trying to confirm what one has read), or it may be a simple directionality problem. In either case, a scaffold like running the finger beneath the text can help, or the edge of a note card can be used to guide the child. *It is important to wean the child off using either the finger or the note card eventually, as these crutches can interfere with fluency later on.*

Note also that that the texts used for repeated readings are always familiar and are at the child's independent reading level (to be discussed in content area four: Assessment).

Spelling Development

One area of instruction that spans kindergarten and beyond is spelling instruction. This section will describe spelling instruction for primary and upper elementary students that you need to know for the test. The terminology associated with spelling instruction will be presented first, before examples of analysis and instructional methods.

The terms *prephonetic, phonetic, transitional,* and *conventional* are used in many of the test registration bulletins to characterize the spelling stage in which a student's spelling can be categorized. An important idea is that children move through each of these stages on their way to becoming proficient in this area of the model. The following are characteristics for each stage that you should know for the test (adapted from Bear & Barone, 1989; Bear & Templeton, 1998; Invernizzi, Abouzeid, & Bloodgood, 1997):

The *prephonetic stage* describes the spelling that one sees in the writing of children who have little to no knowledge of spelling. Here, children will often scribble when asked to spell words because they have not yet learned to associate the sounds that they hear with letters. Later, the scribbling may include discernable lines or symbols that look like regular print. This reflects a child's emerging awareness of the symbolic nature of language. Invented spelling is common at this stage, where children write random symbols or draw pictures of words they are asked to spell. Invented spelling is important, because it will tell you how a child's spelling falls along a continuum of spelling development (from prephonetic to conventional).

The *phonetic stage* begins when the child begins to write letters to represent the dominant sounds he hears in words. Phonetic spellings show development in associating sounds to letters. This stage depends greatly on how much prior knowledge and instruction the child has had in *encoding orthographic letter patterns.* Sounds pretty serious, huh? All that it means is that the child can form the appropriate letters based on the sounds she or he hears and writes down common letter combinations.

The *transitional stage* represents a level where the child encodes all of the dominant sounds heard in the word and *attempts* to include the complexities found in words. Spelling a word like *bread* as *brade* is an example of this stage of development, since the child is attempting to encode a complicated vowel digraph (*ea*) by adding a silent -e to the end of the word. This stage reflects very late development and is a goal of instruction.

The *conventional stage* in spelling is the stage where children spell correctly the majority of words they write. This does not mean that they spell every word correctly, though. Common misspellings at this stage include words like *independance* and *confidant*. In the upper elementary grades, children at this stage of development will use spelling to increase vocabulary, particularly *content-area vocabularies,* as they learn to spell words that use prefixes, suffixes, and roots. A full discussion of this area of spelling instruction will take place when vocabulary instruction is covered later in this chapter.

Table 5.10 illustrates spellings that typify each stage of development (all data are hypothetical).

TABLE 5.10

PREPHONETIC	PHONETIC	TRANSITIONAL	CONVENTIONAL
(scribble drawing)	tr	Tre	"tree"

Each of the spelling data for the word *tree* reflects the spelling stages that you need to know for the test. The first example (prephonetic) for *tree* shows that the child moves from scribbling to encoding (writing) the most dominant sounds heard in the word, which is the consonant blend *tr*. In the transitional stage, the child has successfully encoded all of the dominant sounds heard in the word. The student would need instruction in encoding long vowel patterns to move into the conventional stage.

Activities like words sorts (that end by having the child write the words down in lists) or spelling activities involving writing words in the *-at* family are common. Elkonin **word boxes** are also typical; *though word boxes are never used during phonemic awareness, sound boxes are*. Word boxes help children hear sounds in words where the vowels or other sounds are hard to discern (as in r- control words) by first marking the sounds and then adding the letters (see Figure 5.4).

FIGURE 5.4

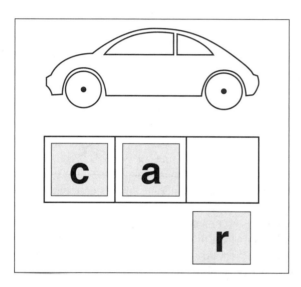

Here, the child has the opportunity to identify the sounds first, make sound–letter associations next, and then spell the words using tiles. This way, they can learn to spell words that are inherently difficult because of the particular features within them. This type of activity is also appropriate for students who are reluctant to spell words because they are afraid that they might misspell them. Word boxes help to elicit a response from the child, because the child can write what she thinks she hears in the word by pronouncing the word to herself and then writing it down. The word boxes can then be used to compare what the child said with what she had written down initially to provide her with a strategy that she can use when spelling unfamiliar words and to reduce her anxiety about spelling.

For questions on upper elementary students, keep in mind that the spelling of one word can reveal how to spell a very similar word. Consider the following (see Table 5.11).

TABLE 5.11

Nature	Natural
Critic	Criticism
Special	Specialist

Teaching words in this manner will help students develop an awareness of how words and their spellings relate to one another. In upper elementary classrooms, children can be taught to spell words based on Greek and Latin roots (see Figure 5.5).

FIGURE 5.5

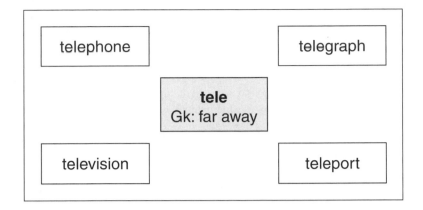

This can take place in the content areas, too. For example, children can be taught to spell scientific terms like *thermal, microscope, thermometer, meter, centimeter,* and *sphygmomanometer* within the context of content area vocabulary instruction.

Vocabulary

Extensive oral vocabulary triggers comprehension. Once a child can decode a word correctly he will comprehend it, because what he has decoded will register meaning in his mind. Consider the written word *cat.* If the word is in the child's oral vocabulary and he understands its meaning, then it is likely to register when the word is decoded for the first time. Vocabulary in upper elementary classrooms is beyond this level, and vocabulary from the sciences can be very elusive. Decoding a word like *entropy* for the first time might not help one comprehend it. Adding its definition as the *second law of thermodynamics* might not help much either, because the words is conceptual in nature and highly specialized. Highly complex words like *antidisestablishmentarianism* present their own challenges, because they are polysyllabic and contain many derivational affixes. Thus, vocabulary in upper elementary classrooms requires a variety of strategies that vary depending on their type and challenges. Without these strategies, comprehending what one reads might not be possible.

To understand the challenges that children face when learning upper elementary vocabulary, you have to know about the five types of words that they may encounter in text. There are four types of vocabulary words to consider here (Armbruster & Nagy, 1992; Dunn & Graves, 1987):

- *Words that they know when reading and that they use in speaking.* These vocabulary words are the most accessible words to children, because the meanings "register" when they read them. For example, when they encounter the word *cat* for the first time and decode it, it is likely that they will understand the word if it is already part of their spoken vocabulary. The only real challenge here is to decode the word correctly and comprehend it.
- *Words they know connotatively or denotatively.* Often, there are differences between a word's *connotative* and *denotative* meaning. Connotation is a word's implied meaning, and denotation is a word's "dictionary definition." Many words that we use in English acquire connotative meanings through use and change, acquiring meaning outside of their dictionary definition. The word *cool* is a good example. The denotative meaning of cool is something "cold to the touch" or "below room temperature." If we hear students say, "Ms. Johnson is a really cool teacher," they are using the word connotatively to mean that the teacher is "hip" or "nice" or "aware." Obviously, if a student is aware of only one type of meaning for a particular word, then they will take away an entirely different meaning of the above sentence. Understanding "Mrs. Johnson is below room temperature" would be a strict denotative understanding of the word *cool.*

■ *Words that they know in reading but rarely use in speaking.* The most obvious examples of such words are those like *heretofore* and *aforementioned.* They represent words that we know in reading, but probably rarely use in casual conversation. As children read more and more varieties of text, they will develop a reading vocabulary that includes words like these, and this collection may exceed their spoken vocabularies. Homographs, too, can present challenges. Knowing whether to say *mínute* or *minúte* depends on context: *Give me a minute* or *that sample is minute* may not be initially discernable to students.

■ *Words that they have seen before in only certain spoken or written contexts.* The target vocabulary of developmental activities are the words that the student knows only in certain contexts and words that are completely unfamiliar to him. Homophones fit this category. These are words that sound the same but are spelled differently, such as, *their, there,* and *they're.* The child might have been saying the word *they're* for years but may not recognize it immediately when reading it for the first time. Confusions in writing may also occur with homophones like *site, cite,* and *sight,* because the child only has a thin grasp of when to use words such as these in particular contexts.

■ *Words that they have never seen before or have never used in speech.* Highly specialized vocabulary words from the content areas, like *entropy,* name concepts that they child might not have any clue about. So, even if words like these are decoded correctly, they will not conjure a familiar idea and register meaning. Structurally complex words fall into this category, and the difference between *denationalization* and *internationalization* might not be immediately recognizable unless the child has particular skills to "get at" the meaning of each word.

Please note that the variety of upper elementary words you will focus on here are ones that are beyond the simple word recognition level. Teaching *word recognition* is different from instructing *word meaning.* In the former, one asks the students to see and say a word; but in the latter, one asks the students to not only see and say the word, but to also understand it. Early on, word *recognition* can be taught by reading the words aloud to the children and having them look at them and write them down. This is also thought to determine their level of vocabulary development; because if they cannot decode the word fluently, then they will not be able to comprehend it while reading.

Early word *meaning* instruction can be taught by simply previewing the passage, pulling difficult vocabulary out, and preteaching the terms to the students before they either read it alone or with the teacher. Reading aloud to children is another early word meaning activity. Here, you reduce the decoding demands on the student by reading to them and discussing any unfamiliar words with them as you go along. Actively questioning and discussion the words with them will help to engage their attention and, hopefully, lead to their understanding of the words in context. Please recognize that the following is **not** an effective way to teach *decoding:* When teaching decoding, have them decode text; when teaching early comprehension, take attention off of decoding and focus it on understanding and context.

These considerations lead us to consider how to instruct higher level vocabulary words, particularly during the reading-to-learn process for children in grades four and above (see Table 5.12).

By the end of third grade, children are expected to be able to successfully decode text, particularly polysyllabic words. We discussed activities associated with polysyllabic words

TABLE 5.12   Vocabulary Development

THIRD GRADE	FOURTH	FIFTH	SIXTH–EIGHTH
Syllabication	*Structural Analysis*	*Roots*	*Etymology*
• Polysyllabic Words	• Inflections	• Greek and	• Word Origins
• Open/Closed Syllables	• Derivations	Latin Roots	• Word History

during the *learning-to-read* process. The important idea to keep in mind from our earlier discussion is that children need to leave the third grade with the ability to syllabicate, because *syllabication* will allow students in upper elementary grades to apply structural analysis to highly complex words.

You also learned about *structural analysis* earlier, when we discussed both *morphology* and *semantics* in Chapter 4. Here is how it applies to vocabulary instruction. Consider these two polysyllabic words: *chimpanzee* and *denationalization.* In the case of the former, syllabicating the word might trigger an image in the child's mind if the word is in the child's spoken repertoire; in the latter example, an image might not come to mind, because the word is not part of the child's spoken vocabulary. Thus, a different set of activities will be required for each word (see Table 5.13).

TABLE 5.13

CHIMPANZEE	DENATIONALIZATION
1. Recognize the letters.	1. Recognize the letters.
2. Syllabicate the word.	2. Syllabicate the word.
3. Say the whole word.	3. Find the base or root word (nation).
	4. Identify suffixes and their meaning (-al, -ize, -ation).
	5. Identify the prefix and its meaning (de-).
	6. Reassemble and say the word.
	7. Check context.

In the case of *chimpanzee,* getting at the meaning of the word is a matter of syllabicating the word and saying it correctly. There is nothing to analyze structurally within the word, because it has no prefixes, suffixes, or root words. *Denationalization,* on the other hand, requires a number of skills that the child must learn in order to comprehend what the word means. To structurally analyze the word, the child needs to be able not only to syllabicate but also to identify base words, roots, prefixes, and suffixes. Prior instruction in each of these areas would have to take place in order to develop the appropriate skills that can be later turned into vocabulary strategies for use while reading.

Root word instruction and instruction in *etymology* can also help to develop a child's vocabulary. There areas have been presented to you already. In the former, having children learn a root word like *tele* and then applying it to a list of words like *telephone, telegraph,* and *telex* will provide them with a tool to access complex vocabulary words. In addition, students can create root word webs and connect them together to see how words relate to one another (see Figure 5.6).

FIGURE 5.6

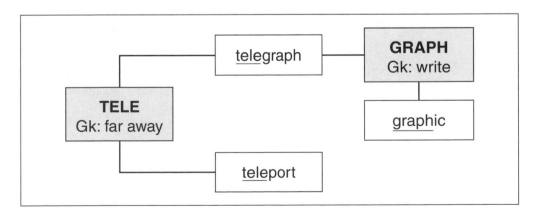

Etymology can also help with teaching word meaning. Activities for etymological studies can be applied to the names of the months or the days of the week (see Table 5.14).

TABLE 5.14

December	Tenth Month
November	Ninth Month
October	Eighth Month
Wednesday	Odin's Day

Such an activity can lead to a discussion of why the calendar only had ten months in it at one time, and who Odin was and why a day in our week is named after him, along with how the spellings of many words give clues to their origins and meanings. Note that looking up words in a dictionary, although an important skill, takes place in a particular context: during research for etymology. These skills must be taught and applied explicitly. Though please recognize that this activity is not used for either word recognition or word meaning, because it is too cumbersome and time consuming. The dictionary is also appropriate when one needs to understand how to pronounce an unfamiliar word that does not follow regular phonics generalizations. For example, *archaeopserinx* and *rhamphorincus* have many letter combinations that are not common in English; therefore, a dictionary will be helpful when determining how to say these words correctly.

At this point, you must be wondering about context. In the test maker's view, context is a wholly unreliable predictor of a word's meaning, so it is deemphasized in this model in favor of relying on the print and the structure of a word to get at its meaning. For some words, though, context is the only way to know which word is correct, or how it is pronounced in a sentence. This is particularly true for homophones and homographs:

- Homographs: The sample is **minute.** Give me a **minute.**
- Homophones: I need to go _____. (*there, their,* or *they're*?)

In each case, the only way to know where to place the stress on the word *minute* depends entirely on context. Similarly, the only way to know which *there* to use is based also on context. Thus, context does play a role in the exam, but it is relegated to this level and should not be your first choice when answering questions on vocabulary.

One important activity to know for the exam that combines print, grammar, and meaning together into one activity is called the *cloze* activity. Cloze activities are nothing more than fill-in-the-blank activities and require children to rely on visual information, syntactic (grammar) information, and semantic (meaning) information to complete the activities. Cloze procedures are also common ways to test comprehension, because they ask students to construct meaning from what they read in order to fill in the blanks with words that make the most sense in the passage (Barnitz, 1998). Here are two examples of them.

Sometimes, cloze activities are used to assess a student's ability to use visual, syntactic, and semantic information to supply correct words within sentences. Consider the example in Table 5.15.

Example one targets a grammar point. Here, it is assessing a student's knowledge of when to use *a* or *an,* and that depends on visual information and her knowledge of English syntax: If the noun that follows the article begins with a vowel, use *an;* if the noun begins with a

TABLE 5.15

EXAMPLE ONE: GRAMMAR	**EXAMPLE TWO: LITERARY TERMINOLOGY**
Give me ____ apple.	Literary _____ are common. They are _____
I bought ____ car.	that compare unlike things. For example, _____
a or *an*	use *like* or *as,* but _____ use neither one.
	analogies, symbols, similes, metaphors

consonant, use *a*. In the second example, relying on semantic clues (called "cues") are required to identify the appropriate word for each blank. This cloze activity assesses a student's knowledge of literary terminology and the vocabulary words related to literary analogies (to be covered in chapter five). In both cases, cloze activities can both assess and teach vocabulary, though their purposes vary depending on the focus on instruction.

A Note on Assessment. Assessment of word recognition and meaning should use the words both in isolation and in context. This will ensure that the child has had the opportunity to demonstrate word recognition skills in both contexts, and the teacher will have a fuller picture of what the child can and cannot do. During oral assessments of vocabulary and reading, the teacher's role is to record the behaviors and to assess the student's ability. No interventions are permitted, like supplying words or helping the student successfully decode the text or print, for either word recognition or meaning assessment.

Comprehension

Recall that fluency is the gateway to comprehension in this model and that by grade three children are expected to be able to decode print fluently. This way, they will have enough attention available to them to have the opportunity to comprehend what they read. The test makers divide comprehension into two categories: *listening comprehension* and *reading comprehension*. Reading comprehension itself is further divided into literal, inferential, and evaluative comprehension. Review the model in Table 5.16 to get a sense of how these areas relate to one another across grade levels.

TABLE 5.16

KINDERGARTEN	FIRST	SECOND	THIRD	FOURTH	FIFTH+
LISTENING COMPREHENSION		READING COMPREHENSION			
		Literal	Inferential	Evaluative	

Comprehension, particularly listening comprehension, is taught early during K–3 instruction, but not during decoding instruction. Since focusing on comprehension during decoding instruction would take attention away from print, it is not part of decoding instruction. Thus, listening comprehension **is** taught to children during the learning-to-read process, though it is done in activities separate from what one undertakes to instruct print. The day might look like this:

■ 9:00 A.M. Decoding Instruction
■ 9:30 A.M. Oral Reading and Listening Comprehension

For example, after decoding instruction, children might be read to for a period of time and then asked to retell the story. Oral retellings are a common means of assessing comprehension. The teacher can direct a question to the children about the plot, sequence, or characters in the story. To ensure the effectiveness of this assessment, the teacher would have to preview and list the most important characteristics that the students must include, along with notes about how much prompting the teacher had to provide to elicit such a response.

Another activity can ask children to draw the stories based upon what they have heard, since having a goal beyond the reading is also important to keep them engaged during the reading. After hearing the story, the children can draw a picture of the main character and his/her adventure. After drawing the picture, the children can narrate their stories to the teacher to foster early literacy development. Not only would such an activity keep them engaged, it would also give children with other learning styles the opportunity to use other abilities to express themselves. In summary, all of these activities will provide the readiness for *reading to learn* once they are fluent decoders of text.

Since comprehension is the primary focus of the *reading-to-learn process* in upper elementary grades, let's look carefully at literal, inferential, and evaluative comprehension once the children are decoding text fluently (see Table 5.17).

TABLE 5.17   Comprehension Development

LATE SECOND–THIRD	FOURTH–FIFTH	SIXTH–EIGHTH
Literal	*Inferential*	*Evaluative*
Factual Questions	How and Why Questions	Fact, Opinion, Propaganda

Literal Comprehension.   Literal comprehension is the most basic level of comprehension. Children learn to answer basic factual questions, like simple wh- questions: who, what, where, and when. Sequences and details are also very important for literal comprehension. That is why having the students list events as they took place in the story is one way that teachers instruct and assess a student's literal comprehension. They are not asked to make inferences nor to evaluate the events at this point, but merely to list the events and the details in order to ensure that they have understood the factual elements presented in the text.

Inferential Comprehension.   Inferential comprehension is a higher level of comprehension. Here, the teacher asks students to make inferences about what they have understood literally. They learn to answer more challenging questions about **how** and **why** things happen in a story. Beyond asking students how and why questions, the teacher can ask them to generate alternative endings to the stories they have read that they have heard and to be consistent with what the main character would probably do. The teacher can then determine whether the literal understandings that the students have were sufficient to make the correct inferential assumptions about the character.

Evaluative Comprehension.   Evaluative or critical comprehension is the highest level of all. Instruction in this advanced area takes place after students are proficient in comprehending what they read or hear both literally and inferentially. Critical thinking involves identifying reason and logic in a text to determine whether the author's point is valid, reliable, and worth considering or whether a work represents fact, opinion, or propaganda. Evaluative comprehension of a literary work would also consider how well each part of the work functions as a whole. This moves beyond merely analyzing character, plot, setting, and the like into asking students to think about whether or not the novel holds together through each chapter of the text, and whether the main and subplot lines are believable and effective when viewed comprehensively.

Nonfiction stories from news articles can also be evaluated for instances of bias and propaganda. Copies of news articles and editorials can be circulated and the students can categorize them into fact and opinion piles and then be asked to justify their decisions. Such an activity will help the students recognize when text contains only facts and when it also incorporates opinions into the passage. Another type of activity asks students to outline the major points found in an article or a speech before having them propose alternative arguments to each point that they have identified. Then, students can propose alternative ideas and research them for the purpose of comparing what they have found with what the author proposed. Comparing and contrasting ideas moves beyond mere literal and inferential comprehension into evaluating ideas. In this way, students learn to be critical readers who can identify facts, opinions, and propaganda in the articles they read.

The type of text being read is the final area to consider in the reading-to-learn stage. The test makers divide texts into two separate categories: narrative and expository. Narrative texts are short stories, novels, and other works of fiction, whereas expository text are informational pieces that include reading in the content areas (science, math, social studies, math word problems, etc.). Text type is important because the organizational patterns of each category is different. Narrative text, for example, has plot, setting, characters, and action. Expository texts often have only lists of details, comparisons, and contrasts or are otherwise hard to understand because they use language in highly specialized ways (e.g., word problems requiring proportions).

Schemata

Schemata is the organizational format of text, and narrative text comprehension *tends to* precede expository text comprehension. This is because children who are reared in homes where they hear stories read to them (even from watching cartoons on television) acquire narrative text schema from direct experience. They learn to anticipate characters, plots, and setting, however rudimentary, through these experiences. Expository text is different. It's organizational pattern, especially in mathematics, may be very abstract. A child who reads a text about different types of butterflies might get lost in the details, because they go into the reading expecting a story but find neither characters and nor action to speak of. They find the text difficult to comprehend, because they lack the mental framework necessary to follow the organizational schemata of the text. Thus, they will have to be taught it explicitly.

Table 5.18 presents the two basic organizational patterns to know for the test.

TABLE 5.18   Story Schema

KINDERGARTEN–EIGHTH GRADE	FOURTH–EIGHTH GRADE
Narrative Schema	*Expository Schema*
• Story Sequence • Story Grammar (plot, character, setting) • Freitag's Pyramid (background, plot, rising action, climax, resolution)	• Details • Sequence • Cause/Effect • Comparison/Contrast • Problems/Solutions

Briefly, narrative schemata includes story sequence, grammar, and something else that you will learn about called *Freitag's Pyramid.* Stories are a part of the life of classrooms from kindergarten through the eighth grade, though in the early grades (where either the foundations of decoding or decoding itself is the focus) narrative schemata is developed mainly through listening and other oral language activities. Expository schemata, on the other hand, is more elusive, because it is not as accessible as narrative schemata. This is because expository schemata involves abstract thinking, understanding cause and effect patterns, and evaluating proposed solutions to described problems. Activities for teaching children to comprehend each type of text differ, yet they all share a common pattern for prereading, while reading, and post reading. Let's look at the basic structure of all schemata activities as they relate to narrative and expository text reading (see Table 5.19). (*Note:* Narrative and expository text activities will be further discussed in Chapters 5 and 6.)

TABLE 5.19

PREREADING	WHILE READING	POST READING
• Prior Knowledge • Advanced Organizing	• Think Aloud • Graphic Organizers	• Literary Response • Research Process

Prereading, while-, and post-reading activities are very important in teaching children to comprehend narrative text. They learn to access their prior knowledge before they read a story, stay engaged in the reading as they read the text, develop story maps while they read, and elaborate and extend their knowledge after they have read something. As students become more and more capable readers, they are asked to focus more and more on story elements, like figurative language, character types, and themes, along with engaging in more challenging tasks like comparing stories cross-culturally and thematically. In short, teaching children to access narrative text schemata is critically important in the reading-to-learn process.

Expository text comprehension is also highly dependent upon schematic patterns. Students need to learn how to read a variety of texts that are organized around lists of details, sequences, cause–effect patterns, and problems–solutions. Prereading, while-, and post-reading activities are very important here, too, since students need to learn how to access prior knowledge and apply it to the text as they read. Furthermore, they need to learn how to make expository text schemata concrete through various types of visual aids, including Venn diagrams, concept maps, and basic outlines. Finally, students need to learn to elaborate and to extend the knowledge that they cull from an expository text though other experiences like the writing and research process (to be discussed in Chapter 6).

CONTENT AREA FOUR: ASSESSMENT

There are two types of assessment to know for the exam. These are individual and group (standardized or norm-referenced) tests. Individual assessment tells you what an individual student can do at one point in time (IRIs) or over time (portfolio evaluation). Group assessments tell you about one moment in time and allows for between group comparisons (individual student and her class, a class with another class, or a school district with another school district).

Informal Reading Inventories (IRIs)

Informal reading inventories include graded word lists and graded reading passages. If you have a fourth grade student, you give the word list first, starting at about a second grade level. You keep moving up the word list, until you find the grade level that frustrates the child (where he or she misses more than 20 percent of the words on a list).

The next step is to have the student read the graded passages. If the frustration level for a fourth grader was at a fourth-grade level, you drop back a grade and start assessing at third grade. You have the child read the passages and note any deletions, substitutions (reading *cat* for *can*), and mispronunciations. After the child reads a passage, you perform the following calculation (Clay, 1993a):

$$\frac{\text{\# of words read} - \text{errors}}{\text{\# of words}}$$

You count any words that were deleted, substituted, or mispronounced as errors. For 100 words read with eleven errors, our calculation would look like this:

$$\frac{100 - 11}{100}$$

This yields a percentage of 89 percent. The percentages correspond to the following reading levels (Clay, 1993a):

- Independent: 100–95%
- Instructional: 94%–90%
- Frustration: 89% and below

The passages usually correspond to books in a series. Green books might be at a level one; yellow books might be at a level two; and red books might be at a level three. If the child's independent level is at the green level, then those books are sent home to be read with the family or read freely in class during sustained silent reading. If the yellow books are at an instructional level, then those texts are used for individual and small group instruction based on the child's need. Finally, frustration books are withheld, until further IRIs indicate that the child is ready to move on to them. In short, today's instructional level books become tomorrow's independent level books; today's frustration level books become tomorrow's instructional level books.

An advantage that informal reading inventories have over other types of assessment is that they are tailored to individual students and therefore reveal individual needs. Interpreting results means considering how the present data reflect progress or regress against other recently administered assessments. IRIs assess students through graded word lists and graded passages and comprehension questions that move from literal to inferential to evaluative.

If the child reads aloud, then the focus is on decoding. If the child reads silently, then the focus is on comprehension. Why? Because of attention. In the former, the child will focus on performance, and there might not be enough memory left over to focus on understanding. Therefore, it is important for you to know what you're assessing: If it's decoding, have them read aloud; but if they are to also comprehend what they have read, then have them reread it silently before asking the questions. Passages that one selects for the miscue analysis should be able to stand by themselves and not depend upon many other units for meaning. Just imagine trying to bake a cake with only half of the ingredients listed. The same is true here: If the passage does not have its own contextual integrity, then it will be difficult for the child to answer any comprehension questions based on the passage.

Miscue Analyses

After the child has read aloud, one performs a miscue analysis. This tells you what *cueing system* the child relies upon when reading. You already learned something about the cueing systems when you learned about cloze activities. Recall that there are three cueing systems to know for the test. The *semantic cueing system* is based on *meaning,* where we look at a multiple-meaning word like *ring* and determine whether it means *to ring a bell* or refers to piece of jewelry. The *syntactic cueing system* helps us figure out the grammatical category of a word in a sentence. The *visual cueing system* (called *graphophonemic* meaning letter–sound correspondence) helps us read words based on the sounds they represent.

After a child reads aloud, the teacher analyzes each substitution to see what cueing system was at work while the child was reading. In Table 5.20, the child's substitution appears above the line; how the text actually read appears below the line. Meaning, Syntax, and Visual correspond to *M, S,* and *V* in the table. The Xs in the boxes below M, S, and V tell you what system was at work at the point of error.

TABLE 5.20   Miscue Examples

EXAMPLE ONE			EXAMPLE TWO			EXAMPLE THREE		
cat car			man boy			cheeseburger girl		
M	**S**	**V**	**M**	**S**	**V**	**M**	**S**	**V**
	X	X	X	X			X	

In example one, the child substituted *cat* for *car.* Since there is no semantic relationship between each word, the M column is blank. Because there is a syntactic (grammatical) relationship between *cat* and *car* (they are both nouns), the S column is checked. And because the words look similar, the V column is checked.

In example two, the child substituted *man* for *boy.* Since there is a semantic relationship between each word, the M column is checked. There is also a syntactic relationship between each of the words (both are nouns), so the S column is checked. However, the V column is left blank, because neither *man* nor *boy* are visually similar.

In example three, the child substituted the word *cheeseburger* for *girl.* Neither the M column nor the V columns are checked, because there is no semantic or visual relationship between these words. The only relationship that exists between each word is grammatical (they are both nouns), so the S column is checked.

Each of these analyses boil down to one thing: *The child does not rely on print <u>enough</u> when reading.* Even when the V column is checked in example one, the child is ignoring the final consonant in the rime. Additional work is needed in that area of decoding. In examples two and three, the child is obviously relying on information beyond the print when decoding text, because the V column was not checked. Thus, print decoding problems abound in the data, and it would be the focus of instruction in all three cases.

Be cautious when looking at any miscue or informal reading inventory data. If the miscue is a simple dialect difference and not a semantic, syntactic, or visual miscue, then it is not considered an error. Exchanging a short vowel for diphthong is a common regional variation. Substituting /peyen/ for *pen* is not a critical error, unless it interferes with comprehension. Therefore, as long as the dialect difference does not detract from a student's reading comprehension, it is not to be targeted as a need for remedial instruction.

Self-corrections can also be analyzed. When a child reads a word incorrectly and then self-corrects it, one can analyze why she did so. The same M, S, V columns are used; and you ask yourself if the child corrected the error based on meaning, syntax, or visual information after she committed the error.

Portfolio Assessments

In contrast to the narrow informal reading assessments, portfolios take a very long view of a child's literacy development: They are collections of artifacts that reflect a child's ability to read, write, listen, and speak. The items are taken from as many sources as possible, so that the portfolio shows a complete and authentic picture of a student's abilities (Courtney & Abodeeb, 1999). The artifacts can include everything from early drafts of writing to audio recordings of the child reading aloud from a favorite book. This way, the teacher can have a complete and "contextualized" view of who the child is, what she can do, and where her needs are. Two portfolio sections that are important for you to know about for the test will be described next. They document reading and writing (Mitchell, Abernathy, & Gowans, 1998).

Reading Sections.   Portfolios can include all of the child's running records, informal reading inventories, miscue analyses, and word lists, so that you and the child can see the progress that the child has made over the year. These documents will also illustrate areas of continuing need that you and the child still need to address. Reading lists are also important. They show the numbers of books and their genres, magazines, and other types of literature that the student is reading in and out of class. This helps both the student and the teacher see progress in the kind and quality of books that the child selects for reading (or avoids). In short, this section should reflect a total picture of the child's reading ability from the beginning of the year to the present moment.

Writing Section.   The writing section collects all of the pieces of writing that the child creates, errors and all. These artifacts can be drafts of poems, complete poems, informal notes, letters to characters from stories, and so forth. They also document all of the work that goes into a paper that the child has written for research projects. This means that all of the pre-writing, the inspirations for writing, including pictures, graphics, and early notes, are part of this section. Drafts and revisions of drafts are also made part of this section, along with comments from the teacher and peers regarding the strengths and needs of the writing. All of these items are important, because they help the teacher and the child see all of the work that went into writing a research paper. Instead of only looking at the final product and assigning a grade to it, portfolios allow one to have a comprehensive view of a child's development. If you have ever felt that a final number on a test or a letter grade was an inadequate means of assessing the real amount of work that went into something that you've done, then you can appreciate the purpose of the portfolio's long view of student development.

Conferences.   Conferences with the child about the portfolio are essential. During these conferences, the teacher and the student discuss the progress that the child has made, along with areas of continuing need. For example, the reading section might show that the child reads a great deal of simple narratives but few expository pieces from journals. The teacher and the student can set goals together to improve this area of the portfolio. Similarly, the writing section will tell both the teacher and the student where the child's strengths and needs lie. For example, the writing might reflect strong organization and a high level of interest but not style. The teacher and the student can discuss this need and make plans for how the student can improve this area of the writing. Subsequent conferences would look at progress in these areas, as well as new ones, as they arise.

Other Portfolio Sections.   The remaining two of the four skills, speaking and writing, can also be included in portfolios. Audio and video records, for example, of public speaking are artifacts that one could collect, along with assessment records of listening comprehension. Later in this chapter, you will learn about reading response journals and learning logs. These types of journals can also be included as part of the portfolio. Here are other items that might be included in the portfolio.

- *Interest Surveys.* Early in the year, it is important to uncover each student's preference for working alone or together on projects, of reading materials, and of topics for future study. This will help the teacher design the learning environment to include specific experiences according to the children's preferences. In addition, knowing the students' preferences and interests will enable the teacher to include the appropriate reading materials in the reading center.
- *Observation Checklists.* Teachers can also use their own observation checklists to gauge student learning. The teacher can note how students behave during SSR or how they answer questions about what they have read. These questions can indicate how well the student tells the teacher about the main idea from what he has read, what facts and details were in the story, what events took place and their order, and words that describe, rhyme, or mean something different in a variety of contexts. These checklists can be used to indicate any problems in reading that can then be targets for small group or individual instruction.
- *Observation Records.* Keeping anecdotal records is also a form of subjective assessment. Noting whether the child is engaged or disengaged during Sustained Silent Reading, for example, will indicate that the child may have a need of some kind in reading assistance. They may not be engaged because they can't find something interesting to read, or because they are not comprehending the book they've selected because it is too hard.

Portfolio Evaluation

Two types of evaluation take place around portfolios. There is student self-assessment and teacher assessment. Student self-assessment has the child reflect on specific areas of the portfolio and identify the strengths and needs in the work (Bottomley, Henk, and Melnick, 1997/1998). Students can select the items that they wish to save in the portfolio based on the elements that show what they have learned or how much growth they have achieved up to this point. The reflections might address whether the student is meeting or has met any stated goals, recognizes her own strengths and needs, and whether any new goals need to be set or revised. This helps the child to develop a sense of inner control and self-direction to set goals and to make plans to meet them (Serafini, 2000/2001). This is a highly personal approach that differs drastically from standardized testing that only shows a child's progress at one moment in time (see Portfolio Assessments, previously discussed).

Students can have a hand in developing the criteria by which their portfolios will be assessed (see Table 5.21). For example, the students and the teacher can work together to develop a list of qualities that should be reflected in the portfolio. They can also establish what shows various levels of progress toward meeting or exceeding the established criteria. It is also important to review the rubric with the students after it has been generated. Doing so will ensure that the students understand how they will be assessed and time can be given to answer student questions and to clear up any misunderstandings.

TABLE 5.21

POINTS	CRITERIA
• 3 Points	• Has met the criteria for punctuating declarative sentences.
• 2 Points	• Has nearly met the criteria for punctuating declarative sentences.
• 1 Point	• Has not met the criteria for punctuating declarative sentences.

The criteria for editing declarative sentences would have to be set and clear for the student, perhaps being posted in the front of the class or at the writing center. In addition, this expectation would have had to have been taught prior to assessment and maybe even agreed upon by class consensus, depending upon how the rubric is designed. As you can see, subjectivity can be a problem with portfolios—with such open and flexible designs and so many eyes looking at the criteria, it can be hard to determine just how objective they are in terms of assessment.

Criterion-Referenced Tests

Criterion-referenced tests are the last type of group assessment that you need to know for the test. The terms associated with these tests include benchmark and rubric (Ediger, 1999). Like the other assessments described in this section, you will have to know how they work, what they tell you about a student's performance, and what is done with the results.

In the first place, criterion-referenced tests look at both product and process. For example, these assessments consider what the child is doing when they write the answers that they write, along with whether or not the answer they've written is correct. Turning to spelling the months of the year, a criterion-referenced spelling test would look at whether the spellings were correct or not and at *how* the child spelled the words:

- Desember
- Febuary
- Janury

The product side of the assessment would be handled through the benchmark score for the test, while the process side would be viewed through preselected rubric criteria. Here is how it works.

A benchmark score for spelling the months of the year might be set at "twelve out of twelve" for third graders in the spring of the year. This means that third graders must be able to spell all of the months of the year correctly before they start grade four. We can up the stakes a bit by stating that children who have not reached this critical benchmark will have to repeat third grade until they can do so. Obviously, you'll be assessing all of your students right from the start of the term to see how far along they are progressing toward that benchmark score, so that you can help those students who appear not to be making progress. This is where the rubric criteria comes in.

If a perfect score on spelling the months of the year is the exit criteria for third grade children, teachers will want to know who is performing at or below these expectations and what to do to help them. Using a rubric can help. Rubrics typically rate students in terms of early, developing, or advanced stages of proficiency. If you assess the children in spelling the months of the year, you can begin to develop a view of which children are early, developing, and advanced based on their score and the *spelling processes* they use. The first item is obvious; the second one needs some explaining.

To achieve a twelve out of twelve on the spelling test, students must not only spell the words correctly but also must capitalize each of the words. The spellings of *January, February,* and *December,* for example, have some odd features about them. *January* has an odd vowel pattern ("ua"), *February* has a silent -r; and *December* ought to have the letter *s* in it, not *c*. Based on this information, spelling development criteria could be set for who is early, developing, and advanced (see Table 5.22).

TABLE 5.22

EARLY	• Does not capitalize the months of the year or does so infrequently. • Spells the words by dominant sounds only (e.g., dsmbr).
DEVELOPING	• Capitalizes most of the months of the year correctly. • Developing spelling patterns (e.g., desember).
ADVANCED	• Capitalizes all of the months of the year correctly. • Frequently spells the months of the year correctly, with very few exceptions (e.g., Febuary).

As you assess the children through out the year on their way toward spelling all of the months of the year perfectly, you can use this rubric to see how they are doing and what they need. For example, if you have two children who consistently get a six on the spelling test, you can figure out why that is so. For the first child, it might be only because they do not capitalize the months of the year. Fixing that will bring them nearer to the benchmark. For another child, capitalization might not be the issue; instead, it is with spelling "er" at the end of some words and with writing all of the sounds not heard in the word (e.g., February). Criterion-referenced assessments are useful for identifying strengths and needs in children and for helping them to reach particular benchmarks in their development. They take both product and process into account.

Norm-Referenced Tests

Norm-Referenced Tests locate a student's score on the normal curve against the performance of other students in the same normative group who are of the same age, grade level, and demographic group. Scores tell teachers how well a child is performing in relation to these other statistical people who have taken the same test. When a teacher reviews norm-referenced scores from English, she can compare her children's level of English comprehension with the performance of their peers on the same exam. They are also considered to be less subjective because of their objective assessment of a group of students under the same conditions. This allows one to compare the performance of a given student with the scores of other students in the class, district, state, and nation.

The terms that you need to know for norm-referenced reporting include raw scores, percentile ranks, grade equivalent scores, and scaled scores.

■ The raw score on a spelling test is simply the number correct out of the number of items given. A child who spells six months correctly has a score of six out of twelve. In short, the raw score is simply the unaltered number correct.

- Percentile rankings are different from raw scores. They make comparing the individual to the group, and a group of individuals to other groups of students, much easier. The scale can go from one to ninety-nine, and you locate the student's raw score on this scale to figure out how much "better" one student did in relation to other students. A student who spelled all of the items correctly would be said to have scored "in the ninety-ninth" percentile, meaning that she did better than 99 percent of the people who took the test. A student who scored zero did worse than 99 percent percent of the people who took the test. Finally, a score in the fiftieth percentile means that the student did "half-as-well" (or "half-as-bad," depending on your perspective) as other students.
- Grade equivalent scores describe a student's academic performance, telling us the grade and achievement levels from one *academic year* to the next. For example, a fourth grade student's score of 5.9 tells us that the fourth grader performs *like* a fifth grader who is in the ninth month of the academic year (May), though we cannot say that the child is "ready" to do fifth grade work. Remember that grade equivalent scores are based on the September to May calendar and that September is the first month and May is the last month in this system. Note also that grade equivalent scores will only tell you about the individual's performance in relation to other individuals; it is not appropriate for group descriptions.

When you encounter questions about what norm-referenced tests do and do not do, keep this spelling example in mind. Furthermore, if you are asked about how you would report results to parents or other caregivers, keep in mind that they are not experts. Pick answers that make thinks very concrete for parents to understand, yet retain the correct ideas. For example:

Your child scored in the ninety-ninth percentile, yielding an above-average, grade-level equivalent score of 10 out of twelve items. You should be proud.

would need to be amended to

Chris got all twelve items right on his spelling test. This means that he scored better than 99 percent of other students who took the test. Since most fourth graders only get ten items correct on the test, his perfect score means that he is doing better than most children his age. You should be proud.

Other terms to know are *reliability, validity,* and *conditions.* Reliability means that a test will provide the same result each time it is given. Giving a spelling test by having the students spell the words aloud before their peers isn't reliable, because it will produce different effects for each student. Content validity means that you have a test that measures what it says it will measure. Having students spell *December* by asking them to spell "the name of the twelfth month of the year" is not valid, because it tests memory and spelling together. Finally, conditions must be the same among all tests if one is going to compare scores. If one group of literature students use their notes for a quiz, but another group cannot, then you may not compare the scores of each group because the tests conditions are different. The scores will not mean the same thing, even if the tests are reliable and valid.

CONTENT AREA FIVE: INSTRUCTIONAL CONSIDERATIONS

Something that makes answering questions about literacy instruction difficult is knowing what the test makers are really asking (see the example at the top of page 127).

You have to understand the writing process to answer the question, but you also have to understand the principles behind instructional activities, like preplanning, to really get it. To understand why D is correct, you need to know how to implement activities in the classroom and how to preplan them. In the question above, you are asked to implement an activity in the classroom for the first time. Because the writing process involves many steps (see content area

A fifth grade teacher wishes to implement the process approach to writing in her classroom. Which of the following statements best represents the action that the teacher should take first?

   A. Consider the grammar points that the students know already and the ones that they will need to learn through the activity.
   B. Plan to have the students brainstorm topics that they might like to write about before attempting the first draft.
   C. Prepare the students to work together to develop a rubric so that they can participate in how the writing project will be scored.
   D. Demonstrate each step of the writing process for the students first and then work with them to carry out the steps together.

ten), you must first model the whole process for students. If not, then any content that you try to teach them will be lost in the confusion of trying to figure out how the activity functions and what the expectations are. So, for any questions on implementation, be sure to look carefully at answers that have modeling as an option. To make this process easier for you, ten key principles will be elucidated for you. These principles will help you to answer questions like these (where all the options look good).

   1. *Understand how to plan activities.* There are three things to consider when planning activities. What will I have the students do before, during, and after the activity?

   Before: One method that is affective for helping students to comprehend what they read takes place before they even approach the text. Having students generate questions before and as they read, for example, will keep them actively engaged in the task of understanding (Langer, 1981). Without questions to guide them through the story or information, they may lose interest or otherwise become disengaged during the process of reading the story. Posing and answering question, then, keeps active reading alive. Pretesting is also a good starting point in the planning process. Pretesting tells one how much students know about a topic before it is introduced. This helps guide the teacher in planning based on what the children know and do not know about a topic. For example, in a unit on dinosaurs, the teacher can introduce a topic and then have the children work in pairs to list what they already know about them. If the children already know enough about the types of dinosaurs that existed, then the teacher can scale her instruction up based on this information. If anticipatory questions will be used, then writing answers to the questions that the teacher expects to hear from the students is also a good place to begin.

   During: The test makers believe that learning occurs best when students participate completely in the learning process, especially in gaining and constructing understanding. Student interest is most important in this model of learning. Having the students pose their own questions and then have the opportunity to answer these questions while they read will keep them actively engaged in the learning process. The teacher's role is to ensure that the learning environment will allow for such endeavors. In sum, because the goal is to have students become independent learners, students must learn to pose and answer their own questions, along with identifying ways to identify resources to satisfy their intellectual curiosity.

   After: Groups of students can work together to answer questions about who, what, where, why, and when after reading a story. Writing answers to these questions when applied to the story will teach students a strategy that they can generalize to other passages that they will read independently. These activities are enrichment activities, where the teacher helps students to elaborate and extend their knowledge using other forms of communication (speaking and writing) to do so.

   2. *Know how to adapt materials for different learning styles.* Teachers need to adapt a variety of instructional materials to meet the needs to their students and their diverse interests and learning styles. Academic learners, for example, may be able to rely on the textbook entirely to gain understanding. Visual learners, however, might need more graphic organizers to ensure understanding, while auditory learners might need small group discussions and lectures on tape to help them comprehend the material. Finally, kinesthetic learners may need hands-on activities and active demonstrations, like highlighting details or creating graphic organizers, to remain engaged in their own learning. Teacher must preplan their lessons based on who their students are and what their learning styles demand.

3. *Recognize the difference between deductive (direct) and inductive instruction.* Direct instruction compartmentalizes learning the section language into distinct and discreet parts. One learns skills in the language one at a time until it has been mastered. This is also called the "bottom up" approach, where students are taught to decode words, identify sentence structures, and other "parts" of the language first. (*Note:* This type of instruction is favored for decoding.)

Inductive approaches are different. Inductive approaches teach academic concepts indirectly. In a deductive approach, the teacher simply presents the concept and then directly teaches it to the students. In inductive instruction, the teacher creates a situation where the students must arrive at the concept that the teacher instructs in the same way that detectives solve crimes. For example, when teaching a grammar point, the teacher might write two examples on the board in the form of a cloze activity.

- I gave the student ___ apple.
- I bought myself ___ new car.

Here, the students are supposed to supply the correct article in the space. Once they do so, they might then be asked to generate the rule: *An* is used before words starting with vowels; *a* is used before words beginning with consonants. The students can then present the rule, along with examples of their own based on the inductive examples. This type of instruction helps students see themselves as capable of solving problems on their own and actively engages them in more rigorous levels of thinking. (*Note:* This type of instruction is not favored for decoding.)

4. *Use metacognition.* Metacognition means "thinking about thinking." When studying for your exam, for example, you may have to stop sometimes and think about whether or not you've understood an explanation. If not, then you reread the passage and ask yourself if you think that you've understood it. If the concept is still unclear, then you may consult another source or ask a qualified person to help you. But you do not quit. That is because you have metacognitive processes that help you to answer your own questions and to motivate you to find solutions.

Metacognitive process need to be modeled for students and can be as minimal as simply asking questions of one's self while reading, or can be as concrete as writing down questions based on the headings and subheadings in a text and then writing down answers to these questions while reading. For example, if one wants to have students self-monitor their own reading and ask themselves if what they're reading makes sense or who the main characters are, then the teacher must explicitly teach this skill through modeling, guided practice, and independent practice.

5. *Use multisensory techniques.* Learning to recognize letters is often accompanied by multisensory techniques. For example, children can be asked to trace felt or fuzzy letters to reinforce the shapes using another sense to do so. This is especially true for letters that are hard to visually discriminate because they are orthographically similar. The idea to keep in mind is that if the concept being taught orally or visually doesn't stick, then try another sense rather than just repeating the ineffective approach over and over again.

This type of technique can be expanded to upper elementary levels, where children are asked to highlight relevant details in a story. They are using kinesthetic and visual skills to make abstract concepts concrete.

6. *Use ability grouping for skills and heterogeneous groups for strategies.* In general, grouping students, whether heterogeneously or homogeneously, will require preplanning. The teacher must consider how to configure the groups, how to populate them, and then how to assign specific goals and tasks to each member of the group to ensure that all members make positive contributions to the effort.

Homogeneous grouping will help meet the needs of readers who are not at the same level as their classmates. This will reduce feelings of inferiority that might otherwise arise if they are placed in situations where their needs are constantly exposed but not addressed. They may feel more comfortable expressing themselves in this type of environment, too, and become more independent learners as a result. Homogenous grouping will also allow opportunities to meet the needs of advanced students who can receive developmentally appropriate materials that take their interests and abilities into account.

Heterogeneous grouping is effective for cultivating a sense of appreciation and sensitivity in diverse classrooms. The key is to structure the groups to play to each of the students individual strengths, so that each member can utilize his or her talent to the fullest and not be made to feel inferior. For example, activities can be structured for the group such that each student, regardless of whether he or she is an academic, visual, or kinesthetic learner, can use his or her talent to the fullest.

7. *Understand individual instruction and mini-lessons.* Individual tutoring may be very effective for remedial instruction. This is because needs can be identified and addressed very quickly, something that might not be possible in small- or whole-group instruction. Instruction can also be tailored to the student's individual strength. If the child is a visual learner, for example, activities can be developed to target this child's strength and make the process of learning easier for him or her. Feedback is corrective but supportive in this model, since the goal is to encourage the student to continue learning and applying whatever skill or strategy that the teacher is modeling.

Planning lessons for individual children begins by addressing the most immediate need of the child in reading, while also aiming the child toward the next level of development. For example, if a child is stuck at the level of blending in phonemic awareness, you address that need. In addition, you also try to aim the child toward the next level of development (segmenting). By doing so, the child will continue to make progress on a continuum of development.

After targeting any need, you should have the child practice the ability in context. Though instruction typically occurs separate from context, the goal is to have the child be able to apply the skill or strategy in a real situation. For example, if sorting words with the rime -at, the final step is to have the child try to read -at words in decodable text. So, after studying and practicing the skill apart from context, be sure to provide the student with the opportunity to practice in a real context. This will lead to independence.

8. *Plan units and other field trips carefully.* When planning units, define learning goals early on. For interdisciplinary units that unite one or more content areas, it is important to determine the learning objectives for each discipline and to define them clearly. The teacher must state in advance what skills the students are to acquire through the unit and how they will connect one area to another. The teacher may ask herself questions about the goals and then answer them concretely before proceeding with the planning of the unit.

Consider a field trip to view art. As part of the preplanning, the teacher will consider how to activate the students' prior knowledge before leaving on the trip. In addition, she will also think about how to have the students remain engaged during the activity. To satisfy these goals, the teacher might begin with a discussion of concepts they have learned about art and list the concepts on the board. Then, the students will generate a list of questions that they will write in their learning logs and apply to the art that they view. When at the museum, the students can jot down notes about the characteristics they've learned about and how they apply to the real art that they are viewing. When they return to class, the students can work together to answer the questions in their learning log, before having a whole-class debriefing on their original questions and the answers.

To assess the students' understanding further, the teacher can ask the students to develop their own art exhibition. They can create pictures based on the concepts that they've learned about and then display them in class. In this way, the students will be able to use all of the four skills (reading, writing, listening, and speaking) for the learning experience, along with demonstrating their understanding of the elements of art that they have learned about.

9. *Know how to select texts.* One of the most important guidelines for selecting multicultural literature is to ensure that the culture is presented accurately and realistically. Wide variety of genres, both fiction and nonfiction, are a must; and they should also represent all reading levels (independent and instructional). Recent and award-winning books are always good candidates to support the goals of the curriculum. Be sure to consider the grade level here. If the students are emergent readers, then pick books that will support phonemic awareness and letter recognition. Decodable texts with regular phonics patterns would be appropriate for developing readers. Finally, wide varieties of literature should be available for fluent readers. All of the texts should be of high interest in all cases.

Equity is another important consideration. Equity is different from equality. Equality means simply having enough books about girls and boys in the classroom. Equity means that one has analyzed each text to ensure that the representations are accurate, nonstereotypical, and help the children aspire to become whatever they want to become based on their interests and skills rather than on societal preconceptions. Selecting books that reflect unbiased views are also important, along with ensuring that the texts show both genders in a variety of nontraditional roles. This is because one wants students' aspirations to be based on their desires and abilities, rather than on someone else's stereotypical expectations for them.

10. *Teach skill to strategy.* This pattern always begins with assessing a student's skill level. Once they have the skill then they can learn to apply it. Think about syllabication. First, the skill must be developed; then it must be converted into a strategy that students can use when reading text with lots of polysyllabic words in them. This pattern is true for anything on the test. Reading techniques are no exception. The pattern is to develop prereading strategies, like finding out what they know about a subject and what want to know about a subject before reading about it, because it focuses students' attention and gives them a skill that they can apply to other passages. Furthermore, it will cue the students into what kinds of strategies to use when reading the passage to answer their questions. Post-reading activities, like having them list what they have learned after reading the passage, engages them in actively comparing what they thought they knew and what they wanted to know in relation to what they have read.

This notion should also extend to teaching English language learners. Try to view answers along the lines of the four skills, *reading, writing, listening,* and *speaking* and align the activities in this manner (see Table 5.23).

TABLE 5.23

READING	Concepts about Print Phonemic Awareness Decoding Instruction Comprehension Instruction CALLA Approaches
WRITING	Language Experience Approach/Writing Process
LISTENING	Total Physical Response
SPEAKING	Communicative Approaches

Literature

DOMAIN TWO: LANGUAGE ARTS

CONTENT AREA SIX: GENRES OF CHILDREN'S LITERATURE

Rather than make grade-level assignments of texts, just divide the texts according to *learning-to-read* literature and *reading-to-learn* literature (see Table 6.1).

TABLE 6.1

LEARNING TO READ		READING TO LEARN			
Emergent	*Developing*	*Tales*	*Fiction*	*Biography*	*Poetry*
Wordless	Pattern	Traditional	Realistic	Autobiography	Narrative
ABC	Decodable	Folk	Historical	Biography	Lyric
Sounds		Fairy	Fantasy		Limerick
Picture		Fables	Sci Fi		Haiku
Books		Myths			
		Epics			
		Legends			
		Allegories			

Learning-to-Read Literature

Wordless Books. Two varieties of wordless books may be targets of questions on the test. Vocabulary books present pictures of concrete nouns and verbs (actions) without words to stimulating oral vocabulary development without the burden of print. Many of them are organized by genre and can be used with initial English language instruction to develop an oral repertoire. Picture stories also include concrete nouns and verbs, but they tell a simple story in pictures. They might depict an activity like going to the zoo and show what happened before, during, and after the activity. The goal is to teach basic story schema (event sequences) and oral language before introducing print.

ABC Books. Books that teach the alphabetic principle (one letter, one sound) teach children the alphabet through pictures and upper- and lowercase letter representations. The letter *Aa* appears on a page, along with a picture that corresponds to the letter name, like *ape.* The texts can be used in concepts about print activities, where the teacher and student point to each letter and then associate the letter with a familiar picture. Many of these texts include fuzzy letters to provide children with tactile sensations during multisensory tracing activities to reinforce letter recognition.

Letter-Sound Books.   These books present upper- and lowercase letters with pictures that represent other sounds associated with letters. For example, it is logical that *A is for ape,* but there are other sounds associated with the letter, too: *ant, aunt,* and *apple.* Letter-sound books move beyond teaching simple letter names into more complicated sound–letter associations. Some of the texts can include sound–letter associations that are not as transparent. Short vowel sounds, for example, can be communicated through pictures that illustrate that *A* is also for *aunt* and *apple.* They can also be made part of kinesthetic activities, where children act out the pictures they see to associate sounds and letters with actions. The *Zoo Phonics* series is an example, where a gesture is taught along with a particular letter and its sound (Aa = ape).

Picture Books.   These books include richly detailed pictures and text. Often, the pictures support the print and offer early readers supported understanding through text and images. These books are ideal for reading aloud to children because the pictures are captivating and the text is imaginative. Books like *Where the Wild Things Are* and *Where the Sidewalk Ends* are examples. (*Note:* These books are **not** favored for decoding instruction, because the test makers believe that pictures may take the children's attention away from print and delay their knowledge of phonics.

Pattern Books.   Pattern books include pictures that support text that is presented with a predictable pattern (see Figure 6.1).

FIGURE 6.1

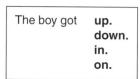

The pattern changes with the picture and the final word in the sentence. The texts are favorable for teaching concepts about print (book concepts, directionality, word matching, etc.), but they are not favorable for teaching early decoding. The test makers believe that the child will simply memorize and apply the pattern throughout the text, because the pattern and the pictures supply too many cues for the child to follow and attention is taken away from relying exclusively on print.

Decodable Books.   These texts are favored on the exam for early decoding instruction. They include decodable elements as seen in the sentence: The *cat sat* on the *mat.*

Typically, decoding instruction takes place with some isolated element of phonics, like identifying blends in the initial positions of words or digraphs in the final positions of words. In the example, it should be obvious to you that the rime -at is the focus of instruction. After teaching the isolated phonics element, decodable texts are used to reinforce the focus of isolated instruction within the context of reading. This way, the part can be taught in isolation and reinforced again in print within the context of "reading" decodable text. Needless to say, these texts are tightly controlled to ensure that the child must focus on the print in order to decode the text. The most severe decodable texts include no pictures, because the pictures may draw a child's attention away from the print. Computer-based texts are similar in that they are meant to reinforce elements of phonics that have been instructed in isolation.

Reading-to-Learn Literature

Let's turn now to the reading-to-learn texts. Texts for teaching children reading-to-learn skills include fiction and nonfiction. The stories include themes that will appeal to the child's age. They can, for example include simple lessons on why obedience is a value to more complex presentations on facing divorce, family illness, or living with a family member who has a disability. Age-appropriate themes are an important consideration, since you do not want to aim to low (and lose interest) or too high (and be "above their heads"). The literary elements of these texts will not be discussed at this point, since these features are part of content area eight. Each type of text has subgenres within it, and you should know their general characteristics for the test.

Traditional Literature. Traditional literature presents stories deeply rooted in the culture from which they are drawn. They can reflect the values, symbols, and worldviews important within a given culture. This makes traditional literature ideal for comparative analyses of animal symbols found in Native American literature (for example), Greek fables, and Chinese folktales. Similarly, themes from Asian traditional stories can be analyzed for their collectivism and individualism with respect to the traditional literatures of western cultures.

Folktales. Folktales are stories that began as part of oral traditions and then because part of cultural narrative. The trickster figure embodied in Brer Rabbit, a figure from Southern literature, and his adventures exemplifies a character who began as oral tradition who then becomes part of a cultural story, where one's wits play a very important role in one's survival. Folktales can provide a glimpse of a culture's worldview at a given time in history.

Fairy Tales. Fairy tales are also cultural stories, though they include magical elements and depict struggles between good and evil. Think about Little Red Riding Hood, where the innocent Red travels to Grandma's house to perform a good deed and is stalked by the wolf. Hansel and Gretal is another example of a fairy tale. The original Grimm's versions of these stories are far more violent and, well, *grim*, than you might imagine (our versions are pretty sanitized). They were meant to inspire obedience in the reader through fear, and other "lessons."

Fables. Fables use animals to teach moral lessons to children. Esop's Fables are widely known. His writings from Ancient Greece include anthropomorphized animals who have human attributes and human experiences. These stories lend the reader some distance and objectivity when seeing how the animals make choices before reflecting on one's own experience. "The Tortoise and the Hare" is a memorable example of a fable, along with its theme of "slow and steady wins the race."

Myths, Epics, and Legends. These stories are long narratives that celebrate the heroism of a culture and its extraordinary deeds. Myths often reveal a cultures religiosity and tell not only about life but also about the role that gods and goddesses played in human events according to their worldview. Epics, like the *Iliad,* include historical elements and stories of actual battles recast within the framework of an epic. Legends may also tell magical stories of heroism, and they often include figures like kings, queens, and knights or other archetypal figures. They may also explain concepts like *chivalry* and demonstrate how one is to behave in the role of knight, king, or serf.

Allegories. Allegories are also cultural stories where the "surface" story actually tells another "deeper" story through symbolism. The *Wizard of Oz* by L. Frank Baum is an example. On the surface of the story, one learns about Dorothy who encounters a Cowardly Lion, a Tin Man, and a Scarecrow on her journey down the yellow brick road that leads to the Wizard. Few readers may be aware that Baum was actually telling a political allegory of the William Jennings Bryan populist campaign. Dorothy symbolized the undecided voter, the Tin Man represented industrial workers, the Scarecrow was the agricultural demographic, and the Cowardly Lion was Candidate Bryan (who needed courage to win).

Realistic Fiction. This type of fiction offers readers plots and themes that mirror real life. The stories are believable and describe people engaging in activities and dealing with situations that one finds in everyday life: family conflict, growing up, managing friendships, or rites of passage. Rather than relying on fantasy, they portray situations that readers can place themselves into and explore how they might react if given similar choices to those of the characters in the story. Narratives such as *A Separate Peace* tells the story of two friends, one who is gifted and one who is not, and an injury that befalls the talented friend that may have resulted from the other character's jealousy.

Historical Fiction.　Historical fiction conveys a sense of a history surrounding an event. One learns about an event and the times through setting descriptions, conflicts, and character choices. *The Chosen* by Chaim Potok is an example. The reader learns not only about the struggles and expectations of American Orthodox and Hasidic Jews in the creation of the state of Israel after World War II, but also about its effects on both communities as witnessed through a friendship. Through the story, the reader learns about the historical context through characters that the reader can relate to.

Fantasy Stories.　Fantastic stories can also be about ghosts, horror, mysteries, and so forth, though science fiction is most recognizable. Science fiction stories are distinguishable from other types of fiction through the setting, which is often other worldly or set in the future, because it relies heavily on yet-unrealized technologies to carry the story. The themes do not necessarily have to be outlandish, as they can be about love, friendship, or other realistic topics. Some can also be socially critical, like *The Hitchhiker's Guide to the Galaxy,* where a manic-depressive robot "put up" with humans and other aliens on a variety of bitingly critical "adventures."

Nonnarratives.　These texts are topical and informational. They offer readers information about health, history (first flights, space explorations), historical figures, athletes, and so forth. Nonnarratives can serve as an introduction to content area texts because they often include tables of contents, glossaries, and indices. They also enable modeling of how to read expository text, which will also help the transition from pure narratives to informational texts.

Biographies.　They tell readers about the life of an author or a historical figure (autobiographies are written by the author him or herself). The question that one always has about biographical writings is, just how objective are they? Often, they present only the best or worst attributes about a person, and they can be very subjective and skewed. In children's literature, they tend to emphasize themes like hard work, perseverance, and "staying in school." They are meant to inspire rather than titillate.

Poetry

Poetry also appears on the exam, though your ability to interpret poetic forms is the primary focus of the exam. Poetry relies on its form and figurative language to convey meaning to the reader. The rhythm and rhyme of a poem can captivate a reader, and the language can stimulate our five senses (touch, taste, hearing, smell, and sight). For the test, it is more important for you to know how to interpret themes and moods based on the devices used in poem than it is to tell the difference between a lyric poem and a haiku. Therefore, I have included here only a brief description of poetic forms found in elementary classrooms. We will spend more time on poetic devices in the next content area.

Narrative Poems.　Narrative poems tell a story and present us with a sequence of events. We will dissect one for you when you learn about the features of literature in content area eight. Narrative poems are distinct from lyric poems. Lyric poems contemplate a singular mood or feeling and captures it in verse. They can also ponder animals or other things. Here is one that uses *free verse:* unrhymed verses organized into a stanza or stanzas:

> **Congestion**
> *Stuffed up*
> *Drip-Drip*
> *Sniffle-Snort*
> *Menthol Scarf*
> *Sleep.*

Limericks.　Limericks are humorous poems of five lines, where lines one, two, and five rhyme and have the same length, and lines three and four are shorter and have their own rhyme scheme. Here is a limerick appropriate to the task at hand.

I once had to prep for a test.
I felt that I'd never get rest.
With coffee in hand,
I'd thought I go mad,
'Till resolving to just do my best.

Haiku.[1]   A haiku is a brief poem that invites meditative insight. It functions like a flash of light that suddenly reveals something previously unseen, unfelt, unthought, or unimagined.

Yes, the palm tree green
something else that will always
remain far from me.

This particular English translation employs seventeen syllables, which is the conventional length of a haiku, arranged by some practitioners in three lines: five syllables, seven syllables, five syllables.

The traditional haiku contains a reference to nature, especially an image that reveals the season or time of year. Most importantly, a haiku involves a conflict, stated or implied, that is to be resolved by the reader. In this poem, the conflict is between the typical human response to nature's beauty—to befriend. At first a reader might not understand the poem because it says something positive but discusses something negative: distance and longing. After further meditation on the brief poem, an insight is possible—that human needs and wants are not always realized. A new respect for nature is the ultimate hope of this haiku.

Modern haiku may use fewer or more than seventeen syllables, and a reference to nature and season may be absent. But there is always a surprise in a haiku, a shock, a fresh awareness and new understanding.

Plays

Since questions on plays will probably be limited, we will spend very little time on them. What differentiates a play from the rest of the literature that we have discussed is that meaning is conveyed through character dialogue, action, and stage directions. We learn about the characters' state of mind by what they say and do on stage. Event-centered plays focus on the drama and action of the plot. Character centered plays focus on one or two main characters and the challenges they face: One accompanies the main character on his or her journey through a number of events. Greek plays come in two varieties: comedies and tragedies. Comedies amuse the audience and can satirize human vices and foibles. Tragedies, on the other hand, are designed to arouse sympathy from the audience for the main character who usually meets a tragic end due to some character flaw beyond his or her control.

CONTENT AREA SEVEN: FEATURES OF LITERATURE

The majority of the questions that you will face on literature will ask you to apply concepts to passages to demonstrate your understanding of prose and poetic devices. The passages may be of only one line or may be an entire passage or poem. You are less likely to face questions of mere definition.

Instead, you will have to know the definition and how it applies to a passage to reveal character motives, symbolism, mood, and the like. These types of questions can be challenging to prepare for, because the test makers have an infinite selection of prose and poetry from which to choose. The best way to learn the material is to be armed with a few powerful examples of each literary devise and know them well enough to apply them to the exam. If you have

---

[1]Section contributed by John Mitchell.

the time, spend a couple of Sundays with the *New York Times Book Review*. Their reviews dissect a variety of fiction, nonfiction, and poems and will help you prepare for the exam.

Story Schemata

Freytag's Pyramid captures the basic organization pattern of elementary literature. It has five steps, including exposition, rising action, climax, falling action, and resolution (denouement). Table 6.2 shows how each step functions in works of literature:

TABLE 6.2   Freytag's Pyramid

EXPOSITION	RISING ACTION	CLIMAX	FALLING ACTION	RESOLUTION
Background Information	Events Building to a Climax	Culminating Event	Events after the Climax	The Final Action That Resolves the Conflict
Narration Setting Foreshadowing Characters	Types of Conflict	Realistic Fantastic Hyperbolic	Symbols and "Truth" revealed	Theme Revealed

If you recall the movie *The Dead Poet's Society,* Robin William's character in the movie had his students rip something similar out of their books, so that they could read and understand literature on their own. But since it may appear on the exam, let's explore each aspect in detail.

Exposition.   Exposition provides us with background information. We often learn about the type of narration that will occur in the story. First person narration tells the story through the eyes of a central character. Third person narration tells the story from the point of view of an observer/nonparticipating character. Omniscient narration is different, because the author provides a "God's eye view" of the story and uses narration that is above and removed from the text. One question that is always a good one to ask is whether the reader can trust the narrator. On the subject of *The Great Gatsby,* many Ph.D. dissertations could be written on whether one can trust the narrator's observations about Gatsby, because there is conflict about just how subjective his reporting of events actually is.

The setting (where and when a story takes place) may also be established early on. The story may take place in one room of a house, at a school, and any other place that you might imagine. Science fiction stories are usually recognized as such because the settings are fantastic and employ descriptions not found in regular life. Descriptions of the setting might also provide use with elements of foreshadowing. In Poe's *Fall of the House of Usher,* the reader is treated to a lengthy description of the Usher home, complete with a gloomy exterior and a crack that runs down the length of the house, from the roof to the foundation. This description of the setting indicates that there is a flaw in the family that will probably result in a tragedy for the Usher family.

One of the most famous descriptions of setting that occurs during exposition is from Crane's *The Open Boat* (Crane, 1898), a story about four men (an oiler, a cook, a correspondent, and a captain) trapped in a small dinghy at sea:

> None of them knew the color of the sky. Their eyes glanced level and were fastened upon the waves that swept toward them. (p. 715)

Here, the reader learns of the chaos in which the characters are immersed because they cannot tell the difference between the ocean water and the sky above them.

Characters may also be established during exposition. There are two types of characters to know for the test. Protagonists are the main characters, and antagonists are the characters who provide opposition to the protagonists. Supporting characters help the protagonist on his or her journey or otherwise move the story along into subplots, provide comic relief, and so forth. We also learn about the protagonist's and antagonist's motivations and behaviors through their interactions with supporting characters in the story. One difference between literature for children and adolescents resides in how changing the characters are. Static characters, who are either good or evil, tend to populate children's literature, but characters found in adolescent literature may grow, change, and evolve into multidimensional characters.

Rising Action.   As the story moves out of exposition, the action rises. We learn about the type of conflict that the characters will face, whether it is realistic or fantastic. There are four types of conflict that you should be able to recognize for the test:

- The character in conflict with another character.
- The character against nature.
- The character against the "gods."
- The character against himself.

The dialogue and events may surround these types of conflicts and lead us to a culminating event. Students can be asked to predict and speculate upon the nature of the conflict, and then read the climax to see if they were correct or not.

Climax.   The culminating event is the climax of the story, when the action reaches its highest level. Based on the four types of conflicts described earlier, the character finally has it out with his or her antagonist, or has a showdown with nature or the "gods," or at last has a defining emotional conflict. Please note that modern literature plays with this framework quite a bit. One frustrating aspect that you may remember from Literature 101 is the way that Faulker tended to end his story at the point of climax, never offering the reader any resolution. That was probably not because he couldn't think of a way to end the story; instead, his preoccupation might have been with the interior motivations and psychological characteristics of his characters, rather than their simple actions and "what they did."

Falling Action.   After the climax, "truths" about the characters are often revealed. Mysteries and detective stories are certainly famous for this, where the reader sees the fallout of the detective's having exposed who committed the crime about which the story has revolved. The reader also learns whether we have been treated to static or multidimensional characters as we see how they respond to the climax that they have just endured.

Resolution.   The *denouement* is the resolution of the story. This is where many author's reveal their point to us. We tend to get the theme (meaning or moral) of the story at the end, and we also learn if the story will end to our satisfaction or in disappointment. Themes can be as simple as *they lived happily ever after* or as complex as what we will see when we look at *The Old Man and the Sea* when we discuss simile, metaphor, and symbol in Other Devices in Literature, the next section.

Other Devices in Literature

Allusions.   Allusions are references to other famous stories within a given work. Bible stories often find their way into literature, but so do children's stories. Much of the popular movies that we watch are little more than allusions to stories that we enjoyed as children. The movie *Pretty Woman* might be described as an allusion to *Cinderella,* where the Prince (Richard Gere) rescues a "fallen" Cinderella (Julia Roberts). Similarly, *Good Will Hunting* can also be characterized as a retelling of the frog-prince story, only here it is a psychologist (Robin Williams) who "kisses" the frog, Will (Matt Damon), and turns him into someone employable.

Flashbacks.   Flashbacks give us background information and insights into character motivations. In *Slaughter House Five* by Vonnegut, the reader is treated to a character named Billy who can travel through time. He does so in his mind, as his past and present experiences move back and forth through his mind, until we finally learn of the central event in his past (the bombing of the civilian town of Dresden in World War II) that has left him distressed. Faulker also uses flashbacks extensively in *The Sound and the Fury* where the opening story is told from the point of view of a mute and mentally challenged character whose mind moves from the past to the present and back again as he encounters natural cues from his environment.

Analogy, Similes, Metaphors, and Symbols.   Authors use a number of devises to describe elements in their stories. Similes are explicit comparisons of one thing with an unlike thing and use *like* or *as* in the comparison. Metaphors are often implied comparisons between two unlike things, though they can be direct statements or conveyed through symbol. Similes are pretty straightforward. You probably have said one at some point in your life:

- I'm as hungry as a horse.
- It's raining like cats and dogs.

You have probably also uttered a metaphor or two, as well:

He has the attention span of a flea.

Extended Metaphors.   Extended metaphors are far more complex than similes are because they rely on a collection of symbols to convey their meaning. Hemingway's *The Old Man and the Sea* provides an example of an extended metaphor conveyed through symbol. For those of you who have not read the story in a while or missed it somehow or avoided it on purpose, here is a brief synopsis:

An old man gets in a small boat and goes fishing on the ocean for what might be his last trip (he's pretty old, remember). He catches the fish of a lifetime and spends many pages bringing it in. It is so big that he has to keep it next to the boat. As he returns home, his prize fish is attacked and destroyed by sharks. All that is left of his wonderful fish is the skeleton. The old man sails one way and the skeleton floats to another part of the island. Later, the skeleton washes on shore and some tourists see it. They comment that a storm must have killed the fish.

Elements from the story can be considered as symbols of things outside of the story. At one level, there is the old man, his fish, the sharks that attack it, and the bones that are left. Beneath these elements are possible symbols that develop into an extended metaphor and symbol (see Figure 6.2).

FIGURE 6.2

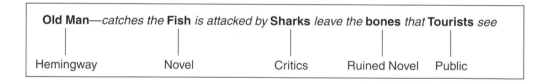

Beneath the symbols of the old man, the fish, sharks, bones, and tourists, we find a metaphor about life and what can happen when we pursue our goals and dreams. If we extend the metaphor further, we can even relate it to our own experience (see Figure 6.3).

FIGURE 6.3

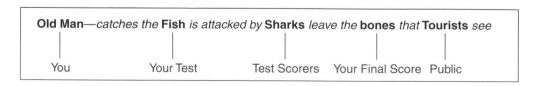

Before you get too depressed about this extended metaphor, keep in mind that Hemingway once said that *The Old Man and the Sea* was "just a fish story."

Themes.   Themes represent the main idea that the author explored in the work. Often, teachers select literatures for their classrooms based on age-appropriate themes, which explains why you might find themes like obeying adults, being nice, and helping out present in preadolescent literature and themes of conflict resolution, relationships, and coming of age in adolescent literature. In *The Old Man and the Sea,* one theme is that no one beyond the person who struggles to achieve a goal sees the difficulty inherent in the task or experiences the disappointment when it doesn't work out. Keep in mind that themes are also cultural. Other cultures that prefer more collectivist themes might argue that such a disappointment is to be expected if one wants to venture out on to the ocean of life all alone.

Poetic Elements

Like elements from literature, you need to prepare for questions that ask you to apply your understanding of poetic devices to lines or entire passages of poetry. To ensure that you understand what selected terms mean and so that you can also bring an example with you to the exam, we will explore several terms common to all of the exams. In addition, we will dissect a sample poem, and present mood, setting, imagery, and theme.

Assonance.   Assonance is a poetic device that repeats a syllabic sound in short intervals to make it memorable.

> *The black cat snapped back: attack!*

This verse is an example of assonance in action.

Alliteration.   Alliteration is like assonance, but it repeats a consonant over and over again in verse. Here is a famous alliteration:

> *Peter Piper Picked a Peck of Pickled Peppers.*

The repeated consonant sound /p/ gives the line its alliterative quality.

Onomatopoeia.   Onomatopoeia is a devise that uses a word that closely resembles the sound it captures.

> The ball *swished* through the net.
> The car went *vrooom!* as it accelerated.

Personification.   Personification assigns human qualities to things and objects.

> *The scorpion tattoos its way across the desert*
> *And stops periodically to unfurl its tail*
> *To claim victory over so much sand.*

Figurative Language.   Simile and metaphor are common devices used in poetry and were discussed earlier in literature.

Poetic Elements Illustrated

To give you some practice in reading and analyzing poetry, we will present a poem for you in *Tupparian* (e.g., bad) verse and describe it in terms of mood, setting, imagery, and theme.

The Drs. Are Out

10,000 trumpets in my head they did blow!
In search of a cure, hence did I go.
Advice from the schooled is all I would need;
Their help I would ask, their help I would heed.

OPEN YOUR MIND the neon did read, while
I relished the though of my newfound lead.
As he sharpened his saw, he said, "by the way,
For you a lobotomy—done free today."

ACK! I screamed and ran 'till I stood
Under a sign that read Dr. Good.
"Good is the name," he thrust his hand out.
"A headache, indeed! Hated mother no doubt."

I thought to myself, as he started to hop,
If this next one can help, then dead I will drop.

His name was quite simply Dr. Phil (O'Sophy),
A friend of the famous Ms. Oprah Winfree.
"I have your answer," he shouted with glee,
"A brand new Mercedes I'll buy just for me!"

With newfound disgust I walked slowly on.
An aspirin I took. My headache? Soon gone.

Mood.   Poetic mood is much like our own, personal moods. Humans can be happy, joyous, sad, depressed, dark, and so forth and so can poems. The language, structure, and descriptions in the poem convey these elements to us. Here, the mood of this poem is playful but a bit cynical. It opens with a narrator who is, despite his pain, hopeful and filled with expectation but ends with resignation and disillusionment.

Setting.   The setting is a journey down the road of self-discovery. The only description of the setting is hyperbolic (exaggerated). A neon sign that reads OPEN YOUR MIND is obviously absurd.

Parody, Satire, and Hyperbole.   Elements of parody and satire fill the poem. Parody describes writing that mocks a recognizable literary style, and satire makes fun of human foibles and fallibility. Dr. Seuss's style is parodied here. The sing-songy rhyme, ridiculously ironic characters, and social "message" are all contained in this world of lobotomizing psychiatrists, hopping psychoanalysts, and goofy pop psychologists. Satire occurs when a human weakness is held to ridicule. Here, it is the common desire of seeking help from others for problems that might be solved on one's own that is satirized.

Imagery.   Imagery is conveyed through figurative language. The poem opens with a metaphor where a headache is linked to 10,000 blowing trumpets without the use of *like* or *as* to accomplish the analogy (which would make it a simile). Onomatopoeia is also present. *Ack!* is a nonsense word that captures what a scream sounds like (for the narrator, anyway). The descriptions of the people in the poem are ironic. For example, Dr. Good isn't.

Theme.   The theme of the poem is revealed at the end, when the narrator discovers that the only cure for his "headache" is to learn to do for him or herself. Another theme might include the fact that there is often a difference between reality and expectation, and that can only be learned the hard way sometimes.

CONTENT AREA EIGHT: INTERPRETING LITERATURE

This content area covers prereading, during-reading, and post-reading activities that teachers use in the classroom before children read, as they read, and after they have read. It is easiest to view the activities like this (see Table 6.3):

TABLE 6.3

PREREADING	DURING READING	POST READING
Prior Knowledge	Strategies	Enrichment Activities

Let's look at each state of reading in detail.

Prereading Activities

The purpose of all prereading activities is to set a purpose for reading a text and to activate prior knowledge (Langer, 1981). That's because students need to stay engaged during the reading (purpose) and to use their background knowledge to comprehend what they encounter (prior knowledge). Good prereading activities will set the purpose and activate background knowledge, so that students can confirm and deny assumptions they have about a topic, anticipate what is to come, and stay focused throughout the reading.

Making predictions is appropriate for any age. This is because it cues the students to begin thinking about what they are going to read and to see if what they predict can be confirmed or denied by the text. In short, engaging the reader's attention and cognition and previewing the text will improve comprehension and retention of the information.

Generating questions to be answered will keep the students actively engaged in the learning process (Carr & Ogle, 1987). The questions draw upon their newly revealed prior knowledge that is both correct and incorrect. They will be able to test their prior knowledge against the lesson and to correct any misunderstandings that they might have about the subject.

In these ways, their reading will be purposeful; and they will try to find answers to the questions that they have generated. Having a personal stake in reading the material is a great motivator. Finally, they can also amend any faulty reasoning or misunderstandings, especially if their questions were based on wrong ideas about the content.

Following are prereading activities for emergent and fluent readers that appear often in the registration bulletins.

Book Walks. Book walks ready children for stories that they are going to hear in small or whole groups. The teacher shows the students the cover and asks them to report what they see and to offer statements about what they think the story will be about based on the cover and the title. This prompts students to listen to the story with the purpose of confirming or denying what their initial impressions were about the topic. Again, engaging attention and cognition in this way will improve the students' comprehension and retention of the information that they hear during the reading.

Introducing chapter books to upper elementary students can also employ a book walk. For example, though students may be accustomed to reading short stories and short informational pieces, the first time they encounter a book with a table of contents, chapters, and an index may be startling. To ease their entry into this new world, the teacher can model all of the parts to the students in a whole-group presentation, and help them understand the purpose of the table of contents, the chapters, the glossary, and the index. Then, she or he can let the students look through the book together in small groups to get a sense of how the book is assembled and to discuss its format. Doing so will enable the students to use the book as a tool and not be hindered by the new change in format.

Anticipation Guides.   Anticipation guides (Duffelmayer, 1994; Duffelmeyer & Baum, 1992) contain true and false statements that students evaluate prior to reading a passage. After they read the text, they revisit each of the questions and reevaluate their original assumptions. For example, prior to reading a passage on sea life, students can answer true–false questions about the passage (see Table 6.4).

TABLE 6.4

1. Whales are fish.	True	False
2. Lobsters and cockroaches share a phylum.	True	False
3. Sharks never sleep.	True	False

After answering the questions, students read the passage and revisit their answers to see how many of their preconceptions were true and how many were false. As a prior knowledge activity, anticipation guides (like all prereading activities) set a purpose for the reading to keep the children engaged and also cue their minds to be receptive to the reading. Finally, they reevaluate their original understandings making this a prereading, while-, and post-reading activity.

KWL Activities.   This acronym stands for *Know, Want to Know,* and *Learned* (Ogle, 1986). The K and W portions are the prereading activities, where students list everything that they know about a topic and then generate questions that they want answered before they read (see Table 6.5).

TABLE 6.5

KNOW	WANT TO KNOW	LEARNED
Segmenting is the highest level of phonemic awareness.	What activity is used to develop segmenting?	Elkonin Boxes are frequently used for segmenting instruction.

After they read the text, they complete the *Learned* column and revisit the *Know* column to ensure that what they thought they knew before the read the text was in fact correct. Any unanswered questions become topics of further investigation, and the teacher and students can work together to identify outside resources to answer those questions. This activity ensures that the reading will be purposeful and that students learn how to pose and answer their own questions. They also see how to undo misconceptions or how to fill in gaps in their understanding by reading.

SQ3R.   This acronym stands for *Survey, Question, Read, Recite,* and *Review.* Like KWL, this activity covers prereading, while reading, and post reading and is used mainly with expository (content area) text (Tadlock, 1978). *Study skills* are also taught using expository schema. Since many chapter books use titles, headings, and subheadings, teachers often use SQ3R to make the schema of expository text not only concrete but also a useful scaffold for teaching. SQ3R asks students to **survey** the titles first. During the *Survey* portion, students preview the text to see how the information is organized. They can learn to skim the selection to get the gist of the information, and scan it for certain phrases to see what kinds of relationships will be drawn. Students can be directed to look at transitional phrases to identify relationships among ideas in the paragraph (see Table 6.6).

After surveying, they then turn each heading into **questions** that they write down in their note books. As the students **read** the text, they answer the questions that they have generated from the headings. After reading, they **review** their questions and written answers to ensure that they have answered them sufficiently. Finally, they **recite** their answers to the questions by

TABLE 6.6

because, since	if, then	before, after	first, second
Cause/Effect	Contingency	Transition	Sequence

reading the question and covering their written responses. They compare what they remember to what they wrote in this last step. This activity is also an excellent one for prereading activities for expository text, because it cues the students into what they will be reading about and prepares their minds for the information.

During-Reading Activities

Literacy in the content areas is also important. For example, when solving word problems in math, the teacher could ask the students to write their solutions down in the form of statements or steps in sentences. This way, the teacher can see the students' thought processes at work, rather than just look at the product the student arrived at after solving or attempting to solve the problem.

Note Taking. This technique is applicable for expository text. The kinds of activities to select are ones that move beyond passively listing details or copying quotations. Instead, one wants to have students develop questions to be answered as the student reads so that the activity is an active one that requires both metacognitive strategies, self-monitoring, and learning how to pose and answer questions as one reads a text. The activity can be as minimal as asking the students to note questions in the margins of copied passages they read to listing questions to be answered in their learning logs.

Students may have to learn that there is a difference between recording information and analyzing/evaluating it (Kesselman-Turkel & Peterson, 1982). T-Journals are an example: One draws a large "T" on a piece of paper and writes the topic across the top of it. In the first column, the teacher and students work together to pull ideas out of a text and list them. In the second column, the teacher and the students evaluate each of the ideas in the first column and write their responses (e.g., whether they think the point is fact or opinion or worse). In this way students can learn the difference between extracting information and evaluating information.

Outlining. After taking notes, the information can be assembled into an outline. The advantage of an outline is that it will help the student see how main ideas and supporting details relate to one another. Figure 6.4 shows an outline applied to the literacy section of Chapter 4 of this text.

The topic is literacy and the main ideas are listed in items I through IV: CAP, phonemic awareness, decoding, and fluency. Supporting ideas are listed within the main ideas. For example, CAP is further subdivided into items A through D: book concepts, sentence concepts,

FIGURE 6.4

TOPIC: LITERACY INSTRUCTION

I. Concepts about Print
   A. Book Concepts
      1. Cover
      2. Title
   B. Sentence Concepts
      1. Direction
      2. Return Sweep
   C. Word Concepts
   D. Letter Names

II. Phonemic Awareness
   A. Matching Sounds
   B. Discriminating Sounds
   C. Blending Sounds
   D. Segmenting Sounds

III. Decoding Instruction
   A. Letter Sounds
   B. Onset/Rime
   C. Phonics Rules
   D. Syllables

IV. Fluency

word concepts, and letter names. Any subordinate ideas that clarify the supporting ideas are listed numerically. Continuing with CAP, items A and B have two subordinate ideas to clarify them. Each of the supporting ideas could have been supported by subordinate ideas throughout the outline.

Graphic Organizers.   Graphic Organizers are effective for teaching a strategy that students can use to diagram the schema of expository text to aid in their comprehension. Recognizing these organizational patterns will also help students with critical thinking because it forces them to organize the details into recognizable categories and to then judge their validity. When studying an historical event, for example, students can be shown a time line of events with pictures to support each area of the time line. Doing so will ensure that students will have a guide to rely on as they read the story.

Graphic organizers are also helpful in reducing confusion that students may encounter when engaging in unfamiliar or complex expository text. They are able to see relationships and can grasp the structure of the information before they attempt to embark upon abstract journeys of understanding. The concrete nature of the information displayed visually will also keep the students on task and hopefully engaged throughout the teacher's explanation and during the activity.

In the content areas, students can use graphic organizers to guide their identification of key concepts and how they relate to one another (see Table 6.7).

TABLE 6.7   A Graphic Organizer for Biology

PLANT AND ANIMAL CELLS

Differences	Similarities	Differences
Cell Structures: Plants	Organelles:	Cell Structures:
• Cell Wall	• Mitochondria	
• Vacuoles	• DNA	
	• Cell Membranes	

Summary:

Graphic organizers can also help students use dominant and subordinate categories of words that show the relationships among the concepts they name. Students can generate a list of everything that they know about a topic and then arrange the information to show how the terms relate to one another (see Figure 6.5).

They can also add to their web, make changes to their understanding, and compare them to see how the relationships are the same or different. To extend vocabulary after reading, teachers can discuss words found in the story with the student. They can discuss synonyms and

FIGURE 6.5

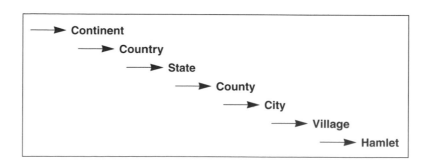

antonyms to words that they have learned about in the reading. Such an activity will enrich their reading vocabularies by first associating new words to words that they already understand. Later, when they encounter these new words in print and decode them correctly, they will have the oral definition in mind and the term will register when they read it for the first time.

Venn diagrams can help students understand expository texts that compare and contrast details about various subjects because they force students to categorize information by similarity and difference.

Guided Reading.   Guided reading teaches reading skills and strategies to individual or small groups of students (Manzo, 1975). Here, one uses each stage of the reading process (prereading, while reading, and post reading) to assist students. For example, with the child or children, the teacher can conduct a prereading activity to draw upon the children's background knowledge and prepare them for reading. Vocabulary can be pretaught or clarified. Questions to be posed and answered while reading can be generated. In addition, strategies to repair information breakdowns can be decided upon (Let's syllabicate when we come to a big word and look for its meaningful parts). Kinesthetic activities can also be incorporated into these activities, as the teacher can have the students highlight important phrases or details within photocopied paragraphs to enhance their understanding and work on specific skills as they read their paragraphs.

Think Alouds.   Think alouds are also good metacognitive activities for students to use while reading (Babbs & Moe, 1983). They can be taught to self-question their way through narrative text to learn how to monitor their own understanding independently. The teacher models how to pose wh- questions to the passage (Who is the main character? What are they doing?), sequencing questions (What happens first and next in this paragraph?), and inferential questions (Why is that character so sad?). Teaching students how to think through a passage metacognitively is an important strategy to know for the test.

Post-Reading Activities

After students read a text, they can also elaborate and extend their understanding of the material and the ideas that they encountered (Bauman, Seifert-Kessel, & Jones, 1992). They are also known as *enrichment activities* to be used with students who have understood what they have read.

Literary Responses.   Responding to literature is meant to elaborate and extend understanding of both concepts and vocabulary. There are questions that one can ask before, during, or after one has read narrative text (Shanahan & Shanahan, 1997). Table 6.8 shows questions related to characters, setting, plot, and evaluation.

Students can also use these questions as a guide to create visual representations of stories that have been read to them. This is another way to encourage children to develop their comprehension skills early on. This way, they can make the connection between the story that they have just heard and what it represents to them in their minds. The teacher can also have the child describe the picture that a given child has created in order to gauge how well he or she has understood what they have just heard read to them.

For writing, an effective way to have children respond to literature is to ask them to write letters to characters or from characters in stories. This way, they can use details from the text to create accurate letters that a character who is in a war, for example, might write home to his or her family. This elaborates and extends the child's understanding because they have to use their newly gained knowledge in a different form of expression.

Another enrichment activity has students elaborate their knowledge through literature discussions. Literature discussions are a good post-reading activity, because people always take away a variety of interpretations from whatever they read. This activity capitalizes on that fact and allows students to share their points of view with the group, without fearing that their interpretation is simply wrong or not worth considering.

TABLE 6.8

CHARACTERS
- Who are the characters in the story? How are they described?
- Which characters are the antagonists? How do you know that?
- Which characters are the protagonists? How do you know?

SETTING
- What is the setting of the story like? Is it realistic or fantastic? Why?

PLOT
- What is the plot of the story? It realistic or unrealistic?
- Who causes the problem in the story?
- What other problems do the characters face?
- How are the problems solved?

EVALUATION
- Would you have solved the problems like this? Why or why not?
- What did you like/not like about the characters? Why?
- Is this a story you would read again or recommend to someone? Why?

Reader's Theater.   The purpose of oral language activities is to use another skill to support reading. Mainly, students use discussions to elaborate and extend their understanding by sharing ideas with one another. The same idea is true when students have the opportunity to dramatize their understandings through activities like reader's theater.

Having students role play how the main character made good decisions can help children learn about their own values, assumptions, and beliefs. Role playing can also help children learn about different points of view. After reading about a historical period of time, for example, children can assume different roles. Some students can be characters from the period and others can be interviewers. The students can take turns interviewing one another and learn the different points of view of the characters in the story.

Students can also learn to connect with works of literature personally. When pretending to be characters in the stories students not only learn about story elements, but also how to think and maybe empathize with the characters in the stories that they dramatize. They can also write alternative endings to the stories and then perform them. To accomplish either of these ends, students must integrate the four skills of reading, writing, listening, and speaking. In short, having students propose and develop their own versions of stories can also reinforce their understanding of literature. They can be rated on how consistent their versions are with what the characters in the story would actually do.

Question–Answer Relationships.   Many content area textbooks contain passages with comprehension questions at the end of the section. The comprehension questions typically move from literal to inferential to evaluative. Students need to learn strategies to answers these types of questions. The techniques usually involve skimming the passage first to get the gist, reading the questions at the end, and then reading the passage to answer the questions. When answering the questions, the student can consider where they will find their answers. There are four types of questions associated with QAR (McIntosh & Draper, 1995):

- Right There   (literal)
- Think and Search   (literal)
- Think It Through   (inferential)
- On My Own   (evaluative)

Students read the question and then decide if they will find the answer right in the text or if they will have to answer it using details from the text and their own impressions. Such an activity helps them to use metacognition to self-monitor their understanding as they read the text and to extend their understanding by answering these types of questions and satisfying their demands (Mesmer & Hutchins, 2002).

Motivating Children to Read

Goal setting and rewards are important considerations. Setting goals means discussing the plan with the child and working together to perform reach tangible goals, like reading a certain number of pages per night, bringing magazine articles from home to be read in class, and so forth. Rewards can be as simple as a token like a star or as public as posting their work on the board to highlight their individual accomplishments, though you are better off considering community-based methods of motivation here. Book clubs are an example, since they stimulate interest. They get to discuss books that they enjoy with one another while also engaging in the self-selection of literature based on what they want to read.

Motivation is also required if the child is stuck in one particular genre. Anecdotal records may indicate that a student only chooses books from the same genre, series, topic, or author thereby limiting their exposure to new formats, vocabularies, and concepts. Certainly, goal setting is an option here, though another approach might be worth considering. For example, the teacher can select texts within the child's range of tastes and interest in order to expand their selections and have them take risks with more challenging books.

Fostering Appreciation

Enjoyment of reading is extremely important, because students who avoid reading at all costs do not improve. One way to help unmotivated or struggling readers, beyond identifying their needs in decoding, fluency, or comprehension, is to ensure that they have high-interest materials available to them at or near their independent reading level. The interest value of the material might draw them into the process of learning to read, and having it at their independent reading level will allow them to succeed.

Fostering appreciation of literature occurs by reducing external demands on students. For example, taking time to read aloud to students from a novel without asking them to write papers on the topic or having any other expectation for them beyond listening and enjoying the story may help foster their appreciation of reading. This is because there are no demands on the students to produce reports and the like, thus reducing the likelihood of resentment or anxiety concerning the assignment. Here, they can simply enjoy hearing the story for the sheer pleasure of it.

Sustained Silent Reading (SSR) is another option (Krashen, 1993; Trelease, 1995). Here, students select high-interest texts independently and read them for twenty minutes per day without interruption or papers due at the end. Being allowed to discuss stories afterward with other classmates can also help them to develop interest in and enjoyment of literature. Another by-product of sustained silent reading and reading for pleasure itself is that one's vocabulary will also increase. Since they will see words used in different ways in a variety of contexts, they will elaborate and extend their personal lexicon and have a greater source upon which to draw when reading new texts.

Written and Oral Communications

DOMAIN THREE: COMMUNICATIONS

This chapter presents the final domain about written and oral communications (domain three). The content areas of this domain include writing applications (content area nine), the writing process (content area ten), the research process (content area eleven), the editing process (content area twelve), and verbal and nonverbal communications (content area thirteen). As in the previous domains, you will be asked to apply the information in these content areas to texts or dialogues.

CONTENT AREA NINE: WRITING APPLICATIONS

This content area concerns applications of writing, including the form, function, and content of narratives, expository essays, persuasive essays, and research reports (see Table 7.1).

TABLE 7.1

NARRATIVES	EXPOSITORY ESSAYS	PERSUASIVE ESSAYS	RESEARCH REPORTS
Freytag's Pyramid	Informational Patterns	Persuasive Patterns	Research Designs
• Plot Outlines	• Schema	• Objective Data	• Focus Question
• Setting Descriptions	• Facts	• Authority Statements	• Analysis Method
• Character Descriptions	• Objectivity	• Testimonials	• Data Collection
• Sequences	• Main Ideas	• Emotion and Logic	• Data Analysis
• Chronology	• Supporting Ideas	• Call for Action	• Findings
			• Recommendations

Narrative Writing

The important function of narrative writing is to tell an interesting story and, in the words of Mr. Kopesky, my eighth grade English teacher, "to delight and entertain." Narratives contain rich descriptions of setting, character, and plots that are fully developed, consistent, and resolved.

You will find narrative writing easy to remember if you recall Freytag's Pyramid. The steps include: *exposition, rising action, climax, falling action,* and *resolution* (denouement). Try to remember what would take place during the writing of each stage of this model. For example, during *exposition,* the students will be doing character sketches and plot outlines to ensure that they will have richly developed characters, setting descriptions, and an interesting and engaging plot. During *rising action,* the students can sketch the chronology of events to ensure that there are no sudden or illogical shifts in the story. The *climax* can also be written in a way that is consistent with all of the characters, their actions, and the plot, so that the effect is powerful and believable. Finally, during falling action and the resolution, students can write themes that express the main point of their story.

Expository Writing

Expository pieces are designed to inform or persuade and can take a number of different formats and serve a variety of purposes (see Table 7.2).

TABLE 7.2

DEFINITION	CAUSE/EFFECT	COMPARE/ CONTRASTS	PROBLEM/ SOLUTION	NARRATIVE ANALYSES
Describes a theme or process.	Explains how and why something happens.	Explains similarities and differences.	States a problem and describes solutions.	Analyzes characters or literary elements.

The function of any one of these expository formats is to provide a balanced and factual account of the information without arguing for or against a particular position. Learning to separate fact from opinion is important here, because students must learn how to substantiate their claims with objective facts and use unbiased sources. Summary or precis writing is another type of expository essay, where one locates the main and supporting ideas in a piece and summarizes them quickly and faithfully in one's own words.

Persuasive Writing

Persuasive writing uses a formula of gaining attention in the opening sentence or paragraph, organizing objective data, authoritative quotes, and emotional testimonials to make a case, and then calling for action at the end (changing one's position, voting a particular way, etc.). The function of these essays is to move someone to act or to cause change. Undoubtedly, you are familiar with persuasive arguments, though you may not be able to name the form yet. Consider any request for a donation to a cause.

> [Emotion] 1,000,000 children die of starvation every year. [Fact] 1,000,000 children could be saved with $1.00 worth of food. [Logic] For less than the price of a fast-food cheeseburger, you could save the life of a child. [Call to Action] Won't you please donate one hundred cents toward a child's life?

The content of persuasive pieces includes logical and subjective arguments and reasoned and emotional appeals to move someone to take the position of the author or to do what has been asked. In the example above, emotional arguments are offered (child starvation) along with logical arguments (feeding them is inexpensive). The persuasive piece ends with a call to action (donate 100 cents toward a child's life). The format is standard and may appear on the exam as a paragraph followed by questions that ask you to identify the correct element in a multiple-choice question. Please note that persuasive items need not be this dramatic. Having students write letters to school board members or to the media on a particular issue like the dress code are additional examples of how persuasive writing is used in classrooms.

Research Reports

Research writing has the format of posing a question, explaining a method to answer it, presenting data and data analysis, offering findings, and making recommendations. Students can create in class opinion surveys on a variety of topics, administer them, and collect and analyze the data. They can then write up their findings and present them to the class both in writing and in speeches. You will learn about the research process in greater detail later in this section.

Summary and Precis Writing

Also known as precis writing, summaries include all of the major elements presented in a complete work. A student simply lists the major topics in their sequence without attention to the minor details in a work.

CONTENT AREA TEN: THE WRITING PROCESS

The general process for writing that appears over and over again on these test has five steps: brainstorming, drafting, editing, revising, and publishing. You must know not only what purpose each phase serves, but also what occurs within each step (see Table 7.3) (Hoffman, 1998).

TABLE 7.3

BRAINSTORM	DRAFT	EDIT	REVISE	PUBLISH
Quick Write	Outline	Organize	Transitions	Conference
Web	Draft	Clarify	Grammar	Layout
Sketch	Focus	Expand	Mechanics	Print
Discuss		Contract	Spelling	Present

Each step in this approach to writing is modeled for the students. The process can also be made part of the daily routine so that it becomes something natural for the students to carry out independently and in small groups. Students can participate in establishing the criteria to be used to evaluate the final product.

Brainstorming

Brainstorming is the prewriting phase. Students generate ideas based on how the purpose has been set for the writing. For example, they might be responding to literature to analyze a character's actions, or they might be working on a narrative piece that places a main character in a new setting with a new challenge. The following activities are common during brainstorming. The *Catcher in the Rye* will be the vehicle through which we will illustrate these elements.

- *Quickwrite.* Students write for a sustained period of time and either list or write continuously in stream-of-conscious sentences to generate as many ideas as they can before trying to draw a topic or an outline out for the first draft from what they have written. No attention is paid to grammar.

  Holden Caulfield is conflicted confused drop out antihero . . .

- *Webs.* Students can also make webs and maps to sketch out the ideas before them. A central topic is placed in the center of a circle on a page and details and ideas can be connected to it to show how details relate to the central concept. For example, a main character's name can be written in the center and all of his or her attributes can be listed (both good and bad) so that a complete sketch is before the student (see Figure 7.1).

FIGURE 7.1

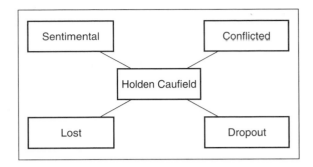

Students can be paired or grouped heterogeneously to discuss their ideas without fear of criticism, since all ideas are on the table at this point in the process.

Drafting

The next step in the process is to develop the draft. Students can organize outlines and try to list dominant and subordinate ideas first before writing the draft. Paragraph frames that scaffold writing a paragraph can also be used. They look like this:

1. *Topic:* Holden Caulfield is lost in nostalgia and sentiment.
2. *Details:* He drops out of school because he is disillusioned by the choices in life and longs to keep life still and unchanging as what one finds in a museum.
3. *Conclusion:* It is a story of a character's inner conflict with the external world and a longing for stability.

Students can share and discuss their outlines and drafts and receive feedback about what to expand or contract to make the piece more effective and interesting.

Editing

Editing occurs when the draft is read silently or aloud to help shape the piece into an appropriate format. Sequences are verified and ideas are strengthened with details and quotations. The idea is to ensure that all of the details and events have been completed and organized effectively. Extraneous ideas are also eliminated during this phase of the writing process.

Revising

Revision occurs at the paragraph, sentence, and word level, where transitions, grammar, mechanics, word choice, and spelling are reviewed. Checklists for these items are common, and grammar points are often taught separately before they are applied to the writing. We will review the principles of revising writing in content area twelve. For now, just accept that revisions of grammar occur here and nowhere else.

Publishing

The work is completed and can be turned in for rubric evaluation, self-evaluation, or conferencing. Students can also read their work one more time to ensure that it is complete. The students' writing can also be combined into a classroom journal and used during parent–teacher conferences so that caregivers can see the progress that their child has made throughout the term. Polished items can also become part of a class magazine, journal, or other presentation to be shared among classmates or other students in other classes or grades.

CONTENT AREA ELEVEN: THE RESEARCH PROCESS

The research process is complex, and it is important to break it down into manageable parts to help the students be successful on the task. Making the process as systematic as possible with clearly defined goals will ensure that the students have the opportunity to stay on task and to develop skills that they can transfer to new, future projects and to work independently. The process parallels the writing process that you just reviewed, with some important additions and considerations. Let's look at them next.

Teaching Student Researchers

What is the goal of instruction? Answering this question will help the teacher determine what items are most important to include in the classroom for research projects.

The most effective way to teach the research process is to use the skill-to-strategy approach. This means that students will have had the research process modeled for them in steps, along with an immediate opportunity to apply these steps in context as a learning strategy. For example, if the students are to locate information from a periodical journal, the teacher must model the process first, have the students practice it together, and then independently to see if they can actually carry out the task alone. Linking what is taught in class with what they will then carry out in real life as closely as possible will increase the chances of their acquiring the skill.

Structuring the Research Process

The following information will be helpful for both oral and written reports if you are asked how to structure the research process for students

- *Pose the question.* One of the easiest ways to help students narrow their topics is to have them pose the topic as a question to be answered. In this way, students can learn to recognize whether the question is too broad or too narrow to answer. Because it is easier to answer a question, students can try to find and narrow a topic by posing an answerable question. Asking a question like *Why are there so many poor in the word?* is not as answerable a question as *Why is the poverty rate in South Minneapolis so high?* Teaching students to refine their research questions is an important part of the research process.
- *Identify the focus of research.* This asks students to consider their question and what specific steps they will take to conduct the research to answer it. If they are going to answer questions about poverty in South Minneapolis, they need to look at job, education, and other data to investigate their questions. Library and Internet resources must be identified and roles that define who will find the information must also be stated if the students are working in a group.
- *Identify the resources.* Students also need to decide about what kinds of resources they will consult (e.g., living people, books, journals, Internet, etc.). Learning how to create categories is an extremely important aspect of this stage of the research process. Higher order thinking skills are required to arrange the information logically and to decide upon what to include or exclude. Furthermore, students must learn how to draw relationships between categories and to synthesize the information into an assembled, coherent whole. They must also learn how to summarize the main points from the research they read.
- *Ensure that there is a multiplicity of materials.* If students are to complete a research project, having multiple copies of popular journals will ensure that students have better access to resources in the classroom to meet the expectations of the assignment. Students can be asked to conduct opinion surveys in class about various subjects and to then write up their findings in a report. Students will then go into the research. After finding, reading, and noting the information, they return to the group to present their findings.
- *Gather the information.* To help students locate information for research projects, students need to begin to plan the research strategies carefully. This includes listing all of

the key terms and ideas related to their topic. Doing so will enable them to search the Internet and other data bases using these key words and ideas and will provide them with a wealth of sources that may relate to their topic.

- *Develop the outline.* Once the information has been gathered, it is time for the students to synthesize it into an outline. The outline will force the group to decide upon the ideas to be kept or excluded. For example, if the students are researching "Ocean Life," they can compare and contrast their outlines to ensure that they are on task (see Table 7.4).

TABLE 7.4

GROUP ONE	GROUP TWO
I. Sea Mammals	I. Coral Reefs
II. Crustaceans	II. Algae
III. ~~Fresh Water Perch~~	III. ~~Tourist Places~~

Items I and II from both groups would be kept; the extraneous items would be excluded.

- Students should also learn how to use graphics in their research. Separate activities can be conducted to teach them this process. For example, students can conduct their own classroom research, collect data, and then present it in the form of a table. They can learn how to label and caption the table and how to incorporate the graphic into a written report. Other activities for tables include whole-class activities where the teacher and students generate list characteristics and categories of a subject that they are studying (birds, mammals, and fish for example), and the categories become part of a table's headings. Other considerations include text density, use of verbs, and bulleting information telegraphically.

Plagiarism

Plagiarism is wholesale copying of text out of books, newspapers, and so forth and dropping the copied material into your paper without indicating that it is a quote and without citing the source. Even if you change a few words here and there, it is still plagiarism if it looks too much like the original or if the ideas are not truly yours. Here is an example of plagiarism:

> Plagiarism includes wholesale copying of text out of books, newspapers, and so forth and dropping the copied material into your paper without indicating that it is a quote and without citing the source.

Here, only one change was made (*is* to *includes*) and no reference is given. Basically, you must cite the source when using the ideas, opinions, theories, actual spoken or written words, or data that are not part of common knowledge. Common knowledge includes any facts that any reasonable person would know; proprietary knowledge pertains to facts that are revealed through research or other hard work:

1. There are twelve months in a year. (common knowledge)
2. There are five essay formats that you must know for NES exams (proprietary knowledge)

The first item is something that everyone knows; the second item is not something that the average person would know. Once you can recognize the difference between common and proprietary knowledge, you have to know how to use sources in your writing. Quoting material correctly is the only acceptable way to avoid plagiarism. This is accomplished through direct and indirect quotations. The way that one cites direct and indirect quotations depends on two factors:

- Is the source primary or secondary?
- Are you using APA or MLA style?

Let's deal with primary and secondary sources first, before APA and MLA style. Primary sources are the original documents from which you draw the quote; secondary sources are books, analyses, and so forth from which you draw a quotation that *they used in their book from an original source.* If you are writing a paper on the U.S. Constitution and you have a copy of it in front of you, then you are using a primary source and you would cite it as such.

Alternatively, if you are using a hypothetical book called *The Boosalis Guide to the U.S. Constitution* and you quote from the constitution out of my sections that analyze it, then you are using a secondary source for your U.S. Constitution paper. Plus, you have to give my book and me a citation. Why? *Because I did the hard work in finding and dissecting portions of the constitution for you, and you have to give me credit for that!* Dictionaries, encyclopedias, CD-ROMs are often loaded with secondary source material, so you have to be very careful when quoting from them.

How you format in-text quotations and citations depends on the style you are using. There are a number of different styles: Chicago, Turabian, APA, and MLA. APA stands for the American Psychological Association, and MLA stands for Modern Language Association. The registration bulletins do not state which type of style you need to know for the test, so let's use the most popular ones: APA and MLA. (It is most likely that the test will refer to MLA, by the way.) Table 7.5 shows a comparative table for APA and MLA in-text quotations.

TABLE 7.5

APA IN-TEXT CITATIONS	MLA IN-TEXT CITATIONS
Primary Sources	*Primary Sources*
Boosalis (2004) provides an overview of APA and MLA style.	Boosalis's *Beating Them All!* provides an overview of APA and MLA style.
There are two primary ways to cite sources: APA and MLA (Boosalis, 2004).	There are two primary ways to cite sources: APA and MLA (Boosalis).
Secondary Sources	*Secondary Sources*
According to Chris Boosalis, "There are two primary ways to cite sources: APA and MLA" (as quoted in Johnson, 2004, p. 23).	According to Chris Boosalis, "There are two primary ways to cite sources: APA and MLA" (qtd. in Johnson 23).

When referencing a quotation in APA, you simply give the single or primary author first and the year of publication. If there are multiple authors, then you list them:

Boosalis, Boosalis, Boosalis, and Boosalis (2004) state that . . .

If you use the multiple-authored work in other parts of your document, then you can shorten the reference using *et al:*

Boosalis et al. (2004) state that . . .

The Latin phrase *et al.* simply stands for "and others." If there are other works with the same authors under different titles, you cite them as follows:

Boosalis et al. (2004a) state that . . .
Boosalis et al. (2004b) state that . . .

Quoting secondary sources in APA style simply gives the quotation and cites the secondary source this way:

According to Chris Boosalis, "There are two primary ways to cite sources: APA and MLA" (as quoted in Johnson, 2004, p. 23).

This means that the quote of mine that you are using in your paper was found in Johnson's 2004 work on page 23.

MLA style is different. Look at the Table 7.5 and note the differences. You should see that no year is given—only the source and the page number at the end of the quote. Note how this is handled in both primary source examples. Secondary sources are handled in way that is similar to APA, but the abbreviation "qtd. in" is used instead of the whole phrase.

Developing a reference list also differs in APA and MLA. First of all, in APA the list of books and journals at the end of the paper used as sources of information for writing the article is called a reference list; however, in MLA style, it is called a work cited list. Second, the way that books, journals, and electronic media are cited differ, too (see Table 7.6).

TABLE 7.6

APA REFERENCE LIST	MLA WORKS CITED
Book, Single Author	*Book, Single Author*
Boosalis, C. N. (2004). *Beating them all!* Boston: Allyn & Bacon.	Boosalis, Chris N. *Beating Them All.* Boston, Massachusetts: Allyn & Bacon, 2004.
Book, Multiple Author	*Book, Multiple Author*
Boosalis, C. N., Boosalis, C. N., & Boosalis, C. N. (2004). *Beating them all!* Boston: Allyn & Bacon.	Boosalis, Chris N., Chris N. Boosalis, and Chris N. Boosalis. *Beating Them All.* Boston, Massachusetts: Allyn & Bacon, 2004.
Journal Article	*Journal Article*
Boosalis, C. N., Taghavian, A., & Myrhe, O. (2003). The role of CBEST scores. *The California Reader, 37,* 22–36.	Boosalis, Chris N., Alex Taghavian, and Oddmund Myrhe. (2003). "The role of CBEST scores." *The California Reader.* 37.1 (2003): 22–36.
Websites	*Websites*
Boosalis, C. N. (2003). Beating them all. Retrieved January 1, 2004, from http://www.beatingtherica.com	Boosalis, Chris. Beating them all. 1 November 2003. 1 January 2004. http://www.beatingtherica.com
CD-ROM	*CD-ROM*
Dissertation Abstracts (SilverPlatter, CD-ROM, September 2003 release)	*Dissertation Abstracts.* CD-ROM. Silver Platter. Sept. 2003.

APA bibliographies have the following general format for books:

Last Name, First Initial, Middle Initial. (Year). *Title in italics.* City of Publication: Publisher.

The book title is in italics and only the first letter in the sentence is capitalized. Proper nouns and words after colons are also capitalized, but the rest are lowercase:

Beating them all: Thirty days to success in English literature.

Journal articles follow roughly the same format. The title is not italicized—*but the name of the journal is.* Furthermore, the volume number of the journal is given and so are the page numbers at the very end.

Websites are cited by offering the date of retrieval, along with the URL. Because Websites change rapidly, it is important to state the date that you visited and extracted the material from the site because it might disappear eventually.

MLA bibliographies, on the other hand, have a number of distinguishing characteristics. Books are cited as follows:

Last name, First Name, Middle Initial. <u>Title Underlined.</u> City, State of Publication: Publisher, Year.

Journal articles in MLA are referenced as follows:

Last name, First Name, First Initial. "Title in Quotation Marks." <u>Journal Title Underlined</u>. Volume, Number (Year): Pages.

Websites in MLA are cited like this:

Last Name, First Name [if any]. Title of Page. [Date Created:] Day Month Year. [Date Visited:] Day Month Year. URL

Evaluating Sources

A valuable resource for evaluating sources is called ACTS. It stands for *accurate, credible, timeliness,* and *sources.* Each element of the acronym offers you criteria by which to evaluate and select resources. Each element is explained next.

Accurate.   The sources that you choose should be unbiased. A test of reasonability means looking for slanted or propagandized information and then maybe rejecting it. For example, when writing an article on the dangers of obesity, information provided to you from *Living the Fried Life* might not present the same type of information that *Cholesterol Today* might. Therefore, checking for political or other biases is important when determining reasonability.

Credible.   You have to judge whether the source is a credible one. To do so, you have to check the author's credentials and understand how the journal, paper, or editors select items to include in their publication. For example, articles in *Newsweek* are probably more reliable than articles found in *The National Enquirer.* The reputations of these journals are different, the selection criteria are different, and so are the motivations. In academia, the most respected journals are those that use peer-review processes, where an author submits a work and the editor sends it out for review by leading figures in the field. Those "peers" determine whether the article becomes a publication or not.

Timeliness.   Timeliness means that the information hasn't gone stale. For example, if you are writing an essay on effective diets for students and your sources are from 1900, then your information will miss over 100 years of new information on the topic. In short, you have to ensure that your information is accurate and timeliness is one good way to judge a source.

Sources.   The final element is to look for where the source gets its sources. Just because an article appears in a leading journal does not mean that it is unbiased or completely factual. One must look at the sources listed to see if they are outdated, biased, or problematic in some way. Furthermore, one must be careful not to mistake an editorial (deliberately opinionated) with a news report (deliberately unopinionated), because the sources for each type of writing will differ. A common classroom activity capitalizes on this fact: Teachers can photocopy five editorials and five news items without the titles and ask the students to judge whether they are factual or opinionated. Doing so will help the students to develop their evaluative reading skills. In any case, the sources one uses in a research report should use objective data in the same way that you intend to use objective data: to present a credible, accurate, and reasonable article.

CONTENT AREA TWELVE: THE EDITING PROCESS

Editing and revising writing occur before publishing a work. Editing involves organizing paragraphs, supporting and clarifying ideas, and providing transitions between paragraphs. Revising addresses sentence structure (grammar), mechanics (punctuation), and spelling. Only the major ideas that appear in the registration bulletins will appear in this section (see Table 7.7).

TABLE 7.7

ORGANIZATION	Introduction Thesis Body Paragraphs Conclusion
STYLE	Parallelism Redundancy Passives Transitions
GRAMMAR	Subject/Verb Agreement Comma Splices Run-on Sentences Sentence Fragments

Organization

When reviewing student essay data, look for organizational patterns in the essay and within each paragraph. What you are looking for is the basic five-paragraph essay that uses an introduction, thesis, body paragraphs, and conclusion. Within each paragraph, you are looking for topic sentences, sequenced supporting details, and a concluding sentence (see Table 7.8).

TABLE 7.8

INTRODUCTION	There are three stages in spelling development.
THESIS	The stages are prephonetic, phonetic, and transitional. Each one has different characteristics and activities.
BODY PARAGRAPH	Prephonetic spelling is the first and earliest stage of spelling. It is characterized by scribbling lines or using symbols arbitrarily to represent letters. Letter/sound activities help students move to the second phase of spelling development.
BODY PARAGRAPH	Phonetic spelling is the second stage of spelling development. A child's spelling of the dominant sounds heard at the beginnings and endings of words typify this stage. Learning to encode medial sounds through letter–box activities are common at this developmental level.
BODY PARAGRAPH	Transitional spelling is a later stage of spelling development. Here, the child encodes all of the major sounds heard in the word, but may need additional work in spelling patterns. This will help the child move into the conventional stage of spelling.
CONCLUSION	The prephonetic, phonetic, and transitional stages are part of spelling development, and each one has its own characteristics and required activities.

When you review student data on the test, look for the five essay components and at the structure of the body paragraphs, since they may reveal needs that you will have to identify in multiple-choice or short-answer questions. (Essay outlines or paragraph frames would be appropriate for developing organizational skills.)

Editing Paragraphs

Your knowledge of internal paragraph structure, organization, and the transitional phrases between them will be areas of assessment. You will certainly be asked multiple-choice questions on some aspect of this subject, and you may even be asked to write an essay about it. The data set might look something like this:

> **MY FAVORITE MEMORY**
> My best memery are about last chrismas. When I got a brant new bicicle. I rode it every day. When the snow melted. I saw it at ericks bike shop it was really cool, like the one that evel kenevels got. its biger than my old bike. My freind mike jumped it at taft park and he skined his knee. My dad told me that I'd havto be real carefull on my bike cause santa isn't enshured. I wanto jump my bike real high to like evel. Thats why I like this memery the best.

During the revising stage, you would ignore the sentence, style, and spelling problems and focus only on the paragraph's internal structure. Clearly, there is a topic sentence (*My best memery is about last christmas*) and a concluding sentence (*Thats why I like this memery the best*). There are problems with the order of the ideas and there are also extraneous details in the paragraph that would have to be taken care of during the editing phase of the writing.

Story Frames

As students become more and more proficient in writing single words, sentences, and lengthier writings, structure developmental writing activities are used. The most common tool used for this purpose is the paragraph frame (Lewis, Wray, & Rospigliosi, 1994). Story frames provide a scaffold to transition students from simple ideas about writing words and sentences to writing full paragraphs. The frames provide and outline that the teacher creates and the students complete (see Figure 7.2).

FIGURE 7.2

> My favorite memory is _____. It is about
>
> _____. Also, _____. Thus,
>
> _____ is my favorite memory.

Transitions between paragraphs might also be areas of instruction using either paragraph or story frames. Consider the following adverbs and how and when they are used (see Table 7.9).

TABLE 7.9

LINKING ADVERBS	COMPARATIVE ADVERBS	CONTINUATION ADVERBS	SUBSTITUTION ADVERBS
• Alternatively	• Similarly	• Furthermore	• Instead
• On the other hand	• Likewise	• In addition	• Rather

Transitions explicitly link ideas within and between paragraphs. For example, they link ideas, compare ideas, continue ideas, and substitute ideas.

Revision of Grammar and Mechanics

You may also be asked to review student writing for style (see Table 7.10).

TABLE 7.10

PARALLELISM	*Swimming and to run are my favorite activities. Swimming and running are my favorite activities.
REDUNDANCY	*Students need to write. Students need to study. Students need to learn. Students need to write, study, and learn.
PASSIVES	*The book was read by the boy. The boy read the book.

If the organizational pattern of the sample data looks okay and the paragraphs are sequenced properly, then you may have to look at the style. Problems with parallelism are easy to identify. In Table 7.10, the writer has not used the same form of the words that are in the subject. Redundancies are also easy to spot, since the data may show a student who is writing the same words or phrases over and over again throughout the paragraph. Passive voice sentences are pretty simple to find, too. Look for the characteristic "was + verb" and a "by phrase": "The dog **was walked by his owner.**"

Grammar.   Table 7.11 shows common grammar errors that you can spot in data sets.

TABLE 7.11

SUBJECT/VERB AGREEMENT	*He walk to his house yesterday. He walked to his house yesterday.
COMMA SPLICES	*He walked to his house yesterday, he had dinner with his family. He walked to his house yesterday, and he had dinner with his family.
RUN-ONS	*He walked to his house yesterday he had dinner with his family. He walked to his house yesterday. He had dinner with his family.
FRAGMENTS	*When he walked home yesterday. He had dinner with his family. When he walked home yesterday, he had dinner with his family.

If the verbs do not agree with the subject in number or tense, then they show areas of need. Comma splices, too, might be present. A comma splice occurs when a student "staples" two complete sentences together, instead of using a period to end one sentence before beginning another or joining them together with a conjunction. Run-on sentences are similar to comma splices, only lazier. Here, the writer not only leaves off a conjunction but also forgets to supply a comma. Sentence fragments are usually sentences that begin with what's called a subordinating conjunction. You'll know them when you read them because the thought seems incomplete.

Given these examples, go back to the opening paragraph, My Favorite Memory, and try to find the agreement, splice, run-on, and fragment problems in the paragraph. You should be able to identify at lest one of each variety quite easily.

Mechanics.   Mechanics (punctuation) is listed as an area of assessment on the exam. You will most likely see data sets to be analyzed for the major areas of mechanics, so let's apply some of the principals to the sample paragraph.

My best memery are about last chrismas. when I got a brant new bicicle. I rode it every day. When the snow melted. I saw it at ericks bike shop it was really cool, like the one that evel kenevels got. its biger than my old bike. My freind mike jumped it at taft park and he skined his knee. My dad told me that I'd havto be real carefull on my bike cause santa isn't enshured. I wanto jump my bike real high to like evel. Thats why I like this memery the best.

Capitalization.   In English, we capitalize the first word of each sentence. Clearly, this student is having difficulty with that as seen in the sentence fragment in sentence two. Proper nouns are also capitalized in English, and the student missed Christmas, Erick's Bike Shop, and Evel Knievel.

Punctuation.   Commas are used in the following instances. In a series of three or more nouns or adjectives, use commas:

The flag of the United States is red, white, and blue.

Use commas to link independent clauses before *and, but, nor, for,* and *or:*

I saw it at Erick's Bike Shop, **and** it was really cool.

Use semicolons *instead of and, but, nor, for,* and *or* to join independent clauses:

I saw it at Erick's Bike Shop; it was really cool.

Use semicolons before words like *however, therefore,* and *thus:*

I want to finish this section on grammar; however, I have lots more to type.

Use apostrophes to show possession and contraction:

- Evel Knievel's (possession)
- That's (contraction of that is)
- It's (contraction of it is)

Word Choice.   There are two types of words to be aware of: Those that are easily confused, and those that are gender biased.

Confused Words.   Many lists of easily confused words exist. They include words like accept/except; affect/effect; borrow/lend; can/may; two, to, and too; their, there, and they're; its/it's; sit/set; and data/datum.

In the paragraph, the student has several word confusions. Its and it's are confused: *It's bigger than my old bike* reflects the proper form, because the child is contracting "it is." The student is also contracting words erroneously: *Have to* is contracted as *havto,* and *want to* is contracted as *wanto.*

Avoiding Gender Bias.   No gender biases are present in the paragraph. You should know how to read for and how to amend instances of gender bias. In the first place, it is best to write in nonspecific terms:

A. Any lawyer who is worth **his** fee must be honest.
B. Any lawyers who are worth their fees must be honest.

Sentence A is biased, because it sounds as if all lawyers are men. The problem is corrected in sentence B by using the plural form which renders the sentence gender unbiased.

Words like *weathermen, mailmen, policemen,* and *firemen* are also outdated. Use these types of words instead:

Forecasters   mail carriers   police officers   fire fighters

Spelling.   Please review Chapter Two for more information on how to characterize this student's writing in terms of prephonetic, phonetic, transitional, and conventional spelling.

CONTENT AREA THIRTEEN: INTERPERSONAL COMMUNICATIONS AND PUBLIC SPEAKING

This final content area is about nonwritten communications. The bulk of the material covers preparing, delivering, and evaluating informational, persuasive, and dramatic speeches. There may be general questions about human communications (interpersonal and mass), but these areas tend to be subordinate to your understanding of the basic elements of public speaking.

Oral and Written Language Differences

Similarities and differences between oral and written communications exist (Akinnaso, 1982). Both types of communication must consider the audience and their level of knowledge, experience, and expectations. Both also employ descriptions, main ideas, supporting details, and organizational principles and transitions. However, they differ in how much latitude one has in expressing complex ideas. Writing can be read and reread for clarification, but spoken language disappears the moment the utterance leaves ones lips. This plays a role in how we use short, powerful examples, summative graphics, and even body language when we speak.

Elements of Oral Communication

Communication involves a sender who encodes a message for a receiver who hears the message and decodes (Barker, 1990). We decode messages for etic information (what is said on the surface) and for emic information (what is said beneath the surface).

Types of Interaction

Interpersonal, small group, public, and mass communications affect the level of interaction and feedback that a receiver may offer to the speaker (Luft, 1984). In all instances, both etic and emic information and nonverbal signals will influence how the listener decodes the message. Following are different sender/receive configurations to know for the test.

Dyadic Communication.   This is basic two-person, interpersonal communication. The amount of feedback is high, and the sender can tailor his message for the listener and adapt his communicative style based on how well the listener seems to receive the information. Active (participatory) listening includes analytic, supportive, reflective, and evaluative listening.

- Analytic listening is hearing and understanding the message that one receives. Questions are for clarification, and the interaction is straight forward. Participation is to ensure that misunderstandings are few and that clarification requests are common.
- Supportive listening is different from pure analytic listening. While clarification questions will occur here, the listener shows solidarity with the speaker and encouragement to validate what the speaker is saying. In short, the feedback one offers to the speaker is supportive and encouraging.
- Reflective listening combines analytic and supportive listening. Here, the listener clarifies both verbal and nonverbal cues to ensure understanding; and the listener may also interact and restate ideas back to the speaker to demonstrate understanding. Reflective listening may be either supportive or nonsupportive, depending on whether one agrees with what one is hearing.
- Evaluative listening is the most critical listening of all. One listens carefully for opinions stated as facts, inconsistencies, or flaws in logic. Feedback can be highly critical, and

respondents may need to learn how to offer critical feedback in a way that is nonjudg-mental and impersonal, yet honest and straightforward. Learning about when to offer evaluative criticism to a speaker may also be necessary, as certain times for criticism may not be as favorable as other times. For example, telling a speaker that he is not doing well *during* the speech may not be received very well.

Small-Group Communication.   Small-group communication relies on the same types of listening (analytic, supportive, reflective, evaluative) but it can be less interpersonal, because one must take cues from more than just one person (Beebe & Masterson, 2000). In addition, this type of communication may differ from dyadic communication because the roles may be assigned externally (Benne & Sheats, 1948). For example, the role of the leader may be desig-nated with the responsibility of keeping the focus of discussion on task. In the classroom, stu-dents will need to learn how to use summary statements to move from one point of discussion to the next and how to build consensus among all members of the group. Listeners, too, play a role in the interaction, as they need to have the opportunity to ask clarificating questions dur-ing the small-group discussion. The teacher's role in this instance is to ensure that all ideas will be entertained without criticism or evaluation, perhaps until the students are asked to decide upon which ideas to present as their best ones.

Public and Mass Communications.   These types of communication are less interpersonal and there are fewer opportunities for providing feedback or seeking clarification directly from the source. The speaker must take this fact into consideration to ensure that messages are clear and that it is not lost by nonverbal and other interference that can distract the listener or reduce the impact of the speech.

Types of Speeches

There are four types of speeches to know for the exam: extemporaneous, informational, per-suasive, and interpretive.

Extemporaneous Speeches.   Extemporaneous speeches can be either informational or per-suasive, but they tend to be brief, on-the-spot deliveries that can be word-for-word reading from one's notes to a group of listeners or a speech invented off the top of one's head. The key to the success of speeches of this nature is knowing how to select and present information suc-cinctly in a summative format for an audience.

Informational Speeches.   These speeches follow the same format that you learned about in written communications. They can describe cause and effect, problems and solutions, details and demonstrations, and so forth. Facts are presented and summarized, and the goal is to inform the audience about a subject rather than to persuade them to take one position or another.

Persuasive Speeches.   Persuasive speeches are delivered to move an audience to act or to take a particular position on a subject. Knowing the audience is very important because the speaker must tailor the message to them. The message must be adapted to their level of knowl-edge, belief system, and to their logical or emotional hot buttons. The format is to first gain their attention and then to establish a connection with them. The body of the speech moves from one compelling point to the final, most compelling point. Then, the speaker makes a final request for action. We will discuss persuasive techniques shortly under *preparing speeches*.

Dramatic Interpretations.   These are soliloquies taken from dramatic plays. Shakespeare's plays are obvious selections. The expectation of the audience is different from what one finds in informational or persuasive speeches. Since the delivery of the dialogue is what will carry the speech, the words must be delivered powerfully and vividly. Furthermore, the passage that one selects must be one that can be delivered in this manner. The effectiveness of the rendition will depend on how well one delivers the speech both orally and physically, because lavish descriptions and poignant adjectives and adverbs are usually absent from the text.

Preparing Speeches

The formula for preparing speeches is the same as what you saw in the writing process. There is brainstorming, drafting, editing, revising, and presenting. Outlines are essential during drafting. Main ideas and summaries are extracted and organized according to an informational pattern (cause and effect, problem solution, etc.) or in the persuasive format.

Knowing the audience is paramount. If you do not consider what they already know, then the speech may come off as either condescending or over their heads. The message must be tailored to their logical or emotional expectations. This will help the speaker to get the audience to accept or what he or she is asking them to consider (e.g., multiple points of view or a singular call to action).

If the speech is persuasive, one can make an argument using either inductive or deductive reasoning. Induction presents facts to an audience and then asks them to deduce the point with the speaker, whereas deduction offers the point first and then the ideas that support it. In either case, the speaker has to make a choice about which type of reasoning will be used in order to organize the body of the speech effectively.

The level of objectivity is another important consideration to be made during the drafting of the speech. The least subjective evidence often comes form statistical data that shows why something is numerically true. Each statement that the speaker makes can be bolstered by objective data to make the case factually powerful. Using quotes from authority figures is another way to support arguments, but they are more subjective. The reputation of the source that the speaker selects is what provides support to one's argument. Listeners do take a person's credibility into account when hearing a speech, so authoritative quotes can be very helpful.

Common ground and "bandwagoning" are the most emotional techniques that one can use. Here, the speaker tries to get the listeners to buy into the position by showing that the speaker and the audience are on the same page. This technique can be effective if the audience might be repelled by a pro or con position on a issue. Testimonials are a common parts of these techniques. Quotations from people who are "just like you" are used to support ideas and to move the audience from a position of resistance to acceptance before they are asked to "join the crowd."

Delivering Speeches

There are a number of considerations for delivering a speech to know for the exam. The test makers want you to consider volume, rate, and tone. Volume is good for emphasizing and distinguishing main from supporting ideas. Rate can be varied, too. Obviously, a normal rate of speech is expected, but speaking more quickly or slowly at selected points in the speech can increase the dramatic aspects of the presentation and make them more compelling. Tone is also very important. It, too, can be varied for effect, though a speech can be rendered incoherent or frivolous if the wrong tone is selected. If the topic is serious, then the tone should also be serious—the audience takes its cue for how to receive the information from the speaker, and they might not know what to think if the tone does not match the topic. Finally, speeches delivered in a monotone voice might help some members of the audience sleep but do nothing for the message that one is trying to communicate to them.

Because nonverbal information is also communicated during speeches, it must be considered carefully. Gestures can be used for emphasis, though to many gesticulations or nervous ticks can be highly distracting for the audience. Proxemics (social distance) is another important nonverbal consideration. Moving closer to the audience connotes intimacy, and moving away from the audience increases coldness and standoffishness. One must be careful to use the appropriate proxemics when delivering a speech to an audience or when speaking interpersonally. Finally, eye contact is important and can be cultural. Generally, maintaining eye contact is the way one conveys forthrightness and certainty in Western culture, so it must be used for a Western audience.

The discussion of nonverbal behaviors leads us to cultural considerations. For many cultures, certain gestures that westerners use for nonverbal politesse are offensive to other groups. Pointing with one's index finger, for example, might be used for emphasis in one culture but constitute an offensive gesture in another. Proxemics is another cultural variable. Some cultures may favor intimate distances, and others may favor space. Eye contact, too, can not be assumed to be the same cross-culturally. Looking down or away from a speaker may be an indication of deep respect rather than disinterest.

Evaluating Speeches

The role of the audience is to interpret and evaluate a speaker's message. The audience can listen critically to detect any contradictions or gaps in logic found in a speech. Problems with public speaking include:

- Relying on cliches to carry a message: *The early bird catches the worm.*
- Begging the question (assuming facts without first establishing them): *If you don't send in your entry, you won't win!*
- Including nonsequitors (connecting unrelated ideas together): *Preparing for exams is difficult, and I need to feed my dog.*
- Overgeneralizing (extending facts beyond their boundaries): *All lawyers are crooks.*
- Associating cause and effect erroneously (post hoc ergo procter hoc): *Crimes increase with every full moon!*

The audience must also separate fact from opinion: Were the statements supported with logic or emotion? Were facts drawn from reliable and unbiased sources? Finally, effectiveness is judged by the effect of the speech. If it was an informational speech, did it inform? If it was a persuasive speech, did it persuade? If neither of these goals were achieved, then the speech can be said to have failed in its purpose.

World History[1]

DOMAIN ONE: EGYPTIAN, INDIAN, MESOPOTAMIAN, CHINESE, AND HEBRAIC CIVILIZATIONS

TABLE 8.1   Domain One Content Summary: Ancient Civilizations: 5000 B.C.–500 A.D.

	EGYPT	INDIA	MESOPOTAMIA	CHINA	HEBREW
GEOGRAPHY	• Egypt is located in northern Africa. • Nile River.	• Located in southern Asia. • Himalayas lie to the north & the Indian Ocean to the south. • The Indus and Ganges are major rivers.	• Farming, raising cattle, sheep, etc. • To the north-west are the Taurus Mts. and to the east lie the Zagros Mts. • Persian Gulf to the south.	• China is located in far eastern Asia. • Huang He or Yellow River and the Chang Jiang or Long River. • Divided into two parts.	• Israel is located on the eastern shores of the Mediterranean Sea. • Bounded on the east by the Arabian Peninsula.
HISTORY/ GOVERNMENT	• Old, Middle, and New Kingdoms	• Empires ruled by emperors with supreme authority • Chandragupta Maurya united India in 320 B.C.	• Akkadian Empire in 2350 B.C. • Babylonian Empire in 1790 B.C. • Kassites Empire in 1600 B.C. • Median Empire in 612 B.C.	• As early as 5000 B.C. farmers growing rice. • Xia and Shang Dynasties. • Three social classes. • Legalism	• The Jewish Bible dictated the behavior of the kings and people.
RELIGION/ ARCHITECTURE/ ART	• Believed in many gods but the Sun God, Re, was their chief god. • Pyramids were built beginning during the Old Kingdom.	• Hinduism is one of the oldest religions—the Vedas are the holiest books. • Buddhism was founded by Siddhartha Gautama.	• Main god was Enlil—wind, rain, storms. • Mud-brick temples called ziggurats. • Ea was another major god of wisdom and waters.	• Shang Di main god. • Ancestor worship. • Oracle bones. • Filial piety. • Great Wall.	• Practiced monotheism or belief in one God. • The Ten Commandments. • Israel and Judah. • Torah. • Old Testament.

(continued)

[1]Chapter contributed by Sam Marandos.

TABLE 8.1   Continued

	EGYPT	INDIA	MESOPOTAMIA	CHINA	HEBREW
SCIENCE	• 365-day calendar. • Three seasons.	• Doctors set broken bones and helped women give birth . • Used the base-ten system in math.	• Made the first wheels and wheeled carts. • Built reservoirs, canals, and dikes. • Cuneiform writing.	• Chinese writing. • Bronze ritual vessels, weapons, chariots, and walled cities.	• Built towns. • Specialized as weavers, spinners, dyers, potters, metal-workers.
CULTURE	• Children were valued as gifts from god.	• Mohenjo-Daro and Harappa were two major cities of ancient India—located in the Indus Valley.	• Three classes: upper, middle, and low. • Sumer • Babylon	• Each region of China has its own dialect and culture. • Family was basic unit.	• Abraham left Mesopotamia for Canaan at God's request. • Jacob was Isaac's son—also called Israel.
IMPORTANT PEOPLE	• Menes Cheops • Tutankhamen • Thutmose III • Hatsepsut	• Ashoka • Siddhartha Gautama	• Gilgamesh • Sargon • Hammurabi	• Nugua • Yu • Hou Ji • King Wu • Confucius	• Saul • David • Solomon • Moses
ECONOMY	• Agricultural • Trade	• Farming, raising cattle, sheep, and goats	• Agriculture • A merchant class appeared.	• Farming and raising stock.	• Farming • Trading • Nomadic

CONTENT AREA ONE: EGYPTIAN CULTURE

TABLE 8.2   Time Line of Events

5000 B.C.	Egypt was organized into two kingdoms
4000 B.C.	First written Egyptian books from papyrus.
3100 B.C.	King Menes unites both Egyptian kingdoms.
2750–2260 B.C.	Old Kingdom period.
2061–1784 B.C.	Middle Kingdom period.
1570–1070 B.C.	New Kingdom period.
1379–1362 B.C.	Akhenaton accepted only one god.
1120 B.C.	Ramses III, the last of Egypt's pharaohs, died.
1922 B.C.	The discovery of King Tut's tomb.

Geography

Egypt is located along the northern shores of Africa on the Mediterranean Sea. It is a long strip of land between the latitudes 24 and 31 degrees north. The north-flowing Nile River has been the center of life for Egyptians because its yearly floods bring a fine layer of sand and clay, or silt, which makes the land productive. The Nile River runs the whole length of more than one thousand kilometers and forms a very long strip of land that is cultivable. The Nile River Valley does not exceed fourteen kilometers in width. The rest of the Egyptian landscape is desert.

History/Government

The Sahara desert to the west, the Nubian Desert to the south, the Red Sea to the east, and the Mediterranean Sea to the north afforded early Egyptians with natural protective barriers from invaders. Thus, by 5000 B.C. Egyptians had banded together into two kingdoms: Upper Egypt and Lower Egypt. Upper Egypt made up the southern part from the first cataract to the source of the Nile River. Lower Egypt made up the northern part which was bounded in the north by the Nile Delta. By 3300 B.C., both Upper and Lower Egypt had their own kings. About 3100 B.C. the king of Upper Egypt, Menes, decided to unite both kingdoms. He was victorious, and he became the king of both regions. King Menes is credited with the design of a new double crown to signify the union of the two regions. The family of King Menes made up the first dynasty to rule Egypt. In all there were thirty dynasties, or series of rulers, from the same families.

Historians have divided the history of Egypt into three periods. The Old Kingdom lasted from 2750 to 2260 B.C. It was during this period that the Egyptians built the great pyramids. King Zoser, sometime during the 2600s, decided to have a special burial made for himself. He called upon his chief advisor, Imhotep, who was also an architect to design such a burial place. King Zosher started the age of pyramid building. The Middle Kingdom lasted from 2061 to 1784 B.C. during which time the Egyptians excelled in art, architecture, and literature. The New Kingdom lasted from 1570 to 1070 B.C. during which time the Egyptians expanded their power into neighboring regions and built an empire. It was during the New Kingdom period that the Egyptians began calling their kings pharaohs.

Religion and Architecture

According to Egyptian thought, at first there was chaos. From the chaos emerged the sun who was covered with sand and is thought to have emerged from water. This sun is referred to as Ra, Atum (perfect being), or Khepri. Ra was later combined with another god to form the most powerful Egyptian god, Amon-Ra. Osiris was another important god who was thought to have created the Earth. Later he was assassinated by his brother Seth. Osiris had a son named Horus by his wife Isis. Osiris is well known as the god of the dead or the afterlife. Hapi was the god who controlled the Nile's flooding and was highly regarded. Anubis was the jackal-god and believed to be the illegitimate son of Osiris. Other Egyptian gods included Hathor, the goddess of love, and Thoth, the god of wisdom.

The Egyptians prayed to numerous gods for the things that they wanted out of life. They also believed in an afterlife and planned for it. The pharaohs and nobility spent their lifetimes planning for the afterlife. They began with small tombs that expanded into the architectural marvels we now know as the great pyramids of Egypt. The pharaohs wanted to make sure that their wealth, positions, and servants remained with them so that they could have an advantage in the afterlife. To guide the dead in their voyage to the afterlife, Egyptians put together a collection of prayers in what is known as the *Book of the Dead*. The pyramids were constructed in order to house the bodies of the pharaohs, the bodies of their servants, their wealth, and other objects of importance to them. The pyramids were thought to be impregnable from the outside in order to keep people from disturbing the peaceful rest and wealth of the pharaohs. However, the pyramids were breached through the ages and only a few remained untouched until the twentieth century.

The Egyptians believed that the body must be protected from decay if it was to enjoy such things as eating, drinking, dancing, or other pleasures in the afterlife. As a result, they embalmed the body in order to protect it from decay. This embalming process took about forty days. They treated the body with natron, a kind of salt, to dry it out. The mummified body was wrapped in 400 yards of linen strips before being placed in the coffin which had the face of the dead person crafted on the outside. The coffin was placed in the burial room of the pyramid which was then sealed. Air shafts were designed to allow air to come into the pyramid and to allow the king's soul to fly to heaven.

The pyramids were flat structures piled one on top of each other. Usually a pyramid was about one mile long with a 133 foot high wall of stone. There were fourteen doors in the wall but only one could open. The king's body lay about eighty feet below ground. About eighty pyramids survived into the present. The Great Pyramid of Cheops, built at Gizeh, was considered as one of the Seven Wonders of the Ancient World. In 1922, King Tutankhamen's tomb was discovered in the Valley of the Kings untouched by robbers. The tomb was full of treasures and provided the modern world with a glimpse of King Tut's life and times. King Tut was only nine when he became the pharaoh or king. He died when he was nineteen. King Tut's tomb had four rooms full of furniture, clothing, and jewelry. There were beds, chairs, vases, musical instruments, baskets of food, figures of Egyptian gods, model ships, and chariots. Additionally, there were three coffins set one inside the other which were covered with gold. These treasures have allowed us today to get a glimpse into the Egyptians' past.

During the New Kingdom, King Akhenaton (1379 to 1362 B.C.) accepted only one god rather than multiple gods. He prayed to Aton, the sun god. After the death of this pharaoh, the Egyptian clergy returned to the worship of many gods. It was also during this period that the use of underground tombs instead of pyramids were favored by the pharaohs.

Science

The early Egyptians observed the heavens very closely and were able to design a 365-day calendar. This calendar had 12 months of 30 days each with 5 extra days added to make it 365 days in total. This helped them to plan for the Nile's yearly flooding and planting of a variety of crops.

Ancient Egyptians used hieroglyphic writing, which made use of pictures, to record important information using the papyrus plant which grew along the Nile River. Written records indicate that Egyptian doctors treated patients with bone fractures and breaks with splints and casts. The doctors also had knowledge of various drugs to treat different diseases. Additionally, the doctors were knowledgeable in sewing wounds and performing surgeries.

Culture

At the top of the social structure of Egyptian society was the King or Pharaoh. Egyptians believed that their kings were gods and as such had ultimate authority over them. The kings owned everything. Below the kings, Egyptian society was divided into three classes. The upper class was made up of priests, court nobility, and landed nobility. The priests were made up of both men and women whose primary duties were to perform religious ceremonies. The court nobility was made up of people who acted as advisors to the King and Queen. The landed nobility was made up of people who managed the King's and Queen's estates. Women of this class were very important because land and property passed from mother to daughter.

The middle class was also made up of men and women who were traders, merchants, and skilled artisans. Professional people such as scribes, teachers, artists, doctors, and pyramid planners and builders were also included in the middle class.

The lower class was subdivided into free laborers and slaves. The free laborers had few rights and lived poorly in mudbrick homes. The slaves were usually prisoners of war and were made to work on farms and build roads, irrigation canals, and other building projects, such as the pyramids. It was possible for lower class people to rise to positions of respect and honor if they were smart and ambitious.

Children were highly valued by Egyptians because they believed that they were the gifts of their gods. In Egyptian art, children are shown with their parents playing games and having fun. They played such games as leapfrog, wrestling, and tug-of-war. Children of the upper class also learned how to read, write, do math, and study literature. The work week for Egyptians was ten days in length with one day off. They worked from sunrise until sunset. During their time off from work, Egyptians liked to listen to music, dance, and attend parties. Men and women wore makeup and jewelry. Women wore long, sleeveless dresses made from cotton while the men wore knee-length linen skirts with or without short-sleeved shirts.

Important People

Menes was the king who united Upper and Lower Egypt into one nation or empire and thus is a key individual in Egyptian history. King Cheops is well known for the great pyramid that he built, which became one of the Seven Wonders of the ancient world. King Tut is well known today because of the treasures found in his tomb in 1922 and the light they shed on ancient Egyptian life. Other Egyptians are also well known. Hatsepsut became pharaoh during the New Kingdom when she took over the reins of government from her nephew Thutmose III. She ruled Egypt for twenty years. During this time she restored old temples, built new ones, built a great temple for herself, built obelisks, expanded trade, and improved life for her people. She did not seek to expand power outside of Egypt. After her death, her nephew, Thutmose III, took over power and became one of Egypt's most successful military leaders and one of its mightiest pharaohs. He led military excursions into Syria, Palestine, and south to modern day Sudan. As a result, he brought Egypt great wealth from all of these nations.

Economy

Egypt's economy was dependent on the yearly floods of the Nile River. Through careful planning and use of the 365-day calendar, Egyptians were able to plant varieties of seeds that they harvested for home consumption as well as for trade. The Egyptians built irrigation ditches to carry water to the fields and invented the plow in order to till the soil. As such, farmers became the backbone of the Egyptian economy. All work done for the kings by the upper, middle, and lower classes was paid for in food, such as bread, beer, and milk.

Trade and yearly gifts from conquered nations also helped Egyptian society. Goods such as wheat, copper, lead, gold, ivory, ebony, leopard skins, rare woods, and others were traded for the goods of Egypt or given as yearly gifts. Slave labor also helped Egypt with public buildings, the pyramids, obelsisks, temples, irrigation projects, and farm work.

CONTENT AREA TWO: INDIAN CULTURE

TABLE 8.3   Time Line of Events

1500 B.C.	Migrations into India and introduction of Hinduism.
563 B.C.	An Indian prince, Siddhartha Gautama, was born. He later became the founder of Buddhism.
320 B.C.	India's first empire under Chandragupta Maurya.

Geography

India is located in southern Asia. The area it fills is called the Indian subcontinent. To the north of the Indian subcontinent lie the tallest mountains, the Himalayas. Two great rivers begin in the snowy peaks of the Himalayas. The rivers are the Indus River and Ganges River. The Indus River spills over every spring and the old layer of soil is enriched with a new layer of silt. Early farmers in this region grew barley and other grains in this rich soil.

History and Government

The Indus Valley civilization is over 4000 years old. However, it wasn't until the 1920s that British archaeologists began studying a site that had been uncovered in the 1850s while the British were building a railroad in the area. The site is called Mohenjo-Daro and is located about 600 miles southwest of Harappa. Other sites representing some sixty villages were also unearthed and have provided us with an insight into the people who populated the Indus Valley. Mohenjo-Daro and the other cities represent the Harappan civilization. Besides Mohenjo-Daro, there were the cities of Harappa and Lothal. The early civilization of Mohenjo-Daro and the other cities ended in mystery around 1500 B.C. Archaeologists found evidence of sudden death and unburied bodies suggesting either a devastating earthquake or an invasion.

About 1500 B.C. there were great migrations of people into India. The newcomers brought with them new ideas and vastly different customs. These invaders are known as Aryans which means "noble." These individuals came from eastern Europe and western Asia. Because they had horses, the Aryans were better fighters. They introduced the chariot to India. In time they became farmers and raised such crops as barley and wheat. They lived in small villages in the countryside.

The Aryans brought with them a new social order. Using their holiest books, the Vedas, they divided their society into four social classes with each class assigned a special job. These social classes worked together in similar fashion as the human body. The Brahmans, who were the priests and scholars, made up the head. The Kshatriyas, who were the rulers, made up the arms. The Vaisyas, who were the merchants and professionals, made up the legs. The Sudras, who were the laborers and servants, made up the feet. This social class structure was the precursor to India's caste system. Below all the other castes were the untouchables who did all the unpleasant work in Indian society. Individuals assigned to a specific social class worked within their groups and could not change from generation to generation. This caste system was the foundation of Hinduism in India.

India was united in 320 B.C. by Chandragupta Maurya in India's first empire. He, his son, and grandson were ruthless rulers who expanded their empire into what is today southern India and western Pakistan. Chandragupta's grandson, Ashoka, killed hundreds of thousands of people until he discovered the Buddhist religion. He became a strong convert and issued a number of edicts in Buddhism's behalf. He sent missionaries throughout Asia to spread the teachings of this religion. One of his edicts called on people to show "obedience to mother and father." After his death, India became a land of small kingdoms.

In 320 A.D., Chandragupta I became the ruler of a small kingdom in the Ganges Valley. He conquered some of the other kingdoms and started the Gupta Empire. Much of what is known about this empire comes from the writings of a Chinese monk, Faxian, who traveled across India and collected his writings in the book of *Fo Kuo Chi* or the *Record of Buddhist Kingdoms*.

Religion/Architecture/Art

The people of the Indus Valley, as represented by the remains and artifacts found in Mohenjo-Daro, had an elaborate religion. Numerous female statues attest to the fact that the people worshipped a goddess. In sculptures and carvings, it is shown that people burned incense or candles and animals played a part in the religious ceremonies. Because of the existence of a huge bath house with living quarters, it is suggested that a priestly class existed which lived in great luxury. The Aryans, who invaded India about 1500 B.C., brought with them Hinduism. Hindus worship three main gods: Brahma the Creator, Vishnu the Preserver, and Shiva the Destroyer. There were also many lesser gods. The Hindus believe that people live many lives and after the body dies, the soul returns to life in a new body. This rebirth is known as reincarnation.

Another great religion that took roots in India is Buddhism. The Buddha, or "Enlightened One," is believed to have been an Indian prince who sought knowledge about life. After traveling and studying with Brahman priests, the prince felt that he finally understood the meaning of life and began teaching the Four Noble Truths: (1) Suffering is a part of life. (2) Wanting things brings suffering. (3) People can find peace by giving up wants. (4) Following eight basic principles, called the Eightfold Path, can lead to peace. He thus became Buddha. His actual name was Siddhartha Gautama. After Buddha's death, his followers kept preaching and the founding of a new religion, Buddhism, came to life. Eventually it spread over all of Asia.

Science

Writing was used by the people of the Indus Valley. We know this by the seals that they left with writings on them. It is evident that craftsmen and merchants knew how to read and write. However, the writings have not been deciphered by archaeologists. Baked bricks were used for building houses and paving the streets and baths instead of sun-dried bricks.

During the Gupta domination, Indian doctors used inoculation to help people fight diseases. Indian doctors also grafted skin and set broken bones. Indian mathematicians developed the base-ten number system that we use today.

Culture

The city of Mohenjo-Daro was laid out in blocks and the streets were paved and lined with different types of shops. Houses here faced inward toward interior courtyards. The houses were made from a white marble stone. Staircases suggest that families spent enjoyable evenings on their rooftops where the air was cooler. The houses had indoor toilets and some even had baths. The streets of the city had sewers which carried the waste water from the city.

Most of the people lived in small huts in villages around Mohenjo-Daro. Two-story homes were used by the upper class in the city to live in luxury with rooms for servants and guests. Their homes had baths with waterproof tiles. Their furniture was made out of wood which was decorated with bone, shell, and ivory inlays. The wealthy also had ornate pottery, bronze tools, silver pitchers, and gold jewelry. Different forms of toys were also made for the amusement of children. Balls, marbles, toy carts, and rattles were found in abundance. In addition, each home had a chute whereby the trash could be emptied into bins and collected by city workers.

When the Aryans invaded India, they brought with them the Sanskrit language. Many Indian languages of today, including Hindi, have their roots in Sanskrit. Sanskrit was a sacred language to the Aryans because they believed it to be the language of the gods.

Important People

Siddhartha Gautama was an Indian prince who was born in 563 B.C. and became the leader of a new religion called Buddhism. Chandragupta Maurya was a ruler who in 320 B.C. united India and formed the Maurya Empire. His grandson, Ashoka, came to embrace Buddhism and called on people to adopt peaceful ways of living. Chandragupta II ruled India during its golden age. He supported many artists and writers including Kalidasa, an author well known for his poems and plays.

Economy

Farming appears to be the basis of the economy and subsistence of this civilization. Trade was also part of the economy in the Indus Valley. Grain appears to be the main staple that was used and traded due to the existence of a granary and heavy stone weights suggesting that large amounts of grain was being weighed by an organized labor force.

Two seaports existed in the Indus Valley which were used to trade with the Sumerians. It is possible that sailboats were used by the people of the Indus Valley to travel the Arabian Sea while camels and ox-drawn carts carried goods to other parts over land. Their ships probably used the monsoon winds to cross the Arabian Sea carrying such items as gems, sesame oil, and cotton. Proof of contact between the Indus Valley people and Sumerians lies in the unearthing of Indus Valley seals in the ancient city of Ur and several other Sumerian cities.

CONTENT AREA THREE: MESOPOTAMIAN CULTURE

TABLE 8.4   Time Line of Events

4000–3000 B.C.	Tribes settled and built cities.
2900–2400 B.C.	Sumerians had city-states.
2500 B.C.	Sargon I united all the city-states.
1760 B.C.	Hammurabi united lower Mesopotamia into Babylonia.
1600 B.C.	The Hittites conquer Babylonia.
1200 B.C.	The Hittite kingdom collapsed and smaller states emerged.
729 B.C.	Babylonia was conquered by the Assyrians.
605–550 B.C.	The Chaldean Empire emerges.
550 B.C.	Cyrus the Great establishes the Persian Empire.

Geography

Mesopotamia is part of the Fertile Crescent, which in ancient days included parts of what are now the countries of Syria, Turkey, Lebanon, Jordan, Iraq, and Israel. On the west the region bordered on the Mediterranean Sea and on its southeastern part lies the Persian Gulf. The Mountains form the northwest border and the Zagros Mountains lie to the east. Cutting through this region are two rivers, the Tigris and Euphrates. A fertile region of land lies between the two rivers, thus the name Mesopotamia or "land between the rivers." This region provided people with plenty of water and good land on which to grow food. Therefore, people changed from hunter-gatherers to farmers.

History and Government

Because it took a lot of planning to construct their irrigation systems, their ziggurats, and other public buildings, large numbers of ancient Sumerians had to live together. This required the writing of many laws in order for people to work together in harmony. Ancient Sumer became a civilization made up of a number of independent city-states. Each city-state had its own leaders and its own government. At the earliest period, the leaders would get together and make laws to govern their cities. As time passed, individual monarchs or kings provided the leadership needed. The kings had control of all aspects of Sumerian society, including religion, agriculture, and building plans. Because Sumerians believed that their gods chose their kings, many legends were told about their kings. The best known legend is the one about Gilgamesh who ruled the ancient city of Uruk sometime between 2700 B.C. and 2500 B.C. Gilgamesh sought to learn the meaning of life and thus traveled widely to find out. As a result he had many adventures. People built stories around these adventures.

Around 1000 B.C., new empires sprang up in ancient Mesopotamia including Assyria and Babylonia. Adad-Nirari, the king of Assyria, conquered northern Mesopotamia and expanded his rule all the way to the Mediterranean Sea. In 745 B.C., King Tiglath-Pileser III extended the empire by conquering Babylonia. However, he had to contend with many rebellions because he and his people were despised by those he conquered. The conquered people were forced to relocate and give up their lands and their wealth. The empire was thus weakened and the Chaldeans with the help of the Medes managed to overthrow the Assyrians.

The new Babylonian Empire established complex trading networks with Egypt, Greece, and other nations. Nebuchadnezzar, who ruled from 605 to 562 B.C., is best known for the hanging gardens of Babylon. He was also a great military leader who expanded his empire into Syria and Phoenicia. He also attacked and burned the city of Jerusalem. As a result, he sent thousands of Jews to Babylonia as slaves. The Babylonian Empire came to an end under King Nabonidus, who was highly unpopular. Babylonia was invaded by Cyrus the Great, king of Persia.

Religion/Architecture/Art

The ziggurat was the largest building constructed by the ancient Sumerians. It was a huge mud-brick temple. The architects of the ziggurat constructed it in layers, one on top of the other. Each succeeding layer was smaller. At the top was located the shrine dedicated to each city's special god. The Sumerians worshipped many gods. Their main god was Enlil who controlled the wind, storms, and rain. The second most important god was Ea, who controlled the waters and was the god of wisdom. Different gods stood for different things. The ancient Sumerians believed that if they prayed to their gods they would provide them with good harvests. They explained such phenomena as the floods as signs that their gods were displeased with them.

Science

The farmers of Mesopotamia developed a system of irrigation made up of connected ditches, canals, dams, and dikes in order to move water where it was needed. This irrigation system also helped farmers to control water during flooding periods by diverting the water to areas away from their fields and villages. They also built reservoirs to store excess water which was used when the rivers subsided. The farmers in Sumer also invented the wheel, which made it possible to build wheeled carts. Domesticated animals pulled the carts, which could be used to transport building materials for houses, move goods, and also to travel easier. The Sumerians also built the first sailboats that they used for travel and commerce.

To mark their farming boundaries, the ancient Sumerians used a land unit called the *iku,* which equates to our *acre.* In order to keep track of transactions, Sumerians also invented the quart as a means of measuring wheat and barley and thus were able to keep records. The need to keep records led Sumerians to their greatest innovation which was writing. Scribes used wet clay to create clay tablets which were imprinted with their writing. These tablets were baked and stored as records. Their writing made use of wedge-shaped symbols and is called *cuneiform* writing.

King Nebuchadnezzar encouraged many priests to become astronomers who were able to study the heavens and heavenly bodies. They were thus able to design calendars based on their observations. The Babylonians also divided the hour into sixty minutes just as we do today. In mathematics, they created the concept of place value.

Culture

Due to the large food surpluses, Sumerian society became stratified. Three social classes made up their society. At the top were the king, priests, and other important people and their families. The middle and largest class was made up of artisans and merchants, including carpenters, bricklayers, doctors, and scribes. The lowest class in Sumerian society was made up of slaves who were either prisoners of war or people who were enslaved for punishment. Slaves could become free after a period of time.

Men had more authority in Sumerian society because they controlled their households and could divorce their wives for any reason. Women, however, could serve as leaders and many did serve as religious leaders. Women were allowed to own property, to divorce cruel husbands, and to run their own businesses.

Under Babylonian rule, Mesopotamia came under the laws created by Hammurabi. His Code of Hammurabi covered all areas of conduct, including the family, the rights of individuals (including women), the conduct of professionals, the economy, and the military.

Important People

Sargon of Akkad is said to have been the son of sheepherders who spoke Akkadian. Later he gathered an army and founded the city of Akkad. He went on to conquer Uruk, Ur, Lagash, Umma, and northern Mesopotamia. He also conquered other lands reaching as far as Egypt. He is said to have created the world's first empire.

Hammurabi became the ruler of Babylonia in 1792 B.C. He conquered all other people around him, including the Assyrians, and ruled Mesopotamia as one great empire. He maintained a strong centralized government. He appointed governors to help him rule, had judges all over the empire to met out justice, created a tax system with tax collectors, and created the Code of Hammurabi. In his Code, Hammurabi's laws covered religious issues, property rights, duties of professional workers, irrigation, military service, crime and punishment, marriage and family.

Gilgamesh was a ruler who sought the meaning of life. The *Epic of Gilgamesh* is a well known collection of stories in poetry style.

Nebuchadnezzar was the king who ruled the Babylonian Empire. Under his rule, he expanded the empire to the borders of Egypt, expanded trade throughout the region, and encouraged the growth of astronomy and mathematics.

Economy

By about 3000 B.C. the city-state of Uruk was made up of some 60,000 people. This concentration of so many people made it possible to carry on agriculture on a grand scale. The farms produced an immense supply of food, which created a surplus. This led to a division of labor with some people specializing as craftworkers, metalworkers, merchant, and managers. Their food surpluses of wheat, barley, and copper tools allowed the ancient Sumerians to trade with people throughout the Fertile Crescent. They usually traded their surplus food for needed resources, such as wood, salt, precious stones, and raw tin and copper. Later leaders of Mesopotamia carried on trade with Egypt, Greece, Phoenicia, and others.

CONTENT AREA FOUR: CHINESE CULTURE

TABLE 8.5   Time Line of Events

4500 B.C.	Chinese farmers grew millet.
3500 B.C.	Chinese women raised silkworms and weaved silk cloth.
2205–1766 B.C.	China ruled by the Hsia.
1500–1027 B.C.	China ruled by the Shang dynasty.
1027–256 B.C.	The Zhou dynasty rules China.
221–206 B.C.	China is centralized by the Qin emperor.
140–87 B.C.	Wu Di, of the Han dynasty, brought peace and prosperity to China.
100 A.D.	Invention of paper.
618–907 A.D.	Printing was invented under the Tang dynasty.

Geography

The vast majority of China's people live south of Shanghai. In this part of China, people rather than machines do most of the work. Rice is the dominant crop, and rice farming requires more labor than other crops. Farmers have learned to use every bit of land possible to feed the large population, using terraces to create more farmland. The warm climate of southern China allows farmers to have two and sometimes three harvests. Wheat is the most common crop of northeast China. The land is similar to what you might find in Kansas, but is much more crowded. North China's severe winters limit the growing season to about half the year. Western China is less populated than Eastern China. West of the wheat fields is the Gobi Desert. The few people who live on this barren, rocky land are nomads who raise cattle, sheep, and goats. Many continue to live in felt tents called yurts, while others live in simple clay homes. The Himalayas begin their rise south of the Gobi.

History and Government

Prehistoric Period.   Like other ancient civilizations, Chinese civilization also started along a river, where plenty of water was available for the people, animals, and crops and the soil was rich and sandy, making it easy to work with their simple tools. By 10,000 B.C., a group of people called the Yangshao had settled near the Huang He River in north central China. Another river, the Wei, joins it and together they form a bend like an elbow.

About 3000 B.C., another culture, the Lungshan, developed in northeast China. These people were also farmers who grew wheat and millet and raised cattle, sheep, pigs, and dogs. They hunted, fished, and gathered wild foods. Eventually, the Lungshen moved to the south of China because it rained there and they were able to raise rice. The Lungshen were an advanced civilization who harvested silk from silkworms and used it to weave fine silk fabrics.

The Xia and Shang Dynasties (2000 B.C.).   According to one Chinese legend a man named Yu, a great engineer, became the leader of the Chinese people. When floods covered most of the good land, it is said that Yu the Great dug deep into the rivers forcing them to hold more water and thus cause the waters to recede. The farmers were again able to continue with their farming. Yu the Great founded the first Chinese dynasty, the Xia. Information about the Xia comes primarily from legend because there were no written records at that time. The Xia ruled for 300 years. Its last king, Chieh, was an evil person who was overthrown by another leader called Chang Tang. His reign began the Shang Dynasty. The Shang used war chariots and bronze weapons, a new technology that helped them to take control of China. The Shang ruled China from 1766 to 1122 B.C. The rulers of the Shang Dynasty, over a period of time, were able to organize the Chinese people, became skilled engineers, and built great walled cities. Within the walls of the cities lived the rulers, priests, and warriors. Their skilled craft-workers lived outside the walls, and the farmers lived in villages along the rivers. Archeological evidence shows that in the capital city of Anyang, the Chinese used cowrie shells for money. During the Bronze Age, the Chinese used metal coins for currency. Around the 1600s B.C., Shang craftsmen learned how to mix tin and copper to produce a new, stronger metal, bronze, which was used for weapons, pots, plates, pottery, spears, and chariots.

The Zhou Dynasty.   In the early 1100s B.C. a group of people living in the Wei Valley helped the Shang rulers to patrol the borders guarding against invaders from the west. However, one of their leaders, King Wen, decided to try and establish his own dynasty by overthrowing the Shang. He was not successful but his son, Wu Martial, succeeded in 1122 B.C. Wu Martial instituted his own dynasty called the Zhou.

The Zhou kings controlled China through a system of feudalism. They placed their relatives and other favored individuals in positions of power and in charge of the land as the new nobility living in walled cities and owning the surrounding land. Chinese peasants or serfs had to pay these people in order to use the land. The new nobles then paid the king a portion of what they collected from the peasants. They were like kings themselves, and in time they warred against each other. In order to raise good crops, the nobles hired well-educated people and skilled workers to help them build flood control projects. They also hired tax collectors to collect taxes from the serfs. Scholars were hired to keep records of the transactions. Because in different regions of China people spoke different dialects, the Zhou rulers decided to use picture writing in order to make sure that everyone understood what was communicated to them. As such, they helped to unify the Chinese.

By 771 B.C., the Zhou Dynasty had lost most of its power as powerful lords controlled the land. They rebelled and drove the Zhou rulers out of the capital. The Zhou moved their capital to Luoyang and officially they still ruled China until 256 B.C. The real power, however, had shifted to the powerful lords. This period of time was chaotic for China because the powerful lords fought one another for control and advantage.

Many learned men tried to bring peace to China at this time of chaotic conditions. One of the better-known individuals was Confucius (551–479 B.C.). Although he was born into nobility, Confucius and his family were very poor. His parents died when he was young and Confucius grew up as an orphan. He studied very hard and became the leading scholar of his time; his ideas became the foundation of Confucianism, and his teachings still continue to influence the Chinese.

Confucius believed that five different relationships existed between people: husband and wife, father and son, older and younger brother, friend to friend, and subject and ruler. He further stated that the foundation of each relationship depended upon three virtues: sincerity, loyalty, and mutual respect. The first three relationships deal with family. Confucius taught that children should respect their parents all of the time. The end result has been generations of Chinese living together in one household. Children not only had their parents in their home but also their grandparents and even aunts and uncles. Families usually stayed together in one place because their ancestors were buried nearby. When a son married, he brought his bride to his father's home. Confucius went on to parallel his view of the family with that of the rulers. He taught a ruler should act like a good father to his subjects. On other matters, Confucius said that government should be based on virtue or goodness and not on punishment and laws. Also government officials should get their jobs because they were educated and qualified and not just by having good family connections.

Other groups of people sprang up all over China preaching their own ideas and ideals. The Moists believed in universal equal love for everyone because it would help to bring about lasting peace. The Legalists preached that people were bad by nature and that strict punishment for breaking the laws should be imposed. Another group, the Daoists, believed that people were neither good nor bad and should live a simple life in harmony with nature. Confucianism and Daoism are both responses to the upheavals of the Dynastic Cycle, where an empire would rise and then fall and plunge the society into chaos. Both systems attempt to solve this problem, particularly after the fall of the Zhou Empire.

Confucianism proposes having a very rigid social hierarchy to maintain social order. These rules ensure that each person understands his or her place in society and the duties that he or she must carry out. For example, leaders exist to lead in a benevolent manner and followers exist to carry out the wishes of the leader in loyal manner. The leader has power only so long as he rules in a just and fair manner; if not, his power can be taken away.

Daoism, on the other hand, posits that nothing can be done to prevent dynastic cycles, except learning how to live harmoniously with one's self and within nature. The goal is to avoid major social changes because major social changes disrupt the harmony and the natural flow of life. One small change, for example, may result in unintended consequences; therefore, it is better to do nothing than to try to impose social orders upon a world that has its own flow of energy.

In 256 B.C., the Qin state attacked and defeated the last Zhou emperor. Ten years later, in 246 B.C.. a man from Qin by the name of Cheng challenged all other lords and won. His rule began the Qin Dynasty, which lasted only fifteen years. Cheng changed his name to Qin Shuhuangdi and took on the new title of emperor. In the short span of time that the Qin Dynasty lasted, Qin Shuhuangdi, to maintain effective control, organized the empire into thirty-six provinces, which in turn were divided into districts. Each province was assigned a governor and a defender. He also set up and headed a state bureaucracy. The emperor decided to hire people on the basis of merit rather than family connections. The new employees were given salaries and were strictly supervised. Below the emperor were other officials, such as the eleven chamberlains who looked after the emperor's household and three dukes who controlled the army. Qin also set up measurement standards for the whole empire and improved written language so that all people in China understood it. He also did away with the feudal system and allowed everyone, including the peasants, to purchase and own their own land. Qin is also responsible for burning many books that did not support his way of thinking. The works of Confucius and others were the targets of censorship. Qin is also credited with building the Great Wall of China. He used a forced-labor group of some 300,000 men to build the wall, which is 1,500 miles long and thirty feet high. The purpose of the wall was to keep invaders out and also to keep peasants from leaving their farms. Although Qin was a cruel emperor, he is given credit for unifying China. To this day China has retained its name which has its roots in the name Qin or Ch'in.

The Han Dynasty

After the death of Qin, the peasants and army became dissatisfied and revolted against the Qin Dynasty. The first Han emperor, Han Gaozu, decided that the empire could not be ruled by Legalism only. Therefore, he surrounded himself with scholars and other educated people to rewrite some of the old writings of Confucius and others from memory. He also combined the thinking of Legalism and Confucianism into one and ruled by example and not through the use of punishment.

Another emperor, Wudi, who ruled China from 141 to 87 B.C., sent out his armies on the road to conquest and expansion of the empire, and added lands in southern China, North Korea, North Vietnam, and the Gobi Desert regions. Wudi sent out an explorer further west to find out about other people. His representative, Zhang Qian, brought back tales from people all the way to modern-day Afghanistan. This interested Wudi, and he is given credit for the growth of the Silk Road where merchants could take their goods and trade with other regions.

Religion/Architecture/Art

The early Chinese believed in numerous and individual gods that they felt helped them in their everyday life. There were gods that controlled the sun, moon, stars, rivers, and mountains. Their supreme god was Shang Di, who communicated directly with their priests. Ancestor worship was also practiced by the ancient Chinese. Ceremonies were held whereby oracles were asked to consult with dead ancestors in order to find out about their future.

Science/Innovations

The Chinese made the first books about 3,000 years ago by using brush and ink on sheets of bamboo and silk. They then bound them together to make books. The Chinese also invented paper money in order to make trade easier. About 1600 B.C., during the Shang Dynasty, metalworkers learned how to make bronze from copper and tin. As a result, new works of art became possible. Early Chinese used a potter's wheel, and they baked strong, durable pottery in kilns.

During the Han rule, paper was invented by beating mulberry bark fibers and mixing them with other fibers and water. These were spread out and allowed to dry into paper sheets. Han rulers also were the first to introduce the use of iron-tipped bamboo poles for deep drilling. Han writers produced brilliant works in the areas of mathematics, medicine, and poetry. It was during this period that Sima Jian wrote the complete history of the Qin Dynasty.

Culture

Most Chinese lived in farming villages that were located along rivers. The people had to work together on flood control and irrigation systems in order to use the land properly and to raise the crops that they needed. Important people lived in cities in ancient China. As a result, a stratification of society took place. Chinese society was made up of the rulers and their families who enjoyed a privileged existence. Then came the priests who saw to their religious needs. The warriors came next, and they provided the security that people needed. Skilled craftsmen provided the services required of their professions or line of work.

Important People

Yu, the "Great Engineer," a leader of the Lungshan, helped his people to work cooperatively together on flood control and irrigation projects and founded the first great Chinese dynasty, the Xia, in 2000 B.C. Emperor Qin founded the Qin Dynasty and unified China. He improved written language, built up a bureaucracy to rule China, and began the construction of the Great Wall.

TABLE 8.6

COMPARISON	HAN DYNASTY	ROMAN EMPIRE
Period	• Founding in 206 B.C. • Existed for four centuries. • Ended in 220 A.D.	• Roman Empire was founded in 44 B.C. • Ended in 250 A.D.
Culture	• Chinese of this period used many inventions like the wheelbarrow, the pulley to move heavy loads, the use of bellows for furnaces. • The emperor rode in collapsible carriages made possible by the use of sliding metal ribs. • The invention of paper made possible the spread of literacy. • Used paper to write poetry, mathematics books, dictionaries, government reports, and a large-scale census. • Zhang Heng invented the earthquake weathercock to predict earthquakes in 132 A.D. • The Han Dynasty stood for order and stability with support for Confucian principles, which are still followed today in China.	• There is archeological evidence on a wool weaving that Romans did trade with the Han dynasty. • Romans during this period sent their legions into the surrounding areas and conquered Europe and its various civilizations. • Roman power extended into the Middle East and Africa. • Roman legions also invaded and controlled Great Britain. • The Romans built aqueducts, bridges, and roads. • Romans traded widely throughout the vast empire. • Life was leisurely for the wealthy, who engaged in business, education, the arts, etc. • The social structure included the wealthy class; merchants, artisans, and farmers made up the lower classes; slaves were at the bottom of the social scale.
History	• Expanded into barbarian territory in the northwest. • Controlled the Silk Road trade route. • The Han Dynasty unified China and allowed government to perpetuate itself. • Wu Di was the emperor with the longest reign, which lasted 54 years. • Emperor Wu is responsible for the expansion of China to its present size. • Emperor Wu declared war on the nomadic people known as Xiongnu in 133 B.C. in order to protect China's northwest frontier. • Han influence spread far and wide until a coup by Wang Mang in 9 A.D. • Han rule reemerges with Guangwu Di as the emperor in 25 A.D. and lasted for 32 years. • At the end of the first century A.D. the house of Liu which dominated the Han Dynasty came to an end and a series of child rulers followed. • Liu Xie was the last emperor of the Han Dynasty and he abdicated the throne in 220 A.D.	• Augustus Caesar was responsible for bringing about the *Pax Romana* or Roman Peace beginning in 27 B.C. and lasting until 180 A.D.

Economy

Ancient Chinese people were primarily farmers who raised a variety of crops. Farmers raised millet and rice as staple foods. They designed and built irrigation systems to protect their crops. They also traded with other surrounding people such things as silk fabric, pots, plates.

CONTENT AREA FIVE: HEBRAIC CULTURE

TABLE 8.7   Time Line of Events

1250 B.C.	• Moses leads the Hebrews out of Egypt.
1025 B.C.	• Saul becomes the first king of the Hebrews in Palestine followed by David.
977–937 B.C.	• Solomon, the son of David, rules Palestine from Jerusalem.
722 B.C.–66 A.D.	• Jews were ruled by different people.
66 A.D.	• The Diaspora or scattering of Jews by the Romans.

Geography

Israel is located along the eastern seaboard of the Mediterranean Sea. Five geographical areas dominate the land of Israel. The northern mountainous section is the Galilee region. Mount Meron is located in the central part of Galilee and represents the highest point in Israel. The Plain of Esdraelon is a densely populated region and a highly productive agricultural area. The coastal plains contain most of Israel's major cities, industries, and commerce. The Negev is a triangular desert region and extends to the southern end of the Dead Sea. The Judean and Samarian hills run north and south throughout most of Israel.

With such a variety of regions, Israel supports a variety of agricultural produce, including citrus fruits, bananas, cotton, tobacco, grapes, dates, figs, olives, almonds, and avocados.

History and Government

Abram was a man who lived in the ancient city of Ur. He and his family believed in one God. The Bible tells us that God spoke to Abram and told him to take his family and move to the chosen land. He traveled with his family to a place called Shechem. Here Abram and God made a covenant or special agreement whereby Abram promised to be faithful to God, and in return God promised to give Abram's descendants the land of Canaan. Abram's name was changed to Abraham, which means "father of many nations." He is said to be the father of the Jewish people through his son Isaac and father of the Arab people through his son Ishmael. After a time, Abraham's son Isaac came to be called first Jacob and then Israel. It is through his name that all of his descendants, including his sons, came to be called Israelites. Each of his twelve sons led his own tribe.

When famine came to their land, many Israelites left their homes and traveled to Egypt to work. Here they were enslaved. In 1225 B.C. Moses, one of their leaders, led a revolt against the Egyptians and led his people out of Egypt in what has been called the Exodus. During the Exodus, God spoke to Moses on top of Mount Sinai and gave him the Ten Commandments. The Ten Commandments became a set of laws about responsibility and duty to God and to each other. The Ten Commandments also became part of the teachings of Judaism, the religion of the Jewish people, and later to Christianity and Islam.

The stories of Abraham, Moses, the Exodus, and the return to Canaan make up the first five books of the Hebrew Bible or Torah. Historians rely on stories told in the holy Bible in order to trace the history of the Israelites. In 1250 B.C., Moses led the Israelites out of bondage from Egypt. God had given Moses great powers to use against the Egyptians, who were reluctant to let the Israelites leave. Outbreaks of disease, plagues, infestations of lice, frogs, and locusts were used by Moses to convince the Egyptian pharaoh to let his people leave for their promised land, Canaan. According to the Torah, the holy book of the Israelites, Moses parted the waters of the Red Sea in order to let the Israelites escape the wrath of the pursuing Egyptian soldiers. The waters receded after all of the Israelites had crossed safely, and the Egyptian army drowned. The Israelites spent forty years wandering in the wilderness under Moses's leadership. This journey of forty years is known as the Exodus. The Israelites finally made it to their promised land but were plagued with unfriendly neighbors.

The Monarchy.   When the Israelites arrived in Canaan they set up a loose confederation among the different tribes. To be their leader, they selected Saul as their first king in 1020 B.C. Saul tried to keep the Philistines, a warrior group, at bay but was unable to do so. The Torah tells us that they used a giant of a man called Goliath to terrorize the Israelite army. For forty days Goliath would go out in the field and challenge the Israelites to send a man out to fight him. A young boy named David heard Goliath's challenge and decided to take him on, with King Saul's blessing. David used a sling to defeat Goliath. The Philistines fled from the Israelites, and David became a hero. This caused King Saul to become jealous, and he tried to kill David. Upon Saul's death, David became king of the Israelites. During his reign, he united the twelve tribes even more closely than before, the Philistines were defeated for the last time, and he made Jerusalem the capital city of the Israelite nation. David died in 961 B.C., and his son Solomon became the king. Solomon was a very wise ruler who made treaties with Egypt and other surrounding people that ensured Israel's safety. He also built many palaces, forts, and temples, including the great temple in Jerusalem.

Two Kingdoms.   Upon Solomon's death in 922 B.C., the various tribes quarreled among themselves. This led the northern tribes to form their own kingdom, name their own king, and make Samaria their capital. This kingdom retained the name of Israel. The southern tribes created their own kingdom and named their kingdom Judah with Jerusalem as its capital. The two kingdoms existed peacefully, side by side, for over 200 years. Although politically divided, the two kingdoms still shared the same religion.

Conquest of the Two Kingdoms and the Reign of Priests.   Israel was invaded and conquered by the Assyrians in 721 B.C., and Judah was conquered by the Babylonians in 587 B.C. The Jewish people were treated harshly and many were made slaves. A group of influential Israelites, called prophets, kept telling the people that the reason they found themselves in this accursed situation was that they had broken their covenant with God. The prophets preached for the people to stay with God's word and the future may be brighter and the Israelites enslaved in Babylonia and elsewhere may someday be allowed to return to their homeland.

   After fifty years of enslavement in Babylonia, King Cyrus of Persia, in 540 B.C., allowed the Israelites to leave Babylon for their homeland. Once back home, the Israelites rebuilt the temple in Jerusalem and allowed their priests to help govern them. The Torah became the guiding light of the Jewish people from the 400s B.C. onward until 200 B.C.

Revolt of the Maccabees.   In 200 B.C., the rule of the Torah came to an end as Syrian rulers took control of Israel. These Syrian rulers imposed Greek ideas and culture upon the Jews. Some Jews liked the ideas and culture of the Greeks but many rejected them. When the Syrian ruler Antiochus came to power in 175 B.C., he forced the Jews to adopt and practice Greek customs including worshipping Zeus and other Greek gods. However, this caused a lot of anger and frustration among many Jewish people. One Jewish priest named Mattathias and his five sons challenged the Syrians by organizing a revolt. Mattathias' son, Judah Maccabee, became the leader of the insurrection and fought the Syrians for two years. In 164 B.C., the Maccabees, a name used to identify all the rebels, drove the Syrians out of Israel and Israel became a free nation for the next eighty years. The temple in Jerusalem was rededicated with a special service that is still carried on in December of every year called Chanukah.

Religion/Architecture/Art

From the time of Abraham and the founding of Israel, the Jewish people have worshipped one true God, Yahweh. This belief in one God is called monotheism and has impacted Western civilization heavily. Their religion is called Judaism and their holy book, the Torah, contains the first five books of the holy Bible. The Torah contains the sacred history and laws of the Jewish people. The Torah contains the books of Genesis, Exodus, Leviticus, Numbers, and Deuteronomy. Starting in 400 B.C. the Jewish people's religion, Judaism, has defined the laws by which they should live their lives.

Science

The Israelites built magnificent temples to their God and many other government buildings. The Hebrews developed the Old Testament, which sheds light on the history and customs of that period of time.

Culture

The Jewish people from their beginnings believed in one God. Their beliefs were eventually collected and written down in their holy book, the Torah. Their lives have been closely attached to the teachings of the Torah and the worship of God. For the most part, Israelites were a group of farmers, nomads, and sheep herders who strived to make a home for themselves. For centuries they suffered at the hands of many conquerors. They experienced slavery and control over their lives by many different groups of people. However, their strong belief in their God and their Judaic religion allowed them to persevere and survive.

Most of the cultural practices and beliefs of the Jewish people were borrowed from the civilizations of Mesopotamia and other Fertile Crescent people. Even the Hebrew language was adapted from the Canaanites, and some of their proverbs can be traced back to the early Phoenicians. Men practiced farming and often intermarried with other groups of people and pretty much accepted the social and economic traditions of Canaan. The Israelites kept their patriarchal family units intact and also their individuality. It was this individualistic nomadic spirit of individual rights that kept them apart from the other peoples of the Near East. Their zeal for ownership of all goods in common and close ties to their clansmen influenced the economic and social values of the Israelites.

Important People

Abraham was the founder of Israel and is considered the father of the Arabs as well. He made a covenant with God whereby he promised to be faithful to God in return for God's promise to give Abraham's descendants the land of Canaan.

Moses was the leader of the Israelites who led them out of bondage from Egypt and gave the Jewish people the Ten Commandments.

King Saul was the first king of the Israelites upon their return from bondage in Egypt. King David was the second king of the Israelites and is credited with building the great city of Jerusalem. King David also wrote many psalms to the glory of God. He is also credited with killing Goliath, a huge man in the Philistine army, with a sling.

King Solomon was the son of David and was known for his wisdom. He built the great temple to God in Jerusalem.

Economy

The economy of the Israelites depended on agriculture, a nomadic existence, and the raising of animals. Agricultural produce included a variety of vegetables, and nomads specialized in the raising of animals. Nomads found it difficult to change their customs and ways of doing things because, in the pastoral society in which they lived, economic decisions were made based on custom and habit rather than on changing conditions. In Hebrew cities, people engaged in different types of work, including some becoming carpenters, wool merchants, potters, spinners, dyers, metalworkers, and weavers. Trading with the Phoenicians and others was carried on. Mining of copper and other metals also helped the Israelites.

DOMAIN TWO: KUSH, GREEK, AND ROMAN ANCIENT CIVILIZATIONS

TABLE 8.8   Ancient Civilizations 5000 B.C.–500 B.C.

	KUSH	GREECE	ROME
GEOGRAPHY	Located where modern-day Sudan is in Africa.	Greece is located in eastern Europe and is part of the Balkan Peninsula. It is made up of the mainland and many islands in the Aegean and Ionian seas.	Today, Rome is the capital city of Italy. It is located on the Tiber River near the Tyrrhenian Sea. It is the seat of the papacy of the Roman Catholic Church.
HISTORY/ GOVERNMENT	• Numia, in ancient times, was called Kush. It was an area ruled by Egypt for almost 2000 years.	• Stone Age • Minoans • Myceneans • The Dark Age • Renaissance • Athens and Sparta • Hellenistic Greece	• Romulus and Remus founded Rome in 753 B.C. • Early Rome was a kingdom of two classes. • Republican Rome was established in the 4th century B.C. • Imperial Rome became the capital of the then-known world. • Germanic tribes invaded Rome in 410 A.D. and 455 A.D. leaving it very weak.
RELIGION/ ARCHITECTURE/ ART	• Much of the religion of Kush was similar to that of the Egyptians. • Arts and crafts included vases, bowls, bracelets, and earrings made of gold and silver.	• Greeks believed in many gods but they recognized twelve main gods who lived on Mount Olympus. Zeus and his wife Hera were the ruling gods. Others included Athena, Artemis, Ares, etc.	• Romans borrowed the concept of the Greek gods but renamed them. Jupiter was the equivalent of the Greek god Zeus. Their gods presided over all aspects of Roman life. • Roman architecture was borrowed from the Greeks. Columns, domes, beams, and arches were added to their buildings.
SCIENCE	• Kush was rich in iron ore. As such, iron tools and weapons were made and traded.	• Copper and tin were mixed to make bronze. • They developed a system of writing.	• Built many public buildings, especially temples and sports arenas. • Romans were great engineers who built canals and roadways throughout their empire.

TABLE 8.8 **Continued**

	KUSH	GREECE	ROME
CULTURE	• The culture of Kush remained primarily like that of Egypt. The court ceremonies, religious practices, and language were those of Egypt.	• Ancient Greeks functioned around their beliefs in many gods. They enjoyed life by involving themselves into religious ceremonies, sports, music, and trade with countries in Africa, Asia, and Europe.	• Romans borrowed many cultural ideas from the Greeks. The ideas of artists, sculptors, scientists, and philosophers were taught to roman children by Greek teachers.
IMPORTANT PEOPLE	• Kashta • Piankhy • Taharqa	• King Minos • Solon • Leonidas • Pericles • Aeschylus, Aristophanes, Euripides, and Sophocles—wrote during the Golden Age. • Phillip II • Alexander the Great	• Romulus and Remus • Scipio • Lucius Sulla • Julius Caesar • Augustus Caesar • Virgil
ECONOMY	• Kush was rich in gold and ivory that was highly prized by the Egyptians. • Additionally it traded ostrich feathers, perfumes, oils, and exotic animals with Egypt. • Iron tools and spearheads were traded for luxury items from India and China.	• The ancient Greeks raised grapes and oil. • Small amounts of wheat and barley were also raised. They traded for other goods from other lands. • They were also good seafarers and colonized many areas from which they took what they needed.	• Trade and travel were easier for the Romans and other peoples of the Italian peninsula because the mountains and hills were less rugged than in Greece. • People traded with each other. • Volcanic ash provided some areas with rich soil to plant crops.

CONTENT AREA SIX: KUSHITE CULTURE

TABLE 8.9 **Time Line of Events**

2000 B.C.	• Egypt bought gold and cattle from Kush.
1400 B.C.	• Egypt invaded Kush and required it to pay tribute.
1070 B.C.	• Egypt was too weak to keep control of Kush.
750 B.C.	• Kashta conquers Lower Egypt.
654 B.C.	• Assyrians drove the Kushites from Egypt.
591 B.C.	• Kush moved its capital from Napata to Meroe.
350 A.D.	• Meroe was conquered by the neighboring kingdom of Axum.

Geography

Ancient Kush was the area now known as the Sudan, which is located just south of Egypt in Africa.

History

Kush flourished as a civilization between 700 B.C. and 150 A.D. The people of Kush had been Egyptian subjects, and in 750 B.C. they decided to take over all of Egypt. The period that they ruled Egypt is known as the 25th Dynasty. About 630 B.C., Egypt was attacked by outside powers and the Kushites were not able to defend Egypt. They, therefore, retreated back to their original territory. Their capital city of Meroe was an important center with valuable iron ore deposits.

Religion/Architecture/Art

All three of these aspects were similar to those of ancient Egypt.

Science

The Kushites learned how to mine iron ore and then refine it into a number of iron products, such as spear points and knives.

Culture

The culture of Kush was similar to that of Egypt.

Important People

The Kushite ruler named Kashta attacked and conquered Upper Egypt in 750 B.C. Later, his son Piankhy attacked and conquered Lower Egypt. Shabaka, Piankhy's successor, became the first pharaoh of Egypt.

Economy

The economy of Kush depended on trade with Egypt, Arabia, India, and other parts of Africa. Kush traded iron tools and spearheads for the goods that it needed from India and China. Gold and ivory was also traded especially with Egypt. Wild animals and bird feathers were items that were highly prized by Kush's trading partners.

CONTENT AREA SEVEN: GREEK CULTURE

TABLE 8.10   Time Line of Events

6000 B.C.	• The island of Crete had been settled.
1600–1400 B.C.	• Crete had become a great power under the Minoan civilization.
1900 B.C.	• The Mycenaeans invade the Greek mainland.
1400–1200 B.C.	• Mycenae and Troy become important trade powers in the Aegean.
1100 B.C.	• The Dorians invade Greece.
750–338 B.C.	• The Hellenic Age.
594 B.C.	• Solon is elected as chief magistrate of Athens.
490 B.C.	• The battle of Marathon with the Persians.
480 B.C.	• Xerxes burned the Acropolis.
460–429 B.C.	• The Golden Age of Pericles.
431 B.C.	• The Peloponnesian War between Athens and Sparta.
336 B.C.	• Alexander becomes king of Macedonia; start of the Hellenistic Age.
323 B.C.	• Alexander the Great dies in Babylon from fever.

Geography

Greece is the southeasternmost region on the European continent. It is defined by a series of mountains, surrounded on all sides except the north by water, and endowed with countless large and small islands. The Ionian and Aegean seas and the many deep bays and natural harbors along the coastlines allowed the Greeks to prosper in maritime commerce and to develop a culture which drew inspiration from many sources, both foreign and indigenous. The Greek world spread out to many settlements around the Mediterranean and Black seas. During the Hellenistic period, it spread as as far east as India.

The mountains, which served as natural barriers and boundaries, dictated the political character of Greece. From early times the Greeks lived in independent communities isolated from one another by the landscape. Later these communities were organized into poleis, or city-states. The mountains prevented large-scale farming and forced the Greeks to look beyond their borders to new lands where fertile soil was more abundant. Natural resources of gold and silver were available in the mountains of Thrace in northern Greece and on the island of Siphnos, while silver was mined from Laurion in Attica. Supplies of iron ores were also available on the mainland and in the Aegean islands.

History and Government

Stone Age.   During the Stone Age (10,000 B.C. to 3000 B.C.), Greece was settled by people from the Near East as well as Central Europe.

Minoans.   The Minoan civilization was established in Minos, Crete. Crete is an island just south of mainland Greece. About 1900 B.C., the people of ancient Crete began to build great palaces which functioned as centers for religion and government. The palace at Knossos was three stories high occupying about 185 acres of land. The palaces were decorated with paintings depicting the daily life of the people. The Minoans placed a lot of significance and value in dancing, music, and sports. The Minoan civilization was destroyed either by an earthquake or a major fire.

Mycenaeans.   The Mycenaeans were a people who lived near the coast of the Peloponnesus. They traded with the Minoans and as a result they had adapted some of the Minoan ways, including religious beliefs. They also imitated and changed the Minoan art styles and pottery to suit their tastes. They adapted Minoan writing to Mycenaean, which became the early form of Greek writing. The Mycenaeans built great palaces; but unlike the Minoans, they built walls around them to protect them. The Mycenaeans founded many colonies along the Mediterranean. Their civilization weakened after 1100 B.C.

The Dark Age.   The period 1100 B.C. to 800 B.C. is known as the Dark Age because much of the Minoan and Mycenaean inventions, learning, and political power waned. Greeks, in general, went back to simpler ways of life.

Renaissance.   This period lasted from 800 B.C. to 500 B.C. and was characterized by renewed interest in colonization and the spread of Greek culture around the Mediterranean and Black Sea areas.

Athens and Sparta.   Many city-states were founded during the Renaissance period. This period is accentuated by the building of the cities high on hills and surrounded by high walls. These cities made up large communities called poleis, or city-states. Among the best known are Athens and Sparta.

The city-states were first ruled by tyrants. These tyrants were individuals who took control of the government and made decisions for the people. Later, the city-states decided how they wanted to be governed. For example, Athens allowed all propertied men to assemble and make the laws for the community. This laid the foundation for our later democratic societies. Other city-states decided to have a king or wealthy individuals run the government, as in Sparta. Sparta's ruling group was called an oligarchy.

Persian Wars and the Golden Age of Greece.   From 540 B.C. to 479 B.C. Persian armies had invaded the Middle East and taken over many Greek colonies. The Persian king, Darius I, decided in 490 B.C. to invade Athens. At the plain of Marathon, the Athenians defeated the Persians in a single day's fighting. A messenger was sent to Athens to tell the Athenians about the victory. This messenger ran for twenty-six miles nonstop and dropped dead after announcing the victory. Our modern Olympic games had their beginnings from this heroic act.

The son of Darius I decided to invade Athens again in 480 B.C. in order to revenge his father's defeat. Athens allied with Sparta in order to defeat the Persians. Three hundred Spartans led by their king Leonidas held the Persians at bay at Thermopylae to give the Athenians time to prepare to fight off the invaders. All three hundred Spartans died and their deed lives to this day. The period from 479 B.C. to 431 B.C. is known as the Golden Age of Greece. Pericles, an aristocrat, led Greece for fifteen years. It was during this time that the Parthenon was built on the Acropolis. It celebrated the Greek victories over the Persians.

Hellenistic Greece.   In 338 B.C., Athens and her ally, Thebes, were defeated by a strong king from Macedonia, an area just north of Athens. This was Phillip II whose armies defeated Athens and her allies in the Battle of Chaeronea. This gave Phillip II control of most of the Greek peninsula and allowed him to unify the former city-states. Phillip II respected Greek culture and wanted to make sure that Greeks did not fight each other. He decided to turn the Greeks attention towards the Persian Empire, which controlled many former Greek colonies. His plans were to free those Greek colonies. However, he was assassinated in 336 B.C., and his 20-year-old son Alexander became king.

Alexander consolidated his control over the Greek city-states, and in 334 B.C. he and his army crossed the Hellespont Strait into Asia Minor. Once he defeated the Persian king, Darius III, he went on to free the former Greek colonies and also to conquer new lands. Wherever he went, he established democratic rule. He and his soldiers intermarried with women of the areas that he conquered. He built many cities, naming them after himself, which became great centers of learning. In this way, Alexander was responsible for spreading Greek culture and knowledge throughout the then-known world.

The period of Alexander's conquests and several centuries afterwards is known as the Hellenistic Age. During this time the people he had conquered learned to speak the Greek language and accept the Greeks' religion. His empire was multicultural, stretching from the Danube River in Europe to the middle of India.

Religion/Architecture/Art

During Greece's Golden Age, Pericles invited experts in the building trades and artists to come to Athens and create new works of art. New temples were designed with new columns. They used three different styles of columns: the Doric, Ionic, and Corinthian. The Corinthian was the most decorated and detailed column of the three. Other buildings included theaters, gymnasiums, and public buildings of all kinds and shapes. The new buildings were painted with murals depicting Athens' history and mythical heroes and heroines.

Early Greek sculptors made bronze and marble figures that were rather stiff and too formal in design. However, by the fifth century B.C. sculptors like Phidias made use of the natural lines of the human body. In the fourth century B.C. another sculptor, Praxiteles, improved on Phidias' carved figures in grace and poise.

Writers proliferated during this period. For example, Herodotus, purported to be the first historian, wrote his book *History of the Persian War* and provided geographical information about the then world. Thucydides, another historian of the same period, wrote *The History of the Peloponnesian War,* which has become a model for other historians. The Greeks also invented drama. Writers like Sophocles wrote plays to entertain people. He wrote plays about tragedies and serious events. His contemporary, Aristophanes, wrote comedies or plays with humor.

Science

During the Golden Age, Pericles invited many scientists from around the Mediterranean to come to Athens and study nature and human behavior. One of the better-known scientists was Hippocrates, who wrote that illnesses come from natural causes. He advised people to eat healthy with well-cooked meats, wheat bread, and lots of vegetables. The Hippocratic Oath is the creed that modern medical practitioners promise to follow.

It was during the waning years of the Golden Age that great teachers, now called philosophers, lived and worked in Athens. Socrates, in 399 B.C., became a well-known teacher and philosopher who taught the youth of Athens to question everything around them, including their leaders. His questioning technique has come down to us as the Socratic Method. One of his students was Plato, who followed in Socrates' footsteps in criticizing the leaders of Athens. He started the Academy, a school where students and other philosophers could learn the lessons necessary to live well and be governed well. His school provided information on how to be a good citizen which called for a well-informed and responsible citizenry. One of Plato's students was Aristotle who sought to discover knowledge firsthand. As a result, he wrote about and discovered knowledge in such areas as law and economics, astronomy, zoology, botany, and sports.

During the Hellenistic Period, teachers learned to use advanced mathematics. Archimedes taught geometry and figured out how to measure the circumference of a circle. He also discovered the rule of specific gravity, which has become known as Archimedes' Law. Another scientist, Aristarchus, used mathematics to demonstrate how the earth moved around the sun. It was during this period that Euclid wrote his book, *The Elements,* which is still the basis for the study of Plane Geometry. Eratosthenes was the scientist who estimated the circumference of the earth and drew the first lines of longitude and latitude on a world map.

Culture

Greeks were individualistic in many ways and developed their own styles of living. The city-states of Sparta and Athens exemplify the different cultural ways of life. In Sparta, boys and girls were taught that exercising the body was good for them because it made them stronger and wiser. Boys at the age of seven were sent away to camps for physical training while the girls stayed at home to learn how to manage the household. Girls, however, were trained in gymnastics and running. Women in Sparta had more privileges and rights than anywhere else in ancient Greece. Their other major duty was to give birth to strong sons in order to serve their community. Boys trained until the age of 18 and served in the military until age 30.

Spartan society was very closed because Spartans did not want to see their society change. As such, they did not go far and did very little trading with others. Athens was very much unlike Sparta. It required its young men to serve in the army only during war. All adult men could participate in government decisions. Democracy had its beginning here. All male citizens would gather to make an assembly that made its decisions according to majority rule. One of its leaders, Solon, influenced the citizenry towards democracy around 594 B.C. Another Athenian leader, Cleisthenes, further strengthened government by the people by allowing all free men over the age of twenty to fully participate in the government.

However, not everyone was included in this democratic process. Women and slaves had no say in the government process. Greeks, from early on, felt a connection among themselves and thus a had a strong cultural identity.

Important People

Pericles was an important leader who ruled Athens during the Golden Age. He was responsible for many public buildings, temples, gymnasiums, and so forth being constructed during this period, including the Parthenon. Socrates, Plato, and Aristotle were influential philosophers who did much to educate people in the areas of critical thinking, law, government, ethics, and the responsibilities of the citizenry.

Alexander the Great was the Greek leader who spread Greek learning throughout the then-known world. He was a great military strategist who won almost all of his battles. His military tactics are still studied by our modern military leaders.

Economy

The Greek economy depended upon trade with other people. The soil is not adequate for large-scale farming, so the Greeks had to look around the Mediterranean for goods that they needed. They were able to raise some crops, such as wheat and barley, as well as vegetables. However, olives and grapes became important exports. Athens, early on had become the center of learning and many people came to study, thus adding to the economy of Greece. Other centers of learning were added later during the Hellenistic Period, such as Alexandria, Egypt, where Greek learning and influence spread.

CONTENT AREA EIGHT: ROMAN CULTURE

TABLE 8.11   Time Line of Events

2000–1000 B.C.	• Indo-European tribes move into the Italian peninsula.
750 B.C.	• The founding of Rome.
509 B.C.	• The Roman patricians revolt against the Etruscans and set up the Roman Republic.
390 B.C.	• The Gauls invade and burn down Rome.
280 B.C.	• Pyrrhus defeats the Romans and makes peace.
264–146 B.C.	• The Punic Wars between Rome and Carthage.
219–202 B.C.	• The Second Punic War takes place under the Carthaginian General Hannibal.
100 B.C.	• All lands along the Mediterranean were under Roman rule.
March 15, 44 B.C.	• The Ides of March; Caesar is murdered.
31 B.C.	• Octavian defeated Antony and Cleopatra at Actium.
27 B.C.–180 A.D.	• Pax Romana.
476 A.D.	• Rome falls to barbarians.

Geography

Rome today is the capital city of Italy. It is centrally located on the Tiber River, which has served as a portal to the Tyrrhenian Sea. Rome was originally built on seven hills. In ancient times, Rome was the seat of power for the mighty Roman empire. The Italian peninsula is an area less rugged than Greece and more blessed with land that has a rich soil. The volcanic activity on the peninsula helped to enrich the soil and farmers were able to grow crops. Because Italy had few good harbors, it limited the various groups of people of the peninsula to trade with each other rather than trade across the sea. So, as Rome grew to become a great power so did its willingness to expand trade outside its borders.

History and Government

People from central Europe began to move into the Italian peninsula as early as 1000 B.C. They settled just south of the Tiber River. Here they raised a variety of crops, including peas, barley, beans, wheat, grapes, figs, olives, and many different kinds of vegetables. They also raised animals such as goats and sheep for their wool which they wove it into fabric for clothing. These early people were the ancestors of the Romans and came to be known as the Latins.

A small group of Latins built a village in one of the hills along the Tiber River in the eighth century B.C. This village later became the city of Rome. Rome became a central city due to its location and was able to trade with other people throughout the peninsula. The surrounding hills and country provided Rome with natural protection from would be enemies while at the same time providing its people with plenty of wood and stone to begin building.

Early legends about Rome's founding tell the story of twin brothers who were left to die by their great-uncle and were raised by wolves. When they grew up, they fought and defeated their great uncle, set up their grandfather as king, and left to find and build their own city which became the city of Rome.

An influential group of people called the Etruscans, who lived in northern Italy, gained control of Rome in about 600 B.C. They brought to Rome an infusion of Greek ideas and customs that they had learned from trading with Greek colonists. For about a hundred years Rome was ruled by a king. However, the Romans were unhappy with their Etruscan overlords and they rebelled. Upon gaining their freedom, they decided to form a republic.

The Roman Republic. The Roman Republic began in 500 B.C. and ended with the establishment of the Roman Empire in 44 B.C. The Romans of this period set up a form of government that was slightly different from the Greeks'. They set a representative Roman government made up of an assembly of elected officials. These officials, in turn, elected two consuls to rule over them. The idea of having two consuls was to provide a checks and balances situation where neither of the two consuls could gain too much power. In time of emergency, a dictator could be selected to make decisions but his term of office was only for six months.

Besides the assembly, there was another body of officials who advised the consuls. This body made up the senate. To become a senator you had to belong to the patrician social group. The patricians were the descendants of the original settlers and founders of Rome. The rest of the people belonged to the plebeian social class and were thought to be of lesser importance. In time, however, the plebeians decided that they did not have as much influence in their society as the patricians, so they revolted. In turn they created official positions called tribunes to help make decisions much as the patricians helped the two consuls. The patricians became alarmed at this development and decided to concede a number of privileges to the plebeians. These changes included having the tribunes sit in on senate meetings and have veto power over decisions. Unwritten laws were also written down so that everyone would know what their rights and responsibilities were. These changes allowed both groups to become somewhat equal in stature.

Beginning around 500 B.C., the Romans subdued all peoples in the Italian peninsula. Rome at this time became very interested in overseas trade with its neighboring states. As a growing power, Rome wanted to control the trade routes throughout the western Mediterranean Sea. However, the city-state of Carthage, located in northern Africa, also wanted to control the trade routes of this same region. As a result, Rome and Carthage fought three wars, known as the Punic Wars. While one of Carthage's generals, Hannibal, was busy invading the Italian peninsula from the north and across the Alps with elephants, a Roman general by the name of Scipio decided to attack lands in northern Africa that belonged to Carthage. Hannibal had to abandon his attack on the Italian peninsula and rush home to defend Carthage. In 202 B.C., the Romans defeated Hannibal in the town of Zama and Carthage gave up.

However, hostilities did not end until 146 B.C. when the third Punic War was fought. This time the Romans laid waste to the city of Carthage and sold its inhabitants to slavery. By this time the Romans also controlled Greece, Macedonia, and southwestern Asia. To rule such a great expanse of territory, the Romans appointed governors to rule and collect taxes.

Roman Dictatorship. Under the Republic, Rome controlled a huge area of the then-known world, from whom they collected huge amounts of taxes. This tax money went to the wealthy, who became richer, and the poor became poorer. As a result civil disobedience and rebellions took place between the rich and the poor. In 82 B.C., a leader by the name of Lucius Sulla decided to end this strife and conflict. He made himself into a dictator and ruled for three years.

Sulla retired after three years, and the Romans went back to their practice of choosing two consuls to rule them. It was during the turmoil of this period that a popular general, Julius Caesar, used his military power to gain political power. With the support of two other influential men, Pompey and Crassus, Caesar was chosen as consul. In 60 B.C., these three men decided to join their political might in a union called the First Triumvirate in order to rule Rome. Caesar went on to win a great victory for Rome against Gaul. He conquered Gaul and extended Rome's frontiers northward to include modern-day France and Belgium. He also crossed the English Channel and invaded England. For these successes, Caesar became very popular with the people of Rome. However, certain senators did not like the power that he had gained so they conspired to reduce or destroy his power. They ordered him to come back to Rome without his army. Caesar brought his army and upon crossing the Rubicon River, he broke the long-standing law of Rome that no Roman army should cross the Rubicon. Many senators and Pompey fled to Greece where Caesar pursued and defeated them. Upon his return to Rome in 46 B.C. he declared himself dictator for life. At this point the senate became concerned that Caesar was planning to make himself king. This they did not like. A small group of senators, led by Marcus Brutus, one of Caesar's best friends, conspired to murder him. So, when Caesar came to the senate without his bodyguards, he was stabbed over and over again on March 15, 44 B.C., which is also known as the Ides of March.

After the death of Julius Caesar, civil war broke out between his supporters and the supporters of the senate. Caesar's grandnephew, Octavian, and Marc Antony, a Roman general, defeated the armies of the senate. Octavian and Antony divided the Roman Empire into two sections with Octavian keeping the western part and Antony the eastern section. However, Antony had different plans and conspired with Cleopatra, the queen of Egypt, to take over the whole Roman Empire. In 31 B.C., Octavian met the forces of Antony and Cleopatra in a sea battle near Actium and defeated them. Antony and Cleopatra fled to Egypt where they both committed suicide. The Roman senate then appointed Octavian the ruler of the whole Roman Empire. They gave him the title of Augustus Caesar, or "respected one."

The Roman Empire.   Augustus became Rome's first true emperor, but he never used that title. Instead he called himself *princeps,* or first citizen, of Rome. A period of peace began in 27 B.C., called the Pax Romana, and lasted until 180 A.D. Augustus passed laws making it possible for more people in the empire to become Roman citizens. He wisely chose efficient and just people to govern different provinces as governors. He built good roads throughout the empire that allowed people to travel better and also allowed the Roman legions to move quicker. Roman legions, about 6000 soldiers to a legion, guarded the Roman Empire and helped to unite all people. Augustus also modernized Rome by building new government offices, libraries, temples, and public baths.

Religion/Architecture/Art

The Roman religion borrowed heavily from the Greeks. Their main god, Jupiter, shared many of the characteristics of the Greek god Zeus. The Romans at first worshipped their gods without images. They felt that their gods were there for them without having to have statues or to build temples in their honor. Due to the influence of Greeks and Etruscans, the Romans eventually started to build temples and sculpt statues of their gods in human form. Their gods had different functions and personalities. Janus was worshipped as the god of beginnings, and Vesta was the goddess of the hearth. Priests and priestesses served the many gods of the Romans in fancy temples.

During the period of Pax Romana all kinds of buildings went up in Rome including the Colosseum which was completed in 80 A.D. The Colosseum was used by the Romans for entertainment where gladiators would fight to the death or fight with animals. The Romans made improvements to Greek architecture during this period by adding domes, arches, and murals to their buildings. The Romans also built aqueducts to connect canals, which brought water to the cities.

Science

The Romans developed writing during the seventh century B.C. They adopted an alphabet used by their neighbors, the Etruscans. Their language became the Latin language and is the basis for many languages used today. Two forms of the Latin language developed during the Roman civilization. The first was a literary form used mostly in writing. The second was a simplified or vernacular form used in everyday life. One of the great writer's lived during Rome's Golden Age of Latin literature from 100 B.C. to 14 A.D. His name was Cicero. He wrote many speeches, letters, and essays. Another great writer of this period was the great poet Vergil. He wrote the epic story, *The Aeneid,* telling about a Trojan hero named Aeneas who goes on to find the city of Rome after the destruction of Troy by the Greeks.

The Romans were also great engineers who built a network of roads that allowed goods and the armies to move quickly throughout the empire. The Romans were also great city planners. They designed and built cities around a central public square called the forum. In the forum area were the public buildings, which were built from marble. Important scientists of the Roman period were primarily Greeks. The well-known Greek astronomer Ptolemy recorded everything that was known about astronomy. Another Greek scientist was the Greek physician Galen who was the most famous physician, next to Hippocrates.

Culture

Roman society was divided up into a number of social classes. The wealthy patricians and plebeians made up the upper class, which owned most of the land. They lived in their own houses that sometimes also served as their places of business. Their homes were very large with a number of rooms to accommodate the members of the family, servants, and slaves.

All other citizens, like farmers, artisans, merchants, and so forth made up the lower classes. These groups of people lived in apartment-style dwellings. The apartments were sometimes made up of just one room and whole families lived crowded in them. The social class at the bottom were the slaves. Since they were not considered citizens of Rome, they did not enjoy all of the benefits of Roman society. Their owners controlled the lives of the slaves. Slaves were sometimes freed upon the death of their owners and became free citizens of Rome.

Men controlled the family in Roman society. Women made some of the household decisions but their influence was limited. Even though women could own their own property, they had no say in their government decisions.

Important People

Julius Caesar was the brilliant general who added the vast area of Gaul and Britain to Rome's great empire. He tried to make himself king and was assassinated by a group of senators on March 15, 44 B.C., on what is known as the Ides of March.

Augustus Caesar was the grandnephew of Caesar who defeated Antony and Cleopatra and consolidated Roman rule in what has been called the Pax Romana that lasted several centuries.

Economy

The Romans were at first farmers who were blessed with areas of fertile soil and plenty of water. Volcanic ash had enriched the soil and allowed for an abundance of vegetables, wheat, barley, olive oil, wine, and other products to be grown and traded with neighboring tribes at first and later with other city-states outside of the Italian peninsula.

Eventually, the Romans made many conquests and their economy became more global in scope. They used slaves to work the land and do other types of work. They controlled the trade routes of the Mediterranean Sea and were able to collect taxes from throughout the empire. Precious metals flowed to Rome from many of its provinces. The rich enjoyed all kinds of luxuries from different types of food to luxurious homes, clothing, furniture, and other household items.

To feed the poor and the armies, Rome had to depend upon their provinces to provide enough wheat. If there was not enough wheat to go around, emperors had to contend with riots. The largest Roman industry was mining of marble and other materials that they used to make pottery, glassware, weapons, and tools. Precious metals, such as gold and silver, were mined in Greece and northern Italy and lead and tin were mined in Spain. These metals were used to trade with other people in foreign regions.

DOMAIN THREE: CHINESE (LATE), JAPANESE, AND AFRICAN CIVILIZATIONS

TABLE 8.12   Chinese (Late), Japanese, and African Civilizations

	CHINESE	**JAPANESE**	**AFRICAN**
HISTORY	• 220 A.D. end of Han dynasty. • Buddhism introduced in China 343. • Emperor Wen rebuilds the Great Wall. • 618–907 the Tang Dynasty. • 907–959 short-lived dynasties. • 1200s China ruled by the Mongols. • 1275–1292 Marco Polo visits China.	• Jomo culture. • Honshu become the first ruling family. • Nara becomes the first capital city. • Kyoto becomes the capital city in 8th century. • Appearance of the samurai and shogunate government in 12th century. • Ashikaga shogunate. • Tokugawa shogunate. • Feudalism. • Treaty with the U.S.	• A number of kingdoms flourished in Africa during this period: • Ghana—1054. • Mali—thrived for over 400 years. • Songhai—1464. • Kingdom of Zimbabwe. • Kanem-Bornu. • Hausa states. • Benin.
GEOGRAPHY	• China divided into north and south by the Qin Ling Mts. • Huge plain in the north allowed invaders into China. • Highest peak in the world is Mt. Everest.	• Made up of group of islands. • Honshu is home to 80% of the people. • Japanese Alps. • Mount Fuji.	• Second largest continent. • Africa is divided into four ecological regions. • Fertile coastal land can be found at the very northern and very southern part of Africa. • Sahara and Kalahari deserts. • Savanna bushes and grasses. • Lush rain forest near the equator. • Niger, Nile, Zambezi, and Congo are main rivers.
ART/ ARCHITECTURE	• Use of nature for themes in art. • Use of ceramics.	• Religious temples. • Woodblock print techniques in art.	• Built libraries and stone houses. • Mosques were built.
SCIENCE/ INNOVATIONS	• Poetry and printing. • Discovered gunpowder. • Irrigation systems. • Use of canals. • Use of gunpowder.	• Poetry, like haiku. • Samisen music instrument. • Dances. • Diaries. • Rock gardens.	• Mining of precious metals.

TABLE 8.12   Continued

	CHINESE	JAPANESE	AFRICAN
RELIGION	• Buddhism. • Daoism. • Confucianism.	• Multiple gods. • Shinto. • Buddhism. • Zen.	• Islam.
SOCIAL AND ECONOMIC SYSTEM	• Farming predominates. • Large landholdings by wealthy and strong.	• Wrestling contests. • Ceremonies. • Peasants made up most of the population. • Shoguns were the military leaders. • Merchants carried on trade. • Farming.	• Traders. • Gold, copper, tin, iron, ivory. • Salt. • Farming.
CULTURE	• Peaceful and harmonious coexistence with nature. • Search for peace and freedom.	• Buddhism had a great influence on Japan's culture. • Zen art stressed. • Tea ceremony. • People are part of nature.	• Swahili culture had its own language and included many religions and ways of life.
IMPORTANT PEOPLE	• Li Bo—the most beloved poet. • Emperor Wen organized public projects. • Kublai Khan the Mongol leader.	• Prince Shotoku encouraged the spread of Buddhism. • General Oda Nobunaga unified Japan in 1591. • Tokugawa Ieyasu established the shogunate of Tokyo in 1605.	• Mansa Musa advertised the wealth of Mali. • Uthman dan Fodio united the Hausa states.

CONTENT AREA NINE: LATER CHINESE CULTURE

Geography

The Han Dynasty controlled an area that is one-third of modern China. Throughout history, the eastern half of China was the area where population growth and important events took place. The cities of Nanjing, Luoyang, and Changsha are located here. This eastern region of China is divided by the Qin Ling Mountains, thus creating northern and southern China. The people in these two regions have had very little if any contact with each other. Geographically, China was not only divided but also protected from invaders. The Himalayas protected China from the southwest and the Taklimakan Desert from the west. From the east China was protected by the Pacific Ocean. However, China was unprotected in the north where a huge plain left it open to invaders. Mount Everest is the highest peak in the world at 29,028 feet and is located on the Himalaya Mountains of southwest China.

History

Invasion from the north, finally brought an end to the Han Dynasty in China and in 220 A.D. China splintered into small kingdoms. It took almost 300 years for a strong leader to come forth and reunite the Chinese Empire. Yang Jian, an official in northern China, took over power and proclaimed himself the emperor of northern China in 581 A.D. In the next eight years, he invaded and conquered southern China as well. He went on to rename himself as Emperor Wen, and he started the Sui Dynasty. He helped to unify the empire by accepting three different systems of thought which were prevalent during that time. Since Buddhism was practiced by many Chinese and the emperor himself, he recognized its teachings. Buddhism had been imported from India and a Buddhist monk, Kumarajiva (343–413) directed thousands of Chinese Buddhist monks to translate the Buddhist texts and preachings so that common people would understand them. By 477, there were about 10,000 Buddhist temples and over 150,000 Buddhist monks in China. He then allowed the teachings of Confucianism and Daoism to proliferate. As a result, the people were happy and unity was the end result. Emperor Wen also instituted a number of other changes in order to unify China. He brought back many traditions that had been forbidden before, he repaired and rebuilt the Great Wall, he built a grand capital city at Changan, he began building the Grand Canal between the Huang He, or Yellow River, and the Chang Jiang, he set up schools for people to learn calligraphy, he founded many colleges, and Chinese classics were collected and copied in order to preserve them.

The Sui Dynasty lasted only two reigns. The last Sui emperor, Yangdi, had exhausted the military with too many campaigns and too many building projects by the people, which caused unrest and rebellion. One general, Li Yuan, captured the Chinese capital and declared himself emperor, bringing in the Tang Dynasty.

The Tang Dynasty (618–907) brought a lot of prosperity to China. For the first one hundred years China became the cultural center of East Asia. This was the most cosmopolitan period than in any other period before the onset of the twentieth century. During the reign of the first two emperors, Gaozu and his son Li Shimin, China was divided into 300 prefectures under their control. To collect taxes, both emperors allotted equal amounts of land to all males. In return for their allotments of land, farmers were required to serve in the Chinese army. There were also auxiliary troops made up of Turks, Khitans, Tanguts, and other non-Chinese people.

The Tang, in 630, decided to fight their former allies, the Turks, and they gained a lot of new territory. The Tang emperor Taizong as a result also acquired the new title of Great Khan. The Tang continued to conquer new lands and expanded their empire as far east as modern Afghanistan.

From 646–683, Emperor Gaozong took the throne as the third Tang ruler. However, he was in poor health and his wife, Empress Wu, became the power behind the throne. When the emperor died in 683, Empress Wu kept power to herself on behalf of her two young sons. Then in 690, she decided to proclaim herself emperor. The new dynasty was known as the Zhou. Empress Wu is the only woman in Chinese history to hold the title of emperor. She managed to hold on to her throne until 705 when she was deposed at eighty years of age.

From 907 to 959, there were five short-lived dynasties. In 960, Zhao Kuangyin founded the Song Dynasty. Zhao ruled by the name of Emperor Taizu. He and other early Song rulers limited the power of the military in order to prevent rebellions. The Song dynasty made use of civil examinations in order to attract talented people to their administrations. Also during this time agricultural technological advances increased the production of rice and created a great population growth. The population of China grew to more than 100 million people.

During the 1200s, China was invaded and slowly conquered by the Mongols under the leadership of Genghis Khan at first and then by Kublai Khan, a grandson of Genghis Khan. With this conquest came the end of Song domination of China. The Mongols instituted the Yuan Dynasty which was marked by a government made up of foreigners. Since the Mongols controlled a vast area from eastern Europe to Korea and from Siberia to India, trade and communications increased. Many foreigners came to China bringing new ideas, medicines, and food. One of the foreigners was Marco Polo. Marco Polo lived in China from 1275 to 1292. Marco Polo took the knowledge of the Chinese civilization back to Europe, which eventually resulted in the Age of Exploration by the Europeans. However, most Chinese found life under the Yuan Dynasty very difficult because the Mongols taxed the people very heavily and took some of the land away from the peasants. As a result, there were frequent rebellions. In 1368, a Chinese leader, Zhu Yuanhang, managed to defeat the Mongols and instituted the Ming Dynasty. He became known as the Hongwu Emperor. He ruled China with an iron hand for the next thirty years. He is said to have been a cruel emperor. Eventually, his son, Zhu Di, took over control of the empire in 1402. He led many military incursions against the Mongols and spread his influence into Vietnam.

The Ming Dynasty was overthrown by peasant rebellions and a new warlord became emperor. This new dynasty is known as the Manchu Qing Dynasty and lasted from 1644 until its downfall in 1911.

Art and Technology

The Chinese made great strides in the area of poetry and painting. Both of these areas dealt with the theme of harmony between man and nature. Paper money was also invented by the Chinese. Woodblock printing also made its appearance first in China. Various types of books were available, including the teachings of Confucius and books on law, science, mathematics, and medicine. Gunpowder was also invented by the Chinese.

Religion

Buddhism was introduced into China during the Han dynasty. Buddhism took hold in China because it offered hope for peace. It taught Chinese to meditate in order to achieve enlightenment and thus be able to achieve inner peace.

Social and Economic System

China's economic system at this time included the ownership of land by aristocratic families. Small farmers had been forced to work the fields of the large landowners. Merchants also thrived in China. The Chinese printed the first paper currency to make it easier to carry. Trade relationships had been established between a number of cities.

Culture

Chinese culture evolves around long-established traditions dealing with farming, religion, and the search for enlightenment. Religions like Buddhism, Daoism, Confucianism, and others were well received by the Chinese because they were all characterized by an emphasis on peace and freedom.

Poetry and painting were highly valued by the Chinese. Both poets and painters sought to portray harmony with nature. Chinese society was stratified with an upper class that included the emperor and his family and the poor people in the lower level. Religious people, merchants, and the military made up the middle class.

Important People

Emperor Wen was the leader who rebuilt the Great Wall of China. He also brought Taoism to China. He encouraged great public works, such as the Grand Canal, which provided work for the Chinese population and the expansion of agriculture. Kublai Khan, a Mongol, conquered and ruled northern China for a period of time. He tried to conquer south China, which was then ruled by the Song Dynasty, but was unsuccessful. Zheng He was a court official who made seven voyages to the Middle East and the east coast of Africa.

CONTENT AREA TEN: JAPANESE CULTURE

Geography

Japan is an island country in Asia made up of a group of islands. It is surrounded on the west by the Sea of Japan, on the north by the Sea of Okhotsk, on the southwest by the East China Sea, and on the east by the Pacific Ocean. Japan is a very mountainous country with 86 percent of its land covered by hills and mountains. The islands of Japan are actually mountain peaks. These mountains were formed by volcanic activity with about fifty volcanoes still active. As a result, there are almost 1,500 earthquakes each year.

The largest island is Honshu where about 80 percent of the people of Japan live. Japan's tallest mountains, the Japanese Alps, are located here with the tallest peak being the well-known Mount Fuji. Japan is blessed with many rivers, but they are not navigable because they are short and swift. The Japanese use these rivers to irrigate their fields and to generate electrical power. Only about 20 percent of Japanese land is suitable for farming.

Since Japan is surrounded by water, it remained in isolation and free from invasion from other Asian people. The Japanese were also able to contain new ideas and changes within their islands because of their isolation.

History

Hunter-gatherer groups of people lived in Japan over 10,000 years ago. The first Japanese culture was called the Jomo and it flourished around 8000 B.C. Anthropological findings of fishhooks and harpoon points show that these people used the surrounding waters to fish, but they also gathered and hunted on land. The Jomo culture lasted until 200 B.C. when it was replaced by the Yayoi. These people settled in Honshu where the soil was rich and rice became a very important crop. The Yayoi culture was replaced by the "tomb culture," so-called because of the clay figurines of soldiers and horses that have been excavated. After 400 A.D., one of the groups of people on Honshu became much more powerful than the others. As a result, this family became the first ruling family of Japan with its first emperor said to be descended from the Sun Goddess. The same ruling family still functions in Japan today. During the 600s, Korean Buddhists exported Buddhism to Japan where the Japanese Soga clan accepted it as a unifying influence for the Japanese people. Buddhism was welcomed primarily because people felt that Shinto did not provide for all of their spiritual needs. So, the two religions were accepted side by side.

The government of Japan began to change in similar fashion as that of China. The emperor of Japan announced that all property outside of the capital was his property. He then went on to divide the land into small plots, and he appointed clan leaders to oversee them. In this way, the emperor strengthened his government and also was able to collect taxes from the land.

The government decided in 710 to relocate its capital to Nara in the Yamato plain where both religion and art flourished.

Cultural imports began to arrive in Japan from continental East Asia around 300 B.C., starting with agriculture and the use of metals. These new technologies eventually helped build a more complex Japanese society, whose most remarkable and enduring structures were huge, key-shaped tombs. Named for these tombs, the Kofun period endured from the early fourth to the sixth century A.D.

In the middle of the sixth century, Japan embarked on a second phase of extensive cultural borrowing from the Asian continent—largely from China. Among the major imports from China were Buddhism and Confucianism. Buddhism was particularly important, not only as a religion but also as a source of art, especially in the form of temples and statues. Although Buddhism eventually became a major religion of Japan, some evidence indicates that the Japanese initially were drawn more to its architecture and art than to its religious doctrines.

As the Heian court reached its height of cultural brilliance, however, a class of warriors (samurai) emerged in the provinces. In the late twelfth century, the first warrior government (known as a shogunate) was established at Kamakura. Japan entered a feudal era of frequent wars and samurai dominance that would last for nearly four centuries, first under the Kamakura and then under the Ashikaga shoguns.

The culture of the Kamakura period (1185–1333) is noteworthy particularly for its poetry, prose, and painting. Although the Kyoto courtiers lost their political power to the samurai, they continued to produce outstanding poetry. The warrior society contributed to the national culture as well. Anonymous war tales were among the major achievements in prose. Painters produced narrative picture scrolls depicting military and religious subjects such as battles, the lives of Buddhist priests, and histories of Buddhist temples and of shrines of Japan's native religion, Shinto.

The Kamakura shogunate ended with a brief attempt to restore imperial rule. Then in 1338 the Ashikaga shoguns established their seat near the emperor's court in the Muromachi district of Kyoto. During the reign of the Ashikaga (known as the Muromachi period), which lasted until 1573, Japan again sent missions to China. This time they brought back the latest teachings of Zen Buddhism and Neo-Confucianism, as well as countless objects of art and craft. Zen Buddhism, which had been introduced from Korea, became popular. In 1603 a third warrior government, the Tokugawa shogunate, established itself in Edo (present-day Tokyo), and Japan entered a long period of peace that historians consider the beginning of the country's modern age. During this era, known as the Tokugawa period (1603–1867), Japan adopted a policy of national seclusion, closing its borders to almost all foreigners. Domestic commerce thrived, and cities grew larger than they had ever been. In great cities such as Edo, Osaka, and Kyoto, performers and courtesans mingled with rich merchants and idle samurai in the restaurants, wrestling booths, and brothels of the areas known as the pleasure quarters. These so-called chonin, or townsmen, the urban class dominated by merchants, produced a new, bourgeois culture that included seventeen-syllable haiku poetry, prose literature of the pleasure quarters, the puppet and kabuki theaters, and the art of the wood-block print.

Japan's seclusion policy ended when Commodore Matthew Perry of the United States sailed into Edo Bay in 1853 and established a treaty with Japan the following year. The Tokugawa shogunate was overthrown in the Meiji Restoration of 1868, and Japan entered the modern world. During the early years of the new order, known as the Meiji period (1868–1912), Western culture largely overwhelmed Japan's native heritage. Ignoring many of their traditional arts, the Japanese set about adopting Western artistic styles, literary forms, and music. By the end of the Meiji period, however, the Japanese not only had resuscitated many traditional art forms but also were making impressive advances in modern styles of architecture, painting, and novels.

Since the beginning of the twentieth century, Japan has moved steadily into the stream of international culture. Japan's influence on that culture has been especially pronounced since the end of World War II (1939–1945). Japanese movies, for example, have received international recognition and acclaim, and Japanese novels have been translated into English and other languages. Meanwhile, traditional Japanese culture has flowed around the world, influencing styles in design, architecture, and various crafts, such as ceramics and textiles.

Religion/Art/Architecture

The religion of early Japan was based on the worship of nature and is called Shinto. This religion has a cadre of gods with the main one being kami, the Sun Goddess. Later, Prince Shotoku, in 593 A.D., was influential in getting the Japanese to accept Buddhism right alongside with Shinto.

Japan's oldest indigenous art is handmade clay pottery, called Jomon, or cord pattern, pottery. Produced beginning about 10,000 B.C., it marked the beginning of a rich ceramic-making tradition that has continued to the present day. During the Kofun period, sculptors fashioned terra-cotta figurines called haniwa that depicted a variety of people (including armor-clad warriors and shamans), animals, buildings, and boats. The figurines were placed on the tombs of Japan's rulers.

When Buddhism arrived in Japan, its architecture and art profoundly influenced native styles. Horyuji temple, built near Nara in the early seventh century, has the world's oldest wooden buildings, as well as an impressive collection of Buddhist paintings and statues. During the Nara period, many new temples were erected in and around the city. The most famous temple is Todaiji, where an approximately 16 meter (53 foot) Daibutsu (Great Buddha) statue is housed in the world's largest wooden building. Possibly inspired by the temples of Buddhism, a distinct style of Shinto architecture began to develop. Drawing on native traditions such as raised floors and thatched roofs with deep eaves, Shinto produced artistically fine structures such as the Ise Shrine and the Izumo Shrine.

After the emperor's court moved to Heian-kyo in 794, the construction of Buddhist temples continued. Many were now built in remote areas, where they were designed to blend harmoniously with their natural settings. The esoteric Shingon sect of Buddhism arrived from China creating a demand among Heian courtiers for the visual and plastic arts of Shingon. These included mandalas (diagrams of the spiritual universe used for meditation) and paintings and statues of fantastic beings, sometimes fierce with extra limbs or heads. Beautifully appointed residences (called shinden residences) also began to appear at this time. These rambling structures opened onto raked-sand gardens, which featured ponds fed by streams that often flowed under the residences' raised floors. Although no examples of shinden residences exist today, narrative picture scrolls from the late Heian period depict these residences of the courtier elite.

During the early Kamakura period, Nara-era traditions of realistic sculpture inspired a sculptural revival that produced dynamic, individualized figures. But probably the finest products of Kamakura art were narrative picture scrolls.

Architecturally, the Muromachi period is best remembered for the construction of Zen temples. Notable examples are the so-called "Five Mountains" temples of Kyoto, which were situated mainly around the outskirts of the city to take advantage of the mountain scenery that borders Kyoto on three sides. These temples became the settings for most of the best dry landscape gardens (waterless gardens of sand, stone, and shrubs) constructed in Muromachi times

Many schools of painting flourished during the Tokugawa period, including one that used Western techniques such as shading and foreshortening to produce the illusion of space and depth. The most popular by far, however, was genre art, or art depicting people at work and play.

One of the greatest architectural works of the Tokugawa period was the Katsura Detached Palace, built in the seventeenth century. Its clean, geometric lines had a powerful influence on post–World War II residential architecture in many foreign countries. By contrast, the mausoleum of the shogun Tokugawa Ieyasu at Nikko, built during the same period, is extraordinary for its elaborate decoration.

Among Japan's best-known modern architects is Tange Kenzo. His buildings won international fame and include the Hall Dedicated to Peace at Hiroshima and the main Sports Arena for the 1964 Tokyo Olympics.

Science/Innovations

Throughout most of their history, the Japanese people have written poetry and prose in both Chinese and Japanese. This section deals mainly with literature written in the Japanese language.

Japan's earliest literary writings are simple poems found in the country's oldest existing books, the Koji-ki (Records of Ancient Matters, 712) and the Nihon shoki (Chronicles of Japan, 720) of the early Nara period. The mid-Nara period witnessed the compilation of Manyoshu (Collection of Ten Thousand Leaves), an anthology of some 4,500 poems written in the seventh and eighth centuries. Courtiers wrote most of the poems in Manyoshu, the great majority of them in the five-line, thirty-one-syllable waka (or tanka) form. Kakinomoto no Hitomaro, the best known of the poets, also wrote in a longer form that makes up a small percentage of the poems in the anthology. Some of the poems are celebrations of public events, such as coronations and imperial hunts, but even at this early time Japanese poetry was primarily personal. Its two main subjects were the beauties of nature, especially as found in the changing seasons and in heterosexual romantic love.

During the Heian period, court poets, using the waka form exclusively, reduced the range of poetic topics. Proper subjects had to meet the poets' ideal of courtliness (miyabi) and demonstrate a sensitivity to the fragile beauties of nature and the emotions of others, an aesthetic known as mono no aware. The Kokinshu (Collection of Ancient and Modern Poems, begun in 905) set the standard for all future court poetry. Meanwhile, the invention of the kana syllabary (in which each symbol represents a syllable) enabled the Japanese to write freely in their own language for the first time. (Previously, most writing was in Chinese.) The invention of kana also stimulated the development of a prose literature. Court women took the lead in writing prose, using forms such as the fictional diary and the miscellany, a collection of jottings, anecdotes, lists, and the like.

Sometime in the late sixteenth century, Japanese musicians began playing a three-stringed, banjolike instrument called the samisen, which had originated in the Ryukyu Islands. Both the kabuki and puppet theaters adopted the instrument as an accompaniment, and it was also played frequently by geisha, a class of professional female entertainers that emerged in Tokugawa times.

In the modern era, the Japanese wholeheartedly embrace Western classical music. Japan has produced some of the world's leading classical performers, conductors, and composers. Modern Japanese dance draws on both traditional and Western styles and includes the avant-garde buto dance form.

In the Tokugawa period, townsmen living in the great cities produced most of Japan's major literature. Haiku, consisting of just the first seventeen syllables of the waka, became a means for expressing emotional insights, or enlightenments, especially when composed by a master such as Basho. Even today, haiku enjoys enormous popularity in Japan. Although the modern age has seen important developments in poetry, the novel is the literary medium that has enjoyed the most artistic success.

CONTENT AREA ELEVEN: AFRICAN CULTURE

Geography: Africa is the second largest continent in our planet. It has a number of distinctive regions:

1. The coast—Only in the extreme north and south are there coastal plains which are fertile enough for agriculture to thrive.
2. The desert—There are two huge deserts in the middle of Africa. The Sahara Desert is the world's largest and is located in the northern region of Africa. The Kalahari is located in the southern region.
3. The savanna—This region is located near the deserts and is made up of short bushes and short grasses.
4. The rain forest—This region is located near the equator where it receives a lot of moisture. It is made up of lush, green forests.

Four rivers traverse the African continent. They are the Nile, the Niger, the Congo, and the Zambezi.

History

Sub-Saharan Africa.   A number of different civilizations sprang up in sub-Saharan Africa:

1. The kingdom of Ghana developed around 400 A.D. in the area occupied today by Sudan. From the writings of Arab geographers, Ghana was an extensive empire with a strong central government that was controlled by a king. The form of government was that of a theocracy because the people believed that the king was partly divine and could communicate with their gods. Ghana produced a lot of gold; and in times of inflation, the king would withhold some of it in order to strengthen the economy. The capital city of Ghana was Kumbi-Saleh. One of the towns housed the king and his household, and merchants and others lived in the other. Small mud houses served as dwellings for the people who raised crops to support those in the towns. In 1076, the Muslim Berbers called Almoravids decided that the people of Kumbi-Saleh were wicked and they wanted to convert them to Islam. As a result they attacked and took the city. However, the people of Ghana took it back.

2. Ghana was conquered by an army from one of its provinces led by Sundiata. This province expanded into a larger empire called Mali. Mali prospered between 1235 and 1468. Sundiata was an ambitious leader who expanded the empire of Mali to include rich gold and salt mining regions. Sundiata was highly regarded by his people.

Another great leader of Mali was Mansa Musa, who decided to take a trip to Egypt in order to advertise the wealth of Mali. He spent so much gold in Egypt that the value of gold in

Cairo dropped very low and did not recover for a period of twelve years. Mali's capital city was Timbuktu, a center for the study of manuscripts. The women of Mali, according to the Muslim traveler Ibn Batuta, were allowed to go out in public and did not have to follow the wishes of their husbands. The women proved to be highly educated.

3. The Songhai province was a part of the Mali empire. However, when Mali weakened the king of Songhai attacked and took over Timbuktu in 1468. Sonni Ali began his reign, which lasted for thirty-five years. One of his generals took over the empire upon his death in 1493. His name was Askia Mohammed and he, too, reigned for thirty-five years during which time he expanded the empire to encompass most of West Africa. Askia set up a good tax and communications system. He also encouraged people to obey the Muslim religion. The Songhai empire under Askia was the best organized and efficient of all civilization of West Africa.

4. The kingdom of Zimbabwe was located where Rhodesia is now. The city of Kilwa was located here. This was a rich area because of the gold fields located nearby. The city of Kilwa was a well-planned city with fancy homes, town squares, walkways, palaces, and a number of mosques. This city was a very important trading center.

5. Kanem-Bornu was a small kingdom located east of Lake Chad. Its first king began a dynasty that ruled this kingdom for more than a thousand years. Its king converted to Islam in 1085 but its people were free to pursue other religions as well. Idris Alooma became its better-known ruler. He ruled Kanem-Bornu from 1580 to 1617. This king built up his cavalry to look like the European knights. This cavalry was well trained in the use of guns and the king himself led them. As a result, Idris Alooma was sought after by kings of other kingdoms. Kanem-Bornu eventually weakened and its last ruler was killed in 1846.

6. The Hausa were a group of people who lived in the area occupied today by Nigeria. These people were highly independent and lived in separate city-states. They enjoyed trading with the empires of Mali, Songhai, and people of the African rain forest. A leader of the Fulani people, Uthman dan Fodio, united the Hausa city-states in the early 1800s.

7. In the forested area of southern Nigeria existed the Benin kingdoms who were ruled by kings called Obas. At first the Obas ruled and shared power with a council of elders. However, in the fifteenth century Oba Eware the Great consolidated his power in Benin and created a powerful army. This allowed him to become more powerful than the council of elders. The Obas were more than political or military leaders, they were also the religious leaders of Benin. The Obas very carefully recorded their history on cast bronze plaques that have survived through time to provide the modern world with important information about Benin.

8. About 500 B.C., a people called the Bantu, made up of a number of groups of people—the Kikuyu, Zulu, Tonga, Xhosa, and Shona—lived in West Africa. As their numbers multiplied and their villages became overcrowded, they began their migrations to other parts of the continent. Some moved to East Africa, others moved to Central Africa, and still others to South Africa. The reason they moved to other places was to settle in new areas where life would be less harsh than where they lived. In East Africa, the Bantu developed an economy based on trade. They became middlemen for African goods, which were traded with the Arab merchants in the Indian Ocean area. East African ports became centers for Africans, Persians, Indians, Arabs, and southeast Asians who came to trade. In time, many Bantu became laborers, shopkeepers, dock workers, and brokers, all of whom adopted and integrated cultural ways and customs from the other cultures they came into contact with. It was in this way that the Islamic religion spread into Africa and the Arabic language found its way into the well-known Swahili culture of East Africa.

East Africa.   It was in East Africa that the Bantu learned how to grow crops such as yams, rice, coconuts, bananas, and others from the Asians who came to trade. By 1400 A.D., Bantu-speaking people lived in all areas of sub-Saharan Africa. In South Africa, Bantu people raised sorghum, cattle, and sheep. They also became excellent craftsmen in the use of iron, wood, ivory, and other metals. Because gold was discovered and its value recognized, the Bantu developed their own mining methods. The rich gold deposits allowed for the development of Zimbabwe, a great kingdom, during the period 1000 A.D. to 1300 A.D.

Central Africa.   In Central Africa, south of the Congo River, the Bantu people became excellent boat builders because of the forested region in this area. The Bantu people here, known as the Kongo, also developed weaving and woodcarving. The Congo Basin was a rich forested area with a variety of animals. As a result, the Kongo people involved themselves in other pursuits which included hunting. The Great Rift Valley, which was 4,000 miles long, had plenty of water and dry grasslands allowing for cattle grazing and for raising of a variety of crops. Because the Kongo people had so much in terms of natural resources, they concentrated on building and developing their culture. As a result, they developed the earliest system of government in the sub-Saharan region.

Portuguese Contact.   The Bantu people's civilizations and accomplishments suffered many setbacks and disasters once the Portuguese began their period of exploration into these areas beginning in the 1400s A.D. The brisk and profit-driven trade business of East Africa and Zimbabwe was taken over by the Portuguese, who used the profits to benefit Portugal. The Kongo people suffered even more because the Portuguese involved them in the Atlantic slave trade.

Art/Architecture

The kingdoms discussed above all dealt in trading commodities such as gold, tin, iron, and so forth. As such, their art was represented in cast bronze plaques and other such plaques. The rulers, officials, and other important people lived in stone houses and the poor people lived in mud huts.

Science/Innovations

These civilizations were able to mine the ores from the ground and process them into finished goods that they could trade with others. Armaments were designed for military purposes and weapons were produced from metals that these people mined.

Religion

Many of the people of Africa believed in many gods at first. However, all of the civilizations of Africa came into contact with Arabs who introduced them to Islam. So, many rulers and their families became Muslims even though their poor subjects may have worshipped different gods.

Social and Economic System

All of these kingdoms had rulers who enjoyed all the amenities of life. Below them were the artisans, merchants, and soldiers who carried on the economic activities and protection of the empires. At the bottom of the social classes were the poor people who tilled the land or worked the mines in order to feed the people in towns and provide the goods necessary for trade.

Important People

There were a number of leaders who proved to be strong willed and able to keep their empires intact as pointed out above. Mansa Musa went on a spending spree in Egypt with gold in order to advertise the wealth of Mali. Uthman dan Fodio united the disorganized Hausa states into a strong empire.

DOMAIN FOUR: MEDIEVAL AND EARLY MODERN TIMES: 500 A.D.–1500 A.D.

TABLE 8.13   **Medieval and Early Modern Times: 500 A.D.–1500 A.D.**

	ARABIAN	MESOAMERICAN	ANDEAN
GEOGRAPHY	• A peninsula located between Asia and Africa. • Rich in oil. • Mostly a desert region. • Has water transportation routes.	• Region bounded in the east by the Caribbean Sea and on the west by the Pacific Ocean. • Mountains traverse the length of this region. • The Yucatan Peninsula is a forested jungle area.	• Mostly mountainous region along the west coast of South America. • Andes Mts. dominate the region.
HISTORY	• Ubar civilization. • Arab culture. • Moslems. • Mohammed and the Koran. • Mecca as the holy city.	• Many Indian groups lived in this region. • Olmecs. • Maya Empire. • Aztec empire. • Tenochtitlan.	• Incas. • Empire of 12 million people. • Road builders. • Emperor ruled. • Land belonged to the state.
ART/ ARCHITECTURE	• Mosques dominate. • Arab architecture. • Paved streets. • Pottery making.	• Temples. • Basketry, weaving, embroidery, metal work. • Sculpturing, painting—relief carvings.	• Temples.
SCIENCE/ INNOVATIONS	• Concept of the zero. • Medicine. • Astronomy.	• Astronomy. • Medicine.	
RELIGION	• Mohammed. • Many nomads believe in a number of gods. • Most of the Arabs are Muslims. • Ramadan.	• Believed in human sacrifice. • Priests had great power. • Worshipped the sun.	• Believed in human sacrifice. • Priests had great power. • Worshipped the sun.
SOCIAL AND ECONOMIC SYSTEM	• Arabs live in close-knit extended family units. • Women tend to the household chores and raise the children. • Most of these people are nomadic, raising animals. • Farming is also practiced. • Complex banking system. • Trade associations and joint-stock companies.	• Indian life centered around the tribe. • After marriage a man was given a plot of land. • The land would be passed on to his son. • There was no private ownership of land. • Raised corn, tomatoes, squash, avocados, and beans. • Used conquest of other people to provide slave labor.	• Indian life centered around the tribe. • After marriage a man was given a plot of land. • The land would be passed on to his son. • There was no private ownership of land. • Raised corn, tomatoes, squash, avocados, and beans. • Used conquest of other people to provide slave labor.

CONTENT AREA TWELVE: ARABIAN CULTURE

Geography

Arabia is a peninsula located between Africa and Asia. In fact, it forms a sort of bridge between the two continents. It is bounded on the northwest by the Mediterranean Sea, the west by the

Red Sea and Africa, the southeast by the Arabian Sea, and the east by Asia and the Persian Gulf. Along its coasts there are fertile regions but in the middle is mostly desert with oases. These oases provide water from the ground.

History

At an early time in the Arabian Peninsula a civilization thrived at Ubar from 900 B.C. to 500 A.D. Because water became scarce, so did Ubar's existence. People in the Arabian Peninsula lived in areas where there was water. The sources of water were called oases. The people were nomads and traveled from one oasis to the next. Arabia was also criss-crossed by various trade routes taken by merchants and traders of that period. So, maintaining water wells at different oases helped to serve not only the people who lived a nomadic life but also the traders and merchants. The nomadic families of the Arabian Peninsula called themselves Arabs, which was the name of their language.

In order to survive in these desert regions, the Arabs lived in close-knit families or groups and formed tribes with each tribe led by a sheikh. The sheikh was the judge and jury in times of family or tribal conflicts. Some of the Arabs lived around the oases and others lived in villages. Many were farmers or herders of animals.

By the seventh century, many prosperous cities dotted the coastline of the Arabian Peninsula. The city of Mecca was one such prosperous place, and it was here that the prophet Mohammed was born in 570. At an early age he worked for a wealthy widow and traveled with the caravans. On these travels he met and talked to people from various places and with different beliefs. These contacts influenced his philosophy and religious beliefs. He eventually married his rich employer and had four children. His marriage also provided him with the leisure time he needed to reflect upon his beliefs. By the age of 40 he began having visions that led him to believe that the one true God, Allah, had selected him as his prophet. In 622, Mohammed left Mecca and traveled to Medina. His departure from Mecca is a holy event for the Muslims. After Mohammed's death, his preachings and beliefs were recorded in the holy book, the Koran.

Arab influence grew as Islam spread throughout the Arab world. Muslims were able to conquer the Persian and Byzantine empires. Wherever they went, Arabs gave people a choice of converting to Islam or paying a head tax. However, Christians and Jews were exempted because the Arabs believed that their God was one and the same. In time, the Arabs were able to conquer Egypt, northern Africa, and Spain.

Art/Architecture

Great columns and arches were part of the buildings of mosques and palaces. They also used domes and minarets from where the Muslim faithful could be called to prayer. Luxurious furnishings were also available. Tiled mosaics, pottery making, rug weaving, jeweled metal work all added to the artistic genius of the Arab culture.

Science/Innovations

A banking system and trading associations allowed the Arabs to become prosperous. Muslim traders also made use of the compass and the astrolabe a number of years before Europeans did. The concept of zero in mathematics also came from the Arabs. Arabs also established hospitals and medical schools in many major cities. Arab doctors were able to diagnose a number of diseases and even perform surgeries.

Religion

Some of the nomads had many gods or idols that they worshipped. They also believed in spirits that could inhabit a person and even objects. However, there were some who believed in the existence of one God. Most of these people today are Muslims and follow the teachings of Islam.

Social and Economic System

Because of the desert conditions, Arab families lived together with children, grandchildren, and grandparents. The men made the decisions, and the women tended the household chores and the raising of children. Their economy was based on raising herds of animals and on farming. The nomads traded camel meat and milk for grain from the villagers. Merchants traded such items as sugar, tea, carpets, cloth, and weapons.

As part of the Islamic culture, Arabs organized a complex banking system with central banks and branches. People could do business in this way when they were far from home. They also formed trade associations and developed joint-stock companies. People would pool their money for a trade expedition that would last several years.

CONTENT AREA THIRTEEN: MESOAMERICAN CULTURE

Geography

Central America is a narrow strip of land that connects North and South America. It is part of the North American continent. The *cordilleras,* a series of mountain ranges, run north and south along all of Central America. On both sides of these ranges are located areas of lowlands covered with rain forest and swamps.

History

The "mother civilization" of Central America is that of the Olmecs. They were a group of people who as early as 1500 B.C. were cultivating all kinds of plants including squash, maize, and beans. The Olmecs also fished and hunted wild animals in the forests. Besides farming, hunting, fishing, and gathering, the Olmecs traded with other people in the nearby regions. The oldest Olmec city is located at San Lorenzo where huge stone columns have been discovered. They also used basalt rock that weighed many tons in order to carve human heads without the use of metal tools. To honor their gods, Olmecs built temples for them on top of pyramids. They also invented picture writing, their own number system, and a calendar.

A neighboring civilization, that of the Mayas, borrowed Olmec ideas as early as 500 B.C. The Mayan civilization included more than one hundred cities and spanned a huge area that included todays Mexico, Guatemala, Belize, Honduras, and El Salvador. Their greatest accomplishments took place during the Classic Period, which dates from 300 A.D. to 900 A.D. During this period, the Mayan architects and builders built pyramids, palaces, stone temples, and plazas.

The Aztecs/Mexicas were the native American people who dominated northern Mexico at the time of the Spanish conquest led by Hernan Cortez in 1521. According to their own legends, they originated from a place called Aztlan, somewhere in north or northwest Mexico. At that time the Aztecs (who referred to themselves as the Mexica or Tenochca) were a small, nomadic, Nahuatl-speaking aggregation of tribal peoples living on the margins of civilized Mesoamerica. Sometime in the twelfth century they embarked on a period of wandering, and in the thirteenth century settled in the central basin of Mexico. After continues battles with other tribes, the Aztecs finally found refuge on small islands in Lake Texcoco where, in 1325, they founded the town of Tenochtitlan (what is today Mexico City). The term Aztec, originally associated with the migrant Mexica, is today a collective term, applied to all the peoples linked by trade, custom, religion, and language to these founders. Fearless warriors and pragmatic builders, the Aztecs created an empire during the fifteenth century that was surpassed in size in the Americas only by that of the Incas in Peru. As early texts and modern archaeology continue to reveal, beyond their conquests and many of their religious practices, there were many positive achievements including the formation of a highly specialized and stratified society and an imperial administration, the expansion of a trading network as well as a tribute system, and the development and maintenance of a sophisticated agricultural economy, carefully adjusted to the land and the cultivation of an intellectual and religious outlook that held society to be an integral part of the cosmos. The yearly round of rites and ceremonies in the cities of Tenochtitlan and neighboring Tetzcoco, and their symbolic art and architecture, gave expression to an ancient awareness of the interdependence of nature and humanity.

Art/Architecture

The art and architecture of the Indian civilizations of Central America included carved figures, stone temples, and some of the largest pyramids in the world. They also had their distinctive pottery, murals, and stone monuments.

Science/Innovations

Indians of this region burned and slashed parts of the rain forest in order to carry out farming. They also knew that the ash would fertilize the soil and last for about three years. After that, the land lay fallow for several years before it was used again. The Indians of this area, especially the Mayas, knew how to use mathematics and astronomy. They created their own calendar, and they used their own number system, which included a symbol for zero. They also watched the night sky and recorded the movements of the planets, especially Venus. By watching the stars they developed a 365-day calendar that helped them to keep track of planting, harvesting, and seasonal changes. They also had their own writing alphabet and made use of the bark of wild fig trees to make paper.

Religion

All three Indian groups believed in gods of the sun, rain, and other aspects of nature. The main god of the Aztecs was Quetzalcoatl, and they made human sacrifices to him. An interesting cultural characteristic shared by both the Mayan and Aztec civilizations was the integration of both government functions and religious practices.

Social and Economic System

All three Indian civilizations carried on farming as their main preoccupation. They all traded with other people for the things that they needed. The war-like Aztecs also raided other tribes and took their lands, had them pay homage, and enslaved the captives.

All of the cities of the Mayas had their own king whereas the Aztecs had only one emperor to rule them. The Aztecs had a stratified society with the emperor on the top social ladder followed by the nobles who helped him, then came the soldiers. Below these upper three groups were the masses made up of farmers, merchants, and artisans. In Aztec society young girls were allowed to go to school just as the boys did and were even allowed to own property and become religious leaders.

CONTENT AREA FOURTEEN: ANDEAN CULTURE

Geography

The Andes Mountains traverse the western regions of South America. On the western side of the Andes is the Atacama Desert and to the east is the Amazon River basin. Most of South America lies within the tropics.

History

The Inca civilization was located up high in the Andes Mountains in what is now Peru. The first group of Incas settled in the city of Cuzco about 1200 A.D. Their ruler also gave them their name, the Inca. The Inca were not a peaceful people, and they raided and conquered their neighbors. By 1532 when the Spanish arrived, the Incas ruled over an area that included the present-day nations of Peru, Ecuador, Bolivia, Argentina, and Chile.

Art/Architecture

Temples to their gods made of stone.

Science/Innovations

To rule their empire, the Incas built two major roadways connected with shorter ones. They used stones where it was feasible and carved steps on steep mountainsides. They also used rope bridges across deep canyons.

Religion

The Inca religion was based on many gods related to the sky and nature.

Social and Economic System

The Incas had a stratified society with the king and his nobles at the top followed by the soldiers, farmers, merchants, and artisans. In the center of each city were located the government buildings where accountants kept records of the number of people in the empire and the goods that were produced and traded. Because they had no alphabet or number system, they used knotted strings, or *quipus,* to keep records. Most people worked on government-owned farms while others worked as artisans, farmers, and merchants. To support the empire, all households had to pay a labor tax. To keep things running smoothly throughout the empire, the Incas used to train those that they conquered in their ways and send them back to their people.

CONTENT AREA FIFTEEN: EUROPEAN CULTURE

TABLE 8.14   Europe during the Middle Ages: 500 A.D.–1300 A.D.

HISTORY	• Fall of Rome in 476. • Clovis and the Franks. • Charles Martel. • Pepin. • Charlemagne and the Holy Roman Empire. • England.
SOCIAL AND ECONOMIC SYSTEM	• Feudalism permeated European society.
ART/ARCHITECTURE	• Great cathedrals were built.
RELIGION	• Christianity spreads.
SCIENCE/INNOVATIONS	• Warfare changed by the introduction of the horse and later guns.

When Rome fell to the barbarians under Odoacer in 476 A.D., a new era began in European history and lasted until about 1450. This period of time has been called the

Medieval Period or Middle Ages. The conquering barbarians divided up Europe into different kingdoms.

France

One of the kingdoms established by a Germanic group called its people the Franks. Beginning in 481, a fifteen-year-old king led the Franks for the next thirty years. His name was Clovis and he was responsible for enlarging his kingdom and bringing the Franks Christianity.

Rome was still the center of Christianity and many of the new kingdoms that sprang up in Europe adopted Christianity and many of the early laws and traditions of the Roman civilization. Many monks formed their own groups and lived in monasteries. The monks are responsible for preserving the cultures and customs of ancient Greece and Rome, as well as the church.

After Clovis's death, a new line of rulers came forward to rule the land of the Franks and to expand their power throughout Western Europe. Charles Martel was the king who defeated the Muslim invaders from Spain at Tours in 732. His son, Pepin, took over as king in 751 with the blessings of the Pope of Rome. Pepin's son, Charlemagne, became king in 771 and ruled for forty-eight years. His reign was marked by many campaigns against the Lombards in Italy, the Avars, and Slavs, and others. The conquered people were forced to accept Christianity. In 800 A.D., Charlemagne went to Italy with his army to help Pope Leo III with a rebellion. As a result of this support, the Pope crowned him emperor. In this position he yielded great power to rule and to strengthen the church. After Charlemagne's death, his sons divided the empire into small kingdoms. However, they had to contend with foreign invaders such as the Magyars, Muslims, and Vikings. Their kingdoms became weakened as a result, and the people were without protection.

England

England, the island nation, also suffered greatly from invasions, particularly those from the Vikings. For thirty years, Alfred the Great, an Anglo-Saxon king, fought the Vikings and held them at bay.

A claim to the throne of England by William, Duke of Normandy, in 1066 caused the invasion of England. So, on October 14 of that year, he took over England in the bloody battle of Hastings. He came to be called William the Conqueror and ruled England with an iron hand. He set up a feudal system and divided up England among his followers. Large estates called fiefs were given to his soldiers who became his vassals. These vassals swore an oath of loyalty to him and promised to provide the king with soldiers, called knights, for military duty. Thus the people in England and France felt protected from invaders.

In the eastern Roman Empire, called the Byzantine Empire, civilization went on after the fall of Rome. The Byzantine emperor became the head of the eastern Christian church. The city of Constantinople was the seat of political as well as religious power. The Emperor Justinian built Hagia Sophia as the counterpart of St. Peter's church in Rome.

Social and Economic System

The feudal system created a new social and economic system in Europe. The king was at the highest level followed by the nobility, who were the king's vassals. The king's vassals, or lords, had their own local vassals who owed allegiance to them and the king. Soldiers, called knights, were also included in the nobility because they belonged to that social class. The lords built castles in order to protect the people during war and the knights became the champions for the lords. At the bottom of the social scale were the poor masses. They were mere slaves called serfs.They became bound to the land that they lived on.

Other people moved into towns in order to pursue different types of life. At first towns had disappeared with the fall of the Roman Empire but five hundred years later, or about 1000 A.D., cities began to spring up as a revival of trade took place. In the towns people specialized as blacksmiths, bakers, weavers, and shoemakers. These craftsmen from the different trades organized themselves into guilds or unions. As a result, young people wanting to pursue a trade had to become apprentices first, then journeymen who were paid for their work, and finally masters who were allowed to join a guild.

Women at this time came under the protection of their fathers or husbands and had few rights. They received no education but were trained by their mothers to take care of the home and bear children. Women were no better off in the Byzantine Empire. In the Byzantine Empire, or eastern Roman Empire, the government had set up schools and libraries for male students who belonged to the upper classes to study the classics. Most Byzantine people were poor farmers.

Art/Architecture

Most art and architecture dealt with religious themes. Great cathedrals and churches were built. The western churches had fancy church exteriors where the Byzantines had plain looking churches on the outside. On the inside, the western churches made use of statues to represent the holy people of the church whereas the Byzantines created works of paintings called icons.

Religion

The Church of Rome ruled the Christian kingdoms of Europe. Christianity spread to all European kingdoms between 800 and 1300 A.D. The church was organized into a hierarchy starting with the local parish and parish priest at the lowest level. A number of parishes together made up a diocese, which was controlled by a bishop. The dioceses were grouped into provinces, or archdioceses, and were controlled by archbishops. Above them were the cardinals, who acted as advisors to the pope. The pope, meaning "father," was the supreme leader of the church. In monasteries, monks and nuns had their own organization with abbots and abbesses running the operation of the monasteries. The church became all powerful to the extent that kings had to bend to their power or face excommunication. To gain salvation, people had to pay one-tenth of their produce each year in terms of money, goods, or free labor. This was called a tithe. In the Byzantine Empire, the emperor was at first the head of the church. However, the bishop of Constantinople eventually gained power to become the patriarch.

The Catholic Church called upon all Christians to undertake a series of crusades in order to liberate the Holy Land from the Muslim infidels. In total there were seven crusades beginning in 1096 and lasting until 1300. These crusades allowed Europeans to be exposed to Arab culture. The Arabs were great merchants and traders where the Europeans had lost touch with the outside world. As a result of these contacts, crusaders gained new ideas about government, science, trade, and so forth. This started Europeans thinking about their lives and conditions. It started a spark that lighted the way to the Renaissance.

Science/Innovations

After about 1100 A.D., education shifted from the monks in the monasteries to universities, which became guilds for students and teachers in towns. They studied philosophy, religion, medicine, and law. Women were not allowed to participate.

War technology came about during the Middle Ages. When Martel encountered the Muslims, he only had foot soldiers to fight horse-mounted soldiers. He, therefore, asked his vassals to purchase horses and be trained to use them in wartime. Heavy armor was also introduced together with longbows whose arrows could penetrate armor. Also, the introduction of gunpowder and guns came about in the 1320s.

CONTENT AREA SIXTEEN: CHRISTIANITY AND ISLAM

TABLE 8.15   Medieval and Early Modern Times: 500 A.D.–1500 A.D.

	CHRISTIANITY	ISLAM
HISTORY	• Jesus was the founder. • People believed Jesus to be their long-awaited messiah. • Jesus used the teachings of the Torah and emphasized the Ten Commandments. • Jesus was accused of treason and crucified. • Jesus' Resurrection from the dead convinced his followers that he was the messiah.	• Muhammad was the last messenger of Allah. • Muhammad's teachings are included in the holy book, the Qur'an. • Muhammad's followers are called Muslims. • Muslims believe in the five pillars. • There are over 1 billion Muslims in the world.
FOUNDERS	• Jesus of Judea.	• Muhammad of Mecca.
PEOPLE	• 12 Disciples.	• Caliphs.
IMPACT	• Became the largest religion in the world.	• There are over 6 million Muslims in the U.S.

Christianity

History.   Jesus is the founder of Christianity. He was born in Bethlehem, Judea, about 5 B.C. He was divinely conceived by his mother, Mary. His father was Joseph, a carpenter by trade. He is regarded by his followers as the redeemer and the son of God. Our information about Jesus comes from the Gospels. His teachings drew from the teachings of Jewish beliefs. He taught people to live by the Ten Commandments. He also told people to love one another and be kind and compassionate even toward their enemies. All of his teachings emphasized aspects of the Jewish Torah. Because his followers believed him to be the messiah or deliverer, many Jewish leaders did not accept him and neither did the Romans who occupied Palestine. In 33 A.D., while Jesus celebrated the Jewish festival of Passover with his disciples, he was arrested for treason against Rome. He was tried and was crucified. After his death, his followers believed that he came back from the dead in an event called the Resurrection. As a result, his disciples and other followers spread the word of his resurrection and teachings and a new religion, Christianity, came into existence.

Islam

History.   The followers of Islam believe that their faith always existed and that a number of their prophets tried to reveal it to people, but it was the prophet Muhammad who is given credit for finally bringing it to the people. Muhammad was born in Mecca about 570 A.D. He taught people that there was only one God and his name was Allah. His followers came to be known as Muslims. His teachings are in their holy book called the Qur'an. Muslims follow the five basic acts of worship known as the five pillars. The five pillars include:

- Belief in one God and that Muhammad is the last messenger of God.
- Muslims must pray five times a day and must visit a mosque, their temple, on Fridays.
- Muslims must give a part of their earnings to the poor each year.
- Fasting during the daytime must be practiced during Ramadan, the ninth month of the Islamic calendar.
- Muslims must make at least one pilgrimage to Mecca, the holy city located in Saudi Arabia.

There are about 6 million Muslims in the United States today and more than 1 billion worldwide.

CONTENT AREA SEVENTEEN: THE RENAISSANCE, REFORMATION, AND ENLIGHTENMENT

The Renaissance

The Renaissance was an awakening or rebirth of consciousness among Europeans who had been entrenched in the feudal system for a number of centuries. This new awakening began in Italy and created the following:

1. By 1450 the bubonic plague had come to an end after claiming one-third of Europe's population.
2. The Hundred Years' War between England and France came to an end in 1453.
3. Many cities grew rapidly and urban merchants grew wealthy.
4. The crusades had provided Europeans with new ideas and new inventions in the areas of mathematics, astronomy, medicine, and trade.
5. Italian artists brought new styles and techniques to the Renaissance.
6. Christian humanists like Thomas More and Desiderius Erasmus wrote refreshing books about utopian life, greedy merchants, quarrelsome scholars, crime, corruption, and war.
7. William Shakespeare brought the Renaissance to England, where he became a famous playwright.
8. Queen Elizabeth I in England became a patron to artists and writers.
9. The German inventor Gutenburg invented the printing press and was able to print whole books at a low price. This allowed many people the luxury of buying and reading books, articles, newspapers, and magazines.
10. The invention of printing also produced the Bible in the vernacular and, as such, people were able to read the Bible on their own.
11. Scholars of this period helped to undermine the feudal system of Europe by placing a lot of emphasis on personal or individual achievements.

The Reformation

During the Renaissance movement, the Church of Rome was greatly weakened because of the new emphasis on the secular and on the individual instead of the religious. The popes of Rome during this period were corrupt. They became patrons of the arts and spent huge amounts of money. The popes also took personal pleasures and even fought in wars. All of these factors caused people to call for the reformation of the church. When a friar named Johann Tetzel began selling indulgences, or pardons for the sins of people, in order to collect money to rebuild St. Peter's Cathedral in Rome, Martin Luther decided to take the church to task. He decided to publish ninety-five theses, or formal statements, attacking the selling of indulgences. This action began the Reformation movement aimed at reforming religious establishments.

Martin Luther was viciously attacked by the pope and the Holy Roman emperor who was a devout Catholic. Luther and his followers decided to separate themselves from the Catholic church and declared themselves to be Lutherans. In 1529, certain nobles and princes of Europe decided to support Luther against the Catholic Church. These protesting individuals came to be called Protestants. England's King Henry VIII decided to become Protestant after the pope of Rome declined to grant him a divorce from Catherine of Aragon so he could marry Anne Boleyn. The English Parliament passed the Act of Supremacy, which made Henry the head of the Church of England.

John Calvin instituted his own religious ideas in Geneva, Switzerland, and founded another Protestant church called Calvinism.

As a result of these protests, the Catholic Church decided to reform itself. Between 1545 and 1563, Catholic bishops and cardinals at the Council of Trent decided on several doctrines on ways to reform the Catholic faith. The first reform had to do with church finances and others dealt with such issues as the spread of Catholicism and the attempt to halt the spread of Protestantism. This attempt by the Catholic Church to correct a number of its practices has been called the Counter Reformation.

The Age of Enlightenment

During the 1600s and 1700s, many philosophers started to look at the beliefs of the ancient civilizations, primarily Greece and Rome, and came to the conclusion that the new Europe that emerged during the Renaissance period was much better and much more superior in terms of the exploration of unknown lands, new trade routes, and new scientific discoveries. In general, learning during this time seemed to have taken great strides. The humanist philosophers of this period included such individuals as Voltaire, Francois Marie Arouet, Pierre Laplace, Denis Diderot, John Locke, Jean-Jacques Rousseau, Isaac Newton, and many others. They helped to usher in a heightened period of learning called the Enlightenment or Age of Reason. Jean-Jacques Rousseau's *Declaration of the Rights of Man,* for example, expounded on the belief that the laws of any country or society reflected the expression of the general will of the people and not the monarchs or rulers of countries. Also during this time, scientists made many discoveries in the areas of electricity and magnetism, chemical equations in chemistry, and new theories about the solar system. This Enlightenment era emphasized the use of reason as a new approach to solving problems and helping to bring about progress and change. Rulers, such as Frederick II of Prussia, Catherine the Great of Russia, and Joseph II of Austria, bought into the Enlightenment ideas and helped their people to discover new ideas and new ways to make life more interesting. For example, Catherine the Great (1762–1796) imported musicians, architects, and many intellectuals to Russia from western Europe in an effort to help Russians learn new ways. Joseph II of Austria went so far as to abolish serfdom, allow for former serfs to own their own land, and provided for religious freedom for all his people and their religions.

Upheavals in thought emerge that cause both secular and scientific shifts with far-reaching impacts and consequences. One major shift is in the notion of reason as the most important faculty a human beings possess, beyond any other capacity they have. A second, and perhaps more important shift, is the discovery of the scientific method: Using reason and deduction, it is possible for human beings to know their world objectively and understand its laws and functions. Obviously, these two important shifts have impacts on religion because they place importance on the human being and move away from a mechanized, "god-centered" universe.

The roots of the Enlightenment are primarily French and middle class. Economic shifts also made much of this possible.

These enlightened philosophes made extravagant claims, but there was more to them than merely negations and disinfectants. It was primarily a French movement because French culture dominated Europe and because their ideas were expressed in the environment of the Parisian salon. Therefore, it was basically a middle-class movement. They nevertheless labored for man in general, as well as for humanity.

Clearly the feudal edifice was crumbling, but there was no real antagonism between the bourgeoisie and the aristocracy as yet. One can detect the bourgeoisie struggling for freedom from state regulations and for liberty of commercial activity. It is also evident that a wave of prosperity brought a greater degree of self-confidence to the bourgeoisie. Great fortunes were made in every town. Mercantilism was loosening its hold on the economy. By 1750, the reading public came into existence because of increasing literacy. Yet the philosophes lived a precarious life. They never knew whether they would be imprisoned or courted. Yet they assumed the air of an army on the march.

Intellectual Setting

From the seventeenth century the philosophers inherited the rationalism of Descartes, but the impulse of natural science alchemized into the Enlightenment. Newton had discovered a fundamental cosmic law that was susceptible to mathematical proof and applicable to the minutest object as well as to the universe as a whole. Maupertuis and Voltaire made Newton's law common property by 1750. John Locke had denied innate ideas and derived all knowledge, opinions, and behavior from sense experience. Condillac carried this to its conclusion by insisting that even perception was transformed sensation.

So the traditional anthropocentric view of the universe lay in ruins and with it the anthropomorphic conception of God. Hence Montesquieu, Voltaire, the encyclopedists, and physiocrats created the synthesis of social science that was based on past progress. All of this was done in an atmosphere of religious, political, and economic controversy. Biblical criticism came from Hugo Grotius. Political economists, shocked by the difference between prosperous Holland and backward Spain, first posited precious metals as the source of wealth, then commerce, and then agricultural production (as developed by the physiocrats).

In all this controversy, social science was beginning to yield evidence—the critical and historical method of Pierre Bayle. Exotic travel literature had its effect as well. It supported the positivist, experimental mentality of the eighteenth century. It brought the aura of the "noble savage" into prominence. There was a moral sense in natural man. Rousseau and the encyclopedists succumbed to this idea. But that was not the case with Montesquieu and Voltaire. By 1750 the social sciences had already become inductive, historical, anthropological, comparative, and critical.

Method

There was great faith in the instrument of reason rather than mere accumulation of knowledge. Doctrinal substance was not as important as overall philosophy. We need to keep this in mind if we want to understand the Enlightenment. It was not so much Descartes "reason" but rather Newton's laws—not abstraction and definition, but observation and experience were points of departure. What placed the stamp on the Enlightenment was this analytical method of Newtonian physics applied to the entire field of thought and knowledge. Order and regularity came from the analysis of observed facts, and the real power of reason lay not in the possession but in the acquisition of truth. So pure analysis was applied to psychological and social processes. From here on out the doctrine of historical and sociological determinism (the application of the principle of causality to social science) was generally accepted. Many historicists have ridiculed this naive scientific positivism. By facile dogmatism, the philosophes frequently ignored their own method.

Their new ideal of knowledge was simply a further development of seventeenth century logic and science. But there was a new emphasis on

- The particular rather than the general.
- Observable facts rather than principles.
- Experience rather than rational speculation.

The philosophers' faith in reason remained unshaken.

Enlightenment and Religion

It was an age of reason based on faith, not an age of faith based on reason. The enlightenment spiritualized the principle of religious authority, humanized theological systems, and emancipated individuals from physical coercion. It was the Enlightenment, not the Reformation or the Renaissance, that dislodged the ecclesiastical establishment from central control of cultural and intellectual life. By emancipating science from the trammels of theological tradition, the Enlightenment rendered possible the autonomous evolution of modern culture. Diderot said, "If you forbid me to speak on religion and government, I have nothing to say." Hence natural science occupied the front of the stage.

Most of the philosophes wrote on natural science. To Diderot, d'Holbach, and the encyclopedists, all religious dogma was absurd and obscure. LeMettrie and d'Holbach were consistent determinists. Voltaire disagreed with them and said they had a dogmatism of their own. Diderot, too, insisted on the free play of reason. But he was an unashamed pagan and believed in a kind of pantheism or pan-psychism, not pure atheism or materialism. He was humanistic, secular, modern and scientific. He expected from his method a regeneration of mankind.

English deism, however, was more pervasive in the Enlightenment. It emphasized an impersonal deity, natural religion, and a common morality of all human beings. Deism was a logical outgrowth of scientific inquiry, rational faith in humanity, and the study of comparative religion. All religions could be reduced to worshiping God and a commonsense moral code. There was a universal natural religion.

David Hume rejected the notion of a universal natural religion. Natural religion held that people are guided by the dictates of reason and that these dictates would remain true in all places, at all time, and for all people, much like Newton's laws and notions of cause and effect.

Hume was skeptical because human motivations interfere with our notions of cause and effect, and we are often driven by impulses. How can one make accurate predictions about cause and effect, where humans are concerned, when one's true motivations might never be pinned down? Quite simply, you can never know true cause through reasoning, because universal laws do not apply to human behavior.

These notions affected the philosophy of the Enlightenment. How could ideas like natural rights, self-evident truths, and universal laws of morality exist if we can never really know anything for certain? Hume's skepticism pertained to rational religion, an oxymoron: Since religious experience is rooted in passions, hopes, and fears, how could one determine absolute, objective truth? Quite simply, one cannot, and religions may be socially necessary but always laking scientific validity.

Voltaire is in the middle between the materialism of the Encyclopedists and the skepticism of Hume. His ruthless and comic deflation of theological sophism prevented him from recognizing the deepest drives of Catholicism. He conveyed the power of intellect to his generation, but also saw the limitations of reason. Reason was, after all, a poor instrument, but it was the only weapon that raised man above the animals. He believed in the argument from design or "first cause." But this no longer sufficed Diderot and Hume. Voltaire accepted the classical ideal of the brotherhood of man and the universal morality of man. He was essentially a humanist—the greatest humanist of the Enlightenment. He had not the depth of David Hume or Immanuel Kant, but they could not have done his work. Voltaire had only one absolute value: the human race.

The central theme of the Enlightenment is the effort to humanize religion. All philosophers rejected original sin. Here Pascal became a problem for them. For Pascal used their method of analytic logic to prove the existence of original sin and the utter inability of the unaided human reason to solve the problem without accepting the authority of faith. How do you explain the "double nature" of mankind? It becomes intelligible only through the doctrine of the fall of man. Pascal haunted Voltaire all his life. The cruel laughter of the Candide could not suppress the problem of evil. In the upshot he accepted Pascal's analysis of human nature. By becoming an agnostic, he became prisoner of Pascal's argument—reason without faith ends in skepticism.

Rousseau had a more original solution to Pascal's problem. In his two discourses he painted a picture of depravity of society that would have delighted Pascal. If he accepted degeneration, how was he to explain radical evil? He discovered a new agent of degeneration—the "fall of man"—not god or individual man but society. Thus salvation comes through the social contract. Man must save himself. In social justice is the meaning of life. It was neither a theological or metaphysical solution but a modern solution.

History

The Enlightenment rescued history from the antiquarians and the philologists: Voltaire, Hume, and Gibbon. Pierre Bayle was the real founder of historical criticism and the intellectual father of the historians of the Enlightenment (*Historical and Critical Dictionary,* 1697). To get at the reliable and incontrovertible facts of history was for him not a point of departure, but an end in itself. His *Dictionary* was a record of errors and historical falsehoods. He transformed the dictum that history was nothing more than a record of crimes and misfortunes of mankind. He did for history what Galileo did for science.

Historical truth could only come from the objective examination of the human record. The Enlightenment ideas made meaning out of this record. Empirical causation and human solidarity, despite incessant warfare and the idea of progress, made a conceptual mastery of the chaotic and meaningless facts of history. Enlightenment historians applied the whole culture of their age to the past. Not the "unique event" of Leopold von Ranke, but the evolution of generic man—the spirit of the times and nations—are the essence of history.

At the base of Voltaire's conception of civilization lay the great monarchies of Europe with their institutions, their quests for power, but also their promotion of economic welfare, the basis of cultural progress. Voltaire believed in the republic of scholars and in the primacy of ideas in historical evolution. Ideas were the motive force. Thus he became the prophet of progress. But how does one reconcile progress and the universality of human nature? Human nature reveals itself only in historical evolution. Progress is the gradual assertion of reason. To some degree, this was didactic history.

Hume also accepted the uniformity of man and failed to grasp the irrational factors in human history. But he too asserted the primacy of ideology. Yet this static view began to change. He believed neither in reason or in progress and was profoundly occupied with the historical process—that is, with change as such. He put facts above theory and the unique aspects were more significant than the common occurrence. Hume, of course, was horror struck with Voltaire's sweeping generalizations.

Social Science and Political Thought

The philosophes did not discover the natural rights theory, but they made it the foundation of ethical and social gospel. They introduced natural rights into practical politics. They gave natural rights the dynamic force that revealed its explosive energy in the French Revolution. But their argument moved steadily away from metaphysics toward empiricism—away from reason toward experience. Liberty of the person, security of property, and freedom of discussion were less rooted in abstract reason than in commonsense views of fundamental human needs, impulses, and inclinations. In spite of the utopianism of Rousseau, the rest had a sense of reality. Reason is still primary, but it is not insurrectionary or bloodthirsty. Only in society could man realize his full potential. They believed in the social function of knowledge. Except for Rousseau, none of the philosophes agitated for a radical transformation of society. All of them, like Voltaire, defended enlightened absolutism.

Montesquieu published his *Spirit of the Laws* in 1748. He expressed here real hatred of despotism, clericalism, and slavery. Being a member of the petit noblesse, he called for an "intermediary corps" and fundamental laws to temper the monarchy. His former colleague magistrates called it restitution of the ancient constitution. So, he influenced both the aristocratic reactionaries, who wanted to revitalize feudal estates and parliaments, and the honest liberals who idealized English constitutionalism with its principle of separation of powers that was the basis of modern constitution making. This book was the first study in ideal sociological patterns. He advocated the examination of a variety of constitutional forms to discover the republic and its inner law. A network of interacting forces, if altered, affect the equilibrium of the whole structure. He is the founder of the typology of constitutional patterns.

The Encyclopedists had a more dynamic conception. But they also believed in metaphysical norms to which societies must conform. Hence natural religion, natural morality, natural rights, and natural economies should prevail. They also popularized the idea of progress, stated more clearly later by Turgot and Condorcet. They used the Leibnitz idea of continuity.

The Physiocrats shared with the philosophes a rationalist, hedonist, and utilitarian outlook. Natural rights were thought to be necessary for economic progress. They were opposed to the rivalry and jealousies of mercantilism. They reduced all social science to economics. Quesnay started with an examination of the agricultural situation in France. He wanted protection for agriculture and promoted the Third Estate. But agriculture came first and liberalism second. He thought there should be harmony between positive laws and natural laws and that this harmony could be established via reason. The sovereign was to be a "legal despot." This vague utopian constitutionalism was a regressive step from the ideas of Montesquieu.

Rousseau rejected all compromise with contemporary society. He called for a moral reformation, a revival of religion, and a purification of manners. He passionately asserted the moral and legal equality of man, the sovereignty of the people, and the authority of the general will. He wanted a return to primitive simplicity. While he realized that his "state of nature" never existed, he asserted that self-knowledge was the source of his proofs. In two discourses he exposed his unlimited personal individualism. Yet in the social contract, we get the glorification of unlimited absolutism of the state. Freedom for Rousseau is the submission to the law which the individual has imposed on himself. It is a voluntary consent to a necessary law. By entering this state, men gain the enlargement of their perceptions and capacities. Political and intellectual freedom is worthless for man, if he does not have moral freedom. The function of the state is to bring about legal and moral equality.

Physical, intellectual, and economic equality are beyond human remedy. The state, according to Rousseau can interfere with property only if legal and moral equality is jeopardized. Later, he posits that the young must learn the compulsion of things but be protected from the tyranny of men. All must obey the general will as a law of nature, not as an alien command but because of necessity. This is only possible if society makes the laws that it obeys. Hence a radical political and social revolution is necessary. He demanded man's mastery over nature and projected a moral rationalism. Without a doubt, we are here on the road to Immanuel Kant.

The Enlightenment also touched the American colonies where Thomas Jefferson and Benjamin Franklin were greatly impressed with the new ideas coming from Europe. In fact, Franklin kept in touch with a number of philosophers, especially those in France. Both Franklin and Jefferson were enlightened individuals themselves with a variety of talents in the areas of science, government, inventions, intellectual endeavors, and political ideas. Both of these men were very influential in getting the American colonists to revolt against British rule by using arguments such as those of John Locke who had written that the people had the right to abolish an abusive government and establish a new one. That's what the American colonists did. It was Jefferson who headed a committee that wrote the Declaration of Independence for the American colonies on July 4, 1776.

The American Revolutionary War and the new age of Enlightenment also brought changes to France where the people revolted against a nobility that had lost touch with the peasants. The French government had spent a lot of its resources helping the American colonies in their struggle against the British. Coupled with the poor harvest in 1788, the poor people of France had enough. The nobles paid no taxes and enjoyed the good life while the poor people had to still pay taxes, had to contend with food shortages and higher food prices, as well as mounting unemployment and starvation. When King Louis XVI decided to call the legislative branch of France's government into session in order to raise taxes in 1789, the Third Estate of the Estates General broke away from the other two and formed a separate branch called the Assembly. The Assembly represented all people except the clergy (First Estate) and the nobility (the Second Estate). It forced King Louis to do away with government by absolute rule and agree to a constitutional monarchy. However, when King Louis gathered soldiers near Paris in July of 1789, the people became concerned that the king was going to renege on his promise for a constitutional government and they decided to storm the Bastille, a prison which contained arms and political prisoners, on July 14, 1789. This attack and take over of the Bastille was the beginning of the French Revolution. A month later, August, the Assembly adopted its Declaration of Rights of Man and of the Citizen guaranteeing all citizens their natural rights of "liberty, property, security, and resistance to oppression."

A period of terror followed the execution of the King Louis and his queen Marie Antoinette together with thousands of nobles. This period was brought to an end when General Napoleon Bonoparte decided to step in; and in 1804, he brought Pope Pius VII to Paris to witness his coronation as emperor. Napoleon went on to attack Great Britain but his navy was defeated on October 21, 1805, by Lord Nelson at the battle of Trafalgar. This defeat caused Napoleon to turn his attention towards central Europe. Napoleon was able to:

1. Get the Holy Roman Emperor, Francis II, to give up his imperial title.
2. Controlled all of Italy with the exception of the Papal States.
3. Set up puppet states in Holland, Portugal, and Spain.
4. Defeat the Prussians and Russians and signed the Treaty of Tilsit making Russia and France allies.
5. Take the Polish lands away from Prussia to create the Grand Dutchy of Warsaw.
6. Defeat Austria and take some of Austria's territories in 1809.
7. Set up a number of codes or laws regulating trade and commerce. These included the Civil Code, the Code of Commerce, and the Penal Code.

Napoleon's attempt to unify continental Europe met with resistance from Russia and Great Britain who together with their allies battled against Napoleon. The end of Napoleon came at the hands of the British who sent him to the island of Elba. He later returned but was finally defeated at the Battle of Waterloo on June 18, 1815. Napoleon abdicated the throne, and King Louis XVIII returned to power in France. Great Britain and Austria, on the one hand, and Russia, with Prussia on the other, held a meeting known as the Congress of Vienna on June of 1815. The purpose of this Congress was to come to terms on how to contain France.

Thus, the period of Enlightenment was a time when drastic changes took place in thinking, learning, science, and politics. However, some of the changes that took place during this time were not long lasting for many of the poor who found themselves in the same predicaments as before once new monarchs and leaders took over in enlightened countries.

The Congress of Vienna (1814–1815)

A number of changes took place in Europe as a result of Napoleon's defeat:

1. The Holy Roman Empire ceased to exist.
2. A German confederation of thirty-nine states was created.
3. The Habsburgs retained control of Italy. However, the Italian peninsula was divided into a number of duchies which were controlled by different rulers. This caused many people to yearn for the unification of all of Italy. Italian nationalism grew rapidly, as a result of the action of the Congress of Vienna to divide Italy under different rulers.
4. Poland was portioned off by Russia, Austria, and Prussia.
5. Prussia was given the Rhineland territories.
6. Islands in the Ionian Sea were given to Great Britain.

France experienced four different periods of changes, which included:

■ The Restoration period (1814–1830), which was brought to an end by the July Revolution of 1830.
■ The July Monarchy (1830–1848), which was brought to an end by the February Revolution in 1848.
■ Second Republic (1848–1852), which ended when Napoleon III took over power.
■ Second Empire (1852–1870), which was brought down by the Franco-Prussian War in 1870.

Two Revolutions in Great Britain

The Age of Enlightenment brought changes not only to France but also to Great Britain. Two revolutions of a different kind took place here:

1. The agricultural revolution: During the 1700s the British farmers began producing greater amounts of crops thanks to new methods in farming. These new methods included:

   A. Crop rotation replaced the outdated three-field system used during the Middle Ages. Under the old method, one field was planted with one crop, like wheat, and a second was planted with another, like oats. The third field was allowed to stay fallow. Every year they switched crops. However, with the new crop rotation system, a field was allowed to stay fallow every third year. Animals could be raised in this field during this time while the soil regenerated itself. In this way, British farmers were able to raise new crops, such as turnips or clover. Also they began raising more and more animals such as cattle and sheep. Food became abundant for the masses of people that lived in burgeoning cities.

   B. Farm tools greatly improved during this time as well. A man by the name of Jethro Tull developed the horse drawn seed drill in the 1730s which allowed for consistent spacing and depth in planting of seeds. This spacing allowed farmers to break up the soil more often and thus give the seeds more air and water in order to grow more sturdy and productive.

   C. A new system of enclosure during the 1600s and 1700s allowed the wealthy to purchase the small plots of land that belonged to the poor farmers. This allowed the wealthy to have large farms around which they placed enclosures or fences. Once fenced the landowners could use the land as they wished. As a result, new methods allowed these large farms to produce an abundant amount of crops.

2. The Industrial Revolution: Because of Great Britain's growing population, there was a demand for more food and other goods, such as clothing. To meet this demand, inventors came up with new ways to increase the manufacturing of goods. As a result, a number of inventions helped to bring about what is called the Industrial Revolution. The social structure of Europe was transformed as a result of the Industrial Revolution, because the new economy weakened the position of artisans who controlled the production of goods during the feudal period. The political life of Europe also changed because it increased the power of the urban middle class. Some changes included:

   A. John Kay invented the flying shuttle in 1733 which allowed one person on the mechanical loom to do the work for two. Other inventors brought similar changes to the manufacturing of goods.

   B. Capitalism, as defined by British economist Adam Smith, took hold in Great Britain. This new form of economic thought called upon people to invest their capital or money in many enterprises thereby allowing inventors, companies, and other individuals to use their resources not only to benefit themselves but others as well.

   C. Cities attracted many people from the farms because the factories needed an ever growing number of workers. The cities became overcrowded and living conditions for many were miserable as recorded by writers like Charles Dickens of that period of time.

   This Industrial Revolution allowed Great Britain to become the industrial workshop and role model for the rest of the world. The inventions and ideas about agriculture and government spread to other nations. In many nations it caused inequities to occur and new oppression against the poor to take place.

The 1800s also brought great changes in the medical field. Individuals like Louis Pasteur discovered how germs were responsible for the spreading of various diseases and the demographic trends that ensued as a result. Prior to this time there were plagues and other diseases that caused many deaths in Europe. However, with the discovery of the germ theory by Pasteur, medical science was able to search for ways to control the spread of diseases. New treatments and new drugs were pioneered to help people.

United States History[1]

UNITED STATES GEOGRAPHY

The United States is divided into five regions: Northeast, Southeast, Middle West, Southwest, and West.

The United States is located in the western hemisphere. It makes up a portion of the North American continent. It stretches from the east coast 3,000 miles to the Pacific coast in the west. It is bordered in the north by Canada, in the south by Mexico, in the west by the Pacific Ocean, and the east by the Atlantic Ocean and the Caribbean. The United States is made up of fifty states with Hawaii being the only noncontinental state. The United States has a variety of climate and weather conditions. It is also rich in minerals and other natural resources.

CONTENT AREA EIGHTEEN: NATIVE AMERICANS

The first Americans to come to the North and South American continents came from Asia, according to scientists. For thousands of years human beings moved from Africa to Europe, then to Asia. Some 12,000 years ago or longer, a land bridge existed between Siberia and what is today Alaska. This land bridge was covered by glaciers. Animals, like the mammoth, resembling a giant elephant, were hunted by the early people in Siberia. Ancient hunters moved across the Bering bridge chasing after the mammoths. Slowly their numbers increased and they moved southwardly into North, Middle, and South America. The movement of people from Siberia to North America is just a theory. Not enough tangible evidence exists that this is the way it happened. However, most scientists, or rather archaeologists, believe in this theory.

Each group of people who moved to the new continents had their own customs and traditions or cultures. All of these individuals were at first hunters. However, a thousand or so years after their arrival, great changes took place as the climate warmed and the glaciers started to melt. Also the mammoths, saber-toothed tigers, horses, and camels disappeared. As a result, the ancient Americans had to turn to gathering for their food needs and also learned to hunt smaller game as well as fish. Eventually, Native Americans, or American Indians, learned to plant seeds and harvest them when they were ripe. This development turned Indians into farmers. Archaeologists provide evidence of this event that dates back from 7000 to 5000 years ago. The most important food that they grew was corn, or maize. They grew and harvested squash, pumpkins, beans, avocados, and twelve kinds of corn.

With the development of farming, Native Americans began to form into tribes, developed their own religions, and specialized in certain kinds of work or trade. Surplus food was used for trade with other tribes.

All Native American tribes had their own oral storytelling traditions whereby they passed on stories of creation. Native Americans were very close to nature. They respected the physical

---

[1]Chapter contributed by Sam Marandos.

world and all animals. They felt a kinship with the animals, and they called them brothers. They gave thanks for the animals that they killed to use for food, footwear, utensils, clothing, and so forth. Some of their oral stories told of how the earth was created so that living things would be able to live on it.

Northeastern and Eastern Woodland Native Americans

Northeastern and Eastern Woodland Native Americans lived in the forested regions of the New England states and the eastern seaboard, where natural resources provided for basic needs, and hunting for small game was common.

The Iroquois.   The Iroquois lived where New York state is now located. Fur trading was an important activity for them, and their towns were large, ranging from 500 to 2,000 people. The League of Five Nations included members from the Mohawk, Oneida, Seneca, Onondaga, Cayuga, and Tuscarora tribes. Around 1640, the Iroquois would wage war on the French over trade disputes and enlist the aid of the English colonies. The French, in turn, would ally themselves with other tribes who had been pushed out by the Iroquois and wage war with them. In 1701, the Five Nations settled their disputes with all parties: They retained their rights to the fur trade, but agreed to avoid conflicts with other tribes and with France. The United States disbanded the league in 1784, after some tribes sided with the British during the American Revolution.

The Cherokee.   The Cherokee lived in what today is Georgia and Tennessee. They made their homes from twigs, branches, and mud. They were farmers who grew squash, corn, and beans. Historically, the Cherokee aided the British both during their conflict with the French and during the American Revolution. After signing treaties with the United States in the early 1820s, the Cherokee adopted many forms U.S. government, including an elected chief and a congress consisting of a senate and house of representatives, and a constitution. When gold was discovered on Cherokee lands, Georgia tried to have the Cherokee removed through either force or purchase. The Cherokee Nation passed laws protecting their lands from sale, but the Georgia government confiscated the land anyway. Though the U.S. Supreme Court found the seizure unconstitutional, President Andrew Jackson sent no army to enforce the ruling.

In 1835, Cherokee lands were put up for sale by leaders, causing great internal strife among members of the tribe. Eventually, federal troops forced unwilling members from their lands. The Trail of Tears refers to their exodus and subsequent deaths from diseases and marauders during their travel to Oklahoma. Once in Oklahoma, the Cherokee reinstituted their government, along with several other tribes. Later, the Cherokee would side with the Confederacy during the Civil War and have their government dissolved after the conflict.

Mound Builders in the Midwest

The Mound Builders created pyramid-shaped mounds in the eastern and central United States from 1000 B.C. to 700 A.D. The mounds served a variety of purposes, from burial chambers to public spaces and plazas.

The Hopewell Culture.   As the result of networks of trade, cities arose and the Mound Builders created tombs for their chiefs and centers for their religion. The Hopewell people populated these areas from 200 B.C. to 400 A.D., and their mounds still stand as reminders of their culture.

The Mississippian Culture.   In the 750s, the Mississippian culture emerged as maize growers who created their towns by mound building. They also created enormous temples, the most impressive of which is the Cahoka City in St. Louis, Missouri. The population of the city may have reached as many as 20,000 members.

The Southwest Native Americans

The Pueblo people lived in the cliffs in the dry, stony mountain ranges of northwestern New Mexico and northeastern Arizona. They were maize and bean growers, as well as basket and pottery artisans. The Pueblos are also known for resisting Spanish occupation and for driving Spanish missions from their territory in 1680. Eventually, they would fall under Mexican control and, later, U.S. control after the Mexican War in the 1800s.

The Plains Indians

The plains lie east of the Rocky Mountains and occupy the central United States. In early history, the plains supported large herds of bison, and the Plains Indians hunted them as their main food source. The characteristics of the Plains Indians have been exploited in film, and most of us can recognize their pipes, dances, drums, and headdresses when we see them.

The Blackfoot. The Blackfoot were nomadic bison hunters who followed herds into the plains from Canada. They get their name from the ash they used to stain their moccasins. The Blackfoot had conflicts with other hunting and farming tribes in the plains, and the other tribes would often band together to defend themselves against their attacks. The organization of the tribe was by band, with each band having its own chief. They thrived on mobility and constructed portable villages so that they could leave an area quickly.

The Mandan. Not all Plains Indians were nomadic herdsman. Some tribes, like the Mandan, turned to agriculture and grew maize. The Mandan became expert farmers and built a great nation in the plains of Missouri. They lived in sod-built circular homes that could hold as many as 60 people. Buffalo hunting twice a year was also a source of sustenance and conviviality, as well as tools, clothing, and arrowheads. As with the Blackfoot, the labor was divided, where the men did the hunting and the women skinned the animals, making household items.

Eventually, the Plains Indians would be joined by other tribes from the eastern woodlands as Europeans moved into their lands.

Northwest Indians

The inhabitants of this region crossed the Bering Sea land bridge that existed during the Ice Age prior to 10,000 B.C., and became the paleoindians who would populate the North, Central, and South Americas. Climate affected the cultural development of Native Americans who stayed in the Pacific Northwest, depending on whether they lived in the coastal or the mountain regions.

The coastal Native Americans, like the Makah, who were whalers, and the Chinook settled in permanent housing made of cedar. With plentiful food sources from the ocean and rivers, as well as nuts and roots, these tribes tended to settle and stay in one place, since they were not following herds of animals around on the plains. Not surprisingly, fish were a staple food and religious rites arose to honor the fish they would catch. Dugout canoes were also common. Socially, they observed class and demonstrated their wealth by throwing lavish parties and bestowing gifts upon the attendees.

Native Americans who lived along the mountain ranges were more nomadic, traveling to the coast for food in summer and gathering nuts and roots in autumn. While on these journeys, they carried portable shelters with them. When winter would come, they would dig large pits and live in underground shelters.

California Indians

In general, we can discuss Native American living in the interior and along the coast of California. Paleoindian hunter-gatherer traditions of hunting, fishing, and gathering foods persisted throughout the interior of California for thousands of years. Life in villages was simple and involved thatch-roofed homes in the temperate climate. Coastal Native Americans, on the other hand, hunted the sea from canoes developed a trade in shells, and tended to be less nomadic, given their circumstances. In short, region and climate have a marked impact on the behavior of a given tribe and what it must do to survive.

The Northern Modoc. These hunter-gatherers lived on pond seeds, hunting, and fishing in the northern intermountain region. They summered in brush huts and wintered in brush and reed huts. The Modoc were also expert weavers, making everything from cradles to mats to baskets. The Modoc did not welcome European settling, and eventually there was a clash resulting in the Modoc War of 1872.

The Central Nisenan. The Nisenan people lived in the central valley around Sacramento. The Ninsenan who lived near rivers depended on them and developed a distinct way of life, where dome-shaped homes collected into 500-member villages. Hunting small game, fishing, and gathering foods was the common way of life for the Ninsenan, and they developed canoes and boats as a form of fishing technology. Other Ninsenan tribes lived in the hills and depended on seasonal foods, which they gathered. Ninsenan society consisted of a chief and male and female shamans who cured the ill and resolved conflicts. Religous practices centered around the harvest. The Gold Rush affected their existence negatively, as many were killed and driven from their lands when more Europeans began to inhabit and settle Northern California in search of gold.

The Southern Diegueño. The San Diego area of California has had inhabitants for centuries. Around 1769, the Native Americans living there discovered Father Junipero Serra, a Jesuit priest. Fortunately for Father Junipero, these natives were friendly. Father Junipero built the Mission San Diego with their help and named the people the Diegueño. They were primarily hunter-gatherers who fished, hunted small game, and gathered fruits, nuts, and berries. The Diegueño did not stay friendly forever and began to resent occupation, eventually burning down the San Diego mission.

CONTENT AREA NINETEEN: THE AGE OF EXPLORATION AND COLONIZATION

The Renaissance, or rebirth of knowledge, that took place after the end of the Middle, or Dark, Ages also awoke Europeans' curiosity about the rest of the world. They thus began to search for ways by which they could discover what lay over the hill. Italian city-states had an idea about the Middle East but knew that the Muslim rulers would not allow them to make inroads into their region. However, a man by the name of Marco Polo did make a journey into Asia and ended up in China. When he returned some twenty-four years later, he had some fabulous tales to tell. He also brought back with him a different type of cloth—silk. Up to this time even kings and queens of Europe wore clothes made from cotton. Polo also brought back with him samples of spices that Europeans did not have. These items created a lot of interest. Polo also brought back gunpowder, which in time gave western European nations an advantage in warfare. Europeans, as a result of Marco Polo's exploits, sought to reach the Far East by water, thinking that it was safer and shorter. Prince Henry the Navigator of Portugal sent Diaz along the shore of western Africa in order to find a route to India and China. Diaz got as far as the Cape of Good Hope before rough seas forced him to return home in 1488. In 1497, another Portuguese explorer, Vasco da Gama, followed in Diaz's route and was successful in rounding the Cape of Good Hope and making it to India. He came back to Portugal with a ship full of spices.

Following Portugal's lead, Spain also tried to find a way to the Far East. An Italian sailor by the name of Christopher Columbus tried to convince King Ferdinand and Queen Isabella to fund his voyage to the Far East by sailing the ocean to the west. Up to this point, many Europeans felt that the earth was flat. Columbus figured that the earth was more rounded. So, if you sailed west, you would arrive in the east. After various attempts, Ferdinand and Isabella provided Columbus with three ships, the *Niña,* and *Pinta,* and *Santa Maria.* Columbus sailed on his first voyage on August 3, 1492, from Palos, Spain. On October 12, 1492, after sailing for three months and with his crew ready to revolt, Columbus sighted land. He did not know then that he had discovered a new world. By his calculations, he figured that Asia was about 3,000 miles from Europe. In reality it is about 13,000 miles. So, Columbus named the inhabitants of

San Salvador "Indians" because they resembled people from the East Indies. Columbus made a total of four voyages to the new world.

A man by the name of Amerigo Vespucci who had been sent to validate Columbus' claim and that of others that they indeed had found a way to Asia. Vespucci went back to Europe certain that what had been discovered was not Asia. On a newly published map by German cartographer Martin Waldseemuller, the new land was named America in honor not for Columbus but for Amerigo Vespucci. Table 9.1 shows a chart of early interest in lands beyond Europe and its surroundings.

TABLE 9.1   Age of Exploration

NAME	COUNTRY	AREA EXPLORED	PERIOD
Brendan	Ireland	An unknown land.	About 500 A.D.
Leif Eriksson	Sweden, Norway, and Denmark	Vinland or wine land because there were many grapevines	1000 A.D.
Marco Polo	Italy	China	1271–1295
Bartholomeu Dias	Portugal	Cape of Good Hope	1488
Christopher Columbus	Spain	San Salvador, other Caribbean Sea islands, and along the shores of Central America	Four voyages in 1492–1493; 1493–1496; 1498; 1502–1504
Vasco da Gama	Portugal	India	1497–1499
Amerigo Vespucci	Portugal	Venezuela to Argentina	1499
Vasco Nunez	Spain	Pacific Ocean	1513
Balboa and Ponce de Leon	Spain	Florida	1513
Ferdinand Magellan	Spain	Circumnavigated the globe	1519–1522
Hernando Cortes	Spain	Aztec Empire of Mexico	1519
Francisco Pizarro	Spain	Inca Empire of South America: Peru, Ecuador, Bolivia, and Argentina	1531–1533
Cabeza de Vaca and Esteban	Spain	Texas, told about The Seven Cities of Gold	1536
Francisco Vasquez de Coronado	Spain	Arizona, New Mexico, Texas, Oklahoma, and Kansas	1540
Hernando De Soto	Spain	Florida, Georgia, North and South Carolina, Tennessee, and Alabama	1539

In 1494, the Spanish and Portuguese petitioned the Pope of Rome to divide the world between these two countries because of their discoveries. The Pope drew a Line of Demarcation showing the sections to be claimed and explored by Portugal and Spain. In 1513, Ponce de Leon went in search of a mythical fountain of youth in what is now Florida. He was killed there by the natives. In the same year Balboa crossed the expanse of Panama and gazed upon the Pacific, or Peaceful, Ocean.

Spain sent other explorers from its headquarters in Cuba to explore the new world. In 1519, Ferdinand Magellan sailed along the shore of South America and was able to round the tip of South America through what is today called the Strait of Magellan. He and his three ships sailed for many months. His crew got sick with scurvy and a number died. Finally, in March of 1521, Magellan and his crew reached the Philippine Islands. In a skirmish on one of the islands, Magellan was killed. In September of 1522, Magellan's remaining crew of eighteen sailors returned to Spain on the ship *Victoria*. Magellan's trip confirmed what Columbus believed—that the world was round and one could sail west and end up in the east.

Hernando Cortes, another Spanish explorer, set off from Cuba to explore along the coast of what is now Mexico. Once on shore, he heard stories of untold riches. He burned his ships so that his men could not go back to Cuba and with 900 men marched inland. He discovered the Aztec Indian civilization Tenochtitlan in what today is Mexico City. The Aztec Emperor Motecuhzoma was fearful of Cortes because of an ancient prophecy. He gave Cortes gold and silver to leave but Cortes would not. The end result was that Cortes and his men destroyed this Indian civilization and went on to establish the colony of New Spain.

To the south, another Spaniard, Francisco Pizzaro, encountered the Inca civilization along the Andes Mountains of South America. When the emperor of the Incas, Atahuallpa, refused to give up his religion and subjugate himself to the king of Spain, Pizarro took him prisoner. Atahuallpa was eventually killed, even though he gave the Spaniards riches in gold and silver. The Spaniards then went on to destroy this Indian civilization and enslave the people.

Two other explorers, De Soto and Coronado, searched the American Southwest for the mythical Seven Cities of Gold but never found them. In 1541, De Soto and his men reached the banks of the Mississippi River.

New Spain and the Spanish Empire

The area explored by Cortes eventually was named New Spain. Spain eventually expanded its power into Central and South America. It introduced slavery into many of these areas. The Native American populations were forced to work for them. The Spanish also exerted their influence into Baja California and then into Alta California.

By 1580, Spanish power was at its heights and many thousands of Spanish people lived in North and South America. However, hostilities between Spain and England caused Spain to send its mighty armada, or armed ships, to attack England. The English had smaller and more maneuverable ships and were able to evade the Spanish armada. Bad weather and rough seas in the English Channel destroyed most of the armada. This event in 1588 caused the weakening of Spain as a world power and helped England and other nations to compete for colonies in the New World (see Table 9.2).

TABLE 9.2   French, English, Dutch and Other Explorers

NAME	COUNTRY	AREA EXPLORED	PERIOD
John Cabot	England	Newfoundland	1497
Giovanni Verrazano	France	New York Bay and Hudson River; mapped North American coast	1524
Jacques Cartier	France	Discovered the St. Lawrence Gulf and the St. Lawrence River	1534
Sir Francis Drake	England	Pacific coasts of North and South America; claimed the coastal lands of what is now California for England; first Englishman to sail around the world	1577
Sir Walter Raleigh	England	Roanoke Island; Virginia Dare was the first English baby born in America	1587
Samuel de Champlain	France	Founded the city of Quebec; explored region of New England; made maps and drew pictures	1603
Henry Hudson	Holland	Sailed up the Hudson River in his small ship the *Half Moon;* explored eastern coast of North America	1609
Father Marquette and Louis Joliet	France	Discovered the Mississippi River to the mouth of the Arkansas River	1673
Robert de La Salle	France	The first European to travel the whole length of the Mississippi River all the way to the Gulf of Mexico; claimed the whole Mississippi Valley for France	1682

CONTENT AREA TWENTY: THE ENGLISH COLONIES

A group of Englishmen formed the London Company in order to help in the colonization of America. In 1606, they sent a group of colonists to start a settlement in Jamestown, Virginia. They reached their objective on April 26, 1607, after eighteen weeks at sea with 120 men. The leaders of this settlement were Christopher Newport and Captain John Smith. In a short time a number of men had died, the settlement was running out of supplies, and they did not have water nearby. The Indians proved to be unfriendly, and the whole area seemed unhealthy. Christopher Newport sailed for England to get more supplies. By December 25, 1607, only fifty-three people were still alive and Captain John Smith had gotten help from the Powhatan Indians. It happened that Captain John Smith had been captured by these Native Americans and was about to be killed when the daughter of the chief, Pocahontas, intervened and saved his life. The Powhatan became friends of the colonists. In 1608, Newport returned to Jamestown with more settlers and two women. However, by 1609, only about sixty people remained alive due to sickness and hunger. In time, however, Jamestown became a successful settlement and the growing of tobacco flourished.

Another group of settlers called Pilgrims came to America and settled at Plymouth, Massachusetts. Their reason for coming was primarily religious in nature. They wanted to get away from persecution in England and petitioned the king to allow them to settle in the new world. They boarded the ship *Mayflower* and in 1620 set out on their voyage. Once they arrived, but before they disembarked, they decided to draw up a document to help them make rules and laws to live by. This is known as the Mayflower Compact, or agreement.

The Native Americans of the area befriended the Pilgrims and helped them to survive their first year. An Indian by the name of Samoset introduced the Pilgrims to Squanto, who had traveled to England and spoke English. Samoset also introduced the Pilgrims to Chief Massasoit of the Wampanoag Indians. They all became friends. In 1621, the Pilgrims and the local Native Americans came together to have a feast to celebrate the Pilgrims' first year in the New World and to give thanks to God for helping them. This became the first Thanksgiving celebration.

Another group called the Puritans settled near the Pilgrims. They too had left England in order to be able to worship God in their own way. They settled in their colony called the Massachusetts Bay Colony in 1630. Later the Plymouth Colony and Massachusetts Bay Colony became one. Boston became the main city of this colony.

Other groups of Native Americans were also encountered by the colonists. Among them were the Iroquois, a powerful group who were successful at war with other tribes and were also excellent merchants. They allied themselves with the English and Dutch early on and prospered into the early 1700s. The Iroquois were divided into five tribes and were called the Iroquois League. Their government was a loose confederation from which our Articles of Confederation borrowed substantially. Another important feature of the Iroquois was that women played a very important and prominent role in tribal government. The women were allowed to choose the tribal *sachems,* or leaders, as well as the religious leaders. Another group of Native Americans made up the Illinois Confederacy. This group belonged to the Algonquian language group.

Other colonies were founded by the English and other European nations as shown in Table 9.3.

The thirteen English colonies can be grouped into the New England Colonies, the Middle Colonies, and the Southern Colonies. Each of the regions where the colonies were located had its own characteristics. First, each region was settled by people from different parts of Europe. The New England Colonies were founded and settled by the English. Native Americans in the New England region were alarmed by the intrusion and expansion of Europeans into their territories. The Middle Colonies were settled by the French, Germans, Scots, Irish, and some free Africans. The Southern Colonies were settled by the English, French, Scots, and African slaves. The colonies differed by the industries they pursued. The New England Colonies depended upon fishing, shipbuilding, and whaling. The Middle Colonies depended on farming, flour milling, shipping, and trading. The Southern Colonies engaged in farming

TABLE 9.3   The English Colonies

COLONY	FOUNDERS
New Hampshire (1623)	People from Massachusetts
New York (1624)	Dutch set up trading posts there. England took this colony in 1664.
Connecticut (1633)	People from Massachusetts
Maryland (1634)	Lord Baltimore found it as a heaven for Catholics
Rhode Island (1636)	Roger Williams
Delaware (1638)	Swedish settlers. It became part of Pennsylvania in 1681.
New Jersey (1640)	John Berkeley & George Carteret
Pennsylvania (1643)	William Penn as a colony for Quakers
North Carolina (1653)	People from Virginia
South Carolina (1670)	People from Virginia
Georgia (1733)	James Oglethorpe

and trade. The Middle Colonies were the breadbasket colonies because of their specialty in planting and raising wheat. The Northern Colonies developed the first schools and school systems. The Southern Colonies came to depend on slave labor in order to raise tobacco and cotton in large plantations. The slavery issue would eventually become a national issue and would divide the nation.

CONTENT AREA TWENTY-ONE: THE AMERICAN REVOLUTION AND THE BIRTH OF THE UNITED STATES

The relationship between England and her American colonies became strained during and after the French and Indian War, which began in 1754 and lasted until 1763. The British made use of their colonists to fight the French and their Indian allies. George Washington was a 21-year-old officer who fought for the British against the French in the Ohio valley. By the year 1759, the British were successful in repelling and even defeating the French in some of their skirmishes. The British General Wolfe led his men on an attack against the capital city of New France, Quebec. The attack was successful and the French capital was captured. Due to the success of this battle, the British were able to defeat the French, and in 1763 the Treaty of Paris was signed whereby the French ceded all of Canada to the British.

During this war, the British treated the colonists fighting for them as inferior. British officers were rude and arrogant towards the colonial officers like George Washington. The British also used bad language in their daily dealings with the American colonists, which caused many colonists to disrespect them. Colonists also felt that their colonial government and merchants were not treated fairly by the British. There was, as a result, a feeling of resentment towards the British from the colonists who felt that they should be treated like all full-fledged British citizens.

After the French and Indian War, the British decided that the American colonies should help Britain pay for the cost of the war. George Grenville, the chief minister for King George III, asked the Parliament to pass the Sugar Act in 1764. The Sugar Act placed a tax on molasses, a product that was widely used by the colonists. Colonists in Massachusetts, like Mercy Otis Warren and her brother James Otis, were the first to speak out against this new form of taxation. They both felt that this was unjust and greedy on the part of the British. Some people agreed with these two individuals but others did not. There were many colonists, called Loyalists, who were still loyal to the British. They felt that the tax was justified because Britain had to pay for its expenses to defend the colonists. However, the tax generally caused further resentment toward the British.

Next, the British decided to forbid colonists from settling between the crest of the Appalachian Mountains and the Mississippi River. In this way they did not have to pay to protect the colonists from Indians. In 1765, Grenville and Parliament passed the Stamp Act in order to raise more money to protect the colonies. This act required American colonists to pay for stamps on all legal documents and printed materials, like newspapers. The colonists decided to boycott or protest this new act. They argued that since colonists had no representation in Parliament, they should not be taxed. Although many colonists were angry at the British Parliament, some colonial governments like the one in Pennsylvania decided to send Benjamin Franklin and a group of other representatives to England to plead their case in Parliament. Franklin made it clear to the English Parliament that the colonists would fight if the British sent soldiers to collect the new taxes. The British lawmakers refused to accept Franklin's request and chose to ignore the others' warnings. In the colonies, Benjamin Franklin with James Otis and other concerned colonists decided to have a meeting to discuss common interests and action to take against the Stamp Act. This meeting, held in New York City in 1765, had representatives from nine of the thirteen colonies. The end result was that the representatives in a united voice asked colonists to refuse to buy goods that required stamps. Upon hearing of the Stamp Act Congress, Grenville and Parliament backed down. Grenville fell from power, and the new leaders repealed the Stamp Act. However, in 1767 Parliament decided to reassert itself and imposed taxes on tea. Protests followed this action. The Parliament reacted by sending troops to the American colonies. By 1770 there were 9,000 soldiers quartered in the thirteen colonies. Also in 1770, the "Sons of Liberty" and the "Daughters of Liberty"—protest groups of colonists—led protests against the British Parliament that they felt was trying to take away their rights and their freedom.

The British continued their taxation strategy by imposing the Townsend Duties in 1770. A group of colonists had gathered on Boston Common to protest the British Parliament's actions. British soldiers fired upon them and four colonists were killed, including an African American called Crispus Attucks. This skirmish is known as the Boston Massacre.

In 1773, a group of Boston colonists dressed as Mohawk Indians boarded a ship in Boston Harbor and threw all of the tea it was carrying into the harbor. In Edenton, North Carolina, fifty-one women led by Penelope Barker carried out a similar action. The British government had sent this tea to the American colonies to sell at discounted prices. As a result of these actions, the British Parliament passed the Coercive Acts of 1774 to punish the colony of Massachusetts. At the urging of Samuel Adams, a leader in Massachusetts, Committees of Correspondence formed among the colonists to protest these actions and to help spread the news more quickly throughout the colonies. Delegates were sent to Philadelphia where the First Continental Congress had formed. The delegates tried very hard to find some kind of solution to the Coercive Acts but came up empty.

As the Continental Congress was coming to an end, the colony of Massachusetts decided to train its militia members to become Minutemen, or fighters ready to take action in minutes. In April 1775, British General Thomas Gage had heard reports that a group of colonists, called Patriots, had stored weapons in nearby Concord and that two important leaders of the Sons of Liberty, Samuel Adams and John Hancock, were staying in the town of Lexington. He sent 700 British soldiers to arrest the Patriots and confiscate the weapons. When the British soldiers arrived in Lexington, the Minutemen were waiting for them. In an exchange of fire on April 19, 1775, eight Minutemen were killed and some others were wounded. The British then marched on to Concord to get the weapons. However, the Minutemen had been warned and had moved the weapons. When the British arrived at Concord, they could not locate any weapons. They then marched back to Boston. The Minutemen ambushed the British as they went along and some seventy-three soldiers died while there were ninety-three casualties among the Minutemen. Lexington and Concord marked the beginning of the armed struggle between Britain and its American colonies.

Second Continental Congress

In 1775, a second Continental Congress was set up because violence had broken out between the British and the colonists at Concord and Lexington. This Congress published a statement titled *A Declaration of the Causes and Necessities of Taking Up Arms*. This statement was not intended as a declaration of independence but rather expressed the feelings of the delegates that the British government was not treating them as British citizens. An Olive Branch Petition had been sent to King George III asking him to repeal all of the unfair laws that were causing problems between Britain and its American colonists. While King George III contemplated what to do, the colonists made preparations for war.

The delegates to the Second Continental Congress asked all colonies to send men to Massachusetts to form a Continental army. It appointed George Washington as the commander of this new army. Each colony also contributed money for the support of the new army. The army consisted of 14,500 men. Some of these men had flintlock muskets and others had come with spears and axes. These soldiers had no uniforms but were experienced fighters who had fought frontier wars. Their way of fighting was similar to that of Native Americans. In small groups they would hide, fire, and run. The British army consisted of professional soldiers with good training and new weapons. The British also hired mercenaries to help them, like the German Hessians and American Indians.

CONTENT AREA TWENTY-TWO: THE WAR FOR INDEPENDENCE

Although the American colonists were engaging the British in skirmishes, they still hoped for a fair settlement whereby they would still remain British subjects. However, several events caused many colonists to feel that only full independence would satisfy them.

While in England, Benjamin Franklin met John Paine, a tax collector who had lost his job, and advised him to come to the American colonies. Paine followed the advice and in January 1776 published a pamphlet entitled *Common Sense,* which urged the colonists to revolt against the British and win their independence. Then on June 7, 1776, a delegate from Virginia, Richard Henry Lee, gave a speech in which he declared that the colonies should be independent and that the colonies no longer owed any allegiance to Britain or its king.

Still, some of the colonies hoped for a peaceful and just solution before declaring their independence. While the delegates to the Second Continental Congress decided to wait for a month before taking formal action to declare the colonies independence from Britain, a committee was formed to write a declaration. Thomas Jefferson, Benjamin Franklin, John Adams, Roger Sherman, and Robert R. Livingston served on this committee. However, it was Thomas Jefferson who did most of the writing. He divided the Declaration of Independence into four parts:

Part 1. Listed the reasons behind the declaration.

Part 2. Jefferson listed the colonists' beliefs about government.

Part 3. Discussed the colonists' grievances and unfair treatment of them by the British government.

Part 4. He stated all the reasons as to why the colonies ought to be free.

The Declaration of Independence was approved by the Congress on July 4, 1776, and the American colonists had declared their independence.

What Groups Were Involved in the Revolutionary War?

There were groups of colonists who remained neutral during the conflict. There were some who remained loyal to the British crown. The rest supported the independence movement (see Table 9.4).

TABLE 9.4   Groups Involved in the Revolutionary War

CHURCH GROUPS	• Anglican Church—members in the northern and middle colonies remained loyal to King George III while members in the southern colonies supported independence. • Congregationalists—made up the largest group in the colonies and supported independence. • Presbyterians and Baptists in the northern colonies supported independence while many in the south remained Loyalists.	• The Quakers, or the Society of Friends, was one group that refused to participate. They believed in a peaceful resolution of the conflict.
WOMEN	• Some women helped by making goods that had been boycotted. • Some formed groups to raise money for the cause. • Some decided not to get married to any man who had not proved himself a patriot. • Some remained Loyalist.	Other women took part in the fighting for independence: 1. Phillis Wheatley wrote poems in support of independence. 2. Mercy Ottis Warren wrote a play to support the Patriots. 3. Abigail Adams urged her husband to give women a voice. 4. Mary Ludwig Hays took over firing a cannon during the Battle of Monmouth after her husband was killed. 5. Mary Slocumb fought at the Battle of Moores Creek Bridge.
NATIVE AMERICANS	• Most Indians stayed out of the fighting. • Indians in the Ohio Valley helped the British. • Some of the Iroquois in the Hudson River area fought with the Patriots.	• Some Indians saw themselves as separate from both sides of the conflict and decided not to participate.
AFRICAN AMERICANS	• Some free African Americans, like Peter Salem, fought with the Patriots. • About 5000 African Americans fought with the Continental army.	• Some enslaved African Americans joined the Patriots after they were promised freedom. • Other enslaved African Americans were enticed to the British side and formed the Ethiopian Regiment.

Foreign Governments Help the Patriots

Some European countries and individuals who did not like the British decided to help the American colonists. These included:

1. Casimir Pulasky and Thaddeus Kosciuszko, Polish officers.
2. Marquis de Lafayette, a young French noble.
3. Johann de Kalb and Friedrich von Steuben, German soldiers.
4. The French government sent ships, weapons, and soldiers to help the colonists.
5. Jorge Farragut, a Spaniard by birth, fought in both our nation's army and navy.

The War Ends

In 1777, General John Burgoyne with 5,000 soldiers marched south from Canada hoping to divide the colonies into two. However, at the Battle of Saratoga, General Horatio Gates was able to rout the British with his Continental army.

In December 1777, George Washington had set up headquarters at Valley Forge, Pennsylvania. Thousands of his men were without boots, while others were sick and some died. There was also not enough food to feed the soldiers properly. With the help of Friedrich von Steuben, the soldiers at Valley Forge were changed into a well-disciplined unit ready to fight once the winter was over. Many Patriots such as John Paul Jones (the military hero), Francis Marion (the Swamp Fox), George Rogers Clark, and many others fought and won battles for the American colonies.

In 1780, the British army invaded and captured Charleston, South Carolina. From there they traveled northward into North Carolina and eventually Virginia. In 1781, the British army under General Charles Cornwallis had set up headquarters at Yorktown, Virginia. Here the British were engaged by the Continental army with the help of the French. The French blocked Chesapeake Bay so that the British fleet could not send supplies to Cornwallis. On October 19, 1781, the British army surrendered to George Washington and his army. It was not until September 3, 1783, that the Treaty of Paris was signed and the American colonies were recognized as free and independent.

The American Revolutionary War was a significant influence on Latin American countries who were under the control primarily of Spain and to a lesser degree Portugal. The Revolutionary War inspired Mexicans, for example, to declare their independence from Spain, beginning with the uprising in 1810 led by a Mexican priest, Miguel Hidalgo. It took eleven more years for Mexico to win its independence.

CONTENT AREA TWENTY-THREE: THE ARTICLES OF CONFEDERATION AND THE U.S. CONSTITUTION

TABLE 9.5 Comparison Chart

	ARTICLES OF CONFEDERATION	U.S. CONSTITUTION
EXECUTIVE	• Did not have an executive.	• The president became the chief executive with a cabinet of advisers.
LEGISLATIVE	• The Continental Congress was created to carry out legislative and executive matters: 1. Congress did not have the power to tax. 2. Congress did not have the power to create a national army. 3. Congress could not regulate foreign or interstate commerce. 4. Each state had one vote in Congress. 5. Nine out of 13 votes were required to pass laws.	• Congress was created with two houses: 1. House of Representatives with a membership of 435. Representation was based on a state's population. 2. Senate with a membership of 100. Representation was based on equal representation—2 senators from each state.
JUDICIAL	• There was no judicial branch. • Judicial functions were left to each state.	• A judicial branch was created: 1. The Supreme Court became the highest court with 9 justices. 2. Created 12 federal courts of appeals. 3. Created 90 federal district courts.

The Articles of Confederation were written as early as 1776 but were not approved until 1781. The Articles of Confederation gave our country its first constitution. It was, however, a weak government from the very start. The central government depended on the states good will to function properly. Each state had its own militia and its allegiance was to that state. Each state also printed its own money, which might or might not be recognized by the other states. There was no executive branch to enforce any of the laws passes by the congress. Individual states created their own constitutions; however, these constitutions were not to the liking of everyone. It was evident in the 1780s that the way our country was functioning was not right. Something had to be done because the conditions were chaotic. Many influential men like George Washington, Benjamin Franklin, James Madison, Thomas Jefferson, Alexander Hamilton, military officers, lawyers, merchants, and others felt the need to establish a strong central government in order to strengthen our country. These men came to be called Nationalists. They decided to meet in Philadelphia, Pennsylvania, in 1786 to discuss ways to strengthen our nation. However, only twelve delegates showed up from five states. So, it was decided to meet again in the summer of 1787.

Meanwhile the state of Massachusetts felt it necessary to impose a heavy direct tax on its citizens in order to help pay its debts. This caused an uprising known as Shay's Rebellion. People refused to pay their taxes and drove off the tax collectors who came after them. Petitions to the state courts were thrown out, and the rebels closed those courts down. This rebellion convinced people in other states that there was a need for change in the structure of our government. In 1787, delegates started flowing in to Philadelphia. At first their primary mission was to strengthen the Articles of Confederation. However, as the discussions continued, the delegates split into two factions, one that favored strengthening the Articles and those who felt that they had to start reinventing the national government from scratch.

James Madison and some of the others who wanted to make over the government proposed what is called the Virginia Plan by which:

1. The national congress would be bicameral (have two houses).
2. Representation in both houses would be based on a state's population. This meant that the larger states would have more representatives in both houses.
3. The new government would have an executive and judicial branch.
4. The new government would have the right to tax its citizens.
5. The new government would have veto power over the states.

Other delegates to this convention, which came to be known as the Constitutional Convention of 1787, feared some of the aspects of the Virginia Plan. They instead came up with their own New Jersey Plan by which:

1. Congress would be given the right to tax.
2. The national government would have an executive and a judicial branch.
3. The Congress would be unilateral (one house) and each state would have one vote.
4. This plan would leave most of the power to the states.

The convention became deadlocked over the two plans. However, the delegates persevered and on July 16, 1787, they arrived at a compromise known as the Great Compromise. It called for:

1. The legislative branch was to be bicameral (two houses) per the Virginia Plan.
2. The House of Representatives would have membership based upon the population of each state, and the Senate would have equal representation—two—from each state. Representatives would be elected every two years, and senators would be elected every six

years. Congress as a whole was given the power to coin new money, declare war, provide for an army and navy, regulate commerce, and carry out relations with other countries.

3. Congress was not given the right to veto state legislation.

4. A three-fifths compromise was reached in regard to the enslaved people in the south. African Americans and Indians were excluded from participating in government.

5. The new constitution created a checks and balances, or separation of powers, system whereby each branch of the national, or federal government, would check each other's powers so that none of them became too powerful.

6. The president's term of office was established at four years, but he could be reelected as many times as the voters approved.

7. The president would be elected by the lectors of the Electoral College. This was an indirect way of electing the president by having the voters vote for electors from each state who would get together to vote and elect a new president.

8. The judicial branch would be made up of nine justices with one of them selected to be the chief justice. Justices would be appointed by the president with the consent of the senate. Justices would hold their offices for life during good behavior.

Not all of the delegates were in support of the Constitution. However, most Nationalists like George Washington, James Madison, Alexander Hamilton, Benjamin Franklin, and others decided to support the Constitution—they came to be called Federalists. The Federalists, especially Alexander Hamilton, came to believe in a loose rather than a strict interpretation of the Constitution because it would allow the federal government to intervene in such areas as the economy. Those who were against the Constitution came to be called Anti-Federalists. These two opposing groups had to convince the voters to take the position of being for or against the Constitution. In order for the Articles of Confederation to be removed and the Constitution to replace them, nine states had to ratify or approve the Constitution.

By 1790, all thirteen states had ratified the Constitution. The Constitution was approved after the Federalists agreed to some changes and the addition of a Bill of Rights. The Bill of Rights, or first ten amendments to the Constitution, was approved in December of 1791.

When elections were held in the fall of 1788, most of the candidates elected were Federalists. George Washington was elected as the first president of the United States, and John Adams was elected the vice president. Washington was inaugurated in New York City on April 30, 1789. As soon as he took over the government, Washington began to appoint the members of his cabinet. He chose Thomas Jefferson, the author of the Declaration of Independence, as his secretary of state. He chose Alexander Hamilton as his secretary of the treasury. Henry Knox was selected as secretary of war and Edmund Randolph as attorney general.

In 1790, the United States got its official capital by the passage of the Residence Act of that year. It designated a ten-square-mile piece of land on the Potomac River, named the District of Columbia, as the site of the new capital. An African American inventor and mathematician, Benjamin Banneker, was commissioned to survey the area. A Frenchman, Charles L'Enfant, was the artist and architect who developed the city's plan. The government was now in place and the Constitution of the United States empowered it to deal with its problems.

CONTENT AREA TWENTY-FOUR: PERIOD 1789–1830

George Washington became president of the United States in 1789 and served two terms. He was elected by the electoral college in both cases. However, by 1796 political parties had emerged. Each party provided a list of its candidates for president and vice president, and the

TABLE 9.6

PRESIDENT	INTERNAL AND EXTERNAL PROBLEMS	OTHER ISSUES
George Washington (1789–1797)	• Chose Jefferson as secretary of state. • Chose Hamilton as secretary of the treasury. • Chose Henry Knox as the secretary of war. • Chose Edmund Randolph to be his legal adviser. • Internal problems began between Jefferson and Hamilton. • Jefferson believed in states rights and Hamilton believed in a strong central government; Jefferson's followers became known as anti-Federalists and Hamilton's followers became known as Federalists. • Jefferson saw a nation of farmers and Hamilton saw a nation of cities.	• A banking system was set up under the guidance of Hamilton. • Printing and coining of money was begun. • Jefferson, Hamilton, Knox, and Randolph made up the first Cabinet. • Hamilton and his followers started the Federalist Party, which included John Adams, John Jay, and Henry Knox. • Jefferson's followers started Democratic–Republican Party, which included George Clinton.
John Adams (1797–1801)	• Won the election by 4 electoral votes over Jefferson. • Jefferson became the vice president.	• Adams was the first president to occupy the White House in Washington, D.C.
Thomas Jefferson (1801–1809)	• Engineered the purchase of the Louisiana Territory in 1803 from Napoleon Bonaparte. • Sent Lewis and Clark to explore the Louisiana Purchase. • Lewis and Clark were helped by a Native American guide named Sacagawea. • Zebulon Pike was also commissioned to explore the western part of the Louisiana Purchase. • Pike's exploration made settlers want to move to the Northwest Territory but Native Americans became violent. • The Shawnee chief, Tecumseh, warned settlers to stay away.	• Writer of the Declaration of Independence. • Robert Fulton's steamboat, the *Clermont,* sailed up the Hudson River.
James Madison (1809–1817)	• Shawnees had formed a confederation to fight Americans and the British gave them guns. • The Shawnees were defeated by the Governor of the Indiana Territory, William Henry Harrison, in the Battle of Tippecanoe in 1811. • Americans blamed the British for the trouble with the Native Americans. • The War of 1812 began. Captain Oliver Hazard Perry defeated the British fleet on Lake Erie in September 10, 1813. • The British burned Washington, D.C., in August 1814. • General Andrew Jackson won an astounding victory over the British in December of 1814 in the Battle of New Orleans.	• The British impressed American sailors into service in their navy. • William Henry Harrison led a force of Americans into Canada and defeated the British and their Native American allies in the Battle of Thames on October 5, 1813. Tecumseh died during this battle. • The War of 1812 made Americans very proud of themselves for being able to stand up to the greatest power on earth. • Francis Scott Key wrote the poem "The Star-Spangled Banner" while watching the attack on Baltimore during the War of 1812. This poem became our national anthem. • Erie Canal project was begun.
James Monroe (1817–1825)	• Ushered in the Era of Good Feelings for Americans who felt a wave of patriotism. • Annexed West and East Florida from Spain. • He announced the Monroe Doctrine on December 2, 1823, which warned other nations to stay out of the affairs of the western hemisphere.	• A border between the U.S. and Canada was set by President Monroe and the British.

TABLE 9.6 Continued

PRESIDENT	INTERNAL AND EXTERNAL PROBLEMS	OTHER ISSUES
John Quincy Adams (1825–1829)	• Jeffersonian Republican • Son of Abigail and John Adams • Negotiated the Adams–Onis Treaty with Spain in 1819 by which Florida became part of the U.S. • Largely wrote the Monroe Doctrine.	• Adams won the election of 1824, even though he had fewer popular votes than Andrew Jackson. This came about because the election was thrown into the House of Representatives because no candidate had enough electoral votes. The House of Representatives voted to elect Adams.
Andrew Jackson (1829–1837)	• Seventh President. • U.S. made up of 24 states. • First president to come from the frontier. • Was thought of as a "common man." • Sectionalism was a problem in 1828. • John C. Calhoun, the vice president, resigned over the issue of sectionalism and states' rights. • Indian Removal Act of 1830 called for the removal of all Native Americans from east of the Mississippi to west of the Mississippi. • Although Supreme Court Chief Justice John Marshall ruled that Cherokees should remain in their lands and be protected, President Jackson sent in the soldiers to have them removed to the west. This journey to the Indian Territory, in 1838, has been called the Trail of Tears because of the Native Americans' suffering. • Jackson fought against the Bank of the U.S. In the Supreme Court case of *McCulloch v. Maryland,* John Marshall ruled that Congress had the right to create the bank and states had no right to tax the national bank. Marshall justified his ruling by using Article I, Section 8 of the Constitution, which stated that Congress has the right "to make all laws necessary and proper." • President Jackson, however, vetoed the rechartering of the bank, which forced it to close its doors in 1836. • Jackson was seen as a strong and stubborn man who embodied the spirit of the frontier.	• All white American men could vote by this time. Previously it had been only white men who owned property. This helped Jackson win the election. • Jackson believed that the national government should allow the states to take care of economic development. • Henry Clay, speaker of the House of Representatives, supported an American System whereby the federal government would be involved in helping the states to build roads, canals, colleges and universities, etc. • The followers of Jackson changed their party's name from Democrat–Republicans to Democrats. • South Carolina passed the Nullification Act in 1832 in order to void the Tariff of 1828 passed by Congress. Jackson did not go along with this and South Carolina threatened to secede from the Union. Jackson asked Congress to pass the Force Bill of 1833, which forced South Carolina to collect the tariff taxes. Since Congress reduced some of the tariff duties, South Carolina voided the Nullification Act.
Martin Van Buren (1837–1841)	• Severe depression followed Jackson's eight years in office. • Van Buren was not strong like Jackson. • The Panic of 1837, brought about because of the closure of the Bank of the United States, caused many people to lose their jobs and many lived in poverty. • The depression was still going on during the election of 1840 and Van Buren lost.	

electors had to vote on those candidates listed. In today's elections things have changed. Each political party now chooses its candidates through primary elections held by each at different times every four years. The winners from each party are then nominated to be their party's candidate for president.

The Louisiana Purchase

The western boundary of the United States in 1783 was the Mississippi River. The American frontier was the land between the Appalachian Mountains and the Mississippi River. The settlement of this frontier allowed the United States to expand westward. Pioneers like Daniel Boone led the way to westward expansion. Boone and a friend named John Finley discovered the Cumberland Pass that led them over the Appalachian Mountains into what is now called Kentucky. Two major Indian groups, the Cherokee and the Shawnees, called Kentucky their home. They captured Daniel Boone a number of times and let him go with the warning for him not to come back to Kentucky. However, Boone kept going back. His exploits and the kind of land he had explored caused many Americans to want to move there. Boone advertised Kentucky as a beautiful and bountiful land where thousands of buffalo roamed. As early as 1775, Boone had led a group of settlers through the Cumberland Pass and into Kentucky. They began cutting down trees and brush in order for wagons to pass. This became the Wilderness Road used by pioneers.

When pioneers reached the Mississippi River, they found that they could go no further because the land on the west side of the river belonged to Spain. However, when Thomas Jefferson became president in 1801, he dreamed about the United States being able to expand all the way to the Pacific Ocean. So, when he heard that Spain had given the area called Louisiana back to the French, he sent representatives to Napoleon Bonaparte offering to buy the area for $10 million. Bonaparte was hard pressed by war at home and in the colonies in the Caribbean, so he made a counteroffer to Jefferson. He offered the whole of Louisiana for $15 million. On April 30, 1803, an agreement was reached and the Louisiana Purchase became a U.S. territory.

Jefferson immediately commissioned Meriwether Lewis and William Clark to take an expedition into this new territory and to make a report of their findings. Lewis and Clark gathered a group of thirty men and in 1804 left St. Louis and traveled up the Missouri River. Lewis and Clark were befriended by a Shoshone woman named Sacagawea. She was able to act as an interpreter for them and served as their guide. She got her brother, Cameahwait, to supply the explorers with horses.

Lewis and Clark traveled down the Snake and Columbia rivers all the way to the Pacific Ocean. The expedition, called the Corps of Discovery, arrived back in St. Louis in September of 1806 bringing with them maps, drawings, seeds, birds, other animals, and reports about the vast expanse of land. The maps, showing important passes through the mountains, helped pioneers to later find their way to the Pacific Ocean.

Another explorer, Zebulon Pike, left on his expedition in 1806 to explore the southwestern portion of the Louisiana Purchase. Pike's expedition followed the Arkansas River all the way to present-day Kansas where he and his men were able to observe the prairie full of thousands of buffalo. Traveling further westward, Pike came upon one of the peaks of the Rocky Mountains, which he described as "blue mountain." Today that peak is known as Pike's Peak in his honor. Finally, the expedition ended up on the northern section of the Rio Grande where Pike and his men were taken prisoner by Spanish soldiers. They had trespassed onto Spanish territory. After spending a short time in jail, the governor in Santa Fe allowed Pike to leave. In leaving, Pike noted the trail to follow to get back to Santa Fe, which he described as being in dire need of manufactured goods. After the news got around, American traders headed for Santa Fe to sell their goods.

The War of 1812

Many settlers felt the urge to move westward upon hearing of the many stories that were told by the Pike and Lewis and Clark expeditions. However, Native Americans did not want the settlers to come and settle on their lands. Trouble began in the Northwest where the British still had a lot of influence with the Native Americans. The British sold rifles to Indians like the Shawnee. Their leader Tecumseh and his brother Tenskwatawa, otherwise known as the Prophet, were trying to unite the tribes to fight the incursion of U.S. settlers into their lands. Tecumseh tried to organize the tribes of Kentucky and Tennessee into a confederation in 1811. Upon hearing this information, the governor of the Indiana Territory, William Harrison, decided to move 1,000 soldiers near the Shawnee town called Prophetstown. The Prophet feared that the soldiers were about to attack and urged the Indians to attack first in what is called the Battle of Tippecanoe on November 7, 1811. The battle was inconclusive but Prophetstown was destroyed and the Native Americans went on a rampage attacking settlers. U.S. settlers were enraged and blamed the British. They decided that the United States should attack Canada and drive the British from all of North America. All sections of the United States were eager to attack the British because on the high seas the British navy boarded U.S. ships and impressed (forced), many sailors into the service of the British ships.

In June 1812, war was declared by the Congress. On September 10, 1813, the U.S. Captain Oliver Hazard Perry engaged the British on Lake Erie and defeated them.

William Harrison led 3,500 soldiers on a raid into Canada. On October 5, 1813, Harrison's forces defeated the British at the Battle of the Thames. The Indian leader Tecumseh was among the dead, since Native Americans fought on the side of the British. In August 1814, the British retaliated by invading Washington, D.C., setting fire to the White House and other important government buildings.

The final battle was fought at New Orleans where Andrew Jackson put up a heavy resistance. The British with 5,000 soldiers were unable to defeat Jackson's army. What either side did not know was that the British and the U.S. settlers had signed a treaty in Europe two weeks earlier on December 24, 1814, and the Battle of New Orleans wasn't necessary. However, this battle made Americans proud of themselves at being able to stand up to such a great power as Britain. It was also during this time when the British were attacking Baltimore that Francis Scott Key wrote his famed "Star Spangled Banner." The end result was that President James Madison was able to negotiate a new border for the United States, got Spain to allow west Florida to be annexed by the United States, and to give up east Florida to the United States. The War of 1812 allowed the United States to feel pride and at the same time to expand and secure its borders from Spain, Britain, and France.

The Missouri Compromise

As the nation began to spread westward, the issue of slavery gained prominence. When the Missouri Territory, which was part of the Louisiana Purchase, asked to become a state in 1919, many settlers were opposed to allowing slavery. At the same time, Maine had petitioned to become a state as well. Henry Clay, a congressman from Kentucky, offered a compromise to this situation. He proposed that Missouri come into the Union as a slave state and Maine as a free state. The remainder of the territories would be considered as they applied for statehood. This compromise worked well for almost thirty years.

The Monroe Doctrine

In 1823, President James Monroe decided to further strengthen the United States against foreign powers by proclaiming the Monroe Doctrine, which warned ambitious nations from trying to expand their influence and power in the Americas. This doctrine has been used a number of times since.

The Industrial Revolution

The economy of the United States was growing steadily even before the War of 1812. However, after the war, the economy took off. Where goods were made primarily by hand before, now machines were taking over mass producing goods for the country. This Industrial Revolution changed the way people thought, the way they lived, and the way they did things in general.

A spinning machine invented in England was carefully studied and memorized by Samuel Slater, a young factory worker who decided to come to the United States in 1789. The spinning machine changed the way textile factories produced cloth. This new technology was known only in Great Britain, and the British government kept people from taking the technology outside of its borders. Slater, however, was successful in taking the technology with him by memorizing it. When he arrived in the United States, Slater designed and made the first spinning machine in America for a textile mill in Rhode Island owned by Moses Brown. The Industrial Revolution was thus begun in the United States.

Eli Whitney was another American inventor who came up with the idea of mass producing identical parts. That way, parts did not have to be done one by one by hand. The invention of interchangeable parts for manufacturing goods and machines allowed for specialization by workers who would make only part of a machine or a piece of clothing while others made the other parts. This new approach to making goods caused prices of goods to drop.

Francis Cabot Lowell was able to follow the same method that Slater did by visiting Britain and memorizing the machines he observed. Between 1810 and 1812, he was able to build his own factory where he combined spinning, dyeing, and weaving under one roof.

Men, women, and children were hired to work in these factories. More and more factories were built, and new arrivals to the United States were able to find jobs in them. Factories were mass-producing goods but had a difficult time transporting them to markets. At the same time western farmers could not take their produce to markets quick enough either. The New York legislature in 1817 was convinced of the need, and the Erie Canal project was started. When the canal was finished in 1825, it opened the way for New York City to become the leading trade city in the nation.

The Congress of the United States also saw the need for better transportation routes and decided to fund the building of the National Road, which was to run from the Atlantic coast to Ohio. The National Road was completed in 1841 and joined the eastern and western United States.

At the same time that the National Road and the Erie Canal were being built, a man by the name of Robert Fulton brought out his steamboat, the *Clermont*, in 1807. Another, the *New Orleans*, was built in 1811. Ten years later, there were steamboats sailing along the many lakes and rivers of our nation.

In 1830, Peter Cooper built the first locomotive and named it the *Tom Thumb*. The building of railroads accelerated after 1830 and helped to move manufactured goods from the factories quicker and in greater quantities.

Jacksonian Democracy

Andrew Jackson became the seventh president on March 4, 1829. He was the first president who was not wealthy, and he was also the first president to have been raised on the frontier. He distinguished himself in the army and became a war hero during the War of 1812 against the British. He also had the reputation of being very tough and hard as a hickory tree. He was nicknamed Old Hickory by his soldiers. People also thought of him as one of them, a common man, and therefore worthy of their votes. While president, he fought for the common people who voted for him. He voted against the establishment of a national bank because he felt that it would only serve the best interests of the wealthy. Jackson's presidency was marked with serious divisions between himself and his vice president, John C. Calhoun of South Carolina. Calhoun was an advocate for states' rights whereas Jackson believed in the preservation of the Union. Calhoun decided to resign his office over the issue of states' rights.

During 1830s, the Congress decided to remove some Indian tribes and transport them to reservations in Oklahoma. Some tribes, like the Seminoles, fought the idea of moving, but in the end many were killed and forced to move anyway. The Cherokees in the Southeast tried to fight their eviction from their lands by going to court. John Marshall, the Supreme Court's

Chief Justice, issued a ruling that stated that the Cherokees should remain in their lands and be protected. However, President Jackson moved them by force in 1838 to Oklahoma, known as the Indian Territory. The Cherokees had to march some 800 miles to their new homes. Some 4,000 of them never made it. This journey has been called "The Trail of Tears."

U.S. settlers had always dreamed about moving the country's border all the way to the Pacific Ocean. They called this their Manifest Destiny. It was not surprising, then, that settlers spread all over the continent tried to colonize and settle as many areas as were open to them. In 1820, Moses Austin went to Texas and asked for permission to remain there. He died before permission could be granted. However, his son Stephen F. Austin went ahead with his father's plan and settled in southeastern Texas. He brought many settlers to this area once Mexico became independent from Spain in 1821. When the Mexican government saw the great numbers of U.S. settlers coming to Texas, they became fearful and decided to stop any more from coming. The Mexican government passed laws in 1830 preventing any more settlers from coming and imposing more taxes on those who had already settled there.

In 1834, General Antonio Lopez Santa Anna became dictator in Mexico. He sent his soldiers into Texas to enforce the new Mexican laws. This new development angered the U.S. settlers, and they decided to fight. In February 1836, General Santa Anna moved his army close to the small town of San Antonio. A number of U.S. settlers had taken shelter inside the Alamo, an old Spanish mission. Among them were Davy Crockett (the frontiersman), James Bowie, and William B. Travis. After thirteen days of siege and fighting, Santa Anna breached the walls on March 6, 1836, and killed 189 American Texans. He only spared the lives of women and children.

Texas leaders, meanwhile, had declared the independence of Texas and had elected David G. Burnett as their president with Sam Houston as the commander of the Texas army on March 2, 1836. On April 21, 1836, Sam Houston's forces fought with Santa Anna's at the Battle of San Jacinto. Sam Houston was victorious and even captured Santa Anna. Santa Anna was set free after he agreed to allow Texas to be free. Sam Houston went on to become president of the Texas republic twice before its admittance to the Union in 1845.

Oregon, Utah, and War with Mexico

Missionaries had made their way to Oregon and Utah as early as 1834. They had sent letters back east describing the beauty of the land, its mountains, and its valleys. American settlers decided to move to this part of the continent beginning in 1842. The route the settlers used to get to Oregon became known as the Oregon Trail. It took almost six months for the settlers to arrive at the Willamette Valley in Oregon. In 1846, President James K. Polk decided that he needed to have a clearcut boundary between that part of the Oregon Country that U.S. settlers began calling their homes and the part that belonged to the British. A treaty was agreed to setting the boundary at the 49th parallel.

In 1847, a group of Mormons under the leadership of Brigham Young decided to settle in the Great Salt Lake valley where they felt safe from other settlers due to their religious practices and beliefs. They originally tried to settle in Illinois but they had met with hostility because of their practice of multiple marriages. Their leader and prophet Joseph Smith was killed there in 1844. Once Young and his Mormons settled in their new homes, they worked hard and made the desert blossom. The area settled by the Mormons was called the Utah Territory, and Young became its first governor. Later it became a state of the United States.

In 1846, meanwhile, the Mexican army had crossed the Rio Grande and attacked a U.S. patrol, killing sixteen soldiers. This angered the United States, who sent an invading force under General Winfield Scott to attack Mexico. This force arrived in Mexico by sea landing in the city of Veracruz. After a year's fighting, the two sides signed the Treaty of Guadalupe Hidalgo in 1848. Under the terms, the United States was able to purchase California, Utah, Nevada, and parts of New Mexico, Wyoming, Arizona, and Colorado for $15 million. Later on in 1853, the United States also made the Gadsden Purchase, thereby expanding U.S. territory to its present size with a total of forty-eight states. It was also during this time, 1848, that gold was discovered in California, causing that territory to swell with new settlers.

CONTENT AREA TWENTY-FIVE: CALIFORNIA— BEFORE AND AFTER THE GOLD RUSH

The expansion of the United States to include territories that extended to the shores of the Pacific Ocean caused some consternation or concern for many in our country. Both the South and the North looked upon this new area as an opportunity to expand their economic interests. Gold discovered in California and huge silver deposits in Nevada invited the interests of both sections of our country because in the vent of hostilities wealth was a necessary resource. Events prior to the discovery of gold and after the Gold Rush are very important to the understanding of our country's history and growth.

The Acquisition and Settling of California

In 1519, the conquistador known as Hernando Cortes conquered the mighty Aztecs of Mexico and established New Spain. After establishing Spain's claim to New Spain, Cortes sought to find the Strait of Anian, a waterway that was said to connect the Atlantic and Pacific oceans. This strait would have made it possible for the Spanish to take a shortcut to Asia. Cortes, therefore, sent an expedition north from Mexico's west coast in search for the Strait of Anian. In 1535, he and some of his men sailed north along the coast of Baja California. He claimed this area for Spain. He was not able to find the Strait of Anian because he returned to Spain.

The first European explorer to explore the area of present-day California in detail was Juan Rodriguez Cabrillo, another Spanish explorer, who in 1542 discovered San Diego Bay. Cabrillo had set sail from the Mexican port of Navidad with the purpose of exploring Alta, which means high or upper, California. Cabrillo did make contact with the Chumash Indians on San Miguel Island. While there he fell and hurt himself. He sailed north even farther but was forced to return to San Miguel Island because of his injury and there he died.

In the 1560s, Spain found it necessary to try to explore California for several reasons. First, the Spanish needed a good port in order to anchor its galleons returning from Asia and the Philippines. The Spanish sailors made use of the ocean currents and winds in order to steer the galleons to Alta California instead of Mexico. Here they would rest and be able to continue their trip to Mexico. While here the sailors replenished their water, made needed repairs to the galleons, and gathered a fresh supply of food. Secondly, English pirates, like Francis Drake, attacked many of the Spanish galleons, which carried gold and silver. In 1577, Francis Drake had sailed from England and went around the Strait of Magellan at the tip of South America in order to reach the west coast and eventually California. While here he attacked successfully several Spanish galleons and took large quantities of gold. This was shocking to the Spanish because no other nation had sailed this side of the Pacific Ocean. They felt the need to make their claim to the land along the west coast, including Alta California. They, therefore, sent Sebastian Vizcaino on an expedition to map the coast of Alta California in 1602. Vizcaino was successful in his mapping activity and sailed into Monterey Bay. He recommended this bay as being a good harbor for Spanish galleons. However, the Spanish for the next 165 years lost interest in Alta California because settlers did not want to go that far away from Mexico City and also because there were physical barriers to be overcome.

During the 1760s King Carlos III found out that the Russians had begun to explore the Pacific Northwest. The Russians were hunting sea otters for their furs and moved along the coast as the sea otter herds moved. They needed to set up camps in order to rest and replenish their food supply. One of the camps they set up was Fort Ross just north of present-day San Francisco. This move by the Russians raised King Carlos's interest in claiming all of Alta California for Spain. He, therefore, ordered that the Spanish to travel to Alta California and set up religious settlements called missions. In this way people besides the religious fathers would be attracted to this new land and come to settle.

The Mission Period: 1769–1823. Following King Carlos's orders, Jose de Galvez as governor of New Spain decided to send three expeditions to Alta California. One of these expeditions was by sea and the other two by land. Governor Galvez chose Gaspar de Portola to lead one of the land expeditions while the other was led by Captain Fernando Rivera and Lieutenant Pedro Fages. They traveled north to Alta California in 1769. Accompanying Portola's expedition was Junipero Serra, a Franciscan priest who wanted very much to Christianize the Indians. Captain Rivera and Lieutenant Fages arrived in what today is San Diego in May of 1769 while Captain Portola and Father Serra arrived in July. It was father Serra who erected a large cross to celebrate their arrival and also to mark the spot where the first mission would be built. Father Serra named this first mission San Diego de Alcala. This mission, like all the others built later, had a central patio with a fountain at the center and was surrounded by other buildings and protected by a double gate. Some of the buildings and other special areas included those buildings required by the priests, laborers, shops, storehouses, a water supply, and a cemetery. The church was the main building and was built to be sturdy and to last a long time. The padres managed the mission, which became like a mini-kingdom.

Portola, meanwhile, traveled on to look for Monterey Bay. However, his journey proved to be difficult and he ran out of food. He returned to San Diego and did not attempt to look for Monterey Bay until the following spring. This time he found Monterey Bay.

Another Spaniard, Juan Bautista, heard of Captain Portola's journey and difficulty in getting to Monterey, so he decided to lead a group of thirty families through the Sonoran Desert area to San Diego and then on to Monterey. The group reached Monterey in March of 1776. However, the journey proved to be very difficult and the physical barriers too overwhelming, so for a long period of time supplies and people had to come to San Diego and California by ship from Mexico.

When Captain Portola made his second trip to find Monterey Bay, Father Serra followed him a short time later. Father Serra set up the second mission, which he called Mission San Carlos Borromeo de Carmelo. Captain Portola claimed the land for Spain and built a presidio nearby where the soldiers would be housed. Father Serra's plan was to attract the Native Americans to come to the mission where he would teach them to farm the land around the mission and also to learn other kinds of crafts. These skills would allow the Indians to be self-sufficient. When more missionaries came to the missions founded by Father Serra, they would help the Indians with their training and education in the Christian religion. The Indians were very curious and came to the missions. They adopted the Spanish offerings of clothing and European-style foods, helped the padres or fathers to build churches and other mission buildings, they helped to plow the land and harvest the crops, and they made it possible for the missions to be self-sustaining. Father Serra's plan was to build a series of missions following the coast of California where they would have fresh water for watering the fields and would be close to Native American villages in order to attract the villagers. After all, it was the objective of the Catholic Church and the missionaries to Christianize the Indians, whom they saw as children of God. Father Serra was able to build nine missions, before his death, out of a total of twenty-one. He was also instrumental in introducing a number of trees and vegetables to California missions. He planted orange trees, lemon trees, fig trees, and olive trees. In addition he introduced the planting and harvesting of beans, pumpkins, red peppers, onions, garlic, corn, melons, peas, and squash. He also sent for almond, walnut, apple, peach, plum, and pear trees. The padres introduced plows and used oxen to pull them. They planted wheat and other grains. Wheat was turned into flour by Native American women, who were taught by the Spanish to use the metate and mano to grind the seeds. The flour was used for bread. The padres also introduced a number of animals such as cattle, sheep, and horses to California. They also taught Indians to weave the wool into cloth and to sew clothing of different types as well as blankets. Grape vineyards were also planted and wine and raisins were the end products.

Some of the Native Americans saw a number of advantages in living and working in the missions. These advantages included (1) the mission provided daily nourishment, (2) they were also provided with clothing, and (3) the new Spanish culture seemed intriguing. Some Indians, however, tried to leave the missions because they found life difficult because (1) they were harshly punished by the padres, (2) manual labor at the mission was monotonous, and (3) their schedules were very rigid and had to be followed. The Native Americans who had agreed to work and live in the missions were not allowed to leave. Those who tried were brought back forcibly by the soldiers. Soldiers were usually stationed nearby in the military installations called presidios. It would have been better if the padres had treated the native people more humanely because they provided all the labor required in the missions. There were very few Mexican or Spanish settlers to work on the missions and mission lands. So, even though many look at the period of the missions nostalgically, it was a hard time for the Indians in many ways. With the missions spreading, their traditional ways of life were destroyed, and many died with this growth. Some missions had as many as 2,000 Indians.

Lieutenant Fages, meanwhile, was keeping himself busy in Monterey but he also had his thoughts on the settlement of California by the Spanish. He wrote a letter to the Viceroy of Mexico stating that five missions had been built and some Spanish settlers had come. He told the viceroy what a nice climate California had and the abundance of wild game. He also informed him about another bay where there was a need for the Spanish to settle. This was San Francisco Bay. The viceroy was persuaded to send Captain Juan Bautista de Anza to California from Sonora. There were many Spanish settlers in Sonora, and they were willing to go and settle in California. Captain Anza chose a small group of soldiers, a priest named Father Garces, and a friendly Indian guide to try and get to California from Sonora. After a number of hardships the group was able to make it to Mission San Gabriel. From there Captain Anza went back to Sonora and brought back a party of settlers whom he led to San Francisco Bay region to settle. Settlers brought with them sheep, cows, horses, goats, and small calves; and they built a settlement around San Francisco Bay in 1776. With this settlement, Spain was able to claim California as its own.

Mexican California

On September 15, 1810, Father Miguel Hidalgo began an uprising against the Spanish in Mexico. It took twelve years for Mexico to win its independence from Spain. While the Mexicans struggled for independence, the people of California, calling themselves Californios, did not participate. Since Spain decided to stop sending supplies to the Californios, other countries like Russia, Portugal, and England immediately began trading with them. The Russians built Fort Ross in order to expand their fur trading activities and expand their influence in California. They brought some settlers to Fort Ross together with cattle, sheep, hogs, and horses. Russians used Fort Ross for tanning hides but they also built ships, tiles, and barrels.

England and the United States also began sending ships to trade. U.S. settlers from the east did their own hunting of seals and otters in Alaska but they would on many occasions come south and trade with the Californios, even though the Spanish forbade the practice. After Mexico won its independence, these foreign countries were encouraged by the Mexican governments to come and carry on trade in California.

The prosperity of the missions made some Spanish settlers and officials in Mexico and Spain very jealous because the missions represented a sort of self-sustained feudal society with the padres in strict control. The Spanish king in 1813 tried to have the lands controlled by the padres for ten or more years reverted back to the Native Americans. However, there was a change of heart and the mission lands stayed in the hands of the padres for a few more years. The status of California changed after Mexico finally won independence from Spain in 1821. California was proclaimed a territory of the Republic of Mexico in 1825. This change allowed some Californios to use their influence with the Mexican authorities to try to limit the power of the missions. The Mexican government in 1833 decided to allow the California Indians to leave the missions and allowed Californios to settle the lands.

The Rancho Period.   With the demise of the missions, land grants became very important to Californios. Some of the old Spanish soldiers had been given grants by the Spanish king, and they in turn had used the land to raise cattle. With Mexico's independence from Spain and the downfall of the missions, the Mexican government gave out more land grants in order to encourage settlers to move to California. As a result, great ranches, or rather *ranchos,* sprang up for a period of time through the 1840s. The *rancheros,* or ranchers, built homes on their land grants from adobe with whitewashed walls and tiled roofs. Workers on the rancho rode horses and helped the rancheros to raise their cattle. Cattle were used for food, their hides traded as if they were money, and a number of items were made from them including shoes, boots, and beds. Cattle tallow, or fat, was used to make candles and soap. People on the ranchos lived pleasant lives and enjoyed many activities. Rodeos were frequent and so were *fiestas,* or social celebrations. They also had contests as to who was the most skillful in riding horses, and they also raced for entertainment and fun.

Americans Come to California. As soon as Mexico became independent from Spain in 1821, ships from the United States made frequent visits to Monterey and San Francisco. These ships were whalers, and the sailors enjoyed coming ashore in the former Spanish settlements in order to rest and get fresh food from the California missions. Stories about California were taken back to the United States where the interest of shoemakers and others was aroused. They sent ships to California to get hides. The ship owners hired young men to trade for hides. Some of these young men were encouraged to stay in California, convert to Catholicism, and become Mexican citizens. These men married California women and settled there working for shipowners.

Another group of U.S. settlers came to California by land in November of 1826. These men were trappers and were led by Jedediah Smith. He and the other trappers had crossed the Colorado River and followed its banks until they reached a Mohave village where they were told that they must cross the Colorado River again and go through the Mojave Desert in order to reach any of the California settlements. Smith and his men, guided by two Indian men, traveled on the southern part of the San Bernandino Mountains, through a green valley to Mission San Gabriel. While at the mission, Smith sought permission for him and his men to stay in California. However, Governor Echeandia did not like to see U.S. settlers coming to California and he jailed Smith and his men. Some U.S. ship captains came to the governor and asked him to release Smith and his men. The governor told Smith to leave California and not to come back. Smith led his men back towards the United States but instead of following the same route they had originally used to come to California, the traveled northwest. After a short distance they came upon the Central Valley of Caifornia. The Spanish had not gone into the valley because they did not think it had good land for growing crops. As a result, few people knew what the great Central Valley was like. While traveling north, Smith found many opportunities to trap beavers and other animals which he found in great supply. He also noted the many rivers and creeks that dotted the Central Valley. The local Indians proved to be very friendly and did not bother him and his men. With his supply of furs, Smith decided to cross the Sierra Nevada Mountains with two of his men. After a hard journey, he was able to reach the Great Salt Lake. He only rested for a few days before starting back with a new party of trappers. This time he followed his first route to reach California but he came across an unfriendly group of Indians and most of his men were killed. He and some of his men did manage to get to Mission San Jose. The governor again had him arrested, but again he was helped by U.S. ship captains. Upon his release he decided to go through the great Central Valley and go northward towards the Oregon Territory. He and his men crossed the Sacramento River where Red Bluff is located today and went through the Trinity Mountains. They reached the ocean and eventually Fort Vancouver. From there Smith went on to the Great Salt Lake. After a while Smith got restless and decide to go back to California again. This time he and his party took the Santa Fe Trail. While traveling through the desert looking for water Smith was attacked by Native Americans and was killed. Jedediah Smith is an important figure in the history of California because he pointed the way for others to come and settle in California by using at least two routes that he explored. He also let settlers know about the beautiful Central Valley that was teeming with game and different types of plants. At this time, the United States was a new nation made up of twenty-three states. However, there were U.S. settlers in both Washington and Oregon.

U.S. settlers had begun many settlements as they traveled west. One of these was Independence, Missouri. Here, people who wanted to go west would stop and get supplies. Then they would travel to the Spanish settlement of Santa Fe. The Spanish welcomed the Americans who brought goods to trade. From there, Mexican traders would take goods, such as furs, to Los Angeles by following the Old Spanish Trail. Some of the goods were taken also to San Diego by following the Gila River Trail. There the furs would be shipped to China where they were traded for silk. The silk was welcomed by U.S. settlers, and they paid a good price. U.S. trappers also made their way into California, sometimes with permission granted by the Mexican authorities and sometimes without. Trappers found that if they went to the great Central Valley no one knew that they were there. So they could trap animals and get their hides and leave. To get to the Central Valley, they would first go to Independence, Missouri, and get provisions. Then they would follow the Oregon Trail to the Great Salt Lake. From there they followed the California Trail over the Sierra Nevada where Lake Tahoe is and into the Central Valley.

As a result of these many contacts and intrusions by ships, trappers, and traders, California was advertised as a land of opportunity. A man by the name of John Marsh heard the stories about California and decided to go there. Once he reached Los Angeles he was permitted to stay because of his medical training and knowledge. He had to become a Mexican citizen and also convert to Catholicism. In 1838, Marsh was granted permission by the governor to establish his own ranch. He did so on land near the foot of Mount Diablo. The home that he built was the first ever built by a white man in the great Central Valley. Some Native Americans welcomed Marsh because he was good to them.

During the same year that Marsh came to the Central Valley, 1839, another man named John Sutter sailed up the Sacramento River in three boats. He came to California because he heard great stories about opportunities that could get him rich. Originally, Sutter came from Switzerland where he heard many stories about the United States. He was an opportunist and wanted to become rich. So, he traveled to the United States and settled in Missouri where many of his countrymen had made their homes. It was here that he heard of California from merchants and traders. He decided that he wanted to go there. He, therefore, traveled west and ended up in Fort Vancouver, which was part of the Oregon Country. From there he boarded a ship and went on to the Hawaiian Islands where he stayed for five months. However, he still dreamed of California. At his first opportunity he took charge of a trading ship sailing for Alaska. He thought that he would be able to reach California from there. While in Alaska, he was able to trade his fur for a good price. He then took the ship and sailed south towards California. On July 2, 1839, Sutter sailed into San Francisco Bay. He stayed there only two days because he was told to go to Monterey and pay the customs tax. While in Monterey, Sutter pleaded with Governor Alvarado to let him stay and settle in California. He told the governor that he had been a soldier in the Swiss army. He was willing to become a Mexican citizen and he wanted to start a settlement in the great Central Valley. Governor Alvarado listened to Sutter's proposition very carefully because the Native Americans of the Central Valley used to raid Spanish settlements. He figured that with Sutter's army training, maybe Sutter could take care of the problems with the Indians. He, therefore, granted Sutter permission to stay in California and allowed him to choose land along the Sacramento River.

Once he got permission to stay, Sutter took three boats and loaded them with tools and supplies. He took along the Hawaiian men and their wives who had come along with him and a small party of other men and sailed up the Sacramento River passing by John Marsh's ranch. Sutter and his party sailed on to a place where the Sacramento and American rivers joined. Here he set up camp. He had to send his men back to Yerba Buena, or San Francisco, to get more supplies, tools, horses, and cattle. In 1840, Sutter chose a small hill about two miles from the Sacramento River and one mile from the American River. He chose the hill to built his home with adobe bricks because the area flooded. Around his home the Hawaiians built their own grass huts similar to those they had in Hawaii. Sutter hired many Indians to help him build a number of buildings using adobe bricks. He also taught Native Americans to take care of his animals, horses and cattle. Sutter showed them how to make the adobe bricks and then had them build a wall around his home and his buildings. On the top of the walls were placed cannons to protect the settlement. This place included workshops, stables, granaries, storehouses, and places where visitors could spend the night. This settlement was named by Sutter as New Helvetia but is now known as Sutter's Fort in Sacramento.

Sutter was an enterprising man. He hired men who had a variety of skills. He needed blacksmiths, coopers, carpenters, Mexican cowboys, tanners, hunters, trappers, and others. His settlement prospered just as did John Marsh's ranch.

Soon other Americans decided to come to the rich Central Valley of California. A group of men, women, and children started such a journey from Independence, Missouri, in 1841 under the guidance of a man named Bartleson. With him Bartleson took a young man named John Bidwell as his secretary for record keeping. When the group reached Soda Springs, most of the families decided to go on the Oregon Trail to Oregon first before they felt safe to turn south toward California. Bartleson and John Bidwell, however, convinced one family to go with them using the California Trail. The Bartleson–Bidwell party and the family of Benjamin Kelsey made their way towards the Sierra Nevadas. However, Bartleson and some of the men who had accompanied the party decided to slip away during the night and left Bidwell and the family alone. They started over the mountains but ran out of food. They had to kill one of the mules in order to survive. A short time later they came upon the foothills of the San Joaquin Valley where game was plentiful. As they traveled towards the valley, they met up with a Mexican vaquero, or cowboy, who worked for John Marsh. John Marsh welcomed them at his ranch and Bidwell and his party were granted permission by the governor to stay in California. The Kelsey family, made up of Benjamin, his wife Nancy, and their young daughter Ann, settled on land where the city of Stockton is located today. Ann Kelsey has the historical distinction as being the first pioneer child to come to California by land. John Bidwell went on to New Helvetia where John Sutter took a liking to him and made him his main helper.

Just before Bidwell came to see John Sutter, a Russian from Fort Ross came to see him. Sutter was invited to go to Fort Ross to talk with the Fort's commander. The Russians had decided to sell Fort Ross after being there for some thirty years. A deal was struck whereby Sutter would send supplies to the Russians in Sitka, Alaska, each year for four years. Sutter was overjoyed over the deal because the fort came with four boats, different kinds of tools, cannons, guns, bullets, and gunpowder. In addition, the Russians left behind their sheep, goats, and hogs. All of these items were desperately needed in New Helvetia.

In March of 1844, two American explorers came to New Helvetia. John C. Fremont and his guide Kit Carson had been sent by the U.S. government to explore the western region of the continent. These two men had found a new pass through the Sierra Nevada's that eventually became known as Kit Carson Pass and from there they followed the American River to Sutter's settlement. Fremont and Sutter had a falling out, and Fremont left with his party and traveled southward. He crossed the mountains through the Tejon Pass, traveled through the Mojave Desert, then on to the Old Spanish Trail and eventually reached Santa Fe through the Santa Fe Trail. When eastern settlers heard about Fremont's travels, more and more people became excited about coming to California. Other U.S. settlers, like Peter Lassen, came to California to start a new life. Lassen set up his home and ranch in northern California. Mount Lassen and Lassen Park are named in his honor.

In 1845, there were rumors of war between the United States and Mexico. It was during this time that John C. Fremont came to California for a second time. While traveling north in the great Central Valley, he received a communication from the U.S. government that caused him to turn back and make camp sixty miles north of Sutter's Fort. Soon there were other groups of U.S. settlers setting up camps nearby. There was talk of war, and settlers wanted California to be a part of the United States. When war between the United States and Mexico started on June 14, 1846, a group of settlers who had taken General Vallejo as a prisoner decided to set up a government for Americans in California. They decided to design their own flag, which consisted of a white canvas with a painted red star in one corner, a painted grizzly bear in the middle, and a strip of red flannel with the words "California Republic," on the bottom. This became the Bear Flag of California, which they raised in Sonoma.

Meanwhile, three U.S. ships sailed into Monterey Bay under the command of Commodore Sloat. On July 7, 1846, Commodore Sloat ordered that the Mexican flag be taken down and the U.S. flag be raised in its place. When the Bear Flag group in Sonoma heard what Commodore Sloat had done, they took down the Bear Flag and raised the U.S. flag in its place.

On July 15, 1846, another ship came to Monterey under the command of Commodore Robert F. Stockton. He took over command of the situation from Commodore Sloat. At the same time, John C. Fremont had organized some volunteer trappers and settlers into an army. He called them the California Battalion. John Bidwell was one of the men who joined Fremont's army. This army went around California raising the flag of the United States, including the settlement in Los Angeles where there appeared to be some resistance. Fremont sent a messenger to Commodore Stockton, who was in San Francisco. The commodore set sail for San Diego planning to attack the resisters from the south. At the same time a group of men under Stephen Kearny, who was a general in the United States Army, sent word that he too was coming overland from New Mexico. General Kearny's men engaged the Californians under Andres Pico in the mountains near San Diego. In what is known as the Battle of San Pascual, the Californians withdrew. General Kearny turned his men towards the Los Angeles settlement with the help of 180 men that Commodore Stockton had sent. The U.S. flag was raised over Los Angeles on January 10, 1847, after a brief encounter with the resisting Californians. On January 13, 1847, Andres Pico and his men surrendered to John C. Fremont and the war was over.

The war between the United States and Mexico lagged on until a treaty was signed in February of 1848. As part of the settlement of 15 million dollars, the United States was given control of New Mexico, Texas, and California.

The Gold Rush Period

More people started to come to California in 1846. One group that left Illinois included the Donner family and the Reed family. They traveled by wagon train to Fort Bridger, Wyoming. There they heard of a shortcut trail to California. It was called Hastings Cutoff, and this route took the group along the south side of the Great Salt Lake. Once they had done that, they had to go across the Salt Lake Desert. By this time they were behind schedule and winter was approaching. In October they began crossing the Utah and Nevada deserts. When they reached the foot of the Sierra Nevada, they were tired and decided to rest, thinking that the weather would stay fair. That was not the case. It started to snow, and the snow became deeper and deeper. When they reached a lake, known today as Donner Lake, they decided to build cabins and wait out the weather. They ran out of food and began eating their animals, animal hides, and the bark of trees. Many of them became sick and died. Some say that some of the people resorted to cannibalism.

In the middle of December, fifteen people decided to brave snow that was twenty feet deep. A number of them died in the attempt, but some made it to a rancho. From there word was sent to Sutter's Fort for help. People came and rescued the Donner Party members who had survived. What befell the Donner party did not stop other settlers from coming to California. Many used the Santa Fe Trail and on through the Old Spanish Trail to make it to the great California Central Valley.

John Sutter, meanwhile, dreamed of building a sawmill so that he could turn redwood trees into lumber and sell it to the new settlers. He asked one of his blacksmiths to make the machinery needed to be able to cut the logs into planks. John Sutter decided to form a partnership with a carpenter friend of his called James Wilson Marshall. The deal was for Sutter to supply the machinery needed and Marshall to build the saw mill. Sutter and Marshall decided to locate their mill on the south fork of the American River. In order for the saws to run, water was needed with enough force to turn them. However, the river's bed had accumulated a lot of gravel. So, Marshall and his men decided to dig the gravel out of the way and make a small canal called a millrace in order to give water the force it needed. Above the small canal Marshall would build a small dam so that when he opened the gate of the dam water would rush down the small canal and provide the force necessary to run the saws.

Marshall and his Native American diggers worked hard day in and day out in order to clear the gravel and rocks to make the canal. He also used water gathered behind the dam to wash some of the gravel out of the canal. By January 24, 1848, the canal and the millrace were just about completed. As Marshall was inspecting the work done on the canal and millrace, he noted something shiny on the bottom of the ditch. He reached down and picked up several pieces of the shiny material. They felt like metal and had a yellow color. Marshall had never seen gold ore before and wasn't sure what he was looking at. He decided not to let anyone else know about the yellow flakes until he had time to think. Next morning he went back to the ditch where he had found the flakes. There were more of them. He tried to break them but they were hard as metal. This convinced him that what he had found was gold. He tried two other tests to make sure of his find. First he put lye on the yellow flakes to see if their color changed. It didn't. Next he put several flakes in the fire to see what would happen. Again the flakes were unscathed. These two tests convinced Marshall beyond any doubt that what he had found was really gold.

John Marshall rushed to tell Sutter of his finding. He met Sutter in his room where he took out an old rag with small yellow flakes no bigger than the size of peas. After both men tried several other tests, they decided that it was indeed gold that they had found. The next day, Sutter went to Sonoma to look for himself. He was not too excited about the gold because he had other grander plans for the valley. He wanted people to come and take up farming and ranching. If it was announced that gold had been discovered all of his workers would leave his employment and go searching for gold. He had to plan carefully.

He met with surrounding-area Native Americans and offered them clothing, shoes, knives, and flour in return for the rights of twelve square miles surrounding the mill. He then told his workers at the mill about the gold discovered. He raised their wages and asked them to keep quiet about the gold for at least six weeks. Meanwhile he sent a messenger to the U.S. governor in Monterey asking him to grant Sutter the mining rights to the area he claimed. However, since no treaty had yet been signed with Mexico, the governor told him that he did not have mining rights.

Word of the gold got out. Some say it was John Marshall who let it be known. Others said that Sutter himself had told John Bidwell about the gold's discovery. Bidwell was not interested in that kind of gold. He believed that wheat was the kind of gold that was needed. Others say that the son of one of the workers at the sawmill told a wagon driver about the gold and sold him some flakes. The driver went to Sutter's Fort and bought some supplies with those flakes at Sam Brannan's store. On May 15, 1848, Brannan went to Coloma and found some flakes of gold that he placed in a small jar. Then he traveled to Portsmouth Square in Yerba Buena, San Francisco, and shouted that gold had been discovered on the American River. The Gold Rush was on! Men left their work and went looking for gold. Word spread throughout California, Oregon, and Washington. Men left their work there, too, and came to California to look for gold. The news reached the United States and then the whole world. People came streaming in from many places. Some came by land and others by ship. By the spring of 1849, there were hundreds and even thousands of people who were rushing to the gold fields of California. They came to be known as the forty-niners. These men came primarily from the United States but there were others who came from England, France South America, Hawaii, China, and Germany. Three settlements became towns almost immediately. These were the towns of San Francisco, Sacramento, and Stockton. All three towns became overcrowded without enough housing for all newcomers. Tents were set up by the hundreds to provide the housing needs of the forty-niners.

The forty-niners did not stay long in any one place but proceeded to the foothills, rivers, streams, and creeks looking for the yellow metal. The little ranch of Tuleberg, owned by Captain Charles Weber, filled up with tents and eventually was renamed Stockton. Some 35,000 people came to California in 1849 to search for gold. This surge of people had a very catastrophic effect on John Sutter and his dreams. People took supplies and tools from him without paying him. His workers left him. His land was taken by the forty-niners, who without paying, settled on it. Sutter moved to his Hock Farm on the Feather River with his family trying to survive. He appealed to the courts for help but he did not get it. Eventually, after his home burned, he moved to Pennsylvania. For many years he sought compensation from the U.S. Congress but received none. Sutter died at the age of 80, a very poor man.

The forty-niners who found gold had to work very hard to get it. They used flat pans to pan gravel and sand in order to find the gold, the weight of which is as much as eight times as much as sand and gravel. It would settle on the bottom of the pan. Others used a cradle box with an iron grate onto which they would scoop shovels of sand and gravel. Then water was thrown into it to wash out the sand and gravel through a hole while the gold, being heavier, stayed at the bottom of the cradle box.

The forty-niners kept looking for easier ways to get the gold. They built cradle-like boxes that were about a thousand feet long. They called them *long toms,* and they would set them in a stream where water ran through them all of the time. The miners would shovel the sand and gravel into the long tom, and at the end of the day they would collect whatever gold was at the bottom.

Other means of getting gold included a damlike setup where the water was collected and then allowed to flow down a slope where it picked up speed and force and finally came out an iron nozzle. They pointed the nozzle at small hills and washed down the gravel in order to get to the gold. Troughs were used to collect the sand and gravel. The troughs were outfitted with strips of wood that caught the gold nuggets. This was called hydraulic mining. This kind of mining contaminated rivers and streams, and to this day mercury from those areas still pollutes our water supply.

Forty-niners searched for gold but they needed places to stay. These camps or towns that sprang up were also lawless places. Places like Placerville and Jackson had different names during the Gold Rush Period. Placerville was known as Hangtown and Jackson was called Bottle Springs. Other mining camps were known by names such as Chinese Camp, Rattlesnake Bar, Spanish Dry Diggings, French Camp, and many others. These places had no roads and could be reached by foot or horseback. Mules and donkeys were also used. Food had to be transported from great distances. Food cost a lot of money in these camps. The Spanish Californians saw an opportunity to mine gold in another way. They had large herds of cattle, and they found that miners would pay high prices for fresh meat. Since most of these large herds were in southern California, Spanish cowboys would herd them to northern California. This cattle drives caused a lot of damage to Native Americans because the cattle would eat all of the seeds that the Indians used for food. The Native Americans, however, could not keep the Spanish Californians from moving the cattle through their territories. Once the cattle were brought to the gold fields, they were allowed to eat the grasses that surrounded them. The cattle were slaughtered and pack mules were used to transport the fresh meat to the miners. The Spanish Californians would carry bags full of gold back to southern California after each drive. Some were robbed and killed on their way back.

Miners would use gold dust to pay for their food and other supplies. One pinch of gold dust was worth one dollar. Miners sent their money to towns where storekeepers would keep their gold safe. During the winter period, the miners spent their time in towns where they used up their gold or gambled it away. Some miners were robbed of their gold and there were frequent holdups of stagecoaches carrying gold. It has been recorded that many African American slaves were able to save enough gold for themselves to be able to buy their freedom. One such slave was Moses Rogers, who was able to save enough money to buy and own two gold mines. Another was Robert Anthony, who bought his freedom and then went on to open his own quartz mill. With the money he made, he was able to help other slaves to buy their freedom.

Some of the forty-niners who were not lucky in the fields flocked back to towns like San Francisco. Sam Brannan, for example, built stores to sell supplies to miners and became wealthy. Another man was Levi Strauss, who made canvas for tents and coverings for wagons. However, when he was unable to sell all of his rolls of canvas, he decided to use the canvas to make pants with stronger pockets whereby miners could put their gold ore in them without tearing. These pants came to be known as Levis.

Life in the towns like San Francisco was not always pleasant because gangs used to hold up and rob people and most often commit murders. These gangs also set frequent fires to buildings and destroyed many businesses. To get rid of these gangs, Sam Brannan got together a group of trusted men and formed a vigilante committee. This committee was very effective in getting rid of the gangs. They did this by arresting men who committed these crimes; known criminals were persuaded to leave the city; and all newcomers came under the scrutiny of this vigilante committee. Soon, other towns had similar vigilante committees to help make their towns safe places. However, what was needed was law and order. All Californians, including Spanish Californians, felt the need for California to become a state in order for it to have law enforcement to keep everyone safe.

The Gold Rush brought many changes to California. Some were good and others not so good. Most men who came to search for gold became very lonely. Therefore, they sought to make their new communities like the home regions they had left. As a result, many churches were built during this period. One African American minister, Darius Stokes, is said to have founded fourteen churches. Churches made the miners feel at home. Newspapers were also begun. Sam Brennan started a newspaper and later joined with another, *The Californian,* which had begun in Monterey in 1846. The new paper was called the *Alta Californian.* There were also theatrical presentations because forty-niners enjoyed going to plays.

In order for California to become a state, the people had to make some changes in order for the U.S. Congress to begin proceedings. To make these changes, men met in each town to choose representatives who would go to Monterey to help set up rules and regulations as a prerequisite to a state constitution. These representatives met in Colton Hall on September 1849. This was California's first constitutional convention.

CONTENT AREA TWENTY-SIX: PERIOD OF REFORM (1830–1860)

The period between 1830 and 1860 is best known for some important events and changes in U.S. society. Horace Mann in Massachusetts, as the secretary of the board of education, began to tout the idea of a free public education system where all children could benefit from a free education. He pushed for the building of public schools, the training and hiring of full-time teachers, and the opportunity for children to get an elementary and high school education. Those that would benefit the most were the white boys, some white girls, and free African American children who had to attend separate schools from white children. Children of slaves were not given the opportunity.

This period also marked the differences between the different regions of the United States. Slavery predominated the economic system of the South. The issue of slavery caused many debates and divided people who felt it necessary to support slavery as an economic issue and those who wanted to do away with it as a moral issue. The latter group came to be called abolitionists. The Quakers were the first group to support the abolitionist movement. Other people like William Lloyd Garrison used his newspaper *The Liberator* to call for the abolition of slavery. Another newspaper, called *Freedom's Journal,* was founded and written by African Americans. Harriet Beecher Stowe published a book entitled *Uncle Tom's Cabin,* which influenced many people's attitudes toward slavery in 1852. Frederick Douglass, a fiery African American speaker, made many speeches against slavery. Sojourner Truth also traveled and spoke against slavery. The Underground Railroad was one means by which abolitionists and free African Americans were able to encourage many slaves in the South to escape and become free in the North.

Women like Elizabeth Cady Stanton, Susan B. Anthony, Lucretia Mott, Sojourner Truth, and many others decided that it was time for women to have the same rights as men, including suffrage, or the right for them to vote. They met at Seneca Falls, New York, on July 19–20, 1848, to outline their concerns and agenda. Stanton went on to proclaim that "all men and women were created equal." Women in the South felt that they were no better off than the African American slaves. The master of the plantation was the patriarch who ruled everyone around him including women, children, and slaves. Sojourner Truth became a speaker for African American women and was also involved in the women's rights movement of the 1840s and 1850s. Harriet Tubman was another African American woman who became involved in the Underground Railroad.

Some rights were won, and women in Wyoming, for example, even got the right to vote. Few women had been allowed to attend colleges and universities in the 1820s, but by the 1890s there were several thousand who had successfully graduated from these institutions. Elizabeth Blackwell was the first woman to earn a medical diploma, and she went on to practice medicine in 1850 New York City. Similarly, Maria Mitchell became a professor of astronomy at Vassar College in 1865. Women did not make real gains until 1920 when the Nineteenth Amendment granted full suffrage rights.

CONTENT AREA TWENTY-SEVEN: THE CIVIL WAR AND RECONSTRUCTION

TABLE 9.7   The Civil War

COMPARISONS	NORTHERN STATES	SOUTHERN STATES
POPULATION (1860)	• 19,000,000. • Northerners owned no slaves in 1860; large numbers of immigrants made their homes in the North.	• 11,000,000 with 4,000 being slaves. • 75 percent of Southerners did not own slaves; only 3 percent owned 20 or more slaves while the other 22 percent owned one a only a few. • Very few new immigrants came to the South so Southerners came to depend more and more on slave labor.
ECONOMY	• Industrialization opened up new opportunities for people, especially recent immigrants who were able to find jobs in factories. • Industrialization made many people wealthy. • 1,170,000 workers. • Bank deposits of $207 million.	• The South depended on a few crops raised in large plantations that were worked by African slaves. • Tobacco and cotton provided Southerners with their cash needs. • 111,000 workers. • Bank deposits of $47 million.
CONFLICT	• Northerners saw all southerners as slave owners. • They also fought hard to keep new territories free from slavery. • Abolitionists and free slaves attacked the South's social, educational, and economic systems.	• Southerners were threatened by the wealth of the North and its ability to attract newcomers, thereby expanding their work force. • They resented Northerners for keeping them from expanding their holdings to new territories. • They did not like what the abolitionists were trying to do. • Tariffs imposed by the North on manufactured goods needed by the South caused a lot of friction.

Due to its rapid expansion beginning in 1783, the United States encountered a number of issues that eventually led to war between the southern and the northern states. The issues included:

1. The industrialization of the New England states caused an imbalance in the economies of the northern states and the southern. The southern states came to depend on slavery for cheap labor and on crops that required extensive territory.
2. The United States as a whole had benefited from territory it took from Mexico and the ceding of the Oregon Territory by Great Britain. The midwestern states were experiencing great population growth, especially from Germany. The southern states felt threat-

ened by the ever-expanding economy of the northern states and the large growth in population in the Midwest. The population of the southern states remained stagnant, however, and its territorial expansion was questioned. These differences between the regions were the underlying causes of the Civil War.

3. The North also benefited politically because it was most populous, thus giving the northern states an advantage in the number of Representatives they had in Congress and also in the Electoral College.

4. Tariffs imposed by the North on needed manufactured goods hurt the South economically.

5. The Compromise of 1850 worked out by Henry Clay caused a lot of anger on the part of northerners because it included the Fugitive Law. This law stated that as part of the Compromise of 1850, any runaway slave had to be returned to its owner no matter if the runaway slave had made it to northern or free states. People helping slaves to run away from their owners were to be punished and fined. Northern abolitionists were greatly dissatisfied.

6. In 1854, Congress passed the Kansas–Nebraska Act, which made a change to the Missouri Compromise. Under this new law, Kansas and Nebraska were given the opportunity to vote on whether they wanted to become free or slave states. Many settlers decided to go to Kansas in order to cast their votes one way or the other. This caused a lot of bad feelings; fighting broke out among the two groups and some 200 people were killed.

7. The Supreme Court of the United States was asked to decide a case where a slave, Dred Scott, asked for his freedom after his owner died. His argument was that his owner had taken him to live in Illinois and Wisconsin, of which one was a free state and one a free territory. The Chief Justice of the Supreme Court who rendered the decision was Roger B. Taney. His decision was as follows:

   A. Dred Scott was a slave and had no rights.

   B. Dred Scott was property since he was a slave.

   C. The Missouri Compromise was unconstitutional because it kept some people, the southerners, from owning property.

8. The acquisition of large tracts of land such as the Louisiana Purchase gave the North a vast advantage over the South. The North had the money and industrial resources necessary to build railroads to these new regions. Since most immigrants to the United States settled in the North, people from the North settled in the new territories mainly because railroads and other means of transportation allowed them the ease with which to resettle themselves from the east to the new west. The railroads, especially, allowed goods and services to flow from the North to the West and thus benefitted northerners at the expense of the South, where slavery predominated and only a few crops were raised. These crops were usually sent abroad to Europe. The South felt threatened by this expansion of the North's economic and industrial might.

9. Abraham Lincoln, who was a lawyer and later a congressman, believed that the government had no right to end all slavery but could contain it where it already existed.

Other issues emerged as causes of the Civil War:

1. Lincoln ran for the U.S. Senate against Stephen Douglas in the election of 1858. In a number of debates, Douglas stated his support for the Kansas–Nebraska Act whereas Lincoln argued that slavery had to end and should not be allowed to spread to the West. Douglas won the election.

2. The question of slavery was an issue during the presidential election of 1860. Lincoln ran as the Republican candidate, and Stephen Douglas ran as part of the Democratic Party. Some southerners supported another Democratic candidate, John Breckinridge of Kentucky, who believed that slavery should be allowed all over the United States. Many southerners feared that if Lincoln was elected, he would not allow them to expand in the West. On November 6, 1860, Lincoln won the presidency.

3. South Carolina seceded from the Union when Lincoln was elected president. Other southern states took the same action. These states declared their own government and

called it the Confederate States of America under their newly elected president Jefferson Davis. Some people advised Lincoln to let the southern states go. Constitutionally, President Lincoln felt that South Carolina could not take such action. He felt that the Union had to be kept as one.

4. On March 4, 1861, Lincoln received an urgent message from the officer in command of Fort Sumter. This fort was in the hands of the Union but was located just offshore from Charleston, South Carolina. The message implored the president to send urgently needed supplies, otherwise the fort would be turned over to the southern states, or Confederacy. Lincoln decided to send supplies to the fort. However, Jefferson Davis decided to take over the fort before the supplies arrived. So, on April 12, 1861, Confederate troops fired upon Fort Sumter. That was the immediate cause of the Civil War.

Political Parties.

TABLE 9.8   Political Parties

NAME OF PARTY	WHAT IT REPRESENTED	WHO SUPPORTED THE PARTY
DEMOCRATIC PARTY	• In the North, the Democratic Party supported the right of the voters of new states to choose whether they wanted to be a free or slave state. • In the South, the Democratic Party wanted to see that slavery expanded into the new territories.	• People from a variety of backgrounds supported the Democratic Party. • Urban area voters and especially Catholics went along with the Democratic vision. • Also some southerners gave their support.
AMERICAN PARTY OR KNOW NOTHING PARTY	• The American Party was anti-slavery and anti-Catholic. • The members of this party were highly nativist and anti-foreign. • They did not like the new immigrants from Ireland and Germany. • They tried to influence legislation making it more difficult to be a naturalized citizen.	• Supporters of the Know Nothing Party were primarily those who were middle class with a fear of so many foreigners coming to the U.S. • Other supporters included Protestants who were in fear of losing jobs to newcomers from Ireland and Germany.
REPUBLICAN PARTY	• The Republican Party was against slavery and against Catholics. • Republicans had a nativist attitude similar to the Know Nothing Party.	• The Republican Party was supported by Protestants, people in the New England region, middle-class people, professionals, farmers, and small businessmen.

The 1850s also saw changes in the political spectrum of the United States. The Whig Party faded away because the issues that brought about its appearance in the 1830s were no longer relevant. In its place arose two new parties. One was called the American Party or Know Nothing Party, which was anti-slavery, highly "nativist," and anti-Catholic. The members of this party were primarily Protestants who felt that they were the "natives" and were, therefore, fearful of a wave of new immigrants coming to the United States during the period between 1846 and 1854. The second party that evolved from the Whig Party became known as the Republican Party. It shared views similar to those of the Know Nothing Party but had wider support from Protestants; working middle-class people especially in the New England States; and farmers, professionals, and small businessmen. The old Democratic Party survived and was supported by a collection of diverse groups mainly in the North, but it also had support in the South. All three parties took sides on a number of issues that divided the country and shortly led it to war.

John Brown's Raid. John Brown was an abolitionist who had carried out raids in Kansas. On October 16, 1859, he decided to raid Harper's Ferry, a federal arsenal in the state of Virginia. His plan was to grab weapons and ammunition and pass them on to the African American slaves who would use them to rebel and free themselves. John Brown's action was supported by the abolitionists in the North. The commander of Harper's Ferry, Colonel Robert E. Lee, had been alerted and was ready for John Brown and his men. In the attack that ensued, half of Brown's men were killed, two of his sons lost their lives, and John Brown himself was hanged. This action by John Brown and his men caused southerners to feel resentment towards the northerners who supported him and furthered the divisions that were already obvious between the two regions.

Battles of the Civil War. Bull Run was the first major battle fought in Virginia. Surprisingly, the South won the battle. This worried many northerners who felt that the North had the upper hand from the start. Lincoln was hard pressed to do something. He blockaded the South in order to keep it from getting supplies from European nations. Lincoln also appointed General George McClellan to be the commander of the Union army in the East. Lincoln's strategy was to follow a plan recommended by General Winfield Scott, which was to surround the Confederate States and squeeze them to the point that they surrendered. Table 9.9 below shows just a sample of the hundreds of battles fought during the Civil War.

TABLE 9.9   Some Battles of the Civil War

BATTLE	LOCATION	DATE	WHO WON
Fort Henry and Fort Donelson	Mississippi	February 6, 1862	General Grant for the Union.
Monitor vs. Merrimack	Chesapeake Bay, Virginia	March 9, 1862	A Union victory at sea.
Shiloh	Tennessee	April 6–7, 1862	General Grant for the Union.
Memphis	Tennessee	April 6, 1862	Captain David Farragut for the Union.
Seven Days' Battles	Virginia	June 25–July 1, 1862	General Lee and General Stonewall Jackson defeat the Union forces under McClellan.
Antietam	Maryland	September 17, 1862	General Lee and General McClellan fought a bloody battle but neither side won.
Chancellorsville	Virginia	May 1863	Union General Hooker and General Lee fought—Lee won the battle. General Stonewall Jackson died from his wounds.
Vicksburg	Mississippi	July 3–4, 1863	Union forces take Vicksburg.
Gettysburg	Virginia	July 3, 1863	Union forces won the battle.
Chickamauga	Georgia	September 19–20, 1863	The Confederate army won the battle.
Chattanooga	Tennessee	November 23–25, 1863	The Union army won the battle.
Bentonville	North Carolina	March 19, 1864	The Union army won the battle.
Savannah	Georgia	December 21, 1864	Captured by General Sherman for the Union.
Appomattox	Virginia	April 9, 1865	General Lee of the Confederacy surrenders to General Grant and the Civil War is ended.

During the Civil War, many changes were taking place in U.S. society:

1. Women did not fight in the war but they carried out other duties to help in the war effort:
   A. Women went to work in factories.
   B. They oversaw businesses, farms, and, in the South, they ran the plantations.
   C. They oversaw to supplies and clothing for the soldiers.
   D. Women like Clara Barton and Sally Tomkins took care of the wounded as nurses.
   E. A few of the women worked as spies for both the South and the North.
2. The Emancipation Proclamation was issued by President Lincoln on January 1, 1863, for a number of reasons:
   A. Freeing the slaves, Lincoln reasoned, would cause a great hardship for the South and thus shorten the duration of the war.
   B. The British would look more favorably on the North because they were against slavery.
   C. Freeing the slaves would also encourage many of them to rebel or run away from the South and join the northern army.
3. The Gettysburg Address in 1863 by President Lincoln was an inspirational speech that inspired people in the North to try harder to keep the Union intact.
   A. The speech honored the soldiers who defended the Union.
   B. He expounded on the timely virtues of liberty and equality.
   C. He spoke of "government of the people, by the people, for the people."
4. President Lincoln limited the rights of people in the North during the war, which made the federal government stronger.
5. Many African Americans freed themselves and helped others to freedom during the war.
6. Draft laws were passed to get men to serve their country as soldiers.

President Lincoln was assassinated on April 14, 1865, while attending a theater performance at Ford's Theater in Washington, D.C., with his wife Mary Todd Lincoln. This was just five days after General Lee's surrender at Appomattox. His assassin was John Wilkes Booth, who later died himself. Lincoln's death was a blow to both the North and the South. Lincoln was a compassionate leader who wanted to unite the states again. To do that, he planned to be fair in his treatment of the South.

Reconstruction Period

As soon as the war was over, Congress passed legislation to help the former slaves:

1. By 1865, the slaves had been freed. However, later on in 1865 the Thirteenth Amendment, which did away with slavery, was added to the Constitution of the United States.
2. Congress also set up the Freedmen's Bureau in 1865 to help the former slaves and some white people to build a better future for themselves and their families.
   A. The Bureau provided for education whereby many former slaves learned how to read and write.
   B. The Bureau funded the building of 4,000 new schools and provided trained teachers.
   C. The Bureau had plans to provide former slaves with farms and supplies of their own, but it did a turnaround and allowed the former plantation owners to have their lands back.
   D. The former slaves had to look for jobs, so they turned to sharecropping.
3. Vice President Andrew Johnson became president upon Lincoln's death. He tried to heal the nation and follow in Lincoln's footsteps:
   A. He pardoned those Confederates who pledged loyalty to the Union.
   B. State governments were allowed to hold elections and take up the business of running their states.
   C. The southern states were also to ratify the Thirteenth Amendment and void secession, and state war debts were forgiven.
   However well intentioned President Johnson's plan of Reconstruction was, the South did not want to accept it. The southern state governments decided to do what they wanted.

4. Southern governments, instead of following President Johnson's Plan for Reconstruction, started limiting the rights of the African Americans. Laws labeled black codes were passed taking away some of the rights of former slaves.

   A. African Americans were not allowed to vote.

   B. They could do only certain kinds of work.

   C. If they could not find work, they could be forced to work in fields without pay.

   D. Some southern states did not allow former slaves to travel freely.

   E. The Ku Klux Klan, or KKK, an organization made up of southern whites, terrorized African Americans by breaking into their homes, beating them, and even committing murders.

   F. During this time segregation laws, known as Jim Crow laws, called for the legal separation between African Americans and whites. This meant that African Americans had to sit separately in public places, transportation systems, bathrooms, educational institutions, and so forth. These Jim Crow laws caused many suspected criminals or perceived troublemakers who were African Americans to be lynched illegally by angry white mobs.

   G. As the relations between African Americans and whites deteriorated in the South, many African Americans began to speak out against the discrimination and prejudices they were experiencing. African American leaders like W. E. B. DuBois denounced all political, economic, and social discrimination against African Americans. Meanwhile Mary White Ovington helped to organize the National Association for the Advancement of Colored People, or NAACP. This organization has helped many African Americans throughout the United States to fight prejudice and discrimination to this day. It also has been instrumental in helping to pass legislations that have benefited African Americans politically, socially, and economically.

5. In March of 1866, the Congress decided that President Johnson's Plan for Reconstruction was inadequate, and the members of Congress passed their own plan. A Civil Rights Act was passed granting African Americans equal rights. In addition, the Congress passed the Fourteenth Amendment protecting all citizens, including African Americans and naturalized citizens, from having their rights restricted by state governments.

Congress also passed the Military Reconstruction Act of 1867, which divided the South into five military districts. These districts were assigned a general who would govern them while delegates were selected to gather and create new state constitutions. In order for the southern states to be accepted back into the Union, they had to guarantee all citizens their freedoms, allow African Americans to vote, and ratify the Fourteenth Amendment to the U.S. Constitution.

In order to rein in the power of the president, the Congress passed the Tenure of Office Act, which restricted the power of the president to fire a government official without the permission of the U.S. Senate. This Tenure of Office Act brought on a lot of tension and hostility between Congress and the president. When the president tried to fire Secretary of War Edwin Stanton, the House of Representatives decided that it was unconstitutional for him to do that, so they started impeachment procedures against President Johnson. In 1868, the proceedings moved to the U.S. Senate, where the president was tried. However, the Senate did not find the president's action severe enough to find him guilty and President Johnson retained his office. However, his power and influence was greatly diminished.

In 1869, Congress proposed the Fifteenth Amendment to the U.S. Constitution, and it was ratified in 1870. This amendment stated that a citizen could not be denied the right to vote by a state government or the federal government "on account of race, color, or previous condition of servitude." This amendment had been passed with the hope that African Americans would vote for Republican candidates, because it was shown during the presidential election of 1868 that African Americans in the South who had been allowed to vote did vote for Ulysses S. Grant, who won the presidency by a very narrow margin.

A final piece of legislation that allowed the Union to reconstruct the South was the U.S. Supreme Court's decision, *Texas v. White* in 1869, that stated that the Congress had the right to reconstruct the governments of the former Confederate states. As a result of this ruling, radical Republicans were able to push their agenda in redistricting the political and social boundaries of the South with the help of African Americans.

Reconstruction of the South.   Radical Republicans decided that if their plan for reconstruction was to be successful, they had to have Republicans elected to state offices in the South and federal officials selected to carry out the plan had to be individuals willing to help the radical Republicans. To accomplish the task, northern Republicans moved to the South carrying their suitcases, after which they were labeled carpetbaggers, in order to make sure that the wishes of the Congress were carried out. These carpetbaggers were joined by white southerners, called Scalawags, who had converted to being Republicans in order to influence the economic development of the South. As a result, a number of changes took place:

1. A number of African Americans were elected to public offices in the South.
2. Economic development was supported and more railroads, banks, and businesses appeared to help in this development.
3. Debt peonage, or labor contracts, was instituted by planters whereby former slaves were given money that they had to work off by signing a labor contract. This was very similar to slavery because it forced many poor African Americans to work for former white planters in order to pay off the money they had been loaned. It was very difficult for them to pay their debts, and the debts became larger and larger.
4. Not wanting to sign labor contracts, many African Americans tried to grow crops on rented land. The land belonged to white farmers who would allow the African Americans to raise crops, and then they would share the profits. This practice is called sharecropping. When the crop was sold, the landowner would get one-third to one-half. The sharecropping system arose in the South as a result of a disruption in the previous arrangements of the southern labor force.
5. A number of African Americans and white farmers became tenant farmers whereby they would pay cash in order to rent a piece of land. To get equipment and supplies until harvest time, these tenant farmers had to agree to sell their crops to a local merchant.
6. Sharecropping and tenant farming were two methods by which African Americans were able to survive economically during the period after the Civil War.
7. In the election of 1877, President Hayes' re-election was in the hands of southern Democrats. He decided to remove all federal troops from the southern states and allow for former Democrats to regain complete control of the South in return for their support of his reelection. This deal became known as the Compromise of 1877. It brought about the end of Reconstruction and the return of control of the South by southern whites.

CONTENT AREA TWENTY-EIGHT: EXPANSION INTO THE LAST WEST (1865–1900)

This region included the Great Plains, which stretched from Canada to Mexico and from the Rocky Mountains eastward to almost the Mississippi River. This region includes the states of North Dakota, South Dakota, Oklahoma, Kansas, Colorado, Montana, part of Texas, Nebraska, and Wyoming. The invention of the cotton gin also motivated the settlement of southern regions west of the Mississippi because the raising of cotton required more land and cheaper means of production.

Also included in this region was the Great Basin, which lies beyond the Rocky Mountains. This area was made up of such states as New Mexico, Nevada, Idaho, Arizona, and Utah. Later, it also included California and Oregon.

The Last West was first settled by miners who searched for silver and gold. Lodes, or large deposits, of silver were first discovered in South Dakota, Colorado, and Nevada. In 1873, Virginia City, Nevada, had the largest and richest lode in the history of mining. Miners would rush into an area where a discovery was made and stay until they could find no more silver or gold. Then they would move to somewhere else. However, with each location, farmers and settlers had remained behind and continued to live on the land after the miners had left.

The Cattle Kingdom: The 1770s and 1880s

The Plains proved to be a wealthy region for the raising of cattle. The short grass that grew on the Plains was good for cattle raising. For cattlemen to raise large herds of cattle, they needed large expanses of land. This brought them into conflict with Native Americans. Many battles were fought between the Plains Indians and the cattlemen. These Indians were able fighters who were skilled horsemen. Plains Indians had become skilled horsemen once they learned to domesticate horses that were first introduced to the area by Spanish explorers of the southwestern United States. They were able to use their spears and bows and arrows successfully at first because the cattlemen had only single-shot guns. Later on, the Indians were supplied with guns by U.S. settlers who sought to benefit themselves. This caused an escalation in the fighting between the Native American tribes and the U.S. settlers and cattlemen. Eventually, the Indians lost and many tribes were wiped out.

In a short time, however, the Colt revolver and repeating rifles were invented and used by the cattlemen and other white men. Soon, the buffalo were being killed by the hundreds and the Indians' way of life was being destroyed. Between 1850 and 1885, some 50 million buffalo were killed. The Native American tribes were slowly defeated as their way of life was altered by these events.

Cattlemen of the 1870s and 1880s ruled the Great Plains. They raised cattle and then would drive them to railroad centers to be shipped to the East where the growing population hungered for beef. Towns like Abilene, Dodge City, and Ellsworth became large cattle towns in Kansas. Famous cattle trails, like the Chisholm Trail, allowed cowboys to drive cattle to the cattle towns to be shipped by railroad to the East. The cattle towns needed law and order, so they hired people like Wild Bill Hickok to be marshals and protect people.

The Cattle Kingdom started to decline when too many cattle grazed on the Plains. Some cattlemen kept smaller herds and in order to protect their lands put up barbed wire around it. This restricted the growth of large herds. Prices for cattle also began to drop drastically, forcing many cattlemen to go out of business. Railroads had expanded to many areas where cattle could now be loaded directly into railroad cars and shipped east. Thus the long cattle drives came to an end. Farmers also trekked westward into the Great Plains and further restricted the use of the land for raising cattle.

Farming on the Great Plains

Farmers who settled on the Great Plains learned to drill wells in order to get enough water to farm and raise their crops. Windmills made of wood and later steel were used to bring the water to the surface. Once the water was pumped to the surface, farmers dug irrigation ditches to transport the water where it was needed. The farmers also used barbed wire to keep cattle out of their fields. The increase in the number of farmers allowed the Last West to be settled.

The federal government also encouraged the settling of this vast region by:

1. The Morrill Land-Grant Act of 1862—This legislation allowed people to purchase government-owned land for a small amount of money. The federal government gave 140 million acres to the states. The states in turn sold the land to banks and speculators for as little as fifty cents per acre. The banks and speculators sold the same land to settlers for prices ranging from $5 to $10 per acre.
2. The Homestead Act of 1862—The federal government itself sold 160 acre plots of land directly to individuals, including immigrants, for a $10 registration fee. These people, called homesteaders, had to build a home and live on the property for five years before they could claim ownership of the land. Many immigrants and African Americans took advantage of this offer of free land and moved into the western lands. Many women also were able to file for homesteads on their own.

CONTENT AREA TWENTY-NINE: AN INDUSTRIAL NATION

TABLE 9.10   The Rise of Industrial America

	RURAL AMERICA	INDUSTRIAL AMERICA	NATIVISM	INVENTIONS
IMMIGRATION	• Many people moved from the farm to the cities looking for jobs. • Machinery made it possible for farmers to work large areas of land with minimal help.	• Steady immigration from foreign countries into the United States.	• Backlash against foreigners because they provided cheap labor and took away jobs from U.S. workers.	• A number of inventions helped to bring about changes on the farm. • The expansion of railroads allowed many immigrants to settle in the western lands.
GROWTH	• Many farm hands and children of farmers moved into the cities for jobs, because they had been replaced by time-saving farm machines.	• Factories allowed for more people to have jobs. • Mass production of clothes, shoes, etc., allowed more and more people to be able to afford to buy them.	• People from countries such as Greece, Italy, Turkey, Japan, China, Germany, Austria, Hungary, Russia, Mexico, and countries of Latin America poured into the United States beginning in the late 1880s.	• Aqueducts and pipes were used to transport water from the reservoirs to individual houses, apartments, office buildings, and businesses. This made it possible for many people to live in the cities.
LIFE	• Children attended one school with one teacher teaching them. • In the cities children went to different schools, and they had different teachers for different classes and grades.	• New housing projects near factories and apartment houses allowed workers to live in better conditions. • Parks, libraries, newspapers, books, movie theaters, etc., allowed people to live a better life. • Children went to school.	• Chinese workers were restricted because they were used by businesses as strike breakers.	• Bicycles came into use, which allowed people to enjoy the outdoors more. • People spent more time with their families at parks and other recreational facilities like social clubs. • Sports like baseball, football, and hockey also helped people to enjoy life.
PEOPLE	• Farmers found life easier because with new machinery they were now able to produce more without quite such hard work and long hours. • Life on the farm became more enjoyable for farming families.	• Adult classes taught people the English language, American culture, and American government. • Labor unions appeared to help people get better working conditions and better pay. • Women had more leisure time on their hands because of inventions like the washing machine, sewing machines, and others.	• Stricter naturalization requirements were put into place to make it harder for foreigners. • The language and culture of the United States was greatly emphasized to foreigners.	• The invention in 1844 of the telegraph by Samuel F. B. Morse allowed people from the East to communicate with people in the West. • The invention of the telephone by Alexander Graham Bell allowed people to communicate long distance.

Industrial America (1877–1916).   Factories existed in the United States since the early 1800s. However, it wasn't until after the War of 1812 that factories became very important. The northern states were able to build many factories primarily because there were many rivers whose waters could be used to run the machines in the factories. Northern businessmen also invested in expanding their factories, whereas southerners invested their money to buy land and slaves. With a number of inventions, factories began to mass-produce cloth, shoes, boots, and other products. These factories employed hundreds of thousands of workers.

The building and expansion of railroads also helped to industrialize our country. The railroads carried raw materials to the factories, and they also transported manufactured goods to people around the whole nation. By 1861, railroads reached just beyond the Mississippi River and communication with the west was done by the invention in 1844 of the telegraph by Samuel F. B. Morse. In 1862, Congress decided to connect the East with the West. The job was given to the Union Pacific Company and the Central Pacific Company. The Union Pacific began its westward trek from Omaha, Nebraska, while the Central Pacific started eastward from California. These companies received large grants of land to build the railroads. By 1869, these two companies had met their objective.

The railroad lines came together near Ogden, Utah, and thus the transcontinental railroad was born. Railroads made it easier for people and goods to be transported great distances. People who wanted to move west and establish themselves as farmers, ranchers, or other business enterprises could do so easily. The railroads also made it easy for mining companies to transport ore from mines to many ports where it was transferred to factories and made into steel and other iron products. In 1873, Andrew Carnegie used the Bessemer process, used first in England, to produce steel at a low cost. Steel allowed the United States to make larger machines and better trains and ships. These improvements helped the United States to become an industrial nation.

Oil production was another industry that helped the United Sates become a world industrial power. John D. Rockefeller started the Standard Oil Company, which found ways to locate and drill for oil successfully throughout the United States. This oil was refined and used for many purposes. Machines used oil to run more smoothly and last longer. Kerosene and grease were also converted from oil into products that were sorely needed by many businesses and individuals.

At first, water power was used to run the machines in factories. Later steam engines improved on the process. However, a man by the name of Thomas A. Edison discovered the use of electricity, and electric power became an important source in designing new machinery more efficiently and at a low cost. The discovery of electricity also led to the invention of the telephone by Alexander Graham Bell in 1876. By 1915, telephones could be used to carry their messages all the way from the East to California in the West.

Henry Ford was another entrepreneur who sought to make machines that could make life more interesting for people. He began toying with the idea of a "horseless carriage" and invented the first automobile. He used ideas from other inventors to build automobiles with interchangeable parts. He built his first factory in Detroit, Michigan, with an assembly line that allowed his workers to assemble the automobiles much faster. By 1914, Henry Ford was able to make 146 cars per hour using his assembly line.

This period of industrial growth was made available by the many inventions designed by individuals who sought ways to reduce the time required to produce goods in great quantities. In this way, goods would be available to all people because they would be more affordable.

Population Growth.   Until 1880, most of the immigrants to the United States came from European countries like England and Germany. After the 1880s, many people immigrated to the United States from other European countries like Greece, Italy, Austria, Turkey, Hungary, and Russia. Immigrants also came form other parts of the world like China, Japan, Mexico, and Latin America. These newcomers found jobs in factories, mines, farms, ranches, and other businesses. As a result of these migrations of people into our country, the United States was able to grow very rapidly in terms of population but also in terms of becoming a very powerful industrial nation. In return for their contributions to the growth of the United States, the government made sure that it provided these newcomers with schools for themselves and their children. Adult classes taught people the English language, U.S. culture, and U.S. government. In time these people applied and became naturalized citizens. Individuals also helped immigrants in special ways. For example, Jane Addams founded the Hull House in Chicago where working mothers could leave their children for the day while they went to work. Other activities at Hull House included reading and cooking clubs for older children and for adults. Addams also was instrumental in pushing for legislation that made milk safe for children and for laws to protect women. Other organizations sought to help the poor and needy of the cities by opening houses for home care.

To accommodate the huge number of people, cities had to design and build cheap housing close to where they worked. The result was the building of apartment buildings that were roomier and safer than older unsafe buildings. The new buildings used concrete reinforced with steel rods to ensure the buildings' strength. Steel was also used to make the framing for the buildings strong and durable. Other buildings, such as hotels, were also built to accommodate the needs of individuals such as travelers and business people. Business buildings of every kind and style were also built to house the offices and places of business for many companies and individuals. In 1885, the first skyscraper was built in Chicago. It was called the Home Insurance Building; New York's Flatiron Building was built in 1902.

The growing populations of the cities also needed fresh water. This demand cause cities to drill wells for fresh water in some places, but large reservoirs were built in other large cities like New York City. Aqueducts and pipes were used to transport water from the reservoirs to individual houses, apartments, office buildings, and other businesses. With the availability of water, the cities set up fire departments.

Other changes allowed people to move faster and more easily to places of employment or just for travel. Cities built subways to allow people to travel underground; street cars traversed the central areas of cities, elevated railroads were built, and electric-powered streetcars made their appearance by the late 1890s.

The United States was becoming a multicultural nation through cultural diffusion: the infusion of many ideas that impacted our culture. The Chinese gave us paper for our newspapers and books; the Germans invented the printing press; the raising of wheat and weaving came to us from the Middle East; and many other wonderful inventions were brought for us to enjoy.

Nativism.   Nativism, the idea of restricting immigration, reappeared again during the 1880s. Nativism had first appeared during the 1850s when U.S. citizens tried to restrict Chinese immigrants. Nativists in the Midwest demanded that the English language and U.S. culture should be emphasized in adult classes followed by stricter citizenship education courses for those who wanted to become naturalized citizens. In 1885, nativists were influential in getting the labor contract laws repealed in order to keep people like the Chinese from being recruited to come to the United States. Many businesses and companies also made it a practice to bring in foreigners to do the jobs that striking workers were unwilling to do. This caused many citizens to become hostile toward foreigners. In 1894, Republican senator Henry Cabot Lodge organized the Immigration Restriction League, whose primary purpose was to require immigrants to pass literacy tests as a condition of admittance to the United States.

Family Life.   During this industrial expansion, family life took on some interesting characteristics: Families would gather and have dinners together; they would be together usually in the morning and evenings. Children in the cities attended different schools: The younger children attended elementary schools, and the older attended high schools. Each class had its own teacher. Schools were not located in the same area for all children. Children living on farms usually attended the same school, and a single teacher taught all grade levels. During this time, children were now looked upon as consumers rather than as producers. During colonial times

parents had many children because they needed workers for their farms, otherwise the family would not prosper.

Women found more time on their hands because of new conveniences. Inventions like gas and electric stoves made it possible to cut the amount of time needed for cooking, because they did not have to collect wood or wait for the wood to burn before they could cook. Cooking now took only a fraction of the time. Women also did not have to spend a lot of time canning because factories now canned and produced every type of food imaginable. Water for washing clothes, the dishes, and taking baths was now available at the turn of the faucet. No longer did women have to transport water from a distance. These new inventions and conveniences allowed women to join clubs, read magazines and newspapers, and carry on recreational activities with their families. Popular games like baseball became a national sport after the Civil War. Shortly thereafter, football, basketball, and hockey were games enjoyed by all. Additionally, people rode bicycles for enjoyment and recreation as well as attending concerts, visiting libraries, museums, and theaters.

U.S. Farms Change.   Changes were also evident on the farms. Starting with the invention of the steel plow, farmers were able to till larger areas and produce more. Machines for cutting crops like grain were also invented. Threshing machines made it possible for farmers to separate the kernels of grain from the stalks and also to bundle and tie the cut grain. After 1900, farmers saw the appearance of tractors, which they could use to do much of the hard work. Machinery made it possible for farmers to work large areas of land with minimal help. This caused many farm hands and members of farm families to move to the cities for jobs. By 1920, people in the cities greatly outnumbered people on the farms. Interesting enough was the fact that farmers produced an abundance of food to support the growing populations of the great cities while the city people made machines and other products needed by farmers. This created an atmosphere of interdependence among the two groups.

Prohibition Groups and Purity Crusaders.   There was a revival of the Temperance Movement in the late 1800s. It was supported by the Prohibition Party (1869), the Women's Christian Temperance Union (1874), and the Anti-Saloon League (1893). The agenda of the Temperance Movement included opposition to drinking and opposition to immoral activities.

Appearance of Socialism and Labor Unions.   During the 1890s, almost 90 percent of U.S. citizens were not sharing in the great prosperity of the United States. Most workers were just making ends meet. They were poor, and they knew it. A new economic and political philosophy made its appearance at this time in the form of socialism. Socialist ideas were spread through the teachings of a German, Karl Marx, who saw inequities between the profits reaped by rich and the prevalent conditions of the poor workers. Some Americans sympathized with some of the tenets of socialism but most of them were reluctant to embrace socialism. U.S. workers turned instead toward labor unions for help. In 1869, the Noble Order of the Knights of Labor was organized in Philadelphia. People from all walks of life and every type of work were encouraged to join this labor union. Under the leadership of Terence Powderly, this labor union won some good labor reforms that included:

- Equal pay for equal work.
- An eight-hour work day for workers.
- An end to the long hours of child labor.

The Knights of Labor became involved in a conflict with railroad owner Jay Gould, who in 1885 tried to reduce workers' wages. Union members insisted that the union take a stance against this action by Gould. Upon its members' insistence, the union decided to act and was successful in getting Gould to back away from the wage cut. As a result, the membership in the Knights of Labor skyrocketed to over 700,000. Eventually, the union became involved in a number of other strikes and was not successful. As a result, the union lost members and began to decline. By the 1890s this union had almost disappeared.

A new union formed in 1886 under the leadership of Samuel Gompers. It was called the American Federation of Labor or AFL. This union differed from the Knights of Labor. The AFL organized workers by skill or trade into smaller unions. The issues that were important to this union were wages, working hours, and working conditions. The union did not encourage African Americans to join; however, they were allowed. The union also did not want women to join.

A number of union strikes took place between 1881 and 1900. The main issues included wages, hours of the work day, and the opportunity of workers to organize into unions.

Well-known strikes include:

- The Haymarket Strike of 1886—The main issue was the eight-hour work day. Scabs, or strike breakers, had been hired to do the work of union members. Police officers were brought in to keep the peace between the two groups. However, someone threw a bomb into a police formation in Chicago's Haymarket Square, killing seven policemen. This caused the authorities to hang four leaders of the union and imprison others. However, the individual responsible for throwing the bomb was never found. The governor of Illinois eventually pardoned those union leaders who were jailed.
- The Homestead Strike of 1892—Union workers at a Carnegie plant in Homestead, Pennsylvania, called for a strike when Henry Frick tried to roll back wages. Frick decided to call in a private police force, called Pinkertons, to break up the strike. Violence broke out between the Pinkertons and union strikers. A number of people were killed on each side. Eventually, the union called off the strike and the Carnegie plant remained nonunion until the 1930s.
- The Pullman Strike of 1894—This strike involved the railroad industry and the American Railway Union led by Eugene V. Debs. George Pullman, the inventor of the Pullman railroad sleeping cars, had built a town and cheap housing for his workers. People were able to pay for the housing with their wages. However, the depression of 1893 forced Pullman to lay off workers and drastically cut the wages of the remaining workers. However, the cost of housing remained the same as before. The workers went on strike to call attention to this inequity. The strike, however, disrupted railroad services, including the delivery of mail. The railroad asked the federal government to intervene because of the disruption of mail delivery. President Grover Cleveland sent in the army to keep orders. In the process a number of people were killed. Eugene Debs was jailed for six months, and the union became disorganized and finally fell apart.

These strikes laid the foundation for government opposition to unions. As a result, unions were strictly limited for the next thirty years.

Other Protests.   A populist revolt took place in the 1890s that united people from different ethnic and racial backgrounds. White and African American farmers had a common cause. These farmers did not share in the wealth of industrial America. Tariffs had been instituted against imported goods in order to strengthen goods raised or manufactured in the United States. These tariffs helped the industrial factory owners by protecting them against foreign competition. Because of the reduction of foreign competition, manufactured goods' prices at home rose higher for workers. Farmers were not happy with these prices, but at the same time they did not want foreign food products to enter the United States. At the same time, foreigners who wanted to buy U.S. produce abroad could not do so because they did not have enough U.S. currency available to them. Either way, farmers were unhappy with tariffs.

African Americans became interested in higher education at this time. By 1900 there were several thousand college graduates from over thirty African American colleges. Booker

T. Washington was one such graduate. In 1895 he made a speech at the Atlanta Exposition where he sought to encourage African Americans to seek help to improve their social and economic status. Because of his peaceful approach, Washington was consulted by the president of the United States and other business people on issues involving race relations.

Another issue with farmers was the supply of money available at home. Following the Civil War, the federal government had taken a lot of paper money out of circulation. This caused a deflation to occur, a dropping of prices. This made farmers very unhappy because they were not able to make ends meet financially. Two groups evolved out of this issue over currency. Those who favored deflation wanted money to remain scarce, but those favoring inflation wanted to increase the amount of money in circulation. The deflationists were able to convince the federal government to do away with the bimetallic standard that permeated our nation. Until 1873, the United States made gold or silver coins, including certificates that could be turned in for either gold or silver. Starting in 1873, however, the deflationists influenced the government to adopt a gold standard for its currency. Farmers were not happy with this development. They wanted a free silver currency whereby the government could coin silver dollars in order to increase the money supply.

In 1866, Oliver H. Kelley organized the Patrons of Husbandry, or the Grange for short, in order to help farmers with their issues. The Grange became popular because it was able to address some of the farmers' concerns, including prices for goods, fees paid to railroads, and the formation of cooperatives whereby farmers could buy goods in large quantities and therefore save money. The Grange's influence began to wane when farmers decided to support other organizations who supported free silver as a basis of the national currency. The farmers turned to the Greenback Party to help them with this issue.

The Farmers' Alliance party replaced the Greenback in the 1880s. This Alliance stood against railroad monopolies that caused farmers to pay high prices and fees. The Alliance proved successful in convincing legislators to pass laws regulating the railroads, increasing the circulation of currency, passing antitrust legislation, and providing farmers with credit.

The Farmers' Alliance proved to be a boon to women as well because many women served as officers of the organization and participated in public speeches. One of the most popular speakers for the Farmers' Alliance was Mary Elizabeth Lease, a Kansas lawyer, who was able to deliver hypnotizing speeches while at the same time winning support for women's political rights.

The federal government was not successful in helping farmers to deal with their plight. The presidents of this period did not have the political clout necessary to make many changes, although they were able to pass some legislation regulating certain monopolies. As a result, the Farmers' Alliance was able to win some political offices in the South.

In 1892, the Alliance organized its own political party, the Populist Party. This party called for the increase of money circulation, the change from a gold to a free silver standard, a graduated income tax, and ownership of the transportation and communication systems by the government.

In 1896, the Populists selected William Jennings Bryan, a silver advocate, to be their candidate for president, while the Republicans selected William McKinley, who supported the gold standard. Bryan lost the election because he failed to win much support in the urban and industrial cities and states. The Republican Party also had the advantage of having the support of voters in large urban states. In 1900, prices of gold fell and Congress, as a result, again voted to make gold its standard of currency.

The period between 1877 to 1900 was coined the Gilded Age by Mark Twain because it was a period of widespread corruption in government and business. It was also a period when the federal government, under the leadership of weak presidents, failed to solve the many political, economic, and social problems that plagued our country. Our country appeared to be still troubled by sectional politics three decades after the Civil War had united the South and the North.

CONTENT AREA THIRTY: THE SPANISH–AMERICAN WAR AND WORLD WAR I

The United States began to trade more heavily with other nations in Europe and in Asia. Clipper ships were used during the mid-1800s to sail around the tip of South America to China and later to Japan. In 1842, the United States had a treaty to trade with China. In 1852, the United States sent Commodore Matthew C. Perry to Japan to see if the Japanese wanted to trade. After some tense discussions, the Japanese agreed to a trade treaty.

The United States also gained some additional territory. In 1867, Secretary of State William Seward made an agreement to purchase Alaska and the Aleutian Islands from Russia. In the 1890s gold was discovered in Alaska. This caused a rush of thousands of people to Alaska. Besides gold and other resources, Alaska provided a wealthy fishing area for many fishermen. Alaska became a state in 1959.

The Hawaiian Islands were also taken over in 1898 and made a territory; Hawaii became a state in 1959. Pearl Harbor became an important Pacific port for the United States. Midway and Wake Islands were also taken over by the United States and have provided good ports for trade and military activities.

Cuba asked the United States for help against Spain in 1898. The United States used the explosion of a U.S. warship, the *Maine,* as an excuse to go to war against the Spanish. The warship was located in the Havana, Cuba, port when it exploded. The United States blamed the Spanish and declared war. U.S. soldiers, led by the likes of Theodore Roosevelt, won a number of battles against the Spanish. When the treaty was signed, Cuba became an independent nation and the United States took the Philippine Islands as a territory. It was not until July 4, 1946, that the Philippine Islands became independent from the United States.

The United States found it difficult to send ships and men to the Caribbean from the west coast during the Spanish–American War. The sailing time took months. After the war, the United States purchased a strip of land across Panama, which it called the Canal Zone. In order to make this purchase, President Theodore Roosevelt helped Panamanian rebels fight for its independence from Colombia. Panama became an independent republic and immediately gave the United States a temporary grant of a ten-mile-wide strip of land. Through this strip, the United States built the Panama Canal, which took ten years to complete. When completed in 1914, the Panama Canal made it possible for merchant and military ships, as well as ocean liners, to travel from the east coast to the west coast in a fraction of the time it previously took to travel around the tip of South America.

President Theodore Roosevelt's tenure of office was marked with interventions in a number of Latin American areas. To strengthen U.S. influence in the western hemisphere, Roosevelt issued his Roosevelt Corollary in December of 1904, which stated that the United States was no longer interested in expanding its territory. He wanted to assure nations of the hemisphere that the United States only wanted to be a good neighbor with them. However, his actions in Panama, the Dominican Republic, and other areas caused the other Latin American governments to feel resentment and mistrust towards the United States.

Progressive Era Reforms: 1900–1920

A number of reforms that took place in the 1890s continued into the early 1900s. These reforms included:

1. Urban Reforms
   - Political machines had taken over many urban cities and were able to influence the outcome of elections, regulations, and new laws. Civic-minded individuals and organizations tried to reform this kind of practices by supporting law-abiding candidates (Starr, 1985).

- Progressives also were instrumental in getting cities to take over utilities that were privately controlled and usually provided services at a high price. In taking over the utilities, city governments were able to offer the services at more affordable prices (Fehrenbacher & Snyder, 1964).
- Mayors, such as Hazen Pingree, felt that welfare services should be provided for the people, especially those who were poor, so he provided people with public baths, public parks, and work-relief programs (Jackson & Schultz, 1972).

2. Reforms at the State Level
- Reform-minded legislators and governors tried to make things better for people. Reformers like Governor Robert La Follette of Wisconsin and Governor Hiram Johnson of California helped to pass laws that made state governments more efficient (Olin, 1968). They passed state labor laws, safety laws, and factory legislation to help U.S. workers. La Follette was also influential in bringing about the direct primary whereby voters could select candidates for upcoming elections (Burgchardt, 1992).
- Labor reformers sought to establish labor relations departments to help employers and employees resolve their differences through arbitration (Fisher, 1953).

3. Reforms at the Federal Level
- Legally binding arbitration legislation was passed and supported by people like President Theodore Roosevelt when conflict arose between the United Mine Workers in 1902 and the owners (Scamehorn, 1992).
- In 1906 the Pure Food and Drug Act and the Meat Inspection Act sought to require labeling on food and a rating system for meat (Libecap, 1992).
- Antitrust legislation forced many companies like Standard Oil and the American Tobacco Company to reorganize because they did not serve the good of the public (Abrams, 1963).
- The National Reclamation Act of 1902 was passed in order to protect scarce water resources (Abrams, 1963).
- The Eighteenth Amendment, known as the Prohibition Amendment, which was passed in 1919 but repealed in 1933, sought to ban the making and selling of liquor (Hamm, 1995).
- Women's suffrage was another reform that had begun decades earlier. Women's movement leaders like Susan B. Anthony, Carrie Chapman Catt, Alice Paul, and others fought for the right of U.S. women to vote (Cullen-Dupont & Frost, 1992). Women demonstrated by the thousands in many cities. They held rallies and made speeches throughout the nation. They volunteered their services during World War I. On August 26, 1919, the Nineteenth Amendment to the U.S. Constitution was ratified, giving women the right to vote (Brown, 1993).

World War I

TABLE 9.11 Europe's Alliance's during World War I

ALLIED POWERS	CENTRAL POWERS	NEUTRAL COUNTRIES
Serbia	Germany	Norway
France	Austria–Hungary	Sweden
Great Britain	Ottoman Empire	Switzerland
Belgium	Bulgaria	Spain
Russia		Albania
Italy		Netherlands
Greece		
Romania		
Finland		

In 1914, war broke out in Europe. Secret treaties between various countries in Europe had created some volatile situations. The immediate cause of World War I was the assassination of Archduke Francis Ferdinand and his wife Sophie. Austria-Hungary believed that Bosnians were behind the assassination. It, therefore, insisted that Serbians apologize and meet certain demands. When Serbia balked at these demands, Austria-Hungary declared war. As a result of alliance agreements Germany and Austria-Hungary were on one side and Russia, England, and France were on the side of Serbia. Germany declared war on Russia first and then decided to declare war on France as well. Germany tried to get to France by invading Luxembourg and Belgium. When this invasion took place, Great Britain decided to declare war on Germany. Other countries took sides in this conflict. The Ottoman Empire, which included Turkey, decided to fight on the sides of Germany and Austria-Hungary, known as the Central Powers. Italy joined the Serbian side, known as the Allies.

The United States did not want to participate in this war. Woodrow Wilson, our president, did not want the United States to be drawn into this conflict and tried to keep the United States neutral.

It proved a difficult task for the United States to remain neutral. First the English stopped U.S. merchant ships from carrying goods to Germany. This angered Americans. German submarines, on the other hand, attacked and sank U.S. merchant ships carrying goods to England. Some sailors were killed in these actions. The United States asked Germany to stop attacking U.S. ships but Germany refused. Americans came to view Germany and its leader, Kaiser Wilhelm, as very militaristic and frightening. U.S. public opinion was also swerved against Germany when a Germany U-boat sank the British passenger liner, the *Lusitania,* on May 7, 1915. About 1,200 passengers died, including 128 from the United States.

Great Britain, meanwhile, intercepted a telegram sent to Mexico by Germany's foreign secretary, Arthur Zimmerman, in which Germany promised that if Mexico were to fight on the side of the Central Powers and attack the United States, Mexico would be able to reconquer its lost territories of Texas, New Mexico, and Arizona. In March 1917, another event took place in Russia that caused many Americans to side with the Allies. The Russian Czar Nicholas II was overthrown by revolutionaries, the Bolsheviks. This fitted well with Americans who disliked autocratic rule. The final act that caused the United States to enter the war was the sinking of three ships by German U-boats, the *City of Memphis, Illinois,* and *Vigilancia.* On April 6, 1917, the U.S. Congress passed a war resolution, which President Wilson signed, thus declaring war on Germany and the Central Powers.

Thousands of U.S. soldiers, under the command of General John J. Pershing, fought in the war in Europe. The government called upon all U.S. citizens to help in the war effort. Citizens from different ethnicities joined together in this war effort. Some helped in factories, some grew food and supplies for the war effort, and others fought in the front lines in Europe. Many African Americans enlisted to fight in the war and others went to work in factories to help with the production of war goods.

The U.S. Congress passed the Selective Service Act in May of 1917 in order to draft young men into military service. Twenty-four million men registered for the draft by the end of 1918, but only 3 million were chosen to be drafted. There were other individuals who volunteered to participate in the war effort in Europe. Women volunteered to serve as nurses, telephone operators, clerks, and drivers.

Events during the War

- In Russia the Bolsheviks took over the government under the leadership of Vladimir Lenin and set up a Communist government. A civil war within Russia forced Lenin to make peace with Germany. This allowed Germany to bolster its attack on France.
- When the German armies were within fifty-six miles from Paris, France, the U.S. armed forces came to the aid of the French. On August 8, 1918, the Allied Powers using newly invented tanks, fought the German forces at the Battle of Amiens. The Allies were able to stop the German advance. Although Germany sent feelers for an end to the war, the

Allies decided that total surrender was required. With 500,000 American troops and 100,000 French troops and the support of airplanes dropping bombs from the air, the Allies moved in for the final assault. On November 11, 1918, the war was over and the Kaiser had fled Germany.

■ The United Sates lost 50,000 soldiers; the French lost over a million soldiers, the British lost 900,000 soldiers. Overall, there were 8 million deaths among the soldiers and sailors; there were also 20 million civilian casualties across Europe.

The Versailles Treaty.   The Treaty of Versailles was signed by the Allied Powers on June 28, 1919. The United States, however, did not declare the war officially over until July 2, 1921. President Wilson had been disappointed by the treaty because he had hoped to win some concessions from the Allied Powers:

1. He wanted to give German colonies self-determination.
2. He wanted to establish collective security through the creation of a League of Nations. However, the U.S. Congress refused the idea, even though the other Allied countries voted for it.

The Treaty of Versailles required that reparations were to be paid by Germany to the tune of $33 billion. This caused a humiliation for Germany, and Germany never forgot this.

The 1920s and 1930s.   The 1920s brought a renewed emphasis on isolationism in the United States. U.S. citizens had become disillusioned with the United States' participation in the war and wanted our country to totally withdraw from international affairs of any kind. Nativism again reappeared. Nativists came to believe that people from foreign countries could not be trusted to be loyal citizens. As a result, the Congress in 1921 passed legislation limiting the number of immigrants coming into the United States to 350,000. Again in 1922, the Congress slashed immigration to 164,000. Many nativists wanted to specifically restrict the immigration of people from southern and eastern Europe because most of those people were Catholics.

A number of changes took place in the United States during this time:

1. In the area of women's rights, women were now being able to serve on juries, the government provided money for prenatal and infant health care, and women could vote.
2. Thousands of African Americans moved to the North to fill job vacancies during the war. However, they found discrimination and prejudice in the North as well.
3. During the 1920s, the Republican Party took and held onto the White House.
4. The 1920s became the era of jazz music. During this era the behavior of people, especially the young, changed dramatically. With the advent of the automobile, young people did not have to meet at their homes. They could now travel to other places. Young women began dressing in more revealing clothing, wore makeup, and adopted new behaviors that were encouraged by young men.
5. The convenience of cars allowed greater freedom for women who could now drive to do their shopping. Women also bought new sewing machines, vacuum cleaners, and other machines to help them.
6. Movie theaters began showing movies with sound starting in 1927. Studios like Warner Brothers and Columbia began making big money from ticket sales.
7. Sports became a great pastime for Americans, and many sports figures became heroes.
8. The 1920s saw the birth of fundamentalism, a religious movement that led to the Scopes trial in Dayton, Tennessee. The American Civil Liberties Union (ACLU) defended John T. Scopes over the issue of creation versus evolution.

9. The 1920s also saw a renewed effort by the Ku Klux Klan to recruit new members. The KKK terrorized not only African Americans, but also Catholics, Jews, and other groups. Its power came to an end by the end of the 1920s.

10. Other important events of the 1920s included chain stores, radios, increased migration of people, and increased leisure time.

In other parts of the world, like Italy, fascism took hold as workers revolted because of bad economic times. Italy's middle class later supported the rise of Benito Mussolini because he promised to put an end to this widespread worker revolts.

The 1929 Stock Market Crash.   The 1920s was a period of prosperity for some people. For others, it was very difficult. However, many who were hard pressed did a lot of buying on newly established personal debt or credit. Farmers had invested in new machinery, and production was very high during the war years. After the war, prices began to fall quickly because there was no less demand for food. As a result, farmers could not meet their payments for land and machinery that they had purchased. Additionally, factories went into a slump and factory workers saw their wages plummet. In other areas of the economy, like mines and the textile mills of the South, things were not going so well. All of these factors should have been interpreted as signaling bad times ahead, but people did not see them clearly. Starting in October 1929, the Dow Jones average dropped twenty-one points in one hour. The following day many investors started selling instead of buying. Stock prices began to fall rapidly. Other people began selling their stocks as well. By November 13, the Stock Market had lost over $30 billion. The aftermath of the Stock Market crash affected all sectors of the economy:

1. Over 4 million people lost money on investments.
2. Workers were laid off because of factory closures.
3. Thirteen million people were unemployed by 1932.
4. The Gross National Product fell from $103 billion in 1929 to $56 billion by 1933.
5. Farm prices fell; restaurants and small businesses closed; household workers were dismissed by the wealthy; banks closed; international trade, banking, and manufacturing suffered great losses; the world settled in for a worldwide depression.
6. Conditions on the Great Plains worsened by continued drought that created a dust bowl. This caused a great exodus of hundreds of thousands of people from Oklahoma, Kansas, Texas, and other states of that region.
7. Children began to suffer from malnutrition and poor health.
8. Men and women felt ashamed because they were without work.
9. Discriminatory practices increased against African Americans.

Surviving the Effects of the Depression.   People tried many ways to survive this gloomy period during the 1930s:

1. People swapped work with their neighbors.
2. People depended on things that they could do for themselves in order to survive. They raised their own chickens, raised vegetables, used wild berries for jelly. People lived together in crowded conditions and helped one another in many ways.
3. Religious and charitable organizations banded together to form soup kitchens in order to feed many hungry people.

The "New Deal."   President Herbert Hoover tried to get the economy going again through a number of measures such as the Hawley-Smoot Tariff, which did not work, and the setting up of the Reconstruction Finance Corporation to give credit to banks. Nothing seemed to work. For the 1932 presidential election, the Democrats nominated Franklin Delano Roosevelt as their candidate. He proposed the New Deal—a program aimed at reconstructing the economy and creating jobs for people. He was elected president. His first actions included:

1. Creating the Federal Deposit Insurance Corp on June 16, 1933. Roosevelt asked Congress to close all banks and asked that it pass the Federal Deposit Insurance Corporation legislation, which insured individual deposits up to $5,000. This action reassured people that they could once again do business with banks. The banks were reopened and business began to pick up briskly as people deposited their money instead of taking it out.
2. Roosevelt proposed a public works program to put people to work. Projects included building and repairing roads, airports, sewers, bridges, and many other such projects and activities.
3. New Deal programs included the organization and creation of various work agencies such as the Civilian Conservation Corps (CCC), the Public Works Administration or (PWA), and the National Youth Organization (NYA).
4. In 1935, the Social Security Act was passed that provided retirement pensions and benefits to those 65 years old and older. It also provided unemployment for those out of work and payments to children whose fathers were dead or had left the family without support.

CONTENT AREA THIRTY-ONE: WORLD WAR II

Through the 1930s, events outside the United States became very gloomy and dangerous:

1. Benito Mussolini brought fascism to Italy. Mussolini and many Italians felt short-changed by the Treaty of Versailles that ended World War I. Because of this dissatisfaction, they banded together with other dissatisfied Italians to form the Fascist Party in Italy. Slowly, Mussolini and his backers took over political power in Italy.
2. Adolf Hitler took power in Germany. Hitler had fought in World War I as a private and had been wounded. When the war came to an end, he felt that Germany had been short-changed and treated unfairly. He decided to join the German Workers' Party in 1919. Because he was a fiery speaker, he soon controlled the party. In 1920, this party changed its name to the National Socialist German Workers' Party, or its shorter name, Nazi Party. When the depression hit Germany, Hitler and his party found many unhappy Germans who were willing to join him. In 1933, Hitler used his party's strength in the German parliament to help elevate him to the post of chancellor. He was then given dictatorial powers to help him deal with Germany's economic, political, and social problems. He named his new government the Third Reich. Hitler began to mistreat the Jewish people, blaming them for all of the problems Germany encountered. He put many Jews in concentration camps, where a large number were exterminated in gas chambers. He then sent his troops into the Rhineland and took it over. In 1936, Hitler formed alliances with Italy and Japan. Together these three nations made up the Axis Powers.
3. Japan started on the path of aggression in Asia. The Japanese military embarked on an aggressive policy of conquest in order to be able to use the resources of conquered areas for natural resources that their country lacked. In 1931, Japan invaded Manchuria, a Chinese region rich in minerals. In 1937, the Japanese took over Shanghai, Nanjing, Beijing, and other Chinese cities. In 1941, Japan continued its aggression into Southeast Asia.

Hostilities Begin

France and Great Britain were reluctant to enter into a conflict with Germany or Italy. They followed a policy of appeasement and let Hitler have his way. In 1939, Hitler and Mussolini had helped Spanish insurgents, under the leadership of General Francisco Franco, to take control of Spain. Again France and Britain remained neutral, and only the Soviet Union sent military aid to the Loyalist forces of Spain's King Alfonso XIII. General Franco went on to organize a fascist government that was to last until the 1970s. Hitler turned toward Austria and Czechoslovakia as his next targets. He invaded and took over Austria then demanded that the Sudeten Germans of Czechoslovakia be given self-rule or he would attack. The prime minister of Great Britain tried to dissuade him from attacking. However, Hitler was able to gain the approval of Great Britain and France to annex the Sudetenland with the promise that he would not attack any new areas. He was allowed to do so, and he went on to take not only the Sudeten region but also the whole of Czechoslovakia.

Hitler became overconfident with his ability to take over new territory. In March 1939, he demanded that a corridor of land running through Prussia be given back to him by Poland. Hitler at this point decided to make friends with the Soviet Union, whereby Stalin would guarantee his neutrality in the event war broke out with Great Britain and France. Stalin would, with Hitler's blessing, be able to control eastern Europe. This agreement is known as the Nazi–Soviet Pact.

On September 1, 1939, Hitler attacked Poland. Two days later Great Britain and France declared war on Germany and thus World War II began. Hitler moved very quickly to attack and take over Denmark on April 9, 1940, followed by Norway, France, the Low Countries, Yugoslavia, and Greece. He did this in the short period of two years. Germany tried to defeat Great Britain by attacking by sea and by air. However, Germany was unsuccessful. The British refused to surrender. Hitler, then, decided to go after the Soviet Union, despite his nonaggression pact. In June 1941, he launched his first attack on Russia. He was able to take some three million prisoners, but the winter proved too severe for his troops and many German soldiers died. At this point the Japanese made their sneak attack on Pearl Harbor, and Hitler decided to declare war on the United States.

The United States had tried to remain neutral at first. President Roosevelt, however, had convinced Congress of the need of a two-ocean navy and the need to pass a Selective Service Act. These two actions were approved in 1940 and Roosevelt ordered men to be drafted and trained. On December 7, 1941, the Japanese made a sneak aerial attack on Pearl Harbor, destroying a number of U.S. ships and killing many sailors. This act, and the fact that Hitler had declared war on the United States, was what got the United States into World War II.

Germany decided to attack Russia again in 1942. This attempt at conquering Russia also failed because Soviet troops, with the help of Allied and U.S. supplies, were able to rout the German army. After November of 1942, British and U.S. forces fought a number of battles that forced the Germans out of Africa. Then the Allies landed in Sicily in 1942–1943, thus forcing Italy to surrender. Beginning in June 1944, the Allied armies were able to liberate France, Belgium, and finally Germany through the Normandy invasion, which created a second front and gave the Soviet Union an opportunity to take a breather from the mounting pressure it was experiencing from the German forces. The Allied armies met the Soviet army on the Elbe River in May of 1945.

The Cost of the War in Europe.   Millions of people were killed during this war and the whole of Europe lay in ruins:

1. Fifteen million military personnel were killed.
2. Thirty-five million civilians were killed.
3. Six million Jews were killed by the Nazis in what has been described as the Holocaust.

The War in the Pacific.   Japan had hoped to fight the United States to a standstill whereby the Japanese could negotiate a peace treaty recognizing Japanese hegemony in east Asia. As such, the Japanese moved quickly to conquer such U.S. outposts as Guam and the Philippine

Islands. They also moved on to attack and conquer the British and Dutch colonies throughout Southeast Asia. Then they moved on to the Bismarck archipelago and New Guinea.

In 1942, at Midway Island, however, U.S. aircraft carriers were in a position to attack and defeat a major Japanese carrier force. This dampened Japan's rapid advance in the Pacific. The United States at this time was fighting at two fronts. The strategy was for a major effort on the European theater of the war while maintaining a good fighting force in the Pacific. The United States planned to hop from island to island beginning with the Philippines and moving towards the Marianas. The Marianas could be used as bombing bases against Japan.

On July 16, 1945, the United States had experimented with and detonated the first atomic bomb. This new and destructive weapon could now be used against Japan in order to shorten the war in the Pacific. President Harry S Truman had to make that decision just four months after he took over the presidency, after the death of President Roosevelt in April 1945. President Truman wasn't sure what to do, but after some soul searching and discussions with his advisors, he decided to use the bomb because of two main factors: First, if he just invaded Japan, there would be very heavy casualties. Second, Americans were very bitter toward Japan's sneak attack on Pearl Harbor. Therefore, he ordered the dropping of an atomic bomb on Hiroshima on August 6, 1945. An estimated 70,000 Japanese were killed and thousands of others were injured. A second atomic bomb was dropped on the city of Nagasaki three days later, killing about 40,000 people. Following these bombings, the Japanese decided to surrender unconditionally on August 14, 1945.

CONTENT AREA THIRTY-TWO:
POST–WORLD WAR II AMERICA (1945–1960)

World War II ended in May 1945. However, serious divisions had emerged between the United States, Great Britain, and the Soviet Union. The Soviet Union's behavior toward the areas they had liberated was very disturbing. There was no doubt in anyone's mind that the Soviets intended to stay in those countries and establish communist regimes. A meeting of the "Big Three" took place in July 1945 in a suburb of Berlin called Potsdam. Germany at this point was divided into four occupation zones as follows:

1. The eastern and middle portions were controlled by the Soviets.
2. The northwest portion was controlled by the British.
3. The southeast portion was controlled by the United States.
4. The southwest portion was controlled by the French.

In addition to Germany being portioned among the Allies, the city of Berlin was similarly divided into four occupation sectors. The Big Three also agreed that a four-power tribunal was to be set up at Nuremberg to judge Nazi war criminals.

Because the United States was still fighting the Japanese, President Truman was eager to get the Soviet Union to enter the war in the Pacific to help bring it to an end. The United States had no idea if dropping the atomic bomb on Japan would cause that nation to surrender, so it tried to elicit the participation of the Soviets to help bring an end to war in the Pacific. As a result, President Truman went along with the decisions made at Potsdam. These decisions were to be temporary until a peace treaty could be signed. However, things turned out differently.

At the Peace Conference convened in Paris in the summer of 1946, it was agreed that:

1. Treaties were signed to end the war with Finland, Bulgaria, Romania, Hungary, and Italy.
2. The frontier lines of the Balkans were restored to what they had been in 1939.

3. Greece was to be part of the British sphere of influence, although Greek communists tried to take over and a civil war ensued that brought in the United States. This event caused the United States to institute two new policies in 1947. The first was the establishment of the Truman Doctrine, which pledged aid and assistance to any country whose independence and freedom was threatened by communism. The second policy was the establishment of the Marshall Plan, which sought to provide economic help to those countries whose economies were weakened by the war.

In the spring of 1948, communist East Germany and the Soviets decided to cut off communications to West Berlin, which was surrounded by the Russian occupation zone. The United States organized and carried out the Berlin airlift. This operation involved the sending of food to West Berlin by dropping supplies from the air. This incident caused a worsening of relations between the western powers and the Soviet Union. It was also the beginning of what Winston Churchill labeled the "Iron Curtain" around the countries that the Soviets now controlled. This resulted in cooled relations between the western powers and the Soviet Union and led to the appearance of a Cold War between the communist countries and the western democracies that was to last until 1980. World War II, then, appears to have facilitated the growth of the Soviet Union as a superpower because it was able to capture or destroy the power of traditional leadership groups in eastern Europe.

The Aims of the United States during the Cold War

The United States tried to protect its vision of the democratic elements of government, which included liberty, equality, and representative government. Additionally, the United States wanted a global economy shaped after its own capitalist economy.

The Aims of the Soviet Union and Its Allies during the Cold War

The Soviet Union under Stalin became a totalitarian dictatorship with a strong central government that controlled all means of production in the Soviet state. Stalin also set up similar governments in the satellite states it controlled. A communist ideology pervaded the new Soviet order. The governments of the Soviet Union and other socialist countries depended on an economy whose governments set production quotas for workers. The Soviet Union, for example, started five-year plans by which workers had to meet certain conditions or quotas.

Reaction of Western Democracies to the Cold War

The United States and its allies followed a policy of containment against the Soviet Union and its communist allies. They organized into a new alliance called the North Atlantic Treaty Organization (NATO) in 1949. Its purpose was to help the United States and member European governments against insurgency from the communist states. A number of events took place during the Cold War:

1. China was turned into a communist nation by Mao Zedong in 1949. However, Chinese nationalists under the leadership of General Chiang Kai-shek retreated to the island of Taiwan where he set up a Chinese government. The United States recognized Taiwan as the legitimate China during the Cold War.
2. In 1945, Korea had been divided into two spheres of influence. There was a western sphere and a communist sphere. Korea had been divided at the thirty-eighth parallel of

latitude with Soviet soldiers occupying north of this line and U.S. soldiers occupying south of this line. In June 1950, North Korean troops invaded South Korea. By November 1950, China sent in some of its own troops to help the North Koreans. The United States, with the support of the United Nations, went to the aid of South Korea. U.S. troops were at first led by General Douglas McArthur. The war lasted until a truce was signed in 1953 with Korea still divided.

3. In Vietnam, the communist party under the leadership of Ho Chi Minh declared Vietnam a republic. However, France did not want to let go of its colony and a war ensued. Ho Chi Minh's objective was to keep France from restoring its colonial rule over Vietnam. By the mid-1950s, the United States was providing most of the aid France needed to keep on fighting Minh and his communist rebels. At an international conference in Geneva, Switzerland, in 1954, it was agreed that Vietnam be divided along the seventeenth parallel, giving Ho Chi Minh control of the north. This arrangement was to cause grave consequences in the 1960s and 1970s.

4. During the Cold War, the United States felt it necessary to protect its interests in Latin America. The United States intervened a number of times in the affairs of Latin American countries to protect its interests. In 1959, however, Fidel Castro managed to overthrow the dictator of Cuba and establish his own government. Castro eventually turned to the Soviet Union for economic assistance, and Cuba became a Soviet sphere of influence.

5. Fear of communism in the United States caused some leaders to accuse others of being soft on communism. As a result many lives were ruined. Republican senator Joseph R. McCarthy rose to prominence in politics by making such accusations. Many Americans were blacklisted in a number of industries because of these accusations.

The Postwar Economy

The U.S. economy grew very rapidly after World War II (see Table 9.12).

1. A number of corporations sprang up during this time that brought wealth and power to many people, as well as jobs for others. General Motors, Ford, and Chrysler brought new life to the automobile industry. Franchises created fast food restaurants like McDonald's, Burger King, and Kentucky Fried Chicken. All of these ventures created thousands of jobs. Employment grew in all sectors of the economy but was most pronounced in trade and finance over a period of forty years between 1920 and 1960.

2. Technology brought many changes to U.S. society. The use of atomic power to generate electricity, the invention of transistors to make calculators and computers, the invention of the television, and high-tech machinery for the farms all helped to remake U.S. society.

3. Mass production techniques were applied to housing because the population of the United States was experiencing a baby boom and housing was desperately needed. The new approach to building homes caused prices for homes to become more affordable for many people.

4. Lending companies made it possible for more and more Americans to purchase goods using credit cards. The Diner's Club credit card appeared first in 1950, was followed by the American Express card and BankAmericard.

5. Men's and women's roles became clearer during the 1950s, when it was thought that the role of the man was to get an education, get a job, and support the family. Women were supposed to be satisfied with staying at home, taking care of the house chores, having children, and raising the children. Not everyone was happy with this new contentment and groups of nonconformists, like the beatniks, challenged these traditional roles.

TABLE 9.12

PERIOD	ECONOMIC	SOCIAL	POLITICAL
1950s	• *Brown v. Board of Education of Topeka, Kansas,* declared that "separate facilities are inherently unequal." • AFDC, or Families with Dependent Children, was created to replace the earlier ADC, or Aid to Dependent Children, which had been created in the late 1930s.	• National Education Act in 1958 provided students with money to go into science and math fields. • African Americans still plagued by "Jim Crow" laws.	• Sputnik sent into space by the Soviet Union caused concern in the U.S. because there was fear of an atomic attack. • The U.S. started building bomb shelters. • Cold War is at its height with the communist countries. • NATO, or North Atlantic Treaty Organization, had been created by the U.S. and democratic nations of Europe. This was part of the 1947 Truman Doctrine, which sought to aid those nations threatened by the Soviet Union and its allies.
1960s	• President Kennedy seeks to help the poor and African Americans. • President Johnson institutes his Great Society programs to help all people. These programs were supposed to help eradicate poverty in America. • Federal programs for welfare were expanded. • The Vietnam War causes civil unrest and the economy is dragged down due to its high cost. • Peace Corps Program began under Kennedy to help undeveloped countries. • VISTA began by President Johnson to help people in America.	• John F. Kennedy wins presidency with Lyndon Johnson as vice president and begins his New Frontier programs. • Kennedy was assassinated in Texas on November 23, 1963. • Civil unrest as African Americans sought to gain recognition. • The Civil Rights Act of 1964 tried to bring about fairness and justice for all people. • Poll taxes done away with through passage of the 24th Amendment. • James Meredith seeks to enter all-white university and President Kennedy sends 100,000 troops to protect him.	• The U.S. began its own space program by not only putting men into orbit around the earth but also landing men on the moon. • Neil Armstrong walked on the moon in 1969. • There was a lot of unrest throughout the country carried on by an opposition to U.S. involvement in Vietnam. • Robert Kennedy was assassinated as he sought the Democratic nomination for president. • Richard Nixon defeats Democrat Hubert Humphrey for president. Nixon had announced his Vietnamization policy whereby he would disengage from Vietnam and bring American forces home.
1970s	• Inflation and unemployment are very high during this decade. • Nixon was too preoccupied with international affairs and paid little attention to the economy. • President Ford tried to turn the economy around through his WIN, or Whip Inflation Now, policy. • President Ford's economic policy failed and a recession followed with widespread layoff of workers, and unemployment peaked at 9 percent.	• President Carter sought to bring about an end to discrimination in America. • President Carter introduced new programs for health and welfare. • Carter's administration brought in many women and minority people.	• Nixon widened the war in Vietnam by attacking targets in Cambodia, 1970. This action caused a protest at Kent States University in Ohio where National Guardmen fired and killed four students. • In 1971 Nixon signed the SALT I treaty with Soviet Premier Leonid Breznev. • Before the election of 1972, President Nixon mined North Vietnamese harbors and began the bombing of Hanoi. • Henry Kissinger announced that the U.S. was on the brink of peace a few days before the 1972 election and Nixon was swept into office. • On April 29, 1975, the North Vietnamese who had invaded South Vietnam were successful in taking Saigon. • The U.S. forces were evacuated and the Vietnam War came to an end.

TABLE 9.12   Continued

PERIOD	ECONOMIC	SOCIAL	POLITICAL
1970s *(cont.)*	• In the presidential election of 1976, Democrat Jimmy Carter was able to portray himself as a common man, "a peanut farmer," and was able to win with the help of his running mate, Walter Mondale.		• 58,000 Americans had been killed during the Vietnam War and more than 300,000 wounded. • Before the 1972 elections, Nixon authorized the break-in of the Democratic headquarters that brought about the Watergate scandal. Its end result was the downfall of both Nixon and his vice president Spiro Agnew. • President Nixon resigned on August 9, 1974, and Gerald Ford became president. • Nixon was granted a pardon by President Ford. • In the election of 1976, Democrat Jimmy Carter of Georgia assumes the presidency. • In 1978, President Carter hosts the Egyptian and Israeli leaders at Camp David. • Shah of Iran is overthrown. • In 1979, hostage situation in Iran.
1980s	• Trickle-down economics supported by President Reagan. • Reagan believed that more government did not solve a country's problems. • George Bush promises and then reneges on taxes. • Economy weakened during Bush's tenure. • Microprocessors make their appearance and the computer revolution begins.	• Social welfare programs were attacked as taking away people's dignity. • President Reagan cut back drastically on welfare programs. • Cutbacks in social programs continued under President Bush.	• In the election of 1980, Carter loses the presidency to Ronald Reagan. • Reagan diffuses the hostage situation with Iran. • Mikhail Gorbachev became the leader of the Soviet Union. He tried to reform the Soviet System. Reagan encouraged Gorbachev to make changes.
1990s	• By 1992, the economy is on the upturn. • Stock market has a bull run after Clinton's election. • NAFTA, or North American Free Trade Agreement, is passed by Congress in 1994. • Ross Perot criticized NAFTA because he felt that jobs normally in the U.S. would be relocated to Mexico. • The U.S. helped Mexico's problems with its economy by loaning Mexico $12.5 billion. • President Clinton and Vice President Al Gore help to boost the use of the Internet as an Information Highway.	• President Clinton signed Welfare Reform bill in 1996 which made revolutionary changes to the AFDC program. • Medicare health programs were left intact by President Clinton; however, House Republicans lead by Newt Gingrich wanted changes to be made such as raising premiums for the wealthier recipients. • Block grants were provided to the states in 1996 and states were allowed to decide how to spend the money to help those on welfare.	• During President Bush's tenure, Soviet leader Gorbachev dissolved the Soviet Union on December 31, 1991. • Bill Clinton elected president and had to contend with a Republican-controlled Congress during and after the 1994 Congressional elections. • Republicans were swept into office with their "Contract with America" agenda.

(continued)

TABLE 9.12   Continued

PERIOD	ECONOMIC	SOCIAL	POLITICAL
2000s	• Starting at the end of the 1990s, the U.S. and the global economy take a turn downwards. • The stock markets worldwide lose ground. • President Bush tries to resuscitate the economy by giving tax breaks, hoping that people will spend more money and thus stimulate the economy. • Beginning in 2004, the economy appears to be slowly on the mend. • President Bush's budget for 2004 includes billions of dollars for the rebuilding of Iraq and the continued fighting in Afghanistan. • Thousands of jobs are lost in the United States as companies set up shop in foreign countries.	• Like President Reagan in the 1980s, President Bush sought to bring morality back into American consciousness. • Because of the September 11, 2001, tragedy, many Americans became fearful for their safety, especially when flying to destinations outside of the U.S. • Strict rules on travel are put into place to safeguard the U.S. at home and abroad. • In his State of the Union speech, President Bush stated that he was opposed to same-sex marriages and might seek an amendment to the U.S. Constitution to make the marriage of a man and a woman the only legal marriage.	• A tragedy struck the United States on September 11, 2001. The twin towers of the World Trade Center in New York City were destroyed by terrorists who hijacked two airplanes and then flew them into the twin towers. A third airplane crashed in a field in Pennsylvania, and a fourth hit the Pentagon in Washington, DC. On October 7, 2001, the United States strikes Taliban in Afghanistan. • As a result of the national tragedy, a Home Security Department was created for the protection of the homeland. • Spring 2003, the United States, Great Britain, and a handful of other countries invade Iraq because President Bush believed that Saddam Hussein had weapons of mass destruction. • Saddam Hussein is captured in 2004. • By February 2004, the United States has suffered the loss of over 500 troops in Iraq. • President Bush's approval rating drops below 50% in 2004. • The Democratic nominee for the 2004 election was John Kerry, who was defeated by incumbent president George W. Bush. • By February 2004, President Bush comes under attack that weapons of mass destruction did not exist in Iraq before the war.

CONTENT AREA THIRTY-THREE: CHANGES BROUGHT ON DURING THE 1950s, THE 1960s, AND BEYOND

Americans received the shock of their lives when the Soviet Union launched the first artificial satellite, Sputnik, into space in 1957. People became worried and feared that the security of the United States was in jeopardy because now the Soviet Union could attack the United States with atomic bombs via rockets such as the one that sent Sputnik into orbit. A panic gripped the nation and millions of Americans felt the need to build bomb shelters to protect themselves against atomic bombs. This event forced President Eisenhower to ask Congress to pass legislation, the National Defense Education Act of 1958, to provide low-cost loans for students to become teachers with an emphasis on science and foreign languages. Our government leaders also emphasized the need for the United States to enter the space race against the Soviet Union.

During the early 1960s, there was still prejudice against African Americans that kept them from getting decent jobs with decent pay, and their rights were restricted. African Americans had still not realized the benefits of our democracy that they were entitled to following the Civil War. Even though legislation had been passed in the form of the Thirteenth, Fourteenth, and Fifteenth Amendments to the U.S. Constitution, African Americans were still plagued by "Jim Crow" laws in the South in the 1960s. The civil rights movement of the 1960s brought many people together from all ethnicities in order to provide support for African Americans' rights. The Civil Rights Act of 1964 sought to correct the injustices suffered by African Americans. However, it took a lot of courage by many people to begin to make it a reality. Issues left over from the Reconstruction period included:

1. The civil rights of African Americans. Many African Americans could not sit in certain areas in stores and on buses. They, therefore, organized and took action against these injustices. When the Supreme Court ruled in *Boynton v. Virginia* (1960), that segregation was illegal on interstate buses, the Congress of Racial Equality (CORE) and Martin Luther King supported what was called the Freedom Rides. These Freedom Rides were taken by African Americans to see if desegregation was indeed a reality. While at first it appeared that it was so, African Americans found that in states like Alabama white people turned violent.

2. Equality in education was an issue. African Americans attended separate schools apart from white students. James Meredith decided to break with this practice by trying to transfer to the all-white University of Mississippi in 1962. To ensure Meredith's safety, President Kennedy sent the National Guard. Meredith was allowed to enter and finished his education there in 1963.

3. Jobs and housing were issues. African Americans were not hired for well-paying jobs, even though they qualified. They also were refused housing because of their race. There were many marches by African Americans who sought to bring about change. The Ku Klux Klan tried to frighten and intimidate not only African Americans but also other people who sought to help African Americans.

President Johnson signed into law the Civil Rights Act of 1964, which contained nine Titles. Title I for example, prohibits different voter registration standards for African American and whites. The Twenty-Fourth Amendment to the U.S. Constitution, which safeguarded citizens' rights, especially those of African Americans who had been required by some southern states to pay poll taxes in order to vote was also ratified. This amendment forbade states from collecting poll taxes and thus allowed all citizens access to all national elections. The Congress of the United States also passed the Voting Rights Act of 1965, which allowed the attorney general of the United States to appoint federal examiners to register voters in troubled areas, especially some of the southern states.

Other significant events of this period included:

1. African Americans were discriminated against in the areas of housing, jobs, and education. In many instances, they were segregated from other groups of people. Jackie Robinson became the first African American to break the color line in sports. His success as a baseball player helped to ease the attitudes of other Americans. In 1951, a man by the name of Oliver Brown sued the Board of Education in Topeka, Kansas, in order to get permission to send his daughter to a whites-only school. This case went all the way to the U.S. Supreme Court, which heard arguments from a brilliant African American lawyer, Thurgood Marshall, who was supporting Brown's case. The Supreme Court in *Brown v. Board of Education of Topeka, Kansas,* declared that "separate facilities are inherently unequal." In 1955, the Supreme Court ordered that all schools should desegregate. This caused problems in Little Rock, Arkansas, where African American children wanted to attend whites-only schools. President Eisenhower federalized the Arkansas National Guard and sent in paratroopers to protect the children.

   In Montgomery, Alabama, in December 1955, Rosa Parks refused to give up her seat to a white man on the bus. She was arrested and charged with violating segregation laws. This caused the African Americans under the leadership of Martin Luther King, Jr., to call for a boycott of the bus company in Montgomery, Alabama. The bus boycott was a peaceful demonstration by African Americans, and it illustrated how effective nonviolent direct action can be. The end result was the ruling by the Supreme Court that bus segregation was unconstitutional.

2. Even though the Civil Rights Act of 1964 and the Voting Rights Act of 1965 were supported by the federal authorities, still many African Americans did not enjoy the freedoms enjoyed by other people. As a result many of them turned to radical leaders in order to get their messages across. Malcolm X, for example, created his own Nation of Islam. Others, like Stokely Carmichael, allowed themselves to be jailed many times in

order to call attention to the injustices suffered by African Americans. Still others, like Huey P. Newton, became founders and members of the Black Panther Party. Black Power brought on new calls for changes to take place in order for prejudice and discrimination to end.

The New Frontier

The election of 1960 ushered in the New Frontier program of John F. Kennedy. His administration provided U.S. citizens with a brighter vision of the future by stressing the need for people to volunteer their services in order to improve conditions. He also launched programs to protect the environment, tried to help the poor, and launched a successful space program that eventually put man on the moon. He was also successful in launching the Peace Corps, which trained citizens to go overseas and help people in poor countries. Kennedy also dealt with a number of other significant events:

1. He instigated the Alliance for Progress program to help countries in Latin America, Africa, and Asia improve their transportation and communication systems.
2. Upon assuming the presidency, Kennedy was confronted with the Bay of Pigs invasion of Cuba on April 17, 1961. It proved disastrous for the new president. The United States also appeared very weak to the rest of the world.
3. Nikita Khrushchev decided to erect the Berlin Wall, which caused a lot of conflict between the United States and the Soviet Union for several decades.
4. The United States and the Soviet Union almost went to war when it was discovered that the Soviets were setting up missiles in Cuba. President Kennedy placed a naval quarantine around Cuba in 1962, and the Soviet Union was forced to dismantle the missiles. This crisis led to the signing of the Limited Test Ban Treaty dealing with atomic weapons testing.
5. Vietnam was proving to be a problem area for President Kennedy, and he sent a handful of military advisers to help the South Vietnamese.

On November 22, 1963, while parading in Texas, Kennedy was assassinated and the nation was grief-stricken. The vice president of the United States, Lyndon B. Johnson, took over as president and launched his Great Society programs. In many respects Johnson's programs were similar to what Kennedy had proposed; however, Johnson was able to push many of his programs through Congress. His Great Society programs included:

1. Johnson declared war on poverty and pushed legislation, which created the Volunteers in Service to America (VISTA), which provided people with the opportunity to help the poor in different communities.
2. Johnson signed the Civil Rights Act of 1964 into law. This act was comprised of nine titles. Each title dealt with a number of guarantees that individuals should have no matter what their ethnicity or race. The provisions of this act also empowered the Women's Rights Movement to bring feminist issues to the forefront. The National Organization for Women (NOW) was organized by feminists to help bring about gender equity for women.
3. Johnson supported the passage of the Elementary and Secondary Education Act of 1965 in order to provide help to states based on the number of children from low-income families.
4. With the passage of the Immigration Act of 1965, Johnson helped to do away with immigration quotas, which were discriminatory.
5. President Johnson became entangled in the Vietnam War. He asked Congress to pass the Gulf of Tonkin Resolution, which would grant him the power he needed to do what he wished in Vietnam without the declaration of war. By 1968, there were 543,000 U.S. soldiers fighting in South Vietnam. The war caused many protests by students in universities around the country. Young men refused to serve in the armed forces, and many left the country in order to circumvent the draft. Young people became disenchanted with social conditions in our country and many of them experimented with other ideas and experiences (including drugs).

The Nixon Administration

Vietnam. During the election of 1968, Richard Nixon declared that he had a plan to end the war in Vietnam. He was elected president and proceeded with his Vietnamization policy. He began withdrawing U.S. troops from Vietnam from 1968 through 1972. President Nixon still hoped to win in Vietnam, and he mounted an offensive against the communist sanctuaries in Cambodia. He also initiated the bombing of North Vietnam's capital city of Hanoi and many harbors. A few days before the 1972 election, Nixon announced that the war was coming to an end. He won the presidential election. In 1973, a cease-fire agreement allowed the United States to withdraw from Vietnam. It was not until 1975 that fighting ceased in South Vietnam because the South Vietnamese soldiers continued the fighting without the help of the United States.

Cost of the Vietnamese War. The Vietnam War cost the United States 58,000 deaths, 300,000 wounded, and $150 billion. Thousands of returning servicemen found it difficult to adjust to normal life, the U.S. economy was in shambles, and social conditions underwent an upheaval.

Watergate. Nixon wanted to win the election of 1972 by a large margin against his Democratic opponent. In June 1972, Nixon approved the tapping of telephones at the Democratic National Committee headquarters in the Watergate complex in Washington, D.C. However, the men hired to do the job were discovered and arrested. Nixon tried to cover up the incident but was unsuccessful. He went on to win the election but the Watergate scandal refused to go away. A special prosecutor was named to investigate the incident. When the special prosecutor, Archibald Cox, asked Nixon for the White House tapes, Nixon fired him. To make matters worse, his vice president, Spiro Agnew, had been accused of evading income taxes and had resigned his office. Nixon appointed Gerald R. Ford to become his vice president. In July 1974, the House Judiciary Committee started hearings to look into the allegations against Nixon and the possibility of impeachment procedures. Nixon, feeling that his Republican supporters had deserted him, resigned the presidency on August 9, 1974, and Gerald Ford became president.

The Ford Administration

Once Gerald Ford became president, he decided to heal the divisions cause by the Watergate scandal. He, therefore, issued Nixon a presidential pardon. As a result, Ford lost support among the U.S. people. Because of his action, Ford was not able to steer the country forward. The economy began to stagnate under Ford's leadership, and Ford was unable to keep inflation under control. When the presidential election of 1976 arrived, the voters were not forgiving and as a result Gerald Ford lost the presidency to Jimmy Carter, the Democrat.

The Carter Administration

Jimmy Carter was a very honest individual who tried to bring dignity to the office of president. Some of the events of this administration include:

1. Appointed women and minorities to his staff, because he believed in racial and gender equality.
2. President Carter was influential in getting Anwar el-Sadat of Egypt to visit Israel and begin amiable talks with the Israeli leader Menachem Begin. Both of these leaders were invited to a conference by Carter. They met at Camp David in September 1978. Playing the peacemaker, Carter convinced both leaders to sign the Camp David Accords, which outlined a framework for peace in the Middle East. As a result, Egypt became the first Arab country to recognize Israel's existence.
3. President Carter agreed to return the Panama Canal to Panama by the year 2000. This caused a lot of debate in the U.S. Senate. However, the agreement was narrowly approved.
4. President Carter established diplomatic relations with China in 1979.
5. The most critical event during Carter's administration was the overthrowing of the Shah of Iran and the hostage crisis that followed. An elderly Islamic cleric, Ayatollah Khomeini,

became the leader of Iran. When President Carter allowed the Shah to enter the United States, Iranian students attacked the U.S. embassy in Tehran and took everyone hostage. It was not until January 21, 1981, that Iran agreed to release the 52 hostages. Carter was out of office at that time and Ronald Reagan welcomed the hostages home.

It was during this time period that individual states took the responsibility to improve conditions for all workers. For example, Illinois held a Constitutional Convention in 1970, which sought and did strengthen that state's Bill of Rights by prohibiting discriminatory employment practices.

The Reagan Administration

Ronald Reagan was inaugurated in January 1981, and he began his tenure in office at a time when government had become too bureaucratic and too distant from the people. His administration ushered in a period of conservatism. During the election of 1980, Reagan had attacked President Carter on issues ranging from the handling of the economy and the hostage crisis in Iran. When the election results were in, Reagan had won by a landslide. To Reagan this meant that people agreed with his conservative ideas and wanted less government meddling in their affairs. Reagan dealt with a number of issues, such as:

1. He proposed and followed his economic plan, known as Reaganomics, which was based on the theory of supply-side economics. His first act was to cut taxes in order to stimulate the economy. He cut taxes by 5 percent in 1981, and then 10 percent in 1982–1983. He also proposed the closing of loopholes that allowed some people to not pay their fair share of taxes. He simplified the income tax brackets by reducing their numbers. Many Americans benefited by these changes to the tax code but wealthy Americans benefited the most by having their tax rate drop from 50 percent to 38 percent.

2. President Reagan, as part of his Reaganomics theory, believed in deregulation of business in order for competition to keep a check on prices. His idea was that businesses were spending too much money trying to comply with government regulations, rather than paying for improving their businesses so that more people would have jobs and prices for goods would drop.

3. In 1981, President Reagan announced a new plan, called New Federalism, with the objective of reducing the intrusion of the federal government into the lives of the people. Therefore, he told the states that federal money they received could be spent as they saw fit. This plan gave states the responsibility to help their people but not the money to do it. A recession followed for a short period of time.

4. President Reagan followed a tough line against communism. He recommended that Congress pass legislation to fund his Strategic Defense Initiative known as Star Wars, by which the United States could be protected from a missile attack from the Soviet Union. The Initiative proposed a huge satellite shield be placed in outer space that could knock out incoming missiles before they had a chance to strike land.

5. The United States was involved in a number of regions around the globe. In the Middle East, President Reagan sent Marines into Lebanon as a peacekeeping force. A truck full of explosives rammed through the gate of a Marines barrack, exploded, and killed 241 Marines. President Reagan, because of U.S. reaction to this tragedy, withdrew all U.S. troops from Lebanon.

President Reagan also sent military forces to the island of Grenada where a Cuban-style communist government had been set up. Because there were several hundred U.S. medical students on Grenada, Reagan invaded the island on the pretense of protecting the medical students. The new Grenadian government was overthrown, and free elections were allowed to choose new leaders.

6. Savings and loan banks (S&Ls) were deregulated by Reagan in order to allow them to become more profitable. Some of these S&Ls used risky methods to make money. As a result, a number of these banks went into bankruptcy, losing billions of dollars for the investors.

7. The Iran-Contra Affair was an attempt by President Reagan to use money from arms sales to Iran to bankroll secret missions against Nicaraguan guerrilla fighters known as Contras. When these secret missions and how they were funded became public knowledge, Colonel Oliver North took the blame instead of Reagan.

The Bush Administration

As President Reagan's vice president, George Bush tried to follow in the footsteps of the popular Reagan but found that he could not accomplish the kind of feats that Reagan did. In the election of 1988, Bush was challenged by Democratic Governor Michael Dukakis of Massachusetts. By election day, U.S. voters felt that neither candidate addressed the issues that concerned them. As a result, almost half of eligible voters decided not to go to the polls. George Bush was elected the new president. Some of the events associated with the Bush administration include:

1. The fall and break up of the Soviet Union in 1989. The Soviet leader, Gorbachev, wanted to reform his country because too much money was being spent on the armed forces thus crippling the Soviet economy. Gorbachev decided to allow Soviet eastern Europe to hold free elections. These countries went on to call for their independence from the Soviet Union. Gorbachev allowed these countries to become independent. The Berlin Wall was brought down by East Germans who were allowed free travel to West Germany. As a result, the two sectors reunified into a free Germany. By 1991, the Soviet Union was gone and in its place was Russia with a number of independent commonwealth states. Boris Yeltsin became the president of the new Russia and Gorbachev found himself without a job.

The fall of the Soviet Union allowed people around the world to take a look at the conditions in the former satellites where the communist system had sought to produce goods with little regard to the damage that was done to the environment. Waterways had been highly polluted, factories were dangerous places to work, and natural resources were wasted.

2. During Bush's tenure of office, Saddam Hussein, the dictator of Iraq, decided to invade Kuwait. Because of U.S. oil interest in Kuwait, President Bush asked a number of nations to join him in stopping Saddam from taking over Kuwait. Twenty-eight nations participated in Operation Desert Storm in 1991. The war, also called the Gulf War, lasted only forty-two days before Saddam's forces were forced to leave Kuwait and move back into Iraqi territory. The war was not resolved and left Saddam Hussein in power in Iraq.

3. On the home front things were not going too well for the economy. The unemployment rate had jumped to 7 percent and people were unhappy. To help the economy, President Bush decided to break his election pledge not to raise taxes. Once he raised taxes, people became angry with him. Economic issues haunted Bush in the election of 1992.

The Clinton Administration

Although Bush got high marks for ending the Cold War and the defeat of Saddam Hussein in the Gulf War, it was the economy that concerned most voters in the election of 1992. The 1992 election was a three-way race for the White House. President Bush was the Republican candidate, Bill Clinton was the Democratic candidate, and H. Ross Perot was a third-party candidate who focused mainly on the economy. Bill Clinton won the presidency with only 43 percent of the popular vote but with 357 electoral votes to Bush's 160, and none for Perot. Significant events during Clinton's administration included:

1. He asked Congress for new spending powers in order to jumpstart the economy. His first budget included both taxes and tax cuts. President Clinton added higher taxes to Social Security, income, and gasoline. These actions were not very popular with the people, who saw the rich getting richer.

2. President Clinton sought to provide universal health coverage for all Americans. His wife, Hillary, was appointed to spearhead this move. However, Congress rejected Clinton's health plan.

3. Voters in the Congressional election of 1994 decided to vote in Republicans. The Republicans under the urging of Newt Gingrich, a congressman from Georgia, made a "Contract with America." This contract promised to scale back the government, reduce taxes, and balance the budget. The Republicans scored with the voters, and many entrenched Democrats lost.

4. The congressional Republicans clashed over the budget with President Clinton. However, they proved to be too extreme, and Americans began to mistrust them. As a result, President Clinton's popularity grew.

5. During the 1996 electoral campaign, Clinton was able to get some legislation that suited many Americans through Congress. Bob Dole, a U.S. Senator, was the Republican Party's candidate. He proposed a 15 percent tax cut. However, the voters did not buy into that idea. Clinton was able to defeat Dole because he stuck to the issues that concerned most everyday Americans.

6. During his second term of office, Clinton offered Russia an economic package of $2.5 billion to help Boris Yeltsin bring a free enterprise economy to this former communist country.

7. In South Africa, Prime Minister F. W. de Klerk and the antiapartheid leader Nelson Mandela worked together to help bring apartheid down and allow the South African nation to hold free elections. Nelson Mandela was elected president of South Africa.

8. In the Middle East, Clinton was successful in bringing together the leader of the Palestine Liberation Organization (PLO), Yasser Arafat, and Israeli Prime Minister Yitzhak Rabin. They were able to forge a number of peace accords to help bring peace to the Middle East.

9. In Bosnia, President Clinton decided to participate in a NATO-sponsored bombing of Bosnia in order to force the dictator of that country to stop the ethnic cleansing war that was responsible for thousands of deaths of civilians who were Muslims. A cease-fire was the end result, and Bosnia's leaders were captured and held for trial.

10. The economy started to rebound as the North American Free Trade Agreement (NAFTA) took hold on the North American continent. This agreement was to counter the expansion of the European Union's attempt to organize a single market for a group of nations.

11. Clinton's presidency was rocked by allegations of a sexual nature against President Clinton. Clinton was humiliated by Republicans in the House of Representatives who voted to impeach him. The attempt to remove him failed, and Clinton was able to finish his term of office. His behavior in his involvement with a young government intern caused Clinton's popularity to diminish on moral grounds.

12. President Clinton and Vice President Gore were strong advocates of the new computer technology. They pushed legislation and encouraged people to use this new information highway to learn new skills and become better informed. Millions of Americans took to computing. This new avenue of information allows voters in an election year to check out a candidate's views, history, and experience in order to make a better selection of a candidate who would be best suited for the office sought. In fact, voters today have a variety of sources of information allowing them to check out the backgrounds of all candidates running for any office.

The use of the information highway also allows students in our K–12 system and in colleges and universities to locate different types of information. However, teachers and professors should caution students against using information that cannot be substantiated.

13. President Clinton, like many other public figures of the past, found that the use of compromise in his dealings with Congress and in international affairs proved to be successful. Compromise is essential in many situations where two parties cannot seem to find a common ground for any type of agreement.

The Second Bush Administration: Into the Twenty-First Century

George W. Bush is our current president. He won a contested election in 2000 against Vice President Al Gore. The election results were muddled by vote counting in Florida. The Supreme Court entered the fray and Bush was declared the victor. Like Reagan in the 1980s, Bush based his presidency on conservative values and beliefs. He sought to bring morality back into U.S. consciousness after President Clinton's affair with Monica Lewinsky in the Oval Office.

From the outset of his presidency, Bush sought to call attention to Saddam Hussein in Iraq. He felt that Iraq had weapons of mass destruction. A tragedy struck the United States on September 11, 2001. The twin towers of the World Trade Center in New York City were destroyed by terrorists who hijacked two airplanes and then flew them into the twin towers. Thousands of people died as the buildings collapsed. This caused Bush to create a new cabinet post in the form of the Department of Homeland Security. He also asked Congress to pass new legislation that gave him greater powers to detain people suspected of terrorist activities. He also vowed to hold those responsible for the 9-11 attack wherever they may hide. Terrorist leader Osama bin Laden was targeted as the person behind the attack and efforts were made to capture him. Osama bin Laden was responsible for the organization of terrorist groups like Al-Qaeda and the Taliban of Afghanistan. The United States became involved in Afghanistan where a new government was set up with the help of the United States. U.S. forces bombed of hundreds of caves where terrorists were hiding. Large caches of munitions were discovered and destroyed, but Osama bin Laden eluded capture.

President Bush then went on the offensive against Iraq's leader Saddam Hussein, whom Bush perceived as a dictator who harbored and supported terrorists and terrorist activities. He also accused Saddam of hiding weapons of mass destruction and began preparations for an invasion of Iraq. Other nations of the world urged President Bush to allow inspectors to go into Iraq and prove that these weapons existed. However, President Bush, with the help of Great Britain's Prime Minister Tony Blair, decided to invade Iraq in the spring of 2003. The United States built up its forces in the Gulf region and started bombing Iraq's cities, especially Baghdad. Iraq fell very quickly and Saddam and his army practically disappeared. However, as U.S. troops took over parts of Iraq they were met with resistance from resistance fighters who saw the Americans as invaders. The number of casualties from this type of fighting escalated and is still going on. President Bush asked Congress for $87 billion to help rebuild Iraq. The Congress did pass that legislation. Saddam Hussein was captured in the fall of 2003 hiding in a small underground room all by himself. His sons had been killed earlier by allied soldiers, and his daughters live in exile. Saddam is classified as a prisoner of war and is protected under the Geneva accords. As President George Bush begins his second term, having defeated John Kerry in the 2004 election, it is too soon to list events.

Change to a Global Economy

Beginning in the 1990s, electronic communications brought the world closer together. Countries began to invest widely throughout the world. Trade agreements brought former foes together such as the United States, China, Russia, the Western democracies, some Latin American countries, and so forth, which started looking to each other and elsewhere for fresh markets for their products. What has ensued as a result is the creation of a global economic network. Countries in Africa, some in Latin America, and others in Asia who could not compete in this global network saw their economic growth sink. Even Russia had to depend on the United States and other countries to provide it with monetary assistance in order to achieve some balance in its economy. China had already embarked upon a modernization program based on market incentives upon the death of Mao Tse-tung. This modernization has allowed China to benefit financially and to compete globally.

The U.S. Constitution and the Bill of Rights[1]

DOMAIN FIVE: UNITED STATES *(continued)*

CONTENT AREA THIRTY-FOUR: U.S. CONSTITUTION

The Constitution of the United States begins with the Preamble, or introduction. The Preamble sets the rationale behind the writing and purpose of the Constitution. It lists six reasons for the Constitution's establishment:

1. To form a more perfect union—the Articles of Confederation were weak.
2. To establish justice—it created a federal judicial system.
3. To ensure domestic tranquility—it provides for the creation of national militias to keep the peace.
4. To provide for the common defense—the armed forces protect all states.
5. To promote the general welfare—our government is there to protect its citizens' rights.
6. To secure the blessings of liberty for ourselves and our posterity—for us to enjoy our freedoms that we can pass on to our children.

After the Preamble come four Articles:

1. Article I deals with the Legislative Branch of our government. It consists of ten sections that enumerate the powers of the Senate and House of Representatives. *Note:* The power of the Legislative Branch can be checked by the Judicial Branch through the checks and balances system put into place by our founding fathers where actions of the Legislative Branch can be deemed unconstitutional.

2. Article II deals with the Executive Branch of our government. It consists of four sections that enumerate the powers and duties of the president and vice president. *Note:* The power of the Executive Branch can be checked by the Judicial Branch by allowing the Supreme Court the power of judicial review over decisions made by the president.

3. Article III deals with the Judicial Branch of our government. It consists of three sections that enumerate and explain the powers and duties of our federal courts. *Note:* The power of the Judicial Branch can be checked by the Executive Branch by having the president appoint the Supreme Court Justices with the consent of the Senate.

4. Article IV deals with the various relations between the states. It consists of four sections.

[1]Chapter contributed by Sam Marandos.

A feature of the U.S. Constitution that best embodies the concept of "federalism" lies in the wording of the Tenth Amendment, which states that "The powers not delegated to the United States by the Constitution, nor prohibited by it to the states, are reserved to the states respectively, or to the people." In other words, states can do whatever they wish as long as the Constitution does not prohibit such action or does not reserve it for the federal government.

The Constitution allows for the expansion of the rights and responsibilities of the citizens of our country because the power of the federal government and state governments are constitutionally limited (see Table 10.1).

CONTENT AREA THIRTY-FIVE: THE BILL OF RIGHTS

The Bill of Rights includes the first ten amendments to our Constitution. According to the Bill of Rights, a person accused of a crime has the right to confront his or her accusers and question them in a court of law. The Bill of Rights was added to the Constitution in 1791.

Amendment 1: Provides freedoms of religion, speech, the press, and the right to assemble.
Amendment 2: Provides for the maintenance of a militia and the bearing of arms.
Amendment 3: Prohibits housing of soldiers during peace time.
Amendment 4: Protects people against unwarranted searches and seizures.
Amendment 5: Provides for due process of law and the trial by jury and just compensation for seizure of private property.
Amendment 6: Ensures an accused the right to a fair trial.
Amendment 7: Guarantees a jury trial in civil cases.
Amendment 8: Prohibits inflicting cruel or unusual punishment on anyone.
Amendment 9: Guarantees that the rights of the people under the Constitution cannot be denied.
Amendment 10: Provides that any power not listed in the Constitution or prohibited by it belongs to the states or to the people.

Additional amendments:

Amendment 11: Provides that a citizen of one state cannot sue a citizen of another state in a federal court.
Amendment 12: Spells out the process by which a president and vice president shall be elected and allows a party to nominate its own candidates for those positions.
Amendment 13: Abolishes slavery.
Amendment 14: Guarantees the rights of all persons born or naturalized in the United States. Establishes the number of representatives each state shall have in Congress based on that state's population. It also abolishes the three-fifths compromise in Article I, Section 2. It prohibits any person who has rebelled against the United States from holding federal office, sets the penalty for such a rebellion, and accepts responsibility for all public debt.
Amendment 15: Guarantees all citizens the right to vote.
Amendment 16: Institutes the income tax.
Amendment 17: Allows for the direct election of Senators and the filling of vacancies.
Amendment 18: Bans alcoholic drinks. This is the Prohibition amendment.
Amendment 19: Gives women the right to vote.
Amendment 20: Sets the beginning terms of office for president, vice president, senators, and representatives: January 3rd for members of Congress and January 20th for president and vice president.

TABLE 10.1

	POWERS	QUALIFICATIONS	CHECKS AND BALANCES

EXECUTIVE
"Enforces the laws"
	• Commander in chief of the armed forces
	• With the approval of the Senate, appoints ambassadors, ministers, consuls, justices, and other department heads.
	• With the consent of the Senate, makes treaties with other nations.
	• Commissions all the officers of the United States.
	• Prepares and presents the federal budget to Congress each year.
		• Must be 35 years old.
		• Must be a natural born citizen.
		• Must be a resident of the U.S. for at least 20 years.
		• Serves a term of 4 years.
			• Checks on the Judicial Branch:
			  1. Appoints all federal judges.
			  2. Grants pardons to federal offenders.
			• Checks on the Legislative Branch:
			  1. Can propose and veto laws.
			  2. Can call special sessions of Congress.
			  3. Makes appointments to federal posts.
			  4. Negotiates foreign treaties.

LEGISLATIVE
"Makes the laws"
	• Lay and collect taxes.
	• Borrow money.
	• Coin money.
	• Establish uniform rules for naturalization.
	• Regulate commerce.
	• Provide for the common defense.
	• Declare war.
	• Maintain the armed forces.
	• Make all laws.
		• Members of the House of Representatives:
		  1. Must be 25 years old.
		  2. Must have been citizen of the U.S. for 7 years.
		  3. Must be an inhabitant of his or her state.
		  4. Serves a term of two years.
		• U.S. Senator:
		  1. Must be 30 years old.
		  2. Must have been a citizen of the U.S. for 9 years.
		  3. Must be an inhabitant of his or her state.
		  4. Serves a term of six years.
			• Checks on the Judicial Branch:
			  1. Can impeach and remove judges.
			  2. Approves appointment of federal judges.
			  3. Creates lower federal courts.
			  4. Can propose amendments to overrule judicial decisions.
			• Checks on the Executive Branch:
			  1. Can override presidential veto.
			  2. Can impeach and remove a president.
			  3. Has the power to declare war.
			  4. Has the power to appropriate money.

JUDICIAL
"Interprets or explains the laws"
	• Power of judicial review.
	• Interpret all laws.
	• Final arbiters in cases of conflicts.
	• Reviews cases from lower courts.
		• Appointed by the president with the consent of the Senate.
		• Appointed for life during good behavior.
			• Checks on the Legislative Branch:
			  1. Power to declare laws unconstitutional.
			• Checks on the Executive Branch:
			  1. Power to declare executive actions unconstitutional.

Amendment 21:   Repeals the Eighteenth, or Prohibition, Amendment.
Amendment 22:   Establishes a two-term limit for presidents.
Amendment 23:   Grants three electoral votes to the District of Columbia.
Amendment 24:   Makes poll taxes illegal.
Amendment 25:   Sets the procedure for presidential succession in the event something happens to the president and he is unable to serve.
Amendment 26:   Provides 18-year-olds with the right to vote.
Amendment 27:   Deals with the pay of senators and representatives.

The amendments allow for changes to be made to the Constitution because of changing conditions as time passes and new needs arise. This process allows the Constitution to become more democratic than the original document. Our founding fathers had the foresight to make such a process available because they knew that the future of the country would bring many changes.

All amendments from the Fifth through the Eighth deal with the due process of law, which guarantees all people the right to a fair public trial. Individuals brought to trial are also entitled to a lawyer to defend them, and no individual will be allowed to be put on trial more than once for the same crime because that would constitute cruel and unusual punishment.

Section Four: Elementary Science
CHAPTER ELEVEN

Physical Science[1]

DOMAIN ONE: THE STUDY OF PHYSICAL SCIENCE

CONTENT AREA ONE: PHYSICAL AND CHEMICAL PROPERTIES

This content area will cover both the physical and chemical properties of matter. You will see a brief description of physical and chemical properties before we delve into each of these areas separately (see Table 11.1).

TABLE 11.1

	PHYSICAL PROPERTIES	CHEMICAL PROPERTIES
DESCRIPTION	Describes characteristics of a substance that can be observed without changing the substance.	Describes how a substance reacts with other substances to produce new substances.
EXAMPLES	• Density • Hardness • Color • Freezing point • Melting point • Boiling point • Electrical or thermal conductivity	Chemical Reactivity • Example: Solubility in water. • Example: Reacts to oxygen. • Example: Flammability.

All matter, in other words, all physical things in our world, can be described in terms of its physical and chemical characteristics because all matter is composed of elements. Elements are characterized by their own set of chemical and physical properties. As seen above, physical properties describe the characteristics of a substance that we can observe without changing it. Think of a penny: We can describe its physical density, hardness, and so forth. without doing anything drastic to it. In addition, we can also describe how any substance reacts with other substances to produce something new. Keeping with our penny example, and example of a chemical property of that penny would be the way the penny reacts with oxygen to produce a green finish on it.

Physical Properties

Physical properties, you should recall, are those properties of a substance that can be observed without changing the composition of that substance (see Table 11.2).

[1]Chapter contributed by Erica Seropian Cardey.

TABLE 11.2

PROPERTY	DESCRIPTION
Density	Mass per unit volume: d = m/v.
Hardness	Resistance to scratching.
Color	Visual quality determined to by the absorption and reflection of light.
Freezing point	Temperature at which a substance become solid.
Melting point	Temperature at which a substance becomes a liquid.
Thermal conductivity	Ability to allow heat to pass through.
Electrical conductivity	Ability to allow an electrical current to pass through.

Density is the mass of a substance per unit volume. This is commonly expressed in the following formula:

D = mass/volume

To get a sense of the density, just think of the difference between a one-foot–by–one-foot brick and a one-foot–by–one-foot block of balsa wood. The different densities of each type of matter results in a different weight. Our formula, then, would tell us that the *D* for the brick and the balsa would differ, precisely because the mass is different. This difference exists, despite the fact that the brick and the balsa wood share the same volume (one-foot by one-foot).

Hardness is the ability of a substance to resist scratching. This physical property is most commonly used to describe minerals. Hardness does not describe the breakability of a substance (known as the substance's ability to fracture). An example of substances with differing hardnesses would be diamonds and chalk. A diamond has greater hardness than chalk, therefore chalk can be scratched with a diamond.

The *color* of a substance is easy to observe and is determined by the specific wavelengths of light a substance absorbs, and those that it reflects. Why do we perceive the color black the way we do versus the color red? Because black materials absorb all wavelengths of light and reflect none. The color black is produced when no wavelengths of light are reflected. You will learn more about light when you read content area seven toward the end of this domain.

Freezing point is the temperature at which a substance changes from a liquid to a solid. Conversely, a substance's freezing point can also be thought of as its *melting point*, because it is the minimum temperature that is required for a substance to remain in the solid state. Just think of water versus magma: Both of them can be found as solids and liquids, but the temperatures required to change them into these forms will differ greatly.

Boiling point is the specific temperature at which a substance changes from a liquid to a gas. Both water and lead will boil if enough heat is applied to them; however, the former will boil more quickly than the latter, because its boiling point is at a lower temperature. Let's look at water more closely. When in its solid state as ice and then uniformly heated over a period of time, water will gradually pass through its melting and boiling points. It will successively change from a solid to a liquid to a gas. When the temperature of the substance is graphed as a function of time, the melting and boiling points of the substance can be recognized as plateaus in the graph.

Figure 11.1 describes the freezing plateau and boiling plateau for water in Celsius.

In short, the chart illustrates the boiling point for water, along with it starting point (in this hypothetical case) as a solid. All substances have a boiling point, though some may be much higher and not naturally occurring compared to others.

Conductivity refers to how easily a substance allows either electricity or heat to pass through it. There are two types to know: electrical and thermal.

■ *Electrical conductivity* tells you if something will be a good conductor for electricity. Copper is often used in wire because it is a good conductor—because an electrical current

FIGURE 11.1
Temperature
of a Substance
as a Function
of Time

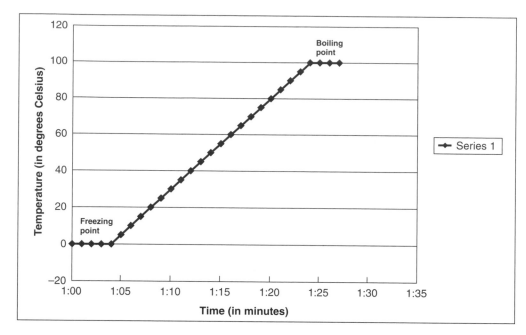

passes easily through the molecules of this substance. Feathers, on the other hand, are not.

- *Thermal conduction* tells you how well or poorly a form of matter conducts heat. The more that a given matter allows its molecules to vibrate and pass heat along to other vibrating molecules through direct contact, the better it is as a thermal conductor. Water is a good thermal conductor. Asbestos, on the other hand, is not, which is why it was used so prevalently as an heat insulator.

With this basic understanding of the physical properties of matter, let's now look at its states.

States of Matter.   Matter can be classified into three physical states or forms (see Table 11.3).

TABLE 11.3

STATE	CHARACTERISTICS	PARTICLE DENSITY	PARTICLE MOVEMENT
Solid	Definite shape and volume.	Particles are packed.	Particles are in tightly virtually fixed positions.
Liquid	Definite volume but no definite shape; they take the shape of the container.	Packed less tightly with some freedom of motion.	Some movement.
Gas	No definite shape or volume.	Space between particles continues to expand.	Constantly expanding.

As you know, matter can change from a solid to a liquid to a gas, meaning that some substances can pass through all three of these states. How is this accomplished? Well, changes in matter result from increases or decreases in the amount of heat within a substance. The addition of heat causes particles to move faster. As particles move faster, their position becomes less fixed. Conversely, as the amount of heat in a substance decreases, the position of particles becomes more fixed. These changes in the "fixed-ness" of particles is the basis of how physical changes in states of matter occur.

The Kinetic Theory of Gases. The pressure of an ideal gas increases when the volume of that gas is decreased and the mass and temperature of the gas remain constant. This is due to the fact that as temperature increases, molecular motion also increases. This results in an increase in the rate of molecular collisions with neighboring molecules and the sides of the container.

The kinetic theory of gases is summed up in Figure 11.2 (assume P is pressure and T is temperature and that mass and temperature stay the same).

FIGURE 11.2

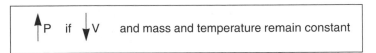

Example: If a balloon filled with gas is suddenly compressed (say squashed by your hands), the volume of the balloon will be smaller than before, but the pressure of the gas inside the balloon will be greater than before.

A Note on Physical Mixtures. To end our discussion of physical properties, please note the following. A mixture contains two or more substances that are not bound chemically. All substances within a mixture maintain their own specific physical characteristics. A mixture can be physically separated back into its original components. An example of a physical mixture is a container that is half-filled with blue marbles and half-filled with red marbles. The blue and red marbles can be physically separated out from one another, indicating that it is a physical mixture.

Chemical Properties

Chemical properties describe how a substance interacts with other substances to form new types of matter, as when we combine hydrogen and oxygen in a particular way to get water (more on that later). These interactions are determined largely by the atomic structure of that substance. It is important to remember that all matter consists of atoms and molecules in various arrangements (see Table 11.4).

TABLE 11.4

TERM	DEFINITION
Atom	The smallest unit of an element that retains the properties of that element.
Element	Substance that has a specific set of chemical and physical properties.
Compound	Substance that consists of atoms of two or more elements that are chemically combined.
Molecule	More than one atom chemically bonded together.

Atomic structures of substances determine its chemical properties. For example, atomic structures make water *water* and lead *lead.* In particular, it is the outer electrons in the electron cloud of the atoms that make up a substance and lead to differences in chemical properties. To understand atomic structure, let's first look at the parts of an atom (see Table 11.5).

TABLE 11.5

PARTICLE	LOCATION	MOTION	CHARGE
Neutron	Nucleus (center)	Clustered tightly with protons.	Neutral—no charge
Electron	Cloud surrounding the nucleus	Orbiting the nucleus with a motion so fast that its exact location is never known.	Negative
Proton	Nucleus	Clustered tightly with neutrons.	Positive

To help you visualize these terms, Figure 11.3 shows how these labels attach to a given atom.

**FIGURE 11.3
Parts of
an Atom**

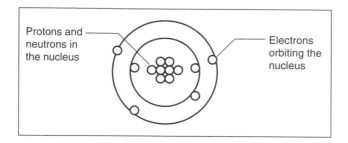

Atoms may be charged positively or negatively, or carry no charge at all. The *neutron,* found at the nucleus or center of the atom, has no charge. *Protons,* tightly packed in with *neutrons,* are also found at the *nucleus* or center of the atoms. Thus, *neutrons* plus *protons* equal an atom's *nucleus.* These subatomic particles are always arranged in a similar way. The overall charge of an atom's nucleus is positive, because the *neutron* is neutral while the *proton* is positive.

Now, as Figure 11.3 shows, electrons move around the nucleus, orbiting in a space called the electron cloud. This area is referred to as a cloud because the motion of electrons is so fast that their exact location within the orbital cannot be pinpointed. The electrons' negative charge cause them to be attracted to the positive nucleus, so the electrons remain relatively close to the nucleus. However, their constant motion prevents them from actually falling into the nucleus.

Atomic Charges: Neutral, Anionic, and Cationic.   The overall charge of an atom depends on the number of protons in relation to the number of electrons in the atom. If an atom has an equal number of protons and electrons, the atom has no net charge and is said to be neutral. If an atom has a different number of protons and electrons, the atom is said to be unbalanced and is called an ion. Ions are considered unstable and react readily with other atoms in an effort to achieve balance or chemical stability. Stable, balanced atoms can also be called "inert" and do not react readily with other atoms.

If an atom contains more protons than electrons, the overall charge is positive and the atom is called a *cation.* Conversely, if the number of electrons is greater than the number of protons, then the overall charge of the atom is negative. These negatively charged atoms are called *anions* (see Table 11.6).

TABLE 11.6

TYPE OF ION	CHARGE	DESCRIPTION
Anion	Negative (–)	More electrons than protons.
Cation	Positive (+)	More protons than electrons.

In addition to having a particular charge, atoms also have mass. We only look at mass in science, not weight, because weight changes with gravity and mass does not. You weigh less on the moon because the gravity force there is weaker, but you still have the same mass. The definition of mass is very abstract and is not likely to be tested. Let's look at mass first. To calculate an atoms mass, you simply apply the formula below:

Atomic Mass: # protons + # neutrons

If you change the number of neutrons that an atom possesses, you only change the mass of an atom, not its charge (recall that neutrons contribute mass to an atom, but have no charge). These atoms of the same element with differing numbers of neutrons (and therefore different masses) are called isotopes.

The isotope atom of an element has the same number of protons (atomic number—to be discussed in the next section) but has a different number of neutrons than another atom of that element (resulting from a different number of neutrons). Explained another way, atoms of the same element can differ in the number of neutrons, each version is called an isotope. Hydrogen, for example, has no neurons at all, while the hydrogen isotope deuterium has one neutron, and tritium has two neutrons. In writing, the isotopes of hydrogen look like this:

Hydrogen	Deuterium	Tritium
$^1H_1$	$^2H_1$	$^3H_1$

Isotope = **same** # *protons,* **different** # of *neutrons*

The Periodic Table

Elements are organized into the periodic table of elements. Each element has its own square on the table that provides specific information about the chemical properties of that element. Elements are further organized in the table by being grouped according to similar properties (see Figure 11.4).

FIGURE 11.4 Periodic Table of Elements

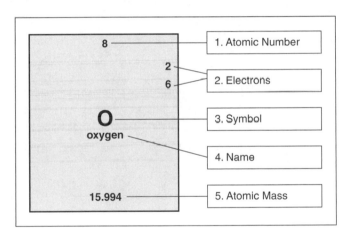

Following are brief descriptions of what the labels applied to an element from the period table tell us.

1. Atomic number tells us the number of protons in the nucleus. In the case of oxygen, there are eight protons in the nucleus.
2. The number of electrons in outer shells (orbitals) is captured by the numbers 2 and 6. This characteristic determines the reactivity of an element (how an element will react with other elements). Oxygen will react with two hydrogen atoms to form water, for example, because oxygen has room in its outer orbital for two more electrons (supplied by the hydrogen atoms).
3. The letter in the center is the chemical symbol. In the case of oxygen, it is the capital letter O, and it is universal for the element.
4. The label below the symbol is the name of the element.
5. Average atomic mass is determined by averaging the masses of isotopes according to their relative abundance (very abundant isotopes contribute more to this average mass than less abundant isotopes).

TABLE 11.7

NOBLE GASES

NONMETALS

OTHER METALS

ALKALINE EARTH METALS

TRANSITION METALS

ALKALI METALS

NEW	1	2	3	4	5	6	7	8	9	10	11	12	13	14	15	16	17	18
ORIGINAL	IA	IIA	IIIB	IVB	VB	VIB	VIIB		VIIIB		IB	IIB	IIIA	IVA	VA	VIA	VIIA	VIIIA

1	1 H 1.00794																	2 He 4.002602
2	3 Li 6.941	4 Be 9.012182											5 B 10.811	6 C 12.0107	7 N 14.00674	8 O 15.9994	9 F 18.998403	10 Ne 20.1797
3	11 Na 22.989770	12 Mg 24.3050											13 Al 26.981538	14 Si 28.0855	15 P 30.973761	16 S 32.066	17 Cl 35.4527	18 Ar 39.948
4	19 K 39.0983	20 Ca 40.078	21 Sc 44.955910	22 Ti 47.867	23 V 50.9415	24 Cr 51.9961	25 Mn 54.938049	26 Fe 55.8457	27 Co 58.933200	28 Ni 58.6934	29 Cu 63.546	30 Zn 65.39	31 Ga 69.723	32 Ge 72.61	33 As 74.92160	34 Se 78.96	35 Br 79.904	36 Kr 83.80
5	37 Rb 85.4678	38 Sr 87.62	39 Y 88.90585	40 Zr 91.224	41 Nb 92.90638	42 Mo 95.94	43 Tc (98)	44 Ru 101.07	45 Rh 102.90550	46 Pd 106.42	47 Ag 107.8682	48 Cd 112.411	49 In 114.818	50 Sn 118.710	51 Sb 121.760	52 Te 127.60	53 I 126.90447	54 Xe 131.29
6	55 Cs 132.90545	56 Ba 137.327	57 to 71	72 Hf 178.49	73 Ta 180.9479	74 W 183.84	75 Re 186.207	76 Os 190.23	77 Ir 192.217	78 Pt 195.078	79 Au 196.96655	80 Hg 200.59	81 Tl 204.3833	82 Pb 207.2	83 Bi 208.98038	84 Po (209)	85 At (210)	86 Rn (222)
7	87 Fr (223)	88 Ra (226)	89 to 103	104 Rf (261)	105 Db (262)	106 Sg (261)	107 Bh (262)	108 Hs (261)	109 Mt (266)	110 Uun (269)	111 Uuu (272)	112 Uub (277)	113	114 Uuq (285)	115	116 Uuh (289)	117	118 Uuo (293)

Atomic masses in parentheses are those of the most stable or common isotope.

| 57 La 138.9055 | 58 Ce 140.116 | 59 Pr (223) | 60 Nd 144.24 | 61 Pm [145] | 62 Sm 150.36 | 63 Eu 151.964 | 64 Gd 157.25 | 65 Tb Terbium 158.92534 | 66 Dy Dysprosium 162.50 | 67 Ho Holmium 164.93032 | 68 Er Erbium 167.26 | 69 Tm Thulium 168.93421 | 70 Yb Ytterbium 173.04 | 71 Lu Lutetium 174.967 |
| 89 Ac (227) | 90 Th 232.0381 | 91 Pa 231.03588 | 92 U 238.0289 | 93 Np (237) | 94 Pu (244) | 95 Am (243) | 96 Cm (247) | 97 Bk Berkelium (247) | 98 Cf Californium (251) | 99 Es Einsteinium (252) | 100 Fm Fermium (257) | 101 Md Mendeleviu m (257) | 102 No Nobelium (259) | 103 Lr Lawrenciu m |

SOLID | Li, Be, B, C, Na, Mg, Al, Si, P, S, K, Ca, Sc, Ti, V, Cr, Mn, Fe, Co, Ni, Cu, Zn, Ga, Ge, As, Se, Rb, Sr, Y, Zr, Nb, Mo, Ru, Rh, Pd, Ag, Cd, In, Sn, Sb, Te, I, Cs, Ba, Hf, Ta, W, Re, Os, Ir, Pt, Au, Tl, Pb, Bi, Po, At, Fr, Ra, La, Ce, Pr, Nd, Sm, Eu, Gd Tb, Dy, Ho, Er, Tm, Yb, Lu, Ac, Th, Pa, U |

LIQUID | Br, Hg |

GAS | H, He, O, F, Ne, Cl, Ar, Kr, Xe, Rn |

SYNTHETIC | Tc, Rf, Db, Sg, Bh, Hs, Mt, Uun, Uuu, Uub, Uuq, Uuh, Uuo, Pm, Np, Pu, Am, Cm, Bk, Cf, Es, Fm, Md, No, Lr |

Note:
The subgroup numbers 1-18 were adopted in 1984 by the International Union of Pure and Applied Chemistry. The names of elements 110-118 are the Latin equivalents of those numbers.

The periodic table lists the atomic number and atomic mass for each element. We can use this information to find out about the atomic structure of each element. This information can be used to find out how many electrons, protons, and neutrons are found in an atom of the element. The list below shows us how the information can be used for this purpose:

1. Atomic number = # of protons (or electrons assuming that the element is neutral)
2. Atomic mass = # of protons + # of electrons
3. # of neutrons = mass # – atomic #

Now that you have some understanding of one element of the periodic table, let's look at the entire table to see how it is organized and what it tells us.

Organization of the Table.   Elements are organized on the periodic table according to their chemical and atomic properties (see Table 11.7).

What's in the Periodic Table?

TABLE 11.8

	LOCATION ON THE TABLE	CHARACTERISTICS
Metals	Left side of the table. Note: All elements to the left of the "stair step" line mark the transition metals.	• Shiny. • Ductile (can stretch into wire). • Malleable (can be shaped). • Conduct heat and electricity. • Copper, Gold, Silver.
Nonmetals	To the right of the metals. Exception: Hydrogen.	• Good insulators. • Do not conduct heat/electricity well. • Phosphorus, Chlorine, Sulfur.
Noble Gases	Far Right: Group VIII of the periodic table.	• Nonmetals that occur naturally as gases. • Do not react readily with other elements. • Helium, Neon, Argon.
Transition Metals	Between metals and nonmetals. *Note:* The "stair step" line distinguishes these metals from the metals and nonmetals.	• Possess some properties of metals and nonmetals. • Silicon, Boron, Arsenic.

Quantities of Atoms

Like most matter found in our world, atoms and molecules not only have mass but weight. We measure then in terms of *moles*. *Mole* refers to the number of particles present, regardless of their mass or volume. A mole is a measurement of quantity only. Moles measure how many particles of something we have. Although moles are usually used to describe the number of atoms or molecules present, you can have one mole of sulfur atoms, one mole of insects, or one mole of apples. Regardless of the substance, one mole always represents the same number of objects or particles you have of something. One mole of a substance is the amount of that substance that contains 6.02×10^{23} particles of that substance. The formula 6.02×10^{23} is also known as Avogadro's number. For example, if you were to take one mole of oxygen atoms and count every individual atom in that mole, you would have exactly 6.02×10^{23} oxygen atoms. Please also note that only neutrons and protons contribute mass to the atom. Electrons do not contribute any mass significant enough to be measured. However, the majority of an atom's volume is due to the electron cloud. A common comparison used to describe the volume of the nucleus in relation to the total size of an atom is a marble inside of a football field.

CONTENT AREA TWO: PHYSICAL AND CHEMICAL CHANGES

Changes of substances can be classified into two types: physical and chemical (see Table 11.9).

TABLE 11.9

TYPE OF CHANGE	DESCRIPTION	EXAMPLE
Physical	No new substances are produced.	Ice melting into water.
Chemical	New substances are produced.	Iron rusting.

Briefly, physical changes are reactions in which no new substances are produced. A physical change *can be reversed,* returning the substance to its original form prior to the reaction. An example of this phenomenon is ice melting into water. Chemical changes, on the other hand, occur when two or more substances react with one another producing new forms of matter. Chemical changes cannot be reversed to return the substances back to their original form. The rust one finds on one's car is an example, where oxidization has occurred. Oxidation is the process where some metals (iron in particular) react with oxygen to produce a new substance—rust.

Because chemical changes are more involved and complex, we will need to spend more time on them. You need to understand the role that chemical bonds play in chemical changes to fully appreciate chemical changes like the process of oxidization.

Chemical Bonds

In chemical changes, substances react with one another as electrons in different elements interact with one another to form chemical bonds. Chemical bonds are the forces that hold compounds together. These bonds form through the interaction of electrons in the outer energy levels of two or more atoms. These interactions result from atoms adjusting to be electrically stable (charges are balanced between protons and electrons).

Balance = # of electrons = # of protons

Electrons orbit the nucleus of an atom in energy "shells." We call these shells *orbitals.* If an atom does not have its outermost orbitals filled with the maximum number of electrons, the atom is said to have an unstable electron configuration. Atoms exchange electrons in the pursuit of achieving a stable electron configuration. Chemical reactions are the result of unstable atoms exchanging electrons with other atoms in an attempt to reach a stable electron configuration. When these atoms are exchanged, existing chemical bonds are broken and new bonds are formed.

Depending on the number of electrons in an atom's outermost energy level, atoms have a tendency to gain or lose electrons. Once electrons are either gained or lost, the atom has become an ion and now has a charge. That charge will be the opposite charge of the atom it exchanged electrons with. These opposite charges attract. This attraction is the force that holds ionic compounds together. There are four major types of chemical bonds that play a role in these changes (see Table 11.10).

Ionic Bonds.   Ionic bonds form when electrons are transferred from one atom to another (see Figure 11.5).

TABLE 11.10

BOND TYPE	BOND CHARACTERISTICS
Ionic	• Electrons are transferred from one atom to another. • Ionic bonds produce **ions** because electrons are either gained or lost, causing the atom to be charged.
Covalent	• Atoms share electrons. • Co- = "share"
Metallic	• Electrons move freely among atoms in "a sea of mobile electrons."
Hydrogen	• Hydrogen atoms are weakly attracted to oxygen atoms producing a weak bond between molecules. hydrogen oxygen ↔ (weak)

FIGURE 11.5

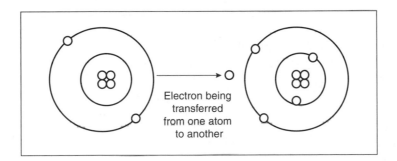

Electron being transferred from one atom to another

Compounds formed in this way are called ionic compounds and usually form when electrons are transferred from a metal to a nonmetal.

Covalent Bonds. In a covalent bond, atoms are attracted to one another through the sharing of electrons to achieve a stable number of electrons. These bonds are weaker than ionic bonds (see Figure 11.6).

FIGURE 11.6

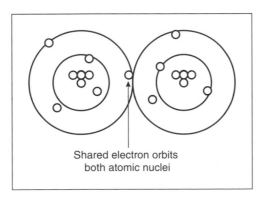

Shared electron orbits both atomic nuclei

Compounds formed in this way are called covalent compounds. Think: *co = share* because in this type of bond electrons are not taken or given away, rather they are shared by both atoms.

Metallic Bonds. As the name implies, metallic bonds are characteristic of metals. Metallic bonds result from electrons moving freely among positively charged cations. Metals do not have a tight attraction to their outermost electrons (known as valence electrons). This quality can be described as a low energy of ionization. The electrons move about freely, not being specifically bonded to any one atom but rather belonging to the metallic crystal as a whole. The negatively charged electrons hold the positively charged cations together (otherwise their like charges would force them apart). Metallic bonds are commonly referred to as a "sea of mobile electrons" (see Figure 11.7).

FIGURE 11.7

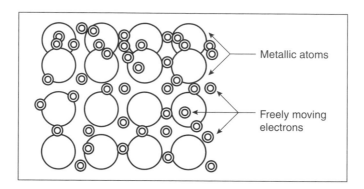

It is this mobility of electrons that makes metals good conductors of heat and electricity. This sea of electrons is very fluid in nature, allowing electricity to pass through easily. The loose structure also allows heat to pass through the metal from one molecule to the next through direct contact. The loose structure is necessary for thermal conduction because as heat is applied and transferred to metal particles, they begin to vibrate. If the metal were tightly structured, the particles would not vibrate as easily, resulting in poor conduction. Substances with rigid atomic structures do not have enough freedom of motion between particles to transmit heat.

Hydrogen Bonds.   In a hydrogen bond, a hydrogen atom of one molecule is weakly attracted to an oxygen atom of another molecule. This occurs because hydrogen atoms have a weak positive charge and oxygen atoms have a weak negative charge. This occurs most commonly in water, but may occur in other substances as well. These hydrogen bonds are the reason that water is cohesive (water molecules "stick" to one another (see Figure 11.8).

FIGURE 11.8

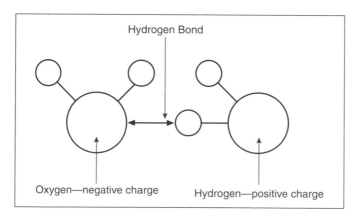

Compounds formed in this way do not have names like ionic and covalent compounds do because compounding does not form a bond. It is just a weak link formed between existing compounds.

Factors Affecting Rates of Chemical Reactions.   Whether a chemical reaction will occur is primarily determined by the molecular structure of the substances involved. However how quickly or slowly those reactions occur is dependent upon several factors:

- *Temperature:* Typically raising the temperature speeds up reactions. This is because increasing the temperature of a substance increases molecular collisions. For example, when water is heated and begins to boil, the rolling movements of the water that are characteristic of it boiling are caused by water molecules moving faster and faster, colliding with each other more frequently.

- *Concentration of Reactants:* A higher concentration of reacting particles also results in an increase in reaction rate due to an increase in the frequency of molecular collisions. For example, acid will corrode a metal more quickly if greater quantities of the acid and metal are present. This is because more acid particles will be colliding with a greater number of metal particles.

- *Particle Size/Surface Area:* The smaller the particle, the greater the surface area of that particle. This speeds up the rate of reaction because it increases the amount of the substance that is exposed for reaction. For example, the same metal in our previous example will corrode more quickly in the acid if it is cut into small pieces. This is because the acid can only collide with particles on the surface of the metal. Smaller pieces have a larger surface area, allowing more of the metal to be exposed to the acid at one time.

- *The Presence of Catalysts:* A catalyst is a substance that allows a reaction to occur at a faster rate without being consumed in the reaction itself. So a catalyst is a substance that is not used up in a reaction, but makes the chemical reaction go faster. The catalyst provides a surface that the reaction occurs upon. For example, hydrogen peroxide is usually stable (not reactive) at room temperature. However in the presence of a catalyst, hydrogen peroxide can break down into water and oxygen.

Naming Chemical Compounds.   Specific rules are followed in the naming of compounds. These rules allow you to decipher a compound's chemical composition solely from reading its name and following the rules of naming.

- The name of the metal goes before a nonmetal (as in sodium chloride).
- Compounds containing no oxygen end in -ide.
- di-, tri-, etc. before the name of an element = # of atoms of that element that are in the compound.
- -ate at the end of a compound name = 3 oxygen atoms.
- -ite at the end of a compound name = 2 oxygen atoms.

Chemical Equations.   Chemical reactions can be recorded as chemical equations. Chemical equations contain the chemical compounds present before the chemical reaction (reactants) as well as the chemical compounds present after the chemical reaction has taken place (products). Chemical equations also indicate the number of atoms of each element and molecules of each compound that are present before and after the reaction. The number of atoms of each element is conserved in the chemical reaction. Atoms cannot be added nor can they disappear. Atoms can only rearrange molecular bonds with other atoms in the equation.

The number of atoms of each element present remains the same on both sides of a chemical equation (see Figure 11.9).

- *Coefficient:* Tells the number of molecules of a compound that are present.
- *Subscript:* Tells the number of atoms of a particular element that are present.

FIGURE 11.9

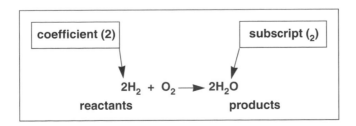

CONTENT AREA THREE: pH

A solution is a specific type of mixture in which the substances of the mixture are evenly distributed among one another. A key characteristic used to distinguish solutions is pH (see Table 11.11).

TABLE 11.11

CATEGORY	PH LEVEL	CHARACTERISTICS	EXAMPLE
Acidic	1.0–6.9	• Contains more hydrogen ions than hydroxide ions and produces hydrogen ions.	• Vinegar
Alkaline (may also be called basic)	7.1–14	• Contains more hydroxide ions than hydrogen ions.	• Sodium Bicarbonate
Neutral	7	• Removes hydrogen ions. • Neither acidic nor alkaline.	• Distilled Water

The three categories of pH are determined by the balance the substance possesses between hydrogen ions (positively charged hydrogen atoms) and hydroxide ions (negatively charged molecules consisting of one hydrogen and one oxygen atom). Recall that ions are atoms that will *either* be charged positively or negatively because they possess an unbalanced number of protons and electrons. An anion is a negatively charged ion, while a cation is a positively charged ion. The symbol for a hydrogen ion is H+ and the symbol for a hydroxide ion is OH-. pH is a scale used to measure the acidity or alkalinity of a substance. pH stands for the power of a solution to yield hydrogen ions (H+):

- **pH** = *power* to yield *hydrogen* ions.
- pH is logarithmic. This is to say that pH 8 is 10 times more alkaline than pH 7, and pH 9 is 100 times more alkaline than pH 7. pH is a negative logarithm of hydrogen ion concentration.

Recall that hydrogen ions are positively charged hydrogen atoms. Also recall that positively charged atoms (cations) possess more protons than electrons. That is why the symbol for a hydrogen ion is H+ (the "+" indicates the charge).

As you can see in Table 11.12, the more hydrogen ions, the lower the pH. PH can be thought of in terms of measuring the concentration of hydrogen ions in a solution.

- High pH = low concentration of hydrogen ions (not very many hydrogen ions in the solution).
- Low pH = high concentration of hydrogen ions (lots of hydrogen ions in the solution).

So to summarize the list above, if a substance has a high pH value, the substance has very few hydrogen ions. It is described as being alkaline. Alkaline solutions have few hydrogen ions because they remove hydrogen ions from a solution. If a solution has a low pH value, it has a lot of hydrogen ions in it. Solutions with low pH values are called acids. Acids have a lot of hydrogen ions because they release hydrogen ions into the solution.

CONTENT AREA FOUR: MOTION AND FORCES

Motions are when an object changes location. An example of this is a ball rolling down a hill. As the ball rolls down the hill, its location is changing, therefore it is in motion. Forces act upon an object to set it in motion. For an example of force, let's go back to our example of a ball rolling down a hill. If that ball was previously at rest (sitting) on top of the hill, a force had to act upon it to start its motion down the hill. The force may have come in the form of a child kicking the ball or the wind pushing it.

Motion

There are a number of factors that you need to understand that effect motion (see Table 11.12).

TABLE 11.12

TERM	DEFINITION
Inertia	An object's resistance to changes in its state of motion.
Displacement	The distance between the starting point and the ending point of an object in motion.
Speed	A magnitude only—no direction.
Velocity	A vector* whose quantity is speed and magnitude is the direction of motion measured in units (m/s = meters per second).
Acceleration	Rate at which velocity changes with time.

*A vector is a quantity (or measurement) that has both a direction and a magnitude.

Inertia is the tendency that all objects have to resist changes in their state of motion. An object at rest will resist being set into motion. An object in motion will resist that motion being halted. If no outside forces act upon an object in motion (forces such as gravity and friction are discussed in the next section), that object will continue indefinitely. The amount of inertia an object has is determined by its mass. Inertia is directly proportional to an object's mass.

More mass = more inertia

An example of differences in inertia is the inertia of a speeding train compared to the inertia of a speeding car. Because the train has more mass than the car, it has a greater force of inertia. That is why it is more difficult to stop the train than it is to stop the car. For the object to stop, the braking force must be large enough to overcome the object's inertia. *Displacement* is the distance between the starting and stopping points of an object in motion. Displacement is independent of the path taken by the object in motion (see Figure 11.10).

FIGURE 11.10

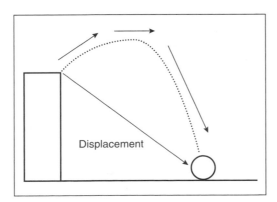

Displacement

Speed is a quantity that has a magnitude only. Speed is not a vector because a vector has both a magnitude and a direction. For example, if we say that a car is traveling 65 kilometers per hour, we have established the car's speed. But we have not indicated the direction in which the car is traveling. If we said that the car is traveling north at 65 kilometers per hour, we have established a vector because we have indicated a magnitude (65 miles per hour) and a direction (north).

Velocity is a type of vector. A vector is a quantity that has both a magnitude and a direction. In velocity, the direction is the direction of motion and the magnitude is speed. Velocity differs from speed in that speed is a quantity that has a magnitude only and no specified direction.

Acceleration is the rate at which velocity changes with time. Acceleration does not necessarily have the same direction as velocity, as in the case of a car braking. Acceleration can be expressed as the change in velocity divided by the interval of time.

Acceleration = change in velocity/time (how long the acceleration took)

Note: The term "change" is often abbreviated with the symbol "delta" or ▲, so the formula above can also be expressed as:

A = ▲ V/time

(where A = acceleration and V = velocity)

Forces

TABLE 11.13

FORCE	DESCRIPTION
Gravity	Force of attraction between all objects.
Friction	Force that resists motion when one material rubs against the surface of another.
Magnetism	Forces between some metal objects that cause them to either attract or repel one another.

These forces can change the motion of an object if they are out of balance. So a change in motion will result when one force is greater than another.

Gravity on earth is experienced as a constant downward pull. This is because the mass of the earth is so large that its force of gravity attracts objects on its surface toward the ground (9.8 meters per second squared, or 9.8 mps^2). Gravity is affected by two factors:

- *Mass:* For the force of gravity between two objects to be strong enough to be noticed, at least one of the objects must have a very large mass.
- *Distance:* The closer two objects are to one another, the greater the force of gravity between them.

Friction is a restrictive force that occurs when one object rubs against the surface of another. Friction forces increase as the roughness of the surfaces involved increases. Friction is the force that eventually stops all objects in motion. If frictional forces were not present, the force of inertia would allow objects in motion to continue in their path indefinitely.

Magnetism involves both attractive and repulsive forces. Objects that possess magnetic properties have two magnetic poles (see "magnetic poles" below) that have opposite charges. Magnetic forces act between two objects that are magnetized. Opposite poles (charges) attract one another and like poles are repelled.

Let's take a moment to revisit charges within the context of forces (you saw this discussed earlier with atoms).

- There are two types of charge: positive and negative.
- Opposite charges attract one another.
- Like charges repel.
- Charges come from atoms possessing a disproportionate quantity of electrons and protons.
- More protons than electrons = positive charge.
- More electrons than protons = negative charge.
- Charge is conserved (it cannot be created or destroyed, only transferred).
- Charge is quantified as the difference between the number of positive charges in a system and the number of negative charges in that system. This is expressed as $+e$ or $-e$.

With those concepts in mind, let's see how they work.

Giving an Object a Net Charge.   Charges cannot be created or destroyed but only transferred. If a system has an equal number of positive and negative charges (and therefore no net charge), a net charge can be produced only by bringing in a charge from outside the system or by removing charge from within the system. Certain materials are more effective than others in transmitting (conducting) an electric charge. There are contingencies on how easily a charge can be transmitted (see Table 11.14).

TABLE 11.14

CLASS	DESCRIPTION	EXAMPLE
Conductors	Easily allows a charge to flow.	Metals
Semi-Conductors	Allows a charge to flow to some extent.	Silicon
Insulators	Charge does not flow easily.	Plastic

Conductors allow a charge to flow freely through them because the outermost electrons in the atoms of a conductor are bound loosely to the atom, allowing the electrons freedom of motion. It is this freedom of motion that is essential to conduction.

Semi-conductors are not useful for conducting charge because the outer electrons in their atomic structures are more rigidly bound than those of conductors.

Insulators are poor at conducting charge because their electrons are bound tightly to the atoms. This rigid structure does not allow electrons the freedom of flow necessary for conduction of charge.

Means of Giving an Object a Net Charge.   There are three primary means of transferring charges: friction, conduction, and induction (see Table 11.15).

TABLE 11.15

MEANS	EXAMPLE
Friction	Rubbing one material against another.
Conduction	Transfer of charge to an object through touching it to a charged object (direct contact).
Induction	Transfer of charge from a charged object to another object by bringing the charged object close to the other object but not touching it.

When two objects are rubbed together, electrons are likely to be transferred from one object to another. This transfer creates a net charge because one object ends up with fewer electrons than protons (creating a positive charge) and the other object ends up with more electrons than protons (creating a negative charge).

Friction occurs when objects rub against one another, resulting in the transfer of electrons from one object to another (see Figure 11.11).

In Figure 11.11, you can see two objects rubbing against each other. As this happens, electrons are transferred from one object to another.

Conduction is the transfer of charge through direct contact. When an object that is charged is touched to a material that is a conductor, some charge is transferred from the object to the conductor. The newly charged conductor takes on the same type of charge as the object (positive or negative).

In Figure 11.12 you can see a charged object in direct contact with a conductor (recall that a conductor is a material that allows an electric charge to pass through it). The charge passes directly from the charged object into the conductor.

Induction is the transfer of charge without directly touching a charged object to a conductor (recall that only conductors will easily transmit charge). In induction, a charged object is only brought very near to a conductor, but not in direct contact. In induction, the newly charged object takes on a charge opposite the charge of the object the charge was transmitted from (see Figure 11.13).

In induction, charge is transmitted by bringing a charged object very close to a conductor.

Magnetic poles—Any object possessing magnetic properties is called a magnet. All magnets have two points called magnetic poles, where most of their strength is concentrated. These two poles possess opposite charges. Just as in the case of electric charges, the opposite poles of different magnets attract each other, and like poles of different magnets repel (see Figure 11.14).

Attractive Force between Oppositely Charged Poles.   Figure 11.14 shows us two bar magnets. Each bar magnet has a positive pole and a negative pole. The oppositely charged poles attract one another, while the like charges repel.

Both electric charges and magnetic poles have a field of force. This is a region surrounding the charge or pole within which the charge may exert force on objects. Within the field of a magnetic pole, the pole exerts force on magnetic objects.

FIGURE 11.11

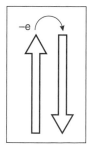

FIGURE 11.12

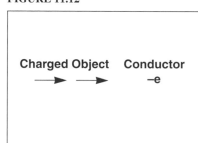

FIGURE 11.13

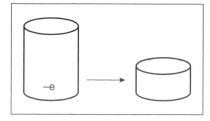

FIGURE 11.14

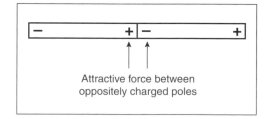

CONTENT AREA FIVE: SIMPLE MACHINES

Simple machines are devices that are used to accomplish work. Work measures the transfer of energy to an object. Simple machines make work easier to accomplish because they exert smaller forces over longer distances to make tasks easier (see Table 11.16).

TABLE 11.16

MACHINE	DESCRIPTION	USE	EXAMPLE
Lever	Bar supported at one point (called a fulcrum) and the level rotates around/upon the fulcrum.	Either multiplies force or multiplies distance and can lift heavy loads with less effort.	• Wheelbarrow • Crow Bar
Pulley	Cable looped around a support.	Multiplies force allowing loads to be lifted with less force.	• Rigging that raises a flag on a flagpole.
Inclined Plane	Sloping surface a load moves upon.	Multiplies force.	• A ramp at a parking garage.
Screw	Incline plane wrapped around a rod.	Multiplies work by moving into or through an object.	• Screw cap on a jar.

A *lever* consists of a bar that freely rotates around one fixed point of support called a fulcrum. Levers are used to lift loads. The force is placed on the opposite side of the fulcrum from the load. The lever multiplies force, allowing heavy loads to be lifted with less effort.

Pulleys are composed of a cable that is looped around a support. Pulleys are usually made of a smooth cable and an easily turned wheel as a support. This reduces friction. The function of the pulley depends on the pulley system:

- *Fixed:* In a fixed pulley system, the support section of the pulley does not move or turn. This pulley system changes the direction of forces only.
- *Movable:* In a movable pulley system, the support of the pulley turns, so the pulley not only changes the direction of force, but multiplies force as well.

An *inclined plane* is a sloping surface that a load is moved along. An inclined plane multiplies force. The gentler the slope, the greater the multiplying effect.

A *screw* is an inclined plane wrapped around a rod. Screws multiply force. A screw can move into or through an object with less effort force.

All of these simple machines depend upon energy. Let's learn about how energy "works" in our world.

CONTENT AREA SIX: ENERGY

Energy can be classified into two basic classes, potential and kinetic (see Table 11.17).

TABLE 11.17

CLASS	DESCRIPTION	EXAMPLE
Potential	Stored Energy	Rock at the top of a slope.
Kinetic	Energy of Motion	Rock rolling down the slope.

Potential energy is energy that is stored. An example of potential energy is chemical energy stored in gasoline. Potential energy is also known as the capacity to do work.

Kinetic energy involves motion. An example of kinetic energy is water cascading down a waterfall.

As an object is in motion, the amount of energy the object has transitions from potential to kinetic. Imagine a rock rolling down a slope as an example (see Figure 11.15).

FIGURE 11.15

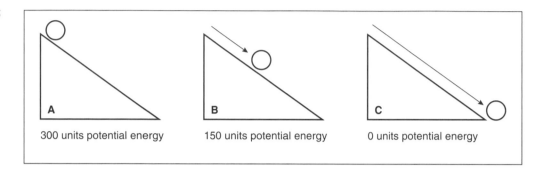

300 units potential energy   150 units potential energy   0 units potential energy

Measuring Energy and Work

Energy is measured in units called joules. Joules are also used to measure work. The unit for work is the same as the unit for energy because work involves a transfer of energy. One joule is the amount of work done when one Newton of force pushes or pulls an object 1 meter. Work is calculated with the following equation:

Work = Force × Distance

or

W = f × d

So for work to be done, an object has to physically move. That means that no matter how much energy you exert pushing on a wall, if the wall does not move, you have not done any work. This also means that by definition, moving your pencil from the right side of your desk to the left side is by definition, more work than taking a multiple-choice test!

Forms of Energy

Besides the two classes of energy that we can describe in terms of kinetic and potential, there are forms of energy to know. These forms of energy are more specific divisions within the two basic energy classes of potential and kinetic (see Table 11.18).

Solar energy is energy that is radiated from the sun. The energy takes many forms, including light and heat. Solar energy can be collected and used for heating. Solar cells are devices that can convert solar energy to electrical energy.

Chemical energy is potential energy that is stored in the bonds of molecules. When a chemical reaction such as combustion takes place, these bonds are broken as atoms rearrange into different molecular configurations forming new substances. When these bonds are broken the chemical energy changes form into kinetic energy.

Electrical energy is kinetic energy that is the result of moving electrical particles. Electrical energy is useful because it can be transformed into other forms of energy.

Magnetic energy is the force that causes some metals to be either attracted to or repelled from other metals. Any material that possesses magnetic energy is called a magnet. Magnetic

TABLE 11.18

FORM	DESCRIPTION	EXAMPLE
Solar	Energy from the sun.	Solar collectors used to heat water.
Chemical	Energy stored in matter.	Fuel such as gasoline.
Electrical	Energy of moving electrical particles.	Powers household appliances.
Magnetic	Force exerted by magnetized objects that either attracts or, due to the magnetic properties of the other magnetized iron filings, repels objects within their field of force.	Bar magnet attracts iron filings to it.
Nuclear	Energy that is stored in the nucleus of an atom.	Atomic nuclei can be split in a nucleus of an atomic process called nuclear fission, releasing energy.
Sound	Energy that travels through material and air as vibrations.	Plucking a guitar string generates sound waves.
Light	Energy that travels as visible waves.	Light bulb.
Electromagnetic	All energy that travels through space as waves, light waves, microwaves, or radio waves.	X-rays, gamma rays, infrared rays.

energy produces a field of force around magnetized objects. Magnets exert force on other magnetized objects within this field.

Nuclear energy is potential energy that is stored in the nucleus of an atom. When the nucleus is split, the potential energy is released, becoming kinetic energy. This energy is used to produce electricity.

Sound energy is kinetic energy that travels as waves. These waves travel as vibrations through solids, liquids, and gases. Sound waves cannot be seen, but are heard as vibrations in our ears.

Light energy occurs in the form of visible energy waves. Light energy is kinetic and can be produced by transforming other forms of energy such as chemical and electrical energy.

Electromagnetic energy is any energy that travels through space in the form of electromagnetic waves. Electromagnetic energy is also called radiation. The entire range of electromagnetic energy is called the electromagnetic spectrum. This spectrum ranges from high-energy gamma rays to low-energy radio waves. The only electromagnetic energy that we can see is visible light.

Energy Transformations

Energy transformations occur when one form of energy transfers to another form. An example of an energy transformation takes place when wood is burned. Chemical energy is stored in the wood. Combustion converts this chemical energy to heat and light energy as the wood burns.

As energy changes form, the total amount of energy present after the transformation is exactly equal to the amount of energy before the transformation. This is called the Law of Conservation of Energy:

Energy cannot be created or destroyed. Energy can only change form.

Heat and Temperature

Difference between Heat and Temperature.   Heat and temperature are two terms that we tend to use interchangeably, but they actually have two very different meanings. Heat is the amount of energy that is transferred from an object at a higher temperature to one of a lower temperature. (Recall that heat is a result of kinetic energy. Also recall that energy cannot be created or destroyed, it can only change form and be transferred from one object to another.)

Temperature is a measure of the kinetic energy of the molecules in a substance (see Table 11.19). (Recall our discussion of heat and kinetic energy from the previous paragraph.)

TABLE 11.19

SYSTEM	SYMBOL	DESCRIPTION
Celsius	°C	water freezes at 0°C and boils at 100°C.
Kelvin	K	0 K = absolute zero.
Fahrenheit	°F	System most commonly used in the United States.

Celsius. The Celsius scale is based on two temperatures—the freezing and boiling points of water. The freezing point of water is set at 0°C and the boiling point is set at 100°C. The difference in temperature between these two points is divided into 100 equal intervals. Each interval is 1 degree Celsius.

Kelvin. The Kelvin scale is also called the absolute scale. Zero on the Kelvin scale is equal to –273.15°C (–459.67°F). Zero Kelvin is also known as absolute zero; the theoretical point at which all kinetic molecular motion stops. The Kelvin scale is measured in Kelvins (not degrees Kelvin).

Fahrenheit. Fahrenheit is the temperature scale most commonly used in the United States. On the Fahrenheit scale, water freezes at 32°F and boils at 212°F.

Note: There are standard ways to convert temperature among these measuring systems. The formulae are shown in Table 11.20; none of the test bulletins state that you need to know them, but it is better to be on the safe side.

TABLE 11.20   Temperature Conversions

Fahrenheit to Celsius	°C = (°F – 32) × 0.555	60°F
Celsius to Fahrenheit	°F = (°C × 1.8) + 32	60°C
Celsius to Kelvin	K = °C + 273.15	60°C
Kelvin to Celsius	°C = K – 273.15	60K

Let's look at a few examples of how these temperature conversions can be used.

- Let's take 50°F and convert it to °C
  (50°F – 32) × 0.555 = 32.24°C
- Let's convert 30°C to °F
  (30°C × 1.8) + 32 = 86°F
- 30°C to K
  30°C + 273.15 = 303.15K
- 303.15K to °C
  303.15K – 273.15 = °30C

When substances heat up, particles of the substance begin to move due to the transfer of kinetic energy. The Kinetic Molecular Theory describes this motion.

1. All matter is made of small particles (atoms and molecules).
2. Particles are in constant motion (possess kinetic energy).
3. Empty spaces exist between particles.
4. Particles and the spaces between them are too small to be seen.
5. In each state of matter, particles behave in a characteristic way.
6. Solid particles are packed so tightly together that they can only vibrate back and forth.
7. Liquid particles are slightly farther apart than in a solid. Particles move slightly faster than those in a solid.
8. Gas particles are far apart, and particle movement is rapid.
9. As heat is added to a substance, the particles' kinetic energy increases. This causes the particles to move more rapidly.

As molecules move and behave according to the kinetic molecular theory, the substance undergoes changes in states of matter. An example of a change in state of matter is when an ice cube (which is a solid) warms up and melts into water (which is a liquid). More types of changes in states of matter are described in Table 11.21.

TABLE 11.21

CHANGE	DESCRIPTION
Melting	Liquid to a solid.
Vaporization	Liquid to a gas.
Evaporation	Slow vaporization.
Boiling	Fast vaporization.
Condensation	Gas to a liquid.
Freezing/solidification	Liquid to a solid.
Sublimation	Solid to a gas or gas to solid.

Heat Transfer.   For a change in the state of matter to occur, heat must be either transferred to or from an object. This transfer produces the change in kinetic energy that is (described in the section on kinetic molecular theory that we discussed in the previous section) needed for matter to change states. Heat is transferred from one substance to another in three major ways: conduction, convection, and radiation.

Conduction: Transferred by direct contact.
Convection: Transferred through the movement of heated material.
Radiation: Heat travels as waves.

Conduction—Energy transfer in which vibrating molecules transfer heat along to other vibrating molecules by means of direct contact. An example of heat transfer by conduction occurs when you place a metal spoon in a bowl of hot soup. Vibrating molecules in the hot soup transfer heat to the metal spoon via direct contact. The net effect of this transfer is the heat of the soup is reduced while the heat of the spoon is increased.

Convection—Transfer of heat through the movement of heated material. In an unevenly heated substance, heated portions of the substance displace portions with lower temperatures. An example of convection occurs when a pot of water is placed on a burner. The lower portion of the water heats more quickly because it is closer to the heat source. This heated water rises to the surface, displacing the cooler water at the surface (that is farther away from the heat source), forcing the cooler water across the surface and then down to the bottom of the pot.

Radiation—Transfer where heat travels through space as waves. An example of radiation can be experienced on a warm sunny day. Solar energy travels to the earth's surface in waves.

CONTENT AREA SEVEN: LIGHT

All light is produced by atoms in an excited state. Atoms become excited when their electrons jump to a higher energy level (an orbital farther out from the nucleus). This occurs when an electron absorbs a photon. Atoms readily drop back down to their nonexcited (ground) state. To do this, the electron must drop back down to its original energy level, releasing a photon. It is this release of photons that produces visible light. Photons are the smallest unit of light energy and are considered to have no mass and no electric charge. Photons can be absorbed by electrons causing the atoms to be in an excited state (occupying a greater amount of energy than in their nonexcited state).

Types of Light

Table 11.22 shows the types of light to know for the test.

TABLE 11.22

TYPES OF LIGHT	SOURCE
Incandescent	Glowing wire filament.
Fluorescent	Phosphors glow in a glass tube.
Polarized	All light waves vibrate in the same plane.
Neon	Atoms of a gas are excited.
Laser	Light of only one frequency.

Incandescent light is produced when electricity passes through a wire called a filament. The transfer of electricity raises atoms in the wire to an excited state, causing the wire to glow. This is the process that powers typical household light bulbs.

Fluorescent light is produced when phosphors in a glass tube are raised to an excited state by passing electricity through the tube. Phosphor is a substance that emits light when it is excited by radiation.

Light waves typically vibrate in many directions. They generally vibrate in both vertical and horizontal directions. Polarized light vibrates in a single plane, such as only vertically or only horizontally.

Neon light is also produced in a glass tube. The tube is filled with a gas, and electricity is passed through the tube. When the atoms of the gas reach an excited state, a colored light is emitted. Different gases emit distinctive colors. For example, neon emits a red color and the gas argon emits blue.

Laser light is light of only one wavelength. This light only travels in one direction with photons parallel to one another. This prevents laser light from spreading over distance like other forms of light do. This also gives laser light the unique property of being able to be tightly focused. The energy of a laser can be so tightly focused that it can be used to cut metal or human tissue in delicate surgery.

Interactions of Light with Matter

When light interacts with matter, one of three things can happen:

Transmission: Light passes through a substance.
Absorption: Light enters a substance and is held there.
Reflection: Light strikes a substance and bounces back.

There are many examples of light interacting with matter in our everyday lives. An example of transmission is when light shines through a window. Light is absorbed when it interacts with black clothing. Black clothing appears black because no light is reflected from it. It is completely absorbed by the clothing and changes form into heat energy. Anyone who has worn a black shirt on a sunny day has experienced light absorption. Reflection occurs when the opposite of absorption occurs. Reflection takes place when a surface absorbs no light waves and they are all bounced back. An example of reflection is the reflection of light in a mirror.

When light is transmitted through a substance, transmission may occur in varying degrees. There are three levels of light transmission to know for the test (see Table 11.23).

TABLE 11.23

LEVEL	DESCRIPTION	EXAMPLE
Transparent	Light passes through so you can see through the material clearly.	Clear glass
Translucent	Light passes through but is scattered so you can see through the material but not clearly.	Frosted glass
Opaque	Light does not pass through. The material cannot be seen through.	Wood

Light and sound both possess properties of waves. In the case of light, it behaves as both a particle (as described with photons) and as a wave. Listed below are characteristic properties of waves. All waves behave as shown in Table 11.24.

- Reflect
- Refract
- Exhibit the Doppler Effect

TABLE 11.24

PROPERTY	DESCRIPTION	EXAMPLE
Refraction	Path of light ray is "bent."	Prism
Reflection	Rays strike an object and are released.	Mirror
Doppler Effect	Observed shift in frequency as the source of the waves moves towards or away from you.	Wailing of a siren

Refraction is the bending of light by passing it through another transparent material of different density than the material it was originally passing through. This occurs because as light enters a different medium its velocity changes. This change in velocity is comparable to the change in velocity you would experience if you were running on land and then transitioned into running in water. Your velocity would change because you travel more slowly through water than you do on land. Both direction and wavelength of the light wave changes as a result of this change in velocity.

Reflection occurs when light rays strike an object and are released again. You can imagine this as light waves "bouncing" off of an object. Reflection involves two rays: an incoming ray (incident ray) and an outgoing ray (reflection ray). Reflection occurs when light waves are not absorbed by an object. The greater the reflectivity of an object, the less light is being absorbed.

All waves also exhibit the Doppler effect. The Doppler effect is the effect produced by a source of waves that is moving. In the Doppler effect, observers whom the source is approaching will notice an apparent upward shift in frequency, and those observers from whom the source is moving away will notice a downward shift. The effect is only observable because distance from the source of waves is changing.

Color

Visible light is electromagnetic energy that falls within the narrow range wavelengths that are visible to the human eye. The eye interprets each different wavelength of visible light energy as a different color.

Vision is a sensation produced by an interaction between the eye and the brain. This occurs when the eye is stimulated by visible light waves. Color that is perceived by the human eye is determined by the wavelengths of light that are being reflected. For example, if an object reflects all wavelengths of light equally, the object appears white. This is because the human eye is not capable of separating the spectral colors. Surfaces appear black if they absorb all wavelengths of light and do not reflect any light at all. In the middle of this range are surfaces that absorb all but one particular wavelength of light. The human eye will perceive the surface as the color of the wavelength of light the surface is reflecting. Materials can reflect more that one wavelength of light. In these cases, the human eye and brain mix the wavelengths of light; and the perceived color is a combination of the wavelengths reflected.

All colors observed by the human eye are composed of the spectral colors. Spectral colors are the individual colors produced by each wavelength of visible light. The spectral colors are listed below in order of longest wavelength (lowest energy) to highest wavelength (highest energy). A common acronym used to remember the spectral colors in descending order of wavelength is **ROY G BIV.**

R ed
O range
Y ellow
G reen
B lue
I ndigo
V iolet

Visible light plays a critical role in the plant process of photosynthesis. Photosynthesis is the process by which plants produce carbohydrates using water, carbon dioxide, and light energy. Photons of light are absorbed by chlorophyll molecules in the plant. This raises the atoms in chlorophyll molecules to an excited state. These photons of light are the energy used to power the process of photosynthesis.

Optical Properties of Waves

Light and sound both possess properties of waves. In the case of light, it behaves as both a particle (as described with photons) and as a wave. Figure 11.16 shows the characteristic properties of waves.

CONTENT AREA EIGHT: CONSERVATION OF ENERGY RESOURCES

There are two types of resources to know for the test:

■ Renewable resources, which can be replaced.
■ Nonrenewable resources, which cannot be replaced.

FIGURE 11.16

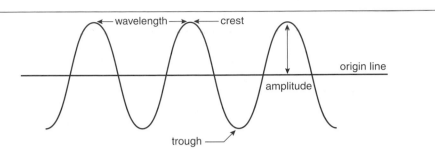

Origin line—indicated medium with no wave traveling through it (not an actual part of the wave).

Crest—highest point of the wave.

Trough—lowest point of the wave.

Wavelength—distance from the crest of one wave to the crest of the adjacent wave.

Amplitude—distance from the origin line to the crest (observed as "loudness" in sound waves).

Frequency—number of waves that pass through a given point in a specified amount of time (observed as "pitch" in sound waves).

Renewable resources are those resources that can be replaced either as they are used, or within a human lifetime. Trees used as lumber or paper production are considered renewable because they can be replaced by new trees that can be planted and grown over a human lifetime. Water is used largely in industry and agriculture. Even though the amount of water that exists in the biosphere is finite, water is considered renewable because it is constantly moving through the hydrologic cycle (water cycle, see Figure 11.17).

FIGURE 11.17
Water Cycle

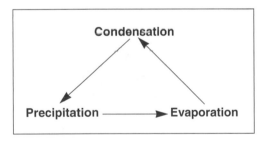

It is important to remember that renewable resources are not in limitless supply. *Renewable* simply means that the resource is replaceable within an approximate time span of seventy-five years.

Nonrenewable resources are those resources that are in limited supply and either cannot be replaced or take millions of years to regenerate. Nonrenewable resources important to human activities include mineral resources and fossil fuels. Minerals such as gold, silver, and iron ore exist on earth in limited supplies. Once human mining operations have exhausted these supplies, recycling of these metals will no longer be an option, it will become a necessity. Fossil fuels, also called hydrocarbons, have become the primary resource used for energy in industrialized nations to generate electricity, power equipment, power vehicles, and to heat homes. The three main types of fossil fuels are petroleum, natural gas, and coal. These hydrocarbons are burned to release light and heat energy.

Fossil fuels are being consumed at an ever-increasing rate. Scientists estimate that global coal reserves will be exhausted within the next 200 years. It is also estimated that the majority of petroleum supplies in the United States have already been discovered.

The use of fossil fuels has serious impacts on the environment. Mining of fossil fuels contributes to erosion and pollution of soils and water. Burning of fossil fuels releases pollutants such as sulfur dioxide and carbon monoxide into the air.

These two types of resources have very different requirements in terms of their management and responsible use. Mismanagement of these resources is sure to lead to irrevocable resource depletion and rampant pollution. Both of these consequences have the potential to render our planet a desolate wasteland no longer capable of supporting life.

CHAPTER TWELVE

Life Science[1]

DOMAIN TWO: STRUCTURE AND FUNCTIONS OF LIVING THINGS

CONTENT AREA NINE: PLANT AND ANIMAL CELLS

Cells are the basic unit of all living things. If anything is smaller or more simple than a cell, it is not alive. So we can say that an atom is not alive, but many atoms together making up a cell is alive. The cell theory summarizes the basic principles of this idea. According to cell theory, the following rules apply:

1. All living things are made of cells.
2. Cells are the basic units of the structures of living things.
3. New cells can only be generated from existing cells. They can not be spontaneously created.

Evolution of Cell Theory

A common theme of science is that significant scientific discoveries are usually the cumulative result of the work of many scientists in many disciplines and different nations over a long period of time. This is a basic concept that you will need to be familiar with. The way in which modern cell theory has been established and altered over time by many scientists is a prime example of the collaborative nature of science. Cell theory is the cumulative result of the accomplishments of many biologists from several nations over a span of 200 years. The evolution of cell theory can be summarized in the following time line. The time line summarizes the events that helped shape the cell theory described above. (*Note:* Do not place too much emphasis on specific dates. Rather, pay attention to the gradual development of the theory.)

- Early 1600s—The microscope is invented in Holland.
- 1674—Anton Van Leeuenhoek is the first person to observe microscopic organisms in water in Holland.
- 1838—Mathias Schleiden concludes from his experiments in Germany that all plants are composed of cells.
- 1839—Theodore Schwann (also in Germany) concludes that all animals are composed of cells.
- 1855—Cell theory is completed when Russian scientist Rudolph Virchow concludes that all cells come from existing cells.

---

[1]Chapter contributed by Erica Seropian Cardey.

Cell Structures

Cells may vary greatly in size and shape, however there are some basic structures that are common to nearly all cells. Cells are classified in two basic ways: prokaryotic versus eukaryotic and, among the eukaryotes, plant versus animal. Prokaryotic cells differ from eukaryotic cells in their size and complexity.

Plant and animal cells differ from one another in both their structure and function. These basic differences will be discussed in greater detail within this section. But first, let's begin to look at the basic functions of these structures so a clear comparison between these different types of cells can be made. The terms in Table 12.1 summarize structures, their functions, and the types of cells these structures can be found in. "Yes" and "no" indicate whether or not the particular structure can be found in that particular type of cell.

TABLE 12.1

PLANT	ANIMAL	PROKARYOTE	CELL STRUCTURE	STRUCTURE FUNCTION
Yes	No	No	Cell wall	Support and protection
Yes	Yes	No	Nucleus	Controls most cell processes and contains the cell's genetic information (DNA will be discussed later in domain two).
Yes	Yes	No	Cytoskeleton	Helps the cell maintain its shape and is involved in cell movement.
Yes	Yes	Yes	Cell membrane	Support and protection.
Yes	Yes	Yes	Cytoplasm	All material within the cell membrane except the cell's nucleus.

The main function of the *cell wall* is to provide structural support and protection for the cell. Most cell walls are made of fibers. The fibers are usually made of carbohydrates and protein. The fiber of plant cell walls is called cellulose. Cell walls are found in nearly all cells except animal cells.

The *cell membrane* is a structure that is found in all cells. The cell membrane is a thin, flexible barrier that surrounds the cell. The cell membrane has two main functions. First, it provides protection and structural support to the cell. Second, the cell membrane regulates what enters and exits the cell. Cell membranes are selectively permeable. This means that the membrane allows certain substances to pass through it, while preventing other substances from passing through.

Cytoplasm is the material that is found within the cell membrane. The cytoplasm includes all of the structures within the inside of the cell. (These are called organelles, and will be discussed further in the next subsection.) The nucleus is the only structure inside of the cell that is not considered to be part of the cytoplasm.

The *nucleus* controls most processes within the cell. The nucleus can be thought of as the control center of the cell, much as the brain is considered the control center of the body. Eukaryotic cells possess a nucleus but prokaryotic cells do not. The nucleus also contains the cell's genetic material (called DNA, to be discussed later in domain two). The genetic material in the cell's nucleus carries the instructions for making proteins and other essential molecules. This process is one of the main functions of a cell. It is important to note that although prokaryotic cells do not have a nucleus, they do have genetic material. The genetic material of prokaryotic cells is located in the cytoplasm instead of being contained in a nucleus.

Prokaryotic versus Eukaryotic Cells

As we have already mentioned, prokaryotic and eukaryotic cells differ in size and complexity. Prokaryotic cells are smaller and lack a nucleus (see Figure 12.1). They also have far fewer

FIGURE 12.1

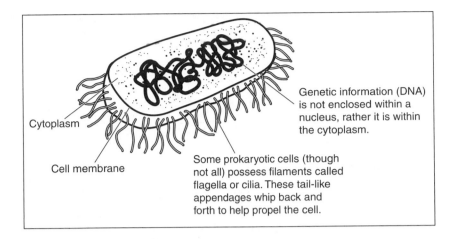

Cytoplasm

Cell membrane

Genetic information (DNA) is not enclosed within a nucleus, rather it is within the cytoplasm.

Some prokaryotic cells (though not all) possess filaments called flagella or cilia. These tail-like appendages whip back and forth to help propel the cell.

specialized structures in their cytoplasm than eukaryotic cells. Prokaryote means "before nucleus". This is because prokaryotic cells existed prior to the development of eukaryotic cells.

Eukaryotic cells are larger and more complex. They have a nucleus and specialized structures within their cytoplasm (see Figure 12.2). These structures are collectively referred to as organelles. Organelles will be discussed in detail in the next subsection of this content area.

FIGURE 12.2

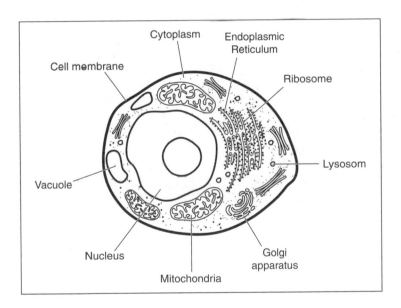

Cell membrane

Cytoplasm

Endoplasmic Reticulum

Ribosome

Vacuole

Lysosom

Nucleus

Mitochondria

Golgi apparatus

Cytoskeleton. The cytoskeleton is a network of protein filaments that help support the cell. The cytoskeleton has two main functions:

- Support the cell.
- Aid in cell movement.

The two primary structures of the cytoskeleton are microtubules and microfilaments. Both structures form networks in some cells.

- Microtubules are hollow tubes of protein. They function in supporting cell structure. They also form tracks that organelles move along. They play a role in cell division (this will be discussed in "Reproduction"). Some microtubules may also extend out from a cell as external appendages that aid the cells in locomotion. An example of this is the "tail" of a sperm cell.

■ Microfilaments are long, thin fibers that are much narrower than microtubules. They aid in the structural support of the cell.

Cytoplasm.   The cytoplasm within the cell houses several types of organelles. It is important to note that the cell's nucleus is not considered to be part of the cytoplasm. Organelles will be discussed in detail next. Organelles are specialized structures that perform specific tasks. The name organelles means "little organs." This is a helpful way to remember what organelles are because they function within cells much as organs do within the greater structure of the body.

Organelles within the Cell

Organelles are specialized structures that perform specific tasks. The name *organelle* means "little organ." This is a helpful way to remember what organelles are because they function within cells much as organs do within the greater structure of the body. Note the various organelles, their functions, and which types of cells they are commonly found in. Notice that very few organelles are found in prokaryotic cells. Recall that a major distinguishing characteristic between prokaryotic and eukaryotic cells is that prokaryotic cells have far fewer specialized structures than eukaryotic cells (see Table 12.2).

TABLE 12.2

| | | | EUKARYOTES | |
| | | Present in Prokaryotes | Present in Animal Cells | Present in Plant Cells |
ORGANELLE	**FUNCTION**			
Ribosomes	Produce proteins	Yes	Yes	Yes
Endoplasmic Reticulum	Modifies proteins and assembles the components of the cell membrane.	No	Yes	Yes
Golgi Apparatus	Processes proteins by attaching carbohydrates and lipids (fats) to them.	No	Yes	Yes
Lysomes	Break down nutrients from food and break down debris in the cell.	No	Yes	Yes
Vacuoles	Store and transport materials in the cell.	No	Small if any at all	Yes
Chloroplast	Performs photosynthesis.	No	No	Yes
Mitochondria	Release energy from stored molecules of food.	No	Yes	Yes

As we look at each organelle in detail, it is helpful to think of the cell as a factory whose primary function is making proteins.

Ribosomes are composed of small pieces of RNA (ribonucleic acid) and protein. Ribosomes use instructions that come from the nucleus to produce protein. As in the case of ribonucleic acid, this idea will be discussed in the section on DNA.

The *endoplasmic reticulum* (ER) is a system of membranes within the cell. The main functions of the ER are to modify the proteins manufactured by the ribosomes and to assemble the parts of the cell membrane. Some ribosomes are free within the cytoplasm, others are fixed to the ER. This is an important idea to keep in mind as we move on to the two types of ER, rough and smooth.

The endoplasmic reticulum has two main sections. Rough endoplasmic reticulum is called "rough" because it is studded with ribosomes. This part of the ER is involved in producing proteins. Proteins produced by ribosomes on the rough ER move from the ribosomes on the rough ER to smooth ER for modification. Smooth ER has no ribosomes on its surface, hence the name "smooth." Smooth ER also caries out other specialized tasks such as producing lipids (fats).

The *Golgi apparatus* further processes proteins. Proteins produced along the rough ER move from the ER to the Golgi apparatus. From the Golgi apparatus, they then travel to their final destinations where they will be utilized by the cell.

Lysosomes are occasionally nicknamed "suicide sacs." They earn this name because they are small organelles that are filled with enzymes. Lysosomes perform two vital functions for the cell. First, lysosomes break down food particles (such as carbohydrates, proteins, and lipids) so they can be used by the cell. Second, lysosomes remove debris from the cell by digesting organelles that are no longer useful. Lysosomes basically digest "worn-out" organelles.

Vacuoles are sac-shaped structures that are found largely in plant cells and to a smaller extent in animal cells and single-celled organisms. Vacuoles may be used by cells to store carbohydrates, water, proteins, or salts. In the case of plant cells, vacuoles also play a role in structural support of plants. Many plant cells have a single, large fluid-filled vacuole. The pressure in the vacuole aids the in the structural support of the plant. Smaller vacuoles are called vesicles. Vesicles are involved in the process of transporting materials within the cell.

Choloroplasts are found primarily in plant cells and are absent in the cells of animals and fungi. Choloroplasts manufacture food molecules for the cell by using energy from sunlight to carry out photosynthesis. (Photosynthesis is the process by which plants use energy from sunlight to make food molecules. This idea will be discussed further in content area fourteen).

The green pigment called chlorophyll is found within chloroplasts. It is this chlorophyll that actually harnesses light energy for photosynthesis.

Mitochondria release energy from food molecules. This energy can then be used by the cell to carry out necessary life functions such as growth and motion. Because mitochondria (mitochondrion is singular, mitochondria is plural) use energy from food to produce energy-rich molecules that are used by the rest of the cell, mitochondria are frequently referred to as "MIGHT-o-chondria" because they are the source of the cell's "might."

CONTENT AREA TEN: PLANT PARTS

Plants have specialize organs just like animals do. The three main types of organs (in plants, we more commonly refer to organs as "structures") or structures are summarized in Table 12.3:

TABLE 12.3

STRUCTURE	FUNCTION
Roots	Absorb water and nutrients and anchor plants to the ground.
Stems	Provide structural support and transport nutrients.
Leaves	Site of photosynthesis and allow carbon dioxide gas to enter the plant and oxygen to exit.

(*Note:* Reproduction and the organs involved in this process in both plants and animals will be discussed in greater detail in content areas twenty-three to twenty-five.)

As a plant grows, *roots* develop a branching pattern that penetrates the soil. Roots grow between soil particles. It is this growth pattern that allows roots to carry out their two primary functions. First, roots absorb water and nutrients from the soil. Secondly, roots provide anchoring and structural support for the plant.

Leaves are broad flat structures whose primary function is to serve as the site of photosynthesis. Leaves also feature pores which expand and contract in order to control the loss of water vapor through the leaves and to allow carbon dioxide to enter (necessary for photosynthesis, which will be discussed later) and oxygen (a by-product of photosynthesis) to be released.

Stems are responsible for transporting nutrients within a plant as well as supporting the main body of the plant. The stem houses the plant's vascular tissue (this will be discussed in the next section), which acts as a go-between, lifting water and nutrients up form the roots and transporting the products of photosynthesis from the leaves to other parts of the plant.

CONTENT AREA ELEVEN: SPECIALIZED TISSUES IN PLANTS

The three major plant organs previously mentioned are made of specialized tissues. The three major tissue systems are summarized in Table 12.4.

TABLE 12.4

TISSUE SYSTEM	FUNCTION	SPECIALIZED TISSUES
Dermal	Outer covering of the plant. • Regulates materials passing into and out of the cell. • Protects against injury.	• Cuticle • Epidermal cells
Vascular	Transports water and nutrients within the plant.	• Xylem • Phloem
Ground	Cells located between the dermal and vascular tissues.	• Parenchyma • Collenchyma • Sclerenchyma

Dermal tissue is the outer covering of a plant. Dermal tissue is usually a single layer of epidermal cells covered by a cuticle layer. Cuticle is the thick waxy layer that protects the plant from injury and excessive water loss.

Vascular tissue composes the transport system of a plant. Vascular tissue acts as a go-between, transporting water from the roots and carbohydrates (the product of photosynthesis) from the leaves. Vascular tissue consists of two types: xylem and phloem. Xylem transports water from the roots to other parts of the plant. Phloem transports nutrients from the roots of a plant to the leaves where they are needed for photosynthesis, and it also transports carbohydrates produced in the leaves by photosynthesis to other parts of the plant.

Ground tissue is located between the dermal and vascular tissue. Ground tissue serves two functions. In leaves, ground tissue cells house large numbers of chloroplasts (recall from the previous section that chloroplasts are the cellular organelles that perform photosynthesis). In other parts of the plant, ground tissue contributes strength and structural support.

CONTENT AREA TWELVE: TISSUES OF BODY SYSTEMS

Complex animals (those composed of many cells) also have specialized organs. Just as in plants, these organs are made of specialized tissues. These organs are further organized into body systems. The body systems work together to maintain homeostasis in an organism. Homeostasis is the maintaining of a consistent environment in the body. Homeostasis involves maintaining a stable nutrient and chemical balance, a stable internal temperature, and a stable chemical composition. Before we examine these specialized organs and the systems that they form, let's look at the types of tissues that these organs are made of.

Animal Tissues

Animals have specialized tissues that perform specific functions just like plants do. The terms in Table 12.5 summarize the basic types of tissue of animals (specifically human) body systems and their basic functions.

TABLE 12.5

TISSUE	FUNCTION	EXAMPLE
Muscle	Controls internal and external movement.	Bicep—arm movement
Connective	Holds organs in place and binds different body parts together.	Ligaments and tendons
Nervous	Directs bodily responses according to messages that are received from the body's environment.	Sensation of pain
Epithelial	Lines the internal organs and covers the body.	Skin

Most animals are primarily made of *muscle* tissue. Muscle tissue controls both internal and external movement as well as voluntary and involuntary movements. An example of internal movement is the muscular movements that direct food along the digestive tract (through the intestines). An example of voluntary muscle movement is moving a leg in order to walk.

Connective tissue serves several functions. Connective tissue holds organs in their proper places. Connective tissue also provides support to the body. Connective tissue that aids in supporting the body takes the form of ligaments and tendons. Ligaments join bones to bones and tendons join muscles to bones.

Nervous tissue directs the body's response to its internal and external environments. Nervous tissue accomplishes this task by receiving messages from the environment. (These messages are called stimuli.) The nervous tissue then analyzes that message before directing a response. (*Note:* The specific cells of nervous tissue as well as specific roles these cells play in larger body systems will be discussed in greater detail in the section on the nervous system.)

CONTENT AREA THIRTEEN: BODY SYSTEMS

These specialized tissues compose specific bodily organs. These organs are further organized into body systems. Each body system carries out specific functions that help the body maintain homeostasis. Table 12.6 summarizes these systems, the organs in the systems, and their functions.

Skeletal

The skeletal system provides several functions.

- Supports the body.
- Protects internal organs.
- Provides for movement.
- Stores minerals.
- Is the site of blood cell formation.

TABLE 12.6

SYSTEM	PRIMARY FUNCTIONS	ORGANS/STRUCTURES
Nervous	Coordinates the body's responses to changes.	Brain, spinal cord, and nerves.
Skeletal	Supports the body, allows for movement, and protects body organs.	Bones, cartilage, ligaments and tendons.
Muscular	Responsible for voluntary movement, movement in the digestive system, and helps circulate blood.	Skeletal muscle, smooth muscle, and cardiac muscle.
Integumentary	Protection from injury, infection, and ultraviolet radiation. Helps regulate body temperature.	Skin, hair, nails, sweat, and oil glands.
Circulatory	Brings oxygen to the body and regulates temperature.	Heart, blood vessels, and blood.
Respiratory	Provides oxygen to the body and removes carbon dioxide.	Nose, pharynx, larynx, trachea, bronchi, bronchioles, and lungs.
Digestive	Converts food into simpler molecules for use by the body and absorbs those molecules.	Mouth, pharynx, esophagus, stomach, large and small intestines.
Excretory	Eliminates waste products from the body.	Skin, lungs, kidneys, ureters, urinary bladder, and urethra.
Endocrine	Regulates processes such as growth, development, metabolism, and reproduction.	Hypothalamus, pituitary gland, thyroid, parathyroids, adrenal glands, pancreas, male testes, and female ovaries.
Reproductive	Produces reproductive cells and houses the developing young (in females).	Females: ovaries, fallopian tubes, uterus, vagina.
		Males: testes, epididymus, vas deferens, urethra, penis.

Bones provide internal structural support for the body much in the same way a steel frame provides support for a building. The rigid structure of bones provides support for delicate organs just as your skull protects your brain. Bones also act as levers that are moved by muscles (review the section in domain one about simple machines for a review of levers). Bones also contain mineral reserves that are important to life processes. Bones are also where the body produces blood cells. Some bones are filled with a soft tissue in their central cavities called marrow. It is this marrow that produces blood cells. The skeletal system also includes joints. Joints are places where one bone attaches to another. Joints are composed of ligaments (recall that ligaments attach bone to bone), a flexible tissue called cartilage, and fluid.

Muscular

All body movement is dependent on muscles. There are three types of muscle tissue (see Table 12.7).

Skeletal muscle is attached to bones. Skeletal muscle cells are large and usually have more than one nucleus. Skeletal muscle is also known as striated muscle because when it is viewed under a microscope, skeletal muscles appear to have alternating light and dark bands. Skeletal muscle is responsible for voluntary muscle movements such as running, dancing, and facial expressions.

Smooth muscle cells have one nucleus and appear spindle shaped under a microscope. Smooth muscle lines hollow body structures such as intestines, blood vessels, and the stomach. Smooth muscle is responsible for involuntary muscle movements such as the movements that cause blood flow and the movements that move food along the digestive tract.

TABLE 12.7

MUSCLE TYPE	STRUCTURE	FUNCTION
Skeletal	Large cells with more than one nucleus, alternating light and dark bands.	Attached to bone, controlled by the central nervous system.
Smooth	Spindle shaped with one nucleus.	Responsible for involuntary movements.
Cardiac	Striated like skeletal muscle but usually has only one nucleus. Not under voluntary control.	Found in the heart only.

Cardiac muscle is found only in the heart. Cardiac muscle has many features in common with both skeletal and smooth muscle tissue. Like skeletal muscle, cardiac muscle appears to be striated, however its cells are smaller. Like smooth muscle, cardiac muscle cells usually only have one nucleus and are regulated by involuntary impulses from the nervous system.

Nervous System

The nervous system can be thought of as the body's control center. The nervous system controls all bodily functions and controls responses to stimuli from within and outside of the body. The nervous system responds to stimuli by carrying messages called impulses. These impulses are electrical signals that are transmitted by neurons. Stimuli are detected by sense organs such as the eyes, ears, skin, nose, and tastebuds. These stimuli initiate messages that are carried through the nervous system by special cells called neurons.

Neurons are the basic cells that transmit impulses. Table 12.8 summarizes the three types of neurons and their role in impulse transmission. (*Note:* Neurons are classified according to the direction that the impulse is traveling.)

TABLE 12.8

TYPE OF NEURON	CARRIES THE IMPULSE . . .
Sensory Neuron	From sensory organs to the spinal cord and brain (stimulus).
Motor Neuron	From brain to the spinal cord, then on to muscles and glands (response).
Interneuron	Connects the sensory and motor neurons.

Divisions of the Nervous System. Neurons function in coordination with many other organs to form the complicated network we know as the nervous system. The nervous system is divided into two classifications which are summarized in Table 12.9.

TABLE 12.9

BRANCH	ORGANS INVOLVED
Central	• Brain—cerebellum, cerebrum, brain stem • Thalamus • Hypothalamus • Spinal cord
Peripheral	• Sensory • Motor

The Central Nervous System. The central nervous system includes the brain and spinal cord. The brain can easily be considered to be the "switchboard" of the central nervous system. This is because of the approximately 100 billion neurons in the brain, most of them are interneurons (recall that interneurons connect the motor and sensory neurons).

The brain can be divided into five major components: the cerebrum, cerebellum, brain stem, thalamus, and hypothalamus. These components as well as the spinal cord are summarized in Table 12.10 and paragraphs that follow.

TABLE 12.10

COMPONENT	FUNCTION	EXAMPLE OF ACTIVITY
Cerebrum	Controls voluntary functions.	Speech
Cerebellum	Coordination and balance.	Dancing
Brain Stem	Involuntary functions.	Heart rate and breathing
Thalamus	Receives messages from the sensory organs and relays the info to the cerebellum.	N/A
Hypothalamus	Recognizes body temperature, thirst, hunger, fatigue, and anger.	N/A
Spinal Cord	Communicates between the brain and the rest of the body.	N/A

The *cerebrum* is the largest region of the brain. This is the part of the brain that is covered in folds and grooves (this increases the cerebrum's surface area). The cerebrum is responsible for all conscious, voluntary activities. Examples of voluntary actions controlled by the cerebrum are learning and speech.

The *cerebellum* coordinates muscle movements that are commanded by the cerebrum. The cerebellum controls coordination and balance, ensuring that the movements regulated by the cerebrum are efficient. An example of the cerebellum at work is the graceful maneuvers of a gymnast.

The *brain stem* acts as an intermediary between the brain and spinal cord. It regulates the flow of information between the brain and the body. The brain stem also regulates many involuntary functions that are critical to life, such as breathing and heart rate.

The *thalamus* relays information from the sense organs to the brain. The *hypothalamus* registers sensations such as hunger, thirst, anger, and body temperature.

The *spinal cord* functions like a telephone line. This is because the spinal cord serves as the primary communication line between the brain and the rest of the body.

The Peripheral Nervous System. The peripheral nervous system includes all nervous tissue that is not part of the brain and spinal cord (hence the name "peripheral" as opposed to "central"). The peripheral nervous system can be divided into two areas: the motor and sensory areas. These areas are summarized in the Table 12.11.

TABLE 12.11

DIVISION	FUNCTION
Sensory	Transmits impulses from sense organs to the central nervous system (inputs the stimuli).
Motor	Transmits impulses from the central nervous system to the muscles or glands (dictates the reaction to the stimuli).

Nervous Response. The two halves of the nervous system work together to carry out nervous responses. Nervous responses occur when the body reacts to stimuli. Figure 12.3 shows the path that messages follow through the entire nervous system when a stimulus response occurs.

FIGURE 12.3

Sensory neuron → **spinal cord** → **brain** → **spinal cord** → **motor neuron**

Integumentary System

The integumentary system serves four major functions. These functions are:

1. Protects against infection and injury by acting as a physical barrier.
2. Removes wastes from the body.
3. Plays a role in regulating body temperature.
4. Protects the body against ultraviolet radiation.

The integumentary system is comprised of three major body parts. Some of these parts are easily considered to be organs, but it may be more logical to refer to others as bodily features. These organs and features are listed and their functions are summarized in the Table 12.12.

TABLE 12.12

ORGAN/ FEATURE	FUNCTION
Skin	• Detects sensations of heat, cold, pressure, and pain and transmits them to the nervous system. • Protects from the outside environment. • Protects the body against ultraviolet rays. • Regulates body temperature.
Nails	• Protects fingertips and toes.
Hair	• Protects against UV light. • Insulates from the cold. • Prevents foreign particles from entering the body via the nose, eyes, and ears.

The *skin* is the largest part of the integumentary system. It contains sensors that relay messages to the central nervous system in order to convey sensations of pain, pressure, heat, and cold. The skin is composed of two layers, each serving a distinct function.

The epidermis is the outer layer of the skin. The epidermis forms a tough, flexible layer that contains the pigment melanin. Melanin is the pigment that determines the color of skin. It is important to note that there are no blood vessels in the epidermis. Hint: The **E**pidermis is the **E**xterior of the skin.

Beneath the epidermis lies the dermis. If the epidermis plays a protective role, then the dermis fulfills the other roles of the skin. The dermis contains blood vessels, sensory organs, hair follicles, nerve endings, and glands. The dermis helps control body temperature by either narrowing or widening the blood vessels to alter blood flow. Widening the blood vessels increases blood flow, increasing the release of heat. Narrowing the blood vessels decreases blood flow, restricting heat loss.

Nails are primarily composed of a tough protein called keratin. They protect the sensitive tips of fingers and toes. An area of rapidly dividing cells called the nail root is the site from which nails grow.

Hair, like nails, is made of keratin. Hair serves three protective purposes. Hair provides insulation from cold as well as shielding skin beneath the hair from the sun's harmful ultraviolet rays. Hair also functions as a physical barrier that prevents dirt and other particles from entering the body via the nostrils, eyes, and ears.

Circulatory System

Larger (multicellular) organisms are dependent on a circulatory system to transport critical materials such as nutrients, oxygen, and waste products. Circulatory systems vary to some degree depending on the type of animal, but the human circulatory system is composed of the heart, blood vessels, and blood. These three major components of the circulatory system and their functions are shown in Table 12.13.

TABLE 12.13

ORGAN/PART	FUNCTION
Heart	Acts as a pump.
Blood Vessels	Transport system.
Blood	Medium that moves through the transport system. Carries nutrients, waste materials, and oxygen.

Heart.   The heart is composed almost entirely of muscle tissue (recall our previous discussion of cardiac muscle tissue). The heart pumps blood through the body by a steady series of muscle contractions. The heart is divided into two halves. These halves are further divided into two chambers each. Each half is divided into an upper and lower chamber. The upper chamber is called the atrium. The atrium receives blood into the heart. The lower chamber is called the ventricle. The ventricle pumps blood out of the heart. So we can say that the human heart consists of four chambers. These chambers are illustrated for you in the Figure 12.4.

FIGURE 12.4

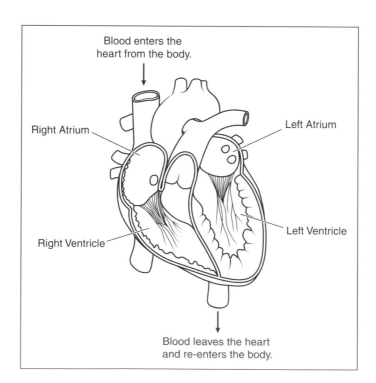

Blood enters the
heart from the body.

Right Atrium

Left Atrium

Right Ventricle

Left Ventricle

Blood leaves the heart
and re-enters the body.

The heart is also equipped with a series of valves that open and close with muscle contractions by the heart. These valves ensure that blood flows through the heart in only one direction. It is helpful to think of blood moving through the heart as traffic moving along a one way street.

Blood Vessels.   Blood travels through the circulatory system via a network of blood vessels. There are three types of blood vessels: arteries, veins, and capillaries. The three types of veins differ mainly in their sizes and whether or not they transport oxygen-rich or oxygen-poor blood. Table 12.14 summarizes the role of each type of blood vessel.

TABLE 12.14

NAME	RELATIVE SIZE	ROLE
Artery	Large	Transport oxygen-rich blood from the heart to body tissues.
Vein	Size Varies	Transport oxygen-poor blood back to the heart.
Capillaries	Smallest	Intermediary between arteries and veins. • Absorb wastes such as CO_2 from body tissues • Brings nutrients and oxygen to body tissues.

These three types of blood vessels work together to bring oxygen-rich blood from the heart (performed by the arteries) to the body's tissues (done by the capillaries) and back to the heart (done by the veins) to begin the process of oxygenation all over again.

Blood is the medium that travels through the organs of the circulatory system. Blood plays several roles in many body systems. Blood transports oxygen, hormones, nutrients, and wastes. With all of these functions, it should be no surprise that blood consists of many constituents. Blood is composed of the following substances:

1. Plasma
2. Blood cells
3. Nutrients
4. Waste products
5. Plasma proteins

Table 12.15 summarizes each blood component and the function that it serves. (*Note:* Many of these components play significant roles in systems other than the circulatory system. However for the sake of continuity, it makes good sense to discuss all of the components of

TABLE 12.15

COMPONENT	FUNCTION
Plasma	Composed of water (90%) as well as nutrients, hormones, dissolved gases and salts, enzymes, and wastes.
Plasma proteins	Specialized functions discussed below.
Blood cells (red and white)	Red: oxygen transport. White: attack foreign substances.

blood at one time. As we discuss other body systems in which blood is significant, you will be reminded to refer back to these items.)

Plasma.   Plasma is the component of blood that deals with all other types of transport except for the transport of oxygen. Plasma contains (and thereby transports) gases, salts, and nutrients. Plasma also contains three types of plasma proteins. Each protein serves a specific function. These functions are outlined in Table 12.16.

TABLE 12.16

PROTEIN	FUNCTION
Albumin	• Substance transport (such as vitamins and hormones). • Regulates blood volume.
Globulin	• Substance transport (such as vitamins and hormones). • Fight infection (to some extent).
Fibrinogen	• Blood clotting.

Respiratory System

The main job of the respiratory system is to control the exchange of carbon dioxide and oxygen between the body and its environment. Before we discuss the respiratory system in any detail, let's first review the basics of respiration.

Respiration.   Respiration is the process in which oxygen and carbon dioxide are exchanged between the air and the body (the exchange takes place specifically using the lungs, the blood and cells of the body). *Note:* Recall from general basic knowledge that when animals breathe air in, the gas in the air that is absorbed and utilized by the body is oxygen. The body then exhales carbon dioxide gas as a byproduct/waste product.

The respiratory system includes six major body parts: the nose, pharynx, larynx, trachea, bronchi, and lungs. To discuss the role that each part plays in the process of respiration, let's trace the path of one breath of air as it passes through the respiratory system.

When the body inhales, air first enters the body through the *nose*. From the nose, air travels to the *pharynx*. The pharynx is more commonly known as the throat. It is the tube shaped structure at the back of the mouth. From the pharynx, air moves to the *trachea*. The trachea is commonly known as the windpipe.

This uppermost section of the respiratory system is equipped with a few "safety features" that render air safe for the delicate tissues of the lungs. Foreign particles such as dust are filtered out by hair in the nose and hairlike structures called cilia in the pharynx. Mucus in the upper region of the respiratory system also traps particles and moistens the air.

After the pharynx, the air moves on to the *larynx*. The larynx is located at the top of the trachea. The larynx houses the vocal chords. The vocal chords are two folds of tissue that vibrate when air moves between them. This vibration produces sounds. This is the action that produces your voice.

Air passes from the larynx to the trachea and into the *bronchi*. The bronchi (bronchus, singular) are two large passageways into the chest cavity. Each bronchus leads to one of the *lungs*. Within the lungs, each bronchus divides into a network of smaller passageways called *bronchioles*. These smaller bronchioles dead end at air sacs called *alveoli* (alveolus, singular). The alveoli are situated in clusters, and can be likened to tiny clusters of grapes. Each alveolus is surrounded by a network of capillary blood vessels. It is at this site within the lungs that the process of gas exchange takes place. We have traced the initial path that air takes into the respiratory system. Let us now take some time to discuss the process of gas exchange within the alveoli. This is an important concept to address because it is the very foundation of the respiratory system's purpose.

Gas Exchange in the Lungs.　　Oxygen that is in the air held in the sacs of the alveoli dissolves in the alveolus' moisture. After this dissolving, it travels through the thin walls of the capillaries (and thus enters the circulatory system—the newly oxygenated blood then carries out the processes already described in the previous section on the circulatory system). Carbon dioxide makes the same trip in reverse—traveling across the thin wall of the capillaries out of the blood and into the air within the alveoli. The carbon dioxide then exits the alveoli following the same path that we traced for inhalation except in reverse (now called exhalation instead of inhalation). This process explains the mechanisms by which animals need to inhale oxygen for survival, and they exhale carbon dioxide. Figure 12.5 summarizes the process of respiration.

FIGURE 12.5

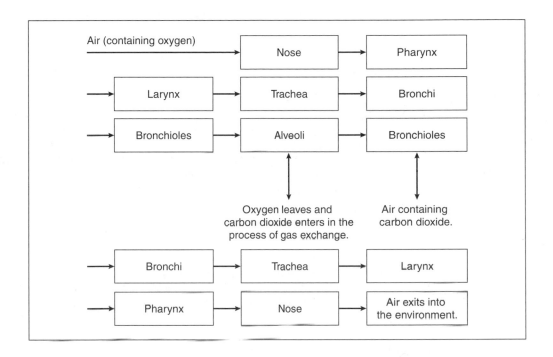

The Digestive System

The basic purpose of the digestive system is to take the large complex molecules of food (recall our discussion of molecules in domain one) and break them down into smaller, simpler molecules that can be used by the cells of the body. Each organ of the digestive system plays a role in the breaking down of food molecules. Table 12.17 summarizes the major organs of the digestive system and their functions. The organs are listed in the order in which they process food as it enters the body. When reviewing Table 12.17 (and discussing the digestive system in general), it is helpful to think of the digestive system as an assembly line that food passes through. At each step in the assembly line, the food is broken down into increasingly smaller particles until the molecules are actually absorbed into the body by the digestive system. Steps (organs) toward the end of the assembly line begin to absorb useful nutrients from the food particles. The final product of this assembly line is waste—those substances in food that the digestive system is unable to absorb.

　　Note: For the purpose of digestion it is important to be aware that an enzyme is a protein that speeds up a chemical reaction. See our description of a "catalyst" in domain one.

　　Let's review some digestion basics that will be helpful to remember as we discuss the organs of the digestive system in greater detail. We must remember that there are two types of digestion. Mechanical digestion is the physical breaking down of food into smaller pieces. This increases the surface area of the food. Recall from our discussion of chemical reactions in domain one that increasing the surface area of a substance increases the rate at which the substance can react in a chemical reaction.

TABLE 12.17

ORGAN	FUNCTION
Mouth	Breaks down food physically (mechanically) via chewing by the teeth and chemically via saliva.
Esophagus	Transports chewed up food to the stomach by muscle contractions.
Stomach	• Breaks food down mechanically by churning and mixing via muscular contractions. • Breaks food down chemically by releasing acids and enzymes.
Small Intestine	Site of most chemical digestion by enzymes. Absorbs nutrients from food molecules.
Large Intestine	Removes water from the remaining undigested material.
Salivary Glands Liver Pancreas	Accessory organs that add secretions to the digestive process.

The second type of digestion is called chemical digestion. Chemical digestion breaks large food molecules into smaller molecules. Because this type of reaction breaks bonds between atoms, it is a chemical reaction. This process is mainly carried out by acids and enzymes. An enzyme is a catalyst (recall our discussion of catalysts in domain one), which is a substance that speeds up a chemical reaction. An enzyme can be defined as a protein that speeds up a chemical reaction (though it is not actually used up in the reaction—it only helps the reaction along).

Mouth.   Food enters the body through the mouth. In the mouth, mechanical digestion is completed by the teeth, which crush and tear the food. Chemical digestion is completed by enzymes secreted in saliva. Saliva also aids digestion by moistening the food.

Esophagus and Stomach.   Once food has been sufficiently processed by the mouth, it travels down the esophagus via muscle contractions and enters the stomach. Swallowing causes muscle contractions in the esophagus to push the food downward.

The stomach is also a site of both mechanical and chemical digestion. The tissue that lines the stomach contains glands that secrete enzymes, acid, and mucus. The acids and enzymes facilitate chemical digestion, breaking large food molecules into smaller, simpler ones. The stomach also performs mechanical digestion as muscle contractions mix and churn the stomach contents.

Small Intestine.   Contracting muscles push the churned up food particles through the small intestine. The small intestine is divided into three regions: the duodenum, the jejunum, and the ileum. Each of these regions has distinct features and functions, which are described for you below:

■ Duodenum—The duodenum is the shortest part of the small intestine. It connects the stomach to the rest of the small intestine. The duodenum is the site of most chemical digestion. Food particles mix with enzymes and fluids that are secreted by the lining of the duodenum as well as enzymes that are secreted by the pancreas and the liver. Recall that the liver and pancreas are accessory organs of the digestive system.

Once the partially digested food (now called *chyme*) has been processed by the duodenum, the break-down phase of digestion is complete and absorption is ready to begin. The chyme is now primarily composed of smaller-sized, simple-nutrient molecules. These nutrient molecules are now in a form that can be absorbed and utilized by the body. The chyme is now ready for absorption.

■ Jejunum and Ileum—The absorption of nutrients takes place in the two lower (and largest) regions of the small intestine. The structure of the small intestine is specially designed to facilitate the absorption of nutrients. The inner lining of the small intestine is covered in circular folds. These folds are covered with tiny projections called *villi* (*villus,* singular). The folds and villi give the small intestine a huge surface area to absorb nutrient molecules. As muscular contractions move the chyme through the small intestine, nutrients are absorbed by the villi and enter the bloodstream through capillaries inside of the villi. At this point, the nutrient molecules can be transported by the circulatory system to the sites in the body where the nutrients will be used.

The nutrients are removed from the food inside the small intestine, but indigestible substances and water still remain and need to be processed further. These remnants of the chyme travel to the large intestine for the final step in the digestion process.

Large Intestine.   The main job of the large intestine is to absorb water from what is left of the undigested chyme. Diarrhea occurs when something interferes with this absorption of water. This is why dehydration is a serious risk associated with the onset of diarrhea. The end of the large intestine marks the end of the digestive system. The waste material that is left at the end of this process is passed through the rectum and is excreted as feces. The human body releases more waste products than feces alone. This process is critical in removing wastes from the body before they can build up to harmful, toxic levels. This process is carried out by the body system that we will discuss next: the excretory system.

The Excretory System

Excretion is the process the body utilizes to eliminate waste products. The excretory system is composed of the skin, lungs, kidneys, ureter, and urinary bladder. The role of each organ in the excretory system is summarized below. *Note:* The skin and lungs will not be discussed further. This is because they have already been covered in detail in the sections in the integumentary and respiratory systems respectively. Recall that the skin excretes sweat, which contains excess water and salts. Also included in sweat is a small amount of a compound called urea. Urea is a toxic compound that is produced when the body breaks down amino acids (the molecule that protein is made of) for energy. The lungs excrete carbon dioxide—a waste product generated in the process of respiration.

The basic organs and their functions in the excretory system are described below (see Table 12.18).

TABLE 12.18

ORGAN	FUNCTION
Skin	Excretes sweat
Kidney	Removes waste products from the blood, generating urine.
Ureter	Transports urine from the kidneys to the bladder.
Urinary bladder	Stores urine before it is excreted.

Humans are equipped with two *kidneys* located along either side of the spine near the lower back. The kidney acts like a filter for removing waste products from the blood. Blood enters the kidney, and waste products are removed from it. These wastes accumulate as urine. The clean "filtered" blood then goes back into circulation (refer to the circulatory system), and urine is transported out of the kidneys through the ureters.

The *ureter* is a tube that leaves each kidney and connects to the urinary bladder. The function of ureters are to transport urine from each kidney to the urinary bladder.

The *urinary bladder* is a sac-shaped organ that holds urine before it is excreted out of the body.

As the body systems work together to maintain homeostasis, the body has two main systems of communication to coordinate processes within the body's systems. The first system, the nervous system, has already been discussed. The body's second communication system is the endocrine system.

Endocrine System

The endocrine system is a series of glands that produce substances called hormones. These hormones are released into the bloodstream. These hormones transmit messages that regulate many body functions and process.

Glands are the primary component of the endocrine system. The specific functions carried by each type of gland are described in Table 12.19.

TABLE 12.19

NAME OF GLAND	PRIMARY FUNCTIONS
Hypothalamus	Controls the pituitary gland and produces hormones that are stored in the pituitary gland.
Pituitary	Produces several hormones that regulate several other glands of the endocrine system and directly regulates certain body functions such as growth.
Thymus	Produces the hormone thymosin, which stimulates T cell development.
Adrenal	Produces the hormones norepinephrine and epinephrine, which help the body deal with stress.
Pineal	Releases the hormone melatonin, which regulates rhythmic processes such as the sleep–wake cycle.
Thyroid	Produces thyroxine, which regulates metabolism.
Pancreas	Produces insulin and glucagons, which regulate glucose levels in the blood (keeps glucose levels stable).
Ovary (in females)	• Produces estrogen and progesterone. • Estrogen—development of secondary sex characteristics (those characteristics other than the actual sex organs such as breast development, higher voice tone, etc.). • Progesterone—Prepares the uterus for supporting and nourishing a fertilized egg.
Testis (in males)	Produces testosterone, which is responsible for the production of sperm and the development of secondary sex characteristics (such as deeper voice, larger body size).

The last two glands mentioned in Table 12.19 are the reproductive glands. They are also called *gonads*. The gonads serve two major purposes. First, the gonads are responsible for secreting sex hormones. Second, the gonads are responsible for producing gametes. These functions are part of the larger system called the reproductive system, which we will discuss next.

Reproductive System

The reproductive system varies greatly from males to females. Because of this fact, they are easier to understand when they are discussed separately.

Let's begin with a discussion of the male reproductive system.

Male Reproductive System.   The primary functions of the male reproductive system are to produce sperm and to produce testosterone, the hormone that is responsible for secondary sex characteristics. Secondary sex characteristics in males include deepening of the voice, facial hair, and increased body size. The main structures of the male reproductive system as well as their functions are summarized in Table 12.20.

TABLE 12.20

ORGAN	FUNCTION
Testes	Sperm production.
Epididymis	Stores fully developed sperm cells.
Vas Deferens	Connects the epididymis to the urethra.
Urethra	Tubelike structure that leads out of the body.
Penis	External organ that houses the urethra.

The *testes* are two organs that are housed in an external sac called the scrotum. The scrotum is outside of the body cavity. It is necessary for the testes to be housed outside of the body cavity so they maintain an internal temperature that is slightly cooler than the internal temperature of the rest of the body. This cooler temperature is necessary for sperm production. Once sperm cells are fully developed, they exit the testes and move to the epididymus.

The *epididymus* is the structure that stores the fully developed sperm cells. From the epididymus, some sperm cells move on to the vas deferens.

The *vas deferens* is a tubelike structure that extends from the epididymus upward into the abdominal cavity. The vas deferens gradually transitions into the urethra.

The *urethra* is the tube leading from the vas deferens out of the body. The urethra is housed in the external organ called the *penis*. As sperm moves through the reproductive tract, it is mixed with fluids secreted by several glands within the reproductive tract. This fluid is called seminal fluid. It mixes with sperm to form the substance semen. Semen contains tens of millions of sperm cells per milliliter. It is this final solution of semen that is released by the penis for the purpose of reproduction.

The Female Reproductive System.   Like the male reproductive system, the female system produces hormones responsible for secondary sex characteristics as well as producing sex cells. However, there are many differences between the male and female reproductive systems. Instead of producing millions of sperm cells each day, the female reproductive system produces an average of just one egg cell per month. Another major difference is that the female reproductive system not only produces the sex cells needed for reproduction, it also houses the developing embryo once conception has taken place.

The main organs of the female reproductive system and their functions are summarized in Table 12.21.

TABLE 12.21

ORGAN	FUNCTION
Ovary	Site of egg production.
Fallopian Tubes	Carries eggs from the ovary to the uterus—site of fertilization.
Uterus	Site where the fertilized egg is nourished and develops.
Vagina	Canal leading outside of the body.

To understand the role that each of these organs plays in reproduction, let's trace the path that an egg takes in the reproductive process beginning with the ovary.

The human body has two *ovaries,* but only one mature egg is produced every month. Mature eggs develop from follicles within the ovary. A follicle is a cluster of cells that surrounds each egg cell. It is interesting to note that a female is born with all of her follicles and egg cells that she will ever have in her lifetime already present. The follicles house immature egg cells until they develop. Although the average female is born with several hundred thousand follicles, only a few hundred ever mature and are released as eggs. About once a month, a follicle gets larger and larger until it finally ruptures, releasing a mature egg. This process of releasing a mature egg for fertilization is called ovulation. Once ovulation occurs, the egg is moved to the Fallopian tubes.

The *Fallopian tubes* connect the ovaries to the uterus. If a sperm is present, the egg may be fertilized as it travels down the Fallopian tube into the uterus.

The Fallopian tube deposits the egg into the *uterus.* If the egg has been fertilized, it will implant into the lining of the uterus. Development of an embryo begins with implantation of the fertilized egg. If fertilization has not taken place, the egg and uterine lining will be discharged from the body via the *vagina* in a process called menstruation.

CONTENT AREA FOURTEEN: BODY SYSTEMS OF OTHER VERTEBRATES

Some body systems differ from humans to other animals with a backbone (vertebrates). You may be required to be familiar with these differences so let's look at them now. Table 12.22 below summarizes some of the major differences.

TABLE 12.22

FEATURE	HUMANS	FISH, AMPHIBIANS, AND REPTILES
Regulation of Body Temperature	Endothermic—Generate and retain heat within their bodies.	Ectothermic—Body temperature is controlled by the external environment.
Respiration	Lungs remove oxygen from the air and excrete carbon dioxide gas.	Gills remove oxygen from water and excrete carbon dioxide gas.
Circulatory System	Humans, birds, mammals, and some crocodiles have a 4-chamber heart.	Amphibians and most reptiles have a 3-chamber heart.
Reproductive	• Mammal, reptile, and bird eggs are fertilized inside of the body. • Most mammals' young develop within the mother's body and receive nourishment directly from the mother's body.	• Fish and amphibian eggs are fertilized outside of the body. • Most fish, all bird, and most amphibian embryos develop inside of eggs outside of the mother's body. • Sharks and some other fish eggs develop within the mother's body and receive nutrients from the yolk of the egg.

Note: Digestive systems vary greatly among different species of vertebrates. To discuss these specific differences in any degree of detail here is not feasible or practical. The important idea to remember when discussing these differences is that the digestive systems of vertebrates feature organs that are specially adapted to their diets. For example, herbivores such as cows and deer consume large quantities of fibrous plant material. These animals have long digestive systems that harbor beneficial bacteria that help digest the tough plant fibers.

CONTENT AREA FIFTEEN: CHEMISTRY OF LIVING THINGS

Recall from domain one that all matter is made of atoms. These atoms are bonded together to form more complex molecules. Also recall from our discussion of tissues and body systems that these molecules are further organized into specialized cells, tissues, body organs, and body systems. When we trace these units of life into their smallest components, atoms and molecules, we find that the basic composition and structure of these substances (their chemistry) plays a vital role in the functioning of basic life processes.

Carbon in Organisms

Carbon is found in many compounds that are found in living things. These compounds form millions of different organic ("organic" meaning "containing carbon") molecules. These organic molecules can be grouped into four types: lipids, nucleic acids, carbohydrates, and proteins. Table 12.23 summarizes the major groups of organic compounds.

TABLE 12.23

MOLECULE	COMPOSITION	FUNCTION
Lipid	Carbon and hydrogen.	• Stores energy, serves as parts of membranes.
Nucleic Acid	Carbon, hydrogen, nitrogen, oxygen, and phosphorous.	• Transmits and stores genetic information.
Carbohydrate	Carbon, hydrogen, and oxygen.	• Energy and structural purposes.
Protein	Carbon, hydrogen, oxygen, and nitrogen.	• Regulates cell processes. • Transports substances. • Muscle and bone formation.

Lipids are composed primarily of hydrogen and carbon atoms. Lipids are used mainly to store energy. Some lipids are also parts of membranes. Lipids are considered to be "hydrophobic," which means that they repel water. Because of this property, lipids can also serve as part of waterproof barriers. Some common examples of lipids are oils, waxes, and fats.

Nucleic acids contain carbon, hydrogen, oxygen, and nitrogen. Nucleic acids store and transmit genetic information. This process is critical in cell reproduction and the manufacture of proteins. Nucleic acids are grouped into two types: deoxyribonucleic acid (DNA) and ribonucleic acid (RNA). These two types of nucleic acids differ in that DNA contains the sugar deoxyribose, and RNA contains the sugar ribose.

Carbohydrates are made of carbon, hydrogen, and oxygen. Carbohydrates are the main source of energy for living things. Some examples of these energy sources include pasta, bread, and whole grains. Plants and some animals also use carbohydrates for structural support. Some examples of these carbohydrates include the tough fiber cellulose that is found in plants and the hard outer shell of most insects (this hard "exoskeleton" is made of a carbohydrate called chitin).

Proteins are molecules that contain carbon, hydrogen, oxygen, and nitrogen. They are large molecules composed of smaller molecules called amino acids. Proteins serve many functions. Some proteins control cell functions and regulate the speed of chemical reactions. Other proteins transport substances into and out of cells (they are called "transport proteins"). Still others play a role in the formation of bone and muscle tissue. Carbon is not the only element or compound that is essential to life processes. Two other compounds that play key roles in the function of living things are water (H_2O) and salt (NaCl).

Water in Living Things

Water is a critical component in all living things because it serves a variety of purposes. Most bodily fluids, including blood, are made mostly of water. Nearly all of the body's chemical reactions must take place in water. If water were absent from the body, these chemical reactions would not take place and the body would subsequently stop functioning. Water also plays an important role in the excretory system. Water is the main component of sweat that is excreted from the sweat glands in order to maintain body temperature in warm conditions. Water is also found in urine—the body's primary waste removal system. Water is also essential to the plant process of photosynthesis.

Salt in Living Things

Salt (meaning compounds that contain sodium) is necessary to life. Sodium carries out many functions. It one of the main ingredients in fluids located outside of the cells (called extracellular fluids). It also aids in the transport of nutrients. Sodium also helps regulate many bodily functions such as fluid levels and blood pressure.

DNA and RNA

Recall from our earlier discussion of nucleic acids that DNA (deoxyribonucleic acid) and RNA (ribonucleic acid) hold a cell's genetic information and transmit that information when a cell reproduces. This is the basic mechanism that is responsible for passing hereditary information from parent organisms to their offspring. DNA and RNA differ from one another in form and function, so let's simplify these concepts by looking at the structure of each one separately.

DNA.   DNA is located in the cytoplasm of prokaryotic cells and in the nucleus of eukaryotic cells. The DNA molecule itself is made of smaller units called nucleotides. A nucleotide is made of three basic sub units: a sugar called deoxyribose, a phosphate group, and a nitrogen-containing (nitrogenous) base. A nucleotide can contain one of four nitrogenous bases: adenine, thyanin, guanine, and cytosine. Nucleotides containing the four possible bases are illustrated in Figure 12.6 and linked together to form one side of a DNA molecule.

FIGURE 12.6

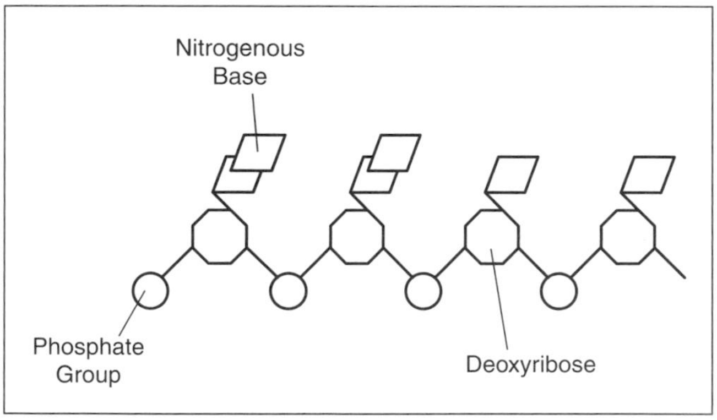

DNA is shaped like a double helix, which looks like a twisted spiral staircase. In the double helix, two strands of DNA are wound around each other. In this shape, the phosphate and sugar forms the backbone of the molecule, and the nitrogenous bases are on the interior of the molecule. These bases form hydrogen bonds with one another, always paring in the same way: Adenine always pairs with thyanine, and cytosine always bonds to guanine.

RNA.   The structure of RNA differs from that of DNA in a few ways. The sugar in its backbone is ribose. RNA also contains the nitrogenous base uracil in place of thyanine. Lastly,

RNA is single stranded, rather than the double helix structure of DNA. There are three types of RNA:

1. *Messenger RNA*—Carries instructions for making proteins from inside of the nucleus to the site of protein synthesis in the cell's cytoplasm.
2. *Ribosomal RNA*—RNA that is found on ribosomes, the site of protein synthesis.
3. *Transfer RNA*—transfers amino acids to the ribosome in the correct order as dictated by the instructions in mRNA.

RNA functions in protein synthesis. Let's look at the process of protein synthesis as a means of overviewing the roles of the three types of RNA. Protein synthesis has two phases, transcription and translation.

- *Transcription*—During transcription, a section of DNA "unzips" to expose the nucleotides. This is used as a template to form a complementary strand of mRNA. The mRNA molecule then travels out of the nucleus to the ribsosome for translation.
- *Translation*—During translation, the ribosome "reads" the instructions of the mRNA to assemble amino acids (which are carried to the ribosome by tRNA) into proteins.

CONTENT AREA SIXTEEN: CHARACTERISTICS OF LIVING THINGS

All living things have a set of characteristics in common that set them apart from nonliving things. These are qualities that a plant and an animal share, but that make them different from fire. Let's look at each distinctive characteristic of living things.

1. *All living things are made up of cells.* Recall our discussion of cells—they are the smallest unit of life. Anything that is smaller than a cell (such as an organelle) is not alive.
2. *Living things reproduce.* Reproduction is the process by which new living things are reproduced. There are two types of reproduction—sexual and asexual. In sexual reproduction, two cells from two different parents unite to form the first cell of a new organism. In asexual reproduction a new organism is produced from one parent. (This will be discussed further in the content area on reproduction)
3. *All life is based on a genetic code.* All living things possess genetic information that is stored in DNA. This information is transmitted from parent to offspring and will be transmitted to future generations when reproduction takes place.
4. *All living things grow and develop.* All living things develop according to their distinctive lifecycles.
5. *All living things must obtain materials from their environment and use energy.* All living things require the taking in of materials to carry out life processes such as growth, reproduction, and basic maintenance. All organisms take materials (such as food and water) from their environments and obtain energy from them. The process by which organisms break these materials down for the purpose of carrying out life processes is called metabolism.
6. *All living things respond to their environments.* The environment of living things is constantly changing. Light, temperature, and living and nonliving things near an organism may change. All of these changes will generate a response in living things. A plant, for example, will wilt in response to a large increase in temperature. An animal may grow a thicker haircoat in response to the colder temperatures of winter.
7. *All living things maintain internal balance.* The process of maintaining this balance is called homeostasis. Changes in an organism's external environment are a constant challenge to homeostasis. An example of the human body maintaining homeostasis in warm temperatures is the excretion of sweat in hot weather to cool down the body's temperature.

CONTENT AREA SEVENTEEN: NEEDS OF LIVING THINGS

Just as all living things have certain definitive characteristics in common, all living things also have a basic set of needs in common.

Food

All living things must take in materials from their environment to be used as a source of energy. For most organisms one of the main materials needed is food. A major exception to this idea is plants. Rather than food, plants must take in water, carbon dioxide gas, and sunlight to perform photosynthesis.

Photosynthesis

Photosynthesis is the process by which plants take several of the compounds that we have discussed as being critical to life processes and convert them into high-energy carbohydrate molecules and oxygen gas. Plants are essentially the only organisms that can "make" their own food in this way. Other organisms must consume carbohydrates because they cannot manufacture them.

Photosynthesis can be summarized in the following equation:

$$\text{Carbon dioxide} + \text{water} \xrightarrow{(light)} \text{carbohydrate} + \text{oxygen}$$

So we can sum up the basic process of photosynthesis by saying that plants harness the energy of sunlight to convert water and carbon dioxide gas into carbohydrates and oxygen gas. Let's look at exactly how this phenomenon occurs.

Recall from our discussion of cells that photosynthesis takes place within the chloroplasts of a plant cell. Also recall that chloroplasts contain a green pigment called chlorophyll. It is the chlorophyll that is responsible for trapping energy from sunlight for the purpose of photosynthesis. Chlorophyll makes a plant appear green because this pigment absorbs some wavelengths of light while reflecting green light. (Recall our discussion in domain one about wavelengths of light and how their reflection and/or absorption determines the perceived color of things.) When these wavelengths of light are absorbed by the chlorophyll, electrons in the chlorophyll are raised to an excited state. This is where the energy comes from to power the chemical reaction of photosynthesis.

Let's look at the two other main needs of living things.

Water

Water has already been discussed as a compound that is necessary for all living things.

Space

All living things require a certain amount of space. The amount of space required varies depending on the organism (compare the space required of a bacteria cell to the space required of a wolf), but all organisms require space to carry out life processes such as feeding, growth, and the excretion of waste.

CONTENT AREA EIGHTEEN: ADAPTATIONS OF LIVING THINGS

Another key characteristic of living things is that as a population, living things change over time. The change in inherited characteristics over time that allows a population to be better suited to its environment is called adaptation. We will discuss the precise mechanics of how this occurs in our discussion of genetics and evolution later on. Here we will discuss the environmental factors that drive adaptation.

The environmental phenomenon that drives adaptation is called natural selection. Natural selection is also known as "survival of the fittest." According to natural selection, individuals that are better suited to their environment are most likely to survive and reproduce, hence being more successful. (This is the ecological definition of a species's success.)

An example of natural selection at work can be seen in a population of antelope. Faster individual antelope are more likely to escape predators. They will then survive and reproduce. Slower antelope will be hunted and killed by predators, removing them from the pool of reproducing individuals. This means that future generations of antelope will inherit traits from the faster, more successful antelope. The end result of this example over time is a population of antelope that is faster and therefore better adapted to its environment.

CONTENT AREA NINETEEN: POPULATIONS IN AN ECOSYSTEM

All populations of organisms occupy a particular role in the larger scheme of an ecosystem. An ecosystem is the total of all living things in a particular place including their nonliving environment. So a typical ecosystem includes plants, animals, bacteria, rocks, soil, air, and so forth.

The number and types of organisms that a particular ecosystem can support varies with the amount of resources available in the ecosystem (specific resources will be discussed in the next content area); however, all ecosystems have organisms interacting with one another. These interspecies relationships can be placed into three basic groups. Each group is a type of symbiotic relationship. Symbiosis is a relationship where two species live closely together.

Mutualism is a symbiotic relationship in which both species receive some benefit from the relationship. An example of a mutualistc symbiotic relationship is that between an oxpecker (a type of bird) and an ox. The oxpecker rides along on the back of the ox, eating parasites off of the ox. Both species benefit—the oxpecker has easy access to a food supply, and the ox has the benefit of having its parasites removed.

Commensalism is a symbiotic relationship in which one species receives some benefit and the other species is neither helped nor harmed. An example of a commensalist relationship is the relationship between a whale and a barnacle. The barnacle attaches itself to the hide of the whale. This does not harm the whale, nor does the whale receive any kind of benefit from the arrangement. The barnacle benefits by obtaining food from the water that passes over the moving whale.

In *parasitism*, one individual receives benefit, while the other is harmed. An example of a parasitic relationship is a tick feeding on the blood of a dog. The tick receives the benefit of food, while the dog may contract diseases from the tick bite.

Other Types of Relationships between Organisms

There are two other types of relationships that occur between organisms in an ecosystem that are not symbiotic. You need to be familiar with them, so let's examine them now.

Competition occurs when organisms of the same or different species try to use a resource in the same place at the same time. A natural resource may be food, light, water, or any other necessity of life.

In *predation* one animal captures and eats another. The animal doing the capturing is called the predator and the animal that is eaten is called the prey.

CONTENT AREA TWENTY: THE FLOW OF ENERGY AND MATTER THROUGH ECOSYSTEMS

Recall from our discussion of energy in domain one that energy cannot be created or destroyed; it can only be transferred. This is also true as food energy is transferred from organism to organism through an ecosystem.

Energy Flow

When we look at energy flow in an ecosystem, we group two main organisms into two groups: producers (also called autotrophs) and consumers (also called heterotrophs). Producers capture energy and use it to produce food (as in the case of plants). Consumers cannot produce their own food and must rely on other organisms for their food. Consumers must "consume" other organisms. Consumers are classified into four basic groups based on what types of organisms they consume (see Table 12.24).

TABLE 12.24

TYPE OF CONSUMER	BASIC DIET
Herbivore	Consumes only plants.
Carnivore	Consumes only animals.
Omnivore	Eats plants and animals.
Detrivore	Feeds on dead matter.

The feeding relationships among producers and different classes of consumers can be graphically illustrated in a food web. A food web illustrates the complex feeding relationships among all of the organisms in an ecosystem (see Figure 12.7). While reviewing this food web, it is important to remember the basics of energy flow in an ecosystem. Energy flows through an ecosystem in one direction: from the sun to producers, then on to consumers.

FIGURE 12.7

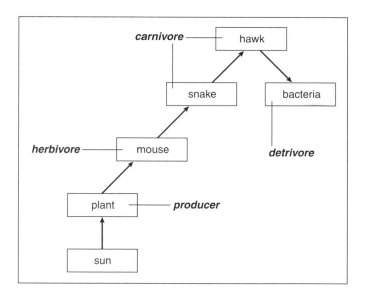

(*Note:* Some food webs show arrows pointing in the direction of energy flow, as this example does, while others point from what is doing the eating to the organism that it is eating, opposite of what this example shows. Be aware of these differences.)

Matter Flow

Unlike energy, matter does not flow in one direction. It is recycled in the ecosystem. Nutrients such as carbon and nitrogen that are found in living things are eventually returned to the soil by detrivores (upon passing through the food web as organisms, they are consumed by higher level consumers). They are then taken up by plants and then reenter the food web.

CONTENT AREA TWENTY-ONE: LIFE CYCLES OF LIVING THINGS

Recall that all living things develop according to distinctive life cycles. Although all living things follow a life cycle, this life cycle varies depending on the organism. Below are some distinct life cycles of organisms that you should be familiar with. Each cycle follows the development of young into adults, but as you can see the appearance and stages of these life cycles vary greatly.

Complete versus Incomplete Metamorphosis

Most insects undergo metamorphosis in their life cycles. (Metamorphosis is the process by which an organism changes shape and form.) There are two types of metamorphosis:

Complete Metamorphosis.   In complete metamorphosis, animals hatch from eggs into larvae. These larvae look and feed differently from adults of their species. The larvae molt (shed their outer covering) several times, finally becoming pupa. This is the stage where the pupa finally develop into an adult. In species that undergo complete metamorphosis, immature individuals and adults of the same species can occupy different parts of the same environment without being in direct competition with one another. An example of an insect that undergoes complete metamorphosis is a butterfly (see Figure 12.8); an example of a reptile is the frog.

FIGURE 12.8

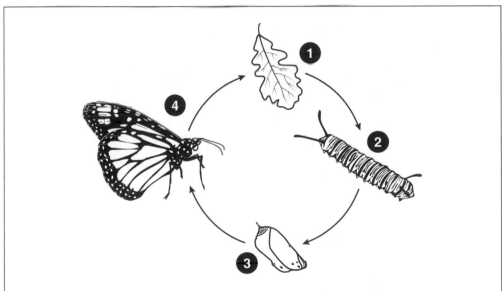

1. Eggs—Adult butterflies lay eggs.
2. Larvae (Larva, singular)—Eggs hatch into larvae. Butterfly larvae are commonly known as caterpillars.
3. Pupae (Pupa, singular)—Larvae develop into pupae, spinning a chrysalis. A chrysalis is the protective covering that houses the developing pupa.
4. Adult—After a period of time developing inside the chrysalis, the pupa emerges from it as a fully formed adult.

Incomplete Metamorphosis.   In incomplete metamorphosis, immature individuals resemble adults and undergo a more gradual series of changes to reach adulthood (see Figure 12.9).

FIGURE 12.9

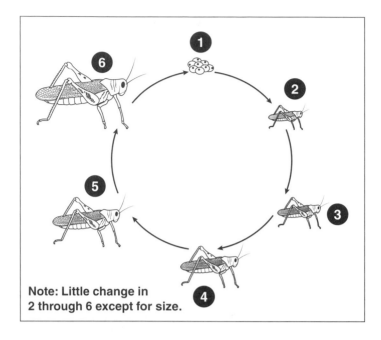

Note: Little change in
2 through 6 except for size.

CONTENT AREA TWENTY-TWO: FACTORS AFFECTING PLANT GROWTH

Plants follow life cycles just as animals do. However many environmental factors affect the growth of plants (see Table 12.25).

TABLE 12.25

FACTOR	PLANT RESPONSE TO ENVIRONMENT	DESCRIPTION
Light	Phototropism	Plants tend to grow towards a source of light.
Gravity	Gravitotropism	Plants tend to grow in response to (usually against) gravity.
Stress	Wilting, yellowing (as a result of nutrient or water deprivation)	Plant growth tends to slow or stop in response to stress.

CONTENT AREA TWENTY-THREE: REPRODUCTION

Recall that all living things reproduce to produce new organisms. This process is accomplished in one of two ways: asexual reproduction and sexual reproduction.

Asexual Reproduction

Asexual reproduction is reproduction that results in offspring generated form one parent. In some forms of asexual reproduction, the parent organism splits in two. In other cases, a smaller part of the parent organism breaks off to form offspring. Asexual reproduction is common in single celled organisms such as bacteria and also in many plants.

Sexual Reproduction

Sexual reproduction involves the uniting of two cells from two different parents to create the first cell of a new organism. The new organism then grows and develops by a sequence of cell divisions from that first cell. Because the new offspring is the result of the union of cells from two different individuals, the new offspring is not identical to either parent. Essential to either form of reproduction is the process of cell division, which we will examine next.

Cell Division in Growth and Reproduction

All types of growth and reproduction depend on a cell's ability to replicate itself. There are two types of cell division: mitosis and meiosis. (*Note:* Before discussing cell division, it is important to be familiar with the term "chromosome." A chromosome is a thread-shaped structure that is made of DNA bound to protein. Chromosomes are the units that pass hereditary information from one generation to the next. Prior to any type of cell division, these chromosomes replicate to form identical chromosome pairs that are called sister chromatids.)

Mitosis. Following are the five stages of mitosis (see Figure 12.10) to know and be able to depict visually for the exam. Ideally, this should be a review for you. If it is not, please consult additional materials such as an eighth-grade biology text for additional support as the space we have been allotted for explanation is limited.

FIGURE 12.10

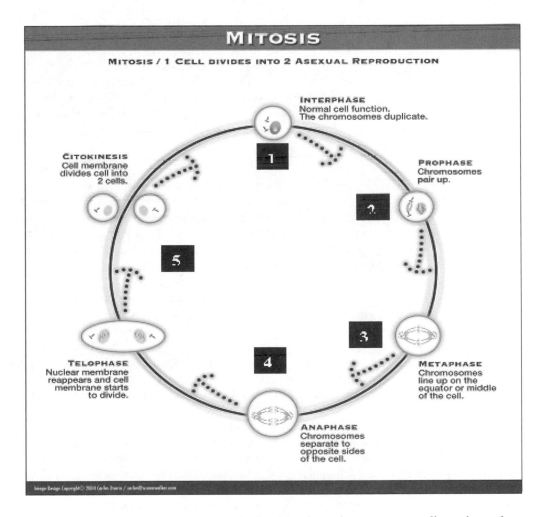

1. **Interphase:** The cell begins DNA duplication where chromosomes replicate themselves during the first state of the process.
2. **Prophase:** During the second stage of the process, the chromosomes pair up and prepare for metaphase.

3. Metaphase: In this stage, fibers extend and attach themselves to the chromosomes.

4. Anaphase: Stretching occurs as the fibers pull the chromosomes to opposite sides of the cell.

5. Telophase and Cytokinesis: During the telophase, the nuclear membrane forms, and then the cell pinches itself in two during cytokinesis, resulting in two separate cells with duplicate chromosome sets.

Meiosis.   Let's look at the process in females first and males second.

FIGURE 12.11

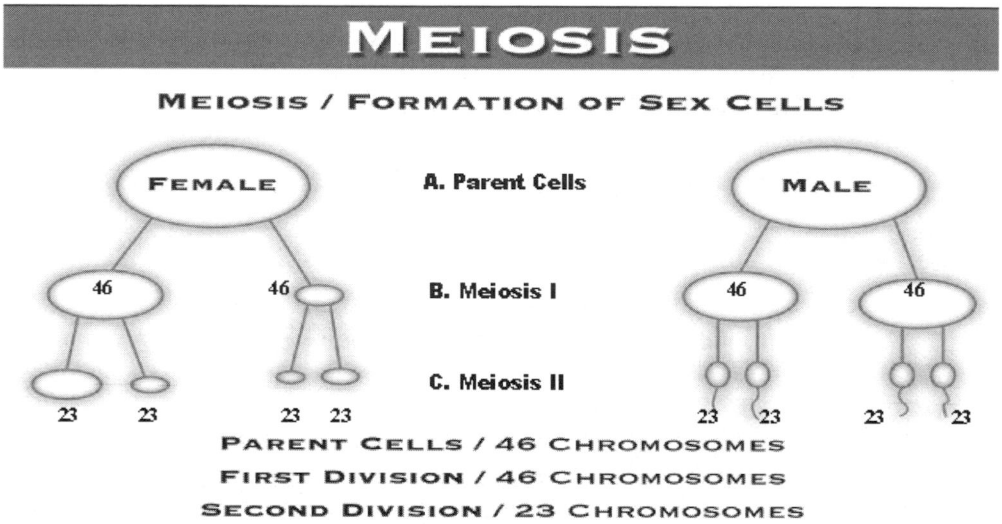

In the female, the parent cells splits into two cells during Meiosis I. At this point, each cell has the same number of chromosomes. During Meiosis II, the two cells split again, yielding four daughter cells with twenty-three chromosomes apiece (see Figure 12.11). *But these four cells are not equal in the female.* Only one cell is usually viable; the others are referred to as "polar bodies" and lack enough cytoplasm to survive and function. This process completes itself before puberty in the female, resulting in a finite number of viable eggs containing twenty-three chromosomes.

In the male, the process is similar, yet different in several important ways. First, the cell splits in Meiosis I and results in two cells with forty-six chromosomes just as we witness in females. However, during Meiosis II, when the cells split again, the result is *not* in only one viable egg; instead, the split results in four potentially viable sperm cells. Of course, not all of the sperm cells may be perfect or function properly, but they do have the potential to donate their twenty-three chromosomes during reproduction. In addition, this process usually *begins* during puberty in males and continues on and on, resulting in a longer reproductive period for males than for females.

In summary, meiosis in females and males results in cell division from a parent cell that begins with forty-six chromosomes and ends with four "daughter" cells with twenty-three chromosomes (half from the original parent cell). In Meiosis I, the same steps are followed with several differences. In prophase, chromosomes pair up with homologous pairs to form a tetrad (two homologous chromosomes or four chromatids). The homologous chromosomes separate (following metaphase). As in mitosis, two new daughter cells are formed after anaphase and telophase. The cells are different from the cells produced in mitosis, however, because they do not have two complete sets of chromosomes (the pairs have separated, remember). These daughter cells then enter Meiosis II and divide themselves in two, resulting in four daughter cells that contain half of the number of chromatids of the parent cell.

CONTENT AREA TWENTY-FOUR: REPRODUCTION OF PLANTS AND ANIMALS

Plants employ both sexual and asexual reproduction (this varies depending upon the type of plant), utilizing both mitosis and meiosis.

Asexual Reproduction in Plants

When plants produce asexually, the offspring are produced by one parent and they are identical to that parent. Asexual reproduction in plants typically involves a smaller part of the parent plant splitting off to form new offspring.

Sexual Reproduction in Seed Plants

As plants have evolved over time, the ability to reproduce by seed is an important adaptation. Seeds allow the sex cells of plants to unite in the absence of water. (Ancient nonseed plants such as ferns require the presence of water for male sex cells to migrate to the female sex cells for fertilization. This is a topic that is covered in upper-level secondary biology; therefore, it is a topic that you DO NOT need to be familiar with.) This adaptation has allowed plants to colonize a greater diversity of habitats independent of water. The paragraph below describes the structures and functions involved in the sexual reproduction of flowering plants.

Male reproductive cells called pollen are produced in the anthers of a flower. This pollen then lands on the sticky surface of the stigma. From there, the pollen grains travel down the style to the ovary where fertilization takes place. The fertilized ovules in the ovary develop into seeds.

Reproduction in Animals

Virtually all animals that are more complex than single cells (such as amoebas and bacteria) reproduce sexually. Recall form previous sections that sexual reproduction involves the union of two cells from different parent organisms to create the first cell of a new organism. The union of the two parent cells takes place in the process of fertilization. Depending on the species of animal, fertilization (where egg and sperm unite) takes place internally, inside of the female's body (as in the case of humans), or externally (as in the case of frogs). After fertilization, the fertilized egg develops into an embryo. This embryo may either develop inside of the mother's body to be released at the end of prenatal development (as in the case of humans, most mammals, and live-bearing fish such as sharks); or the embryo develops in an egg outside of the mother's body as in the case of birds.

CONTENT AREA TWENTY-FIVE: EVOLUTION

We have previously stated that populations of living things change over time. This change over long periods of time is called *evolution*. Evolution is the result of genetic variation. Genetic variation is a change in the genetic information that is transmitted from one offspring to the next.

Sources of Variation

There are two main sources of genetic variation. The first source is genetic variation (also known as survival of the fittest, a concept that we have previously discussed). Please refer to our earlier section on this topic. The other source of variation is actual changes in the genetic material that is transmitted from parent to offspring. This source of genetic variation can be broken into two categories: mutation and random assortment of genes. We will look at each of these categories.

Mutation.   Mutation is any change in the sequence of nucleotides in a DNA molecule. This change may result in a visible difference in the traits of offspring.

Random Assortment of Genes.   Gene assortment results from the millions of different ways that genes may recombine during sexual reproduction. Recall from our discussion of meiosis that chromosomes separate independently of one another and offspring receive half of their chromosomes from each parent. This makes it possible for genes to recombine in offspring in millions of different ways. A simplified example of how this process works is to imagine that each human characteristic were controlled by one chromosome (one segment of DNA). The two chromosomes determining hair color, the two producing eye color, and so forth will all separate independently of each other. They can separate and combine in sex cells in millions of different ways. This is why siblings tend to resemble one another but never look identical to one another (with the rare exception of identical twins).

Evidence for Evolution.   According to the theory of evolution, living things have been evolving on Earth for millions of years. There are three major sources of evidence for this theory that you will need to be familiar with: fossil records, similar (called "homologous") structures of organisms, and matching DNA sequences. Let's look at each of these sources of evidence.

Fossil Records.   A fossil record is the preserved remains of an organism. They are often preserved in rock. Fossils found in different layers of rock show evidence of a gradual change in these organisms over time. The changes observed may either be from simple to more complex life forms or changes that make an organism better adapted to its environment.

Homologous (Similar) Structures of Organisms.   Homologous structures are structures of different species of animals that are very different in form and function but have developed from the same type of tissue in the developing embryo. These structures such as arms, wings, and flippers look different because they have adapted in ways that help different organisms survive in different environments. Similarities and differences between homologous structures can be used to group animals based on how recently they have shared a common ancestor. An example of homologous structures are the front limbs of a dog, a lizard, and the wing of a bird. The structure of the ones in each of these appendages provide evidence of a common ancestor—possibly the fin of an ancient fish.

Similar DNA Sequences.   All living things use DNA and RNA to store and transmit genetic information. This enables scientists to examine DNA sequences and find similarities and differences in organisms at a molecular level. "Reading" the code of DNA allows scientists to trace genetic information over millions of years. This also allows scientists to make connections between animals that may not appear physically to be closely related.

The Opposing Theories of Lamarck versus Darwin

As scientists attempted to unravel the theory of evolution, two major evolutionary theories emerged in the 1800s. In 1806, French scientist Jean-Baptiste Lamarck published his theory on evolution. Fifty years later, English naturalist Charles Darwin published his theory of evolution. Darwin's theory is the theory of evolution that is accepted today. The basic tenets of each of the two theories are summarized below.

Lamarck.   Lamarck proposed that organisms could gain or lose traits or characteristics over their lifetime. According to Lamarck, this change was achieved by the selective use or disuse of organs or appendages. These "acquired" traits could then be passed on and inherited by their offspring. If we used Lamarck's theory to explain why giraffes have such long necks we would say that giraffes that were born with short necks developed long necks by stretching their necks to reach high leaves in trees. These acquired long necks were then passed on to their offspring resulting in a population of long-necked giraffes.

Darwin. Darwin theorized that natural selection has worked over time to result in changes in the characteristics that are inherited by a population. According to Darwin, individuals in a population that are best adapted to their environment will survive and reproduce. This means that their characteristics will be passed on to their offspring. Poorly adapted individuals will not survive, so their characteristics are not as likely to be passed on from one generation to the next. This will result in a population becoming well suited to their environment over time.

CHAPTER THIRTEEN

Astronomy and Earth Science[1]

DOMAIN THREE: THE STUDY OF ASTRONOMY AND EARTH SCIENCE

CONTENT AREA TWENTY-SIX: THE SOLAR SYSTEM

FIGURE 13.1

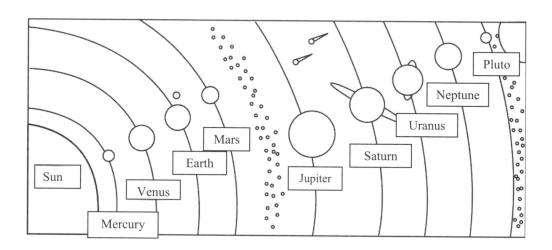

Our planet is part of a larger cosmic system called a solar system. (It is "a" solar system and not "the" solar system because it is not the only solar system in the universe.) Our solar system consists of planets (like our own), planetary moons that revolve around those planets, comets, asteroids, and other miscellaneous debris such as meteors. All of these objects revolve around a central star—our sun (see Figure 13.1).

There are billions of stars in the universe that are similar to our sun. Therefore it would stand to reason that there are potentially billions of solar systems in the universe that function in a way similar to our own. Many of these solar systems have been detected. You will need to be familiar with the basic features and functions of our solar system. Table 13.1 summarizes the major features of our solar system. Masses are given in comparison to the mass of the Earth. The mass of Earth is approximately 6.5 billion trillion tons.

Figure 13.2 contrasts the shape of the near-circular orbit that most planets follow against the elliptical orbit followed by comets and the planet Pluto. Be aware that the elliptical orbit is quite exaggerated for the sake of making a clear comparison.

[1]Chapter contributed by Erica Seropian Cardey.

TABLE 13.1

OBJECT	MASS VS. EARTH	DISTANCE FROM THE SUN	GENERAL DESCRIPTION
Mercury	0.055	57,910,000 km	Heavily cratered with cliffs. Huge range between day and night temps, due to the fact that there is no atmosphere to trap heat.
Venus	0.86	108,200,000 km	Hotter than Mercury due to thick acidic clouds that trap heat. Surface has rolling hills, violent hurricanelike winds, and some active volcanoes.
Earth	1.0	149,600,000 km	Very few craters. Majority of the surface is covered in liquid water.
Mars	0.11	227,940,000 km	Huge canyons and dormant volcanoes. Surface has moderate degree of cratering.
Jupiter	318	778,330,000 km	The largest planet. Has no solid surface. Surface is liquid and gas. Has at least 28 moons that orbit. The "Great Red Spot" is a giant storm on the surface that has been in existence for at least the last several hundred years.
Saturn	95	1,429,400,000 km	The second largest planet. Has no solid surface. Has a pronounced ring system composed of ice and ice-coated rock. Has huge violent storms.
Uranus	14.5	2,870990,000 km	Has no solid surface. Axis is tilted so steeply that Uranus practically rotates on its side.
Neptune	17.2	4,50,000,000 km	Has a similar composition to Uranus.
Pluto	0.002	5,913,520,000 km	Surface appears to be ice and rock. Has one moon about the same size as the planet. Orbits the sun in an oval shaped ellipse rather than a typical near-circular pattern like the other planets.
Comets	Varies significantly, smaller than the planets.	Distance varies due to their noncircular orbit.	Composed of frozen water and other frozen compounds, metal, and rock. Comets orbit the sun in an ellipse (oval), most of which orbit far past Pluto.
Asteroids	Varies significantly, smaller than the planets.	Varies.	Fragments of rock and metal that orbit the sun. Most orbits lie between the orbits of Mars and Jupiter forming the "asteroid belt."

FIGURE 13.2

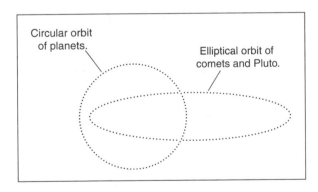

Earth Movement

The Earth, like other planetary bodies, orbits the sun. This movement is called revolution. The Earth also rotates on its axis. The Earth's axis is an imaginary line that runs directly from one pole of the Earth through the center to the other pole. All of the planets have an axis like this and rotate in a similar way. This movement (spinning about an axis) is called rotation. These movements of revolution and rotation result in what we perceive as changes in the time of day and changes in seasons.

Time of Day

Because the Earth rotates on its axis as it orbits the sun, only part of the planet is illuminated by sunlight at any given time. The sun only shines on the side of the Earth that is facing the sun. Due to rotation the actual location of this side is constantly changing.

The length of the day is determined by the rate at which the Earth rotates. One day on Earth is defined as twenty-four hours because that is the length of time it takes for the Earth to rotate once. This is the primary reference used by humans for keeping time. However, problems arise in using this reference to keep track of time globally because different regions of Earth are exposed to daylight at different times in this twenty-four-hour period.

The solution to this problem is the invention of time zones. All the clocks are set to the same time within a time zone. Time zones are set according to degrees of longitude. Longitude is a measurement of how far east or west a location on the Earth is. Longitude is measured using lines called meridians. Meridians are half-circle lines (imaginary lines) that run from pole to pole. Figure 13.3 below illustrates what meridian lines, or lines of longitude, look like when drawn on a map.

FIGURE 13.3

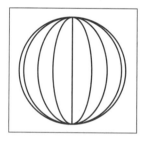

Each time zone is either one hour ahead or one hour behind each adjacent time zone. As you move west across a map, time zones are one hour behind the adjacent time zone to the East. A new time zone starts every 15° of longitude. This creates twenty-four time zones worldwide.

CONTENT AREA TWENTY-SEVEN: POSITIONS OF THE SUN AND MOON

The sun appears to change position throughout the day. We are all aware of the fact that the sun rises in the east in the morning and sets in the west in the evening. The sun appears to be absent from the sky during the night. Near the end of the night, the sun appears to rise in the east again, beginning the cycle all over again. The sun in fact is in a fixed location in our solar system. Its apparent movement is actually the result of the Earth's rotation. The Earth rotates, causing the sun to either be visible or out of sight from any particular location. The moon also appears to rise and set. Although the moon orbits the Earth, the observed effect of the moon rising and setting is also due to the Earth's rotation. As earth rotates, a different section of sky is in view from a particular location. So the Earth's rotation moves the moon into or out of view from a particular location.

Seasonal Changes

The observed appearance of the sun and moon from a particular location not only change with the time of day or night, but they also change with the seasons. In the case of the sun, these changes actually result in the seasons themselves.

The seasons do not result from changes in Earth's distance from the sun. This distance remains relatively constant. Rather, seasons result from the combined effects of the Earth's orbit around the sun and the fact that the Earth's axis is tilted by 23½ degrees. As Earth orbits the sun, this tilt causes different hemispheres (the northern and southern halves of the planet) to be tilted towards or away from the sun at different times of the year. For example, when the North Pole is tilted towards the sun, the Northern Hemisphere (north of the equator) has longer periods of daylight. This is the summer season in the Northern Hemisphere. When the Southern Hemisphere is tilted towards the sun, longer periods of daylight occur in the Southern Hemisphere and the Northern Hemisphere experiences shorter days and longer nights (the summer season in the Southern Hemisphere and the winter season in the Northern Hemisphere). The angle at which the sun's rays hit the Earth also change as this occurs. When either of the poles are tilted away from the sun, the angle of solar rays striking that part of the Earth is very low. The lower the angle, the weaker the rays and the more diminished the heating effect of those rays. These movements are used to mark the beginning of each of the four seasons (see Figure 13.4 and Table 13.2).

The seasons shown in Table 13.2 are the seasons that occur on those dates in the Northern Hemisphere. Remember that the seasons in the Southern Hemisphere are opposite the seasons in the Northern Hemisphere. For example, if December 21 is the first day of winter in the Northern Hemisphere, then it is the first day of summer south of the equator in the Southern Hemisphere (see Figure 13.5). (*Note:* The large arrows indicate solar rays striking the Earth at 90 degree angles.)

The moon also appears to change over the course of time. This is due to the fact that the moon orbits the Earth. It is interesting to note that although the moon revolves around the Earth, it does not spin on its axis. The moon takes about twenty-eight days to complete this orbit. This is where the concept of a month was developed. The appearance of the moon changes due to changes in its location in relation to the sun. This makes more sense if we think of the moon as a giant mirror. Although the moon may appear to glow and we refer to "moonlight," the moon does not generate its own light. The moon reflects light from the sun. This reflection of sunlight

FIGURE 13.4

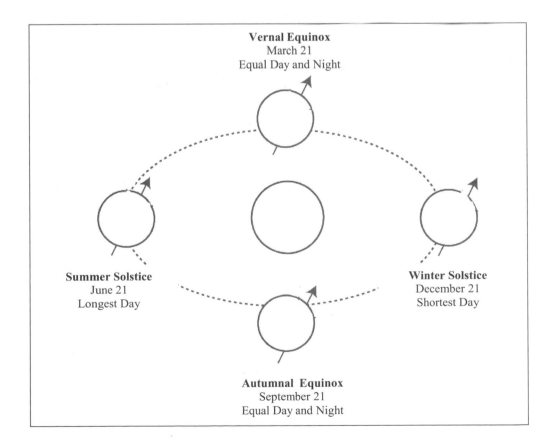

Vernal Equinox
March 21
Equal Day and Night

Summer Solstice
June 21
Longest Day

Winter Solstice
December 21
Shortest Day

Autumnal Equinox
September 21
Equal Day and Night

TABLE 13.2

NAME	SEASON MARKED	DESCRIPTION
Summer Solstice	Beginning of summer in the Northern Hemisphere. Occurs on June 21 or June 22.	The sun's rays strike the Earth at a 90° angle at the Tropic of Cancer. The longest day of sunlight. (Called the "longest day of the year.")
Winter Solstice	Beginning of winter in the Northern Hemisphere. Occurs on Dec. 21 or Dec. 22.	Solar rays strike the Earth at a 90° angle along the Tropic of Capricorn. The longest period of darkness. ("Longest night of the year.")
Autumnal Equinox	Beginning of fall in the Northern Hemisphere. Occurs on Sept. 22 or Sept. 23.	Solar rays strike the equator at a 90° angle. At this time, the North Pole tilts neither towards nor away from the sun. Equal periods of light and dark. Equinox = equal day and equal night.
Vernal Equinox	Beginning of spring in the Northern Hemisphere. Occurs on 3/21 or 3/22.	Same description as autumnal equinox above.

FIGURE 13.5

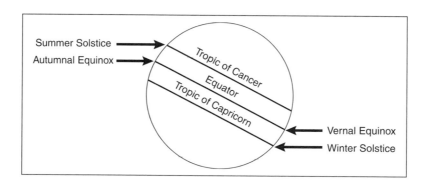

is the only way that we are able to see the moon from Earth. So our view of the moon changes as our view of the illuminated side of the moon shifts. Figure 13.6 below illustrates the difference in sun and moon locations from a full moon to a new moon (where no part of the moon is visible from Earth.)

FIGURE 13.6

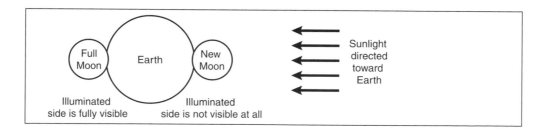

CONTENT AREA TWENTY-EIGHT: OTHER BODIES IN THE UNIVERSE

In addition to the planets and our moon, there are a few other celestial bodies that exist beyond our solar system that you should be familiar with (see Table 13.3). (*Note:* The sun, although located within our solar system, is included in this section. This is because while the sun has been previously mentioned in other contexts, we have not examined it in detail.)

TABLE 13.3

BODY	COMPOSITION	DESCRIPTION
Sun	Hydrogen and helium gas.	The star at the center of our solar system, about which all of the other bodies in the solar system orbit.
Star	Primarily hydrogen and helium gas.	Large, massive body of gases that gives off huge amounts of radiation, much of it as light and heat.
Galaxy	A large group of stars and any bodies orbiting these stars such as comets, asteroids, and planets, as well as clouds of dust and gas (called a nebula).	Galaxies contain billions of stars and gas clouds. A typical galaxy contains 100 billion stars. Estimates vary, but there are at least 50 billion galaxies in the part of the universe that is known. There may be as many as several hundred billion galaxies in the universe.

CONTENT AREA TWENTY-NINE: THE STRUCTURE AND COMPOSITION OF THE EARTH

The Earth's crust is composed of a wide variety of substances. Many of these substances are minerals. A mineral is an inorganic compound (as opposed to *organic,* which would be a compound manufactured by living things, *inorganic* refers to something that is not manufactured by living things). Minerals occur in nature and have a crystal-like structure. Minerals differ in their physical characteristics and in the conditions under which they form. Table 13.4 summarizes the most common types of minerals that you will need to be familiar with. (*Note:* The important idea to take notice of is the differences in the formation and characteristics of these minerals.)

TABLE 13.4

MINERAL	FORMATION	CHARACTERISTICS
Quartz	Forms from cooled "felsic" magma that is high in the element silica.	Colorless or white; impurities produce color. Appears glassy or waxy and has six-sided crystals.
Calcite	Made from calcium, carbon, and oxygen. Mineral may settle out of seawater to form sedimentary rock (a process that will be discussed later).	Colorless or white. Appears glassy.
Mica	Made as rock. Cooled slowly deep within the surface of the Earth.	Appears nonmetallic (does not reflect like a polished metal). Can be broken off into paper-thin parallel sheets.
Ore Minerals	Ores can form in two ways: 1. As magma cools, dense metallic minerals sink to the bottom of the magma forming layers of mineral deposits in the hardened magma. 2. Hot magma or fluids can come into contact with rock, depositing valuable minerals.	Deposits of minerals that metals and nonmetals can be removed from for a profit.

CONTENT AREA THIRTY: ROCKS

Minerals combine to form rocks. Rocks can be grouped into three basic types: igneous, sedimentary, and metamorphic (see Table 13.5). These rocks differ in the way that they are formed and the physical characteristics that they possess.

TABLE 13.5

ROCK	FORMATION	PHYSICAL CHARACTERISTICS
Igneous	Forms when magma (molten rock) cools and hardens.	Igneous rocks always have crystals.
Sedimentary	Forms when sediment (fragments of rock and organic matter) are compressed and cemented together.	Characterized by flat horizontal layers within the rock and visible particles that are cemented together.
Metamorphic	Begins as one of the other two types of rock and then changes due to heat and pressure.	Has crystals like igneous rock and, in some, horizontal layers are visible as bands.

Igneous rocks are formed when molten rock cools and hardens. There are two types of igneous rock: intrusive and extrusive. Intrusive rocks form from molten rock that cools beneath the Earth's surface (called magma). Extrusive igneous rocks form from molten rock that cools on the Earth's surface (called lava). All igneous rocks feature crystals. If the lava or magma cools slowly, then large crystals form. If it cools quickly, then small crystals form.

Sedimentary rock forms when rock fragments, remains of organisms, or minerals that have settled out of water are deposited in layers. Over time, tremendous pressure builds up from the weight of the layers. This pressure compacts the layers together. Cementation occurs when water infiltrates the layers of sediment. The water carries dissolved minerals through the layers, which cement the layers together. Sedimentary rock can be distinguished by visible sediment particles that are lain down by horizontal layers. Examples of sedimentary rock are sandstone and shale.

Metamorphic rock is formed when one type of rock changes form due to tremendous heat and pressure as well as chemical changes. Pressure results from the weight of overlying layers of rock or geologic movements (these movements will be discussed in a later section). Heat may result either from friction due to these geologic movements or from rock coming into contact with magma. Metamorphic rocks may appear layered like sedimentary rock and all metamorphic rocks have crystals like igneous rocks. A common example of metamorphic rock is marble.

CONTENT AREA THIRTY-ONE: LAND FORMS

The surface of the Earth is covered in a variety of land formations. Each type of land form is defined by distinct characteristics. Table 13.6 summarizes the basic land forms that you need to be familiar with.

CONTENT AREA THIRTY-TWO: ROCK- AND SOIL-FORMING PROCESSES

Many geologic processes function to create the rocks and soil in our Earth. We will now look at these processes. When discussing these processes in terms of forming soil, it is important to be aware of the fact that soil is produced from rock that has undergone the processes discussed below. The material from which the soil is formed is called "parent material" or "parent rock."

TABLE 13.6

LAND FORM	CHARACTERISTICS
Mountains	Regions of land pushed up significantly higher than surrounding land. Adjacent mountains with the same shape and structure form mountain ranges.
Rivers	A river is a stream of freshwater that flows along the surface of the earth. Streams feed into small rivers, then these smaller rivers feed into larger rivers to form a river system. All river systems eventually feed into a large body of water such as an ocean or lake.
Deserts	Environment marked by high temperatures and low annual rainfall. Deserts have sparse vegetation. Plants and animals that are specially adapted to high temperatures and little water.
Oceans	Large bodies of water that have salts and other dissolved minerals and compounds. Oceans may reach depths of tens of thousands of meters. Most living things in the ocean inhabit the top several hundred meters of the ocean where sunlight penetrates allowing plants to grow.

Weathering

Weathering is a change in either the physical form or the chemical composition of a rock. Weathering happens to rocks that are exposed at the Earth's surface. There are two types of weathering: chemical and physical.

Chemical Weathering.   Chemical weathering breaks down rocks by changing their chemical composition. Chemical reactions occur between the minerals in the rock, water, acids, and gases such as oxygen and carbon dioxide. An example of chemical weathering is found in some soils that appear red in color. The red color is produced when iron in the soil reacts with oxygen in the atmosphere and the iron oxides. We know iron oxidation as rust.

Physical Weathering.   Physical weathering is also called mechanical weathering. In this type of weathering, rocks are physically broken down into smaller pieces but their chemical composition does not change. Mechanical weathering can result from forces exerted on rocks by plants, animals, ice, wind, and running water.

Erosion and Deposition

Erosion is the process that transports sediments away from the location where they formed. Erosion may move soil or rock fragments. Agents of erosion (forces that power erosion) include moving water, wind, and gravity down a slope. The effects of erosion can be seen in the way that a stream cuts a path through the surface of the Earth and in how rock fragments accumulate at the bottom of a slope. Erosion causes the jagged surfaces of mountains to become more rounded, and the overall level of the mountains to lower over millions of years. Catastrophic examples of erosion at work are mudslides and landslides.

When the agents of erosion cease their movement, the sediment is laid down in its new location. This process is called deposition. Deposition is responsible for the formation of land forms such as beaches. Waves and other types of moving water such as rivers deposit sand and sediment along shorelines to build beaches along rivers, lakes, and oceans. Deposition by wind is responsible for the formation of sand dunes in windswept areas.

Properties of Different Types of Soil

We have discussed different types of rocks, but there are also several different types of soil that form from these rocks as a result of the processes that we have mentioned. Recall that through the processes of chemical and physical weathering, rocks weather to form soils. Table 13.7 below summarizes the basic soil types that you need to be familiar with.

TABLE 13.7

SOIL TYPE	PROPERTIES	FORMATION
Clay	Individual grains are too small to be seen. Has tiny air spaces. Has the ability to absorb large amounts of water (poor drainage).	Weathers from rocks that are rich in the mineral feldspar.
Sand	Large particles can easily be felt and seen. Has large air spaces between the particles (good drainage).	Forms from weathered granite and other rocks that are rich in the mineral quartz.
Silt	Particles are too small to be seen. Texture is between the coarse texture of sand and the super fine texture of clay.	Formed from a variety of weathered minerals. Common in areas where sediment has been deposited by moving water, such as near rivers.

CONTENT AREA THIRTY-THREE: LAYERS OF THE EARTH

There is much more to the composition of the Earth than the rocks and minerals that we have mentioned. These rocks and minerals are limited to the rigid upper layer of the Earth called the crust. The Earth is actually composed of many layers (see Table 13.8).

TABLE 13.8

LAYER	APPROXIMATE THICKNESS	DESCRIPTION
Crust	80km (thicker in areas with mountains, thinner in ocean areas)	Thin rigid outermost layer.
Mantle	2900 km	Divided into two regions, the lithosphere and the asthenosphere.
Lithosphere	15 to 300 km	Composed of the crust and the cool brittle uppermost layer of the mantle (upper mantle).
Asthenosphere	About 200 km	Plastic layer where solid rock flows under great heat and pressure (lower mantle).
Core (outer and inner)	Outer—2250 km Inner—1228 km	Outer—Dense liquid. Inner—Dense solid. The core is made mostly of iron.

Note: Movements of molten material in the liquid outer core is what produces the Earth's magnetic field. Recall from domain one that the Earth is a giant magnet with two magnetic poles just like the poles of a bar magnet.

CONTENT AREA THIRTY-FOUR: PLATE TECTONICS

Through the 1900s a large body of evidence began to surface supporting the idea that the continents were once joined as one super continent (referred to as Pangaea) and have since drifted apart. This theory was proposed in 1912 by Alfred Wegener, and is known as the theory of continental drift. This theory has evolved into the theory of plate tectonics that we accept today.

Evidence of Plate Tectonics

There are three main bodies of evidence that support the idea that the continents broke apart. They are evidence obtained from land forms, rock and fossil records, and plant and animal extinctions. Let's examine each body of evidence.

Land Forms.   The margins of the continents seem to fit together like a jigsaw puzzle. This suggested to Wegener that the continents were once joined and somehow broke apart. More evidence came to light as it was discovered that the age and type of rocks match between coastal areas that were separated by huge expanses of ocean (for example, eastern South America and Western Africa). Mountain chains that end abruptly at coastlines appear to continue on continents on the other side of the ocean.

Fossil Records.   Fossils of the same plants and animals have been found on continents that are separated by oceans. These organisms had no physical ability to swim huge expanses of ocean. This further pointed to the possibility that the continents were once joined.

Evidence of Plant and Animal Extinctions.   Fossil records of plants and animals that lived in a particular area and have since gone extinct yields evidence indicating that the climate of the continents has changed dramatically over time. The climate of the continents millions of years ago was very different from the climate of the continents today. For example, fossilized plant remains have been discovered in Antarctica indicating that the ancient climate there was warm, moist, and swampy. The climate of Antarctica today is too cold to support plants of any kind. This suggests that the continent of Antarctica was at one time located in a region much closer to the equator where the climate would be warmer.

The scientific community did not accept Wegener's theory during his lifetime. This was because while he could provide evidence for the idea that the continents were once joined, he could provide no explanation for the mechanism that drove the continents apart.

Today we now know that Wegener was correct in his theory. The scientific community has taken the discoveries made by Wegener and added to them the discoveries of other scientists in the 1900s to develop the theory of plate tectonics.

Plate Tectonics.   We now know that the Earth's crust is composed of lithospheric plates. This means that the Earth's lithosphere is composed of plates. These rigid plates move over the semifluid asthenosphere. What causes the plates to move over the asthenosphere are convection currents in this layer. Convection currents operate on the basic premise that heat rises and cold sinks. Molten material that is closer to the core is hotter and therefore rises. As it rises, it displaces the cooler material that is closer to the crust. As this material in the asthenosphere moves, so do the plates that are riding on top of it (see Figure 13.7).

The action of plate tectonics results in many effects visible on the surface of the Earth. The geography of the Earth can be attributed to plate tectonics. Continents have the shape that they do because of moving plates either splitting them apart or forcing them together. Each region of the Earth has a specific climate due largely to the fact that plate tectonics has moved regions of land either closer to the equator (causing a warmer climate) or farther away (causing a cooler climate). It is important to note that as plate tectonics continues to shift the location of continents over time, the climates of the continents also continue to change. Though it is also important to note that this movement is slow—usually several centimeters per year—

FIGURE 13.7

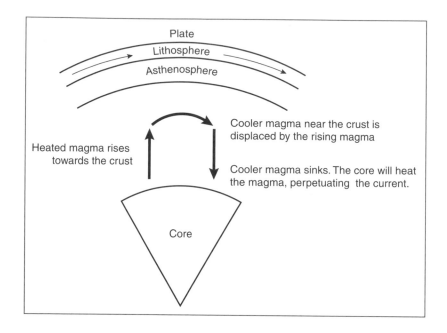

and will therefore take place over millions of years. Plate tectonics is also largely responsible for the geographic distribution of organisms on Earth. As populations of the same species are physically separated due to geography, they gradually adapt to their environments eventually evolving into separate species.

CONTENT AREA THIRTY-FIVE: DYNAMIC EARTH PROCESSES

Plate tectonics is responsible for many gradual changes that occur over millions of years. However plate tectonics is also responsible for some changes that occur more quickly as well. These processes are called dynamic earth processes. There are three major types of dynamic earth processes that you will need to be familiar with: mountain formation, volcanos, and earthquakes (see Table 13.9).

TABLE 13.9

PROCESS	MECHANISM	EFFECTS
Mountains	Two plates pushing against one another, forcing the crust upward.	Changes in the surface structure and topography of the Earth.
Volcanos	Plates either spreading apart or one forces under another causing liquid magma to reach the Earth's surface. May be violently explosive or smoothly flowing.	Mountain formation, deposition of ash, and the formation of igneous rock. Loss of life and property.
Earthquakes	Plates slip against one another after tremendous pressure has built up. This releases energy that is felt as shaking.	May force the crust upward into hills or create huge rifts depending on the plate movement. Loss of life and property.

Note on earthquakes: The location and intensity of earthquakes are influenced by several factors. This is something that you may need to be aware of. There are three factors that influence the intensity of earthquakes. The location at the plate boundary where the slippage first occurs is called the focus. The closer the focus is to the surface of the Earth, the more intense the earthquake will be. Also, earthquakes traveling through less dense materials such as sand will have a greater intensity than earthquakes traveling through more dense materials such as granite. Finally, the degree of slippage will affect the intensity of an earthquake. The greater the amount of actual slippage that occurs, the more intense the earthquake will be because more tension has been released.

CONTENT AREA THIRTY-SIX: FORMATION OF THE EARTH

The young Earth in its early stages of formation was very different from the Earth we know today. You may need to be familiar with how the Earth formed, so let's look at the processes that created the Earth that we know today.

It is believed that the earth formed 4.6 billion years ago. The planets are believed to have begun as clouds of dust and gas that attracted particles to them by gravity. The mass of the earth began to condense and grow as more and more particles were accumulated. About 5 million years after earth's initial creation, the Earth began to heat up. A partial melting occurred that caused the Earth to differentiate into layers. Lighter elements rose to the surface and heavier elements sank to the core. At this time the Earth developed an atmosphere of hydrogen, methane, carbon dioxide, and water vapor. Much of these gases were released by active volcanoes. It was at this time that the Earth's oceans also developed. Over 70 percent of the Earth was covered in water at that time. Over billions of years, the Earth's atmosphere changed to the composition of mainly nitrogen and oxygen gas that we know today. It is believed that the oxygen in the atmosphere was largely produced by primitive photosynthesizing organisms.

CONTENT AREA THIRTY-SEVEN: WEATHER AND CLIMATE

We have discussed in the previous section the fact that a location's distance from the equator impacts overall temperature of that location. However several other factors also play a role in determining an area's weather and climate. Weather takes place in the Earth's atmosphere. The atmosphere is the thick layers of gases that surrounds the planet. Before we examine these factors, it is important to denote the difference between weather and climate. Weather is defined as the general condition of the atmosphere at a particular time and place. Weather changes from day to day and hour to hour. Climate, on the other hand, is the general condition of the weather over many years in a particular region. We can say that climate is the average of weather. Climate does not change from day to day as weather does. We will look at the three major factors that influence weather and climate that you will need to be familiar with: the sun, the oceans, and the water cycle.

The Role of the Sun in Weather

The sun is Earth's only source of heat and light energy. This energy enters Earth's atmosphere and warms the planet. There are two factors that influence how much the sun's rays heat a particular area. The first factor is the angle at which solar rays strike the Earth. The second factor is the length of time the sun shines on a particular area in a day.

When the sun's rays strike the Earth, they strike the equator almost directly. This heats the region intensely because the direct rays spread their energy over a small area. Closer to the North and South Poles, solar rays that strike the Earth are more slanted. This low angle causes the energy to be spread out over a large area, thus heating it less intensely.

The sun will also result in a change in temperature depending on the number of hours of daylight in a region. Temperatures will be warmer in areas experiencing longer days.

This heating of the atmosphere by the sun is also what is responsible for the creation of wind. The creation of winds works on the premise "heat rises and cold sinks." In all forms of matter, things that are heated become less dense because the heat energy in the matter is causing the particles of matter to move faster (the matter expands). (Recall our discussion of kinetic energy and heat in domain two). This is why "heat rises"—less dense materials will rise above materials that are more dense. The opposite is true for matter that is cooler. Particles in cold matter slow down in their movement, causing the matter to become more dense and consequently sink down below matter that is less dense.

Let's apply this idea to wind. Air that receives more solar energy heats up, becomes less dense, and rises above surrounding air masses. Air that is colder sinks. It is this phenomena of warm air and cold air moving due to changes in density that creates wind.

The Role of Oceans in Weather and Climate

Oceans and other large bodies of water affect climate in two ways. The first involves the role of currents. The second way that large bodies of water impact weather and climate is in the fact that they have a moderating effect on weather. Let's look at how this effect works.

Water heats up more slowly than land does. Because of this fact, equal amounts of land and water can absorb equal amounts of radiation and the air temperature over the water will be cooler than air over land. So during hours of daylight, there is a distinct difference in temperature between the air over water and the air over land. Breezes then blow the cooler air from over the water towards land, cooling the air temperatures over the land. This effect is called a sea breeze. In the night, the opposite occurs. The air over land loses heat more quickly. So at night, air over the land is cooler than air over the water. The warmer air over the water then blows inland replacing the cooler air. This process moderates coastal temperatures, making them less extreme.

The Role of the Water Cycle in Weather and Climate

The water cycle is the process by which water moves up from the surface of the Earth, to the atmosphere, and back again. The water cycle impacts weather and climate because this is the process that produces all types of precipitation such as rain, snow, sleet, and hail. Table 13.10 and Figure 13.8 summarize the steps of the water cycle.

The Role of Air Movements and Ocean Currents

Air movements and ocean currents both impact weather and climate. Both types of currents move warm and cold air or water around the planet. Warm air and water currents move from the equator towards the poles (recall that the equator is where the atmosphere is heated the most intensely). Cold air and ocean currents tend to move from the poles toward the equator.

TABLE 13.10

STAGE	DESCRIPTION
Evaporation	Liquid water on the Earth's surface changes to a gas and returns to the atmosphere as water vapor.
Condensation	Water vapor cools and condenses into liquid water droplets in the atmosphere usually as clouds.
Precipitation	Water falls to the Earth as rain, snow, hail, or sleet.

FIGURE 13.8

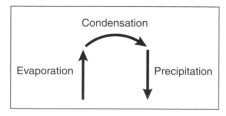

These currents have a chilling effect on climate. Table 13.11 summarizes the basic types of ocean and air currents and cause and effect of each. You will need to be familiar with their causes and the general effect that each has on weather and climate.

TABLE 13.11

OCEAN CURRENTS	CAUSE	EFFECT
Surface Currents	Primarily wind driven.	Warm currents warm coastal climates and cold currents have a chilling effect on coastal climates.
Deep Currents	Driven by changes in density of ocean water. Cold water that has high salinity (high percent of salt and dissolved solids) is very dense and sinks to the bottom, displacing water at the bottom of the ocean and thus powering the current.	Transports large quantities of cold, dense, deep water from the poles toward the equator.

AIR CURRENTS	CAUSE	EFFECT
All Air Currents	Driven by the uneven heating of air in the atmosphere. A convection current is created when warm air at the equator rises and moves towards the poles and cold air at the poles sinks and moves towards the equator.	Transports warm air away from the equator warming climates, and transports cold air from over the poles cooling climates. The net effect is the moderating of global climates.

Storms.   Storms often occur where warm and cold masses of air meet. Some tests require you to be familiar with the phenomena of a thunderstorm. A thunderstorm is a storm that is accompanied by strong winds, thunder, and lightning. Let's look at how a thunderstorm develops.

A thunderstorm develops in three stages.

Step 1 (cumulus stage): Warm moist air rises until the water vapor within it condenses to form a cumulus cloud.

Step 2 (mature stage): Warm moist air continues to rise higher. The cloud becomes dark and rises to a tall column with a flat, spread out top. Heavy rain and, occasionally, hail fall. Strong downward winds are produced as air is dragged downward by the falling rain.

Step 3 (dissipating stage): The storm begins to die out as the down drafts slow and stop and the supply of water vapor in the cloud decreases.

CONTENT AREA THIRTY-EIGHT: BODIES OF WATER

We have spoken a great deal about oceans. The earth has several types of bodies of water besides oceans. It is important to be able to compare and contrast the characteristics of major types of aquatic features. Table 13.12 summarizes the four main types of bodies of water as well as their key characteristics.

TABLE 13.12

BODY	CHARACTERISTICS
River	Water that channels water to either a larger river or a large body of water such as a lake or ocean
Lake	Large body of water (usually freshwater, but not always) that is enclosed by land on all sides.
Ocean	Large body of saltwater that completely encircles the continents and islands.
Estuary	Region where a freshwater source such as a river flows into the ocean. The water in an estuary is saltier than freshwater but not as salty as ocean water.

CONTENT AREA THIRTY-NINE: TIDES

Tides are a phenomena that occurs almost exclusively in the world's oceans. A tide is the daily change in the level of the ocean's surface. The tides are caused by the gravitational pull of the moon. The moon orbits the Earth because the earth's gravity pull's the moon towards it. Just as the earth exerts a gravitational pull on the moon, the moon exerts a gravitational pull on the Earth (though this pull is much weaker). The moon's gravitational pull is the strongest on the side of the earth that is facing the moon. On this side, the gravitational pull causes the level of the ocean surface to bulge. This bulge produces a high tide (the ocean level is higher). This bulge effect also occurs on the side of the Earth that is directly opposite the side facing the moon. At this time the sides of the Earth not experiencing the bulging effect are experiencing low tide (see Figure 13.9).

FIGURE 13.9

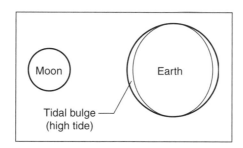

The gravitational pull of the sun also affects the tides in a similar way. However, the strength of this pull is only about one half the strength of the pull exerted by the moon (due to the sun's increased distance from the earth). The sun has the ability to weaken or strengthen the moon's effect on the tides. Recall that due to the tilt of the Earth's axis, different hemispheres of the Earth are tilted towards or away from the sun at different time of the year. This results in tidal patterns being stronger or weaker throughout the course of the year.

CONTENT AREA FORTY: ECLIPSES

An eclipse occurs whenever one planetary body (a planet, a moon, or the sun) passes through the shadow of another. There are two main types of eclipses: solar and lunar eclipses.

Solar Eclipse

A solar eclipse happens when the moon lies between the Earth and the sun, blocking our view of the sun. It is important to note that the moon is about 400 times smaller than the sun, but because it is so much closer to Earth than the sun is, the moon and sun *appear* to be the same size when viewed from Earth. Figure 13.10 illustrates how this happens.

FIGURE 13.10

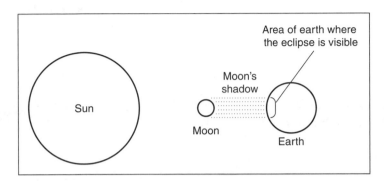

Lunar Eclipse

In a lunar eclipse, the moon and Earth basically switch places in our planetary lineup. For a lunar eclipse to take place, the earth must be between the sun and the moon. The earth casts a shadow on the moon, blocking out the sunlight that would normally be reflected off of the moon's surface. This renders the moon invisible to us here on earth (see Figure 13.11).

FIGURE 13.11

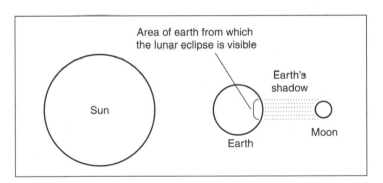

Elementary Mathematics[1]

DOMAIN ONE: NUMBERS, RELATIONSHIPS, SYSTEMS, COMPUTATIONS, AND FRACTIONS

CONTENT AREA ONE: PLACE VALUE

Place value is what allows us to organize numbers, so that they make sense universally. As we examine place value, the key word to remember is value. Imagine the number 5 for a moment. Its value could vary from 5 cents to billions of dollars, depending on where the zeros fall (either before it or after it). In short, numbers or numerals are what we count, but it is where we place them that gives them value. If you will look at your hands, you will see the basis of our system of numeration: 10. Value is based on increasing or decreasing powers of 10 (see Figure 14.1).

FIGURE 14.1   Place Value for 1,234,567,890

1,000,000,000s	100,000,000s	10,000,000s	1,000,000s	100,000s	10,000s	1000s	100s	10s	1s
1	2	3	4	5	6	7	8	9	0

These positions are all to the left of the decimal. They are increasing values for one. They are the "ands" place, as in *tens, hundreds, thousands, ten-thousands,* and so forth. At the right of the decimal are *fractions* or parts of the number one. They are the "enths" place (see Figure 14.2).

FIGURE 14.2

ANDS	ENTHS
Values of One	Fractions of One

Now, consider this number: *.123456789* (see Figure 14.3).

**FIGURE 14.3
Place Value for
.123456789**

10ths	100ths	1000ths
1	2	3
10000ths	100000ths	1000000ths
4	5	6
10000000ths	100000000ths	1000000000ths
7	8	9

[1]Chapter contributed by Charles Jackson.

All of these positions are for numbers *to the right of zero*. Please note that the length of the number does not particularly make the number larger or smaller. For example, compare .2 and .05892. The latter may look like the larger number; instead, it is the smaller. Compare each place starting with the first place to the right of the decimal. In the tenths place we have 2 and 0. Two is larger so .2 > .05892.

A decimal number takes its name from the place where it ends. For example the number above is named one hundred twenty-three million, four hundred fifty-six thousand, seven hundred eighty-nine billionths. Please note that there is no such thing as the "oneths" place. Ones are the basic unit of mathematics and all numbers are either greater or smaller than one.

Powers and Place Value

Now that you have had a refresher on base ten and place value, let's look at *powers* associated with place value and number. *Power* refers to the number of zeros that follow or precede a number, depending on whether it is a number greater than one or a number that is a fraction of one. Exponents are the little numbers near the top of the number that tell us how many zeros we have to add to 1 to reflect its place value (see Figure 14.4).

FIGURE 14.4

1,000,000,000

Place Name	Number	Power of 10
Billions	1,000,000,000	10^9
Hundred Millions	100,000,000	10^8
Ten Millions	10,000,000	10^7
Millions	1,000,000	10^6
Hundred Thousands	100,000	10^5
Ten Thousands	10,000	10^4
Thousands	1,000	10^3
Hundreds	100	10^2
Tens	10	10^1
Ones	1	10^0

Figure 14.5 shows you fractions of one. These are the *nths* place, to the right of zero. They are expressed in *negative exponents*. Remember that these numbers represent *fractions of one* and that *fractions of one* can be expressed with negative exponents.

FIGURE 14.5

Ten*ths*	.1	10^{-1}
Hundred*ths*	.01	10^{-2}
Thousand*ths*	.001	10^{-3}
Ten Thousand*ths*	.0001	10^{-4}
Hundred Thousand*ths*	.00001	10^{-5}
Million*ths*	.000001	10^{-6}
Ten Million*ths*	.0000001	10^{-7}
Hundred Million*ths*	.00000001	10^{-8}
Billion*ths*	.000000001	10^{-9}

You can also see how we can express place value in terms of powers of 10. The positive powers allow us to express whole numbers, and the negative exponent of 10 allows us to express decimal equivalents (the fractions of one). This ability will become especially important as we approach the writing of numbers in scientific notation.

As you walk through the problem below examine it for the use of the associative property of multiplication which allows us to regroup information to make the process easier and also how the value of the decimal place is expressed as a fraction.

$$5.27 \times 3.3$$

$$5.27 \times 3.3 = \left(527 \times \frac{1}{100}\right) \times \left(33 \times \frac{1}{10}\right)$$ Note how the decimal place is expressed as a fraction.

$$5.27 \times 3.3 = 527 \times \left(\frac{1}{100} \times 33\right) \times \frac{1}{10}$$ Using the associative property of multiplication you can regroup the factors in the steps that follow.

$$5.27 \times 3.3 = 527 \times \left(33 \times \frac{1}{100}\right) \times \frac{1}{10}$$

$$5.27 \times 3.3 = (527 \times 33) \times \left(\frac{1}{100} \times \frac{1}{10}\right)$$ Here we apply the rules for multiplication of fractions.

$$5.27 \times 3.3 = (527 \times 33) \times \left(\frac{1}{1000}\right)$$ Now we apply the rules for multiplication of whole numbers.

$$5.27 \times 3.3 = 17390 \times \frac{1}{1000}$$ In this step, we observe the rules for multiplying a whole number and a fraction.

$$5.27 \times 3.3 = \frac{17390}{1000}$$ Lastly we divide as indicated.

$$5.27 \times 3.3 = 17.390$$

CONTENT AREA TWO: SCIENTIFIC NOTATION

Scientific notation is a relative newcomer to the mathematical scene. It is thought that physicists working to define the electrical standards such as volt and ohm were the first to develop it as a sort of mathematical shorthand. Scientific notation is a method that allows us to write extremely large or small numbers easily. It is based on the concept of place value expressed in Figure 14.6. The process is rather simple and involves movement of the decimal point right or left and counting. The methodology as laid out is important so that you understand each step in the process so that you can attack multiple-choice or essay questions on the examination effectively. Copy each step and focus on the reason for the action. This will be helpful if you are faced with an essay question that explores scientific notation.

In Figure 14.6, note how the number is transformed by counting the number of moves it takes to get a number into the *ones* place before adding the exponents to account for the zeros you have removed.

FIGURE 14.6

Compacting a Large Number	Reasoning
289,500,000,000,000	
2.89500000000000	• Move the decimal to the *left* until you have one digit in front of it.
There are **14** total moves.	• Count your total number of moves left, **14** in this case.
10^{14}	• Use that number as your power of 10 exponent.
2.895×10^{14}	• Write as a product of the decimal number and power of 10. Eliminate zeros as needed.

Now try to apply the same procedure on the number in the practice problem below.

Compact this number into scientific notation: 1,259,000,000,000,000

You should have arrived at 1.259×10^{15}. If you didn't, let's examine how the answer was reached. In every whole number a decimal is at the end whether it is written or not.

We move the decimal to the left until one digit remains in front of it and count as we move and use that as our power for the 10. We moved the decimal until we were left with 1.259 and since we moved a total of 15 places to the left we have 10^{15}.

We can also expand a number out of scientific notation into standard notation (see Figure 14.7).

FIGURE 14.7

To expand a number compacted with scientific notation	Reasoning
4.95×10^8	• Reverse the compacting process.
There are **8** total moves.	• Take the power of 10.
4.95	• Write the decimal number.
495000000	• Move the decimal to the *right* the same number of places as the power of 10.
495,000,000	• Add commas as needed.

Expand this number into standard notation: 3.925×10^{11}

You should have arrived at 392,500,000,000. Here is how the answer was achieved. The decimal was taken from where it was and moved 11 places to the right because the power of 10 was 11.

The next thing to learn is how to work with decimals and scientific notation. Review how to compact decimals into scientific notation to reflect extremely small fractions of one. Remember that you have to count the number of zeros behind the decimal point and express the exponent negatively (see Figure 14.8).

FIGURE 14.8

Compact Decimal Numbers	Reasoning
.0000000000532	
5.32	• Move the decimal to the *right* until you have one natural number in front of the decimal. Discard the zeros.
There were **11** total moves.	• Count the total number of moves left you made.
10^{-11}	• Write it as the negative power of ten.
5.32×10^{-11}	• Write it as the product of the decimal number and the negative power of 10.

Compact this decimal number into scientific notation: .000000000000445

You should have arrived at 4.45×10^{-13}. If not, let's examine the process. We moved the decimal to the right until we had one number in front of the decimal, 4.45, and we counted as we moved to determine the power of ten. We moved 13 places so we write the power as 10^{-13}.

Now, let's learn the reverse: How to expand a number in scientific notation into a decimal (see Figure 14.9). Remember to look for negative exponents when deciding the direction in which to add the zeros (either behind or in front of the decimal).

FIGURE 14.9

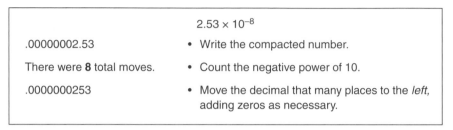

$$2.53 \times 10^{-8}$$

.00000002.53	• Write the compacted number.
There were **8** total moves.	• Count the negative power of 10.
.0000000253	• Move the decimal that many places to the *left*, adding zeros as necessary.

As you now know, the sign in front of the exponent tells you everything that you need to know about where to add your zeros.

Write the following number in standard notation: 7.85×10^{-12}

You should have arrived at .00000000000785. If not, let's examine how it was worked. The power of 10 tells us the number of places to move the decimal to the right. I know from the negative power that I will be creating a decimal. I take 7.85 and move the decimal right 12 places adding zeros as needed.

CONTENT AREA THREE: PROPERTIES OF NUMBERS

Over the centuries people have observed some patterns that have evolved into some basic properties of how rational numbers work. They have been given names—identity, inverse, associative, commutative, and distributive; and they allow us to manipulate numbers, develop equality, and give us methods to prove mathematical principles. The properties seem self-evident mathematically, but in algebra they help us solve equations.

- Identity properties allow us to state positively that a number is what it is.
- Inverse properties of addition show that any number plus its opposite is equal to zero, whereas the inverse property in multiplication allow us to show that any number multiplied by its reciprocal is equal to one.
- Associative properties give us a method of regrouping in addition and multiplication and still have the same result.
- Commutative properties give us the ability to reverse the order of addition and multiplication and still achieve the same answer.
- Distributive properties allow us to spread multiplication over a group of numbers that are added, subtracted, or multiplied.

Mathematical models have been standardized to illustrate these properties. A proper knowledge of the properties of numbers allows us not only to understand the functioning of rational numbers, but also to facilitate our understanding of how equations are solved.

Identity

The property of identity allows us to prove that a number is what it claims to be. Remember that $2 + 2 = 4$? What that means is that 4 *is* the combination of 2 and 2. These mathematical facts can be applied to addition multiplication for both positive and negative numbers (see Table 14.1).

TABLE 14.1

NAME OF THE PROPERTY	ALGEBRAIC MODEL	NUMBER MODEL	MEANING
Identity Property of Addition	$A + 0 = A$	$5 + 0 = 5$	To prove a number is what it claims to be.
Identity Property of Multiplication	$A \times 1 = A$	$7 \times 1 = 7$	To prove a number is what it claims to be.
Inverse Property of Addition	$A - (-A) = 0$	$4 + (-4) = 0$	A number plus its opposite = 0.
Inverse Property of Multiplication	$\dfrac{A}{B} \times \dfrac{B}{A}$	$\dfrac{2}{3} \times \dfrac{3}{2}$	A number multiplied by its reciprocal = 1.

Commutative Property

The next property is the communicative property. It tells us that we can add and multiply numbers in ways that do not change their sums or products (see Table 14.2).

TABLE 14.2

NAME OF THE PROPERTY	ALGEBRAIC MODEL	NUMBER MODEL	MEANING
Commutative Property of Addition	$A + B = B + A$	$4 + 3 = 3 + 4$	The order of addition does not change the sum.
Commutative Property of Multiplication	$A \times B = B \times A$	$2 \times 5 = 5 \times 2$	The order of multiplication does not change the product.

Associative Property

The associative property tells us that the way that we group numbers when we add them doesn't change the sum. The same is true for multiplication (see Table 14.3).

TABLE 14.3

Associative Property of Addition	$(A + B) + C = $ $A + (B + C)$	$(4 + 5) + 6 = $ $4 + (5 + 6)$	The way you group numbers in addition does not change the sum.
Associative Property of Multiplication	$(A \times B) \times C = $ $A \times (B \times C)$	$(2 \times 3) \times 4 = $ $2 \times (3 \times 4)$	The way you group numbers in multiplication does not change the product.

The Distributive Property

The distributive property shows you how to group numbers across processes of addition, subtraction, and multiplication (see Table 14.4).

TABLE 14.4

Distributive Property across Addition	$A \times (B + C) =$ $(A \times B) + (A \times C)$	$2 \times (4 + 5) =$ $(2 \times 4) + (2 \times 5)$	You can use the Distributive Property to rewrite one factor as the sum of two numbers.
Distributive Property across Subtraction	$A \times (B - C) =$ $(A \times B) - (A \times C)$	$5 \times (6 - 3) =$ $(5 \times 6) - (5 \times 3)$	You can use the Distributive Property to rewrite one factor as the difference of two numbers

In the practice problem below, describe steps to the solution, justify each step, and name the property shown.

Problem	Answer	Justification	Property Illustrated
A. 4 + (−3) + (−6)			
B. 5 × 1/5 + 0			
C. 5 × (3 × 2)			
D. 7 × (3 + 9)			
E. 5 × (6 − 2)			

Answers to Practice Problem: (A) 5 Associative Property of Addition, (B) 0 Inverse Property of Multiplication, (C) 30 Associative Property of Multiplication, (D) 84 Distributive Property, (E) 20 Distributive Property

CONTENT AREA FOUR: EXPONENTIAL NOTATION

The use of exponents dates from the late 1400s, but it was Rene Descartes who developed the exponent as we use it today. While examining place value and scientific notation, you noticed we used exponents (or powers) of 10. Students often struggle with this type of notation. This confusion can often be traced to a single illustration often used by the teacher to show students the functioning of exponents: 2^2. Even if you work it incorrectly you get the correct answer. Students get the idea that by multiplying the base and the exponent, a correct answer is achieved. If answering an essay question on exponents it would be useful to point this out, as well as the correct illustration:

BASE^{exponent}

The base is the number that is repeatedly multiplied, the exponent tells us the number of times to use it, so 5^3 means $5 \times 5 \times 5$.

Consider how the base and exponent are related and see if you can devise an essay question that might incorporate your knowledge.

$3 \times 3 \times 3 \times 3$	The exponent tells us how many times to multiply the base.
$(3 \times 3) \times (3 \times 3)$	Group if possible to make your work easier.
81	Multiply

Work through the practice problem for exponential notation, and demonstrate your knowledge of the process.

$$4^3$$

You should have arrived at 64. The problem is worked at the top of the next page.

BASE^{exponent}

4^3

$4 \times 4 \times 4$

$(4 \times 4) \times 4$

16×4

64

In sum, working with exponents "blows them up" and inflates them (provided that they are positive).

Factoring to Primes

Recall that prime numbers are those numbers that cannot be divided evenly by any numbers except 1 and itself. Factoring to primes is the key that opens the door to finding the greatest common factor (GCF) and least common multiple (LCM). GCF and LCM will be essential for you to understand when you learn how to work with fractions. For now, you will only learn about factoring a number to primes. Factoring becomes easier if divisibility rules involving primes are known first.

Basic divisibility rules will make factoring to primes a less threatening process. Each of these rules will help you look at numbers in a different way. Table 14.5 shows you how certain prime numbers have a rule associated with them that can be applied to different numbers.

TABLE 14.5

PRIME NUMBER	DIVISIBILITY RULE	EXAMPLES
2	If the last number is even, then complete number can be divided by 2.	• $12 = 2 \times 6$ • $14 = 2 \times 7$ • (2 and 4 are divisible by 2)
3	If you add the individual digits of the number and the sum is divisible by 3, then the complete number is divisible by 3.	• 15 ($1 + 5 = 6$; 6 is divisible by 3 and so is 15!) $15 = 3 \times 5$ • 1,243,152 is divisible by 3! $1 + 2 + 4 + 3 + 1 + 5 + 2 = 18$
5	If the number ends in zero or 5, then the complete number is divisible by 5.	• 20 and 25 are divisible by 5 • 1,123,712,341,561,456,165 is also divisible by 5!
7, 11, 13, 17, 19, 23, 29, etc.	Test by actually doing the indicated division.	• These primes offer no shortcuts.

The rules that you just learned may help you in any factoring endeavors, so be sure that you remember them. Let's look at how to factor a number to its primes. In copying each step, see how the reasoning carries through the process. It will make the practice problem more beneficial.

TABLE 14.6   Factor 36 to Primes

• 72 is an even number so I know it is divisible by 2: 2×36 • 36 is an even number so I can factor out another 2: $2 \times 2 \times 18$ • 18 is an even number so I can factor out another 2: $2 \times 2 \times 2 \times 9$	• 9 is not an even number so I test it for 3: $3 \times 3 = 9$ • I now have $2 \times 2 \times 2 \times 3 \times 3$ • The number 2 is used three times, so the exponent is 3: 2^3. • The number 3 is used two times, so the exponent is 2: 3^2. • Therefore the answer is $2^3 \times 3^2$.

Now you will combine your knowledge or exponents and skills with factoring to discover how to find the root of a number.

A *base* can also be referred to as a *root*. From that we get the terms such as square root, cube root, 4th root and so forth. Finding a *root* means that we must find the number that is used over and over again. Lets find the cube root of the following example.

$$\sqrt[3]{27}$$

This asks us what number times itself times itself = 27. We know $3 \times 9 = 27$ and that $3 \times 3 = 9$ so we know that $3 \times 3 \times 3 = 27$. What number is repeatedly used? Three! Therefore the cube root of 27 is 3. A quick hint that may make life easier for you: When in doubt, factor to primes and count how many times a number repeats itself.

If we are asked to find the 5th root of 32, $\sqrt[5]{32}$ it would be easier to factor 32 to primes.

$32 = 4 \times 8$
$32 = 2 \times 2 \times 2 \times 4$
$32 = 2 \times 2 \times 2 \times 2 \times 2$

You will see that we have used the number 2 five times. Therefore the 5th root of 32 is 2. Now you will be asked to practice this skill. Using your new found expertise, find the fourth root of 81.

$$\sqrt[4]{81}$$

The root is 3. If your answer differs lets try factoring to primes to see what number is used over and over again.

$81 = 9 \times 9$
$81 = (3 \times 3) \times (3 \times 3)$

I ask myself what number is used 4 times: the answer is 3. Therefore the 4th root of 81 is 3.

CONTENT AREA FIVE: COMPUTATIONS

The operations of addition, subtraction, multiplication, and division allow the mathematical body to function. Multiplication and division are newcomers. Multiplication is a shortcut to the tedious process of repeated addition and repeated subtraction replaced by division. This section will cover these four operations in relation to whole numbers, decimals, and fractions.

As you practice, remember that NES essay questions ask you to *write out your thought processes through math questions as you solve them.* Few people may have actual experience doing that. So, if you are facing essay questions on math, you will want to work through the information in this section as it is presented.

You may need to have the basic vocabulary for operation in whole numbers. If you know this terminology (most people don't), your essays will look more impressive. Furthermore, this obscure math vocabulary may also appear in multiple-choice questions, so let's review the terms (see Table 14.7).

Now that you have some idea about basic operational vocabulary, you need to know the order in which these operations are carried out. It can be compared to a battle plan, and it gives structure to the mathematical process. There is a simple method to commit it to memory. It is an acronym called *PEMDAS,* which stands for *please excuse my dear aunt sally.* Each letter tells you the order to carry out an operation (see Table 14.8).

TABLE 14.7

OPERATION	PART NAME	PART NAME	TOTAL	KEY WORDS
Addition $2 + 2 = 4$	Addend 2	Addend 2	Sum 4	Total, together, after, joined
Subtraction $4 - 2 = 2$	Minuend 4	Subtrahend 2	Difference 2	More than, minus, before, profit, less
Multiplication $2 \times 2 = 4$	Factor 2	Factor 2	Product 4	Of, times, double
Division $2\overline{)2}$ ₁	Divisor (outside) 2	Dividend (inside) 2	Quotient (above) 1	Each, average

TABLE 14.8

ORDER	MEMORY DEVISE	OPERATION	MEANING	EXAMPLE
1	*Please*	**P**arentheses	Do any operation within the parentheses first.	$(2 + 5)$
2	*Excuse*	**E**xponents	Do any calculation involving and exponent.	2^3
3	*My Dear*	**M**ultiplication and **D**ivision	Do any operation involving multiplication or division.	4×5
4	*Aunt Sally*	**A**ddition and **S**ubtraction	Do any operations involving addition or subtraction.	$5 + 8$

Let us apply the order of operations to this problem (see Figure 14.10).

FIGURE 14.10

Please	$\mathbf{(2 + 5)} + (2^3) \times 5$
Excuse	$\underline{(7)} + \mathbf{(2^3)} \times 5$
My	$(7) + \boldsymbol{8} \times \mathbf{5}$
Dear	No Division
Aunt	$\mathbf{(7)} + \underline{\boldsymbol{40}}$
Sally	No Subtraction
	47

One additional rule is the *left to right* rule. If all of the operations are the same, then just forget about "Sally" and work through the problem from left to right:

$$\underrightarrow{2 + 3 + 6 + 11 + 67 + 102 + 5} = 196$$

Rounding Off

Rounding off is a method of making numbers more manageable (e.g., when you don't want to operate all that much). With whole numbers, rounding allows for us to look at the big picture in a general way. For decimal numbers, rounding allows us to deal with nonrepeating and repeating decimals. The process is the same for both with a small twist at the end. Please follow and copy each step of the problem in Table 14.9.

TABLE 14.9

ROUND 1255 TO THE NEAREST HUNDRED	REASONING
1<u>2</u>55	• Underline the place you are rounding off to.
1<u>2</u>55 ↑	• Draw an arrow to the next number to the right. Is the number you are pointing at 5 or larger? (yes or no?)
+1 1<u>2</u>55	• If "yes" add 1 to the underlined number, if "no" leave the underlined number the same.
1<u>3</u>55	• Is this a decimal number? (yes or no?)
"No"	• If "yes" drop all numbers after the one underlined. If "no" change all numbers after the unlined one to zeros.
1300	

Use the example to complete the practice problem below for rounding.

Round 14579 to the nearest thousand.

You should have arrived at 15,000. Here are the steps that were taken to round off:

14579

1<u>4</u>579
↑

+1
1<u>4</u>579

15000

Decimal numbers can also be rounded. We do this to eliminate repeating decimals. Repeating decimals are denoted by a bar over the number or pattern that repeats. The repeat goes on forever. For example:

26.$\overline{6}$	means	26.66666666. . . .
26.$\overline{45}$	means	26.45454545. . . .

Rounding decimals is also useful for decimals that are simply too long to deal with. For example, if you saw that the price of a piece of gum was .2513412341341341, you'd probably go crazy. Much easier just to pay 25 cents. Note the only difference is how numbers are handled after the rounding off has occurred (see Table 14.10).

Apply the same information to the practice problem below:

Round 135.75675 to the nearest thousand*th*.

You should have arrived at 135.757. Let's examine how we arrived at that answer.

135.75675

135.75<u>6</u>75
↑

+1
135.75<u>6</u>75

135.75<u>7</u>

TABLE 14.10

139.<u>9</u>651	• Underline the place you are rounding off to.
139.<u>9</u>651 ↑	• Draw an arrow to the next number to the right. Is the number you are pointing at 5 or larger? (yes or no?)
+1 139.<u>9</u>651	• If "yes" add 1 to the underlined number, if "no" leave the underlined number the same. *(Hint: Don't forget to carry if you have to as in normal addition)*
140	• Is this a decimal number? (yes or no?)
	• If "yes" drop all numbers after the one underlined. If "no" change all numbers after the underlined one to zeros.
140	

Whole Number Operations

Whole number operations include all those wonderful things you learned in elementary school. I'm sure you remember all the endless problems of addition, subtraction, multiplication, and division.

The key to whole number operations is alignment. These operations are dependent upon proper alignment of the place values. One helpful technique is to picture graph paper and imagine one number per square. The "ones" or units are all lined up vertically, then "tens" and so forth. Since multiplication and division are shortcuts some liberties are taken. Note how "carrying" takes place. Again, we know that you know how to do simple math operations like this one; however, many tests with essay questions ask you to write out your thought processes.

$$25 + 103 + 6$$

$$\begin{array}{r} 25 \\ 103 \\ + 6 \end{array}$$ Align the places values so that like will be in line with like.

$5 + 3 + 6 = 14$ Add the ones.

You have made 14. One 10 and 4 ones.

$$\begin{array}{r} 1 \\ 25 \\ 103 \\ + 6 \\ \hline 4 \end{array}$$ Write the 4 in the ones column and carry the 1 to the tens column.

$$\begin{array}{r} 1 \\ 25 \\ 103 \\ + 6 \\ \hline 34 \end{array}$$ Add the tens column. You have not created tens so there is nothing to carry.

$$\begin{array}{r} 25 \\ 103 \\ + 6 \\ \hline 134 \end{array}$$ Add the hundreds column and write the sum.

Go ahead and apply this process to the practice question on the next page, where you will add a column of numbers and demonstrate your understanding the process at each step.

Add the following: 2351 + 35 + 592 + 7

You should have arrived at 2985. If not go back and review the steps illustrated there as we work through the solution together. First remember that position is everything. All numbers in the ones (units) must be aligned. Placing the addends properly we have:

```
 2351
   35
  592
+   7
```

We now add the ones, making tens. The result is 15. We write the 5 and carry the 1 to the next column. We continue the process and arrive at the sum of 2985.

Let's now review the reverse process of the subtraction of whole numbers. Observe how in addition we "made tens," but in subtraction we "break tens" and then "give to the needy."

529 − 53

```
  529        Align the places values so that like will be in line with like.
− 53
```

```
  529        If you have 9 you can give away 3 from that amount.
− 53
─────
    6
```

```
  4          If you have 2 you cannot give away 5 from that amount. Go to the
  5̶29        hundreds column and "give to the needy."
− 53
─────
    6
```

```
  4          You now have 12 and can subtract 5 and write the difference.
  5̶ 12 9
− 5 3
─────
  4 7 6
```

Now apply the steps from the example above to the practice problem. Remember to be careful with the alignment.

Subtract the following: 4389 − 572

You should have arrived at 3817. If not go back and review the steps illustrated there. Remember that placement is everything. The first number stated, 4389 is placed on top, and the 2 of 572 must be aligned under the 9. If I have 9, I can subtract 2. The result is 7. I can do the same with 8 and 7 with a result of 1. However, with the numbers in the hundreds, I must borrow and give to the needy. If I have 3, I cannot give you 5. That is how you arrive at 3817.

Multiplication.   Multiplication of whole numbers can be indicated in a number of different ways:

$$5 * 7 \qquad 5(7) \qquad (5)7 \qquad 5 \times 7$$

Each gives identical results and has the same meaning: multiply five times seven. With a problem like 256 × 64, we can easily see the advantages of multiplication over repeated addition. Just think for a moment: Without multiplication, you'd need to add 256 and its equation 64 times! That's a lot of work and a lot of scratch paper! Here is the process of multiplication illustrated. Follow the reasoning, so that you can write an essay on multiplying if you are asked to do so.

$$
\begin{array}{r}
256 \\
\times\ 64 \\
\hline
\end{array}
$$

$$
\begin{array}{r}
22 \\
256 \\
\times\ 64 \\
\hline
1024
\end{array}
$$
Multiply 256 by 4. Make tens as you did for addition. This is your first partial product.

$$
\begin{array}{r}
256 \\
\times\ 64 \\
\hline
1024 \\
15360
\end{array}
$$
Multiply 256 × 60. Remember that the 6 is in the tens place. You may compensate by inserting a zero at the end of the partial product.

$$
\begin{array}{r}
256 \\
\times\ 64 \\
\hline
1024 \\
+\ 15360 \\
\hline
16384
\end{array}
$$
Add the partial products.

Write the product.

Now try multiplying the next example number in the practice problem. Work through it in steps, just in case you have to write it out on the test.

Find the product of 7059 × 68.

You should have arrived at 480,012.

$$
\begin{array}{r}
7059 \\
\times\ 68 \\
\hline
\end{array}
\qquad
\begin{array}{r}
7059 \\
\times\ 68 \\
\hline
56472
\end{array}
\qquad
\begin{array}{r}
56472 \\
\times\ 68 \\
\hline
56472 \\
+\ 423540 \\
\hline
480,012
\end{array}
$$

Review the steps of multiplication illustrated there if needed. One thing to pay special attention to in the problem is the multiplication with zero and the addition of the number carried to the zero; if a mistake has been made that will be the place to look first.

Division. Division is often difficult for children to grasp because of the numerous steps involved. It can be indicated in a number of different ways:

$$
12 \div 3 \qquad\qquad \frac{12}{3} \qquad\qquad 3\overline{)12}
$$

It involves the skills of estimation, multiplication, and subtraction and certain processes unique to division.

For the rest, you will have to perform division as part of larger questions that may involve several steps (e.g., word problems, tables, graphs, etc.), which should not be a problem because you will (in most cases) have a calculator.

The only challenge may be if they ask you to *estimate* the answer and select from a number of options:

Estimate the answer to the following: 15,667 ÷ 1,333

   A. 8
   B. 9
   C. 10
   D. 7

To figure the answer out quickly, look at the answers and hope that you see ten. $10 \times 1,333 = 13,000$, and 13,000 will divide into 15,666 with a remainder that is less than the divisor. Therefore, the answer is C. Each of the other options will yield remainders that are greater than the divisor, so they are out.

Decimal Operations.   Decimal operations mirror whole number operations with some minor twists involving placement of the decimal. If it has been a while since you've worked with decimals, then you may long for simple examples. Let's begin with simple addition.

Addition and Subtraction of Decimals.   Once again alignment is the key to success. Watch how the place values are lined up. Be sure to align the decimals vertically and add or subtract as if they were whole numbers.

Add 2.3 + .0067 + 364.023

$$
\begin{array}{r}
2.3 \\
.0067 \\
+\ 364.023 \\
\end{array}
$$

Align the decimals so that all place values are to be used like to like. Add "ghost" zeros as needed.

$$
\begin{array}{r}
2.3000\ \textit{(ghost terms)} \\
.0067 \\
+\ 364.0230 \\
\end{array}
$$

Add each column as in whole number addition carrying across the decimal.

$$
\begin{array}{r}
2.3000 \\
.0067 \\
+\ 364.0230 \\
\hline
366.3297 \\
\end{array}
$$

Be sure that the decimal is aligned in the answer (sum).

Add 47.006 + .56 + 8.1

You should have arrived at 55.666. If you did not achieve that answer review the steps presented in the example and double check your alignment of decimals and your use of "ghost" terms in the solution that follows:

$$
\begin{array}{r}
47.006 \\
.56 \\
+\ 8.1 \\
\hline
\end{array}
$$

$$
\begin{array}{r}
47.006 \\
.560 \\
+\ 8.100 \\
\hline
55.666 \\
\end{array}
$$

Let's learn the reverse process now: subtraction. You will see that the process for alignment is the same as for addition of decimals and that subtraction occurs as it does with whole number subtraction.

Subtract 23.08 − .0352

23.08 − .0352	Align the decimals so that all place values are to be used like to like. Add "ghost" zeros as needed.
23.08*00* − .0352	Subtract each column borrowing as necessary as in whole number subtraction.
23.08*00* − .0352 23.0448	Be sure that the decimal is aligned in the answer (difference).

Subtract 25.08 − .8023

You should have arrived at 24.2777. If you did not achieve that answer, review the steps presented and double check your alignment of decimals and use of "ghost" terms. Also re-examine your borrowing across zeros. The solution is presented below:

$$25.08\textit{00}$$
$$-\ 00.8023$$
$$24.2777$$

Multiplication of Decimals. Unlike in addition and subtraction, alignment does not matter when multiplying decimals. You will find that you multiply as with whole numbers. Once you have an answer (product), count the number of places behind the decimal in the factors and move the decimal from right to left in the product the same number of places.

Multiply 28.52 × .05

28.52 × .05	Write the problem. There is no reason to align the decimals.
28.52 × .05 1426	Write the product.
28.52 × .05 14260	Add up the places behind the decimal in the factors.
28.52 × .05 1.4260	Move the decimal from right to the left the same number of places.

Multiply 26.03 × .525

You should have arrived at 13.66575. If you did not achieve that answer review the steps presented and double-check your movement of the decimal in the answer. Remember in multiplication there is no need to align decimals. Double-check your multiplication and carrying across zeros. Here is the solution worked out for you:

$$
\begin{array}{r}
26.03 \\
\times\ .525 \\
\hline
13015 \\
52060 \\
+\ 1301500 \\
\hline
13.66575
\end{array}
$$

Division of Decimals. Having reviewed multiplication of decimals you will now be reminded of the steps of division. You discovered that you placed the decimal as the last step in the process. Division is the inverse of multiplication. Logically then you would deal with the decimal first. The important thing to remember is that you must have a whole number in the divisor. If it is a decimal number move the decimal to the right until it is next to the division brace. Then move the decimal the same number of places under the division brace, adding zeros as necessary.

Divide $3.15 \div .03$

$.03\overline{)3.15}$	Write the problem using the division brace.
$3\overline{)3.15.}$	Move the decimal in the divisor until it is next to the division brace.
$3\overline{)315}$	Move the decimal under the division brace the same number of spaces adding zeros if necessary.
$\dfrac{105}{3\overline{)315}}$	Divide as you would with whole numbers, adding zeros as necessary until the problem has a zero remainder or until the point you are being asked to round off to or the decimal repeats.

Divide $32.882 \div .02$

You should have arrived at 1644.1. If you did not achieve that answer, review the steps and double-check your movement of the decimal in the divisor. Other problem area may be placement of the numbers in the initial setup of the problem. Remember the placement of the numbers is crucial. The number you are dividing by (the number following the $\div$) is placed outside the division brace.

CONTENT AREA SIX: FRACTIONS

The key to all fractional operations is the number 1. One is defined as any number over itself such as:

$$
\frac{2}{2} \qquad \frac{550}{550}
$$

One is what allows us to reduce fractions, write equivalent fractions, change to common denominators, "cross-cancel" in multiplication, and to divide. The top number of a fraction is called the *numerator* and names how many parts of the fraction that you have. The bottom number of a fraction is called the *denominator,* and it denotes how many total pieces of the fraction are available. The various types of fractions are discussed here.

Proper Fractions

Fractions where the numerator is *smaller* than the denominator are referred to as "proper." Some examples are

$$\frac{7}{8} \qquad \frac{2}{3} \qquad \frac{3}{4}$$

Improper Fractions

Fractions where the numerator is *larger* than the denominator are referred to as "improper." Some examples are

$$\frac{12}{5} \qquad \frac{3}{2} \qquad \frac{5}{3}$$

To change an improper fraction to a mixed number, divide the numerator by the denominator. The answer (quotient) becomes the whole number, the remainder becomes the numerator of the fraction, and the number you have divided by (divisor) is the denominator of the fraction.

Example: Write $\frac{15}{4}$ as a mixed number.

$$\frac{15}{4} = 4\overline{)15}$$

The answer would be 3 with a remainder 3. The number you divided by was 4, so you write the mixed number as:

$$3\frac{3}{4}$$

Therefore, the mixed number would be $3\frac{3}{4}$.

Mixed Numbers

As you just witnessed, mixed numbers are a combination of whole numbers and fractions. Some examples are $1\frac{3}{4}$, $4\frac{3}{5}$, and $7\frac{1}{5}$. In multiplication and division of fractions, mixed numbers must be converted to fractions before use. To change a mixed number to a fraction, multiply the denominator by the whole number and add to the numerator (bottom times side, add to top). Then write over the denominator.

Write $3\frac{3}{4}$ as an improper fraction.

$$4 \times 3 = 12, \quad 12 + 3 = 15. \quad \text{The improper fraction would be } \frac{15}{4}.$$

Equivalent Fractions

Equivalent fractions are fractions that name the same amount. For example:

$$\frac{2}{3} \qquad \frac{4}{6}$$

They may appear to be different, but when these fractions are compared, they are identical. Another way to think about it is this: It makes no difference if you ate 2 out of 3 slices of pizza or 4 out of 6 slices, because you still have the same amount of pizza.

Here is a trick to test to see if factions are equal or not:

$$\frac{2}{3} \diagdown \frac{4}{6}$$

Multiply denominator to numerator and denominator to numerator again:

$3 \times 4 = 12; \quad 6 \times 2 = 12.$ Thus, they are both equal.

To discover if two fractions are equivalent, you will cross-multiply and compare the results. If equal, the fractions are equivalent. If not, one will either be greater than (>) or less than (<) the other. Let's see which fraction is larger here:

$$14 \quad \frac{2}{3} \diagdown \frac{4}{7} \quad 12$$

Which fraction is larger? $\frac{2}{3}$. How do you know? Because when you multiply 7×2, you get 14; when you multiply 3×4, you get 12. Since 14 arrives on the other side of two-thirds, it is the larger fraction. (*Note:* Be sure to go in the right direction when cross multiplying, or you'll mess up your answer. The order is always denominator to numerator for both fractions!)

Reducing Fractions

To reduce fractions you need to remove all the fractions of one. One method is to divide the numerator and denominator by the greatest common factor. Another method when the common factor isn't obvious is to factor to primes and remove all fractions of one.

Reduce $\frac{36}{48}$

$\frac{36}{48} = \frac{2 \times 2 \times 3 \times 3}{2 \times 2 \times 2 \times 2 \times 3}$ Factor the numerator and denominator to primes.

$\frac{36}{48} = \frac{\cancel{2} \times \cancel{2} \times 3 \times \cancel{3}}{\cancel{2} \times \cancel{2} \times 2 \times 2 \times \cancel{3}}$ Cancel the common factors, until you can cancel no more.

$\frac{3}{2 \times 2}$ Multiply any remaining factors.

$\frac{3}{4}$ Your answer is the reduced fraction.

Reduce $\frac{28}{36}$

The correct answer would be $\frac{7}{9}$. When factoring to primes you would have $\frac{2 \times 2 \times 7}{2 \times 2 \times 3 \times 3}$. You will note that there are two examples of fractions of one: $\frac{2}{2}$ and $\frac{2}{2}$. Therefore we have $\frac{7}{3 \times 3}$. Multiplying we are left with $\frac{7}{9}$.

Multiplication of Fractions

Multiplying fractions is simple: *top × top and bottom × bottom.* But let's qualify "simple." You can only multiple *fractions!* If the number is mixed, then you have to change it to an improper faction, then top × top and bottom × bottom. For example:

$$\frac{3}{7} \times \frac{2}{5} = \frac{6}{35}$$

Once this step is completed the pattern is simple, just like we said it was: *top × top and bottom × bottom.* This can get complicated if the numerators and denominators are really large, as in:

$$\frac{120}{234} \times \frac{140}{456} = \frac{16800}{106704}$$

As you can see, multiplying 120 × 140 and 234 × 456 will give you really large numbers and take a large amount of time. That's why we have "cross-canceling." It allows you to reduce the fractions before you multiply thus saving time and reducing the potential for mistakes (see Cross-Canceling Common Factors).

<table>
<tr><td></td><td>Multiply $\frac{2}{3} \times \frac{1}{5}$</td></tr>
<tr><td>$\frac{2 \times 1}{3 \times 5}$</td><td>Writing horizontally often reduces mistakes.</td></tr>
<tr><td>$\frac{2 \times 1 = 2}{5 \times 3 = 15}$</td><td>top × top (numerator × numerator)
bottom × bottom (denominator × denominator)</td></tr>
<tr><td>$\frac{2}{15}$</td><td>Write the answer in simplified (reduced) form.</td></tr>
</table>

Now, transfer this knowledge to the problem below.

Multiply $\frac{1}{3} \times \frac{2}{7}$

The answer is $\frac{2}{21}$. If you did not get that answer, go back and review the master pattern for multiplication of fractions. Remember the pattern: top times top; bottom times bottom. Here is the solution worked for you:

$$\frac{1 \times 2}{3 \times 7} = \frac{2}{21}$$

Fractions with Mixed Numbers and Whole Numbers

To offer you a challenge, the next example shows you how to multiply fractions with mixed numbers. Remember: You can only multiply fractions, so all mixed numbers and whole numbers must be converted to fractions before use in multiplication.

<table>
<tr><td></td><td>Multiply $1\frac{1}{4} \times \frac{1}{3} \times 7$</td></tr>
<tr><td>$1\frac{1}{4}$ is a mixed number</td><td>Change a mixed number into a fraction by multiplying the denominator by the whole number and adding to the numerator. Place it over the denominator.</td></tr>
<tr><td>$(4 \times 1) + 1 = 5$

$\frac{5}{4}$</td><td></td></tr>
<tr><td>$\frac{7}{1}$

$\frac{5}{4} \times \frac{1}{3} \times \frac{7}{1}$</td><td>Whole numbers must be converted to fractions before multiplying.</td></tr>
<tr><td>$5 \times 1 \times 7 = 35$</td><td>Multiply the numerators.</td></tr>
<tr><td>$4 \times 3 \times 1 = 12$</td><td>Multiply the denominators.</td></tr>
</table>

$\dfrac{35}{12}$ Write as a fraction (improper in this case).

$2\dfrac{11}{12}$ Change improper fraction to mixed number.

As you do the practice problem, carefully check to see if you have mixed numbers or whole numbers and be sure you change them to fractions first.

Multiply $2\dfrac{1}{3} \times \dfrac{1}{4} \times 7$

If you answer was $4\dfrac{1}{12}$, you did the work correctly. If your answer was $\dfrac{49}{12}$, you didn't change it from an improper fraction to a mixed number. This is the problem worked step by step:

$$2\dfrac{1}{3} \times \dfrac{1}{4} \times 7 \qquad \dfrac{7}{3} \times \dfrac{1}{4} \times \dfrac{7}{1} \qquad \dfrac{7}{3} \times \dfrac{1}{4} \times \dfrac{7}{1} = \dfrac{49}{12} \qquad 12\overline{)49} \qquad 4\dfrac{1}{12}$$

12 goes into 49 four times with a remainder of 1. Write the remainder over the divisor, which gives you $\dfrac{1}{12}$. Now using 4 as your whole, write the mixed number as $4\dfrac{1}{12}$.

Cross-Canceling Common Factors.   You will recall that when we reduced fractions, we factored the numerator and denominator and "canceled" any pairs of numbers found on the top and the bottom. When we multiply fractions, we can apply the same principle to make them easier to work with. Note once again how the number 1 is woven through fraction operations. (Reminder: All mixed numbers and whole numbers must be expressed as fractions.)

Multiply $\dfrac{14}{15} \times \dfrac{5}{7}$

$\dfrac{2 \times 7}{3 \times 5} \times \dfrac{5}{7}$ Factor the numerators and denominators to primes.

$\dfrac{2 \times \cancel{7}}{3 \times \cancel{5}} \times \dfrac{\cancel{5}}{\cancel{7}}$ Identify the fractions of one.

$\dfrac{2 \times 1}{3 \times 1} \times \dfrac{1}{1}$ Replace the fractions of one with 1.

$\dfrac{2}{3}$ Follow the pattern of multiplication.

As you can see, cross-canceling makes finding the reduced answer so much easier.

Addition and Subtraction of Fractions

You probably remember that when you add fractions, you have to make the denominators the same. For example, you can add (or subtract)

$\dfrac{3}{5} + \dfrac{4}{5}$

to get $\dfrac{7}{5}$, but you cannot add (or subtract)

$\dfrac{3}{5} + \dfrac{4}{7}$

yet, because the denominators are not the same. The process to set up fractions for addition and subtraction are the same. The rule in the most basic language is this: When the bottoms are the same you can add or subtract the tops. If the bottoms are not the same, you must find a new bottom. Mathematically it can be stated: When the denominators are the same, you may add or subtract the numerators. If the denominators are not the same, *then you must find a common denominator.* If you know the concept of fractions of one and can count, you have all the skills needed to add or subtract fractions. As you follow the process presented next, note how we use the identity property of multiplication to guarantee that the fraction we end with has the exact same value as the fraction we start with.

Add $\frac{3}{4} + \frac{2}{3}$

$$\begin{array}{r} \frac{3}{4} \\[4pt] + \ \frac{2}{3} \end{array}$$

Rewrite the problem in an easier form to work with.

$$\begin{array}{rc} \frac{3}{4} & 12 \\[4pt] + \ \frac{2}{3} & 12 \end{array}$$

The denominators are not the same, so a new common denominator must be located. *Hint:* When in doubt count by the smaller until the larger will divide it.

$$\begin{array}{rc} \frac{3}{4} \times \frac{3}{3} = & 12 \\[6pt] + \ \frac{2}{3} \times \frac{4}{4} = & 12 \end{array}$$

Ask yourself, $4 \times ? = 12$ and create a fraction of one. Do the same for the second fraction.

$$\begin{array}{rc} \frac{3}{4} \times \frac{3}{3} = & \frac{9}{12} \\[6pt] + \ \frac{2}{3} \times \frac{4}{4} = & \frac{8}{12} \end{array}$$

Multiply the numerators.

Multiply the denominators.

$$\begin{array}{rc} \frac{3}{4} \times \frac{3}{3} = & \frac{9}{12} \\[6pt] + \ \frac{2}{3} \times \frac{4}{4} = & \frac{8}{12} \\[6pt] \hline & \frac{17}{12} \end{array}$$

The denominators are now the same so the numerators may be added.

$\frac{17}{12}$

Is the answer a proper or improper fraction? If proper, reduce if possible.

improper $17 \div 12$

If improper, make into a mixed number and reduce if possible.

$1\frac{5}{12}$

Add $\frac{5}{6} + \frac{3}{4}$

The result should be $1\frac{1}{2}$. If your answer differed, let's examine the solution:

$$\begin{array}{r} \frac{5}{6} \\[4pt] + \ \frac{3}{4} \\ \hline \end{array} \qquad \begin{array}{l} \frac{5}{6} \times \frac{4}{4} = \frac{20}{24} \\[6pt] + \ \frac{3}{4} \times \frac{6}{6} = \frac{18}{24} \\ \hline \end{array} \qquad \frac{38}{24} \qquad 1\frac{7}{12}$$

Subtraction of Fractions. Subtraction of fractions sets up identically to addition. You simply subtract the numerators. There is a twist when it comes to borrowing. Just remember this simple rule: When you have converted to common denominators and need to borrow, subtract one from the whole number and, in the fraction, add the denominator to the numerator. This effectively adds in the one you borrowed without the necessity of converting it to a fraction of one.

$$4\frac{1}{3} - \frac{3}{4}$$

$4\frac{1}{3}$

$-\frac{3}{4}$

Rewrite the problem in standard format.

$4\frac{1}{3} \times \frac{4}{4} = \frac{4}{12}$

$-\frac{3}{4} \times \frac{3}{3} = \frac{9}{12}$

If the denominators are not the same, go through the same steps as if it were an addition problem.

$4\frac{1}{3} \times \frac{4}{4} = \frac{4}{12}$

$-\frac{3}{4} \times \frac{3}{3} = \frac{9}{12}$

If you have 4 you cannot subtract 9, so you must borrow from the whole number.

$\overset{3}{\cancel{4}}\frac{1}{3} \times \frac{4}{4} = \frac{4}{12}$

$-\frac{3}{4} \times \frac{3}{3} = \frac{9}{12}$

Next—To add in what you borrowed, add the denominator to the numerator in the top fraction.

$\overset{3}{\cancel{4}}\frac{1}{3} \times \frac{4}{4} = \frac{16}{12}$

$-\frac{3}{4} \times \frac{3}{3} = \frac{9}{12}$

Now you can subtract the numerators.

$\overset{3}{\cancel{4}}\frac{1}{3} \times \frac{4}{4} = \frac{16}{12}$

$-\frac{3}{4} \times \frac{3}{3} = \frac{9}{12}$

$3 \qquad \frac{7}{12}$

Double check and see if you can reduce (simplify) the remainder.

Subtract $5\frac{1}{2} - \frac{4}{5}$

As a result of your calculations, you should have arrived at $4\frac{7}{10}$. The step-by-step solution looks like this:

$5\frac{1}{2}$ $\qquad$ $5\frac{1}{2} \times \frac{5}{5} = \frac{5}{10}$ $\qquad$ $\overset{4}{\cancel{5}}\frac{1}{2} \times \frac{5}{5} = \frac{15}{10}$

$-\frac{4}{5}$ $\qquad$ $-\frac{4}{5} \times \frac{2}{2} = \frac{8}{10}$ $\qquad$ $-\frac{4}{5} \times \frac{2}{2} = \frac{8}{10}$ $\qquad$ $4\frac{7}{10}$

Division of Fractions

Dividing fractions is just as easy as working with fractions that you multiply. But there is one additional step that you cannot forget. The pattern for dividing fractions is as follows: Once you have converted all mixed numbers and whole numbers to fractions, keep the first fraction the same, change sign of division to multiplication, and flip the second fraction over (reciprocal). Here is the pattern you should remember:

$$\frac{2}{3} \div \frac{5}{7}$$

Same: The first fraction remains the *same*. $\frac{2}{3} \div \frac{5}{7}$

Times: The sign $\div$ changes to *times*. $\frac{2}{3} \times \frac{5}{7}$

Flip: Write the *reciprocal* of the second fraction. $\frac{2}{3} \times \frac{7}{5}$

$\frac{12}{5} \div \frac{3}{4}$	Change any mixed numbers or whole numbers to fractions.
$\frac{12}{5} \times \frac{4}{3}$	SAME, TIMES, FLIP
$\frac{4 \cancel{12}}{5} \times \frac{4}{\cancel{3}1}$	You can cross cancel in the presence of multiplication.
$\frac{16}{5}$	Multiply as indicated.
$3\frac{1}{5}$	If Improper, change to a mixed number and simplify if possible.

Divide $4\frac{1}{2} \div \frac{3}{4}$

You have completed the practice problem and if your answer was 3, you have just graduated from domain one. The solution looks like this:

$$4\frac{1}{2} \div \frac{3}{4} \qquad \frac{9}{2} \div \frac{3}{4} \qquad \frac{9}{2} \times \frac{4}{3} \qquad \frac{(\cancel{3})(3)}{(\cancel{2})(1)} \times \frac{(\cancel{2})(2)}{(\cancel{3})(1)} \qquad \frac{6}{1} = 6$$

Algebra and Functions[1]

CONTENT AREA SEVEN: TERMS IN ALGEBRA

Symbols of operations like addition, subtraction, multiplication, and division are the "action words" of the algebraic sentence; subjects are numbers or letters; and modifiers are the grouping symbols. Like terms of equations can be combined in the same manner that we use conjunctions. Before the fun begins, a brief review of operations with signed numbers is called for.

Addition of Signed Numbers

There are questions associated with adding signed numbers (see Table 15.1).

1. Are the signs the same?
2. If your answer is "yes," add and keep the sign.
3. If your answer is "no," subtract and take the sign of the larger number.

TABLE 15.1

$5 + 3$	Signs are the same.	8	Took the sign they shared.
$-5 + -3$	Signs are the same.	-8	Took the sign they shared.
$-5 + 3$	Signs are not the same.	-2	Took the sign of the larger number.
$5 + -3$	Signs are not the same.	2	Took the sign of the larger number.

Subtraction of Signed Numbers

Subtraction is simply a step of rewriting the problem as addition (see Table 15.2). We redefine the sign of subtraction (minus) as *plus the opposite of what follows* and then follow the rules of addition as stated above.

TABLE 15.2

$5 - 3$	5 plus the opposite of 3	$5 + (-3)$	using addition	2
$5 - (-3)$	5 plus the opposite of -3	$5 + 3$	using addition	8
$-5 - 3$	-5 plus the opposite of 3	$-5 + -3$	using addition	-8
$-5 - (-3)$	-5 plus the opposite of -3	$-5 + 3$	using addition	-2

Multiplication and Division of Signed Numbers

The rules for multiplication and division are the same (see Table 15.3). If the signs are the same the answer is positive, if the signs are *not* the same the answer is negative. (*Note:* Division works in an identical matter with the same rules.)

[1]Chapter contributed by Charles Jackson.

TABLE 15.3

(5)(3)	Signs are the same; the answer is positive.	15
(−5)(−3)	Signs are the same; the answer is positive.	15
(5)(−3)	Signs are not the same; the answer is negative.	−15
(−5)(3)	Signs are not the same; the answer is negative.	−15

CONTENT AREA EIGHT: SOLVING EQUATIONS

Consider these equations: $x + y = 8$ and $x - y = 10$. Our job is to find x and y, so let's review how to arrive at the correct answer together before looking at them individually.

$$
\begin{array}{ll}
x + y = 8 & \\
+\ x - y = 10 & \text{We combine the information we have.} \\
\hline
2x\ \ \ \ = 18 & \text{We divide to discover } x \text{ and to eliminate a suspect.} \\
x\ \ \ \ = 9 &
\end{array}
$$

$$
\begin{array}{ll}
9 + y = 8 & \text{We substitute our discovery into the mystery's pattern.} \\
-9\ \ \ \ = -9 & \text{We subtract 9 from each side of the equation and discover that} \\
\hline
y = -1 & \text{the culprit is } -1.
\end{array}
$$

Here is the process illustrated again.

	Reasoning:
Solve: $2x - 3y = 6$ and $4x - y = 9$	
$2x - 3y = 6$ $-4x - y = 9$	Align like terms so that may be added, subtracted, or multiplied.
To eliminate x I could multiply the whole top by 2. To eliminate y I would need to multiply the whole bottom by −3. Multiplying by 2 is easier.	Examine to see what "suspect" can be most easily eliminated.
$(2)2x - (2)3y = (2)6$ $-\ \ \ 4x - \ \ \ y = \ \ \ 9$	Multiply the whole top by 2.
$4x - 6y = 12$ $-4x - y = 9$	Add to remove the x.
$-7y = 21$ $y = -3$	We divide to discover y and eliminate a suspect.
$4x - 6(-3) = 12$	We now know y and can discover x by substituting and multiplying.
$4x + 18 = 12$ $4x\ \ \ \ = -6$	Subtract.
$x = -\dfrac{6}{4}$, or $-1\dfrac{1}{2}$	Divide and reduce if necessary.

As you begin the practice problem observe how the process removes one variable and moves all numbers to one side of the equals sign and then substitutes to find the remaining variable.

$3a + 4b = 9$ and $2a + 2b = 6$

You should have arrived at $a = 3$ and $b = 0$. If your answer was $-a = -3$, remember that you cannot have an answer with a negative variable in the answer and must multiple both sides of the equation by -1 to resolve the issue. Here is how the problem plays out step by step:

$$3a + 4b = 9$$
$$2a + 2b = 6$$

You could choose to eliminate either the a term or the b term. The results will be identical. For my purposes I chose to eliminate the b term because it involves less work. To do that I multiply through by -2.

$$3a + \quad 4b = \quad 9$$
$$(-2)2a + (-2)2b = (-2)6$$

$$3a + \quad 4b = \quad 9$$
$$-4a + -4b = -12$$
$$-a \qquad = -3$$
$$a = \quad 3$$

Now we substitute back into one of the equations. I choose to use the second one.

$$2a + 2b = 6$$
$$2(3) + 2b = 6$$
$$6 + 2b = 6$$
$$-6 \qquad -6$$
$$2b = 0$$
$$\frac{2b}{2} = \frac{0}{2}$$
$$b = 0$$

Which variable did you choose to eliminate? Did you distribute any multiplication to all terms of the equation? Did you then add or subtract? Once you had a solution, did you substitute back in to find the other variable?

Another way to find out the variables is to solve one of the equations and substitute. Let's take the previous practice problem and see if it works.

Solve: $3a + 4b = 9$ and $2a + 2b = 6$. (*Hint:* Look for the easiest variable to solve for.)

Step 1.
$$2a + \quad 2b = 6$$
$$\quad - 2b \quad - 2b$$
$$2a \qquad = 6 - 2b$$
Solve for a since it is the easiest.

Step 2.
$$2a = 6 - 2b$$
$$2a(\div 2) = 6(\div 2) - 2b(\div 2)$$
Divide both sides of the equation by 2.

Step 3.
$$a = 3 - b$$
You now know what a is equal to.

Step 4.
$$3a + 4b = 9$$
Write the first equation.

Step 5.
$$3(3 - b) + 4b = 9$$
Substitute and distribute.

Step 6.
$$9 - 3b + 4b = 9$$
$$9 + b = 9$$
$$b = 0$$
Solve for b.

Step 7.	$2a + 2b = 6$	Write the second equation.
Step 8.	$2a + 2(0) = 6$	Substitute and distribute.
Step 9.	$2a = 6$	Solve for a.
	$a = 3$	

Now try your hand at solving these two linear equations using the second method:

$x - y = 5$ and $2x + 3y = 0$

You should have arrived at the answer $x = 3$, $y = -2$. If you didn't get that result, compare the steps of your work against the solution to find what needs to be changed.

Solve the easiest equation for the easiest variable:

$$x = y + 5$$

Substitute into the second equation.

$$2(y + 5) + 3y = 0$$
$$2y + 10 + 3y = 0$$
$$5y + 10 = 0$$
$$\underline{-10 \quad -10}$$
$$5y = -10$$

$$\frac{5y}{5} = \frac{-10}{5}$$

$$y = -2$$

Substitute back to calculate x.

$$x = -2 + 5$$
$$x = 3$$

CONTENT AREA NINE: MONOMIALS

Monomials contain only one variable or one self-contained set of variables. The key is to remember that only like terms may be added or subtracted. For example $4ab + 3ab$ are like terms and can be added to equal $7ab$. The following terms may look the same but they are not:

ab^2	a^2b	$(ab)^2$	Lets say that $a = 3$ and $b = 4$. Look at the difference in the values.
ab^2	$(3)(4)(4)$		$= 48$
a^2b	$(3)(3)(4)$		$= 36$
$(ab)^2$	$[(3)(4)][(3)(4)]$		$= 144$

Addition of Monomials

Only ab^2 may be combined with ab^2; a^2b with a^2b; and $(ab)^2$ with $(ab)^2$. They function as place value would in whole numbers.

Add $3n^2 + 2n + 7$ and $8n^2 + 15$

$$\begin{array}{r} 3n^2 + 2n + 7 \\ +\ 8n^2 + 15 \\ \hline \end{array}$$ Align like terms.

$$\begin{array}{r} 3n^2 + 2n + 7 \\ +\ 8n^2 + 0n + 15 \\ \hline \end{array}$$ Insert ghost terms for place holders.

$$\begin{array}{r} 3n^2 + 2n + 7 \\ +\ 8n^2 + 0n + 15 \\ \hline 11n^2 + 2n + 22 \end{array}$$ Add only the like terms. This is as far as one can go unless the value of n is known.

As you practice with the problem below be sure to align like terms.

Add $4y^3 + 5y$ and $7y^2 + 9y + 32$

If you arrived at $4y^3 + 7y^2 + 14y + 32$, your answer is correct. Did you insert ghost terms to fill in the blanks?

$$\begin{array}{r} 4y^3 + 5y \\ +\ 7y^2 + 9y + 32 \\ \hline \end{array}$$ $$\begin{array}{r} 4y^3 + 0y^2 + 5y + 0 \\ 0y^3 + 7y^2 + 9y + 32 \\ \hline \end{array}$$ $$\begin{array}{r} 4y^3 + 0y^2 + 5y + 0 \\ 0y^3 + 7y^2 + 9y + 32 \\ \hline 4y^3 + 7y^2 + 14y + 32 \end{array}$$

Subtraction of Monomials

Subtraction of monomials is as easy as addition. You may need to insert a ghost term to hold a place that is not filled with a like term. Observe what occurs when the sign of subtraction is redefined. In algebra we alter the meaning of the sign of subtraction to read "plus the opposite of." Remember there is no borrowing in monomial subtraction.

Subtract $8n^2 + 15$ from $3n^2 + 2n + 7$.

$$\begin{array}{r} 3n^2 + 2n + 7 \\ -(8n^2 + 0n + 15) \\ \hline \end{array}$$ Align the like terms being careful that the first expression listed is on top. Add ghost terms if you need place holders.

$$\begin{array}{r} 3n^2 + 2n + 7 \\ +\ {-}8n^2 + {-}15 \\ \hline \end{array}$$ Translate the sign of subtraction to "plus the opposite of" and rewrite changing signs as needed.

$$\begin{array}{r} 3n^2 + 2n + 7 \\ +\ {-}8n^2 + {-}15 \\ \hline -5n^2 + 2n - 8 \end{array}$$ Subtract only like terms. This is as far as you can go unless you are given the value of n.

Now, try to apply your understanding to the practice problem.

Subtract $12n^2 + 6n - 15$ from $9n^2 - 2n + 25$

The answer is $-3n^2 - 8n + 40$. If your answer differs, check your steps compared to the solution below paying close attention to the alignment of like terms and the redefinition of the meaning of the sign of subtraction. Did you align the like terms being careful that the first expression listed is on top? Add ghost terms if you need place holders.

$$\begin{array}{r} 9n^2 - 2n + 25 \\ -(12n^2 + 6n - 15) \\ \hline \end{array}$$ $$\begin{array}{r} 9n^2 - 2n + 25 \\ -12n^2 - 6n + 15 \\ \hline -3n^2 - 8n + 40 \end{array}$$

Multiplication of Monomials

Multiplication of monomials is going to look very familiar. You will remember in domain one we discussed the Distributive Property. This property allows us to multiply across addition or subtraction. For example 3(36) can be written as $3(30 + 6)$. When we distribute, we have $90 + 18$, which equals 108. That same principle applies to monomials. Remember, the key idea is Distributive Property. As you look at the problem below observe how each step plays out.

$5(n - 7)$
$5(n) - 5(7)$ the distributive step
$5n - 35.$

Even when it gets complicated in a problem such as this, don't despair. You should fall back on what you know how to do. Remember the exponent tells us how many times to use the base. (*Hint:* Count how many times a variable is used.)

$5(x^2y^3)^4$
$5(x^2y^3)(x^2y^3)(x^2y^3)(x^2y^3)$ Note how the exponent repeats the term.
$5x^8y^{12}$ Observe how the x's and y's are counted.

Let's take these basic skills into a more complicated problem:

Multiply:	Reasoning:
$5y^2(8x^5y^4)$	
40	Multiply the coefficients.
$40x^5y^6$	Add the powers of each variable.

$7n^3(3m^4n^7)$

If you arrived at $21m^4n^{10}$, you are right. If you have a different answer, check the multiplication of the coefficients and the addition of the powers. Did you distribute multiplying the coefficients? Did you add the exponents of like variables? Check those steps as you look at the solution.

$7n^3(3m^4n^7)$ $7(3)(m^4)(n^3)(n^7)$ $21m^4n^{3+7}$ $21m^4n^{10}$

Division of Monomials

Remember fractions? What would you do with a fraction like this: $\frac{8}{4}$? Divide bottom into the top, right? You have just divided your first "monomial." The only tricky part is working with the power, but you know the secret already. If you add the powers in multiplication you must subtract them during division. Multiplication and division are opposite operations after all.

$\dfrac{15a^4b^7}{3a^2b^3c^2}$

$\dfrac{5a^4b^7}{a^2b^3c^2}$ First divide the coefficients if possible.

$\dfrac{5a^2b^4}{c^2}$ Subtract the variables of the like terms. For example $4 - 2 = 2$. So we have a^2, and it stays on top because that's where the higher power was. There was no like term for the c^2, so it stays below and unused.

$$\frac{8b^25d^2}{2b^5d^2}$$

If you arrived at $\frac{20}{b^3}$ you have the correct answer. Did you divide the coefficients? Did you subtract the exponents of like variables? Check these questions against the solution below:

$$\frac{8b^25d^2}{2b^5d^2} \qquad \frac{8b^25d^2}{2b^5d^2} \qquad \frac{8b^2}{2b^5} \times \frac{5d^2}{d^2} \qquad \frac{4}{b^3} \times \frac{5}{1} \qquad \frac{20}{b^3}$$

CONTENT AREA TEN: POLYNOMIALS

A polynomial is an expression that contains two or more terms. For example: $2n + 3m + 7$ is a polynomial because it contains three terms. Remember that an expression has no equals sign, but an equation has one. A polynomial that contains a variable to the first power such as y^1 or y can be a linear equation; if it contains a variable to a power greater than 1 such as y^2, it's not. Polynomials, *like whole numbers,* can be added, subtracted, multiplied, and divided. The method may not seem obvious at first, but it works very much like whole number operations. In addition and subtraction we operate with like terms, in multiplication we distribute, and in division we multiply and subtract. In some ways it makes more logical sense than using the basic operations in whole numbers. For example, there is no carrying or borrowing and that in turn simplifies multiplication and division.

Addition and Subtraction of Polynomials

If one can add and subtract monomials, addition and subtraction of polynomials is rather easy. The rules are the same as with monomials. You must remember to align like terms, use ghost terms for place holders, and remember that there is no carrying in addition or borrowing in subtraction. Be very careful with subtraction—recall that in algebra its meaning changes to "plus the opposite of."

$$(-2x^3 + 5x^2 - 4x + 8) - (-2x^3 + 3x - 4)$$
$$-2x^3 + 5x^2 - 4x + 8$$
$$\underline{2x^3 + 0x^2 - 3x + 4}$$

The answer for the practice problem is $5x^2 - 7x + 12$. If your solution was different, double check your work for the alignment of the like terms and the redefinition of the meaning of the sign of subtraction. Did you use ghost terms as necessary? Did you only combine like terms?

Multiplication of Polynomials

There are two methods that can be used for the multiplication of polynomials. One method will look very familiar because it mirrors the multiplication of whole numbers. The second method uses an acronym to remember the pattern. Let's consider the most familiar one first. You will remember doing problems like this:

$$\begin{array}{r} 235 \\ \times\, 47 \\ \hline \end{array}$$

Remember how we would multiply through by 7 and get a partial product. Then we multiplied by 4 and added our partial products? The process is the same with multiplication of polynomials.

$$
\begin{array}{llll}
a + 3 & a + 3 & a + 3 & a + 3 \\
\underline{a - 5} & \underline{a - 5} & \underline{a - 5} & \underline{a - 5} \\
 & -5a - 15 & -5a - 15 & -5a - 15 \\
 & & \underline{a^2 + 3a} & \underline{a^2 + 3a} \\
 & & & a^2 - 2a - 15
\end{array}
$$

Remember the rules for multiplication of signed numbers (see Table 15.4).

TABLE 15.4   Multiplication and Division of Signed Numbers

The rules for multiplication and division are the same.
If the signs are the same the answer is positive.
If the signs are *not* the same the answer is negative.

Examples:

(5)(3)	Signs are the same, the answer is positive.	15
(−5)(−3)	Signs are the same, the answer is positive.	15
(5)(−3)	Signs are not the same, the answer is negative.	−15
(−5)(3)	Signs are not the same, the answer is negative.	−15

Division works in an identical matter with the same rules.

Multiply: Reasoning:

$(b + 7)(b^2 - 4)$

$$
\begin{array}{l}
b + 7 \\
\underline{b^2 - 4}
\end{array}
$$

Set up the problem in standard form.

$$
\begin{array}{l}
b + 7 \\
\underline{b^2 - 4} \\
-4b - 28
\end{array}
$$

Multiply by the 4 as though it were in the "ones" place.
Remember the rules for multiplication of signed numbers.

$$
\begin{array}{l}
b + 7 \\
\underline{b^2 - 4} \\
-4b - 28 \\
\underline{b^3 + 7b^2 }
\end{array}
$$

Multiply through by the next term.

$b^3 + 7b^2 - 4b - 28$ Add the partial products.

Keep in mind the rules for multiplication of signed numbers as you work the practice problem.

$(a^2 - 5)(a - 4)$

If your answer was $a^3 - 4a^2 - 5a + 20$, you did each step correctly.

$$
\begin{array}{l}
a^2 - 5 \\
\underline{a - 4} \\
-4a^2 + 0a + 20 \\
\underline{a^3 - 0a^2 - 5a + 0} \\
a^3 - 4a^2 - 5a + 20
\end{array}
$$

The FOIL Method of Multiplication of Polynomials

FOIL is the second method of multiplication of polynomials. It's an acronym for a pattern:

First	First Term	$\times$	First Term
Outer	Outer Term	$\times$	Outer Term
Inner	Inner Term	$\times$	Inner Term
Last	Last Term	$\times$	Last Term

Following the multiplication, you add the like terms of the partial products.

$(a + 3)(a - 5)$	First Term $\times$ First Term	a^2
	Outer Term $\times$ Outer Term	$-5a$
	Inner Term $\times$ Inner Term	$3a$
	Last Term $\times$ Last Term	-15
	Combine Like Terms	$a^2 \quad -2a \quad -15$

Division of Polynomials

The easiest type of problem in division with polynomials is when you divide by a monomial (single term). The reason being is that you can set it up as a fraction, and visually it is easier to work. The trick is to remember that each term on the top (numerator) is divided by the one on the bottom (denominator). For example:

$$(8a^2 - 4a) \div 2a = \frac{8a^2 - 4a}{2a} = \frac{8a^2}{2a} - \frac{4a}{2a} = 4a - 2$$

As you can see, $(8a^2 - 4a) \div 2a$ becomes a simple fraction that we can work with:

$$\frac{8a^2 - 4a}{2a}$$

Now, remember all of those properties that you memorized earlier in domain one? This is the distributive property. This property lets us simplify the equation even further:

$$\frac{8a^2}{2a} - \frac{4a}{2a}$$

Look at all those numbers that are divisible by $2a$! See? Now you can cancel and reduce until you are left with

$$4a - 2$$

With tricks like these, you'll have no problem on the test.

$$(9b^3 + 18b^2) \div 3b^2$$

$\dfrac{9b^3 + 18b^2}{3b^2}$ A division problem can be rewritten in fractional form.

$\dfrac{9b^3}{3b^2} + \dfrac{18b^2}{3b^2}$ Each term is to divided by the denominator so the problem can be separated into its individual components.

$3b + 6$ Divide each term by the denominator.

$$(12x^5 - 9x^4) \div 3x^3$$

The answer to the practice problem is $4x^2 - 3x$. Did you divide each coefficient by 3? Did you subtract the exponents of the x terms?

Here are the steps to solution:

$\dfrac{12x^5}{3x^3} - \dfrac{9x^4}{3x^3}$ Rewrite the division problem in fractional form.

$4x^2 - 3x$ Divide each term by the denominator.

Division of a Polynomial by a Polynomial. Division of a polynomial by a polynomial is a little more complicated than dividing by a monomial, but the format will seem very familiar and it will help make the process easier. As with so many operations, with polynomials you will have to be careful with your signs. Remember that when you subtract, signs must be changed because the minus sign has been redefined as "plus the opposite of." One additional caution: You may have to add in "ghost" terms to hold places in the problem as in the example.

To work these problems you will use your old friend from elementary school, the division brace.

$(25a^2 + 15a + 25) \div a + 5$

$a + 5\overline{)25a^2 + 15a + 25}$ First write the equation in standard division format. Remember the number you are dividing by (the one after the sign of division) goes on the outside of the division brace. For the first step ask yourself, "What can you multiply by to get rid of $25a^2$?" $5a$. Write that directly above the $25a^2$. Then multiply $5a(a + 5)$ using the Distributive Property.

$$\begin{array}{r} 5a \ - \ 10 \\ a + 5\overline{)25a^2 + 15a + 25} \\ \underline{25a^2 + 25a} \\ +\text{-}25a^2 - 25a \\ \hline -10a + 25 \end{array}$$

Write your result directly under $25a^2 + 15a$ and subtract. Don't forget that subtraction will change the signs, create $+ -25a^2 -25a$. Do the math and bring down like in whole number division.

$$\begin{array}{r} 5a \ - \ 10 \\ a + 5\overline{)25a^2 + 15a + 25} \\ \underline{25a^2 + 25a} \\ +\text{-}25a^2 - 25a \\ \hline -10a + 25 \\ \underline{-10a + 25} \\ +10a - 50 \\ \hline -25 \end{array}$$

Now we repeat the process. Ask yourself "What can you multiply by to get rid of $-10a$?" The answer would be -10. Why -10? Because you have to take into consideration the sign change when you subtract and it now creates $+ 10a - 50$. Write -10 above $15a$ in the division brace and using the Distributive Property multiply $-10(a + 5)$. Write it under $-10a + 25$ and don't forget that subtraction will change the signs because subtraction in algebra means "plus the opposite of." Write the result as you would with whole number division. You will note we have a remainder.

Write a remainder in fractional form. $\dfrac{-25}{a+5}$

The answer is stated as $5a - 10\dfrac{-25}{a+5}$.

In the following example, you will see how ghost terms are inserted into polynomial division as explained above.

Divide: $(a^3 - a) \div (a + 1)$

$a + 1\overline{)a^3 - a}$ Rewrite the problem using the division brace.

$a + 1\overline{)a^3 + 0a^2 - a}$ Notice that there is no a^2 term. A ghost term must take its place, $0a^2$.

$\begin{array}{r} a^2 \\ a + 1\overline{)a^3 + 0a^2 - a} \end{array}$ What would I multiply a by to eliminate the a^3? a^2. Write it above the a^3.

$\begin{array}{r} a^2 \\ a + 1\overline{)a^3 + 0a^2 - a} \\ \underline{-a^3 + a^2} \\ -a^3 - a^2 \\ \hline -a^2 \end{array}$ Multiply. Now, remembering that the minus sign means "plus the opposite of" change the necessary signs and add.

$\begin{array}{r} a^2 \\ a + 1\overline{)a^3 + 0a^2 - a} \\ \underline{-a^3 + a^2} \\ -a^3 - a^2 \\ \hline -a^2 - a \end{array}$ Bring down as you would in regular division.

$\begin{array}{r} a^2 - a \\ a + 1\overline{)a^3 + 0a^2 - a} \\ \underline{-a^3 + a^2} \\ -a^3 - a^2 \\ \hline -a^2 - a \\ \underline{a^2 + a} \\ 0 \end{array}$ What would you multiply a by to eliminate a^2? $-a$. Why $-a$? Because you have to take into consideration the sign change when you subtract, and it now creates $a^2 + a$.

$a^2 - a$ Check the remainder and, if there is one, write it in fractional form using the appropriate sign.

$(n^2 + 2n + 4) \div (n + 1)$

You should have arrived at $n + 1 + \frac{3}{n+1}$. Did you place the term after the $\div$ outside the division brace? Did you insert ghost terms as needed? Did you consider how to eliminate only the first term? Did you change signs of all terms as you subtracted (step 4 above). Did you repeat these steps as needed? Here is the problem worked step by step for you:

$\begin{array}{r} n + 1 \\ n + 1\overline{)n^2 + 2n + 4} \\ \underline{n^2 + n} \\ n^2 - n \\ \hline n + 4 \\ \underline{n + 1} \\ -n - 1 \\ \hline 3 \end{array}$

$n + 1 + \dfrac{3}{n+1}$

CONTENT AREA ELEVEN: SOLVING ADVANCED LINEAR EQUATIONS

You have experimented with a system of linear equations. Finding a solution to a single linear equation is even easier. To solve a linear equation you will be isolating the variable, step by step, moving all whole numbers to the other side of the equals sign. First distribute, if necessary, and then check each side individually for like terms. Following that, move the like terms of the variable to one side of the equals sign, if necessary, and combine them. Then you will undo any addition or subtraction, and then you will undo any multiplication or division.

$$2n + \underline{3(n - 3)} = 2n - 6 \quad \text{Distribute as needed.}$$

$$\underline{2n + 3n} - 9 = 2n - 6 \quad \text{Combine like terms on each side of the equals sign.}$$

$$\begin{aligned} 5n - 9 &= 2n - 6 \\ \underline{-2n} &\quad \underline{-2n} \end{aligned} \quad \begin{array}{l}\text{Move the variables to one side of the equals sign and} \\ \text{rewrite what remains.}\end{array}$$

$$\begin{aligned} 3n - 9 &= -6 \\ \underline{+ 9} &\quad \underline{+9} \end{aligned} \quad \begin{array}{l}\text{Undo any addition or subtraction using the inverse} \\ \text{operation and rewrite what is left over.}\end{array}$$

$$\frac{3n}{3} = \frac{3}{3} \quad \begin{array}{l}\text{Undo any multiplication or division using the inverse} \\ \text{operation.}\end{array}$$

$$n = 1$$

Try to solve the next equation.

$$2n - 5 + 4 = 7$$

$$2n - 1 = 7 \qquad\qquad \begin{array}{l}\text{Combine like terms on each side of the equals sign} \\ \text{separately. Then move across the equals sign as}\end{array}$$

$$\begin{aligned} 2n - 1 &= \quad 7 \\ \underline{+ 1} &\quad \underline{+1} \\ & \qquad 8 \end{aligned} \quad \begin{array}{l}\text{necessary. To solve an equation for a variable, you must} \\ \text{first undo any addition or subtraction.}\end{array}$$

$$\frac{2n}{2} = \frac{8}{2} \qquad\qquad \text{Then undo any multiplication or division.}$$

$$\begin{aligned} n &= 4 \\ 2(4) - 5 + 4 &= 7 \\ 8 - 5 + 4 &= 7 \\ 7 &= 7 \end{aligned} \quad \begin{array}{l}\text{When the variable is isolated you have discovered its} \\ \text{value. Mentally check to make sure your answer works.}\end{array}$$

$$3n + 3 = 5 - 2n + 23$$

Your answer should be $n = 5$. Did you combine like terms on each side of the = before attempting to solve? Did you undo any addition or subtraction before you undid any multiplication or division? What you did on one side of the = you did on the other?

Here is the problem worked step by step:

$$3n + 3 = 5 - 2n + 23 \quad \text{Distribute as needed (none indicated in this problem).}$$

$$3n + 3 = \underline{5} - 2n + \underline{23} \quad \text{Combine like terms on each side of the equals sign.}$$

$$\begin{aligned} 3n + 3 &= -2n + 28 \\ \underline{2n} &\quad + 2n \end{aligned} \quad \begin{array}{l}\text{Move the variables to one side of the equals sign and} \\ \text{rewrite what remains.}\end{array}$$

$5n + 3 = 28$
$\underline{ -3 -3}$

Undo any addition or subtraction using the inverse operation and rewrite what is left over.

$\dfrac{5n}{5} = \dfrac{25}{5}$

Undo any multiplication or division using the inverse operation.

$n = 5$

CONTENT AREA TWELVE: FACTORING POLYNOMIALS

Factoring with polynomials adds just one small step to solving of a linear equation: Think of it as removing common quantities from each term of an equation. Another way of viewing it is in terms of a multiplication problem. You are finding what was multiplied to get that answer. Consider this problem:

$3x^2 + 9x = 0$

You will notice that on the right side, both contain 3 and x. Factor them out.

$3x(x + 3) = 0$

You now have two equations that you can solve separately. $3x = 0$ and $x + 3 = 0$.

$3x = 0$

Solving the first, you discover that x can equal 0.

$x = 0$

$x + 3 = 0$

Solving the second, you discover that x can also equal -3.

$x = -3$

Both answers are equally valid solutions to the equation; thus, $x = 0$ and $x = -3$!

Keep the process illustrated above in mind as you copy each step and consider the reasoning behind the actions you take.

$4x^2 + 8x = 0$

Each term contains a multiple of 4 and of x

Find the common factors contained in each of the terms of the expression.

$4x(x + 2) = 0$

Remove the common factor from each term.

$4x = 0$

Write each equation and solve separately.

$x = 0$
and
$x + 2 = 0$
$x = -2$

$4(0)(0) + 8(0) = 0$
and
$4(-2)(-2) + 8(-2) = 0$
$16 + -16 = 0$

Check to see if your solutions are correct.

$5x^2 + 20x = 0$

Your solutions should have been $x = 0$ and $x = -4$. Here is the problem worked step by step:

$5x^2 + 20x = 0$
$5x(x + 4) = 0$
$5x = 0 \qquad\qquad x + 4 = 0$
$x = 0 \qquad\qquad x = -4$

Factoring Polynomials That Are the Difference of Two Squares

The difference of two squares is like having twins. One twin is "good" (positive) and the other is "bad" (negative). You can always recognize the difference of two squares in factoring because the terms are perfect squares separated by a minus sign. The examples below will help clarify.

$n^2 - 36$
$a^2 - b^2$
$25y^2 - 81$

In each sample, the first and the last term are perfect squares. Each of the perfect squares is separated by a minus sign. Once you can identify them as the difference of two squares, the pattern to solution is always the same. Notice the pattern that develops when we factor the examples above:

The "good twin" is	and	the "evil twin" is
$(n + 6)$		$(n - 6)$.
$(a + b)$		$(a - b)$.
$(5y + 9)$		$(5y - 9)$.

As you can see the terms are identical except that one is positive and the other negative.

$36b^2 - 9n^2$

You should have arrived at $(6b + 3n)(6b - 3n)$. If not, did you examine each term to see if each were a perfect square?

$36b^2$ is a perfect square $36 = (6)(6)$ and $x^2 = (x)(x)$

$9n^2$ is a perfect square $9n^2 = (3)(3)$ and $n^2 = (n)(n)$

They are separated by a minus sign, so they are the difference of two squares and there is a "good" twin and an "evil" twin: $(6b + 3n)(6b - 3n)$

Factoring a Polynomial with Three Terms

Factoring a polynomial with three terms is "unfoiling." You are given the answer and it will be your job to discover the first, outer, inner, and last terms and to determine what sign of operation (addition or subtraction) to be used. There are some basic patterns that will make your life easier. Consider these polynomials of three terms to see what patterns develop:

$a^2 + 8a + 15$

Because all of the terms are positive, I know that the pattern is $(a + 5)(a - 3)$. How were the numbers 3 and 5 arrived at? Ask yourself, "What two numbers when you multiply them give the answer of 15, but when added result in 8?" The only two numbers that meet that condition are 5 and 3. You will note that all terms are added in the original equation; therefore, all terms are added when the factoring is done.

Now consider this equation:

$a^2 - 8a + 15$

The second term is negative and the third term is positive. If you recall the rules for multiplication of signed numbers, you will recall that there are only two ways to multiply and have a positive result $(+)(+)$ or $(-)(-)$. If both terms were positive then the sign between the first and second terms would be positive. That isn't the case here. Further, if you recall the rules for addition of signed numbers, you will recall that only a negative plus a negative results in a negative. So, when you factor both numbers, the sign must be negative. The pattern in this case would be:

$(a - 5)(a - 3)$

Finally, consider this equation:

$a^2 + 2a - 15$

You will note that in this equation the second term is positive and the last is negative. This calls for an additional strategy. Focus first on the third term: 15. Here, you must ask yourself, "What two numbers if multiplied give 15 for an answer, but if added or subtracted result in 2?" Answering that question will give you the correct sign to use. There are only two possible pairs of factors that will result in 15: 1 and 15, and 3 and 5. Only one of those pairs is two apart, 3 and 5. Now look at the second term. If it is positive, then the larger number of your chosen pair is positive; if negative, the larger number is negative. In this problem your pattern would be $(a + 5)(a - 3)$.

$a^2 - 2a - 15$

As in the previous example, you must ask yourself, "What two numbers multiplied give you –15, but if added or subtracted result in –2?" Answering that question will give you the correct sign to use. Of the two possible pairs of factors that result in 15 only two are apart, 3 and 5. Is the second term negative? If so then the larger of the two factors must be negative. The pattern would be $(a - 5)(a + 3)$.

$b^2 - b - 20$
$b^2 - b - 20$ The first term must be b since $(b)(b) = b^2$.
$(b \quad)(b \quad)$
$b^2 - b - 20$ The only pair of factors that make 20 and are 1 apart are 4 and 5.
$(b \quad 4)(b \quad 5)$
$b^2 - b - 20$ Since the middle term is negative, then the largest of the factors of
$(b + 4)(b - 5)$ 20 must be negative.

$x^2 + 4x - 21$

Here is how the solution is reached:

$x^2 + 4x - 21$
$(x \quad)(x \quad)$ Did you see how x^2 contributes an x to each factor?
$(x \quad 7)(x \quad 3)$ Did you ask yourself what two numbers multiply to make 21, but have a difference of 3?
$(x + 7)(x - 3)$ Did you note in the original problem the $4x$ was positive and the 21 was negative? The only way to get a negative when multiplying is to have opposite signs (positive and negative). The middle term of the original was positive so the larger of the two numbers factored (7 and 3) must be positive.

The Quadratic Equation

Some polynomials are difficult to factor, because we cannot take them apart. To solve difficult polynomials, we must use the quadratic formula (aka quadratic equation) to do so. Let's see how we can actually do this and learn about parabolas while we're at it.

First, here is the standard form for the quadratic formula. You should memorize it.

$$x = \frac{-b \pm \sqrt{b^2 - 4ac}}{2a}$$

You may run into the term *discriminant* on the test. Just in case, here is what it is. See that "stuff" inside the $\sqrt{\ }$? The "stuff" beneath the radical is the *discriminant*. You may also be asked about what the significance is of the discriminant. Well, the discriminant (whatever number you get from taking the square root of $b^2 - 4a$) will tell you the type and number of answers that the quadratic formula will produce. There are three types of discriminant possibilities for you to memorize, just in case you are asked questions about them on the test:

- If the discriminant turns out to be positive, then you will have two solutions when you solve.
- If the discriminant is zero, then you will have one solution.
- If the discriminant is negative, then there are no real number answers to the equation.

Now, if you are asked to apply the quadratic formula to a polynomial, or if you find that you cannot factor a polynomial very easily, then use the steps below to execute the quadratic formula. It may help you solve polynomials more easily. Consider the polynomial below:

$$2x^2 = -x + 6$$

First, ask yourself: "Is this equation in the correct form of $ax^2 + bx + c = 0$?" If your answer is "no," what must you do to put it in the proper form? In the case of $2x^2 = -x + 6$, you must move the $-x$ and the 6 to the other side of the equals sign. This is done in the normal manner as previously explained in this domain. You would add x to both sides of the equation and subtract 6. These two moves result in:

$$2x^2 + x + (-6) = 0$$

Understand that $2x^2 + x + (-6) = 0$ is the same as $ax^2 + bx + c = 0$. Here is how each equation lines up:

$$2x^2 + x + (-6) = 0$$
$$ax^2 + bx + c = 0$$

Here, $a = 2$; $b = 1$ (if there's no number in front of the letter, its always one); and $c = -6$. These letters can now be plugged into the quadratic equation.

Second, it's time to "plug and play." Take the numbers that represent a, b, and c, the polynomial, and plug them into the quadratic formula.

Third, multiply everything inside the radical:

$$x = \frac{-b \pm \sqrt{b^2 - 4ac}}{2a} \text{ becomes } x = \frac{-1 \pm \sqrt{-1^2 - 4(2) \times (-6)}}{2(2)}$$

Fourth, add inside the radical: $x = \frac{-1 \pm \sqrt{1 + 48}}{4}$.

Fifth, arrive at the answer: $x = \frac{-1 \pm \sqrt{49}}{4}$.

Recall the information on the discriminant. Because the discriminant (the number under the radical) is positive (49), you will have two answers.

Sixth, take the square root of 49: $x = \frac{-1 \pm 7}{4}$.

Seventh, show both aspects of the ± sign. To do so, separate the answer into two expressions:

$$x = \frac{-1 + 7}{4} \quad and \quad x = \frac{-1 \, -7}{4}$$

Finally, we solve for each possible answer:

$$\frac{-1 + 7}{4} \quad or \quad \frac{6}{4} = \frac{3}{2} \quad and \quad \frac{-1 \, -7}{4} \quad or \quad \frac{-8}{4} = -2$$

Thus, $x = \frac{3}{2}$ and -2.

Find the values for x in the equation below.

$$-24x + 45 = -3x^2$$

Your answers should be $x = 5$ and $x = 3$. If your results differ, go back and check your solution step by step and refer to the sample problem above.

Before we leave the joys of quadratic equations, we need to end with a brief discussion of parabolas. Parabolas can either be up like a capital U, or down like an upside-down U. The sign of x^2 changes the direction of the parabola. If the sign is negative then it is upside down; if the sign is positive, then it is right side up.

Figure 15.1 shows a graph of the function $y = x^2 - 3$. Since x^2 is positive, the graph is right-side up. Notice how it is like a diver entering a pool, and at the bottom he surges to the top. The bottom of the graph shows the lowest point the diver reaches. This is the minimum or *lower bound* of the graph. A parabola that opens upwards shows a minimum value.

Figure 15.2 shows a graph of the function $y = -x^2 - 3$. Since $-x^2$ is negative, the graph is upside down.

This graph also shows a maximum value. It is like a quarterback throwing a pass. The highest point the ball reaches is the *upper bound,* or maximum value. A parabola that opens down shows a maximum value.

FIGURE 15.1

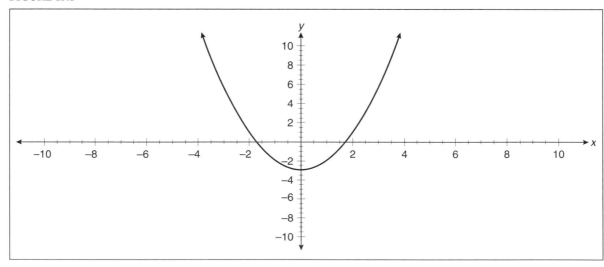

FIGURE 15.2

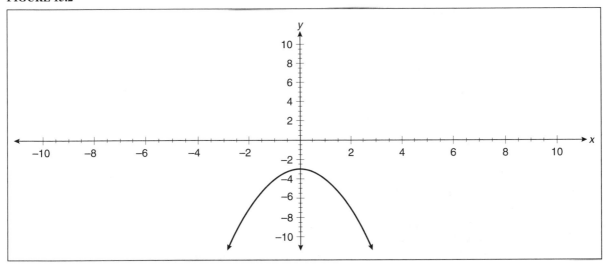

Algebraic Fractions

Surprisingly enough, fractions in algebra are actually easier that with everyday fractions. All the skills you have with them apply, but you no longer have to worry about mixed numbers, common denominators are easier to find, and reducing fractions is a snap. You will see how to add and subtract algebraic fractions first, before learning how to multiply and divide them.

Addition and Subtraction of Algebraic Fractions.   These are the guidelines for working with fractions as you know them. The rule in the most basic language is this: When the bottoms are the same, you can add or subtract the tops. If the bottoms are not the same, you must find a new bottom. Mathematically it can be stated: When the denominators are the same, you may add or subtract the numerators. If the denominators are not the same, *then you must find a common denominator.* If you know the concept of fractions of one and can count, you have all the skills needed to add or subtract fractions.

Let's see how these guidelines work within algebra. Remember that addition and subtraction of fractions set up in the same way, so only one sample will be developed. Consider this problem:

$\dfrac{x+5}{3x} + \dfrac{x+3}{x+1}$ The common denominator would be $3(x+1)$. Multiply each numerator by what is NOT included in the common denominator.

$(x+1)(x+5) + (3x)(x+3)$ You will see that you can rewrite the problem to make your life easier. Multiply as needed.

$(x^2 + 6x + 6) + (3x^2 + 9x)$ Combine like terms as you add.

$4x^2 + 15x + 6$ This is the end result.

The same process would occur with subtraction, except you would be subtracting the term. Be very careful to watch out for sign changes, since we are defining a "minus sign" as "plus the opposite of whatever comes next."

Use your knowledge gained from the addition problem above to do this problem. As you write each step, explain why you are doing it.

$\dfrac{x+5}{3x} - \dfrac{x+3}{x+1}$

Your answer should be $-2x^2 - 3x + 5$. Here are the steps to solution. Compare the steps shown with the explanation above.

$$\frac{x+5}{3x} - \frac{x+3}{x+1}$$

$$(x + 5)(x + 1) - (3x)(x + 3)$$

$$(x^2 + 6x + 5) - (3x^2 + 9x)$$

$$x^2 + 6x + 5 - 3x^2 - 9x$$

$$-2x^2 - 3x + 5$$

Multiplication of Algebraic Fractions.   Remember how we multiply and cancel with regular fractions:

- Multiplying fractions is simple: *top × top and bottom × bottom.*
- You will recall that when we reduced fractions, we factored the numerator and denominator and "canceled" any pairs of numbers found on the top and the bottom. When we multiply fractions, we can apply the same principle to make them easier to work with.
- Remember, when we reduce we factor out and remove fractions of ONE.

$$\frac{3x+15}{x+3} \times \frac{9x+27}{x+5}$$

$$\frac{3x+15}{x+3} \times \frac{9x+27}{x+5}$$
First, factor everything you can to see if you can cross-cancel. Note that 3 is the common factor in the first term and 9 is the common factor in the second. See in the next step how the factoring is shown.

$$\frac{3(x+5)}{x+3} \times \frac{9(x+3)}{x+5}$$
Look for the fractions of ONE: $\frac{x+3}{x+3}, \frac{x+5}{x+5}$.

$$\frac{3}{1} \times \frac{9}{1} = \frac{27}{1} \ or \ 27$$
Write what remains and multiply.

$$\frac{8x+24}{2x+10} \times \frac{x+7}{3x+9}$$

After you cross-canceled and multiplied your result should have been

$$\frac{4(x+7)}{3(x+5)} \ or \ \frac{4x+28}{3x+15}$$

The solution should look like this:

$$\frac{8x+24}{2x+10} \times \frac{x+7}{3x+9}$$

$$\frac{8(x+3)}{2(x+5)} \times \frac{x+7}{3(x+3)}$$
The $(x - 3)$ and the 8 and 2 cross cancel.

$$\frac{4}{x+5} \times \frac{x+7}{3}$$

$$\frac{4(x+7)}{3(x+5)} \quad or \quad \frac{4x+28}{3x+15}$$

Division of Algebraic Fractions. Dividing fractions is just as easy as working with fractions that you multiply. But there is one additional step that you cannot forget. The pattern for dividing fractions is as follows: Once you have converted all mixed numbers and whole numbers to fractions, keep the first fraction the same, change the sign of division to multiplication, and flip the second fraction over (reciprocal).

Same: The first fraction remains the *same.* $\dfrac{2}{3} \div \dfrac{5}{7}$

Times: The sign $\div$ changes to *times.* $\dfrac{2}{3} \times \dfrac{5}{7}$

Flip: Write the *reciprocal* of the second fraction. $\dfrac{2}{3} \times \dfrac{7}{5}$

Let's see how this process applies to division of algebraic fractions. I think you will find things very familiar. We have already touched on multiplication of algebraic fractions, so our only job is to set up the problem correctly. Follow the steps illustrated and compare them with what you already know.

$$\frac{8x + 24}{2x + 10} \div \frac{x + 7}{8x^2 + 40x}$$

$$\frac{8x + 24}{2x + 10} \div \frac{x + 7}{8x^2 + 40x}$$ Treat this like a regular fraction: Same, Times, Flip.

$$\frac{8x + 24}{2x + 10} \times \frac{8x^2 + 40x}{x + 7}$$ Factor if you can to locate fractions of ONE.

$$\frac{(2)(4)(x + 3)}{2(x + 5)} \times \frac{8x(x + 5)}{x + 7}$$ You have these fractions of ONE: $\dfrac{2}{2}$ and $\dfrac{x + 5}{x + 5}$.

$$\frac{4(x + 3)}{1} \times \frac{8x}{x + 7}$$ Multiply top times top and bottom times bottom.

$$\frac{32x^2 + 96x}{x + 7}$$

CONTENT AREA THIRTEEN: GRAPHING FUNCTIONS IN FOUR QUADRANTS

Graphing in four quadrants takes into account that not all solutions to equations fall directly on the number line. To account for that, a graph in four quadrants was devised. Imagine the routine number line starting at zero and expanding horizontally into infinity. All numbers to the right of zero marking moves in the positive direction and to the left moves in the negative. This is called the *x-axis* (see Figure 15.3). Now, picture a second number line at a right angle to the other with the same zero starting point extending vertically into infinity, the values ascending (positive) or descending (negative). This is the *y-axis.*

Since both begin at zero it is referred to as the origin, the starting point. You identify points on the graph by means of coordinates, which are merely directions to get to the "address" on the graph. Each quadrant (quarter) of the graph has a special name and a quality attached to its coordinates.

Coordinates

If you can find directions to someone's house, you can find your way around a graph in four quadrants. Each pair of coordinates (x, y) contains specific information for you to follow. The

FIGURE 15.3

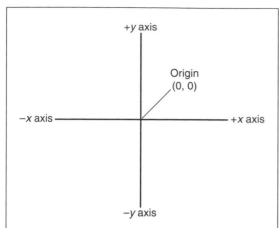

FIGURE 15.4

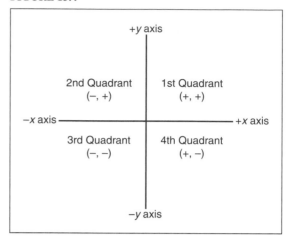

first coordinate is referred to as the *x*, and you move left (negative) or right (positive) from the origin, where the *x* and *y* axes intersect. The second coordinate is called the *y*, and it tells you where to move from the *x* coordinate. If it is negative you move down and if positive you move up.

Finding Line Equations

To find the equation of a line is a more complicated process. To start demystifying it, you need to understand the concept of slope. *Rise* is how far the one moves up or down from a point on the graph and *run* is the distance one moves left or right from that point. A slope can be positive, negative, or zero. It's easier to visualize it. Imagine you are driving a car. There are only so many directions one can drive in the real world. You can drive uphill, downhill, or on level ground. You will need to imagine driving from left to right. If you are driving uphill the slope is positive. If you are driving downhill left to right, the slope is negative. If you are driving on flat ground the slope is 0. If you find yourself driving vertically you are in real trouble, and the slope is declared as undefined.

Each point on a graph has a pair of coordinates. These coordinates are like directions given to drive somewhere in your car. The first direction (coordinate) given is always the *x*, and the second coordinate is always the *y*. When you have two in the same graph and a line runs through them, you can determine the slope of the line using the coordinates of those points. We will call them: (x_1, y_1) and (x_2, y_2). The subscripts are nothing mysterious. They designate only a position. So x_1 means that we are talking about the *x*-coordinate in the first pair, and y_2 means that we are discussing the *y*-coordinate in the second pair.

With this information we can expand the slope formula. Since the rise is the change (difference) in the *y*-coordinates, and the run is the change (difference) in the *x*-coordinates.

$$\text{Slope} = \frac{\text{rise}}{\text{run}} = \frac{y_2 - y_1}{x_2 - x_1}$$

Find the slope of a line passing through the points (1, –3) and (4, 3).

$$\text{Slope} = \frac{3 - (-3)}{4 - 1}$$

$$\text{Slope} = \frac{3 + 3}{4 - 1} \qquad \text{(Remember how to subtract negatives?)}$$

$$\text{Slope} = \frac{6}{3} = \frac{2}{1} \text{ or } 2$$

So the rise is 2 and the run is 1. In other words, from any point on the line, every time you go up 2, right 1 you will hit the line again. When given a whole number as a slope place it over one to test it. For example, if they give you a slope of –6, put it over one: $-\frac{6}{1}$. Now compare it to the picture they give you. From a point on the line, if you go down 6 and right 1 do you hit the line again? If so, that is the correct slope. Now test your skill.

> What is the slope of the line that passes through (–1, 4) and (3, 0)?

Your solution should be –1. If not, check your placement of number according to the slope formula:

$$\text{Slope} = \frac{y_2 - y_1}{x_2 - x_1} = \frac{0 - 4}{3 - (-1)} = \frac{-4}{4} = \frac{-1}{1} \quad or \quad -1$$

With the slope of the line and the point where the line intersects (crosses) the *y-axis*, some very helpful equations develop that can make our life much easier. They are Slope–Intercept, Point–Slope, and Standard form. We choose the form that is easiest given the information and we can move from one form to another.

Slope–Intercept Form of the Equation.   Use this pattern if you are given the slope of the line and the *y*-intercept.
   The master pattern for Slope–Intercept is $y = mx + b$

m is the slope of the line.
b is the point where the line crosses the *y-axis*.

Working with these equations is simply a matter of substitution and solving. You have all the skills to do this.

> Given *m* = 6 and *b* = –4, write the equation of the line in Slope–Intercept form.

$y = mx + 6$	Write the master pattern for Slope–Intercept.
$y = 6x + (-4)$	Substitute the values of *m* and *b* into the pattern.
$y = 6x - 4$	Resolve any problems with addition of negatives.

> Given *m* = 5 and *b* = –8, write the equation of the line in Slope–Intercept form.

After you substituted, you should have the equation $y = 5x - 8$. If not, go back and double-check your substitution.

$y = mx + b$
$m = 5$, place it in the *m*-position, and $b = -8$, place it in the *b*-position.
$y = 5x - 8$

Point–Slope Form of the Equation.   Use this pattern if you are given the slope of a line and one point. This again is a matter of substitution.
   The master pattern for Point–Slope is $y - y_1 = m(x - x_1)$

m	stands for the slope of the line.
(x_1, y_1)	is coordinate of a point on the line.
x and *y*	are the same variables as used in Slope–Intercept form.

If you are given a slope of $-3 (m)$ and a coordinate of 2, 4 (x_1, y), you can write the equation of the line using the Point–Slope pattern, $y - y_1 = m(x - x_1)$. Simply substitute.

$$y - y_1 = m(x - x_1)$$
$$y - 2 = -3(x - [2])$$
$$y - 2 = -3(x + 4)$$

Given the point (–4, 2) and the slope 2, determine the equation of the line in Point–Slope form.

$y - y_1 = m(x - x_1)$	Copy the master pattern for Point–Slope.
$y - 2 = 2(x - [-2])$	Substitute the values of the point and the slope in the appropriate positions.
$y - 2 = 2(x + 4)$	Before distributing, resolve any problems with addition or subtraction of negatives.

Given the point (–5, –7) and the slope –2, determine the equation of the line in Point–Slope form.

The equation in Point–Slope form would be $y + 7 = -2(x + 5)$. If you answer differs, let's solve it together.

$$y - y_1 = m(x - x_1)$$
$$m = -2$$
$$(x_1, y_1) = (-5, -7)$$

place the numbers in the Point-Slope formula

$$y + 7 = -2(x + 5)$$

The Distance Formula.   You have seen that to use the Slope, Point–Slope and Slope–Intercept formulas you plugged the coordinates in where they belonged and things happened in the appropriate order. There are other uses for the coordinates (x_1, y_1) and (x_2, y_2). You can discover the distance of a line and the midpoint of a line using the appropriate formula. These formulas are easy to use. They are what are referred to in this book as "plug and play" formulas.

The distance formula will give you the "length" or distance a line travels on a graph.

$$d = \sqrt{(x_2 - x_1)^2 + (y_2 - y_1)^2}$$

To use this formula, first put the coordinates in the appropriate places; second, use the order of operations to:

- Subtract the coordinates.
- Square the differences you have found.
- Add the results of the squaring.
- Take the square root of the result.

Let's use the coordinates (–2, 3) and (4, 2). Remember these numbers correspond to (x_1, y_1) and (x_2, y_2) respectively, so:

x_1 *is* -2
y_1 *is* 3
x_2 *is* 4
y_2 *is* 2

First, plug the numbers into the distance formula:

$$d = \sqrt{(x_2 - x_1)^2 + (y_2 - y_1)^2}$$

$$d = \sqrt{(4 + 2)^2 + (2 - 3)^2}$$

$$d = \sqrt{(6)^2 + (-1)^2}$$

$$d = \sqrt{36 + 1}$$

$$d = \sqrt{37} \qquad \qquad \text{The distance is the } \sqrt{37}.$$

Now to practice distance formula. Remember this is a plug and play situation. Put the numbers where they belong in the pattern and then crunch numbers.

> Find the length of a line that passes from (3, 2) and (4, 6).

The solution is $d = \sqrt{17}$. Here is how the solution looks:

$$d = \sqrt{(x_2 - x_1)^2 + (y_2 - y_1)^2}$$

$$d = \sqrt{(4 - 3)^2 + (6 - 2)^2}$$

$$d = \sqrt{(1)^2 + (4)^2}$$

$$d = \sqrt{1 + 16}$$

$$d = \sqrt{17}$$

The Midpoint Formula.   The midpoint formula will give you the coordinates of the middle of a line on a graph.

$$m = \frac{x_1 + x_2}{2}, \frac{y_1 + y_2}{2}$$

To use this formula, first put the coordinates in the appropriate places; second, use the order of operations:

- Add the coordinates.
- Divide the sum by 2.

Now let's plug and play with the midpoint formula using the same coordinates: $(-2, 3)$ and $(4, 2)$.

$$m = \frac{x_1 + x_2}{2}, \frac{y_1 + y_2}{2}$$

$$m = \frac{-2 + 4}{2}, \frac{3 + 2}{2}$$

$$m = 1, \frac{5}{2}$$

> Find the midpoint of a line that passes from (3, 2) and (4, 6).

The midpoint of the line is the point with the coordinates (3, 2) and (4, 6): $\left(\frac{7}{2}, 4\right)$

Let's examine how that solution was reached:

$$m = \frac{x_1 + x_2}{2}, \frac{y_1 + y_2}{2}$$

$$m = \frac{3 + 4}{2}, \frac{2 + 6}{2}$$

$$m = \left(\frac{7}{2}, \frac{8}{2}\right)$$

$$m = \left(\frac{7}{2}, 4\right)$$

Graphing a One-Step Inequality. Graphing a one-step inequality works like graphing a regular linear equation with a small difference. That difference is that you will identify a whole group of answers by shading the appropriate area that describes the function of the equation. Consider the equation $y \geq x - 3$. What it states is that y will either be equal to $x - 3$ or greater than $x - 3$. To graph this equation, you would use a very quick trick that will identify where the line crosses the x-axis and the y-axis.

Find the x and y intercept for this equation: $y \geq x - 3$.

First, find the x-intercept (where it crosses the x-axis) by following these steps:

1. Make $y = 0$.
2. Do the calculation(s) and write in terms of x.
3. Put that point on the x-axis.

Plug 0 into the equation, $y \geq x - 3$, to find where the line crosses the x-axis. Since $y = 0$, the equation will now look like this:

$$0 \geq x - 3$$

Then solve for x as you did previously, and read the inequality from the variable.

$$3 \geq x$$

Note on the graph in Figure 15.5 how the line crosses the x-axis at 3.
    Second, find the y-intercept (where it crosses the y-axis) by following these steps:

1. Make $x = 0$.
2. Do the calculation(s), and write in terms of y.
3. Put that point on the y-axis.

Plug 0 into the equation, $y \geq 0 - 3$, to find where the line crosses the y-axis. Since $x = 0$, the equation will now look like this:

$$y \geq 0 - 3$$

Then solve for x as you did previously in Chapter 2, and read the inequality from the variable.

$$y \geq -3$$

Note on the graph in Figure 15.5 how the line crosses the y-axis at -3.

FIGURE 15.5

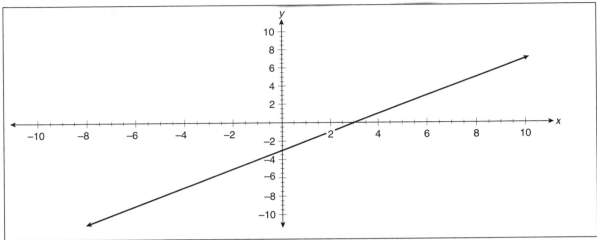

Third, graph the line defined by the *x* and *y* intercepts you placed on the graph. Follow these easy steps:

1. Draw a line extending through the two points you identified. You will use a solid line because you are using a $\leq$ or $\geq$. A solid line indicates that the line is part of the solution. If your equation had only a $<$ or $>$, you would use a dotted line because it is not part of the solution.
2. Shade as necessary to adjust the graph.
   - If the symbol $>$ is used, shade above the line.
   - If the symbol $<$ is used, shade below the line.

In our equation $y \geq x - 3$ note how all possible answers would be $\geq$, so the graph would contain a solid line and be shaded above the line.

$y \leq x - 6$

This is how the inequality works out mathematically:

$y \leq x - 6$

$0 \leq x - 6 \qquad y \leq 0 - 6$

$+6 \qquad +6 \qquad y \leq -6$

$6 \leq x \qquad y \leq -6$

Your graph should look like this Figure 15.6.

FIGURE 15.6

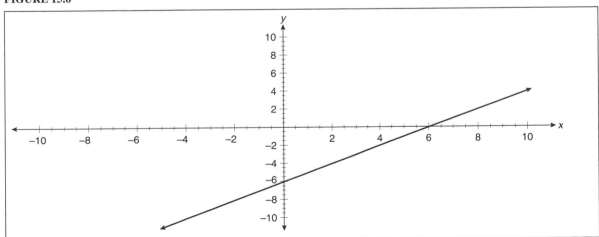

If you found your *x*-intercept as 6 and your *y*-intercept as –6, used a solid line and shaded below the line, you did it all correctly. If not, go back and review the steps presented above.

Finding the Equation of a Line If Two Points Are Known.   If you are given only two points on a line such as (2, 3) and (6, 7) you can find the equation of the line. You will find this process very simple. It's just a matter of channeling information into the proper forms of the equation previously discussed. You will use the slope formula to find the slope of the line, and then either use the Slope–Intercept or Point–Slope patterns. Here are the steps to solution:

- Find the slope of the line using the slope formula.
- If they give you the *y*-intercept, use the Slope–Intercept pattern.
- If they do not give you the *y*-intercept, use the Point–Slope pattern.

Standard Form of the Equation.   If you have the Slope–Intercept or Point–Slope form of an equation, you can easily change it into standard form with the skills you have for moving things back and forth across the equals sign. You have the capability of doing this. You will simply move things back and forth across the equals sign using the inverse operations you used to solve equations.

The master pattern for standard form is $Ax + By = C$.

- *A*, *B*, *C* are real numbers with these exceptions:
  - *A* cannot be zero.
  - *B* cannot be zero.
- The *x* and *y* are the same ones from Slope–Intercept and Point–Slope forms.

Change from Slope–Intercept to standard form: $y = 6x - 4$.

$$y = 6x - 4$$ To write in standard form, both variables must be on the left
$$-6x \quad -6x$$ side of the equals sign. Move the $6x$.

$$y - 6x = -4$$ Check to see that the *x* term comes first.
$$-6x + y = -4$$

Change from slope–intercept to standard form: $y = -5x + 2$.

Did you get $y = -5x + 2$? If so, you did all the steps correctly. If your answer differed, let's work it out together.

$$y = -5x + 2$$
$$+5x \quad +5x$$
$$y + 5x = 2$$
$$5x + y = 2$$

Change from Point–Slope to Standard form: $y - 2 = 2(x + 4)$.

$$y - 2 = 2x + 8$$ First you must distribute.
$$y - 2 = 2x + 8$$ Collect like terms.
$$+ 2 \qquad + 2$$

$$y = 2x + 10$$ You now have the equation in slope–intercept form.

$$y = 2x + 10$$ To write in standard form, both variables must be on the
$$-2x \quad -2x$$ left side of the equals sign. Move the $2x$.

$$y - 2x = 10$$
$$-2x + y = 10$$

Rearrange the variables in the appropriate order for standard form.

$$(-1)(-2x + y = 10)$$
$$2x - y = -10$$

If you have a negative x term, multiply the whole equation through by -1 to resolve it.

Change from point–slope to standard form: $y + 6 = 3(x - 4)$.

Your standard form equation should be $3x - y = 18$. Here is the problem worked step by step for you:

$$y + 6 = 3(x - 4)$$
$$y + 6 = 3x - 12$$
$$ -6 -6$$
$$y = 3x - 18$$
$$-3x -3x$$
$$y - 3x = -18$$
$$-3x + y = -18$$
$$(-1)(-3x + y = -18)$$
$$3x - y = 18$$

CONTENT AREA FOURTEEN: INEQUALITIES

Inequalities

Inequalities, while they often operate like regular linear equations, use a specialized vocabulary and symbols.

$<$	Is less than.
$>$	Is greater than.
$\leq$	Is less than or equal to.
$\geq$	Is greater than or equal to.

Addition and Subtraction Properties.   Just as there are addition and subtraction properties of equality, there are properties for the same operations involving inequalities.

The addition and subtraction properties can be stated as follows:

- Example One: Addition Property of Inequality

    For all real numbers a, b, and c: Example:
    If $a > b$, then $a + c > b + c$ If $6 > 5$, then $6 + 3 > 5 + 3$
    If $a < b$, then $a + c < b + c$ If $3 < 4$, then $3 + 1 < 4 + 1$

- Example Two: Subtraction Property of Inequality

    For all real numbers a, b, and c Example:
    If $a > b$, then $a - c > b - c$ If $6 > 5$, then $6 - 3 > 5 - 3$
    If $a < b$, then $a - c < b - c$ If $3 < 4$, then $3 - 5 < 4 - 5$

To solve an addition or subtraction inequality, you operate as you would for a linear equation using the inverse operation. Remember that addition and subtraction are inverse operations.

To undo addition we subtract, and to undo subtraction we add. Note below in the examples how the inverse operation is used as a method to isolate the variable and solve the inequality.

$$
\begin{array}{llll}
a + 5 < 7 & b - 7 > 9 & 5 \le c - 7 & d + 9 \le 3 \\
\underline{\quad -5 \quad -5} & \underline{\quad +7 \quad +7} & \underline{+7 \qquad +7} & \underline{\quad -9 \quad -9} \\
a \quad\;\; < 2 & b \quad\quad > 16 & 12 \ge c & d \quad\;\; \le -6
\end{array}
$$

Multiplication and Division of Inequalities. It is with the multiplication and division of inequalities that differences with linear equations begin to emerge. You will remember the rules of multiplication of signed numbers. When the signs are the same in multiplication and division the answer is positive, and when not the same the answer is negative. An examination of their properties will show the changes.

   This example shows the properties of inequalities when the value of c is greater than zero. Note the examples carefully because of the contrast that will be pointed out in Example Four.

■ Example Three: Multiplication and Division Properties of Inequalities

   (c is greater than 0)

   For all real numbers a, b, and c ($c > 0$):   *Example:*

   If $a > b$, then $ac > bc$ If $3 > 2$, then $3(4) > 2(4)$

   If $a < b$, then $ac < bc$ If $1 < 4$, then $1(5) < 4(5)$

   If $a > b$, then $\dfrac{a}{c} > \dfrac{b}{c}$ If $8 > 6$, then $\dfrac{8}{2} > \dfrac{6}{2}$

   If $a < b$, then $\dfrac{a}{c} < \dfrac{b}{c}$ If $6 < 9$, then $\dfrac{6}{3} < \dfrac{9}{3}$

   Example Four shows what happens in the multiplication and division of inequalities if the value of c is less than zero (a negative number). Note how the direction of the inequality reverses.

■ Example Four: Multiplication and Division Properties of Inequalities (c is less than 0)

                                          Example:

   For all real numbers a, b, and c ($c < 0$):

   If $a > b$, then $ac < bc$ If $3 > -2$, then $3(-4) < -2(-4)$

   If $a < b$, then $ac > bc$ If $-1 < 4$, then $-1(-5) > 4(-5)$

   If $a > b$, then $\dfrac{a}{c} < \dfrac{b}{c}$ If $8 > -6$, then $\dfrac{8}{-2} < \dfrac{-6}{-2}$ or $-\dfrac{8}{2} < \dfrac{6}{2}$

   If $a < b$, then $\dfrac{a}{c} > \dfrac{b}{c}$ If $-6 < 9$, then $\dfrac{-6}{-3} > \dfrac{9}{-3}$ or $\dfrac{6}{3} > -\dfrac{9}{3}$

   You will notice that in some cases the sign of the inequality reverses.

   To solve multiplication and division inequalities, you use the inverse operation. Remember that multiplication and division are inverse operations. To undo multiplication we divide, and to undo division we multiply. Note below in the examples how the inverse operation is used as a method to isolate the variable and to solve the inequality, being careful to remember that when multiplying or dividing by a negative you sometimes reverse the inequality. Consider the following:

Problem:	$3a < 9$	$\dfrac{b}{2} \ge 9$	$-5c > -25$	$\dfrac{d}{2} \ge 22$
Procedure:	divide 9 by 3	multiply by 2	divide by -5	multiply by 2
Answer:	$a < 3$	$b \ge 18$	$c < 5$	$d \ge 44$

Solve: $-4n < 24$

You should have arrived at $n > -6$. If you have a different result, check against the solution below and watch and especially where the sign reverses when multiplying or dividing by a negative inequalities.

$$-4n < 24$$
$$\frac{-4n}{-4} < \frac{24}{-4}$$
$$n > -6$$

Graphing of One-Step Inequalities.   Graphing of one-step inequalities uses the number line that you are already familiar with, but adds some new notation. A circle is used to indicate where one starts on the number line. An empty circle is used with < and >. The empty circle shows only the starting point and is not included in the solution. In the practice problem above, you would graph it on the number line placing an open circle on the –6 and the arrow would be drawn to the right (see Figure 15.7).

FIGURE 15.7

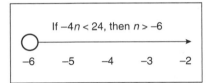

A solid circle is used with ≤ and ≥. The solid circle shows the that the number is included as part of the solution.

Solving Inequalities with Multiple Steps with One Variable.   An inequality with multiple steps and one variable may sound immensely confusing, but look at the example below.

$$2(n + 6) > 18 - n$$

It looks just like a linear equation, and you have all the tools to solve it. One need only remember the steps to solving an equation because, with the exception of the sign reversal that occurs with multiplication and division, they are the same. To prepare to solve this inequality, you will go through two stages: prep steps and solution steps. These are the same steps you would use to solve a regular equation.

- The Prep Steps:
    1. Distribute if necessary.
    2. Collect like terms on each side of the equals sign.
    3. Collect the variable on one side of the equals sign.

- The Solution Steps:
    1. Resolve any addition or subtraction using the inverse process.
    2. Resolve any multiplication or division using the inverse process, being careful with reversing of the sign if multiplying or dividing by a negative.

We will use the sample equation to illustrate the steps:

$2(n + 6) > 18 - n$ Prep Step: Distribute.

$2n + 12 > 18 - n$ Prep Step: Collect the variable on one side of the equals sign.
<u>$+n$ $+ n$</u>

$3n + 12 > 18$ Solution Step: Undo the addition with subtraction.
<u>-12 -12</u>

$\dfrac{3n}{3} > \dfrac{6}{3}$ Solution Step: Undo the multiplication with division.

$n > 2$

Graphing.   Graphing follows the examples above using the number line (see Figure 15.8).

FIGURE 15.8

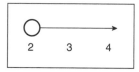

Solving Compound Inequalities with "And" and "Or."   A compound inequality with "and" looks like this:

$-2 < n + 2 \le 4$

A compound inequality with "or" looks like this:

$n - 4 \le 3$ or $2n > 18$

A compound inequality is made up of two inequalities and is connected with either the word "and" or the word "or." To solve either one, you must separate the equations, then resolve them.

We shall tackle the "and" type using the sample problem above.

■ **First,** separate $-2 < n + 2 \le 4$ into two inequalities *reading from the center out.*

$n + 2 > -2$ and $n + 2 \le 4$
<u>-2 -2</u> and <u>-2 -2</u>

■ **Second,** solve each separately using skills from Solving Inequalities to find that:

$n > -4$ $n \le 2$

If you were asked to graph this compound inequality with "and," you would place a empty circle over –4 and a solid circle over 2 and connect the two symbols with a line (see Figure 15.9).

FIGURE 15.9

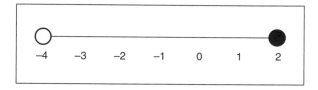

Compound Inequality with "And."

Solve and graph: *Reasoning:*

$-1 < a + 3 < 7$

$-1 < a + 3$ Separate the inequality into two parts reading from the center out.
and
$a + 3 < 7$

$-4 < a$
and
$a < 4$

Solve each inequality separately. In this case subtracting 3 from each side.

To graph, you will use "open" circles because the signs do not include equality. Then draw a line between them.

Solve and graph: $-2 < 2b - 4 \leq 10$

| -2 | -1 | 0 | 1 | 2 | 3 | 4 | 5 | 6 | 7 | 8 |

In the practice problem $b > 1$ and $b \leq 7$. If you have a different answer, let's review the solution and the steps presented above.

$$-2 < 2b - 4 \leq 10$$
$$-2 < 2b - 4 \quad \text{and} \quad 2b - 4 \leq 10$$
$$-2 < 2b - 4 \quad \text{and} \quad 2b - 4 \leq 10$$
$$+4 \qquad +4 \qquad\qquad +4 \quad +4$$
$$2 < 2b \qquad \text{and} \qquad 2b \leq 14$$
$$\frac{2}{2} < \frac{2b}{2} \qquad \text{and} \qquad \frac{2b}{2} \leq \frac{14}{2}$$
$$1 < b \qquad \text{and} \qquad b \leq 7$$

Did you split the inequality into two different parts $-2 < 2b - 4$ and $2b - 4 \leq 10$? Did you solve each separately? When you graphed, did you use an empty circle for $b > 1$ and a solid circle for $b \leq 7$? Did the line you drew cover only the space between the two?

Compound Inequality Using "Or." Next, we shall tackle the "or" type using the same sample problem.

$$n - 4 \leq 3 \text{ or } 2n > 18$$

Solve each *separately* using skills from Solving Inequalities:

$$n - 4 \leq 3 \quad \text{or} \quad 2n > 18$$
$$n - 4 \leq 3 \quad \text{or} \quad \frac{2n}{2} > 18$$
$$+4 \quad +4$$
$$n \leq 7 \quad \text{or} \quad n > 9$$

If you were asked to graph this compound inequality with "or," you would place a solid circle over 7 and the arrow would go left, and place an empty circle over 9 and the arrow would go right. There would be no overlap of answers at all (see Figure 15.10).

FIGURE 15.10

Solve and graph: $3n + 1 < 4$ or $2n - 5 > 7$

$3n + 1 < 4$
$\underline{\quad -1 \quad -1 \quad}$
$\dfrac{3n}{3} < \dfrac{3}{3}$
$n < 1$

Solve each for *n,* first adding or subtracting and then multiplying or dividing.

$$2n - 5 > 7$$
$$\underline{+5 > +5}$$

Solve each for n, first adding or subtracting and then multiplying or dividing.

$$\frac{2n}{2} > \frac{12}{2}$$
$$n > 6$$
$$n < 1 \text{ or } n > 6$$

To graph you will use open circles, since there is no equality indicated. Since this is an "or," the graph will move away from the points indicated.

Solve and graph: $n - 4 < -8$ or $n + 3 > 5$

$$-4 \quad -3 \quad -2 \quad -1 \quad 0 \quad 1 \quad 2 \quad 3 \quad 4$$

You should have arrived at $n < -4$ or $n > 2$. Here is the solution and some checkpoints to help you.

$$n - 4 \leq -8 \quad \text{or} \qquad n + 3 > 5$$
$$+4 \quad +4 \qquad\qquad -3 \quad -3$$
$$n \leq -4 \quad \text{or} \qquad\quad n > 2$$

Did you solve each inequality separately? If you were to graph this answer on a number line, you would have a closed circle over –4 with an arrow going to the left and an open circle over 2 with an arrow to the right.

CHAPTER SIXTEEN

Measurement and Geometry[1]

CONTENT AREA FIFTEEN: TWO- AND THREE-DIMENSIONAL GEOMETRIC OBJECTS

All closed two-dimensional figures in geometry may be referred to as *polygons, poly* meaning "many" and *gon* referring to "side." A polygon is a figure that has many sides. Some polygons have been given specific names based on the number of sides they contain (see Table 16.1).

TABLE 16.1

EXAMPLE OF POLYGON	NUMBER OF SIDES	NAME OF POLYGON
	3	Triangle
	4	Quadrilateral
	5	Pentagon
	6	Hexagon
	8	Octagon

[1]Chapter contributed by Charles Jackson.

A figure with more than 12 sides is referred to as an *n*-gon—"n" stands for the number of sides. If a figure had 23 sides, then it is called a 23-gon.

Some polygons have special names or qualities based upon specific conditions. If you see a figure referred to as *regular* you are being told that all sides of the figure have the same length.

Triangles

Triangles are classified in two ways: by the sides and by the angles (see Table 16.2).

TABLE 16.2

NUMBER OF SIDES	NAME OF TRIANGLE	EXAMPLE OF TRIANGLE
3 equal sides	Equilateral	
2 equal sides	Isosceles	
3 *unequal* sides	Scalene	
3 equal angles	Equiangular Triangle	
One right (90°) angle	Right Triangle	
One angle > 90°	Obtuse Triangle	
All angles < 90°	Acute Triangle	

No triangle has a straight angle—an angle of 180 degrees. The sum of all angles of a triangle is 180 degrees.

Triangle Formulas

Perimeter of a Triangle

Perimeter: Side 1 + Side 2 + Side 3 and label with the measure used.

Perimeter of a Triangle:

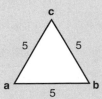

Select angle "a"	Pick an angle. Starting at that angle, add the sides until you have completed a complete "walk" around the triangle.
5 + 5 + 5 15	Write the sum of the sides. Write with the appropriate unit used for measure. If no measurement
15 units	is given, label it in units.

Practice Problem:

Your sum should be 21 units. Here is how the solution was reached:

Perimeter: Side 1 + Side 2 + Side 3
Perimeter = 6 + 7 + 8
Perimeter = 21

Area of a Triangle

Area: $A = \frac{1}{2}bh$ Multiply the base times the height and divide by 2.
Label in square units.

Area of a Triangle:
Find the area of triangle abc:

base = 4
height = 3

$A = \frac{1}{2}bh$	Write the formula.
$A = \frac{1}{2} \times 4 \times 3$	Substitute the values of b and h.
$A = 2 \times 3$	Take $\frac{1}{2}$ of the easiest number.
$A = 6$	Find the product.
$A = 6m^2$	Label the appropriate measure used making it squared. If no measure is given, write the answer in square units.

Find the area of triangle abc:

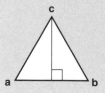

The base is 8 units.
The height is 6 units.

The area of the triangle is 24 square units. Lets examine how that answer was reached:

$A = \frac{1}{2}bh$
$A = \frac{1}{2} \times 8 \times 6$
$A = 4 \times 6$
$A = 24$
$A = 24 \text{ units}^2$

Quadrilaterals

Quadrilaterals are figures with four sides. They are classified and named by their qualities (see Table 16.3).

TABLE 16.3

EXAMPLE	SIDES	NAME OF QUADRILATERAL
	Parallelogram with equal sides	Rhombus
	Parallelogram with right angles	Rectangle
	Rectangle with equal sides	Square

Quadrilateral Formulas

Perimeter of Rectangles and Parallelograms. To find the perimeter of a four-sided figure add the sides.

Perimeter = Side 1 + Side 2 + Side 3 + Side 4

Find the perimeter of rectangle abcd whose length is 6m and width is 8m:

Select angle "a"	Pick an angle.
6 + 8 + 6 + 8	Starting at that angle, add the sides until you have completed a complete "walk" around the rectangle.
28	Write the sum of the sides.
28 meters	Write with the appropriate unit used for measure. If no measurement is given, label it in units.

Find the perimeter of parallelogram abcd:

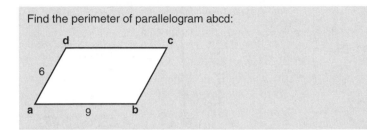

The perimeter of quadrilateral abcd is 30 units. Let's examine the solution:

Perimeter = Side 1 + Side 2 + Side 3 + Side 4
Perimeter = 6 + 9 + 6 + 9
Perimeter = 30 units

Area of Rectangles and Parallelograms. The formula for the area (*A*) of a rectangle or parallelogram can be expressed as base (*b*) multiplied by the height (*h*). It is commonly abbreviated as $A = bh$. Multiply the base times the height (sometimes represented by a dotted line).

Find the area of rectangle abcd:

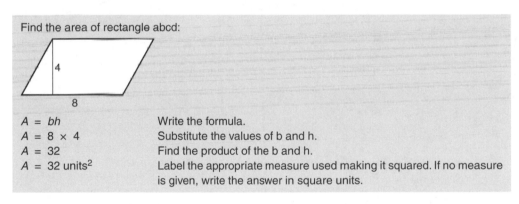

$A = bh$	Write the formula.
$A = 8 \times 4$	Substitute the values of b and h.
$A = 32$	Find the product of the b and h.
$A = 32$ units^2	Label the appropriate measure used making it squared. If no measure is given, write the answer in square units.

Find the area of parallelogram abcd:

The area of parallelogram abcd is 72 square units. Here is the step-by-step solution:

$A = bh$ $\quad$ $A = 9 \times 8$ $\quad$ $A = 72$ $\quad$ $A = 72$ units^2

Area of a Trapezoid. A trapezoid is like a triangle that faced the guillotine. Its head has been removed from its body. The formula can be expressed as:

$A = \frac{1}{2}h(base_1 + base_2)$ $\quad$ The top is usually *base*$_1$; *base*$_2$ the bottom; and *h* indicates the height often indicated by a dotted line.

Find the area of trapezoid abcd:

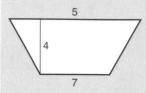

$A = \frac{1}{2}h(base_1 + base_2)$	Write the formula.
$A = \frac{1}{2}4(5 + 7)$	Substitute the values for h, $base_1$, and $base_2$.
$A = \frac{1}{2}(4)(12)$	Find the sum of the top and bottom base.
$A = \frac{1}{2}(4)(12)$	Take one half of the easiest number to cut in half.
$A = 2(12)$	Find the product.
$A = 24$ units^2	Label the appropriate measure used making it squared. If no measure is given, write the answer in square units.

Find the area of trapezoid dcef:

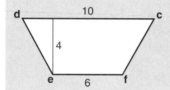

The area of trapezoid cdef is 32 square units. Let's examine the steps to solution of this area problem:

$$A = \frac{1}{2}h(base_1 + base_2)$$

$$A = \frac{1}{2}(4)(10 + 6)$$

$$A = (2)(16)$$

$$A = 32$$

$$A = 32 \text{ units}^2$$

Surface Area of a Rectangular Prism. The great mathematician Polya once held up this shape to his graduate-level class and stated, "You look at this shape and think 'rectangular prism.' I call it a box." Take a clue from Polya and think "box." Before panic sets in, remember this is no more than a series of area problems with the answers added together. If you divide the box into its basic parts, the problem becomes easier. Each box has a front, back, top, bottom, left, and right side.

Top	base × height	(label in square units)
Bottom	base × height	(label in square units)
Front	base × height	(label in square units)
Back	base × height	(label in square units)
Left	base × height	(label in square units)
Right	+ base × height	(label in square units)
Total		(label in square units)

Imagine perfectly wrapping a present for a friend with the least amount of paper. That is the surface area.

Find the surface area of the rectangular prism:

It has a width of 5 inches, length of 6 inches, and height of 4 inches.

Top = base × height
Bottom = base × height
Front = base × height
Back = base × height
Left = base × height
Right = base × height

Write the formula for the top, bottom, front, back, left, and right sides.

Top = 5 × 6
Bottom = 5 × 6
Front = 5 × 4
Back = 5 × 4
Left = 4 × 6
Right = 4 × 6

Substitute in the appropriate values for the base and height of each side.

Top = 30
Bottom = 30
Front = 20
Back = 20
Left = 24
Right = 24
Surface Area = 148

Find the product of each side.

Find the sum of all areas calculated.

Surface Area = 148 inches^2

Label the appropriate measure used making it squared. If no measure is given, write the answer in square units.

Find the surface area of this rectangular prism:

This figure has a base of 6 units, a height of 4 units, and a length of 10 units.

The surface area of the prism is 248 square units.
Let's walk through the solution step by step:

Top	6 × 10	=	60 square units
Bottom	6 × 10	=	60 square units
Front	6 × 4	=	24 square units
Back	6 × 4	=	24 square units
Left	10 × 4	=	40 square units
Right	+ 10 × 4	=	40 square units
Total		=	248 square units

CONTENT AREA SIXTEEN: CIRCLES

Circles are a special case and have a unique relationship involving the circumference and the diameter. We can thank the Greeks for exploring these qualities. They had no calculators, tape measures, or computers but logically arrived at conclusions that have impacted mathematics (see Table 16.4).

TABLE 16.4

MEASUREMENT	DESCRIPTION	SYMBOL
Diameter	The distance across the circle through the center.	d
Radius	The distance from the center to arc of the circle. Two radii equal one diameter.	r
Circumference	The distance around a circle (like perimeter).	C
Chord	Touches both sides of a circle, but does not pass through the center.	ch
Arc	Sections of the curved side of the circle.	⌒
Pi	The circumference of a the circle divided by the diameter. Pi is used mathematically as 3.14 or 22/7; both work, but neither are exactly Pi.	π

Circle Formulas

Circumference of a Circle.   The circumference of a circle is the distance around it. It was originally calculated using only the diameter. Later discoveries showed that it was equivalent to two radii (the plural of radius). The formula can, therefore, be stated in two different ways: One with diameter and one with radius.

Circumference = the product of Pi and the diameter, or $C = \pi d$. Remember that two radii = 1 diameter.

Circumference = the product of Pi and twice the radius, or $C = 2\pi r$.

Find the circumference of the circle (observe the picture to select the formula best suited to your purposes):

8 cm

$C = \pi d$ or π(diameter) or $C = 2\pi r$ or $(2)\pi$(radius)	Write the appropriate formula depending on whether you were given the diameter or radius.
3.14(8)	Substitute in the value for Pi and either the diameter or 2 × radius.
25.12	Find the product of Pi and the prior product if done.
25.12 centimeters	Write with the appropriate unit used for measure. If no measurement is given, label it in units.

Find the circumference of the circle.

The circumference of the circle is 31.4 units.

$C = \pi d$ or π(diameter)
or
$C = 2\pi r$ or $(2)\pi$(radius)
3.14(10)
31.4
31.4 units

Area of a Circle.   Given a radius and the value for π, you can calculate the area of a circle. Remember with area we are determining how any square units would fill the space. It is important to remember the use of exponents here. The formula can be stated as:

Area $=$ the product of π and the radius squared, or π (radius)(radius).

Symbolically is it stated as $A = \pi r^2$.

Find the area of the circle:

$A = \pi r^2$	Write the formula.
3.14 (5)(5)	Substitute in the values of Pi and the value of the radius.
3.14 (25)	Do the easiest multiplication first.
78.5	Find the remaining product.
78.5 units^2	Label the appropriate measure used making it squared. If no measure is given, write the answer in square units.

Find the area of the circle:

The area of the circle is 50.24 square units.
This is how that result was achieved:

$A = \pi r^2$
3.14(4)(4)
3.14(16)
50.24
50.24 units^2

CONTENT AREA SEVENTEEN: THREE-DIMENSIONAL GEOMETRIC OBJECTS

Three-dimensional objects, polyhedrons, are referred to as *geometric solids* or *prisms*. They have specialized names and can be drawn to show specific qualities of the shape (see Figure 16.1). You can find the volume (how much would fill the object) or surface area (how much would cover the object).

FIGURE 16.1

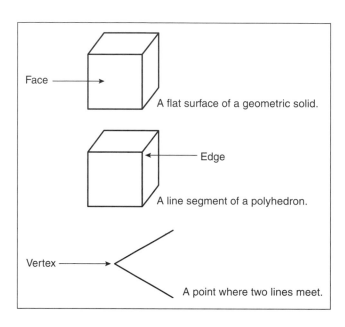

Face — A flat surface of a geometric solid.

Edge — A line segment of a polyhedron.

Vertex — A point where two lines meet.

Geometric Solids

Geometric solids have a certain pattern in common. They use the area of the base as a starting point. The *A* is used to indicate the "Area of the base of the object." Volume is the term used to decide how much space is inside the solid. A helpful trick is to close your eyes and mentally write the formula on a blank wall. During the exam, if you don't remember, focus on a blank wall and imagine it appearing as you wrote it (see Figure 16.2).

FIGURE 16.2

Name of the Solid	Volume Formula	Algebraic Form
Right Solid (Cube or Rectangular Solid)	V = Area of the base (B) × the height.	$V = Bh$
Pyramid	V = Area of the base (B) × the height. Divide the answer by 3.	$V = \frac{1}{3}Bh$

FIGURE 16.2 Continued

Name of the Solid	Volume Formula	Algebraic Form
Cylinder	V = Area of the circle/base (B) × the height.	$V = Bh$
Cone	V = Area of the circle/base (B) × the height. Divide the answer by 3.	$V = \frac{1}{3}Bh$
Sphere	$V = \frac{4}{3}$ × Pi × the radius³.	$V = \frac{4\pi r^3}{3}$

Volume of a Right Solid.   Finding the volume of a cube is easy. First, find the area of the base by multiplying one side by another side. Then, multiply that answer by the height. The only tricky part is to remember to label your answer in the "cubed" (^{3}) measure.

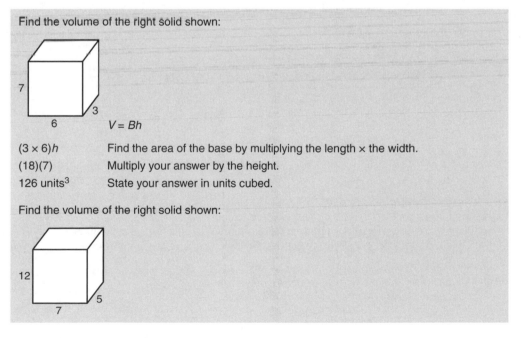

Find the volume of the right solid shown:

$V = Bh$

$(3 \times 6)h$ Find the area of the base by multiplying the length × the width.

$(18)(7)$ Multiply your answer by the height.

126 units^3 State your answer in units cubed.

Find the volume of the right solid shown:

The volume of the rectangular solid is 420 cubic units. Here is the solution to the problem worked step by step for you:

$$V = Bh$$
$$V = (7 \times 5)(12)$$
$$V = (35)(12)$$
$$V = 420 \text{ units}^3$$

Volume of a Pyramid.   The formula for finding the volume of a pyramid is $V = \frac{1}{3}Bh$. You simply perform the same operations for calculating the volume of a cube and then divide that number by 3.

Let's try an example:

Find the volume of the pyramid shown:

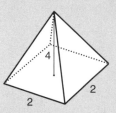

$(2 \times 2)(4) = 16$	Calculate the volume of the entire cube.
$16 \div 3 = 5.33$	Divide the answer by 3 to eliminate part of the cube not included in the calculation.
5.33 units³	Label your answer in the measure³.

Find the volume of the pyramid shown:

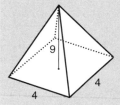

The volume of the pyramid is 48 cubic units.
To arrive at that answer you went through these steps:

$$V = \frac{1}{3}Bh$$
$$V = (\frac{1}{3})(4 \times 4)(9)$$
$$V = (\frac{1}{3})(16)(9)$$
$$V = (\frac{1}{3})(144)$$
$$V = 48$$
$$V = 48 \text{ units}^3$$

Volume of a Cylinder.   The formula for calculating the volume of a cylinder is $V = Bh$. Since the base is a circle, you will have to calculate its area by multiplying 3.14 by the radius² (πr^2).

Find the volume of the cylinder shown:

Pi × radius × radius.	Calculate the area of the base of the cylinder. Since the base is a circle, you calculate the area of a circle by using the formula πr^2.
$3.14(3)(3) = 28.26$ units²	
113.04 units³	Calculate the volume by multiplying by the height, 4, by 28.26.

Find the volume of the cylinder shown:

Note that the diameter is shown as 4 and that you must divide it in half (4 ÷ 2) to get a radius of 2 to perform the calculation.

$$V = Bh$$
$$V = (\pi r^2)h$$
$$V = \pi(2 \times 2)h$$
$$V = \pi(4)(8)$$
$$V = \pi(32)$$
$$V = 3.14(32)$$
$$V = 100.48$$
$$V = 100.48 \text{ units}^3$$

The volume of the cylinder is 100.48 cubic units.

Practice the steps to find the volume of a cylinder. Remember that this is just a process, a pattern that will work the same way each time.

Volume of a Cone.   Find the volume of the cone using this formula:

$$V = \tfrac{1}{3}Bh$$

You find the area of the total cylinder using the formula for the area of a circle and multiply by the height. You eliminate the part of the cylinder not occupied by the cone by dividing by 3, and label your answer in cubic units (units^3).

Find the volume of the cone shown:

3.14(3 × 3)5	Find the volume of the cylinder.
141.3 ÷ 3 = 47.1	Divide the result by 3 to eliminate one-third of the cylinder to form the cone.
47.1 units^3	State the answer in cubic units.

Find the volume of the cone shown:

The volume is 133.97 units^3. Here is how the answer was calculated:

$$V = \tfrac{1}{3}Bh$$

$$V = \tfrac{1}{3}(\pi r^2)h$$

$$V = (\tfrac{1}{3})\pi(4 \times 4)(8)$$

$$V = (\tfrac{1}{3})\pi(16)(8)$$

$$V = (\tfrac{1}{3})\pi(128)$$

$$V = (\tfrac{1}{3})(3.14)(128)$$

$$V = 133.97\overline{3}$$

$$V = 133.97$$

$$V = 133.97 \text{ units}^3$$

Volume of a Sphere.

> Find the volume of a sphere that has a radius of 8 units. Use 3.14 as the equivalent for Pi. If you get a repeating decimal, round to the nearest hundredth. Work carefully and explain your reasoning for each action as you take it.
>
> $$V = \frac{4\pi r^3}{3}$$
>
>

Your calculations should have given you the answer 2143.57 cubic units. If your answer was different, go back and examine the solution.

$$V = \tfrac{4}{3}\pi r^3 \qquad V = \tfrac{4}{3}(3.14)(8)(8)(8) \qquad V = \tfrac{4}{3}(3.14)(512) \qquad V = 2143.57 \text{ units}^3$$

Surface Area of a Sphere.   The formula is $S = 4\pi r^2$. With this pattern and your ability to solve equations, you can manipulate the equation or plug in numbers to find different solutions.

Listed below are all the things you could solve for with the formula for the surface area of a sphere. The first is the original formula, the second is the same formula solved for π, and the third takes the original formula and solves it for the radius.

$$S = 4\pi r^2$$ This is the original equation.

$$\pi = \frac{S}{4r^2}$$ Here the equation was solved for π by dividing both sides of the equation by $4r^2$.

$$r = \sqrt{\frac{S}{4\pi}}$$ Here the equation was solved for r by dividing both sides by 4π and then taking the square root.

To use the same formula ($S = 4\pi r^2$), with numbers, they must either give you the value for S, for r, or for both. If they give you one value, you will have to solve for the other. Just put the value where it belongs and crunch numbers.

Consider this sphere:

It has a radius of 8 units and the value of π is given as 3.14. This is a plug and play situation. Put the 8 in for the r in the original equation and 3.14 for π.

$$S = 4(3.14)(8)^2$$

The next step requires you to remember the rules for order of operations (Please Excuse My Dear Aunt Sally). Exponents take precedence over multiplication. The result is this:

$S = 4(3.14)(64)$

Next step is to be lazy. Do you want to do one decimal multiplication or two? The Commutative Property of Multiplication will allow us to be lazy. We can multiply 4×64 before we multiply by 3.14.

$256 \times 3.14 = 803.84$ units^2.

CONTENT AREA EIGHTEEN: TERMS AND MOVEMENT IN GEOMETRY

Table 16.5 shows the terms necessary for movement in geometry.

TABLE 16.5

Similarity	Geometric figures that have the same shape and same angles, but are not necessarily the same size.
Corresponding Sides and Angles	In two similar polygons, sides, or angles that match up.
Proportionality	Corresponding sides of similar figures in proportion to one another.
Congruence	Figures are said to be congruent if they match in measure and shape, side for side and angle for angle.
Parallel	When two lines in the same plane never intersect. Think railroad tracks and you'll have a good mental image.
Perpendicular	When two lines meet creating a 90 degree angle. Imagine the angle where the wall meets the floor.

Geometric movements of congruent figures can be easily visualized. *Transformations* are the movement of points lines or figures. It is the general category that covers reflections (flips), rotations, and slides.

Reflections or *flips* can be defined as follows: A reflection flips a figure across one of the axis of a graph. The line is referred to as the *line of reflection*. To make the concept easier, imagine a mirror image such as a triangle held against a mirror. Where the edge meets the mirror is the angle of reflection, and what appears in the mirror is quite literally a reflection of the figure.

Rotations are a turn around a given point (for example, the hands of a clock turn around a given point). It is called the *center of rotation*. Take the triangle mentioned above and stick a push pin at one of the angles and rotate it. The push pin is the center or rotation, and each time you spin the triangle you have created a rotation.

Slides move the whole figure (every point) the same distance in a plane. Picture this: You have the same triangle, but now you place it along a ruler placed at an angle on the table top. You move the triangle along the ruler. You have just created a slide.

Reflections, rotations, and slides do not change or alter the size of a figure in any way. The figures are still congruent. Transformations allow us to view geometric figures from different angles or to move them in space.

CONTENT AREA NINETEEN: PYTHAGOREAN THEOREM

A right triangle is a very special figure, mathematically and geometrically. A right triangle consists of three parts: The sides next to the right (90 degree) angle are called *legs* and the side opposite the right angle is the *hypotenuse* (see Table 16.6).

TABLE 16.6

Isosceles	Two 45 degree angles and a right angle. Legs are the same length.	If x is a leg, then the hypotenuse is $x\sqrt{2}$.
30-60-90	Contains a 30 degree and 60 degree angle.	If x is the shorter leg, then the longer leg is $x\sqrt{3}$ and the hypotenuse is $2x$.

The Theorem

If the legs of a right triangle are labeled a and b and the hypotenuse is labeled c, then the squares of the legs added together is equal to the square of the hypotenuse. It can be symbolically shown as:

$$a^2 + b^2 = c^2$$

Given any two sides, you can compute the missing side. This is a plug and play formula, but you have to be ready to use exponents and be able to take the square root. Both of these have been covered previously. We shall work a problem step by step together as a reminder.

Given a right triangle with legs of 8 and 4, find the hypotenuse.

$a^2 + b^2 = c^2$	Write the theorem.
$8^2 + 4^2 = c^2$	Substitute.
$64 + 16 = c^2$	Square what you can.
$80 = c^2$	Add.
$\sqrt{80} = \sqrt{c^2}$	Take the square root of each side.
$\sqrt{(16)(5)}$	Find any perfect square you can.
$4\sqrt{5}$	

Let's try one!

Given a right triangle with a leg of 8 and a hypotenuse of 20, find the other leg.

The answer is $b = 4\sqrt{21}$. The solution is shown below:

$$a^2 + b^2 = c^2$$
$$8^2 + b^2 = 20^2$$
$$64 + b^2 = 400$$
$$-64 \qquad\qquad -64$$
$$b^2 = 336$$
$$\sqrt{b^2} = \sqrt{336}$$
$$b = \sqrt{(16)(21)}$$
$$b = 4\sqrt{21}$$

On some versions of tests you are asked to tell whether an triangle is right, acute, or obtuse. There is a simple method you can apply based on a variation of the Pythagorean Theorem. Often you are only given the length of sides and asked to determine what type of triangle it is.

$$a^2 + b^2 = c^2 \qquad \text{Right}$$
$$a^2 + b^2 < c^2 \qquad \text{Obtuse}$$
$$a^2 + b^2 > c^2 \qquad \text{Acute}$$

Determine whether triangle abc is right, obtuse, or acute:

Leg a = 5

Leg b = 4

Hypotenuse (c) = 6

$5^2 + 4^2$? 6^2 Leg squared + leg squared—Does it equal the hypotenuse squared? Square the terms.

20 + 16 ? 36   Add as needed.

36 = 36   36 = 36, so the triangle is a right triangle.

Determine whether triangle abc is right, obtuse, or acute:

Leg a = 7

Leg b = 3

Hypotenuse (c) = 9

The triangle is obtuse. This is how that determination is made:

$$a^2 + b^2 \; ? \; c^2$$
$$7^2 + 3^2 \; ? \; 9^2$$
$$49 + 9 \; ? \; 81$$
$$58 < 81 \qquad a^2 + b^2 < c^2$$

Therefore, the triangle is obtuse.

Trigonometry: A Quick Refresher

You may be asked questions on trigonometry, which is an offshoot of right-triangle relationships. The most common questions are plug and play ready. The three patterns that you will most likely see are *sine, cosine,* and *tangent.* These measurements relate an angle with two side of the triangle. They are not difficult to calculate, but you must understand how they are related to parts of a right triangle to be able to place the numbers properly. Let's look at those aspects first.

The symbol θ (greek *theta*) is often used to designate the angle. Don't let a symbol panic you; it's like using an *x* for an unknown quantity. The symbol designates which line is opposite and adjacent and which is the hypotenuse. If you move the symbol around on the triangle, you'll change what is opposite and what is adjacent.

Figure 16.3 shows the common formulae that you might encounter on the test.

FIGURE 16.3

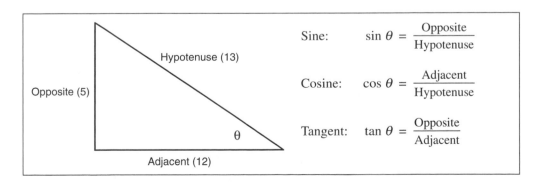

Sine: $\sin \theta = \dfrac{\text{Opposite}}{\text{Hypotenuse}}$

Cosine: $\cos \theta = \dfrac{\text{Adjacent}}{\text{Hypotenuse}}$

Tangent: $\tan \theta = \dfrac{\text{Opposite}}{\text{Adjacent}}$

There is a memory device you can use to remember these relationships: SOH-CAH-TOA. Using the device, you can place the numbers in their proper places. Let's use the triangle in Figure 16.3 and see how it works (see Table 16.7).

TABLE 16.7

Sine	SOH	opposite/hypotenuse	$\frac{5}{13}$
Cosine	CAH	adjacent/hypotenuse	$\frac{12}{13}$
Tangent	TOA	opposite/adjacent	$\frac{5}{12}$

Let's use these relationships to find the sine, cosine, and tangent in the right triangle in Figure 16.4.

FIGURE 16.4

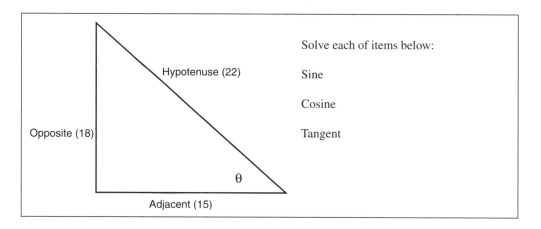

Solve each of items below:

Sine

Cosine

Tangent

You should have identified $\frac{18}{22}$ as the sine, $\frac{15}{22}$ as the cosine, and $\frac{18}{15}$ as the tangent. It's all in the placement!

Techniques in Computation[1]

CONTENT AREA TWENTY: PATTERNS AND THE USE OF FORMULAE

Estimation in whole numbers and decimals allows you to see whether an answer is in the ball-park, saves time, and in multiple-choice tests allows you to eliminate answers and thus improve your chances. Estimation is best accomplished with rounded off numbers. In geometry angles can also be estimated.

Estimating Products

Estimate product of 2577 × 3.8.	Reasoning:
2577 ≈ 3000 and 3.8 ≈ 4	Round off a whole number to the digit farthest left and a decimal to the nearest whole number.
3000 × 4 12,000	Do the Indicated mathematical operation. The sum, difference, product, or quotient will be the estimated answer.

Estimating the Quotient

Estimate the quotient of 4952 ÷ 952.

Your answer should be 5. If not, let's work the problem together.

$4952 \approx 5000$ and $952 \approx 100$

$5000 \div 1000$

5

Estimating Angles

Estimation with angles is best done with visualization using a clock. Picture the angle created at 15 minutes past the hour: That is a 90° angle. From there you may decrease or expand mentally by half. Half of the 90° angle is a 45° and expanded is a 135°. From there various estimated can be made.

[1]Chapter contributed by Charles Jackson.

Estimating Time

Time can be added, subtracted, multiplied, and divided. The only problem comes in carrying and borrowing. Possible essay questions might revolve around the explanation of how time is added or subtracted. Students are so used to carrying one or borrowing one that working with time can be confusing. The conversions are listed in Table 17.1.

TABLE 17.1

1 year	52 weeks
1 week	7 days
1 day	24 hours
1 hour	60 minutes
1 minute	60 seconds
1 year	12 months
1 leap year	366 days
1 decade	10 years
1 score	20 years
1 century	100 years

Watch carefully as the units of time are aligned and what occurs in the process of carrying.

	Add 7 hr. 40 min. + 20 hr. 50 min.
7 hr. 40 min. + 20 hr. 50 min.	Align the problem by units (hours, minutes, etc.).
7 hr. 40 min. + 20 hr. 50 min. 90 min.	Add the minutes.
+1 hr. 7 hr. 40 min. + 20 hr. 50 min. 30 min.	60 minutes equals 1 hour, so take 60 from the minutes and add 1 to the hours.
+1 hr. 7 hr. 40 min. + 20 hr. 50 min. 28 hr. 30 min.	Add the hours.
+1 hr. 7 hr. 40 min. + 20 hr. 50 min. 1 day 4 hr. 30 min.	24 hours equals 1 day, so take 24 from the hours and add 1 to the days.

Add 8 hr. 50 min. + 14 hr. 30 min.

The answer is 23 hours, 20 minutes. Let's examine how we got that answer:

```
   8 hrs.      50 min.
 +14 hrs.      30 min.
  22 hrs.      80 min.      60 min. = 1 hr.
  +1 hr.      -60 min.
  23 hrs.      20 min.
```

Measurement in Standard and Metric Units

An understanding of U.S. standard and metric units is needed before any discussion of length, weight, or mass. Standard units are derived from early English units of measure. The yard was measured from the nose to fingertip, the inch from knuckle to fingertip, and the foot is obvious. All measurement is approximate. No ruler is accurate. As does time, standard measure has quirks that involve borrowing and carrying of units (see Table 17.2).

TABLE 17.2

1 mile	1760 yards
1 yard	3 feet
1 foot	12 inches
1 pound (lb)	16 ounces (oz)
1 ton (T)	2000 pounds (lbs)
1 gallon (gal)	4 quarts (qt)
1 quart (qt)	2 pints (pt)
1 pint (pt)	2 cups (cp)
1 cup (cp)	16 ounces (oz)
1 gallon	768 teaspoons (tsp)
1 dozen	12 things
1 bushel	4 pecks

Metric Units of Measure. Metrics were devised as a method to bring commonality to units of measure and to remove the oddities that occur from country to country in national methods of measurement. They based this method on powers of 10. This would allow for increased commerce between nations. Metric measure has one standardized method no matter if you are working with length, weight, or liquid measure. It uses decimals in place of fractions for partial measures. Since metrics are still not standard measure in the United States, some approximations may be helpful:

- A meter is a bit more than a yard.
- A kilometer is about 3/5 of a mile.
- A kilogram is approximately 2.2 pounds.
- A liter is a little more than a quart.

Know the prefix and you are immediately oriented in the placement of numbers involved (see Table 17.3).

TABLE 17.3

kilo	thousand (1000)
hecto	hundred (100)
deka	ten (10)
meter	the basic unit of measure
deci	tenth (1/10)
centi	hundredth (1/100)
milli	thousandth (1/1000)

Note the standardization and how the use of fractions are avoided (see Table 17.4).

TABLE 17.4

METRIC UNITS OF LENGTH	EQUIVALENTS FOR CARRYING OR BORROWING
meter (m)	The basic unit of length in metrics
1 kilometer (km)	1000 meters (m)
1 hectometer (hm)	100 meters (m)
1 dekameter (dam)	10 meters (m)
1 decimeter (dm)	.1 meters (m)
1 centimeter (cm)	.01 meters (m)
1 millimeter (mm)	.001 meters (m)

METRIC UNITS OF VOLUME	EQUIVALENTS FOR CARRYING OR BORROWING
liter	the basic unit of volume in metrics
1 kiloliter (kl or kL)	1000 liters (l or L)
1 milliliter (ml or mL)	.001 liters (l or L)

METRIC UNITS OF MASS	EQUIVALENTS FOR CARRYING OR BORROWING
gram	the basic unit of mass (weight) in metrics
1000 kilograms (kg)	1 metric ton (t)
1 kilogram (kg)	1000 grams (g)
1 milligram (mg)	.001 grams (g)

You may be asked to perform simple calculations with units of measure, such as inches, yards, and feet. For example, you may have to calculate how many inches are in 8 yards. Here is how to do it:

1 foot = 12 inches 3 feet = 1 yard x inches = 8 yards	First, start out with the information that you know and that you don't know.
$\dfrac{12\ in}{1\ ft} \times \dfrac{3\ ft}{1\ yd} \times \dfrac{8\ yd}{1}$	Second, set up the calculation as a series of fractions.
$\dfrac{12}{1} \times \dfrac{3}{1} \times \dfrac{8}{1}$	Multiply as you would for any fraction.
288 *inches*	State your answer in the terms identified.

Ratio and Proportion

Proportions are an incredibly easy way to solve numerous types of problems where we are comparing a part to a whole amount. We can use this method to solve percent problems, unit rate problems, and a host of word problems. The basic unit of the proportion is a ratio. A ratio is the relationship between two things. They could be numbers, measures, or labels. They are written in a variety of forms: 3 to 5, 3:5, or $\frac{3}{5}$.

All express the same relationship. Other examples of ratios might be scale in drawings and labels such as miles per hour.

Proportion.   A proportion is a relationship between two or more equal ratios. Once the ratio is determined, the pattern must be carried through. For example, if we are calculating kilometers per hour:

$$\frac{60\ km}{1\ hr} = \frac{?}{5\ hr}$$

The equal sign tells us that they are equivalent. As with equivalent fractions, we can cross multiply and maintain the equality: $1 \times ? = 5 \times 60$. Therefore, the missing number is 300.

The basic pattern to solution of proportions is: *Cross-multiply the numbers you can and divide by the number across from the "blank" or variable.* No matter the type of problem to be solved, this pattern will hold true.

In an architect's office, the scale on a set of blueprints is .25 inches. This is 3 feet in the real world. What would a line on the blueprints 4.5 inches long be equal to in the real world?

$\frac{inches}{feet}$	Decide on a relationship and stick to it consistently.
$\frac{.25\ inches}{3\ feet} = \frac{4.5\ inches}{?\ feet}$	Set up the problem as a proportion.
$4.5 \times 3 = .25 \times ?$	Cross-multiply the numbers you can.
$\frac{13.5}{.25} = ?$	Divide by the number across from the blank or variable.
54 feet	Label the answer with the appropriate measure.

Therefore 4.5 inches on the blueprint is 54 feet in the real world.

An artist has created a model of a mural that will be in the reception area of city hall. The scale of a drawing that you are copying to create a mural is 2 inches to 3 feet. How many feet would you have to allow for a 7 inch line?

The line on the drawing represents 10.5 feet in the real world. Let's examine how that answer was arrived at:

$$\frac{inches}{feet} \quad \frac{2\ inches}{3\ feet} = \frac{7\ inches}{?\ feet}$$

$$3 \times 7 = 2 \times ?$$

$$21 \div 2 = 10.5\ feet$$

Any real-life problem where a part is compared to a whole can be dealt with this way.

Unit Measure and Unit Pricing

Unit measure and pricing tells us how much for one of something: How much per hour, how much per pound, and so forth. They are easily computed using proportions. Just be consistent as you set up your proportion.

---

8 pounds of apples are priced at $10.00. What is the price per pound?

$$\frac{pounds}{price} \quad \frac{8}{10} = \frac{1}{?}$$

We now have two equivalent ratios and may cross-multiply and divide to find the price per apple.

The same holds true with measure.

A car travels 300 miles in 5 hours. What is the car's speed in miles per hour?

$$\frac{miles}{hours} \quad \frac{300}{5} = \frac{?}{1}$$

We now have two equivalent ratios and may cross-multiply and divide to find the miles per hour.

Price per item also sets up in a like manner.

> A box of 24 chocolates is priced at $12. How much is each piece of chocolate?
>
> $$\frac{chocolates}{price} \quad \frac{24}{12} = \frac{1}{?}$$
>
> We now have two equivalent ratios and may cross-multiply and divide to find the price for one piece of chocolate.

Proportions and Percents

Proportions and percents have a wonderful relationship that makes our lives so much easier. It allows us to work a whole series of problems with a single method. Used properly, the pattern will place the blank or variable where it needs to be each time. The only trick is remembering the master pattern.

$$\frac{\%}{100} = \frac{is/=}{of/\times}$$

Percent means "by 100s." No matter what the percent is it is always placed over 100. The number related to the "is" or the = is always placed over the number associated with the "of" or times sign. You might be asking yourself why we can do that since we seem to be using unrelated numbers. This is why:

$$\frac{part}{whole} = \frac{part}{whole}$$

In math, *is*, *what*, and *of* have particular meanings for the kinds of operations you must perform. Let's look at *is* first.

> | | |
> |---|---|
> | $\dfrac{?}{100} = \dfrac{?}{?}$ | **What is 40% of 120?**
 Write the "bones" of the pattern. |
> | *What* is related to "is" | Relate the numbers given to parts of the master pattern. |
> | 40 is associated with the % | |
> | 120 is matched with "of" | |
> | $\dfrac{40}{100} = \dfrac{?}{120}$ | Place the information we have using the master pattern. |
> | 40 × 120 = 100 × ? | Since it is a proportion, we can cross-multiply the numbers. |
> | 4800 ÷ 100 = 48 | Divide by the number across from the blank or variable. |
> | Therefore 40% of 120 is 48. | |

> What number is 75% of 180?

The answer is 135. Did your answer differ? Let's examine the basics:

Did you set up a consistent relationship and place numbers in their proper positions?

$$\frac{part}{whole} = \frac{part}{whole} \qquad \frac{\%}{100} = \frac{is}{of} \qquad \frac{75}{100} = \frac{?}{180} \qquad \begin{array}{l} 75 \times 180 = 100 \times ? \\ 13500 \div 100 = 135 \\ 135 \end{array}$$

> | | |
> |---|---|
> | $\dfrac{?}{100} = \dfrac{?}{?}$ | **80 is 40% of what number?**
 Write the "bones" of the pattern. |

80 is related to "is"	Relate the numbers given to parts of the master pattern.
40 is associated with %	
What is matched with "of"	
$\dfrac{40}{100} = \dfrac{80}{?}$	Place the information we have using the master pattern.
80 × 100 = 40 × ?	Since it is a proportion we can cross-multiply the numbers.
8000 ÷ 40 = 200	Divide by the number across from the blank or variable.
Therefore 80 is 40% of 200.	

90 is 60% of what number?

The answer is 150. Did your answer differ? Let's examine the basics:

Did you set up a consistent relationship and place numbers in their proper positions?

$$\frac{part}{whole} = \frac{part}{whole} \qquad \frac{\%}{100} = \frac{is}{of} \qquad \frac{60}{100} = \frac{90}{?} \qquad \begin{array}{l} 90 \times 100 = 60 \times \, ? \\ 9000 \div 60 = 150 \\ 150 \end{array}$$

	What percent is 80 of 320?
$\dfrac{?}{100} = \dfrac{?}{?}$	Write the "bones" of the pattern.
80 is related to "is"	Relate the numbers given to parts of the master pattern.
320 is associated with "of"	
What is matched with %	
$\dfrac{?}{100} = \dfrac{8}{320}$	Place the information we have using the master pattern.
100 × 80 = 320 × ?	Since it is a proportion, we can cross multiply the numbers.
8000 ÷ 320 = 25	Divide by the number across from the blank or variable.
Therefore 80 is 25% of 320.	Be sure to label your answer as a %.

What percent is 75 of 250?

The correct answer is 30%. Did your answer differ? Let's examine the basics:

Did you set up a consistent relationship and place numbers in their proper positions?

$$\frac{part}{whole} = \frac{part}{whole} \qquad \frac{\%}{100} = \frac{is}{of} \qquad \frac{?}{100} = \frac{75}{250} \qquad \begin{array}{l} 100 \times 75 = 250 \times \, ? \\ 7500 \div 250 = 30 \\ 30\% \end{array}$$

Simple Word Problems with Percentages

Word problems aren't difficult just different. Since percentages are ratios and can also be in part/whole format, we can use them to solve many different types of word problems. Look for the key words "is" and "of," and if they cannot be found analyze the problem for something that can be put into part/whole format.

Consider this problem:

Seventy-five percent of the English class passed the test. If 15 students passed the test, how many students were in the class?

The percent is easily located:

Seventy-five percent of the English class passed the test. If 15 students passed the test, how many students were in the class?

You will note that the key words "is" and "of" are not used. So we have to look at finding information that we can put into part/whole format. Ask yourself: If 15 passed, is that the whole class??? It's obvious that some did not pass. So we can identify the part of the part/whole.

Seventy-five percent of the English class passed the test. If 15 students passed the test, how many students were in the class?

The whole must then be all the students in the class.

Seventy-five percent of the English class passed the test. If 15 students passed the test, how many *students* were *in the class*?

We can now set up the problem:

$$\frac{part}{whole} = \frac{part}{whole} \qquad \frac{75}{100} = \frac{15}{?}$$

Seventy-five percent of the English class passed the test. If 15 students passed the test, how many students were in the class?

As you copy the steps, watch for key words and placement of the information.

Seventy-five percent of the English class passed the test. If 15 students passed the test, how many students were in the class?	
$\frac{?}{100} = \frac{?}{?}$	Write the "bones" of the pattern.
75 *is* part *of* 100 15 *is* part *of* some number	Look for the key words "is" and "of" or relationship between a part and a whole. Note how part and whole translate into "is" and "of."
$\frac{75}{100} = \frac{15}{?}$	Write in proportional form using the part/whole format. *Note:* We now have our master pattern.
100 × 15 = 75 × ?	Since it is a proportion, we can cross-multiply the numbers.
1500 ÷ 75 = 20	Divide by the number across from the blank or variable.
Therefore, there are 20 students in class because 75% of 20 is 15.	Be sure to label the answer correctly.

Yesenia answered 25 out of 30 problems on the quiz correctly. What was her percentage on the quiz rounded to the nearest whole number?

Yesenia's score was 83% (rounded to the nearest whole number). Did your answer differ? Let's examine the basics:

Did you set up a consistent relationship and place numbers in their proper positions?

$$\frac{part}{whole} = \frac{part}{whole} \qquad \frac{\%}{100} = \frac{is}{of} \qquad \frac{?}{100} = \frac{25}{30} \qquad \begin{array}{l} 100 \times 25 = 30 \times ? \\ 2500 \div 30 = 83.\overline{3} \\ 83\% \end{array}$$

Percentage of Increase or Decrease Problems Using Proportions

Percentage of increase or decrease problems can be relatively simple if you remember that the change (increase or decrease) is a part of the original whole amount. First you must subtract to find the amount of change, and then place the information into the master pattern.

Note the preliminary step that must be taken:	
What is the percent of change of a television priced at $800 that you paid $500 for?	Reasoning:
$800 - 500 = 300$	Subtract to calculate the amount of change.
$\dfrac{?}{100} = \dfrac{?}{?}$	Write the "bones" of the pattern.
800 is related with the *whole* 300 is associated with the *part* *What* is matched with the %	Identify numbers in the problem associated with part and the whole.
$\dfrac{?}{100} = \dfrac{300}{800}$	Write in proportional form using the part/whole format. *Note:* We now have our master pattern.
$100 \times 300 = 800 \times ?$	Since it is a proportion, we can cross-multiply the numbers.
$30000 \div 800 = 37.5$	Divide by the number across from the blank or variable.
Therefore the percent of change is 37.5%.	Be sure to label the answer correctly.

You win a pair of new shoes for $50 on eBay that originally cost $150 at a retailer. What is the percent of change?

The percent of decrease was 67% (rounded to the nearest whole number). Did your answer differ? Let's examine the solution:

Calculate the change: $150 - 50 = 100$

Set up a consistent relationship and place numbers in their proper positions.

$$\frac{part}{whole} = \frac{part}{whole} \qquad \frac{\%}{100} = \frac{is}{of} \qquad \frac{?}{100} = \frac{100}{150}$$

$$100 \times 100 = 150 \times ?$$
$$10000 \div 150 = 66.\overline{6}$$
$$67\%$$

Discount and Sale Price Using Percentage and Proportion

Finding the discount and sale price is a two-step process. Finding the discount can be done using the proportional master pattern for percentage. You need to remember that the discount is part of the original price. We can, therefore, place it in the part/whole format. To determine the sale price, we must do a simple subtraction at the end of the problem as we subtract the discount from the original price.

A DVD player is regularly $180. It is on sale for 20% off the regular price. How much is the discount? What is the sale price?	
$\dfrac{?}{100} = \dfrac{?}{?}$	Write the "bones" of the pattern.

20 is related to the %   Identify the information using key words or the part/whole concept.

180 is the *whole* amount you would pay

The discount is the *part* you would save

$\dfrac{20}{100} = \dfrac{?}{180}$ Write in proportional form using the part/whole format.
                                  Note: We now have our master pattern.

20 × 180 = 100 × ?   Since it is a proportion we can cross-multiply the numbers.

3600 ÷ 100 = 36   Divide by the number across from the blank or variable.

$36   The discount is the amount you save.

$180 − $36 = $144   The original price less the discount gives you the sale price.

A new laptop computer has a regular price of $3400, but is on sale for 25% off the regular price. How much is the discount? How much is the sale price?

The discount is $850 and the sale price would be $2550. Was your solution different? Here is how the answer was arrived at:

$$\frac{part}{whole} = \frac{part}{whole} \qquad \frac{\%}{100} = \frac{is}{of} \qquad \frac{25}{100} = \frac{?}{3400}$$

25 × 3400 = 100 × ?
85000 ÷ 100 = 850
$850
$3400 − $850
$2550

Chance and Probability

The study of numerical data and the distribution of that data is called statistics. The piece that most concerns us arithmetically is *the measure* of *central tendency*. What that is in less complicated terms is the "typical" term of a set of data. In the language of marketers it could be "the average teen" or "the typical 25-year-old male." How would you arrive at that sort of profile? You arrive at it through a measure of central tendency. There are three major ones to consider: mean, median, and mode.

Mean.   Mean is the sum of the data divided by the number of items (values of the set) added. This may look awfully familiar. You have done it for years. In math, we have called it averaging.

Median.   Median is the middle term in a set of data. This is not to be confused with mean (the average). You can arrive at the median in three easy steps:

1. Arrange the data (numbers) in numerical order (from smallest to largest)
2. Count the number of terms. Odd or Even?
3. Odd: The middle term is the median.
   Even: The average (mean) of the two middle terms is the median.

Mode.   The mode is the term (value) that occurs the most often in a set of data. If no term (value) occurs more often than another, then there is no mode.

Given the data: 3,1,1,8,2,1,3,5,3   Find the mean, median, and mode.

Mean: To calculate the mean, add the terms and divide

$\dfrac{3 + 1 + 1 + 8 + 2 + 1 + 3 + 5 + 3}{9}$ by the number of terms added.

The mean is 3.

Median:	To calculate the median, arrange the numbers in numerical
1, 1, 1, 2, 3, 3, 3, 5, 8	order and find the middle term.
The median is 3.	
Mode:	To calculate the mode, find the term(s) that occur the most
1, 1, 1, 2, 3, 3, 3, 5, 8	times.
1 and 3 occur the most times and an equal number of times.	
The mode is 1 and 3.	

Given the data: 10, 12, 7, 20, 11, 8, 5, 9, 7, 19
Find the mean, median, and mode.

The mean is 10.8, the median is 9.5, and the mode is 7.

Mean: $\dfrac{10 + 12 + 7 + 20 + 11 + 8 + 5 + 9 + 7 + 19}{10}$ $\dfrac{108}{10}$ 10.8

Median: 5, 7, 7, 8, 9, 10, 11, 12, 19, 20 $\dfrac{10 + 9}{2}$ $\dfrac{19}{2}$ 9.5

Mode: 5, 7, 7, 8, 9, 10, 11, 12, 19, 20 7 is the most reoccurring number

Common Statistical Terms

Let's clarify some terms commonly faced by an elementary teacher in the teaching of statistics to children (see Table 17.5). This not a complete list, and your individual state test sites on the Internet should be referenced for additional information.

TABLE 17.5

Probability	A means of describing the likelihood of an event occurring. It can be expressed as the ratio of favorable outcomes to all possible outcomes.
Ratio	A comparison of two numbers expressed as division.
Chance	A method of expressing the likelihood that an event will occur. Chance is expressed as a percent.
Odds	The ratio of favorable to unfavorable events.
Complement	Events that work in tandem.
Dependent events	Events where the outcome of one effects the outcome of the other.
Independent events	Events where the outcome of one has no effect on the outcome of another.
Mutually exclusive events	Events where if one is probable the other is not.
Range	The difference between the largest and smallest of a set of numbers (values).

Probability and Compound Probability

Probability. Probability is expressed as the ratio of the number of favorable outcomes to all possible outcomes. Mathematically the pattern looks like this:

$$probability = \frac{number\ of\ favorable\ outcomes}{number\ of\ possible\ outcomes} \qquad \frac{4}{8}; \frac{1}{2}$$

For example:

What is the probability of rolling an even number when throwing a single die?

A single die has 6 sides. The die contains the numbers 1, 2, 3, 4, 5, and 6.

The number of possible outcomes is 6.

The number of favorable outcomes is 3 (there are 3 even numbers).

Placing these terms into the pattern, we have:

Probability $= \dfrac{3}{6}$ reduce the ratio to lowest terms if possible $\dfrac{1}{2}$.

This means it is probable that in 2 rolls you will get 1 even number.

The chance (which is expressed as a percent) of rolling an even number is 50%.

The odds of rolling an even number are $\dfrac{3}{3}$ or in reduced form $\dfrac{1}{1}$.

Spinners are often used when explaining probability and compound probability in elementary mathematics textbooks.

You have a spinner divided into 8 equal sectors. They are numbered from 1 to 8.
Find the probability, chance, and odds of spinning an even number.

The probability of rolling an even number is $\dfrac{1}{2}$.

The chance of rolling an even number is 50%.

The odds would be $\dfrac{1}{1}$.

Let's examine the answers.

$$probability = \frac{number\ of\ favorable\ outcomes}{number\ of\ possible\ outcomes} \qquad \frac{4}{8}; \frac{1}{2}$$

Chance (which is expressed as a percent): $\dfrac{1}{2} = 50\%$

Odds (the ratio of favorable to unfavorable events: $\dfrac{4}{4} = \dfrac{1}{1}$

Compound Probability.   Compound probability is the probability of independent events occurring in a specified order. Mathematically it can be expressed as the product or the probabilities of each event.

When throwing two dice what is the probability of rolling a 3 on one die and a 4 on the other?

A single die has 6 sides. The die contains the numbers 1, 2, 3, 4, 5, and 6.

The number of possible outcomes is 6 for a single die.

The number of favorable outcomes on one die is 1.

The same holds true of the second die.

The probability of rolling a single number on each die is:

First die: $\dfrac{1}{6}$ Second die: $\dfrac{1}{6}$

The Compound Probability Rule says that to find the probability of these two events occurring at the same time we should multiply the ratios of probability.

$$\frac{1}{6} \times \frac{1}{6} = \frac{1}{36}$$

This means that it is probable that rolling two dice you will roll a 3 and a 4 at the same time 1 out of 36 rolls.

The chance of this occurring is about 2.8%.

The odds would be $\frac{1}{36}$.

You have one spinner divided into 8 equal sectors and numbered from 1 to 8. You have a second spinner divided into 7 equal sections numbered 1 to 7. Find the probability, chance, and odds of spinning an even number on the first spinner and an odd number on the second.

The probability of rolling an even on the first spinner and an odd on the second is $\frac{2}{7}$.

The chance 29% (rounded to the nearest whole number).

The odds are approximately $\frac{2}{3}$.

Here is how the answer was arrived at:

8-Sectioned Spinner:

$$probability = \frac{number\ of\ favorable\ outcomes}{number\ of\ possible\ outcomes} \qquad \frac{4}{8}; \frac{1}{2}$$

7-Sectioned Spinner:

$$probability = \frac{number\ of\ favorable\ outcomes}{number\ of\ possible\ outcomes} \qquad \frac{4}{7}; \frac{4}{7}$$

Compound Probability Rule: $\qquad \frac{1}{2} \times \frac{4}{7} = \frac{4}{14} = \frac{2}{7}$

Chance: $\qquad \frac{?}{100} = \frac{2}{7} \qquad 28.57...\% \qquad 29\%$

$$odds = \frac{number\ of\ favorable\ events}{number\ of\ unfavorable\ events} \qquad \frac{\frac{2}{7}}{\frac{3}{7}} \qquad \frac{2}{7} \div \frac{3}{7} \qquad \frac{2}{7} \times \frac{7}{3} = \frac{2}{3}$$

Be sure to review the chapter on essay writing to be sure that you are prepared for any math essays that may appear on the exam.

Physical Education[1]

CONTENT AREA ONE: BASIC MOVEMENT SKILLS

This content area addresses movement concepts. You learn about body, space, and movement. In addition, you will learn about the difference between locomotor activities (e.g., running) and nonlocomotor activities (e.g., balancing), along with the basic concepts of biomechanics and the ways they affect how the body moves and acts when engaging in physical activity.

Motor Skills

Motor skills include all of the gross motor activities included in games and sports such as running, throwing, skipping, hopping, kicking, batting, hitting, and catching. Each skill has definite stages of progression in skill development from initial stages through elementary and mature stages to the most advanced stages of efficient performance. These stages include attention to the way the child is facing the ball, the pathway that the ball is projected after leaving the child, and the direction the ball takes because of the affect of the skill of the child. The force applied to the ball and the direction the ball takes may denote the level of skill of the child performing that skill.

Motor Development.   Motor development activities are important, because many aspects, like throwing, do not happen spontaneously nor at particular ages. This explains why children of the same age demonstrate different physical and motor capabilities. Maturing children do increase in their motor abilities, but their progress can be increased through practice and training.

Children and adults who are physically active on a regular basis are healthier than those who are not active. There are many reasons for this lack of activity, the most evident being the lack of exposure at an early age to physical skill development activities. If you do not possess the skills to strike a ball, you will probably not play baseball. If you are not skilled in throwing and catching, you will probably not participate in games where those skills are necessary. Children need to learn to throw, catch, jump, and kick when they are young.

If you are going to learn to catch a ball, you have to participate in a developmentally appropriate and logical progression of catching activities. We know that in order to develop physical skills children must spend time practicing those skills. Catching is receiving and controlling an object by the body or its parts. As children learn to catch, they may first fear the ball and pull away to protect themselves. Children progress from catching a ball with their whole body, then with their arms and hands, and eventually with their hands alone.

Stages of Motor Development.   An understanding of motor development will enable you to pick activities that will enhance current skills and foster the development of emerging skills. When looking at motor development, remember to look at both gross and fine motor skills.

[1]Chapter contributed by Leslie Herod.

Gross motor skills involve large muscle movements. Fine motor skills involve the small muscle movements of hands and fingers in coordination with eyes.

There are three distinct stages to the fundamental movement pattern plus the advanced stage:

- Initial—Characterized by the child's first observable attempts at the movement pattern. Many components of the final, mature action may be missing such as a "wind up" or a "follow through" in throwing a ball.
- Elementary—This is a transitional stage in a child's movement development. Coordination and performance improve, and the child gains more control over his or her actions. More components of the final, mature pattern are integrated into the movement, although they may not be performed correctly.
- Mature—The integration of all the necessary and complete movements are coordinated into a well-performed, efficient, purposeful act. The movement resembles the motor pattern of a skilled adult.
- Advanced—The movement pattern integrates all of the component movements of the mature stage of the movement pattern in terms of control and mechanics but also incorporates movement performance acceding the levels of the normal range.

The act of learning to throw a ball takes the child through sequential stages in reaching a mature, efficient performance. In the *initial stage* of throwing, the action occurs mainly from the elbow with a pushing action. The release is forward and downward. The trunk remains perpendicular to the target with little rotation during the throw. The feet remain stationary with weight shifting rearward to maintain balance. In the *elementary stage* the arm swings upward with the elbow flexed in preparation for the throw. The ball is held behind the head and the arm swings forward, over the shoulder, as the trunk rotates toward the throwing side. Shoulders rotate toward the throwing side, and the trunk flexes with the forward motion of the arm. The foot on the throwing side steps forward as the weight of the body shifts forward. The *mature stage* of throwing begins with a preparation for the throw, with the throwing arm swung backward and the opposite elbow raised for balance. The throwing elbow moves forward horizontally as it extends. The forearm rotates, and the thumbs points downward as the trunk rotates to the throwing side in preparation for the release. There is a definite rotation of the hips, legs, spine, and shoulder during the throw. Weight shifts from the rear foot to the foot opposite the throwing arm during the throw.

Locomotor and Nonlocomotor Skills. In order to understand the process of movement education, one must understand the locomotor and nonlocomotor skills. Both are necessary in helping a child reach true movement competency. Movement competency requires the student to first gain basic skills necessary for daily living and child's play and then to develop specialized skills necessary for sports and high-level movement activity. The child gains these competencies through locomotor and nonlocomotor activities. Perceptual motor competency is another consideration related to both types of skill because it concerns balance, coordination, spatial awareness, and knowledge of one's own body.

Locomotor Skills. Locomotor skills are movement of the body from place to place. These skills include walking, running, leaping, jumping, hopping, skipping, galloping, crawling, and rolling. Development of these skills may affect the child's ability to be physically active as an adult. A child who never learns to throw will not be drawn to activities in which throwing is necessary. It is imperative that attention be given to the developmental stages of skills acquisition and in guiding the child though appropriate games and activities that help in gaining proficiency in each of the locomotor skills at a young age.

Nonlocomotor Skills. Nonlocomotor skills are movements performed in one place. These skills include twisting, bending, stretching, pushing, pulling, shaking, and isometric exercises.

Development and participation in these skills better prepare children for the locomotor skills described above. Both locomotor and nonlocomotor skills are necessary in developing healthy, active adults.

Both locomotive and nonlocomotive skills involve aspects of the ability to manipulate objects while in place or while moving from place to place. This ability to manipulate objects during physical activity is necessary in developing spatial awareness and coordination. Manipulation skills include throwing, catching, kicking, bouncing a ball, batting, and hitting an object with a stick or racket. Most of these activities begin with individual practice on a basic level and move to more specialized practice with a partner or a group of people. As skill develops, higher levels of competition can be used in practice.

Biomechanics

Biomechanics is the branch of science concerned with the understanding of interrelationships between structure and function of the human body (or living beings) with respect to the kinematics and kinetics of motion. For some time, the terms "biomechanics" and "kinesiology" were used interchangeably. Biomechanics concerns essential elements (fundamental truths or laws) upon which human movement analyses are based. The first real biomechanics dates back to Aristotle and his study of runners and jumpers in 384–322 B.C. He noted that an animal pushes against the ground to produce movement. Today, high technology is used in studying motion and movement. Physics plays a big role in the study of motion and the application of force upon an object.

Center of Gravity.   Center of gravity is a point about which all the weight of an object can be said to act. Both static and dynamic balance activities (e.g., balancing on a beam, walking the length of a tube) require students to find their center of gravity. Having students engage in a variety of activities that test their ability to find their center of balance will promote the development of this physical education concept.

Force.   The body generates force during physical activity. The action of a force on an object can change the motion of that object. Often the application of force in sports is applied by the human body. Force makes the body use its limbs, shift weight, and maintain coordination. Most activities incorporate a variety of forces in the final completion of the act. Throwing a shot-put, for example, involves clasping, bending, lurching, and throwing. This makes the body use force as a factor for physical development. During physical activities, we generate force.

Motion.   Force applied to an object can create either linear or angular motion. Linear motion is motion in a straight line. Angular motion is movement around a fixed point. Students need to understand how and why one moves in a variety of situations and to learn to use this information to enhance his or her skill. In order to do this they must be able to identify the parts of the body. They need to be acquainted with and practice the scientific principles of Biomechanics, including principles of movement patterns in time, space, and force. Students should be able to analyze their performance and improve movement using self-evaluation and practice. Through maturation and practice of skills, the student should be able to identify and adapt to meet the demands of increasingly complex movement activities and to demonstrate competence in modified versions of a variety of movement forms. The ability to progress through the stages of skill development are important and must follow a progression of those developmental patterns in the stages of development. Skills should progress from simple to complex and allow for practice and competence at each of the levels.

For illustration, the following are general grade-level expectations for biomechanics.

Kindergarten to Second Grade.   At this age level, physical fitness can be developed by expecting the students to run/walk one-quarter mile and run one-eighth mile without walking. They should be able to perform sit-ups according to the requirements in each area of the country and to maintain body fat within appropriate age and sex limits. Body fat is the amount of fat on the body in relation to the amount of muscle. Body fat level are shown in Table 18.1.

TABLE 18.1

MEN	WOMEN
Lean: Less than 8%	Lean: Less than 13%
Average: 8–20%	Average: 13–25%
Fat: Greater than 20%	Fat: Greater than 26%

Students at this age level should be introduced to the concept of cardiorespiratory fitness and the need for aerobic activity in order to achieve a fit heart and circulatory system as well as respiratory system. Students should be able to choose activities that will improve their fitness. Some of the activities that are appropriate for this age would include an obstacle courses, large-group games, jump rope, and aerobic dance.

Grades Three to Five.   The requirements for physical fitness at this age include being able to run one-half to one mile as age increases without walking. The student should be able to perform sit-ups and sit-and-reach according to the requirement in each area of the country. They should also maintain body fat within appropriate age and sex limits. For males, body fat levels should be below 20 percent of the total body weight, and for females, body fat should be below 26 percent of the total body weight. By sixth grade, students should also be able to compare recovery pulse rates with resting pulse rates. Students can identify fitness components related to various activities at this age level and be expected to record fitness goals and personal activity toward achieving those goals. Activities may include keeping a log with daily entries of physical activity and nutrition an be expected to design an exercise program circuit or stations using components of physical fitness.

Grades Six to Eight.   By this time in the students growth and development, they should be able to identify the scientific principles that affect movement. The student can also be expected to analyze and apply knowledge of the opponent's strengths and weaknesses during game situations. They can create games in cooperative groups. Activities to support these accomplishments may include practice and lead-in activities that use movement skills found in their games and movement skill evaluations based on teacher-prepared checklists.

Elements of Movement.   The elements of movement include basic movement skills, such as stepping or shifting weight at a strategic moment, that when put together form a more complex and complete action. The skills listed below are basic but are composed of many elements of movement that take practice and coordination to master. These skills are the basis for many games and sports.

- Throwing—Arm circles back to prepare for the throw, elbow leads in a forward movement, trunk rotates with the throwing arm, and the weight of the body follows through with the motion.
- Catching—Eyes on the ball, arms slightly bent at the elbows and relaxed as the object is brought toward the body when the catch is made.
- Batting or Hitting with a Racket—Eyes on the ball with the elbows in a slightly bent and relaxed position, weight shifts to the front foot upon contact with the ball, and the body follows through to finish the movement after the ball leaves the bat or racket.
- Kicking—Eyes on the ball as the body approaches it with the weight on the nonkicking foot; kicking leg swings forward in a relaxed, slightly bent motion until the foot contacts the ball; and the kicking leg follows through with the motion until it is fully extended in

the direction of the ball. Ball control is enhanced when kicking with the inside of the foot because of the larger surface area of this area of the foot.

CONTENT AREA TWO: HEALTH AND PHYSICAL FITNESS

Fitness is an important part of almost every physical education program. The main objective of a fitness program is to improve cardiovascular performance through cardiovascular endurance. By improving cardiovascular endurance, one improves the amount of oxygen being supplied throughout the body through the bloodstream. Aerobic exercise (movement-type exercise such as running) can increase the heart rate and use of oxygen. Experts agree that heart problems may be diminished by participation in a regular program of physical fitness. Maintaining a training threshold for about twenty minutes three times a week can maintain or improve fitness.

Physical fitness also contributes to improved body composition, which is the ratio of body fat to overall body mass. Strength training develops lean muscle tissue, which uses more calories at rest than fat tissue. A high level of body fat is also a risk factor for disease. Other benefits of a good fitness program include the reduction of stress and the reduced likelihood of injury, disease, and back problems. Fitness education provides programs that help improve an individual's levels in the following areas:

- Cardiovascular endurance.
- Body composition.
- Cholesterol levels in the blood.
- Strength—the amount of force a muscle can exert.
- Endurance—a muscle's ability to contract repeatedly.
- Flexibility—range of motion at a joint.
- Agility—ability to change direction or position quickly.
- Balance—ability to maintain equilibrium.
- Coordination—ability to perform motor activities quickly when needed.
- Power—ability to generate force quickly.

Exercise Plan

A standard, individual exercise plan includes:

- Warm-up (5 minutes): brisk walking or jogging in place followed by static stretching.
- Aerobic workout (25 minutes): bicycling or swimming.
- Cool-down (5 minutes): walking (in or out of water) followed by stretching and flexibility exercises.

Warming up for five minutes will increase heart rate and allow blood to increase its flow to muscles and cells providing the increased amounts of oxygen necessary for increases in activity. Warming up at the beginning of each class prevents student muscular injury. The aerobic portion of the activity will increase heart and metabolic rates and strengthen the cardiorespiratory system. In addition, increasing the metabolic rate will consume body fat. The cool down will enable the heartrate to decrease slowly allowing enough oxygen to continue to be transported by the blood to overextended muscles. PE teachers should also include relaxation exercises at the end of each class to promote the gradual return of student metabolic rates to normal levels. Such relaxation exercises help reduce the physical stress associated with an overly rapid transition from a high level of metabolic functioning to a lower level.

FITT Formula.   FITT stands for frequency, intensity, time, and type. Following are explanations of each principle.

Frequency concerns the number of times that activity of exercise is performed each day. The individual might perform a particular exercise three times a day—once in the morning, once at noon, and once in the evening.

Intensity refers to the amount of effort expended in the performance of each activity or exercise. The individual may slowly perform a particular exercise with little effort and use little strength and energy. However, that same activity might be performed by another individual with great effort and energy, thus expending many more calories and requiring much more of their body.

Time refers to the amount of time the person devotes to the activity or exercise. Is the person going to spend fifteen minutes on an exercise or activity or two hours?

Type is the activity one uses to improve a specific element of health. For example, a person who wishes to increase arm strength would engage in an anaerobic exercise like weight training or push-ups. A person who wishes to increase endurance would engage in an aerobic activity like running wind sprints or running longer and longer distances on a track.

Body Mass Index

The BMI is your body mass index calculated from your height and weight.

$$BMI = kg/m^2$$

BMI is a reliable indicator of total body fat, which is related to the risk of disease and death. The score is valid for both men and women, but it does have some limits. The limits are:

- It may overestimate body fat in athletes and others who have a muscular build.
- It may underestimate body fat in older persons and others who have lost muscle mass.

Nutrition

Protein helps build and repair muscle tissue and is found in meats, fish, nuts, and dairy products. Carbohydrates are a source of energy for the body and are found in breads, cereals, pasta, and other starchy foods. Saturated fats from animal products can be harmful to the body by increasing the amount of cholesterol in the blood vessels, whereas saturated fats from corn or soybean oils are more useful as a source of reserve energy when used sparingly. Vitamins and minerals are found in most properly prepared foods and are only needed in small amounts for aiding the body in normal chemical functions.

The bread, grain, and pasta group, called complex carbohydrates, is energy foods. They provide the main source of fuel and are a better source of energy than simple carbohydrates, which consist of sugars.

Fruits and vegetables provide the body with water, roughage or fiber, vitamins, and minerals. The body is approximately 80 percent water, so it is essential to take water into the body through food. Roughage, or fiber, is the part of a plant that is made of cellulose and is unable to be digested by the human body. This undigested material acts as a scouring pad as it passes through the intestines, cleaning away solid waste, which is then is excreted from the body. The vitamins and minerals are substances that help the body function normally. Vitamins and minerals aid in eyesight, keep hair and skin healthy, and facilitate the production of hormones and other necessary body chemicals. Dairy foods contain calcium for building strong bones and teeth. Bones provide the framework of the body and support muscles as they develop. Dairy products also contain vitamin B_2, which converts food into energy.

The meat group provides the protein necessary for growth and repair of soft tissue. Proteins supply the body with amino acids which are the building blocks for muscle development. Fats, or lipids, are used by every cell in the body to facilitate the use of vitamins. Fats should be consumed in moderation. Water makes up the greatest part of every cell in the body. Water helps the body digest food, transport nutrients, and pass waste. Foods in the food pyramid that are of little use to the body are in the category marked "extras." These foods are high in fats and sugars. Some fats cause high cholesterol that can build up in the blood vessels and eventually block the blood from flowing through that area. If the heart is deprived of the oxygen and nutrients carried in the blood, a heart attack may result. An adult should limit the intake of fatty foods to about fifteen to twenty-five grams of fat each day.

Sugar supplies empty calories and contributes to the development of fat in the body. Too much sugar can lead to obesity, which is a contributing cause of heart disease, diabetes, and some types of cancer.

A maintenance diet is one in which enough calories are consumed to maintain body weight while performing routine daily activities. A reducing diet is one in which fewer calories are consumed than are expended in daily activity. Because the body needs a continuing amount of calories in order to perform, body fat becomes the source of those calories if not enough are consumed during meals throughout the day. As more calories are used by the body than consumed, body fat is reduced and the person loses weight. The only way to lose weight is to consume fewer calories than are expended. The individual can control weight loss and body fitness by increasing the normal amount of exercise and decreasing the amount of unnecessary calories. The type of exercise may depend on the preference of the individual. Weightlifting and strengthening exercises are appropriate for building body mass but aerobic exercises like swimming and running may support cardiovascular endurance over muscle mass. Both choices of exercise will increase the amount of calories used daily and will be instrumental in better body fitness and lowering the BMI.

Our physical health and well-being is affected by exercise, relaxation, nutrition, stress, and substance abuse. Physical health can be improved by being aware of the affects of each of these factors. Exercise can be either aerobic or anaerobic. Aerobic activities include exercises like running, skipping, and jumping, which increase the body's need for oxygen. Anaerobic activity includes exercises like sprinting and basketball that require intense levels of activity for short amounts of time. The more intense the activity, the more oxygen the body requires. The more fit an individual becomes, the more efficient the body will be in the need for oxygen. Aerobic activities also increase the number of capillaries that function in our bodies, because of the increased demands placed on our circulatory system. Another factor to consider in achieving fitness is one's body fat level. Body fat is excess fat that is not necessary for healthy body fitness (see Table 18.1).

Blood Pressure

An individual's blood pressure also contributes to overall good health. Blood pressure is the force of the blood pushing against the walls of the heart and blood vessels. The diastolic rate is the minimum arterial pressure during relaxation and dilatation of the ventricles of the heart when the ventricles fill with blood.

In a blood pressure reading, the diastolic pressure is typically the second number recorded. For example, with a blood pressure of 120/80 ("120 over 80"), the diastolic pressure is 80. This means 80 mm Hg (millimeters of mercury).

"Diastolic" came from the Greek *diastole* meaning "a drawing apart." The term has been in use since the sixteenth century to denote the period of relaxation of the heart muscle.

The systolic pressure is when the heart is contracting. It is specifically the maximum arterial pressure during contraction of the left ventricle of the heart. The time at which ventricular contraction occurs is called systole. In a blood pressure reading, the systolic pressure is typically the first number recorded. For example, with a blood pressure of 120/80 ("120 over 80"), the systolic pressure is 120. This means 120 mm Hg (millimeters of mercury). "Systolic" comes from the Greek *systole* meaning "a drawing together," or a contraction. The term has been in use since the sixteenth century to denote the contraction of the heart muscle.

The optimal blood pressure levels are:

- Diastolic Resting Rate: under 85
- Systolic Resting Rate: under 140

Heart Rate

Heart rate is the number of times the heart beats in a minute. When exercising, it is important to achieve a maximum heart rate in order to increase the strength of the heart. You need to know your resting heart rate and then determine the target heart rate. You can use the following formula to determine your maximum *target heart rate*. The maximum desirable heart rate formula is: 220 – your age = maximum desirable heart rate during exercise.

The optimal heart rate levels are:

- At rest: 40–90 beats per minute
- During exercise: 60 percent of desirable maximum heart rate

Aerobic and Anaerobic Exercise

Aerobic exercise helps your heart and other muscles use oxygen more efficiently. It is an active type of exercise that forces continuous, rigorous movement and heavy breathing. Aerobic exercise stimulates the entire body, burns fat, and strengthens the heart and other muscles. Anaerobic exercise is used primarily for strengthening muscles. One or just a few muscle fibers are exercised in a slow and sustained movement against a stationary object or another muscle group. Anaerobic exercise, like weight training, will also increase one's metabolic rate when at rest resulting in weight loss. As many as thirty to fifty additional calories per day can be consumed by lean muscle, so there is an additional benefit to strength training.

An effective exercise program includes a short warm-up period at the beginning of the activity. The muscles need to be stretched to begin activity in a nonstressful manner. A warm-up of the muscles and joints greatly reduces the risk of injury during exercise and is used for preparing the body for activity while gradually increasing the heart rate. The active or aerobic part of the workout is devoted to some type of active body movement. The activity can change from day to day but should be consistently performed three to five times a week and be active enough to achieve and sustain the target heart rate for at least twenty minutes.

The target heart rate is the rate at which the heart should beat in order to gain strength in the heart muscle. The stronger the muscle, the less it will need to work and the less it will tire and weaken. The formula for finding an individual's heart rate is based on a resting heart rate—the rate at which the heart beats while at rest. Determine the resting heart rate by counting a pulse for a minute while the person is at rest. Choose your level of fitness as 60 percent for beginning, 70 percent for regular exercise, or 80 percent for a competitive athlete. Use the level of fitness number and your resting heart rate in the following equation to find the target heart rate.

220 – your age = maximum heat rate – resting heart rate = (answer)

Take that answer multiplied by the level of fitness = (answer)

Add in resting heart rate to this last answer = Target Heart Rate

The exercise period should conclude with activities like walking and stretching that gradually slow your activity level and stretch muscles to prevent injury and stiffness. The metabolic rate increases during physical activity causing the body to sweat in order to prevent overheating. Dehydration can occur reducing the blood plasma volume. This will in turn lower the blood pressure and reduce the flow of blood to the muscles and skin. Continuous rehydration of fluids is essential during strenuous exercise, especially in excessive heat.

Recognize exercise principles, such as frequency, intensity, and time, to select activities that promote physical fitness. Fitness programs should include purposeful exercise that allows the body to meet the daily demands imposed on it and to continue good cardiovascular circulation.

Benefits of Being Physically Fit

Many people work on physical fitness for the sole purpose of increasing their level of energy. All one has to do is perform an adequate amount of activity, without overdoing it, and eat correctly. Muscles are metabolically active, therefore those who are more physically fit and have stronger muscle tone are those who develop higher metabolic rates, turning their bodies into fat-burning machines.

Consistent participation in activities develops a beneficial connection between the mind and body. When action is requested or required, the brain will agree to the demand and will command an immediate impulse. For those who are unfit, there is no assurance of accurate delivery of the command or the delivery may be delayed by weak mental signal-sending abilities. Thinking makes us smarter, and activities get us thinking. And the more fit we are the better we can think and concentrate. This ability to concentrate and think better transfers to our academic endeavors.

Our bodies are literally held together by a network of muscles and their relative tissues (tendons and ligaments). Weakened muscles cannot hold our skeleton in proper alignment as the body shifts out of its natural position. Physical fitness literally means our body is better able to maintain proper balance and posture. The heart is a muscular pump responsible for the distribution of blood to all areas of the body. When we are involved in activity, our hearts beat at accelerated rates. This acceleration stimulates strength benefits to the heart similar to other muscles.

Instruction

During physical education activities, students need specific and detailed feedback about areas in which they excel and areas in need of improvement. This information can also inform the teacher about how to plan instruction for the students. This way, the teacher can help each student reach individualized goals without planning activities that are too hard for some or too easy for others. Ideally, each student will be assisted in growing to his or her fullest potential.

Teaching Skills

In teaching movement skills to students, a teacher presents the skills using explanation, demonstration, and drills. The instructor must understand the level of skill development for the student and build from basic to more specialized levels gradually. When involved in games or activities using balls, a teacher would start the skills development progression using a larger, lightweight ball and progress to the smaller ball as skill increases. A teacher may present written rules or a description of the activity then provide the students with an opportunity to walk through the activity before expecting competence. Use a variety of methods to demonstrate skills and check frequently for students' understanding. Lower levels of skill development require individual practice with low levels of competition. As a higher skill level is acquired, practice may include a partner or groups of people involving higher levels of competition. Adolescents are sensitive to the embarrassment of failing in a new or difficult skill in front of peers. Allow for success and practice in learning new skills. Often skills practice can take place in sequential, progressive, game-like situations to stimulate student interest and success. Student motivation may be enhanced by allowing for opportunities for choice within the lesson or activity.

Being a member of a team provides many opportunities for social interaction. Students can learn to interact with others and make contributions to the group. The student can develop leadership skills and practice winning and losing gracefully. Getting along with others is a valuable skill that can be promoted in physical education. Social skill in physical education can be improved when taught along with the game or physical activity. Many students who have limited success in other classes may perform best in physical education classes and sports. The teacher should remember that it is important to foster the development of a good self-image along with the student's physical skills. Be careful in situations such as choosing teams that the student is not demeaned or embarrassed by the procedure.

Teachers should remember to include feedback when teaching a skill or activity. Positive feedback tends to be more productive than negative feedback in helping the student to improve. Teachers should also remember that children learn at different rates and according to their individual capacities. Each child should be encouraged to achieve and perform at his or her highest level. A teacher using creative techniques and activities that stimulate the learning environment can achieve this.

CONTENT AREA THREE: INDIVIDUAL AND TEAM SPORTS

Games are usually a contest or activity for amusement that may include many of the fundamental movement skills such as kicking, dribbling, running, and throwing. Team sports are a more organized and competitive activity using team strategy as well as movement skills to achieve a goal, and these include activities like soccer, football, baseball, and basketball. Individual sports involve an individual in competition using movement skill, and these include bowling, swimming, golf, skiing, fencing, and weightlifting. Gymnastics is a very popular type of individual sport. The individual competes but his or her score may be added to the scores of other individuals on their team to compile a team score. One important safety precaution when having students engage in tumbling activities is to ensure that qualified spotters participate in the activity. The greatest risk to students in gymnastics occur from falls and dismounts. Therefore, qualified spotters are required to ensure that students land correctly and thus avoid injury.

There is a difference between play, games, and sports. Play involves creativity and imagination and may not be very physical, but children learn about the world as they play. Play is often spontaneous and unstructured. Games and sport may develop from play as children gradually develop more rules and organization. Often games involve some form of competition, which in turn, fosters cooperation and winning and losing. Developing the skill of gracefully accepting a "win" or a "loss" can be a lifelong lesson that may transfer to all areas of social engagement. Sports refers to organized, formalized games involving physical exertion and strategic thinking.

Sport games can be classified into four categories:

- Court games—Include divided courts (tennis, badminton, ping-pong) and shared courts (handball, squash) where you try to hit an object so that the opponent cannot return it.
- Field games—Games like baseball where you try to prevent the opposing team from retrieving the ball.
- Target games—Games like golf where players are not direct opponents, and games like horseshoe where players are direct opponents.
- Territory games—Games like basketball, football, soccer, and water polo where one team invades an opponent's playing area to score a goal.

Court Games

Tennis is played on a court with one (singles) or two (doubles) players on each side of a net that crosses the center of the court. The singles court is more narrow than the doubles court.

Tennis players use rackets to hit a small, fuzzy ball over a net in order to score points. A point is scored when the ball drops within the boundary of the opposing court and cannot be returned. The first player to score four points wins the game. The game must be won with a margin of two points. The first point scored by each side is called "15." At that point, the score of zero may be called "love." The next point scored after "15" is "30," the next is "40," and then the winning point is "game." If there is a tie score at "40," the score is called "deuce." If the server wins the subsequent point, the score is "add in" (or advantage server). If the receiver wins the subsequent point, the score is "add out" (or advantage receiver). A player must win at least six games over the opponent to win a set. The player winning two out of three sets wins the match.

Field Games

In a typical game of volleyball, there are six players per team set up on a court at one time. A net divides the court in half with players from each team positioning themselves on opposite sides of the net. The players hit a circular ball over the net using any part of their body. Only the serving team scores points when the receiving team is unable to return the ball or to prevent the ball from touching the court surface. The serving team rotates clockwise prior to each change of service. The serving team loses its service right if it commits a fault or fails to get the ball to the opposite court. The serve is then awarded to the opposing team. Each score in a volleyball game is worth one point, and the first team to score 15 points by a margin of 2 points wins the game.

In the game of softball, two teams of nine players compete. The game is played on a field made up of an infield, which is the shape of a diamond with bases located at each of the four corners, and an outfield. The outfield is a large area beyond the diamond-shaped infield. Players on one team position themselves on the field while the opposing team is at bat.

The players at bat may advance around the bases by batting and running in an effort to score. Points, called runs, are scored when a player on the batting team touches all the bases, in order, without being tagged out by a player with the ball in the field. The team scoring the greater number of runs in the allotted innings wins the game. A game usually consists of seven innings. During an inning, one team begins by being at bat until three outs are made by the team in the field. Then the fielding team is given its turn at bat, and the opposing team takes the field.

Target Games

Golf is a game in which a ball is struck with a club from a prepared area, known as the "teeing ground," across fairway and rough to a second prepared area, which has a hole in it, known as the "putting green." The object of the game is to complete what is known as a hole by playing a ball from the teeing ground into the hole on the putting green in the fewest possible strokes. A "round of golf" consists of playing eighteen such holes.

Territory Games

Soccer is a team game played with two teams consisting of eleven players each. The ball is moved along the field by dribbling, passing, and kicking during a game. The object is to score goals. A goal counts as one point and is scored when the ball crosses the opposing team's goal line within the goalie cage. The team scoring the most goals in the allotted time wins. A game is divided into two halves with a rest period between the halves. The game begins with a kick-off at the center circle with each team on its own side of the field. Any player on the field may score a goal and every player should help defend when necessary.

Basketball is played with two teams made up of five players on the court at a time. The players move the ball on the court by dribbling, passing, and shooting. Points are scored when a player shoots the ball through the hoop at the end of the court. A basket may count either two or three points depending on where the shot originates on the court. A completed free throw counts as one point. Free throws are awarded to a player that has been fouled by a member of the opposite team. The team with the most points at the end of the allotted time wins the game. A basketball game is usually divided into two halves with a resting period in between. The game starts with a jump ball at the center court. Cooperative aspects can be integrated into a team sport like basketball. During practice, students focus on passing the ball from their own positions. Passing, unlike dunking, is an element that requires both cooperation and communication. Team dynamics are enhanced when the students learn to strategize together from their positions, as opposed to trying to "slam dunk" the ball every time they receive it.

In a game of football, two teams of eleven players are on the field at one time. The teams move a ball down the field by passing, catching, running, and kicking in an effort to cross the opposing teams goal line and score points. When a team does cross that goal line, it scores a touchdown, worth six points. A kicker sending the ball between goal posts after a touchdown is scored earns an extra point. Three points are earned during a field goal, and two points can be earned in a safety. The team scoring the most points during the allotted time wins the game. The team in possession of the ball plays offense, and the team without the ball plays defense. Both teams line up at the line of scrimmage, which is an imaginary line crossing the field where the ball is placed. Every offensive play from the line of scrimmage is called a down, and the team gets four downs to advance the ball at least ten yards. If successful, the team is awarded a first down with four more tries to get ten yards. A game is usually divided into four quarters with a resting period, or halftime, between the second and third quarters. The game is started with a kickoff.

In field hockey, two teams of eleven players are on the field at one time. The players use wooden sticks to dribble, pass, and advance a small, hard ball along the field to score a goal. A goal is made when a player from one team sends the ball into the goal cage of the opposing team. The goal counts as one point, and the team with the most points at the end of the allotted time period wins the game. Teams may line up in varying formations on their side of the field before the pass back, which begins each half of the game. The game is divided into two halves with a resting period in between. Teams switch playing sides at halftime.

CONTENT AREA FOUR: PHYSICAL GROWTH AND DEVELOPMENT

It is necessary to review various aspects of the human body in order to apply knowledge of human movement and fitness.

Systems of the Body

The skeletal system is the framework that gives shape and form to the human body.

Two or more bones coming together form joints. Joints are connected and held together by strong, tough connective tissue called ligaments. Within most joints is a cartilage, which cushions the joint and absorbs shock. In addition to giving our bodies their shape, the skeleton also stores minerals, calcium phosphate, and calcium carbonate. These minerals are what give our bones their strength.

Until the bones completely ossify, they can be damaged if activities like weight training are introduced too early. Thus, it is important for the physical education teacher to understand when it is appropriate to introduce certain strength activities and when to withhold them.

Muscular System. The muscles in the body are what initiate the movement of the skeleton. There are three types of muscles that make up the muscular system. Skeletal muscles are made of long, elastic muscle fibers and are attached directly to bone by tough, nonelastic tendons. The fibers are strong, can move quickly, but tire easily. Skeletal muscles move the bones through a voluntary action. Smooth muscles control involuntary activities and are not usually attached to bone. Smooth muscle usually moves slowly but has long endurance. They can be found in organs like the intestine, in the urinary tract, and in blood vessels. Cardiac muscle has attributes of both skeletal and smooth muscle tissue because it is strong, moves quickly, and yet has long endurance. Cardiac muscle is found only in the heart.

As a person exercises, the tired skeletal muscles produce lactic acid to make up for an oxygen loss due to overexertion. As the lactic acid builds up, the muscle can become sore and tired. The muscle experiences an oxygen debt until the lactic acid can be replaced by oxygen while resting.

Nervous System. The nervous system is made up of nerve cells called neurons. These cells transmit information throughout the body. The sensory nerves are connected to receptors in the body and send information from the five senses to the brain. The brain sends messages to the muscles by way of the motor nerves. Both sensory and motor nerves are part of the *voluntary nervous system.* The *autonomic nervous system* controls activities such as the heartbeat and digestion and cannot be consciously controlled.

The central nervous system consists of the brain and the spinal cord. The brain has several parts, each with a specific task. The cerebrum is responsible for conscious thought and reactions. It is the largest part of the brain and is separated into a left and right hemisphere. The left hemisphere controls reactions and sensations on the right side of the body and the right hemisphere controls reactions and sensations for the left side of the body.

The cerebellum is located below the posterior to the cerebrum and helps with coordination and execution of muscle activity. The brain stem extends from the base of the brain and is responsible for automatic activity of the heart and respiration. The spinal cord carries impulses to and from the brain and the body.

Respiratory System.   The respiratory system is responsible for bringing oxygen into the body and exchanging that for the carbon dioxide being removed from the body. Oxygen enters the body through the mouth and nose, and travels through the pharynx and trachea to the bronchial tubes into the lungs. The oxygen is exchanged in the alveoli, or air sacs, in the lungs for the carbon dioxide leaving the body. The oxygen travels from the lungs through blood vessels to the heart and is then pumped throughout the body by way of arteries to every cell. The cells use the oxygen in producing energy. One waste product of this process is carbon dioxide, which must then travel through the veins back to the heart and then to the lungs to be exhaled from the body.

Circulatory System.   The circulatory system acts as the transportation system carrying oxygen and nutrition to cells in the body and removing carbon dioxide and other waste. The blood is pumped through blood vessels by the heart. Arteries are the blood vessels that carry blood away from the heart into increasingly smaller vessels until they reach the tiny capillaries. The oxygen–carbon dioxide exchange takes place in the cell, and the waste from the cell is carried away through other capillaries into increasingly larger vessels. The vessels carrying blood back to the heart are called veins.

Maturation

Changes in the body take place during adolescence at different rates for different individuals. All of these changes are controlled by hormones, which are produced in many different glands in the body. Some hormones control changes directly, and others control the production of still more hormones. The pituitary gland, which is located in the brain, is thought to produce the hormone that begins the whole process of change at puberty.

Hormones produced in the pituitary gland travel through the bloodstream to the reproductive glands located in the genital region. The reproductive glands, consisting of the testes in the male and the ovaries in the female, control the changes that occur in the body during puberty. The production of testosterone in the testes of the male is responsible for the secondary sex characteristics that appear during adolescence. It is responsible for rapid growth in muscles mass, production of sperm, and changes in patterns of aggression. Males tend to develop muscle tissue at a much faster rate during puberty than females. It is normal for males to have approximately 10–15 percent less body fat than females during this time.

Puberty begins in the female with the production of a hormone called FSH in the pituitary gland. FSH travels through the bloodstream to the ovaries causing them to begin producing ova and estrogen. Estrogen is the hormone responsible for many of the secondary sex changes occurring in the female. LH, another hormone produced in the pituitary gland, causes ovulation, the process by which an egg or ova erupts from the ovary to begin the menstrual cycle. The hormones produced during adolescence are responsible for many of the physical and emotional differences in the male and female.

Injuries

Many injuries incurred through physical activity can be prevented by a thorough warm-up that includes stretching. However, injuries may still occur. Tendonitis is an inflammation of a tendon that can develop from overuse. A sprain is a stretched or torn ligament at a joint whereas a strain is a stretched or torn muscle. Fractures are breaks or separations in the bone. A good routine of physical activity, including muscle strength, flexibility, and stretching along with the use of proper safety equipment, can help to minimize injuries. Activities and exercise should be age appropriate. Weight training in young children is not recommended because of the possibility of damage to growing bones not yet completely ossified.

Disease

Communicable diseases are illnesses that spread from person to person. They are the most common cause of illness in young children. Germs that cause communicable diseases are found in and on people, animals, food, water, air, and dirt. Most of the germs are carried in human "body fluids"—blood, mucus, saliva, vomit, stool, urine, and discharges from the eyes and skin lesions. Most communicable pathogens are carried on the skin and hair but cause infection by way of penetrating the skin or entering the body by way of the respiratory or digestive systems. Once the body contracts a disease, the immune system usually fights and eliminates the infection without any trouble. Bacteria may infect the body and reproduce at such a rapid rate that the immune system is overwhelmed. At this point, it is necessary to incorporate the use of antibiotics that can aid the body and inhibit the infection. In recent years, however, some forms of bacteria have become resistant to antibiotics commonly employed to resist infection. When antibiotics are used against these strains of bacteria, there is no effect, allowing the bacteria to multiply at a rapid rate and lead to serious complications. It is imperative that antibiotics be prescribed by health care professionals sparingly. If antibiotics are prescribed, the patient must take the entire dosage as indicated by the doctor in order to eliminate all of the invading bacteria and to prevent the possibility of developing a resistant strain. As more resistant strains of bacteria develop, the public faces an increasing health risk by facing infection with the possibility of no antibiotics that will be applicable to that particular infection.

Individuals may be a carrier for a particular infectious disease without their knowledge. Some diseases such as HIV may be without noticeable symptoms. The person may not feel sick or display any signs of the disease but may still be capable of transmitting the disease to other people. Other physical problems affecting children can be chronic or are inherent at birth such as allergies, heart problems, and muscular dystrophy. Diabetes is a type of condition that may develop as the child matures and may be a result of diet or inherited susceptibilities.

It is important to note that different cultures have differing views on the recognition and treatment of various diseases and health problems. As students from other cultures and backgrounds come into the school environment, it is necessary to recognize those differences and to account for them with respect.

Drug Use

A drug is any chemical substance put in the body that causes changes in the mind or body of the user. The drug can be swallowed, inhaled, injected, or rubbed into the skin. Some drugs are used legally as medicines but may be considered illegal if they are misused or abused.

Tobacco.   Many young people start using tobacco to emulate adult behaviors. Tobacco is used by many cultures as a form of hospitality or in religious ceremonies. The use of tobacco, however, is a health risk. Tobacco contains nicotine, which is a poison and causes addiction. The tar found in tobacco is a sticky, dark brown substance that fills the lungs over a period of use and causes inflammation of the bronchial tubes and irritation to the lining of cells, which leads to chronic bronchitis. Smoking paralyzes the bronchial cilia so that particles of tar and other foreign matter cannot be removed. Long-term use of tobacco may result in more devastating affects like emphysema, lung cancer, and even heart disease. Smoking also paralyzes bronchial cilia causing foreign particles to remain in the lungs.

Alcohol.   Alcohol is widely abused because it is inexpensive and easily available. Alcohol is absorbed quickly into the bloodstream from the stomach and small intestine. Approximately seven grams of alcohol can be digested by the body in one hour. If alcohol is consumed at a faster rate than the body can break it down, the level of alcohol in the blood increases and the drinker will experience changes in body control and function.

Stages of Addiction.   The use of drugs and harmful substances follows a similar path leading to addiction:

- Experimentation—Curiosity and occasional use of the substance, usually with friends. The younger the age at which the experimentation begins, the higher the risk of dependency in the future.
- Misuse—Use of the substance becomes more regular or consistent with particular activities.
- Abuse—Use of the substance becomes more frequent and may develop into a habit with some degree of dependency.
- Addiction—Use of the substance on a regular basis. Denial of a problem with the substance. Physical addiction may include illness or pain if the substance is withdrawn from use. Usually, professional help is needed to break the addiction.

There is a difference between addiction and dependency. Dependency is built on an individual's desire for a substance with no physical results occurring if the substance is withdrawn. Addiction is based on a physical need for the substance as well as a strong desire for it. If the substance is withdrawn, the person experiences painful illness or physical reaction to that withdrawal including an increase in heart rate, sweating, tremors in the hands, nausea, and behavioral changes.

A teacher may need to respond to the concerns and questions of parents concerned about their children's possible use of drugs and other harmful substances. One responsible approach would be to discuss the various resources and options available to the family rather than to diagnose a problem.

Decision Making

In order to have good health habits, students need to learn to make good decisions and to set goals over their entire life span. Students need to look ahead and realize that actions they take now will have consequences for the future. This is difficult during the period of adolescents when the individual is focused primarily on the present and has not developed the maturity or experience to anticipate future needs.

Setting goals, and a desire to reach them, is a force that enables students to take control of their future. Goals should be based on the individual's interests, abilities, and values. Basic guidelines for setting goals include:

- The individual needs to understand his or her own strengths, interests, and values.
- Goals should be clearly written, attacking a specific task.
- Goals should be realistic and have a positive affect on the individual.
- Goals need to challenge the individual.
- The individual must have control over the achievement of the goal.

Making good decisions involves a series of steps:

- Define the problem.
- Identify the cause.
- Consider the options and the consequences of actions taken.
- Evaluate the outcome.
- Change the behavior or decision if necessary.

Setting appropriate goals and making good decisions improves an individual's ability interact with others and to respond appropriately to a variety of situations. This increase in individual skills improves a person's abilities in social situations. This in turn can lead to better self-esteem and confidence.

CONTENT AREA FIVE: SELF-IMAGE

In this content area, you learn about the role of physical activity in the development of a positive self-image, and how psychological skills such as goal setting are selected to promote life-long participation in physical activity.

Teenagers often feel awkward, and they look for advice on their appearance and on how they should interact with others. There is plenty of advice available on television, in magazines, and in advertisements telling them how they should look and feel. However, the people illustrated are not representative of the typical teenager.

It is natural for teenagers to notice and be concerned about their bodies. Teenagers need to be given realistic guidance on ways to develop their appearance and activity levels in safe and healthy ways. It is the responsibility of the physical education teacher, and in fact all teachers, to demonstrate important factors in developing strong and healthy bodies that will serve them well throughout life. Being responsible and taking charge of one's health and fitness is empowering. Realistic goals and a plan of action must be developed, in coordination with good accurate information for teenagers, for a healthy plan of action.

CONTENT AREA SIX: SOCIAL ASPECTS OF PHYSICAL EDUCATION

The secret to developing a healthy, lifelong fitness program is to design a program that gives the most fitness benefit with as little pain and as much fun as possible. Working on fitness with friends and peers makes the workout enjoyable and develops social skills within a structured, competitive setting. If students enjoy physical activity because of the social interaction with their peers, they will be much more likely to participate in physical activity throughout their lives.

CONTENT AREA SEVEN: CULTURAL AND HISTORICAL ASPECTS OF MOVEMENT FORMS

Sports, dance, and other forms of movement emphasize attention to the body and breath, liberation from ego, conscious thought, and a path to self-transcendence and equanimity. At their best, sports take the participant in that direction. Ideally, sports and sport participation promote fair play, integrity, nobleness of character, excellence, sacrifice, and self-discipline. But sports can also promote the opposite—cheating, corruption, greed, disrespect for opponents, disloyalty, selfishness, glorification of gratuitous violence, and an attitude that winning is all-important. So there are no uniform consequences for all participants in sports.

Sports and games have played an important part in the weaving of the social fabric of our culture over the ages. As women, African Americans, and other minority groups are accepted into the games of our country, they are accepted into the social structure of our society. Games and sports help us to better understand different people and cultures and to accept them into our lives.

CHAPTER NINETEEN

Child Development[1]

CONTENT AREA ONE: COGNITIVE DEVELOPMENT

Behaviorism

Behaviorism is a theory of animal and human learning that only focuses on objectively observable behaviors and discounts mental activities, where theorists define learning as nothing more than the acquisition of new behavior (Zuriff, 1985).

Conditioning is used as a universal learning process in experiments by behaviorists. Two different types of conditioning yield different behavioral responses:

- Classic conditioning occurs when a natural reflex responds to a stimulus. The most popular example is Pavlov's observation that dogs salivate when they eat or even see food; thus, animals and people are biologically "wired" so that a certain stimulus will produce a specific response (Gormezano & Prosasy, 1987).
- Behavioral or operant conditioning occurs when a response to a stimulus is reinforced. Basically, operant conditioning is a simple feedback system: If a reward or reinforcement follows the response to a stimulus, then the response becomes more probable in the future (Brush, Overmier, & Solomon, 1985). For example, leading behaviorist B. F. Skinner used reinforcement techniques to teach pigeons to dance and to roll a ball down a miniature bowling lane.

There have been many criticisms of behaviorism. Behaviorism does not allow for all types of learning including activities of the mind and thinking and reasoning skills: It does not explain language patterns in children that seem to develop with no reinforcement mechanism; it does not account for transference of these learned patterns to new changes in environment without the necessary application of reinforcement (Uttal, 2000).

This theory is relatively simple to understand because it relies only on observable behavior and describes several universal laws of behavior. Its positive and negative reinforcement techniques can be very effective—both in animals and in treatments for humans. Behaviorism often is used by teachers who reward or punish student behaviors. Some of the important individuals and their theories on behavorism are listed here.

- John Watson was concerned with observable, measurable behavior and those events that stimulate or reinforce the behavior, proposed that a conditioned response means that a child can be taught to respond in a particular way to a stimulus that would not normally elicit that response (Kimble, 1967).

- Pavlov felt that a neutral stimulus, called a conditioned stimulus, may elicit a conditioned response. Pavlov conducted classical conditioning experiments with dogs, finding that

[1]Chapter contributed by Leslie Herod.

they would naturally salivate when the food stimulus is introduced and showing that dogs can be conditioned to salivate in response to any neutral stimulus (Windholz, 1997).

■ Thorndike developed the Law of Exercise—a conditioned response can be strengthened through practice and repetition—and Law of Effect—responses that are rewarded are strengthened and those that are punished are weakened (Thorndike, 1912). These studies led to positive reinforcement of wanted behaviors.

■ B. F. Skinner believed that learning is established through stimulus and response connections, rewards make repeating certain behaviors desirable; thus, reinforcement can establish certain behaviors in children (Skinner, 1957).

■ Sigmund Freud was interested in looking at the relationship between mental functioning and certain basic structures of civilization, such as religious beliefs. Freud believed, and many people after him believe, that his theories about how the mind worked uncovered some basic truths about how an individual self is formed and how culture and civilization operate. According to Freud, what we do and why we do it, who we are and how we became this way, are all related to our sexual drive. Our differences in personality are attributed to different sexual experiences occurring in childhood. Freud attributes personality development in childhood with five stages of development of the sexual drive: Oral, Anal, Phallic, Latency, and Genital. Children focus on different developing stages of sexual desire and as they satisfy needs in those areas, conflict arises leading to development of personality differences in adults. Failure to achieve a satisfactory resolution of conflict at a particular stage will result in the child being fixated in that stage. This fixation at a particular stage is believed to be the cause of many personality and behavioral disorders.

■ Jean Piaget's theory is based on the idea that the developing child builds cognitive structures—in other words, mental "maps," schemata, or networked concepts for understanding and responding to physical experiences within his or her environment (Duckworth & Evans, 1973). Piaget's work is based on four major assumptions (Flavell, 1963):

1. Children are organically inspired to think, learn, and comprehend.
2. Children see the world differently than adults.
3. Children's knowledge is ordered into mental structures called *schemas*.
4. All learning consists of *assimilation* and *accommodation*.

Cognitive development is a result of the child's interaction with the physical world, social experiences, and physical maturation. Children learn through active involvement with their environment. Stage theory states that students develop concepts through a predictable sequence of fixed, but uneven stages.

Piaget's theory identifies four developmental stages and the processes by which children progress through them. The four stages are (Maier, 1969):

1. Sensorimotor stage (Ages Birth–2)—The child, through physical interaction with his or her environment, builds a set of concepts about reality and how it works. This is the stage where a child does not know that physical objects remain in existence even when out of sight, and children exhibit poor motor and verbal skills
2. Preoperational stage (Ages 2–7)—The child is not yet able to conceptualize abstractly and needs concrete physical situations. Children develop language, are egocentric and rigid in their thinking, use semi-logical reasoning and problem-solving skills, and limited social cognition.
3. Concrete operations (Ages 7–11)—The child starts to conceptualize as experiences accumulate, creating logical structures that explain physical experiences. Abstract problem solving is also possible at this stage. Arithmetic equations can be solved with numbers, not just with objects. Learners begin to de-center. Concepts become organized and logical as long as the student is *working with concrete examples and materials*.
4. Formal operations (Ages 11–15)—By this point, the child's cognitive structures are like those of an adult and include conceptual reasoning. The degree of development of

thought at this stage may depend on the students' opportunities for a wide range of manipulative experiences at the operational stage. Students can think in symbolic terms without concrete images and materials; they can reason abstractly and theoretically.

Moral Development

Morality is defined as an internalized set of rules influencing feelings, thoughts, and behaviors in making moral choices. Two basic stages of moral development in children include:

- Morality of Constraint (heteronomous)—Children (age 4–7) see their world through eyes of rules and justice (Piaget, 1932). As they develop, children begin to understand that people make those rules and that there may be many variables in determining what is right and wrong.
- Morality of Cooperation—By about age 10, children look at each new situation and the consequences surrounding their choices before making a moral decision (Piaget, 1932). It may still be difficult at this point to take on another person's perspective or to empathize with another.

One's ability to think develops as the individual matures physiologically and interacts with the environment. Some of the important individuals and their theories on moral development are listed here.

- Abraham Maslow presented a theory based on Levels of Needs. People develop through a hierarchical sequence of needs, where the lower level of needs must be satisfied before the individual can accomplish the higher levels of achievement (DeCarvalho, 1991):
  1. Basic Physiological Needs—Food, water, sleep, and shelter.
  2. Safety—Protected from danger or harm.
  3. Need for Affiliation—To belong and be accepted by others.

Schools have gone to great lengths to help provide for these basic levels of needs so that students may begin the journey of formal education. Schools now have breakfast and lunch programs and have been equipped with metal detectors and guards. There are activities and clubs extending beyond the classroom and the school day that encourage students to connect with other students.

- Eric Erikson's Psychosocial Stages of Development was the basis for his theory of learning, where a person's life can be broken into stages. An emotional crisis at each stage can lead to a positive or negative result, and the result achieved at each stage may determine the pattern for the next stage (Erikson & Evans, 1967):

School Age Stages
  1. Initiative vs. Guilt—Preschool- and primary-school-age children who are treated warmly tend to be able to move away from parents but those who are rejected tend to become more inhibited (Browning, 1973).
  2. Industry vs. Inferiority—Students in the elementary grades who enter school and acquire the academic and social skills necessary for success will achieve a sense of industry, and those who fail will develop a sense of inferiority (Hoover, Marcia, & Parris, 1998).
  3. Identity vs. Identity Confusion—Middle-school-age students strive to find out what they believe in, what their goals, ideas, and values are. Failure to discover these things leads to identity confusion (Lemert, 1999).
  4. Intimacy vs. Isolation—High-school-age students entering young adulthood begin thinking about forming lasting relationships (Ewen, 1998). Children are either able to function independently of parents or are still at some level of parental attachment

according to their level of security. Academic skill acquisition is stressed in the elementary school grades while social interaction is fostered. Schools failing to provide for this struggle to achieve identity in their students risk creating serious psychological problems for the student. Students who are not successful in achieving a solid grasp of identity in the previous stage may have problems forming lasting relationships.

■ L. S. Vygotsky formulated the social cognition learning model that asserts that culture is the prime determinant of individual development, and humans are the only species to have created culture, and every human child develops in the context of a culture (Vygotsky & Luria, 1993). A child's learning development is affected in ways large and small by the culture, including the culture of family environment, in which he or she grows up.

Language and Thought: Development is determined by language, because it is a powerful tool in shaping thought and is essential to acquiring knowledge. A new idea must be *thought* about before any new idea can be formulated. Intellectual expression cannot take place until *thought* and *knowledge* exist. In order to gain knowledge, *language* must be present. During infancy thought and language emerge separately from each other. About age 3, *private speech,* or self-talk, helps children to self-regulate and to control their behavior.

Learning occurs through observation and imitation of more capable peers. There is a continuum of development, where the learner moves onward and upward through the guidance of a more capable peer until she or he becomes independent.

Sociocultural Theory: Children construct their knowledge through culture. The function of a child's cultural development occurs twice—first between people, and then internalized within the child. Language is essential to this development. The child's cognitive growth is socially based and is a shared process involving:

1. Zone of Proximal Development (ZPD)—the distance between a child's actual performance and potential performance, where with guidance by someone more skilled, the child may develop a higher competency and move beyond what she or he was otherwise capable of doing (Lightfoot & Cox, 1997).

2. Scaffolding—a temporary support system from a teacher or older peer to guide the child until a task can be mastered alone (Gergen, 1995). Three essential elements of scaffolding: (a) the use of mediators for learning, (b) the emphasis on language and shared activity for learning, (c) shared activity improves the child's problem-solving ability.

Vygotsky's theories impact learning through curriculum, instruction, and assessment. Since children learn much through interaction, curricula should be designed to emphasize interaction between learners and learning tasks. With appropriate adult help, children can often perform tasks that they are incapable of completing on their own. With this in mind, scaffolding in which the adult continually adjusts the level of his or her help in response to the child's level of performance is an effective form of teaching. Scaffolding not only produces immediate results, but also instills the skills necessary for independent problem solving in the future. Assessment methods must take into account the zone of proximal development. What children can do on their own is their level of actual development and what they can do with help is their level of potential development. Two children might have the same level of actual development, but given the appropriate help from an adult, one might be able to solve many more problems than the other. Assessment methods must target both the level of actual development and the level of potential development.

■ Lawrence Kohlberg emphasized that human beings develop philosophically and psychologically in a progressive fashion.

Moral development occurs in sequential stages as an individual matures in moral reasoning, moving from concrete to abstract (Lapsley, 1996).

1. Preconventional Level of Morality (Ages 4–10)—The first level of moral thinking is that generally found at the elementary school level. Children follow adult instruction on morals based upon consequences. Morality is judged on the fear of being punished

for negative behavior or rewarded for positive behavior. The second stage of this level is characterized by a view that right behavior means acting in one's own best interests.

2. Conventional Level of Morality (Ages 10–13)—Morality is guided by concern about the opinion of their peers and society. This level is characterized by an attitude that seeks to do what will gain the approval of others and is oriented toward abiding by the law and responding to the obligations of duty. Children at this age want to please others while developing their own ideas of what it means to be a good person.

3. Postconventional Level of Morality (Ages 13–Adult)—Morality and ethical choices rise above the laws of society, and individuals form their own ideas of right and wrong based upon internal experience. Many people never reach this level of morality development. This level involves an understanding of social mutuality and a genuine interest in the welfare of others. It is based on respect for universal principle and the demands of individual conscience.

Teachers must recognize that a child in school acts on what is right and wrong based on the child's basic values gained from interaction with significant adults and his or her own sense of self. Teachers must also recognize the impact and importance of interaction and approval of peers. Kohlberg felt that children react differently to moral dilemmas depending upon age, education, and socioeconomic influences.

■ Robert Sternberg (1985) proposed the Triarchic Theory of Intelligence. This theory states that people who are intelligent possess a high level of common sense and will succeed according to their own definition of success by getting the most out of their strengths and adapting to their weaknesses (Sternberg, 1988). The components of intelligence include:

1. Analytical (componential)—The mechanics or components of intelligence such as memory, critical thinking, and problem solving can be measured by traditional intelligence tests.

2. Creative (experiential)—Skills are based on the learner's experiences including the ability to create, design, imagine, or invent. Children with these traits are insightful and creative and may not relate well to academic demands or the structure of school.

3. Practical (contextual)—This can be described as being "streetwise" where one understands how to adapt to the environment to achieve particular goals. There is a combination of adapting one's self; changing the environment; and moving to a brand new environment if one cannot adapt or if one cannot change things.

Teachers need to use lessons and strategies that address all of these intelligences and offer a variety of assessment types to allow their students to demonstrate their strengths.

■ John Flavell's Metacognition describes how, what, and why people know what they know. It is also "thinking about thinking," where one learns how to think his or her way through complex tasks after having learned the process for doing so (Boosalis, 2004). For example, if you have ever found yourself talking yourself through a computer problem before either solving it or calling the help desk, then you know something about metacognition.

For Flavell (1999), adolescents mature into higher levels of metacognition and sophisticated thinking by understanding themselves personally (their strengths, limitations, and differences); the nature of the task before them; and the strategies required to accomplish their goals. As such, teachers should give children the opportunity to learn in each of these domains, so that children can progress in their development. If a teacher ever taught you to skim and scan before reading, for example, he or she was trying to teach you a metacognitive skill to help you become a more independent reader later on in life.

■ Howard Gardner's Theory of Multiple Intelligences suggests there are a number of ways that people have of seeing and understanding the world, and he labels each set of skills that allows individuals to find and resolve the problems they face a distinct "intelligence" (Gardener, 1993a).

This theory provides eight types of intelligence (Gardner, 1993b):

1. Linguistic–Verbal Ability—the ability to think in words and to use language.
2. Logical–Mathematical Ability—the ability to carry out mathematical operations.
3. Spatial Ability—the ability to think in a three-dimensional field and to visualize objects, spatial dimensions, and create internal images and pictures.
4. Bodily–Kinesthetic Ability—the ability and wisdom to use the body and physical skill to control physical motion.
5. Musical Ability—the ability to identify pitch, melody, and tone, as well as sensitivity to rhythms and beats.
6. Interpersonal Ability—the ability to understand others and to interact well with others.
7. Intrapersonal Ability—the ability to understand oneself and to plan and direct one's own life. The spiritual, inner states of being, self-reflection, and awareness.
8. Naturalist Ability—the ability to identify patterns in nature.

Teachers should recognize and plan activities around a balanced combination of all intelligences. Gardner (1993a) suggests a more balanced curriculum that incorporates the arts, self-awareness, communication, and physical education. Teachers need to be aware of the various strengths in each students and to provide activities to encourage those abilities.

■ Albert Bandura's theory of observational learning, sometimes called the social learning theory, says that learning occurs when an observer's behavior changes after viewing the behavior of a model (Bandura, 1973).

The observer will imitate the model's behavior if the model possesses characteristics that the observer finds desirable. Things such as talent, intelligence, power, good looks, or popularity are examples of things that might be considered attractive or desirable characteristics. The observer will react to the way the model is treated and will mimic the model's behavior. When the model's behavior is rewarded, the observer is more likely to reproduce the rewarded behavior. When the model is punished, the observer is less likely to reproduce the same behavior.

Attention and retention account for acquisition or learning of a model's behavior; production and motivation control the performance. Teachers need to remember that students must get a chance to observe and model the behavior that leads to a positive reinforcement. Educators must encourage collaborative learning, since much of learning happens within social and environmental contexts. A learned behavior often cannot be performed unless there is the right environment for it. Educators must provide the incentive and the supportive environment for the behavior to happen.

CONTENT AREA TWO: SOCIAL DEVELOPMENT

We can define personality as the distinguishing characteristics of an individual that make him or her different from anyone else when actions are displayed in a wide range of situations and circumstances. The development of a personality is an interaction between genetic make-up of an individual and his or her environment. Cultural, racial, socioeconomic, educational, social guidance, and health condition could be examples of the forces present in the environment that help shape the personality. Various theorists have proposed differing points of view on the concept of personality development. Freud dealt with personality development from a sexual point of view and was concerned mainly with emotional development. Learning theorists present ideas supporting behavior being modified by experiences. The psychoanalytic development theory proposed by Erik Erikson emphasizes the importance of interpersonal transactions between parents and child and the child's development in a social system. Basically, the individual passes through eight stages during his or her lifetime. These stages are listed below:

1. Infancy (First Year)—this period is characterized by very rapid physical, psychological, and social growth and development. Infants learn to trust others and to care for them. The child begins to explore the physical world. Infants need stimulating and socializing experiences to

aid in developing their personalities. The sense of confidence is established when the infant is able to depend upon caregivers who fulfill their needs. The developmental tasks of infancy include learning to walk, beginning to talk and communicate with others, beginning to have emotional relationships with primary caregivers, learning to eat solid foods, and developing stable sleep and eating periods.

2. Toddler (Ages 1–3)—this stage involves increased motor development, but the child continues to lack skill and judgment so limitations and direction are needed. Children learn basic skills to care for themselves. Failure to learn these skills may make children dependent on others and thus become ashamed of themselves. The child's curiosity increases but his or her verbal and intellectual abilities lag far behind motor development. Frustration often results in temper tantrums. The child must learn to obey rules, and this is a critical period in which the toddler establishes a basic trust in self and a sense of initiative. Piaget suggests that at this age children will begin to understand objects reflexively and then later react purposefully. Children will then make mental symbols of those objects. The developmental tasks at this time include tolerating separation from the primary caregiver, toilet training and control, using words to communicate with others, and becoming less dependent on the primary caregiver.

3. Preschool or Early Childhood (Ages 3–6)—There is tremendous growth in vocabulary at this stage. The child explores his or her world by persistent questioning and uses fantasy during play. The child becomes more cooperative with family and parental demands. A child may take on responsibilities beyond his or her capacity, which may cause conflict and promote a feeling of guilt. The key in this stage is to create a balance between initiative and not infringing on the rights of others. The developmental tasks at this stage include the increasing ability to communicate and to understand others, perform self-care activities, learning the difference between sexes and developing sexual modesty, learning right from wrong, and developing family relationships.

4. School Age (Ages 6–12)—At this stage the child is entering school. Changes occur in personal self-concept, values, and cognitive capacities; and behavior is increasingly influenced by peers. Children acquire social and academic skills. They begin to compare themselves with peers. If they seem to be lacking in skills, they may develop a feeling of inferiority. They have very rigid standards of right and wrong. The developmental tasks at this age include developing social and physical skills needed for games; learning to get along with others; learning behavioral attitudes toward sex; learning basic reading, writing, and arithmetic skills; and developing a concept of self. During the later years of this stage, the child begins to show more maturity as he or she becomes more independent; develops greater muscular strength, coordination, and balance; and acquires the ability to develop and keep friends.

5. Adolescence (Ages 12–20)—The major issues at this stage center around questions concerning the individual's ideas of him- or herself. At this point, the individual will experiment with various roles. If the child does not establish an identity at this stage, he or she may be confused as an adult about roles he or she should be playing. The development tasks at this stage include accepting changes in body and appearance, developing appropriate relationships with males and females, and the sexual role appropriate for his or her age. The child will also become independent from parents and other adults while developing his or her own morals, attitudes, and values. This is a period of emotional upheaval and rebellion, sudden changes of mood, and shifting ideologies. Peer groups are critical in the socialization process. The adolescent needs to find out what sort of person he or she is and what his or her abilities are.

CONTENT AREA THREE: PHYSICAL DEVELOPMENT

Babies and young children learn about their environment through movement and through their senses. They learn how to deal with gravity, to keep their balance, to move their body through space, about time, and about sequence of events.

A child's growth is a continuous process, a gradual sequencing from one stage of physical and mental development to another. There is a tremendous amount of growth and change in a child in the first five years of life. These years are often said to be the most important years in allowing a child to reach their full potential.

By age 2 normal children should be able to walk well, go up and down steps alone, run, and sit in a chair. They are becoming independent in toileting, dressing themselves, and in feeding using a spoon and fork. By this time they can imitate circular motions, turn pages, and kick a ball. In social development, children are very immature with little concept of others as people. They may respond to simple directions, however. Emotionally they are very self-centered, just beginning a sense of personal identity, and often frustrated and negative. At this age, they are just beginning to say words, phrases, and simple sentences with a word capacity of about 270 words. Children will understand simple directions and have a short attention span.

By age 3, children's physical development has improved to allow more advanced running, improved balance to be able to stand on one foot, and the ability to feed and dress themselves adequately. Socially they now recognize and enjoy being with others, they can be expected to take turns with a friend, and they like to "help" in simple tasks requiring little skill. Emotionally children are more easygoing and like to conform. They seem more secure and begin to be more adventuresome as they develop a greater sense of self. Intellectually they can say short sentences and have a vocabulary of about 900 words. There has been great growth in communication, as they tell stories and answer questions.

By age 4, children can skip on one foot, throw a ball overhand, climb a ladder, and cut with scissors. They are able to recognize and draw a "man." Emotionally children are more sure of themselves and begin testing their boundaries. Socially the child plays cooperatively and enjoys other children's company while playing loosely organized group games like tag or duck-duck-goose. Children use complete sentences at this point with a vocabulary of approximately 1,550 words. They engage in coherent conversation and can give name and address. They understand the concept of time; they have learned to generalize, are highly imaginative, and can draw recognizable simple objects.

By age 5, children can hop and skip, have good balance and smoother muscle action, and can print letters. They have established their dominant handedness, and girls seem to achieve a higher level of small muscle control about one year ahead of boys. Emotionally, children are more self-assured, stable, and well adjusted and like to associate with their caregivers. They like to follow rules and enjoy responsibility. Socially, they are highly cooperative and very organized. They can enjoy simple table games at this point and can observe rules and take turns. They will feel pride in accomplishment. Children now have a vocabulary of just more than 2,000 words, can read their own names, and count to 10. They know colors and are beginning to differentiate between fact and fiction. They are highly interested in their environment.

By age 6, children are more skillful with their hands and may be able to ride a bicycle. They start to lose their first teeth and acquire permanent molars. Children are more excitable, impulsive, and changeable and may even seem rude or aggressive at this age. They have begun to read and print letters and simple words. They can read and write numbers and add and subtract single-digit numbers.

At age 7, children demonstrate some elementary skill in bat-and-ball games, skipping, and hopscotch, and can learn to swim or play a musical instrument. They show increased awareness and understanding of the world around them. They are polite and anxious to impress others. At this age, they are expected to read simple words and sentences, print large and small letters, and add within 20 and subtract within 10. A typical personality may be quiet and thoughtful and demonstrate a sense of responsibility.

By age 8, children are physically very lively as sporting skills markedly develop. They can be expected to participate in team sports. Drawings show some proportion and perspective. They can read with understanding, add and subtract three-digit numbers, and begin simple multiplication. Children are self-reliant, sociable, and outgoing. They are active and may be critical of others as they become aware of their own ability to fail. Popularity and success are very important outside the security of their families.

Children at age 9 are very adept with hands and fingers. Special skills and talent in sports and music become evident at this point. The child is well behaved and perserveres in work and play. The child has mastered the basic techniques of reading, writing, and math. Children at this age may be sensible, self-motivated, and more interested in their bodies and about sex.

At age 10, children have a command of the basic skills for personal hygiene, feeding, ball games, and sports. They may begin to assert their independence and enjoy more adult activities and attention. They read well and can write stories to one page in length. This is generally a peaceful age with the child's accepting rules and family.

At ages 11 and 12, the child begins early adolescence. There is rapid physical change with development of pubic hair, breasts in girls, pimples, and gawkiness. Children develop strong sexual feelings with concerns for their own identity and values. They want to be listened to and taken seriously. This is the point when children begin to experiment and take risks. They may question parents, rules, and values. They are impulsive with strong emotions and large mood swings. They can be very self-conscious and want more privacy. Peers are an important influence on behavior as individuals become less dependent on the family.

CONTENT AREA FOUR: INFLUENCES ON DEVELOPMENT

Peer Groups

The influence of peers takes hold as children attempt to establish their own identities away from their families. The influence can be either positive or negative. Thus, learning how to resist negative influences is very important. If the child is already clear about his or her own values, then the child can make better decisions about which behaviors to emulate or avoid.

Ethnocentrism

This is a sociological term used to describe an individual's tendency to view his or her own way of doing things and or making decisions as the right, correct, or best way. Schools in the United States have been accused of being ethnocentric in the way that curriculum is presented and in the way that teachers address students in the classroom. Ethnocentrism can be damaging because it tends to be exclusive rather than inclusive. It is important that teachers try to include all races, religions, genders, and religions when developing curriculum and when addressing students.

Nature versus Nurture

There has been continuing discussion and debate over the question of nature (heredity and genes) and nurture (environment and experience). Children may be born with various physical challenges such as poor eyesight, mental retardation, and some forms of mental illness. However, children's development and ability to cope with those genetic differences may be greatly enhanced or affected by their interaction with the environment as they grow and mature. Perception plays a great role in the individual's personal reality. The world as we know it, and how we react to it, is a result of our selective perception. Effective teachers recognize the effects of student's perceptions on the learning process and promote relevant, realistic expectations. The teacher encourages students to excel and to do their best within a safe and nurturing classroom environment.

Intelligence

Most psychologists agree that intelligence is a trait that is inferred on the basis of observable behavior. The traditional intelligence, or IQ, test is used for predicting future success in school and may be given to children between ages 6 and 16. The two most widely used IQ tests are the *Wechsler Intelligence Scale for Children* and the *Stanford-Binet Intelligence Scale.*

Learning Styles

There are three learning preferences: auditory, visual, and kinesthetic. Knowing the learning preference of each student will help in identifying their needs. Auditory learners require inclusion in discussion and debate. They need to ask questions, summarize, and paraphrase. It is important for auditory learners to recite what they have heard or read. Visual learners need to sit where they can see the teacher and the board. They need to draw, use graphic organizers, and flashcards and be given the opportunity to visualize abstract concepts. They need to read and research. Kinesthetic learners benefit from inclusive activities such as group discussion, role playing, computer work, and other manipulative devices. They learn best through real-life, relevant activities. Kinesthetic learners may need to move about as they are learning. Teachers need to recognize the fact that not everyone learns in the same manner. Teachers need to design lessons that utilize a variety of experiences and approaches.

Motivation

Motivation affects both what is learned and how it is learned. Motivation in students is affected by their goals, beliefs, interests, ways of thinking, and their emotional state. Their ability to learn is also affected by whether the material to be learned is familiar to them. The more a student wants to learn and the more familiar he or she is with the material, the more easily that material can be mastered. Teachers need to facilitate motivation by using strategies that enhance learner effort and comprehension. Effective strategies include purposeful learning activities with guided practice that are relevant to the student.

Metacognition

Metacognition is the ability to know and understand one's own learning and, in doing so, be able to plan, monitor, and evaluate one's own thinking. Learning strategies that can be established to provide feedback on learning include making predictions, checking progress, monitoring performance, and evaluating work. Successful learners can reflect on how they think and learn, thus providing themselves with access to strategies and alternative methods of reaching their goals.

Learning Challenges

Language. Teachers should maintain high learning standards when working with students whose first language is not English. Teachers can use simpler words, use context clues to identify word meaning, model words and phrases clearly and carefully, and actively involve students in the learning process. Learning is most effective when differences in the student's linguistic, cultural, and social backgrounds are taken into account.

Socioeconomic Status. Success in school is specifically related to economic status. Students with a higher socioeconomic status tend toward higher achievement in school and in testing. Socioeconomic status is based primarily on home environment, opportunity for enrichment experiences, and parental expectations. Instruction can be adapted to meet the varying challenges of differing backgrounds. Students with a low socioeconomic status need more encouragement and opportunity to succeed within a structured environment. Students with a higher level of socioeconomic status may be provided with less structure and more material. The level of competition should be minimized. Both groups of students can achieve and should be challenged.

Students with Disabilities.   Students are identified as learning disabled by demonstrating a discrepancy between their measured intelligence and their performance within the classroom. Children do not usually outgrow a learning disability but rather learn coping mechanisms to deal with the disability. Learning disabilities include visual, auditory, language learning, perceptual-motor, attention deficit, and impulsive or hyperactive disorders. Teachers need to recognize these differences within their students and to provide for them. The Individuals with Disabilities Act guarantees all children a free and appropriate education. Students identified with a disability may be integrated into a regular classroom in an *inclusive program;* or they may be *mainstreamed,* where they would receive instruction in a special education program part-time and a regular classroom for the rest of the time. Students may also receive an individualized instruction plans (IEP), which would meet their individual needs within the school routine.

Changing Learning Behavior

Various methods of changing learning behaviors have been successfully employed by teachers. Some things work for all age groups, such as contracts and student logs, modeling, and positive reinforcement. Contracts and logs enable students to think about their behavior and their goals. Modeling is an essential skill for a teacher and requires careful listening, and respectful actions and responses. Reinforcement can be positive in that after reaching agreement on the desired behavior, once that behavior is achieved, a reward is given. Negative reinforcement is appropriate when a teacher is showing a student how to avoid an undesirable consequence.

Methods of changing learning behaviors that work best with children include cooperative learning, content enhancement routines, and inquiry. The teacher encourages active learning where the child is a participant in the lesson by using student ideas and suggestions, praising the student, and answering student's questions. Cooperative learning involves students as they work in a small group to accomplish a task. Cooperative learning encourages students to establish better relationships with others and to solve problems democratically. Content enhancement routines engage students by providing organizational strategies and graphic maps to highlight critical content. The teacher prepares the routines prior to the lesson and then involves the students in developing the organizers together so that the student has a sense of ownership in the lesson. The inquiry method requires planning by the teacher. A problem is presented to the students who then ask questions of the teacher to gain information. The teacher has the students then make probable solutions to the problem. The student is also required to describe the process used in reaching his conclusion.

Environmental Factors

A student reacts to his or her environment depending upon many varying factors. The amount of light in a room, the design of the classroom, noise levels, temperature, and decoration in the room can affect a student's ability to learn. An effective teacher must take into consideration the learning needs of all the students and try to address those needs by creating different environments within the classroom. Small group work, study centers, varying use of light and temperature may help to address the various needs of students in the classroom.

The Arts[1]

CONTENT AREA ONE: VISUAL ART

Visual arts have been a vehicle through which humanity has been able to express basic spiritual needs since the beginning of mankind. A quality work of art succeeds in the purpose for which it was created and is presented with a unique style that is appropriate for its purpose. The artist should demonstrate accomplished technical skill and discipline in the medium with which the work was created. The piece should be distinctive and memorable. All of these criteria should be applied within the historical framework in which the work of art was created. The visual arts comprise categories of painting, sculpture, architecture, and ceramics or pottery. Each of these has its own rules by which to be analyzed and judged.

Painting

Painting is a two-dimensional form of representing reality or arranging color on a flat surface like a canvas or paper, wall, wood panels, or even pottery. Typical media used in painting include oil and acrylic pigments, watercolor, or fresco. Drawing and printmaking are also forms of two-dimensional art using pencil lead, crayons, pastel color, and ink. There are various methods of putting pigment onto canvas and other surfaces. Paint is composed of three components: *pigment,* which is a powdered coloring agent; *binder* or medium, which is liquid that holds pigment together, and a *vehicle,* which is the liquid that aids in the spreading of all paint. The binder that is used affects the characteristics of the paint and affects which vehicle may be used. The process of painting has not changed over time, but the materials and techniques have. Today, artists have many more pigments available to them than they did in the past and a wider variety of binders, vehicles, brushes, and supports.

- *Scrumbling* is a treatment that helps to soften the hard or textured surfaces of a painting. The artist rubs the brush over the surface of the painting to blend colors together and to create a smoother image.
- *Impasto* adds modeling paste to paint to make a thick, lumpy application of paint often showing the brush or palette knife strokes. This adds texture and depth to the application of the pigment.
- *Alla prima* (wet in wet) is a method of painting in a hurried manner. The picture is completed with the first application of paints to the whole picture instead of applying the paint a layer at a time.

[1]Chapter contributed by Leslie Herod.

Metalworking

Engraving is a method of cutting designs or letters into metal with a sharp tool. It has been used for making prints by applying ink over the ingraved area. Money is often made with an engraving process. Prints may also be produced with this method.

Respoussé is a style where a piece of metal is secured to a malleable surface, and the piece is worked from the back (often punched) to create an image on the front of the surface.

Printmaking

Lithography is an example of planographics, where a design is drawn on a surface and then the print is lifted from that surface onto another surface. Rubber stamps are an example of relief printing, where ink is applied to a surface with raised contours and then stamped onto a surface. Potato printing and linoleum block printing are other examples. Etchings and engravings are examples of *intaglio* printing, where ink fills the etch marks and then a metal plate is stamped with great force onto paper. The image is created from the paper being forced into the grooves and absorbing the ink.

Materials

Materials used in producing artistic works that you need to know about for the test include:

- Abrasive—A substance that wears down a surface by the friction of rubbing against it. Abrasives are available in many forms, including powders, compounds, papers, disks, brushes, belts, and more, each most appropriate for certain applications.
- Acrylic Paint—A synthetic paint with pigments dispersed in a synthetic vehicle first used by artists in the late 1940s. They compete with oil paints because of their versatility. They dry quickly, do not yellow with age, and are easily cleaned up using soap and water.
- Airbrush—A precision spray gun attached to an electric air compressor (or other means of air pressure), to spray paints, dyes, or inks. Can be used to apply a wide variation of color with a very smooth application.
- Collage—A work in which pieces of paper, photographs, cloth, and other materials are glued together in an overlapping design.
- Drypoint—A kind of engraving that has a soft, fuzzy line because of the metal burrs.
- Lithography—A method of printing a picture or words from a prepared stone or metal plate.
- Medium—The material used by an artist to produce a work of art.
- Palette—A flat surface used by painters to mix paint.
- Papier-Maché—This is paper soaked in water and flour and shaped into figures.

Technique

Technique is a method of working with art materials to create an art object and can include the characteristics of a medium or the style of a particular artist. Some of the techniques used in producing artwork include:

- Calligraphy—Decorative writing.
- Delineation—Using lines instead of mass to represent an object.
- Depth—The illusion of distance in a flat drawing or painting.
- Design—A plan in which the elements of art and principles of design have been combined to produce a sense of unity.
- Dimensions—A measure of spatial distance. The dimensions are height, width, and depth in a three-dimensional object.
- Distort—To change the way something looks—sometimes deforming or stretching an object or figure out of its normal shape to make it more interesting or meaningful.

- Dominant—The part of a work of art that is emphasized and has the greatest visual weight, is most powerful, or has the most influence.
- Focal Point—The point of interest in a work or art.
- Foreground—The area of a picture that appears to be closest to the viewer.
- Form—All the parts of a structure and the way in which they come together to give a particular meaning. The form of a work is what allows us to derive meaning from it.
- Gradation—A gradual change in value, shape, texture, or color.
- Harmony—Agreement, accord. A blend of compatible elements such as shape, size, and color to produce a pleasing result.
- Horizon Line—A level line where water or land seems to end and the sky begins.
- Intensity—The brightness or dullness of a color.
- Juxtaposition—Being placed close together or side by side to permit comparison or contrast.
- Linear Perspective—Using lines to create the illusion of three-dimensional depth in a two-dimensional work.
- One-Point Perspective—Linear perspective where all lines appear to meet at a single point.
- Proportion—Refers to the relationship of one part to another or to the whole with respect to size.
- Texture—The appearance of or actual "feel" of a surface.
- Sfumato—Technique used in painting to blur or soften the outline by gradual blending of one color into another. Used by Leonardo da Vinci.
- Serigraphy—Known as "silkscreen," a stencil process. A stencil is applied by hand or photographically to a taut nylon screen. Viscous silkscreen ink is then squeegeed through the screen, depositing ink on the paper. A separate screen is required for each color desired.
- Value—Refers to the lightness or darkness of color.
- Vanishing Point—It is the place in linear perspective where the parallel lines seem to meet on the horizon.

Sculpture

Sculpture is a three-dimensional representation of form that may be cut away as in stonework and woodcarving, cast as in working with metals, or built up as in working with clay. Cast sculpture of bronze, silver, plaster, and so forth use molds, where a material is poured in and then takes the shape of whatever has been carved or etched into the interior of the mold itself. Carved sculptures are shaped subtractively, using knives or chisels to gradually remove material until the desired form is left. Mobiles are another form of sculpture, though they are malleable and change into new compositions in space. They seem to interact with the environment as they continue to change form as the air pressure in the room changes.

Architecture

Architecture is a purposeful organization of space to provide a structure for living, working, worshipping, or other needs. Architecture has always responded to the materials available for building and represented the cultural demands and beliefs of the people in the era in which it is built. Architectural design incorporates a very different vocabulary in describing designs and building styles. Terms range from describing arches and columns to actual building styles and time periods in which a particular architectural design was in use. Architectural techniques and practices are also important to understand. Some of the terms that will be useful include:

- Acropolis—The Greek word meaning "high city." Ancient Greek builders chose to build their towns around hills upon which their main temples were placed. The most famous acropolis is in Athens.
- Aestheticism—The belief that the pursuit of beauty is the most important goal. It was prominent in the nineteenth century, now it often carries the connotation of decadence or preciousness.

- Arch—A curved span used in architecture.
- Asymmetrical—Unequal and not identical on either side of a line.
- Barrel Vault—A half-round ceiling made by placing a series of arches from front to back, also known as a tunnel vault. It was developed by the Romans and adopted later by church builders.
- Bauhaus—A German school of design popular in architecture after World War I emphasizing simplified forms and functionalism. Bauhaus buildings are essentially square boxes with windows.
- Column—A freestanding, circular pillar used in architecture.
- Corbelled Arch—A "false arch" bridging a gap by means of overlapping blocks of masonry.
- Feng Shui—The Chinese practice of arranging objects to harmonize with the flow of chi—the vital force believed to be inherent in all things. Feng shui literally means "wind and water." Its principles rest upon the properties of various objects and their relationships on a number of levels to increase or decrease the flow of chi.
- Frieze—A decorative horizontal band usually placed along the upper end of a wall.
- Golden Ratio—Proportion in art, approximately 1.6 to 1, that represents the most pleasing affect.
- Keystone—The central and highest stone in an arch. It holds the arch together by pressing equally on either side.
- Obelisk—A tall, four-sided stone that is usually capped by a pyramidal point.
- Scale—The relative size of an object in comparison with another.

Ceramics

Ceramics or pottery is hollow clay sculpture and pots made from clay and then fired in a kiln under high temperature to make them stronger. Pottery may be functional in nature as a plate, bowl, or vase, or it may serve decorative purposes.

The production of ceramics and pottery uses special clays, glazes, and tools including:

- Bat—A flat even surface used in ceramics upon which clay can be manipulated on a potter's wheel.
- Glaze—A thin coating of minerals that produces a glassy colored coating on pottery after firing in a kiln. Glazing is a technique of painting thin layers of colors again and again to create deep pools of color.
- Grog—An aggregate of prefired clay particles that helps prevent cracking and warping of clay when being fired.
- Kiln—A special oven or furnace that can reach high temperatures and is used to bake clay or melt glazes in the production of ceramic or pottery.

Artistic Expression

Artistic expression has undergone many stylistic changes over the ages. Art is affected by spiritual beliefs, by economic and governmental changes, and by the materials with which the art is created. History of the time in which a work of art is produced should be taken into account when judging and analyzing a piece of art. There are elements of composition that should also be considered when judging art.

Artwork is described using various labels and terminology:

- Anamorphosis and Anamorphic Art—An image that appears distorted, rendering it unintelligible until it is viewed from a specific angle or with a mirror.
- Anthropomorphism—The representation of animals and deities in human form, with human characteristics and behaviors. It appears in as a literary device in fables and allegories and in many animated films.

- Bas Relief—A French term meaning "low raised work." Used in wall sculpture.
- Ersatz—Describes an artificial and inferior substitute or imitation.
- Graphic Design—Mostly for commercial purposes and includes logos, letterheads, packaging, advertisements, signage, and web pages.
- Grotesque—A style of artwork having a fantastically distorted appearance used in ancient ornamentation.
- Mural—A painting made on a wall or building.
- Naturalism—A style in which an artist represents a subject as it actually appears in the natural world.
- Pointillism—A method of painting developed in France in the 1880s in which tiny dots of color are applied to the canvas and appear as shapes when viewed from a distance.
- Relief—Carved or molded artwork in which the figures or objects project from the background.

Elements of Art

Art involves a degree of human involvement—through manual skills or thought—as with the word "artificial," meaning made by humans instead of by nature. In this section, you will learn about the elements of art and how they are used in visual art and design. The elements include lines, colors, shapes and forms, textures, values, and space. Keep in mind that you must learn how to apply them to various pieces of art and that you will need to view different works by different artists to make this chapter effective for you.

Color.   The primary colors are yellow, red, and blue. It is possible to mix all the other colors using combinations of these three colors. Primary colors are basic and cannot be mixed from other elements. Two primaries can be mixed to get a secondary color. Each secondary color on the color wheel is surrounded by two primaries. These two surrounding primary colors are the ones that must be mixed in order to produce the secondary color. *Analogous colors* are colors that stand next to each other on the color wheel or are closely related to each other as in blue, blue–green, and green. Colors can be blended or merged with others to form new colors and techniques. Blending is also called feathering and can give a very soft effect to the painting. Color complements are color opposites. These colors contrast each other in the most extreme way possible. They also help to make each other more active. Color complements are on opposite sides of the *color wheel* (see Figure 20.1).

The color wheel organizes related colors like red, orange, and yellow, next to each other. Colors contrasting one another are placed farther apart (e.g., red and green are opposite, as are purple and yellow). Complementary colors are found directly opposite each other on the color wheel. When analyzing art, look for complementary colors that appear side by side. They create

FIGURE 20.1

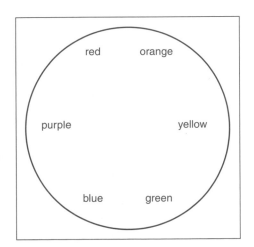

a visual tension for the viewer, because they actually make the eyes strain during the viewing. Often interesting use of color is produced accidentally as color is applied with no conscious preliminary planning.

When looking at paintings, keep in mind that cool colors, like blue and green, tend to withdraw in space and are associated with water, sky, and foliage. They are thought to have a calming affect and often appear to recede. Warm colors, like red and yellow, sometimes called advancing colors, on the other hand, tend to move toward the viewer. An accent can be conveyed with color to increase or decrease emphasis in a composition. An accent can also be conveyed with the use of contour and outline shading.

Color is produced when light strikes an object and then reflects back to the eyes. It has three properties: (1) hue or tint—the color name like red, yellow, or blue; (2) intensity—the purity and strength of a color; and (3) value—the lightness or darkness of a color. *Chroma* is the word used to indicate a color's hue and intensity. *Spectrum* is the whole continuous blending of one color to another and is produced when sunlight is refracted by a prism.

Monochromatic color uses a single color in varying shades. Just imagine a color scheme that begins with black and then gradually becomes gray. Monochromatic colors convey unity and harmony in an artwork. *Achromatic color,* or having no color as in black, white, and gray, can add drama to a piece. Color consists of hue, value, and intensity. Hue is the color itself. Value provides the amount of lightness or darkness of a color, while intensity is the degree of brightness or dullness of a color. Mood and emotion can be communicated using red, orange, and yellow. They are warm colors and may symbolize happiness, hope, or anger. Blue and green are colder and may symbolize despair and depression. Color may also be used to present qualities of illusion. Warm colors tend to expand a piece while cold colors appear to contract a piece.

Line.   Lines can emphasize intimacy or distance. Very sharp and angular lines in works of art suggest less intimacy, whereas very round and supple lines would convey a sense of warmth to the viewer. Curved lines can also convey a sense of unity and flow in a work. When looking at art, pay careful attention to the work and ask yourself if the lines are very sharp and angular or curved and supple. Doing so will help you see if the work suggests division or union or distance or warmth. The axis or axis line is an imaginary straight line that indicates movement and the direction of movement. Background lines that are jagged may convey a sense of tension. Lines that seem to vibrate in the image may indicate a sense of unease or emotional anxiety in the work. Lines may represent or form three-dimensional images or outline a shape. They can be thick or thin, heavy or light, straight or curved, and they may represent various meanings and emotions.

- Dark, heavy lines—anger or depression.
- Light, wispy lines—lightness of spirit.
- Curved lines—movement or softer nature.
- Straight lines—rigidity.
- Horizontal lines—stability and repose.
- Vertical lines—strength and height.

The outline figure or object is the contour. A contour drawing is one in which a continuous line is used to represent the subject matter.

Principles of Design.   The principles of design include various properties that are considered in producing and in analyzing art. The ways that a work of art exhibits and applies these principles can modify the pleasing quality of that work. The composition is comprised of the arrangement of form, color, line, and other elements of art in a particular work. Some principles overlap or oppose others, and some are viewed as more important, more ideal, or desirable than others. There is disagreement on the importance of individual principles among those people who analyze art, but we benefit from understanding and considering all the principles in order to more thoughtfully produce, understand, and judge art and design.

Shape or Form.   Shape is enclosed by space and may be defined by line, color, value, and texture. Shapes may appear to be three-dimensional or flat, conveying only length and width. Shape and form can be created by use of color, line, shading, and texture. It may be geometric or fluid and conveyed as representational or abstract.

Space.   The concept of space in art refers to the distance or area between, around, above, or below things. Space is composed of various qualities. Space can be flat, open or closed, positive or negative, ambiguous or illusionary. Blurred or indistinct shape suggests distance. Overlapping objects establishes their relationship to each other. Overlapping is the simplest way to convey depth, where you show an object in front of or behind another. Foreshortening is a way of changing the shape of something to make one part of it look closer to the viewer than another part. Foreshortening conveys the illusion of depth so that it seems to go back into space. Color graduation suggests depth. Chiaroscuro is the technique of using shading to convey depth of an object in three dimensions.

Negative space drawings use the background as the subject and make objects in the artwork two-dimensional and flat. One concentrates on the space that an object occupies, rather than on replicating the object itself. The artist is free to interpret the object in an unrestrained manner because the goal is not to replicate the object realistically, but to convey its form through the space that it occupies and the space that surrounds it.

Texture.   Texture refers to the surface quality or "feel" of a surface. It may be actual or simulated by shading or using lines.

Value.   Value is determined or presented by the amount of light and dark areas in a work of art. The value of a color may be raised by adding more white and lowered by adding more black. It may represent mood or emotion by using dark areas to suggest depression, despair, or melancholy, or light areas to suggest happiness, hope, and freedom. Value can represent form by using shadows and highlights.

Balance.   Balance refers to the way the elements of art are arranged to create a feeling of stability, harmony, or proportion. It can be symmetrical and formal, or asymmetrical and informal. Size and placement are important aspects in considering the balance of a work of art. Large objects may be balanced by using several smaller objects. Objects placed in a more dominant position may create a feeling of being in or out of balance. The use of line or perspective may create directional forces.

- Symmetry is achieved when one-half of the work of art reflects the other half. A symmetrical work usually creates a sense of formality. Asymmetry is achieved through the use of unequal elements that create balances as when a lighter area is balanced by a darker area. Asymmetrical creation portrays a sense of informality.
- Contrast is the difference between line, color, and texture. It adds variety and increases interest. It is used to stress the differences between two elements of art. Contrast can excite, emphasize, and direct attention to points of interest.
- Dominance is created with the use of color or positioning to call attention to the most important part of a work. Dominance is used to emphasize a point by creating contrast.

Theme and Variation.   The topic or subject matter of the work of art is the theme. The subject matter varies according to the types of themes chosen for the work. Landscapes are works of art that depict scenery such as mountains, valleys, trees, rivers, and forests. Portraits represent a specific person, a group of people, or an animal. Portraits usually show what a person looks like as well as revealing something about the subject's personality.

A still life is a picture of inanimate objects, usually fruit, pottery, flowers, or other common articles.

Rhythm.   Rhythm refers to the repetition of elements in a work of art that may produce a look or feel of movement. Rhythm can be regular (AB—AB) or alternating two qualities or alternating (ABA—CDE— ABA). Progressive rhythm (AB—AABB—AAABBB) is a gradual increase or decrease in elements repeated.

History of Art

The history of art is actually the evolution of mankind. Art was used to explain and express things that were a mystery to man, who used the tools and articles available at the time to produce the work of art. The history of art is a chronicle of the development of religion and the tools created by man to survive.

Historical and Cultural Context.   Art is a fundamental and preliterate human activity. Art illustrates that our need to express our humanity, our being alive, is just as important as our need for food. It is food for the soul. Appreciating and understanding a work of art and the materials used to produce that piece is a window to the culture and spirit of the time in which the work was produced.

   The first known period of prehistoric human culture is the stone age or the stone age of art. The period began with the earliest human development about 2 million years ago.

Paleolithic Period (450,000–10,000 B.C.).   This was the longest phase of human history. Paleolithic people were mostly nomadic hunters and gatherers who lived in caves and used fire and stone tools. Their culture is identified by the stone tools used. Eventually, these people showed evidence of communal hunting. They constructed shelters and developed beliefs centering on magic and the supernatural. They pictured their beliefs in rock paintings, found in the caves they inhabited.

Mesolithic Period (10,000–4500 B.C.).   This period began at the end of the last glacial era, over 10,000 years ago. Cultures included primitive farming and the use of animals as communities were formed. Humans began to manage areas of woodland and to hunt together using the bow.

Neolithic Period (4500–2300 B.C.).   The earliest known neolithic culture developed in southwestern Asia with people settling in villages. These people also cultivated the land and kept domestic animals. They were the first to develop pottery and weaving and to built monuments. The first pottery created was plain, but very soon it began to be decorated. The pottery of this era was distinctive in that the patterns and shapes reflected the various cultures in which they were made. Tombs first began to appear, then elaborate ceremonial sites such as "cursus" monuments and "henges" were built.

Ancient Near Eastern Art (Mesopotamia).   This area of the world developed with more limited range of art as compared to Egypt, because of the conflicts with warring nations and their need for more maintenance in agriculture. The Sumerian people were polytheistic and built step pyramids called ziggurats dedicated to a local god. Sculptures in this area showed long beards on the people's faces. The long beard represented power in their society. Many of the sculptures included mythical creatures, and some of the reliefs demonstrated the use of cuneiform writing in telling the story of battles or proclaiming the power of the ruler.

Japanese Art and Architecture.   Japan has produced art and architecture unique in style since 10,000 B.C. Japan has been invaded continuously over its history and has, therefore, been influenced by many new ideas followed by periods of minimal contact with the outside world. Over time, Japan developed the ability to absorb, imitate, and assimilate foreign elements that complemented its own culture. Painting is the preferred artistic expression probably because the Japanese wrote with a brush instead of a pen. Most Japanese sculpture was associated with religion, but this has declined with the decreasing influence of Buddhism. Japanese have always preferred natural materials and an interaction with the interior and exterior space in their architecture. Japanese art, valued not only for its simplicity but also for its use of color, has had an impressive influence on nineteenth-century Western painting and twentieth-century Western architecture.

Ancient Egypt. Around five thousand years ago, the ancient Egyptians established an extraordinary civilization. Their achievements have impressed and changed the world forever. The pyramids and temples of Egypt are among the most well known. The pyramid was used as a tomb and built of massive blocks of stone in a four-sided structure that symbolizes the sacred mountain and humanity's striving to reach the heavens. The temples of Karnak and Luxor are impressive structures built with huge columned halls and pylon gateways to honor the dead and venerate local and national gods. The buildings and architectural achievements of the ancient Egyptians took a high degree of engineering skills utilizing a large workforce of trained craftsmen and laborers. These buildings were decorated with paintings, carved stone images, hieroglyphs, and three-dimensional statues. The art tells the stories of the gods, pharaohs, common people, and nature. Their beauty and grandeur are still admired.

Bronze Age (2,300–700 B.C.). The people of the Bronze Age erected stone monuments, and their range of metalwork in bronze and gold increased significantly. This is the period associated and named for the people's use of metalwork. Monuments of stone placed in circles like those found at Stonehenge in England and round barrows or cairns, which are mounds raised over the bodies of the dead, dominate this era. There is evidence of settlements of farming families because of the flint tools found. As the period progressed, the settlements became more visible with actual field systems and other land divisions. Many of the earlier monuments had fallen out of use by this time. These changes demonstrate a shift in the way people showed attachment to the land and each other. Metalwork is spread to outlying areas and often "hoarded." This practice may have been the result of disposing of weapons and tools in rivers or bogs as a form of offering to local spirits or as funeral rituals. This may have been the origin of the legend of Excalibur in England.

Iron Age (700 B.C.–A.D. 43). The settlements of this era are marked by hill forts and larger enclosed communities. Tribal ties were maintained through trading, communal labor, and shared conflict. Some of the enclosed settlements seem not to be occupied and could have been used for ceremonial gatherings. Land was divided with boundaries, and conflict occurred because of those boundaries. Weapons and tools were forged from iron that gave the name to this period.

Ancient Greece. Ancient Greece was made up of small city-states, each with their own laws and rulers. The art of ancient Greece was produced in the form of architecture, sculpture, painting, and pottery. People in Corinth made pottery using a watery clay mixture to decorate the pottery. The pots were baked in kilns turning the painted areas black. Unpainted areas turned a light brown color. The pottery and sculpture from this era depicts scenes from Greek life in beautiful black and white detail. For 200 years this pottery was sold throughout the Greek world. Greek soldiers fought to defend themselves from the Persians. The Parthenon was built in Athens in 432 B.C. by the general Perikles. The soldiers had metal armor fashioned into helmets, shields, and leg guards, and carried swords. Yearly festivals celebrating athletics, drama and religious occasions were held in Athens supported by the wealthiest citizens. Greek sculpture and stonework tended to depict man in the most ideal form, stressing the most beautiful or athletic rather than realistic images.

Roman (A.D. 43–410). Military forts developed as Roman invasion of the European and British continents increased. This brought with it more effective methods of communication and new forms of settlement. Planned towns were established and the Roman villa became evident. Many of the tribal leaders adopted the art and forms of the Roman world as they were conquered. The Roman ideal spread through the development of trade in markets, the use of coins with the emperor's head on them, and the reuse by the Romans of the Iron Age sacred sites for ceremonial purposes. Roman art evolved from Etruscan art and has a close relationship to Greek art. The Romans were particularly interested in portraiture—statues that were very realistic in depicting a particular person. The Greeks were interested in ideals and, therefore, depicted individuals in their most ideal form. As the Romans conquered Greece in 200 B.C., their art began to imitate Greek flair for embellishment. The increasing use of the drill, rather than the chisel, made sculpting easier and faster.

The Greeks and Romans appreciated the ideal: men looking beautiful and achieving great feats. The art of this period is particularly important because most of the ideals of Western civilization came from these artistic portrayals. It is important to be able to appreciate and judge a work of art using the elements of art and the principles of design as reference. Other aspects to consider in judging art include the purpose of the work, the culture and era in history in which it was created, the style or the work and the meaning it communicates.

Anglo-Saxon (410–1066).   By the fifth century A.D., the Romans were overwhelmed by colonists and raiders from the North Sea region. Archeological evidence points to rich material traditions in many areas brought about by the existence of networks that brought trade, wealth, and innovation. Vikings were accomplished traders, and they established trade centers and routes that carried goods across much of the known world at that time.

Medieval Art (500–1000).   The art of the early Middle Ages is a mixture of Roman and German influence. However, each area of the world had an impact on the artwork of this period. Medieval art seems even more primitive than its predecessors, as if they were starting over. However, this was a reaction to the devastation caused by the Plague in Europe. Most of art at this time was religious and felt to hold sacred power. The Renaissance art was a "rebirth," as in the rebirth of Greek and Roman artistic sensibilities. Europe experienced a cultural explosion and great value was placed on art. Artists have a history of movements and influences. Artists also develop new aesthetic criteria, to meet the needs of their time. The "outrageousness" of modern or contemporary art exists only in the context of art history.

The Romanesque phase brought energy and excitement to architecture, sculpture, and painting. Architecture had a heavy, substantial, impressive feel. Sculpture was very abstract, combining stiff, formal forms in some places with fantastic carvings of real and imaginary animals and demons in others. In painting, nearly all the art was religious icons, mainly Jesus or the saints presented in frightening or impressive view against gold background. The Romanesque style gradually gave way to the Gothic in about 1100. The most revealing evidence of Gothic architecture is the pointed arch, which was developed in an effort to reach higher and lighter, with walls of glass, reaching up to heaven. Gothic sculpture shows an increased concern for realism and demonstration of emotion. Religious characters are depicted as merciful and compassionate.

Norman (1066–1154).   This period is marked by feudal society. The peasantry worked the land owned by lords who granted land and other goods to the workers in return for goods, rent, and labor. These lords were, in turn, bound to major aristocratic families and ultimately to the crown. The state found it necessary to build many castles and churches in order to maintain control over this system.

Gothic (1280–1515).   The Gothic style began with the architecture of the twelfth century as Europe was moving from the Dark Ages to a new era of prosperity and confidence. Christianity and the age of chivalry influenced the building of magnificent Gothic cathedrals. The most noticeable feature in Gothic painting is naturalism. Some of the painters in the latter period of Gothic style, like Albrecht Durer, were influenced by the Italian Renaissance.

Renaissance (1400–1600). The word *renaissance* means rebirth. The two main components of the Renaissance period are a revival of classical forms originally developed by the Greeks and Romans, and an intensified concern with the importance of the individual as expressed in humanism. The period of history saw an age of great discovery and exploration with a great desire to examine all aspects of nature and the world. Artists were now celebrated as individuals comparable to poets and writers. Painters attempted to portray the real world in their art. They studied the effects of light and perspective. Oil became a new medium for artists and allowed the artist to show characters in a full range of postures and poses and to demonstrate diverse emotional reactions and states. Flemish painters during this period incorporated common objects and animals into their paintings to express a symbolic spiritual meaning. Some of the most celebrated artists of all time, including Leonardo da Vinci, Michelangelo, Donatello, and Piero della Francesco helped define the Renaissance.

Baroque Period (1600–1700). The earliest evidence of the Baroque art occurred in Italy at the end of the sixteenth century and the culminating achievements can be found in Germany and South America as late as the eighteenth century. Baroque art is distinguished by a complex style that is often contradictory. Most work makes an appeal to the senses, often in dramatic ways, and evokes a strong emotional state. Baroque art is often very grand, with sensuous richness, drama, vigorous movement, and tension and is associated with the reinvigoration of the Catholic Church. Using these criteria, much of Hellenistic sculpture could be described as "baroque." The Rococo style of art in the eighteenth century placed emphasis on the carefree lifestyle of the aristocracy rather than on heroes or martyrs. It was characterized by graceful lines and delicate color. Mannerism was a style that portrayed emotion and distortion. Works of art done in this style reflected the upheaval and tension evident in Europe at this time. From the Mannerist style the Baroque inherited movement and motion and from the Renaissance style, solidity, and grandeur, combining the two into a new style.

Realism (1600s). Realism rejects imagination and idealism for close observation and accuracy of reproduction. Caravaggio, a painter in the Baroque period, was representative of the style of Realism.

Restoration (1740–1860). The Restoration period included several different styles in the world of art.

Classicism. Classicism and Neoclassicism are based on the tradition of art of ancient Greece and Rome. The work is characterized by emphasis on form, simplicity, proportion, and restrained emotion.

Romanticism (1700–1800). Romanticism rejected many of the traditions of Classicism and stressed strong emotion, imagination, and rebellion against social conventions. The characteristic attitudes of Romanticism include an appreciation of the beauty of nature, emotion over reason, and the senses over intellect. The art at this time focused on heroes and their passionate inner struggle and spiritual truth, often through themes involving the mysterious or the occult.

Impressionism (1800–1900). The Impressionist style of painting is characterized by an effort by the artist to accurately and objectively record visual reality by using light and color. The artist used small brush strokes while applying unmixed primary colors. Important contributions:

- Claude Monet: French painter with devotion to ideals of movement. His work, *Impression: Sunrise* gave the Impressionist movement its name. He did a series of paintings called *Waterlilies.*
- Pierre August Renoir: Light-hearted themes including *A Girl with a Watering Can, Young Women Talking,* and a series of bathers and landscapes.

Neo-Impressionism, often referred to as Pointillism, is a style of painting in which tiny dots of primary color are used to produce secondary colors. Pointillism is focused on the specific style of brushwork used to apply the paint. The term "Pointillism" was first used with respect to the work of Georges Saurat. Pointillism is considered to have been an influence on the development of Fauvism.

The Twentieth Century

Expressionism (1800–1900).   Expressionism is a style that emphasizes the expression of inner experience rather than a realistic portrayal. The attempt is to depict subjective emotions rather than objective reality. The work demonstrates exaggeration, primitivism, and fantasy by imposing the artist's own personal image of the "true meaning" of an object. Important contributions:

- Paul Cezanne: Concern with form and structure and demonstrated extreme passion within sinister themes as in *The Abduction.*
- Vincent Van Gogh: Vivid and striking color, coarse brushwork and contour form in works such as *The Starry Night, Self Portrait with Bandaged Ear,* and *Still Life with Four Sunflowers.*
- Paul Gaugin: Lived in Tahiti and used vivid color.

Fauvism (1898–1908).   Fauvism is a style of painting that flourished in France for a short time and is characterized by the use of brilliant color applied straight from the tubes in an aggressive manner to create a sense of explosion on the canvas. Important contributions:

- Henri Matisse: sense of formal order in *Woman with the Hat,* uses blues, greens, and reds.

Futurism (1909–).   Futurism was centered in Italy and emphasized the speed, energy, and power of the machine. This movement celebrated change, originality, and innovation in culture and society. Many of the political themes were intended to inspire public anger and to arouse controversy. The art at this time gave expression to the energy and power of the machine age.

Cubism (1907–1914).   This is a school of painting and sculpture in which the subject matter is portrayed by geometric forms without realistic detail. This is a form of abstract art that stresses the abstract form at the expense of other elements in using cubes and cones that overlap and intersect. The cubist style is often flat and two-dimensional, and it presented a new reality in which several sides of an object were depicted at the same time.

Abstraction (1910–).   Spares and colors have an emotional force to explore ideas and sensation in Abstractionist art. Abstract artists select and then exaggerate or simplify the forms suggested by the world around them. Pablo Picasso did this through the use of cubism.

Abstraction is an essentially romantic and spiritual view of art often using animals as innocent representation of nature. Franz Marc painted animals with symbolic colors showing them as at peace and without ego. August Macke was sensitive to form and color in producing gentle scenes using areas of light. Important contributions:

- Franz Marc: *Deer in the Woods, Dog Lying in the Snow.*
- Piet Mondrian: Used geometric figures and only primary colors and straight-sided forms in *Diamond Painting in Red, Yellow, and Blue.*

Minimalism is a formalist style of art in which objects are stripped down to their elemental, geometric form, and presented in an impersonal manner. It is an Abstract form of art that developed as a reaction against the subjective elements of Abstract Expressionism. It was most evident in the 1960s and originated in New York City. Important painters included Ellsworth Kelly and Frank Stella.

Dada (1916–1923).   This was a reaction to artists' disgust for bourgeois values and despair after World War I. This movement sought reality by abolishing traditional culture and aesthetic forms.

Surrealism (1924–).   Surrealism grew out of Dada art and emphasized positive expression. It attempts to express the workings of the subconscious by fantastic imagery and free form. This movement drew heavily on the teaching and writings of Sigmund Freud. Important contribution:

- Salvadore Dali: *Persistence of Memory,* in which everyday objects were distorted as if melting.

American Regionalism (1930–).   Regionalism refers to the work of a group of rural artists, mostly from the Midwest, whose work became prominent in the 1930s. These painters were known for depicting everyday life in the rural plains of the American Midwest. Grant Wood is one of the most well known with his painting called *American Gothic.* Wood also painted landscapes including *Stone City, Iowa,* in which the artist presented a sense of unity and rhythm by repeating the soft round shapes present in the depiction of hills, trees, and bushes. Wood, along with his conservative contemporaries, proposed a social movement aimed at a return to humble agrarian living and modest values. Landscape painting began in the United States during the 1700s. Americans were fascinated with their new surrounds and sought to capture them in art. Instead of using landscapes as a simple background, they became the subject of study— something to be tamed and explored. After the 1930s, landscape painting became a means of rejecting the industrial revolution, suggesting that a return to nature would provide a better way of life for people.

Creative Expression

Students are encouraged to use the elements of art and the principles of design to demonstrate understanding and to communicate meaning in an original work of art. They must select an appropriate medium and master the techniques necessary to better understand and appreciate the complexities and subtitles of that particular form of art. Visual art forms include painting, sculpture, ceramic pottery, architecture, film, photography, and computer art.

Stages of Artistic Development.   Children's art seems to follow patterns and stages in which it progresses as children grow from toddlers into adolescence. The following are the basic stages of artwork in children:

- Scribble Stage. At ages 2–4 years, the drawing is disordered with uncontrolled makings going from light to dark or in circular forms. At this age, the child has little or no control over motor activity. This is a period of exploration of new materials, straight and curving lines, beginning movement from simple gestures into more complex ones. At first, children draw mainly to explore visual–motor experiences, but as they mature, they may tell stories about a scribble as there is a change from a kinesthetic thinking in terms of motion to imaginative thinking in terms of a picture.
- Symbol-Making Stage—At ages 5–9, a child produces shapes so that they'll stand for ideas. Gradually a child recognizes a need for more and more details with color choices no longer being random.
- Pre-adolescent Stage—At ages 10–13, a child is more self-critical and cautious. The child experiences new social pressures with adolescent physical changes and pressures. Expanding awareness bring challenges to a child's self-image and social position. Children may begin to produce art in a more adult fashion. Children at this age may progress in their artistic development only with well-paced instruction and encouragement. Children are

ready to add increasing detail, illusion of depth, subtle coloration, and increasingly sophisticated art techniques and processes.

Art instruction in childhood is thought to be important in enhancing cognitive development across content areas.

CONTENT AREA TWO: MUSIC

Vocal Sound

Sound is produced by an object vibrating at a particular rate of speed. Sound is produced in music by vibrating strings, membranes, columns of air, or by a vibrating solid object like a bell. The *loudness,* or *amplitude,* of a sound is produced by a vibration of sound covering a particular distance in a single wave. If a single sound wave is wide, the sound will be loud. *Pitch* is defined as the frequency of waves of vibration of an object or the number of sound waves during a given amount of time. The higher the frequency, the higher the pitch. *Timbre* describes those characteristics of sound that allow the ear to distinguish sounds that have the same pitch and loudness but a differing number of overtones produced by a vibrating object.

Sound originates from the vibrations of the vocal cords found in the voice box or larynx. When moving air is sent from the lungs through the voice box, the air vibrates the vocal cords. A typical note, such as middle C, requires 262 vibrations of the vocal cords per second. When air is inhaled to fill the lungs, the vocal cords are wide open. When air is exhaled, the cords close slightly. When singing, they vibrate close together. The total vocal mechanism includes the abdominal and back musculature, rib cage, lungs, and the pharynx (throat), oral cavity, and nose. The force of the air causes vibrations in the bones of the face, and in turn creates a resonance in the facial cavities, which amplify the sound. The sinuses, which are the largest cavities, tend to be responsible for the widest range of resonance.

The human voice may be regarded as the first musical instrument of man because it was used as a musical instrument before instruments were invented. It is the only musical instrument common to all musical systems in the world. The sounds produced by the voices of people in differing cultures can be radically different. Compare the high-pitched, nasal qualities produced by the voices of the classical Chinese with the exuberant tonal qualities and pitch of syllables produced by African voices. All man-made instruments are designed to cover a fixed range. The range of the human voice can be extended through practice. One of the unique features of the human voice is that the size and shape of the resonators are under the conscious control of the performer.

A variety of tone colors are produced by this instrument either orally or nasally by the adjustable resonators of the human voice. It would be difficult to duplicate the intensity of feelings the voice puts forth. The extreme flexibility of the control of the frequency, the timber, and the output in the voice make the instrument express all the emotions. The coloring of a tone is made by varying the dimensions of the vibrators and resonators.

As the individual grows and matures, the voice changes because of the physiological changes that occur in the structure of the throat. As a young person passes through adolescence, the pitch of the voice becomes deeper and is especially evident in males. The change in pitch is caused by the lengthening of the vocal cords, or folds, as the larynx becomes larger. The voice may go through several changes as it matures. The first stage of development occurs in early adolescence. As the vocal cords lengthen, the voice has a breathy tone while singing high notes. The voice may crack as the vocalist strains to achieve resonance on high notes that were previously within range.

Elements of Music

The goals of artistic perception are to encourage awareness, involvement, and participation in musical appreciation and performance. It is essential to foster an understanding of the elements of music.

Music is a series of organized sounds consisting of pitch, duration, harmony, and rhythm. Music is an element of time since it exists only during its performance and must be appreciated after that performance only as a memory. Each musical composition consists of rhythm and a beat, which helps to create character for a musical piece. There is a form and texture that is created through the interaction with its elements.

Dynamics.   How loud or soft the music is may change its expressive effect. Terms that describe the dynamics of a piece may include *piano* (soft) to *forte* (loud).

- Adagio—Quite slow.
- Allegro—Fast, cheerful.
- Crescendo—Music gradually gets louder.
- Decrescendo—Music gradually gets softer.
- Forte—The Italian term for "loud," indicated in the musical score by the marking *f*.
- Fortissimo—the Italian term for "very loud," indicated in the musical score by marking *ff*.
- Piano—The Italian term for "soft" indicated by the notation *p*.
- Pianissimo—The Italian term for "very soft" indicated by the notation *pp*.

Form.   Form is the overall structure of music. The sections of music may be repeated or all the parts of the piece may be unique. These phrases or sections may complement each other to create unity or they may contrast in order to create variety. Form is the overall structure, or plan, of a piece of music. AB form has two different sections. ABA form, also called sonata form, has three sections. Rondo form is in ABACABA form.

- Bridge—A section of a song that connects other sections of a song.
- Fugue—A musical composition or technique in which the composer introduces a tune (the theme) while other voices enter at different times playing the same theme on higher and lower pitches. Fugues are usually written for two to four voices. Bach wrote some of the greatest fugues.
- Leitmotif—A musical theme given to a particular idea or main character of an opera.
- Melody—A series of notes that form a tune, phrase, theme, or motive. Repetition is what makes a melody stick in your mind. The melodies you remember are the ones you will like the most. Some melodies are difficult to remember because they don't repeat. Other melodies can be remembered easily because they do repeat.
- Movement—Self-contained section of a larger musical work. A symphony usually has four movements. A piano sonata has three movements.
- Phrase—A melodic idea that acts as a complete thought, something like a sentence. A melody will contain many phrases, just like a story contains many sentences.
- Refrain—The part of the song that repeats, using the same melody and words.
- Sequence—A successive transposition and repetition of a phrase at different pitches.

Harmony.   Harmonies are chords with duration. Chords may consist of two or more notes played at the same time. A chord is defined as simultaneous combinations of three or more tones that constitute a single block of harmony. The chords may vary to create a melody that produces the distinctive sounds of a particular piece of music. Not all music of the world relies on harmony for interest, but it is central to most Western music. Dissonance is created by a combination of tones that sounds discordant and unstable, in need of resolution.

Notation.   Notation is the art of describing music in written form. The *musical score* is a notation showing all the parts of a musical composition. Notes are written on a staff using a clef placed at the beginning of the staff that determines the pitches for each line and space on the staff. There may be a sharp (#) that raises a note a half step or a flat (♭) that lowers a note a half step. Figure 20.2 lists the various types of notes and the duration for which they may be held.

FIGURE 20.2

The staff is broken into measures that mark the time signature at the beginning of the staff. The top number in the time signature represents the number of beats in a measure, and the bottom number tells which note gets a full beat.

Reading Music

Staff. The musical notation made up of five parallel lines and four spaces on which music is written (see Figure 20.3).

Notes. A note is a musical symbol that denotes both pitch and duration. Notes may be solid or an outline with the center left white. Notes are placed on the lines and in the spaces of a staff as shown in Figure 20.4.

Clef Signs. A clef is a symbol at the beginning of the staff to indicate the pitch of the notes in the staff. The treble clef is a notation that puts G above middle C on the second line of a staff. A treble clef indicates that the notes following it will start at middle C and go upwards. Music played in the treble clef notation (see Figure 20.5) is higher pitched than that played in the bass clef notation.

The bass clef is a notation that puts the F below middle C on the fourth line of a staff. A base clef indicates that the notes start at middle C and go downwards. Music played in the bass clef is lower in pitch than that played in the treble clef. The bass clef is indicated in Figure 20.6.

Scales. A scale is an arrangement of pitches from lower to higher according to a specific pattern of steps. *Major, minor, pentatonic* (five notes in an octave), *whole-tone* (based on whole step intervals but with no real starting or ending point), and *chromatic* are five kinds of scales. Each one has its own special sound.

The chromatic scale divides an octave into twelve half-steps (all the white and black notes on the keyboard from middle C to the C above it as shown in Figure 20.7). This is different from the major scale and minor scale, which only have eight tones. A pentatonic scale consists of only five different notes. The two most common possibilities for arranging five dif-

FIGURE 20.3

FIGURE 20.4

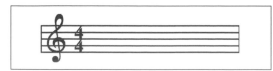

FIGURE 20.5

FIGURE 20.6

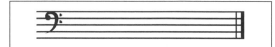

FIGURE 20.7

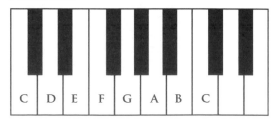

ferent notes to create a scale are major pentatonic and minor pentatonic. Modes are special scales. The major scale and minor scale are modes that we recognize today, but there are many others. If you played all the white keys on the piano from D to the next D one octave higher, you would have the Dorian mode.

A half-step on a keyboard is the distance from one note to the next note, black or white. A whole step on a keyboard is the distance from one note to another with a single key between.

Ledger Line—Treble (Figure 20.8).

FIGURE 20.8

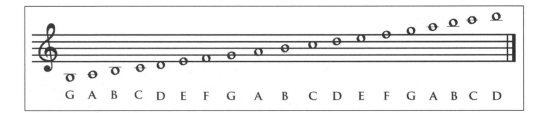

Ledger Line—Bass (Figure 20.9).

FIGURE 20.9

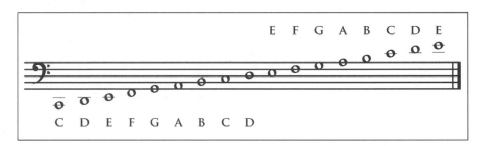

Memorizing Notes (Figure 20.10).

FIGURE 20.10

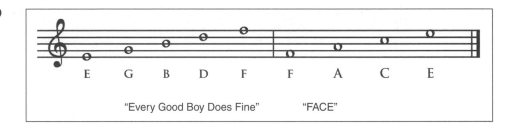

The Measure. The measure is the same as a bar—a rhythmic grouping or metrical unit that contains a fixed number of beats; in notated music, it appears as a vertical line through the staff (see Figure 20.11).

FIGURE 20.11

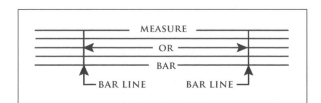

A bar is the same as measure—a way of dividing music into small, organized groups of beats. A vertical line called the bar line indicates the division of measures. Music is usually grouped in two's (duple meter), or three's (triple meter). The downbeat is the first beat of the measure, the strongest in any meter.

Time Signatures.   A time signature is a number that appears at the beginning of a piece of music. The top number tells you how many beats each measure (bar) will have. The bottom number tells you what kind of a note receives one beat. In 4/4 time there are four beats per measure (bar), and the quarter note receives one beat (see Figure 20.12). In 6/8 time there are six beats per measure (bar), and the eighth note receives one beat.

FIGURE 20.12

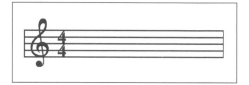

Meter.   The meter is the organization of beats, which is also called a pulse. A waltz is in a triple meter, which is three beats per measure. A march is in duple meter, which is two or four beats per measure. The time signature, usually placed at the beginning of the piece, tells you what the meter will be. The first beat of a group is generally emphasized. A beat should not be confused with a note; a beat may contain one note, many notes, or may be silent (indicated by a symbol called a rest).

Notes, Beats, and Measures.   The beat is noted as a regular pulsation in the music. It is a basic unit of length in musical time. The tempo is the rate of speed at which a musical composition is performed. Tempo is indicated by a tempo marking (usually in Italian), which describes the general speed (and often the mood) of a piece or section. *Allegro* (fast), *andante* (fairly slow), and *adagio* (slow) are common tempo markings.

Key Signatures.   The key signature is made up of sharps or flats and is usually found at the beginning of a musical composition, indicating the key of the piece (see Figure 20.13).

FIGURE 20.13

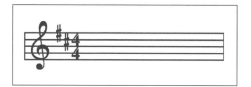

A musical work that is centered around a certain scale or tone is said to have a key. A piece written in C major will usually end in that key. Most music is written in major keys or minor keys. Some pieces are written without a key so that all the tones can be equally important. A flat (♭) is a symbol that lowers the pitch of a note one-half step; sharp (#) is a symbol used to raise the pitch of a note one-half step. The number of sharps and flats indicated in the key signature just after the clef sign indicates the key of the music. A key signature with no sharps or flats is played in the key of C. Modulation is a change of key. Modulating the music occurs when music starts out in a certain key, then changes to a new key.

Identifying Key Signatures.   Each key signature is related to a major scale and its relative minor. With practice, it is possible to memorize the accidentals that are typical of each scale. The accidental can be either a sharp or a flat.

Identifying Key Signatures of Sharps.   The major scale to which it belongs is a half-step above the last sharp (see Figure 20.14).

Identifying Key Signatures of Flats.   The major scale to which it belongs is a perfect fourth below the last flat. In case of more than one flat, tonality is also indicated by the penultimate flat (see Figure 20.15).

FIGURE 20.14

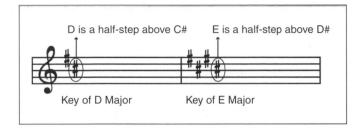

FIGURE 20.15

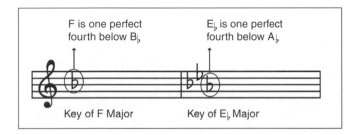

Fourths can be perfect, augmented, or diminished. A diminished fourth is two whole steps or four half-steps. A perfect fourth is two and a half whole steps or five half-steps. An augmented fourth is three whole steps or six half-steps.

Turn. A *turn* is a musical notation indicating a trill and can be shown by the following symbols to indicate the type of trill needed (see Figure 20.16).

FIGURE 20.16

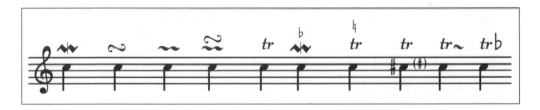

Tonality. Tonality is a central key in a musical composition. If the music moves to a different key, it is expected to return to the original key (called the *tonic*). Tonality gives the listener a "center," providing a context in which melody and harmony have meaning. Atonal music, popular in the twentieth century, has no tonal center.

Identifying Chords. A triad is a common chord type consisting of three pitches built on alternate scale tones of a major or minor scale.

Major Chords. Figure 20.17 shows a triad that may be formed by using the notes of a major scale.

FIGURE 20.17
Major Triads

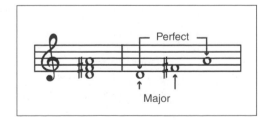

Triads that are formed in major scales on degrees of I, IV, and V are major. Those that are formed on degrees of II, III, and VI are minor.

Minor Chords.   The variety of triads in minor scales is greater because there are three types of minor scales: natural, harmonic, and melodic (see Figure 20.18).

**FIGURE 20.18
Minor Triads**

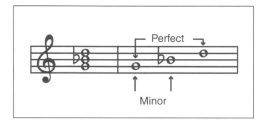

Intervals.   An interval measures the distance between two notes. By counting the number of notes in an interval, we obtain its numerical size. Intervals are always counted from the lower note to the higher one, with the lower note being counted as one. Intervals come in different qualities and size. If the notes are sounded successively, it is a melodic interval. If sounded simultaneously, then it is a harmonic interval.

Tone.   A tone is a sound of definite pitch. The *register* of the music is the pitch location of a group of tones. Tones with high pitches have a high register. Those with low tones have a low register. A flute has a high register; a tuba has a low register.

Pitch.   A melody is created by the changing progression of pitches. *Pitch* is how high or low a note may be. A melody can be created by playing one note at a time while harmony can be added by including chords. The meaning of the melody can be affected by changing the groupings of notes, the rhythm, and duration of notes. A flute has a high pitch; a tuba has a low pitch. The pitch of human voices is described by certain names:

- Alto—Lowest of the female voices.
- Bass—Male voice of low range.
- Soprano—Highest ranged voice, normally possessed by women or boys.
- Tenor—Highest male voice.

Rhythm.   *Rhythm* refers to the relationship of all the notes to the indicated time signature or beat. It includes how long a note is held, how long a break for a rest, and how the notes and rests are counted in relationship to the basic beat. Without rhythm, any song is only a collection of notes.

Note Value.   Notation is the way music is written down. It indicates specific pitches and duration of each pitch. The note value is on the upper staff and the rest value is on the lower staff.
Rests indicate pauses in the music—a rest is a symbol for silence in music. Each rest has a different shape and a specific time value corresponding to a note of the same duration (see Figure 20.19).

FIGURE 20.19

| WHOLE | HALF | QUARTER | EIGHTH | SIXTEENTH |

Rhythm is the way movement is organized in a piece of music, using beat, no beat, long and short sounds, meter, accents, no accents, tempo, syncopation, and so on. It is the controlled movement of music in time.

Tempo refers to the speed of a musical piece. The tempo can affect the music's character and expression by providing contrast in the sections of the music. The tempo exists in time and exists only for the duration of the performance as a reality. Tempo is indicated by a tempo marking (usually in Italian), which describes the general speed (and often the mood) of a piece or section. *Prestissimo* (played as fast as possible), *presto* (very fast), *allegro* (fast), *vivace* (a quick and lively tempo), *andante* (fairly slow; a walking pace or moderate tempo), *largo* (broad; slow and stately tempo; very slow), and *adagio* (slow) are common tempo markings. A steady tempo is indicated by regular pulses. *Syncopation* is hearing beats where you don't expect to hear them; it shifts strong beats to weak beats.

Texture refers to the feel of the music as thick, thin, opaque, or transparent. Music played with a *staccato* motif may sound choppy or brisk. Music played with a *largo* motif may be heavy and smooth. Some general terms for texture include:

- Crescendo—Music gradually gets louder.
- Decrescendo—Music gradually gets softer.
- Motif—Short melodic or rhythmic idea; the smallest fragment of a theme that forms a melodic–harmonic–rhythmic unit.
- Counterpoint—The art of combining two or more musical lines that are to be played or sung at the same time. These lines may be said to be "in counterpoint" with each other. The term is in some ways like polyphony although counterpoint is most commonly used for Baroque music.
- Polyphony (polyphonic)—From the Greek for "many-sounding." Music in which two or more "voices" are heard at the same time. This is different than monophonic ("one-sounding") and homophonic ("like-sounding").

Timbre

Timbre is the unique sound produced by a particular instrument or by combinations of instruments, often called the tone color. It's the quality of sound that makes one instrument or voice sound different from another. For example, a flute has a different timbre than a clarinet. There are families, or groups, of instruments that have similar timbre:

- Woodwinds—Most woodwinds have reeds and are played by blowing into or across the instrument. The flute has no reed and is played by blowing across an opening. Clarinets, oboes, and saxophones are reed instruments that have a single or double reed. The woodwind family is less homogeneous in construction and sound production than the strings; it includes the piccolo, flute, oboe, English horn, clarinet, and bassoon.
- Percussion—Most percussion instruments are played by being struck together or with a mallet, stick, or padded device. African and Southwestern Native American cultures rely heavily on the use of percussive instruments like drums and rattles to enhance their songs created for spiritual, social, or ritualistic functions. Examples of percussion instruments include the piano, drums, xylophone, and symbols. The piano is a keyboard instrument whose strings are struck with hammers controlled by a keyboard mechanism; pedals control dampers in the strings that stop the sound when the finger releases the key.
- Brass—Brass instruments are made of brass or other metals and are played by placing the mouth against a mouthpiece and controlling the air as it enters the instrument. The trumpet, trombone, French horn, and tuba are examples of brass instruments.
  - Euphonium—A close relative of the tuba resembling the baritone horn although its timbre is mellower. It may be notated either at pitch in the bass clef or in the treble clef a major ninth above actual pitch.
  - Trumpet and Coronet—Similar brass instruments notated in the treble clef.
  - Trombone—A brass instrument with a movable slide that allows for changes in notes. It is notated on the bass clef.
- Strings—These instruments are played by drawing a bow across the strings or by plucking them with the fingers or a pick. The violin, cello, guitar, and harp are examples of

string instruments. String instruments comprise the largest section of an orchestra. Without the string section, you would have a band.

- Lyre—Ancient plucked-string instrument of the harp family, used to accompany singing and poetry.
- Harpsichord—Early Baroque keyboard instrument in which the strings are plucked by quills instead of being struck with hammers like the piano.
- Koto—A stringed instrument with flexible tuning and a movable bridge common in traditional Japanese music.

An orchestra is a performing group of diverse instruments; in Western music it is an ensemble of multiple string parts with various woodwind, brass, and percussion instruments. The human voice may also be included in this segment as a musical instrument having a wide variety of range and timbre.

Role of the Conductor

A composer is a person who creates a piece of music by putting sounds together in his or her own way. The conductor then, by means of gestures, leads performances of musical ensembles, especially orchestras, bands, or choruses, following the score written by a composer. It is the responsibility of the conductor to focus and direct the efforts of individual musicians within a band or orchestra into a cohesive group so that they perform together as a single unit. The conductor is able to do this by providing clear directions. A good conductor reads the score of the music, anticipates difficult passages, and then provides detailed guidance for the musicians. The conductor needs to be aware of the combined sound being produced and to regulate that balance by directing band or orchestral sections or musicians. The conductor must lead the musicians without detracting from the overall performance of the group. Conducting patterns are the arm and hand movements by the conductor that create patterns to communicate to the performers the specific beat of the music. The common conducting patterns are 2-beat, 3-beat, 4-beat, and 6-beat; however, there are many others used for special purposes (see Figure 20.20).

FIGURE 20.20

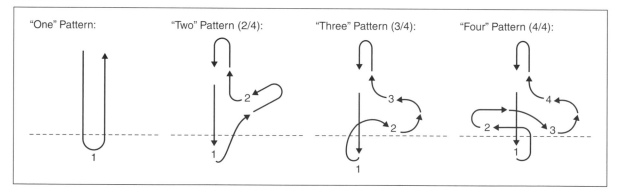

Historical and Cultural Context

Understanding the historical context of music helps in realizing that music is a part of a society and reflects the significant themes of that time. The people of a culture or society have a relationship to their music and the instruments with which they perform that music. Informal instruments used to make music may be functional in that they are often homemade from items commonly used for other tasks. More formal instruments are made primarily for the purpose of making music.

The music created by a particular culture or society reflects the concerns of that people. Blues evolved from African American work songs that expressed depression or sadness. The Gregorian chant evolved in the early Christian era from unaccompanied religious songs and chants. The music of the Renaissance expressed the humanistic spirit of the people by including more voices and instruments in the compositions. Musicians and composers are a product of the their culture and their experience. The music they create communicates that experience.

Music is everywhere. We hear music at the grocery store, at sporting events, at the mall, and in the car. We hear music in hospitals, nursing homes, classrooms, and in church. We hear music from Africa, Europe, Asia, and South America. Music is truly the universal language and knows no boundaries of race, religion, gender, or age. Music is the heartbeat of all life.

Music has been influenced by the historical themes throughout the ages. The spread of Christianity, the influence of the Islamic culture, and the development of the European culture were important in the evolution of the monophonic and polyphonic styles of music in the Middle Ages (450–1450). During this time, Pope Gregory I is generally believed to have collected the music known as Gregorian chant, which was highly approved by the Church. Much later, secular music was sung all over Europe by troubadours.

The Renaissance, from 1450–1600, brought a rebirth of classical learning and a gradual change from the feudal system to the modern state. With the rise of humanism, music began to break free of the Church and a school of composers trained in the Netherlands mastered the art of polyphony in their settings of sacred music. Music was not always written down, however. The madrigal flourished in England at that time. The composers of that period were affected by an increased interest in humanistic learning and the increased patronage of music and wealth. Vocal music during the Renaissance was contrapuntal, where the melody was more important than the words. As music later became redefined, the text of the music became the most important part of the composition.

The Baroque period, from 1600–1750, saw an increasing importance of scientific investigation and the development of the New World. Artificiality and flamboyant, decorative styles were valued in the arts. There was a general rebellion against the melodic contrapuntal styles prevalent in the High Renaissance. Composers employed by monarchs competed in producing music demonstrating great pride, pomp, and pageantry. Johann Sebastian Bach was one of the greatest composers of this period, demonstrating great pageantry in his work.

During the Baroque period music became the foundation for a text and was used to enhance words. It was during the early part of the seventh century that the genre of opera was first created by a group of composers in France and Italy and included great oratorios in the performance. *Oratorios* were usually performed by a soloist backed by a chorus and were religious or spiritual in nature. The instrumental concerto was also common to the Baroque era. Music in this era used more subtle or gradual changes in dynamic levels that occur over longer phrases of the score. This era brought about a full equality of instrumental music as well as an expanding role for music. Choral music continued to be popular at this time and the age culminated in the operas and oratorios of George Frederic Handel of Germany.

The *concerto* was performed in the seventeenth century by ensemble music and employed voices and instruments. In modern times it usually denotes a work in which a solo instrument (or instrumental group) contrasts with an orchestral ensemble. The first movement of the concerto usually includes a cadenza, which is a lively solo passage that occurs near the end of a piece. At first, these solos were improvised. However, composers like Mozart and Beethoven later composed cradenzas for the musicians. During a cradenza the soloist performs while the rest of the orchestra is silent. The solo will often include motives and thematic material that has been used earlier in the music. The orchestra rejoins the piece after a long trill performed by the soloist at the end of the cradenza. This type of solo allows the talent of individual musicians to be presented and lengthens the entire performance while varying the cadence of the piece.

The industrial revolution and the philosophy of Enlightenment in the Classical period brought simpler textures and melodies to music. Musicians retreated from the heavily ornamented styles of the Baroque and embraced the clean, uncluttered style reminiscent of Classical

Greece. At this time, there was a concept of nature in the arts and music played a more social role. The piano became a featured instrument in musical compositions. Vienna became the musical center of Europe and composers came from all over Europe to train in the standard musical forms that continued over the next several decades.

The Classical period reached its majestic culmination with the masterful *symphonies, sonatas,* and *string quartets* by the three great composers of the Viennese school: Franz Joseph Handel, Wolfgang Amadeus Mozart, and Ludwig van Beethoven.

In the Romantic Era, from 1825–1900, there was an increasing importance of science defining a worldview and a growing autonomy for the arts. European nationalism and exoticism helped in changing the status of musicians. There was a rise of program music and increased interest in nature and the supernatural. Artists of all kinds became intent on expressing their subjective, personal emotions. During the early nineteenth century, opera composers turned to folk stories and literature for musical themes.

Giuseppe Verdi and Richard Wagner dominated the field of opera. The invention of new instruments and modifications to existing instruments led to the expansion of the symphony orchestra throughout the century. Taking advantage of these new sounds and instruments, the later Romantic composers created richer and even larger symphonies and concertos. Johannes Brahms and Peter Ilyich Tchaikovksy were from this period.

The twentieth century brought with it phenomenal changes in technology and the advent of instantaneous global communications. This brought about the birth of a "World Music" culture and a widening gap between "art" and "popular" music as ambivalent attitudes toward the musical past increased. Composers explored unusual and unorthodox harmonies and tonal schemes. French composer Claude Debussy was intrigued by Eastern music and the *whole-tone scale,* and he created a style of music called *Impressionism.* Hungarian composer Bela Bartok continued in the traditions of the still strong Nationalist movement and fused the music of Hungarian peasants with twentieth-century forms. *Avant-garde* composers explored the manipulation of rhythms rather than the usual melodic/harmonic schemes. The genre of the symphony continued although modified by this time, and attracted such masters as Gustav Mahler. Many composers like Giacomo Puccini and Sergei Rachmaninoff resisted the temptation for experimentation and remained true to the traditional forms of music. The music called jazz was born sometime around 1895 in New Orleans. It combined elements of ragtime, marching band music, and blues. Jazz incorporated the widespread use of improvisation, often by more than one player at a time. Jazz represented a break from Western musical traditions, where the composer wrote a piece of music on paper and the musicians then tried their best to play exactly what was in the score. In a jazz piece, the song is often just a starting point or frame of reference for the musicians to improvise around.

Ragtime jazz is best exhibited in the compositions of Scott Joplin. Ragtime is a lively, syncopated musical style influenced by marches and polkas to give it a driving beat. The musical roots of ragtime are tied to plantation life.

Rhythms that were part of a musical heritage brought from Africa were incorporated into music. Africa was rich in musical heritage that became a tremendous influence on much of the music that evolved in America after the advent of slavery in the 1800s. The "call and response" pattern that influenced dance in the 1900s also was an influence on the music that supported dance. This wailing, sliding melody in response to the call or holler of a field hand presented itself in the musical tradition that became the blues.

Reggae music became popular in the 1960s. It evolved from the social changes that occurred as a result of the European invasion of Jamaica. Many slaves from West Africa were used to work the large plantations established by the Europeans. Reggae combines both the West African and Jamaican elements of music to produce a lyrical, syncopated form of folk music. Bob Marley was instrumental in the popularization of reggae music as he performed this lively music on electronic instruments.

Sprectstimme is a method of speaking texts at indicated pitch levels. It is a more modern method used when performing works by composers like Alben Berg. Big bands became popular in the 1930s and 1940s. Bands at that time played swing music. "Swing" is produced by the rhythm section. The melody and soloists are allowed to take liberties with the rhythms and phrase their melody as they see fit. Swing music can be written in 4/4 time, although much of it is written in 2/2 time, and sometimes 6/8 or 12/8.

Understanding the effects of culture and the changing attitudes toward music helps us to better understand the styles, idioms, performance media, and purposes of types of music that are part of our multicultural heritage. There is a definite relationship between people and their music.

Students need to be aware of the historical significance of music and the instruments used to produce that music. Our present-day instruments have evolved from those of the past. Musical instruments are created from materials in a cultural context, and the resulting variety of instruments will then influence the music itself. Music has its own forms, periods, and cultural characteristics affected by the social influences of the society in which it is created. Music is a part of our lives and can communicate emotions and satisfy emotional needs. Many people use music as a therapy and derive great personal pleasure from this unique medium for human expression.

Our present culture has many different types of music, which blend and compete with music from other cultures all over the world. We have classified our music into three categories:

- *Popular music* is of most interest to the public and is usually professionally composed and recorded. It can be performed live, in concert.
- *Classical music* is usually from the past or based on past themes and performed by large orchestras. This music may also be recorded and sold to the public.
- *Folk music* has a grassroots, or country, origin and may have a very strong oral tradition. It can be passed from one generation to the next and is strongly influenced by the rural setting in which it is created. It is usually not professionally composed.

Creative Expression

The goals of creative expression are threefold in that they involve encouraging the student in creating, performing, and appreciating in music. Students must develop a wide variety of skills in order to achieve these three goals.

In order to create and perform music, students must first be able to discriminate pitch, rhythm, and the form of music. The student must be a good listener and be able to imagine the overall performance, since it is transitory. Students must acquire knowledge of instruments and musical notation to be able to create original music. Experience in music from various cultures and time periods in history gives the student a context for musical understanding. Performing music can be a rewarding experience fostering sensitivity to musical expression. Singing, playing an instrument alone or with a group, conducting, or listening to music may encourage musical sensitivity, discrimination, and appreciation. As musical acuity develops, students should be better able to analyze and judge the music they hear.

Aesthetic Valuing

In addition to understanding the history and being able to participate in music, a primary goal of education is to be able to judge and appreciate the beauty and the expression of emotions in music. Having the ability to judge and recognize subtle nuances in music may enable students to choose music that is most meaningful to them. It is revealing to note the purpose of the music, the culture in which it was created, and its style. Students can then judge the music as to how well it accomplished or represents each of the criteria in which it was created.

In the Classroom

Many of the goals for creating, performing, and appreciating music can be applied to judging and appreciating other art forms. Students learn to solve problems and overcome obstacles, as they become more accomplished in music. They develop creative skills, learn time management skills, and acquire alternative methods of communication that serve them well throughout life. Music is often a form of therapy that can relieve stress and express repressed feelings.

Teachers can build an appreciation for music by incorporating it into the classroom at the appropriate age level. First-grade students have a limited range of pitches and vocabulary and memory. These students would be most successful learning songs with a limited range of pitches and with repeated phrases. In teaching upper elementary students chordal harmony, it would be best to play songs in three parts on classroom instruments. Upper elementary students can better understand basic concepts of music theory. Appropriate songs for this age group would incorporate simple diatonic and triatonic harmony that helps students gain an understanding of how notes in chords work together.

Music is often used to enhance other art forms. It is taken for granted in the background in performances of other art forms on stage, television, radio, and film. It even helps us relax in elevators. Music is a part of our lives and describes our culture.

There are many different types and styles of music that have evolved over time. Some of the terms used in describing those types of music are listed below:

- A Cappella—Choral music sung without instrumental accompaniment.
- Aria—Lyric song for solo voice with orchestral accompaniment, generally expressing intense emotion and found in opera, cantata, and oratorio.
- Cantabile—Takes its name from the Italian musical term meaning in a singing style. It is a vocal ensemble with a repertoire ranging from Renaissance sacred music and madrigals to contemporary compositions and settings of folk and popular music.
- Cantata—In the early 1700s it was a dramatic madrigal sung by one. It has evolved into a musical composition, often using a religious text, utilizing recitation, arias, and choruses.
- Chamber Music—Ensemble music for up to about ten players, with one player to a part.
- Chorale—A religious hymn or a simple sacred tune sung in unison by a choir. The Lutheran Church first used chorales to enable the congregation to participate in the service. Chorales date back to Bach.
- Concerto—A composition written for a solo instrument. The soloist plays the melody while the orchestra plays the accompaniment. The soloist is sometimes allowed to improvise his or her part in the credenza.
- Overture—An introductory movement, as in an opera or oratorio, often presenting melodies from arias to come. Also an orchestral work for concert performance.
- Round—A song that involves imitation. One section or group sings the melody and another section follows using the same melody but starting at a later interval and overlapping the voice of the first group (as in "Row Row Row Your Boat").
- Scat—To sing words of nonsense syllables, used in jazz. Also called scatting or scat singing.
- Sonata—Instrumental genre in several movements for soloist or small ensemble.
- Symphony—A large musical work consisting of four movements, or sections.

CONTENT AREA THREE: THEATER

Elements of Theater

An essential element of theater is the actual performance. The performance can only be presented with people portraying characters. Acting requires innate talent, craft, and skill. Performers must learn to present themselves to an audience with flexibility and control in a believable portrayal. Another element necessary for theater is the audience. The essence of theater is the interaction between the performer and audience. A theater, dance, or even musical event is not complete unless there are people to see and hear it. Another element of a theater production is the work of the director. This is the individual who is responsible for interpreting the work and bringing life and artistry to the vision of the playwright. The director rehearses the performers and coordinates their actions to make certain that they interpret the text appropriately, intelligently, and excitingly. Familiarize yourself with the following terminology:

- Blocking—The art of moving actors on the stage, a choreography for the people acting on the stage usually done by the stage manager. This involves the physical relationship of each actor to other actors, entrances and exists from the stage, and patterns created by actors to the set.
- Blocking Rehearsal—A rehearsal taking place early in a production schedule where actors write down movements, which may change by opening night.
- Producer—The person responsible for the central creative idea or concept that unifies the work of the director and designers. The production concept acts as the guide for all the elements of the artistic process allowing each designer's work to support and blend with the work of others.

Theater Space. The theater itself is another necessary element to theater. It is the space in which performers and audiences come together. There must be a stage, or some equivalent area, where actors and actresses can perform. It is also essential to have a place for audience members to sit or stand.

The stage is where the essential action occurs. Various types of stages have been employed over history to support the text of the play being presented. A proscenium stage is a permanent structure framed by an arch, and the backstage and the wings are hidden. The performance is only able to be viewed from one side. When the curtain is closed, scene changes can be made out of the view of the audience using a proscenium stage. The space is not easily adapted to other types of staging arrangements. Another type of stage is the thrust. This type of stage forms a catwalk with the stage of three sides. An arena is a circular stage with the audience surrounding it. Arena setting is a configuration of the audience in relationship to the actor in which the audience surrounds the playing area as in "theater in the round." The most informal is the created or found space, which is any space where actors may perform that is out of the ordinary like a parking lot or a field.

Long ago, the stage was tilted or sloped so the audience could see the performers in the rear of the stage. Stage direction was established using this type of stage (see Figure 20.21).

FIGURE 20.21

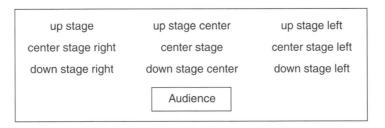

up stage	up stage center	up stage left
center stage right	center stage	center stage left
down stage right	down stage center	down stage left
	Audience	

Terms concerning the stage include:

- Center Stage—The exact center of the floor of the stage.
- Down Stage
  1. The part of the stage nearest to the audience (the lowest part of a raked stage).
  2. A movement towards the audience (in a proscenium theatre).
- Stage Right, Stage Left—Referring to the side of the stage as an actor faces the audience.

Design Aspect. Design aspects in theater include many of the visual effects necessary for an interesting production. These include the costumes, lighting, some form of scenery or background, and sound. Adequate lighting must be sufficient to enable the audience to see the performers or all the other visual affects will be in vain.

The visual aspects of theater are particularly interesting to trace through history because their place in theater production has shifted greatly over time. For example, stage lighting changed dramatically when the electric light bulb came into use at the end of the nineteenth century. The aspects of sound have also changed over time with modern technology. Sound effects in the past were improvised with human ingenuity supplying substitute sounds for the real thing. With the advent of electronic inventions, there are far more elaborate sound effects. Microphones are now used to amplify voice and improve the sound effects.

The purpose of a set is to provide scenery or a background for the actors. It may be an interior of a house or a wooded scene that creates a mood and an atmosphere to augment the written word. The unit set is a permanent scene that may be changed by moving furniture, lights, windows, and doors. A unit set saves time and energy for the stage crew because only smaller items in the scene need to change to show changes in time, mood, or areas. A box set is made up of three walls comprised of flats with a framed ceiling. The flats may be moved or changed to rearrange the scene but it takes time and work for a crew to change the set. A portal set uses downstage flats that are used in all settings but the rear wall flats and upstage wall flats are replaced as scenes change. An environmental set is one that is established among the audience. Some of the terms concerning the design aspects of theater that you need to know to be conversant in talking about theater and theater design include:

- Convention—The tacit acceptance of necessary or customary artificialities as real in a work of art. An example might include background music even though no musicians are visible on stage. The conventions of theater differ depending upon the culture and society in which they evolve.
- Dark Spot—An area of the stage that is not lit.
- Mood—The use of lighting to evoke a particular emotional state in the audience.
- Proscenium Arch—The opening in the wall that stands between stage and auditorium in some theaters; the picture frame through which the audience sees the play. The "fourth wall." In some theaters this arch is elaborately decorated.
- Scene
  1. Location of an action.
  2. In Elizabethan and Jacobean drama, the action on stage between one very brief clearing of the stage and the next clearing of the stage.
- Scenic Designer—The person responsible for authentic sets that portray a particular period in time. A scenic designer must research the time period to authenticate furniture, room design, and decoration.

Text.   The final element essential to theater is the text that is performed. This is the story or event that has been put into dramatic form by a playwright. The playwright develops a script for the performers and director to follow. The text and script must have a focus and a point of view. It must establish the characters in the play, the time period in which the play takes place, the mood of the situation, the actual place where the drama occurs, and the costumes. The terms listed below aid a playwright in developing a script.

- Act—A major division in drama or opera, marked by an interruption in the action of the drama.
- Antagonist—The opposite of the protagonist in a drama. The character or force that resists the protagonist. Conflict results from the protagonist trying to overcome the obstacles imposed by the antagonist.
- Catharsis—A catharsis occurs when an emotional cleansing for the characters and the audience follows a moment of high tragedy at the emotional climax of a play.
- Conflict—The competition between two or more strong characters or concepts in a dramatic work.
- Denouement—The moment in a drama when the essential plot point is unraveled or explained (e.g., "So you see, I couldn't have killed the gardener, because I AM the gardener" [loud organ music, etc.]).
- Exposition—A method of providing information to the audience by the playwright.

- Retrospective Exposition—This explains to the audience what has happened before the play begins. Current exposition gives the audience information about action or events occurring offstage during the play.
- Form—The model or ideal of a particular type of theatrical play, as in a comedic *form*.
- Monologue—That moment when focus is on a single actor who is addressing the audience.
- Motif—A repeated element or thematic idea systematically repeated during a play or film.
- Plot
    1. List of preparations and actions required of technical crews during the performance.
    2. The basic story thread running through a performance/play that gives the reason for the character's actions.
- Point of View—The view from which the story is narrated.
- Protagonist—The leading character or "hero" in a play who has to fight against/oppose the antagonist. This term derives from the theatre of Ancient Greece when the protagonist was the first actor to speak (aside from the chorus). As more "lead" actors were added, they became known as the deuteragonist and tritagonist.
- Soliloquy—A speech by an actor alone on a stage in which the character's thoughts are overheard.
- Subtext—The dramatic implications beneath the text of a script. Basically these are the things that directors and actors must know about the characters that the audience does not need to know explicitly. Subtext may include items like the relationships among characters not evident in the script or the previous lives of the characters.

Plays are categorized depending on the action in the play, the events affecting the main characters, or the time period in which it was first presented.

- Comedy—Historically, this is a play that ends happily. The characters in a comedy are usually less well developed and the language is wittier and lighter than in a drama.
- Dark Comedy—This is a comedy with a distinctly disturbing quality. It may have a macabre theme, or it may relate to the more unpleasant side of life. (Also a play by Peter Shaffer with unusual lighting requirements.) Slapstick is a form of farce employing physical comedy where people get hit, covered in custard pies, or showered with water.
- Drama—The category of literature intended for the stage.
- Elizabethan—Referring to the reign of Queen Elizabeth I (1558–1603). This period included the works of William Shakespeare and Ben Johnson.
- Improvisation—Acting without a script. The actor responds to unexpected stimuli by creating a spontaneous, flexible reaction using anything in the environment for "props" to enhance the performance.
- Jacobean—Referring to the reign of King James I (1603–1625).
- Kabuki—A form of Japanese theater that employs the use of elaborate masks, singing, and dancing in a highly stylized manner.
- Melodrama—This type of play involves sensationalistic plots pitting stereotypical heroes and villains in violent, suspenseful combat. In melodrama, good always triumphs over evil no matter how ridiculous the play's resolution becomes.
- Message Play—Any play that its director describes as "worthwhile" or "designed to make the audience think." Impressive, usually in the daring material attempted.
- Neoclassic Drama—Writers during the Renaissance period attempted to capture the pageantry and mood of Ancient Greece and Rome. In France, writers used rigid verse forms referred to as the unities and enforced a general concern for decorum on stage.
- Pastoral Play—This type of play was popular in Italy during the Renaissance. It was usually set in the countryside and employed satyrs, nymphs, and fairies in music and dancing. It was usually quite light and entertaining.
- Restoration Comedy—Comedic play in of the English Restoration (1660–1700) in which there is debauchery and lustful language.

- Satyr Play—A type of Greek play found in the Classical period that ridiculed the gods, legends, and heroes of Greek theater using obscene or indecent language.
- Tragedy—A tragic protagonist, who often possesses greatness of spirit, commits to a great undertaking in which he or she suffers spiritually, sometimes with great perception, but resulting in death with or without redemption.

History of Theater

The origins of Western drama can be traced to the sixth century B.C. in Greece. Drama in Greek theater was first linked to religious festivals and acted in open-air amphitheaters. The poet Thespis was probably the first solo actor and engaged a chorus of singer-dancers in dialogue. A chorus was used in Greek theatre and was made of a character (or group) representing an element in the drama who comments on the action and advances the plot. The two principal dramatic forms, tragedy and comedy, evolved separately over time. Aeschylus created the possibility of developing conflict between characters by introducing a second actor into the format. His plays demonstrate the paradoxical relationship between humans and the cosmos, in which humans are made to answer for their acts. Sophocles and Euripides were also great playwrights during this period.

Aristotelian theater presented plays demonstrating high levels of intellectual content and a minimum of spectacle. The characters were simple and strong. The plays are usually written in five acts, avoid violence, and do not mix comedy and tragedy. These type of play are attributed to the teachings of Aristotle.

Roman theater developed in the third century. Roman productions were originally based on religious festivals and characterized Roman gods and goddesses. The great playwrights at this time were Plautus, Terence, and Seneca. The Romans adapted Greek dramatic forms and tried to revive them. But with the fall of the Roman Empire in 476 A.D. and the opposition of the early Christian Church, drama almost completely disappeared from Europe. Much of the opposition by the Church was because of the gladiatorial contests and naked dancing. Drama was almost nonexistent by the end of the sixth century.

Medieval drama, when it emerged in the tenth century, was a new creation rather than a rebirth. In the Easter service and the Christmas service, bits of chanted dialogue, called tropes, were interpolated into the liturgy. Drama appeared within the Church itself, as religious narratives were performed by traveling companies to illustrate moral examples of life. Eventually these small plays, sometimes called miracle, passion, or saint plays, grew more elaborate and were presented in larger spaces of the marketplace to larger audiences. Secular elements became evident as artisan guilds took responsibility for the performances. The glorification of God and the redemption of humanity remained primary concerns although local industry was also celebrated.

As the Medieval period gave way to the more humanistic Renaissance, the theater's connection to religion was severed. The secular theaters of Europe, especially in England, encouraged the resurgence of classical tragedy and comedy. The Elizabethan period in England supported theater with larger, well-attended theaters like the Globe. Plays and theater were elevated to their highest literary form during this time by the efforts of Shakespeare, Ben Jonson, and their contemporaries.

Under the Puritan Commonwealth rule of Oliver Cromwell, dramatic performances were banned for the next twenty years. Following the Restoration of the English monarchy in 1660, a new era of more realistic, sophisticated plays became popular. These plays were comedic and made fun of society and social mores. Plays were performed indoors, and women were permitted to be performers for the first time in history.

Renaissance or Elizabethan theater first appeared in Italy during the fifteenth century. These plays were based on Roman figures and styles and featured important concepts such as truth, emphasizing the ideal, proper moral order, and a sense of decorum. This type of theater punished evil and rewarded good. The long narrative dialogues in which a character expressed thoughts to the audience, called soliloquies, were no longer used. The "gallery" evolved during the Elizabethan period and gave rise to tiers of balconies and boxes surrounding the open yard, where spectators with more money could purchase seats with better views and more comfort. Christopher Marlowe and Thomas Kyd were very popular playwrights at the time. The most famous and enduring playwright, however, was William Shakespeare, who had a great effect on both literature and history.

Melodrama became the dominant form of play throughout the 1800s. This was an attempt to appease the audience. They wanted sensationalistic plots pitting stereotypical heroes and villains in violent, suspenseful combat. In melodrama, good always triumphs over evil no matter how ridiculous the play's resolution became.

In its purest form, Romanticism concentrated on the spiritual. It allowed humankind to transcend the limitations of the physical world and body and find an ideal truth. Subject matter was drawn from nature. The romantics focused on emotion rather than rationality. Romanticism produced a large collection of dramatic literature and production that was often undisciplined and substituted emotional manipulation for substantial ideas.

Serious drama of the late nineteenth and early twentieth century emerged from the movement known as Realism. The Realism movement, led by Ibsen, Chekhov, and Shaw, was a response to the melodrama. Realism was an attempt to provide the illusion of nature and deals with ordinary people in ordinary situations in realistic and ordinary settings. The presentation of the play by the actors reflected a closer imitation of reality rather than the overly affected and melodramatic gestures of the past. Stanislavsky, in Russia, promoted the more ordinary and realistic presentation of performance by the actors.

The twentieth century has been an era of experimentation in theater. The antirealistic reaction erupted in a multifaceted movement. The Avant-Garde movement attempted to suggest alternatives to the realistic drama and production. The originator of many antirealist ideas was the German opera composer Richard Wagner. He believed in creating myths. He felt that he should portray an ideal world in which the audience shared the total experience. He tried to depict the soul of the characters rather than their superficial, realistic aspect. Wagner was also responsible for changing the architecture of the theater itself. The stage was similar to other theaters but the auditorium was fitted with a fan-shaped seating area on a sloping floor providing better viewing for all the spectators. He was the first to dim the lights to total darkness during the performance, which was a radical idea.

The Avant-Garde dramatists in the early twentieth century used symbolism, expressionism, and surrealism to portray legends, myths, and dreams in attempting to demonstrate dramatic truth through the manifestation of spirituality, subjectivity, or the unconscious. Much of the Symbolist drama has a mood that is very slow and dreamlike. The intention is to evoke an unconscious response rather than an intellectual one. The sets were suggestive of abstract settings that would create through lighting and objects a feeling of illusion of a real place.

The Expressionist movement, from 1910–1920, explored the more violent aspects of the human psyche. The stage set was distorted and exaggerated with the use of light and shadow to depict a nightmare world. The plots of the plays often dealt with the salvation of mankind.

The Ensemble theater movement of the 1960s abandoned the written text in favor of productions created by an ensemble of actors. The productions relied upon physical movement, unusual arrangements of space, and peculiar language and sounds.

The most popular of the Nonrealistic movement was Absurdism. The Absurdist saw man as lost in the world, trapped by senseless and useless actions. The characters in the play have seemingly irrational and illogical elements that define their actions. Absurdist drama is characterized by viewing the world as alienating and incomprehensible with little cause and effect relationship governing action.

Today, Realism remains the dominant form of contemporary plays. Realistic tendencies are intermingled with techniques borrowed from counterrealistic movements. Psychological realism employing nonrealistic scenic and dramatic devices was used in plays of the 1950s, as in O'Neill's *Long Day's Journey into Night*. Scenery was almost suggestive rather than realistic. European drama at this time was more concerned with plays of ideas. Many plays were based on historical incidents, influenced by war, and explored the moral obligations of individuals to themselves and to society.

Many playwrights in the 1960s and 1970s mirrored society's frustration with a seemingly uncontrollable and self-destructive world. A return to Naturalism occurred in the late 1970s. The focus of these plays is on mundane characters and events. Language is fragmentary, reflecting everyday conversation. This intense focus on a seemingly meaningless part of reality creates a kind of absurdist quality. This quality has combined with a social realism exhibiting a dark humor that has also become popular.

Critical Inquiry

The theater industry is linked with those who comment on it. The job of the theater reviewer is reactive. It can't happen without people putting on plays. It is those plays, taken in tandem with the cultural context, that shape and determine the nature of the criticism, and in turn, the nature of the critics.

A *formalist analysis* of a script is a method of focusing primarily on the text of the script without taking into account the supporting research, theater reviews, or other extraneous information.

Drama and Theater in the Classroom

The goals of educating students in drama and theater are to encourage the development of confidence, creativity, poise, and communication skills. Drama enhances these qualities because it uses both language and body movement in the reenactment of life situations for entertainment and better understanding of the human predicament.

A school curriculum in drama should include development of the vocabulary of theater and development of a criterion for evaluation of drama. Students need to understand terms used in the theater and be able to appreciate a dramatic work.

Drama Curriculum.   A good drama curriculum includes several important elements.

- Acting—Acting involves the student's ability for skillful communication. Acting requires skillful speaking, movement, sensory awareness, rhythm, and oral communication. The actor must practice and rehearse a script before performing in front of an audience. The actor may also perform in improvisation in which a spontaneous, creative, unscripted response results from a problem or unexpected dramatic stimuli.
- Improvisation—the actor responds to unexpected stimuli by creating a spontaneous, flexible reaction using anything in the environment for "props" to enhance the performance.
- Drama—Drama is a reenactment of life situations for entertainment and understanding of human predicaments.
- Theater—Theater involves a more formal presentation in front of an audience. It often includes a script, set, direction, and production. Many people may be involved in the production of the project by not only acting, but by designing sets and costumes, managing the lighting, directing the players and crew, marketing the performance, and arranging the production of the entire process.
- Production—This includes arranging for the entire theater performance. Producers coordinate all the technical aspects of a theatrical presentation.
- Direction—Direction includes coordinating and guiding the onstage activities. Directors guide and inspire the actors, make decisions on set design, costumes, and lighting, and manage the stage crew.
- Playmaking—This involves creating an original script and then staging and performing that story without a formal audience.

Drama Evaluation.   The criteria for judging or evaluating dramatic works commonly includes the following elements to ensure thoughtful reflection. These questions can be asked when considering each of the elements for evaluation.

- Intent—What is the reason for the drama? Does the intent reflect the purpose or theme for presenting the work?
- Structure—Is there a relationship between the various components of a dramatic work? Consider some of these components as balance, sequence, conflict, contrast, design, rhythm, harmony, stress, and transition.
- Effectiveness—What impact does the dramatic work have on the audience? Has the dramatic work succeeded in entertaining, informing, illuminating, persuading, inspiring, shocking, or moving the audience to the degree for which it was intended?
- Worth—Does the dramatic work provide insight, wisdom, or knowledge? A value judgment must be made weighing the importance or worth of the piece.

Creative Expression. The student is encouraged to participate in drama and theatrical performances. Students are involved in creating, performing, judging, and appreciating works in drama. As the student develops skills in acting, directing, and supporting theatrical production, they will better understand and appreciate the characters, environments, and conflict within the production and within the segment of life being reproduced.

Historical and Cultural Context. The student will understand the contributions of storytelling, improvisation, fairytales, folklore, and mythology in the evolution of drama and theater. The "stories" of a culture are often woven into the fabric of performed drama. These histories of a culture add to the diversity and color of the drama from those areas of the world. Japanese Kabuki theater employs the use of masks, singing and dancing in a very stylized manner. Drama and comedy have tried to portray humanity's deepest passion and universal concerns. Medieval drama was primarily religious and performed in cathedrals and monasteries. Until the sixteenth century, most plays and performances in Europe took place in outside open areas like a marketplace or a courtyard. The great Shakespearean plays were originally performed onstage with little or no scenery in a theater but with the spectators merely gathered around the stage on three sides. It wasn't until the seventeenth century that plays and operas were performed with elaborate scenery and indoor lighting. As the values of the middle class were reflected in the nineteenth-century theater, scenery and costumes became more realistic denoting the society's emphasis on the inner and interpersonal conflicts of real people.

Aesthetic Valuing. Theater has had a major effect on literature. Shakespeare, Euripides, Aeschylus, and Sophocles are still being used today in the classroom because of their structure and versatility. Many plays from the past are still being read and performed because of the meaning that they hold. Shakespeare was one of the most effective playwrights. He was able to understand and portray people for who they were and to craft words for each character as no other playwright before or after him. His plays have stood the test of time. Students should be able to judge, evaluate, and appreciate theatrical performances based on the intent, structure, effectiveness, and worth of the play. The details of design principles such as repetition, rhythm, balance, and variation on a theme can be included in the student's discrimination of the characteristics of the work. Changes in lighting, viewpoints, angles, and atmosphere can have a dramatic effect on the visual impression. Changes in lighting technology, such as the use of strobe lighting and holograms, have made recent strides in changing the mood of the performed work of art.

Broadway theater has evolved as a commercial venture named for the boulevard in New York City upon which most of the important theaters present profit-making plays, employing and making star performers, as the play runs for a long period of time. These performances are made to appeal to a wide range of audiences.

Connections, Relationships, and Applications. Theater is a way of expressing everything from feelings to political standpoints. It is a great advantage for students to understand and appreciate theatrical works of art. Theater can help students better understand the importance of historical events in various cultures and time periods. Students develop an appreciation and empathy for others as the take on the roles of various characters with varied backgrounds. Application of what students learn and experience in working in the theater can help them develop skills in problem solving, build confidence and communicative skills, and provide interests in areas otherwise left undiscovered. The development of these skills will serve the student in opening new opportunities for careers and lifelong learning.

CONTENT AREA FOUR: DANCE

Because of its universal appeal, physical and emotional involvement, and history, dance has been an important part of physical education programs. Many of the concepts in a good physical education class also apply to dance. Dance offers students an alternative form of physical expression in which they can express themselves freely. This freedom of expression through movement encourages good self-esteem and mental acuity by combining movement, rhythm, kinesthetic awareness, fitness, and appreciation of cultural and historical differences.

Movements and segments of dance are made up of individual steps, gestures, and beats. All are built upon one another and enhance each other to contribute to the total composition. The "dance" may be enhanced or inhibited by outside influences such as lighting, set design and staging, choice of costumes, and live or electronic musical accompaniment. Forms of dance include the following:

- Rondo: A basic theme is introduced at the beginning of the work and returns between sections of contrasting materials.
- Canon: Movement sequences are first presented by a group of dancers and then restated by other dancers who begin the steps on later counts.
- Collage: A group of movement and thematic ideas that are interpolated into one composition.
- AB form: Similar movement sequences are clearly divided into two large sections without repetition.

Practice, dedication, and focus are essential in training for serious participation in dance. Each practice should begin with a warm-up session consisting of stretches and movements to prevent muscular injury and to prepare the muscles for strenuous activity. Aerobic conditioning exercise is helpful at the beginning of the practice period to build cardiovascular conditioning. The rehearsal period of individual movements, gestures, and phrases of dance would comprise the major portion of the practice period ending with relaxation exercises enabling the individual to return gradually to normal metabolic levels. The rehearsal period stresses the individual characteristics of the steps and dances being performed. Each genre of dance has its own unique technique that must be mastered. Constant exercise and fitness is important in developing a body that is flexible, strong, and fluid in movement. Dedication and commitment to dance is paramount.

Time and Space in Dance

Dance is an artistic form of self-expression that involves the individual in types of kinesthetic movement that include time, space, shape, and force. Time refers to a rhythmic beat or tempo. Space includes the area surrounding the body, which may be involved in the movement of the individual, and the body itself. Shape refers to the positioning of the body to create an image or form. Force is the release of energy that is expressed through movement to the rhythm of the dance. The internal force is exerted through the muscles in the body of the dancer. There is an external force that includes the gravitational pull and restraints exerted on a body in motion. Spatial terms for dance movements or gestures may refer to the size or direction of a movement, or to the extent to which the movement penetrates the surrounding space.

- Range: The size of a movement or gesture through space.
- Direction: The imaginary line along which a dancer moves through space.

- Plane: Spatial areas formed by any two of the three dimensions (e.g., height and width, width and depth).
- Level: Any one of the three horizontal areas into which space is divided in dance.
- Elevation: The ability to jump high into the air and give the appearance of remaining suspended at the apex of the jump.
- En bas: Low, usually in reference to an arm position.
- En l'air: Steps performed in the air or to a leg that is in the air.
- Time: The duration of a dance; a rate of speed as in fast, moderate, or slow; a metric time which is a beat or pulse that guides a performance.
- Adagio: Any dance to slow music; also, part of the classical pas de deux in ballet.
- Allegro: Advancing with a fast or moderate tempo. That part of a ballet class comprised of fast turning or jumping, especially beaten steps, usually follows the adagio.

Dance is one of the most primitive instincts of mankind. Rhythm is the basis of dance, and emotion stimulates the body into movement. Mankind has historically communicated thoughts and desires through dance. Dance has historically been used to express the unknown powers of nature and was often reserved for priests and religious rituals. The use of imagery is employed in dance to inspire and expand rich and articulate movement. Imagery enables a dancer to visualize and internalize the particular qualities of a specific movement. Ancient Greeks, Romans, and Egyptians enjoyed dance for entertainment and expression of ideas. It was in the Middle Ages when the common person enjoyed dance as a celebration. Dance gradually evolved with formalized steps and forms as it became popular to the upper classes in the Renaissance period.

Dance in China dates back nearly 5,000 years. As in most cultures, Chinese dance was linked to expression of life experiences. Chinese dance can be divided into four different categories:

- Ceremonial: For praying to the gods for good harvests.
- Dramatic: For reporting and commemorating historical events.
- Martial: For demonstrating fighting techniques.
- Agricultural: For celebrating work and nature.

Chinese dance was greatly influenced by India about 2,000 years ago as the Silk Road brought Buddhism to China. Bharata Natyam is one of the oldest forms of dance in India and requires extensive body movement, complex rhythms for the feet, and complex facial expression and hand gestures. Japanese Kabuki theater incorporates dance along with masks and operatic spectacle as a form of popular entertainment. The effortless grace of the classical ballet dancer and the refined movement of the Kabuki artist have both affected the cultures in which they evolved. In both cases the appearance and the deportment of the dancers have been emulated in each culture.

Dance in America evolved based on various influences from the tribal religious expression of Native Americans, the dances imported through the African and Caribbean slave trade, and folk dances brought by European immigrants.

The minuet was introduced to the court in Paris in 1650, and it dominated the ballroom until the end of the eighteenth century. Many of the ballets during this period included a minuet. The waltz was first noticed in 1780, and it evolved into one of the most fashionable dances in the courts of Europe.

All historic styles and forms of dance had ratings when performed and would be reported as follows:

- Grotesque: Lowest degree. The dancer was unsteady, movements were imposing while demanding—all skill rather than gracefulness.
- Comic: Second degree. Generally steadier than the first, representing customs, pastimes, or romances of the lower classes.
- Demi-caractere: Third degree. This class exemplified affairs of ordinary life such as a love story or plot, representing the common people.

- Serious: Fourth degree. These were usually found upon the tragic staging. Represented the highest possible degree of skill and elegance.
- Pantomimic: Fifth degree. Ballet. These acts conveyed the entire act through dance with no words.

Ballet is primarily a form of dance that is consciously created rather than spontaneously performed. Ballet evolved from European folkloric dances. Today the character dances of story ballets are one of the primary connections to the folkloric tradition. Ballet also had its origins in Roman pantomime and Italian comedic theater but did not have the essentials of classical ballet until the Academy of Royal Dancing was founded in Paris, France, in 1661. Ballet was then spread to Italy and was included in many operas performed at La Scala in Milan. Since the end of the nineteenth century Russian ballet has often set the standard. One of the most important American choreographers and director of the New York Ballet after World War II was George Balanchine.

In the mid-1800s, a social movement to discover common trends and rituals throughout world societies started as a result of the publication of *Origin of the Species* written by Charles Darwin. This prompted a similar attempt in dance to discover common dance steps and gestures in ritual or cultural dances throughout the world. Curt Sachs studied and wrote about ancient and ethnic dances from all over the world and documented the similarities he found in his book *World History of the Dance.*

After World War II, the traditional aspects of ballet gave way to more abstract interpretation and greater individual expression. Katherine Dunham was an African American woman who studied Caribbean and Brazilian dance and later opened a dance school in Chicago. She is credited with developing an important teaching routine for dance that is still being used today. She used her talents as a dancer, choreographer, and teacher to call public attention to social injustice. In the early 1900s, Isadora Duncan was one of the first choreographers to define movement based on natural and spiritual laws rather than on the formal considerations of geometric space. She created her own free style using natural movements and performed barefoot in loose, flowing tunics. Ruth St. Denis was the first American dancer to incorporate the traditions and practices of the vaudeville stage into the world of serious dance. With her husband, Ted Shawn, she taught and encouraged other great modern dancers such as Martha Graham, Doris Humphrey, and Charles Weidman. These dancers went on to shape and redefine dance in more modern terms.

Martha Graham created a language of angular, percussive gestures displayed in the contraction and release of the muscles of the lower torso. Doris Humphrey based her dance on the theory of "fall and recover." José Limon was a Mexican-born dancer who studied with Doris Humphrey and Charles Weidman and continued the technique based on principles of weight, fall, and recovery in dance. Agnes De Mille and Jerome Robbins included the ballet-type dance in American musical theater. They included folk and jazz in combination with ballet to revolutionize the American musical. Dance is expressed in several distinct categories to be discussed next.

Creative Dance

This is one of the first forms of dance and the one of the most natural for children. Music and its sounds, styles, moods, and expressions are used by the dancer to form a story, express a mood, or to simply release the dancer to move as he or she feels. Creative dance depicts a dancer's feelings through movement.

Modern Dance

There have been two different meanings to the term "modern dance." In the early twentieth century, modern dance referred to ballroom-type dance like the two-step and minuet. Isadora Duncan was to become the mother of the current-day modern dance and by 1913 had reached international fame. Today the term means something different, The term "modern dance" refers to a concept of dance rather than a studio or school. By the 1920s it was a solo or group free-form-type dance that utilized many other styles of dance movement.

The modern dance form evolved due to the restrictions on ballet dancers at the time. Early modern dancers were in opposition to the restrictions of ballet. The use of bare feet was in opposition to the pointe shoe and provided a direct connection with the earth. "Balletic" movements that appeared to defy gravity were revised. Modern dance made the sense of weight visible and explored the use of the floor for falls and other movements on the ground. The form is now very recognizable as the dancer releases inner feelings with outer expression. It works with the teaching of opposites and contrasts such as contract–release, fast–slow, fall–recover. The body is the instrument for expression. Modern dance is based on four principles: substance, dynamism, metakinesis, and form.

Social Dance

Social dance refers to a cooperative form of dance with respect for one's partner and others with whom the dance floor is shared. Many of the dances evolved from quadrilles to schottishe, grand march to polonaise, waltz, and finally, the two-step. Many of these dances are performed to a particular or strict tempo.

Social dance has no real standards or rules. Dancing is a part of living and combines with other aspects of cultural and social life. It is multigenerational and includes dancers of various degrees of skill and experience.

Dances of Other Cultures

Folk dances are dances that have evolved in a particular area and express the culture and music of that area. These dances are as varied as the cultures in which they are performed. Some may be formal with traditional steps and formats and other types may be quite free form and random. Many of the participants wear costumes indicative of the culture in which they live. Dances from all over the world, however, have things in common. The "call-and-response," which refers to the exchange of steps or movements between a soloist and the audience or other dancers, is common to traditional dances of Europe as well as those in Africa.

Structured Dance

The dances in this category have their origins in social dance. Arthur Murray promoted the notion that dancing is steps, and you need to take lessons to be able to dance. Many of the structured dances are made up of combined steps and moves, rather than feeling, connection, or improvisation. These dances include the waltz, jazz, and tap.

Ritual Dance

Ritual dances are often of a religious nature celebrating a significant event or belief common to a particular group of people. The dances have usually been created over time to signify the importance of the coming of a season of the year, recognition of an individual achievement, for inspiration in hunting or war, and to glorify the gods. In Africa, the participants are circled by the audience; however, an audience may not even be necessary. The performances may continue for hours or even days with the inclusion of various religious ceremonies and trances. Ritual dances have been used as a basis for several more modern theatrical performances, but they tend to lack meaning and strength provided by the original setting and history. Trance states have been used in of many world dance forms expressing religious or spiritual rituals in dance. Dances of *Candomblé* and the Whirling Dervishes use trance states as periods of divine contact in which the dancers may experience oneness with the divine. Even the conservative Shakers use trance states in their dances as periods of spiritual cleansing.

Ballet

There are five basic positions of the feet used in ballet: First position: feet in a straight line, heels touching. Second position: feet in a straight line, heels apart. Third position: one foot in front of the other, parallel to it, with heel of front foot in hollow instep of back foot. Fourth position: one foot in front of the other, parallel, but apart. Fifth position: one foot in front of the other, parallel, with heel in front foot touching toe of back foot. These five positions make up or begin many of the more complicated steps and positions that a dancer must assume when performing. Many of these steps have varied little over the centuries. Dancers use a barre to hold onto during the first part of a dance class. The wooden bar runs around the wall of the ballet studio at waist height and helps the dancer find or adjust his or her balance. Alignment is the way in which various parts of the dancer's body are in line with one another while the dancer is moving, and it must be precise and executed with grace and form. Because music and rhythm are the canvas upon which the dance is portrayed, the mood and expression of the music are very important to any of these types of dance.

In addition to the obvious considerations of getting enough nourishment and sleep prior to test day, there are several points you need to keep in mind.

1. *Know the real scores.* Be sure that you know what score you are aiming for on each subtest. Review Chapter 1 and be sure to memorize the tally tables for each of the subtests, so that you can apply them with ease on the day of the test.

2. *Know how to manage your time.* Be sure that you understand the procedures for managing time on your test. If your exam has subtests, it is recommended that you register and take them all at once. That way, you will have a good idea about the content tested on the other tests, and you can begin to prepare for them. If you are taking only one or two subtests, then review the specific plans for each combination of subtests.

3. *Use written and multiple-choice strategies.* Be sure that you know the strategies for the written and multiple-choice sections, and that you have had the chance to practice them on the study guides that you have obtained. (*Note:* In all cases, complete the essays, even if you run out of time on the multiple-choice questions. That way, you can get feedback on your writing and level of content knowledge from the score report that you receive after the exam.)

4. *Dress comfortably and bring earplugs.* Since you can neither control the location of the exam nor its environment, be sure to dress for test success. That means wearing comfortable clothes. A layer or two is a good idea, depending on the season, since you can more easily remove a sweater than ask the test proctor to turn the thermostat down. Foam earplugs are another good idea. They can be purchased at your local pharmacy. One candidate reported that the person next to her sighed constantly during the exam—not loudly, but audibly enough to be a distraction to this particular candidate—and it ruined her experience. So, it may be a good idea for you to use earplugs during the exam in order to ensure that your attention stays focused on the task at hand. Try them out prior to test day. Follow the directions that accompany the package for use.

5. *Be confident!* If you have studied the content and practiced the strategies, then you are in an excellent position to do your best on the exam. Take pride in that . . . and beat the exam!

REFERENCES

Abrams, R. (1963). *The issues of federal regulation in the progressive era.* Chicago: Rand McNally.

Adams, M. J. (1990). *Beginning to read: Thinking and learning about print.* Cambridge, MA: MIT Press.

Akinnaso, F. N. (1982). On the differences between spoken and written language. *Language and Speech, 25* (Part 2), 97–125.

Anderson, P. (1985). Explaining intercultural differences in nonverbal communication. In L. A. Samovar & R. E. Porter (Eds.), *Intercultural communication: A reader* (6th ed., pp. 286–296). Belmont, CA: Wadsworth.

Anderson, S. R. (1985). *Phonology in the twentieth century.* Chicago: University of Chicago.

Armbruster, B. B., & Nagy, W. E. (1992). Vocabulary in content area lessons. *The Reading Teacher, 45,* 550–551.

Asher, J. (1982). *Learning another language through actions: The complete teachers' guidebook.* Los Gatos, CA: Sky Oaks.

Asher, J. J., & Garcia, R. (1969). The optimal age to learn a foreign language. *Modern Language Journal, 53,* 334–341.

Asher, J. L. (1969). The total physical response to second language learning. *The Modern Language Journal, 53,* 1–17.

Babbs, P. J., & Moe, A. J. (1983). Metacognition: A key for independent learning from text. *The Reading Teacher, 37,* 422–426.

Ball, E. W., & Blachman, B. A. (1991). Does phoneme awareness training in kindergarten make a difference in early word recognition and developmental spelling? *Reading Research Quarterly, 26,* 49–66.

Bandura, A. (1973). *Aggression: A social learning analysis.* Englewood Cliffs, NJ: Prentice-Hall.

Barker, L. (1990). *Communications* (5th ed.). Englewood Cliffs, NJ: Prentice-Hall.

Barnitz, J. G. (1998). Revising grammar instruction for authentic composing and comprehending. *The Reading Teacher, 51,* 608–611.

Barnlund, D. (1989). *Communicative styles of Japanese and American images and realities.* Belmont, CA: Wadsworth.

Bates, E., & MacWhinney, B. (1981). Second language acquisition from a functionalist perspective: Pragmatics, semantics, and perceptual strategies. In H. Winitz (Ed.), *Annals of New York Academy of Science conference on native language and foreign language acquisition* (pp. 190–214). New York: New York Academy of Science.

Baumann, J. F., Seifert-Kessel, N., & Jones, L. A. (1992). Effect of think aloud instruction on elementary students' comprehension monitoring ability. *Journal of Reading Behavior, 25,* 407–438.

Bear, D., & Barone, D. (1989). Using children's spellings to group for word study and directed reading in the primary classroom. *Reading Psychology, 10,* 275–292.

Bear, D., Invernizzi, M., Templeton, S., & Johnston, F. (2000). *Words their way: Word study for phonics, vocabulary, and spelling instruction.* Upper Saddle River, NJ: Merrill.

Bear, D., & Templeton, S. (1998). Explorations in developmental spelling: Foundations for learning and teaching phon-

ics, spelling, and vocabulary. *The Reading Teacher, 52,* 222–242.

Beebe, S., & Masterson, J. (2000). *Communicating in small groups: Principles and practices* (6th ed.). Boston: Allyn and Bacon.

Benne, K., & Sheats, P. (1948). Functional roles of group members. *Journal of Social Issues, 4,* 41–49.

Bernstein, B. (1964). Elaborated and restricted codes: Their social origins and some consequences. *American Anthropologist, 66*(5), 55–69.

Bley-Vroman, R. (1986). Hypothesis testing in second language acquisition. *Language Learning, 36,* 353–76.

Bloom, P. (Ed.). (1994). *Language acquisition: Core readings.* Cambridge, MA: MIT Press.

Boosalis, C. N. (2004). *Beating them all! Thirty days to magic score on any exam of elementary literacy instruction for teacher certification.* New York: Allyn and Bacon.

Bottomley, D. M., Henk, W. A., & Melnick S. A. (1997/1998). Assessing childrens' views about themselves as writers using the Writer Self-Perception Scale. *The Reading Teacher, 51,* 286–291.

Brown, J. K. (1993). The nineteenth amendment and women's equality. *Yale Law Journal, 102,* 1–12.

Brown, R. (1973). *A first language: The early stages.* Cambridge, MA: Harvard University Press.

Browning, D. S. (1973). *Generative man: Psychoanalytic perspectives.* Philadelphia: The Westminster Press.

Burgchardt, C. R. (1992). *Robert M. La Follette, Sr.: The voice of conscience.* New York: Greenwood Press.

Bush, F. R., Overmier, J. B., & Solomon, R. L. (1985). *Affect, conditioning, and cognition: Essays on the determinants of behavior.* Hillsdale, NJ: Lawrence Erlbaum Associates.

Cairns, H. S. (1996). *The acquisition of language* (2nd ed.). Cambridge, MA: Harvard University Press.

Canale, M., & Swain, M. (1980). Theoretical bases of communicative approaches to second language teaching and testing. *Applied Linguistics, 1,* 1–47.

Carr, P. (1993). *Phonology.* New York: St. Martin's Press.

Carr, K. S. (1983). The importance of inference skills in the primary grades. *The Reading Teacher, 36,* 518–522.

Carr, K. S., & Ogle, D. (1987). KWL plus: A strategy for comprehension and summarization. *Journal of Reading, 30,* 626–631.

Chamot, A. U., & O'Malley, J. M. (1986). *A cognitive academic language learning approach: An ESL content based curriculum.* Washington, DC: National Clearinghouse for Bilingual Education.

Chomsky, C. (1969). *The acquisition of syntax in children from 5 to 10.* Cambridge, MA: MIT Press.

Chomsky, N., & Halle, M. (1968). *The sound patterns of English.* New York: Harper & Row.

Clay, M. M. (1993a). *An observation survey of early literacy achievement.* Portsmouth, NH: Heinemann.

Clay, M. M. (1993b). *Reading Recovery: A guidebook for teachers.* Portsmouth, NH: Heinemann.

Cohen, A. D. (1996). Speech acts. In S. L. McKay & N. H. Hornberger (Eds.), *Sociolinguistics and language teach-*

ing (pp. 383–420). New York: Press Syndicate of the University of Cambridge.

Cohen, D. H. (1968). The effect of literature on vocabulary and reading achievement. *Elementary English, 45,* 209–213, 217.

Courtney, A. M., & Abodeeb, T. L. (1999). Diagnostic-reflective portfolios. *The Reading Teacher, 52,* 708–714.

Cox, B. D., & Lightfoot, C. (1997). *Sociogenetic perspectives on internalization.* Mahwah, NJ: Lawrence Erlbaum Associates.

Crane, S. (1898). The open boat: A tale intended to be after the fact of being the experience of four men from the sunk steamer Commodor. In P. Lauter (Ed.), *The Heath anthology of American literature* (Vol. 2). Lexington, MA: D. C. Heath.

CSET. (2002–2003a). *Registration Bulletin.* California Commission on Teacher Credentialing and National Evaluation Systems, Inc.

CSET. (2002–2003b). *Registration Bulletin* [and test information]. Retrieved March 23, 2004, from http://www.cset.nesinc.com

Cullen-Dupont, K., & Frost, E. (1992). *Women's suffrage in America: An eyewitness history.* New York: Facts on File.

Cummins, J. (1979). Cognitive/academic language proficiency, linguistics interdependence, the optimal age question and some other matters. *Working Papers on Bilingualism, 19,* 197–205.

Curtis, S. (1977). *Genie: A psycholinguistic study of a modern-day "wild child."* New York: Academic Press.

Decarvalho, R. J. (1991). *The founders of humanistic psychology.* New York: Praeger.

Duffelmeyer, F. A. (1994). Effective anticipation guide statements for learning from expository text. *Journal of Reading, 37,* 452–457.

Duffelmeyer, F. A., & Baum, D. D. (1992). The extended anticipation guide. *Journal of Reading, 35,* 654–656.

Dunn, A. H., & Graves, M. F. (1987). Intensive vocabulary instruction as a prewriting technique. *Reading Research Quarterly, 22,* 311–329.

Ediger, M. (1999). Evaluation of reading progress. *Reading Improvement, 36,* 50–56.

Eimas, P. (1975). Developmental studies of speech perception. In L. Cohen & P. Salapatek (Eds.), *Infant perception.* New York: Academic Press.

Erikson, E., & Evans, R. I. (1967). *Dialogue with Erik Erikson.* New York: Harper & Row.

Evans, R. I. (1973). *Jean Piaget: The man and his ideas.* New York: E. P. Dutton.

Ewen, R. B. (1998). *An introduction to theories of personality.* Mahwah, NJ: Lawrence Erlbaum Associates.

Fassold, R. (1984). *The sociolinguistics of society.* New York: Blackwell.

Fassold, R. (1990). *The sociolinguistics of Language.* Rowley, MA: Newbury House.

Fehrenbacher, D. E., & Snyder, L. L. (1964). A *basic history of California.* Princeton, NJ: Van Nostrand.

Fisher, L. H. (1953). *The harvest labor market in California.* Cambridge, MA: Harvard University Press.

Flavell, J. H. (1963). *Developmental psychology of Jean Piaget.* Princeton, NJ: Van Nostrand.

Flavell, J. H. (1999). Cognitive development: Children's knowledge about the mind. *Annual Review of Psychology, 50,* 21–45.

Gardner, H. G. (1993a) *Multiple intelligences: The theory in practice.* New York: Basic Books.

Gardner, H. G. (1993b). *Frames of mind: The theory of multiple intelligences.* New York: Basic Books.

Gardner, R., & Lambert, W. (1959). Motivational variables in second language acquisition. *Canadian Journal of Psychology, 13,* 266–272.

Gass, S. (1984). A review of interlanguage syntax: Language transfer and language universals. *Language Learning, 34,* 115–132.

Gass, S., & Selinker, L. (1983). *Language transfer in language learning.* Rowley, MA: Newbury House.

Gass, S. M., & Selinker, L. (1994). *Second language acquisition: An introductory course.* Hillsdale, NJ: Lawrence Erlbaum Associates.

Gergen, K. (1995). Social construction and the educational process. In J. Gale & L. P. Steffe (Eds.), *Constructivism in education* (pp. 17–40). Hillsdale, NJ: Lawrence Erlbaum Associates.

Giles, H., & Smith, P. (1979). Accommodation theory: Optimal levels of convergence. In H. Giles & R. St. Clair (Eds.), *Language and social psychology* (pp. 45–65). London: Blackwell.

Goldstein, L. M. (1987). Standard English: The only target for nonnative speakers of English? *TESOL Quarterly, 21*(3), 417–436.

Gormezano, I., & Prosasy, W. F. (1987). *Classical conditioning.* Hillsdale, NJ: Lawrence Erlbaum Associates.

Gray-Schlegel, M. A., & King, Y. (1998). Introducing concepts about print to the preservice teacher: A hands-on experience. *The California Reader, 32,* 16–21.

Hakuta, K. (1974). A preliminary report on the development of grammatical morphemes in a Japanese girl learning English as a second language. *Working Papers on Bilingualism, 3,* 18–43.

Halliday, M. A. K. (1978). *Language as social semiotic: The social interpretation of language and meaning.* Baltimore: University Park Press.

Hamm, R. F. (1995). *Shaping the eighteenth amendment: Temperance reform, legal culture, and the polity, 1880–1920.* Chapel Hill: University of North Carolina Press.

Hennings, D. G. (2002). *Communication in action: Teaching literature-based language arts.* Boston: Houghton Mifflin.

Hoffman, J. V. (1998). When bad things happen to good ideas in literacy education: Professional dilemmas, personal decisions, and political traps. *The Reading Teacher, 52,* 102–112.

Hoover, K. R., Marcia, J. E., & Parris, K. D. (1997). *The power of identity: Politics in a new key.* Chatham, NJ: Chatham House Publishers.

Huang, J., & Hatch, E. (1978). A Chinese child's acquisition of English. In E. Hatch (Ed.), *Second language acquisition* (pp. 118–131). Rowley, MA: Newbury House.

Hyman, L. M. (1975). *Phonology: Theory and analysis.* New York: Holt, Rinehart and Winston.

Hymes, D. (1972). On communicative competence. In J. Pride & J. Holmes (Eds.), *Sociolinguistics.* Harmondsworth, UK: Penguin Books.

Ingram, D. (1989). *First language acquisition.* Cambridge, MA: Academic Press.

Invernizzi, M. A., Abouzeid, M. P., & Bloodgood, J. W. (1997). Integrated word study: Spelling, grammar, and meaning in the language arts classroom. *Language Arts, 74,* 185–192.

Jackson, K. T., & Schultz, S. K. (Eds.). (1972). *Cities in American history.* New York: Knopf.

Johnson, J., & Newport, E. (1989). Critical period effects in second language learning: The influence of maturational state on acquisition of ESL. *Cognitive Psychology, 21,* 60–99.

Joos, M. (1967). *The five clocks.* New York: Harcourt, Brace and World.

Katamba, F. (1993). *Morphology.* New York: St. Martin's Press.

Kellerman, E., & Sharwood-Smith, M. (1986). *Cross-linguistic influence in second language acquisition.* New York: Pergamon.

Kemporson, R. (1977). *Semantic theory.* Cambridge, UK: Cambridge University Press.

Kesselman-Turkel, J., & Peterson, F. (1982). *Note-taking made easy.* Chicago: Contemporary Books.

Kilma, E., & Bellugi, U. (1966). Syntactic regularities in the speech of children. In J. Lynons & R. Wales (Eds.), *Psycholinguistic papers.* Edinburgh, UK: Edinburgh University Press.

Kimble, G. A. (1967). *Foundations of conditioning and learning.* New York: Appleton Century Crofts.

Krashen, S. D. (1981). *Principles and practice in second language acquisition. English Language Teaching Series.* London: Prentice-Hall International.

Krashen, S. (1982). *Principles and practice in second language acquisition.* Oxford, UK: Pergamon.

Krashen, S. (1983). Practical applications of research. Psycholinguistic Research *ACTFL Yearbook.* Lincolnwood, IL: National Textbook.

Krashen, S. (1985). *The input hypothesis: Issues and implications.* New York: Longman.

Krashen, S. (1993). *The power of reading.* Englewood, CO: Libraries United.

Krashen, S., & Terrell, T. (1983). *The natural approach.* New York: Pergamon.

Labov, W. (1972). *Language in the inner city: Studies in black English vernacular.* Philadelphia: University of Pennsylvania Press.

Langer, J. A. (1981). From theory to practice: A prereading plan. *Journal of Reading, 24,* 152–156.

Lapsley, D. K. (1996). *Moral psychology.* Boulder, CO: Westview Press.

Larson-Freeman, D. (1976). An explanation for the morpheme acquisition order of second language learners. *Language Learning, 26,* 125–34.

Larson-Freeman, D., & Long, M. H. (1991). *An introduction to second language acquisition research.* New York: Longman.

Lee, D. M., & Allen, R. V. (1963). *Learning to read through experience* (2nd ed.). New York: Meredith.

Lemert, C. (1999). *Social theory: The multicultural and classic readings.* Boulder, CO: Westview Press.

Lemke, J. *Talking science: Language, learning, and values.* New York: Ablex.

Lenneberg, E. H. (1967). *The biological foundations of language.* New York: Wiley.

Lessow-Hurley, J. (1990). *The foundations of dual language instruction.* White Plains, NY: Longman.

Levinson, S. (1983). *Pragmatics.* Cambridge, UK: Cambridge University Press.

Lewis, M., Wray, D., & Rospigliosi, P. (1994). ". . . And I want it in your own words." *The Reading Teacher, 47,* 528–536.

Libecap, G. D. (1992). The rise of the Chicago packers and the origins of meat inspection and antitrust. *Economic Inquiry, 30,* 242.

Lightfoot, C., & Cox, B. D. (1997). *Sociogenetic perspectives on internalization.* Mahwah, NJ: Lawrence Erlbaum Associates.

Locke, J. (1983). *Phonological acquisition and change.* New York: Academic Press.

Luft, J. (1984). *Group processes: An introduction to group dynamics* (3rd ed.). Palo Alto, CA: Mayfield.

Maier, H. W. (1969). *Three theories of child development: The contributions of Erik H. Erikson, Jean Piaget, and Robert R. Sears, and their applications.* New York: Harper & Row.

Manzo, A. V. (1975). Guided reading procedure. *Journal of Reading, 19,* 287–291.

McCauley, J. K., & McCauley, D. S. (1992). Using choral reading to promote language learning for ESL students. *The Reading Teacher, 45,* 526–534.

McIntosh, M. E., & Draper, R. J. (1995). Applying the question-answer relationship strategy in mathematics. *Journal of Adolescent & Adult Literacy, 39,* 120–131.

Mesmer, H. A. (2001). Decodable text: A review of what we know. *Reading Research and Instruction, 40,* 121–142.

Mesmer, H. A., & Hutchins, E. J. (2002). Using QARs with charts and graphs. *The Reading Teacher, 56,* 20–29.

Mitchell, J. P., Abernathy, T. V., & Gowans, L. P. (1998). Making sense of literacy portfolios: A four-step plan. *Journal of Adolescent & Adult Literacy, 41,* 384–389.

Newell, J. (1984). *Advance organizers: Their construction and use in instructional development.* ERIC Document ED 298908.

Newmark, L. (1966). How not to interfere with language learning. Language Learning: The Individual and the Process. *International Journal of American Linguistics, 40,* 77–83.

Odlin, T. (1989). *Language transfer. Cross-linguistic influence in language learning.* Cambridge, UK: Cambridge University Press.

Ogle, D. M. (1986). K-W-L: A teaching model that develops active reading of expository text. *The Reading Teacher, 39,* 564–571.

Olin, S. C. (1968). *California's prodigal sons: Hiram Johnson and the progressives, 1911–1917.* Berkeley: University of California Press.

O'Malley, E. (Ed.). (1998). *Reading/language arts framework for California public schools, kindergarten through grade twelve.* Sacramento: California Department of Education.

Owens, R. (1984). *Language development: An introduction.* Columbus, OH: Merrill.

Owl. (2004a). *Using American Psychological Association (APA) format* (updated to 5th edition). Retrieved March 23, 2004, from http://owl.english.purdue.edu/handouts/research/r_apa.html

Owl. (2004b). Using Modern Language Association (MLA) format. Retrieved March 23, 2004, from http://owl.english.purdue.edu/handouts/research/r_mla.html

Oyama, S. (1976). A sensitive period for the acquisition of nonnative phonological system. *Journal of Psycholinguistic Research, 5,* 261–284.

Park, B. (1982). The big book trend—A discussion with Don Holdaway. *Language Arts, 59,* 814–821.

Pfaff, C. (Ed.). (1987). *First and second language acquisition processes.* Rowley, MA: Newbury House.

Piaget, J. (1932). *The moral judgment of the child.* London, UK: Routledge & Kegan Paul.

Rasinski, T. V. (2000). Speed does matter in reading. *The Reading Teacher, 54,* 146–151.

Ruesh, H. (1991). *Top of the world: A Novel.* New York: Pocket Books.

Samuels, S. J. (1997). The method of repeated readings. *The Reading Teacher, 50,* 376–381.

Scamehorn, H. L. (1992). *Mill & mine: The CF&I in the twentieth century.* Lincoln: University of Nebraska Press.

Searle, J. R. (1969). *Speech acts.* Cambridge, UK: Cambridge University Press.

Selinker, L. (1969). Language transfer. *General Linguistics, 9,* 67–92.

Selinker, L. (1972). Interlanguage. *International Review of Applied Linguistics, 10,* 209–231.

Serafini, F. (2000/2001). Three paradigms of assessment: Measurement, procedure, and inquiry. *The Reading Teacher, 54,* 384–393.

Shanahan, T., & Shanahan, S. (1997). Character perspective charting: Helping children develop a more complete conception of story. *The Reading Teacher, 50,* 668–677.

Skinner, B. (1957). *Verbal behavior.* New York: Appleton Century Crofts.

Stahl, S. A., & Kuhn, M. R. (2002). Making it sound like language: Developing fluency. *The Reading Teacher, 55,* 582–584.

Starr, K. (1985). *Inventing the dream: California through the progressive era.* New York: Oxford University Press.

Stauffer, R. (1980). *The language experience approach to the teaching of reading* (2nd ed.). New York: Harper.

Sternberg, R. J. (1988). *Advances in the psychology of human intelligence.* Hillsdale, NJ: Lawrence Erlbaum Associates.

Strickland, D., & Morrow, L. (1989). Environments rich in print promote literacy behavior during play. *Reading Teacher, 43,* 178–179.

Tadlock, D. F. (1978). SQ3R—Why it works, based on an information processing theory of learning. *Journal of Reading, 22,* 110–113.

Taylor, B. (1975). The use of over generalization and transfer learning strategies by elementary and intermediate students in ESL. *Language Learning, 25,* 73–107.

Taylor, M. (1992). The language experience approach and adult learners. National Centers for ESL instruction (ERIC Document Reproduction Service EDO-LE-92-01). Retrieved May 21, 2003, from http://www.cal.org/ncle/digest/langexper.html

Thorndike, E. L. (1912). *Education, a first book.* New York: Macmillan & Co.

Trelease, J. (1995). Sustained silent reading. *California English, 1,* 8–9.

Turner, D. (1978). *The effect of instruction on second language learning and second language acquisition.* Paper presented at 12th Annual TESOL Conference, Mexico City, April 1978.

Turner, E., & Rommetveit, R. (1967). The acquisition of sentence voice and reversibility. *Child Development, 38,* 650–60.

Uttal, W. R. (2000). *The war between mentalism and behaviorism: On the accessibility of mental processes.* Mahwah, NJ: Lawrence Erlbaum Associates.

Vacca, R. T., & Vacca, J. L. (1989). *Content area reading* (3rd ed.). Glenview, IL: Scott, Foresman.

Van Allen, R., & Allen, C. (1970). *Language experience and reading.* Chicago: Encyclopedia Britannica Press.

Vygotsky, L. S., & Luria, A. R. (1993). *Studies in the history of human behavior: Ape, primitive, and child.* Hillsdale, NJ: Lawrence Erlbaum.

Whorf, B. L. (1956). *Language, thought and reality: The selected writings of Benjamin Lee Whorf.* Cambridge, MA: MIT Press.

Williams, J. P. (1980). Teaching decoding with an emphasis on phoneme analysis and phoneme blending. *Journal of Educational Psychology, 72,* 1–15.

Windholz, G. (1997). Ivan P. Pavlov: An overview of his life and psychological work. *American Psychologist, 52,* 941.

Wolfram, W., & Johnson, R. (1982). *Phonological analysis: Focus on American English.* Washington, DC: Center for Applied Linguistics.

Wysocki, K., & Jenkins, J. R. (1987). Deriving word meanings through morphological generalization. *Reading Research Quarterly, 22,* 66–81.

Yopp, H., & Yopp, R. (2000). Supporting phonemic awareness development in the classroom. *The Reading Teacher, 54,* 130–143.

Zuriff, G. E. (1995). *Behaviorism: A conceptual reconstruction.* New York: Columbia University Press.

INDEX

Please note that topics are indexed by domain, in the same order as domains appear in the text.

LANGUAGE ARTS

SOCIAL STUDIES

SCIENCE

HUMANITIES